"This is a book proclaiming the Word of God."

—*Prof. Asher S. Kaufmann, Hebrew University of Jerusalem, The Temple Mount – Where is the Holy of Holies?*

"This will intrigue casual readers into diving into the Scriptural commentaries."

—*The Reverend John F. Mangrum A.B., M. DIV., S.T.D.*

"Keeps you absorbed from first page to last."

Rabbi Samuel M. Silver, D.D. Temple Sinai of Delray Beach, FL

"A first-class treatment of the subject in a man-on-the-street style. He will reach many people with the Truths in his book."

Earnest L. Martin, Ph.D. Director, Associates for Scriptural Knowledge

"Jesus and the Third Temple offers a powerful new interfaith bridge to Christians and Jews."

— *Dr. Joyce Starr, Kissing Through Glass: The Invisible Shield Between Americans and Israelis*

Jesus and the Third Temple

The Complete Guide to the Ancient History and Secret Rituals of the Red Heifer Ceremony

Why Building the Third Temple in Jerusalem is a Jewish Right and a Christian Imperative!

Jesus and the Third Temple

The Complete Guide to the Ancient History and Secret Rituals of the Red Heifer Ceremony

Robert Reiland

Your Own World Books
Silver Springs, NV

jesusandthethirdtemple.com
yowbooks.com

COPYRIGHT

Jesus and the Third Temple: The Complete Guide to the Ancient History and Secret Rituals of the Red Heifer Ceremony

No part of this book may be reproduced or transmitted in any form or by any means, graphic, electronic, or mechanical, including photocopying, recording, taping, or by any information storage retrieval system, without the written permission of the publisher.

Copyright © 2007/2008 by Your Own World, Inc.
All rights reserved.

Your Own World Books
Third Edition - September 2008
ISBN-10: 1-59772-036-4
ISBN-13: 978-1-59772-036-6
jesusandthethirdtemple.com

YOUR OWN WORLD BOOKS
an imprint of Your Own World, Inc.
Silver Springs, NV USA
www.yowbooks.com
SAN: 256-1646

Dedication

The Principal Figure of this Book

To all those who love the Lord, and to all those who will then love Him when they meet Him.

Table of Contents

Foreword by Professor Asher S. Kaufman....................xii

Introduction....................xviii

Part I - Shekhinah Departure Event....................1

1. "His" Story....................3

2. The Event....................15

3. Impressions....................27

Part II – Examining the Departure Event....................35

4. Archaeological Comments....................37
    Assumptions....................38
    The Open Gate....................39
    What "City?"....................39
    Where was the "Miphkad Altar?"....................40
    Who Shut Which Gate?....................47
    Oregano and Red Stuff....................52
    Please Stay Downwind....................54
    Line of Departure....................55
    Where the "Fault" Lies....................58
    The Truth about Watergate....................61
    Some Obvious Arguments....................61

5. Some Updated Bible Stories....................67
    Why Gethsemane?....................68

  Now, What about this "Jesus?" 71
    What Judeans and Romans were Thinking 73
    Where was The Crucifixion? 75
    Evidence in The Temple 81
    Not your ordinary "Veil" 82
    If You Had Been There 83
  Keeping His Schedule 86
  Caiaphas; Should we "judge" him? 87
  The Character of God 88

6. Prophecies Seen in This Event 91
  More Heifers for the Unclean 91
  Closed Door Policy 94
  Fulfilling the Feasts 98
    Pesach (Passover) 98
    Hag Hamatzah (Unleavened Bread) 98
    First Fruits 99
    Shavuot (Weeks or Pentecost) 102
    Rosh Hashanah (New Year) 102
    Yom Kippur (Day of Atonement) 103
    Sukkoth (Booths) Feast of Tabernacles 103
  Christian Interpretation of Jewish Feasts 104
    New Testament Reference – Old Testament Sources ... 110
  When did those "Two Days" Start? 113
  Olivet, a Holy Mountain 120
  The Divine Number 122
  Another Divine Number 123
  And, yet Another Divine Number 123
  What if Israel had Repented? 124

7. "Signs and Wonders" 127
  Signs of the Jewels 128
  Signs Above the City 129
  A Sign to be Seen, but not Heard 130
  A Time of the Signs 130

A Woe in the Darkness 131
"Sign" of the Disappearing Signs.. 133
"Drawing the Lots".. 135
"The Crimson Strap"... 136
The Two "He-Goats"... 137
"The Westernmost Candle"... 138
"The Logs for The Altar" 138
"The Breads" 139
"The H'ekhal doors" 139
How Jews Regarded the Signs... 139
Is "The World" Learning? 144
The "Good News" is: 146

Part III – Rebutting Critics and Skeptics..159

8. The Controversy..161
The Accusations.. 162
The Resistance 166
Scriptural/Historical/Archaeological Evidence 169
Some Missing Pieces 170
You Shall Know The Truth... 173

9. The Debate..179
Ezekiel's Prophecy: The Glory Withdrawal 179
Whose "House?".. 182
Rending of The Veil 190
What, then, did the Centurion See? 194

10. Will the Real "Chosen People" Please Stand? 197
It's Not to Worry!.. 200
Something to Think About!.. 201
Can a "Jew" Love The Lord? 201
Father, Forgive Us! 205
Messiah, Son of Joseph – and a Carpenter! 208

11. The Debate Continues 213
So, who Believes in Signs? 213
"The" Unanswered Question 216
Understanding the Cohens and The Trinity 217
How Many "Gods" did You Say? 218
References and Bibliography for: Shekhinah Departure 219

Part IV – The Red Heifer and The Law 223

12. Do Christians Need The Law? 225
References and Bibliography for: Do Christians Need the Law? 259

13. The Forgotten Sacrifice 261

14. "Pictures" from the Red Heifer 271
"Practically Perfect" — Verse 2 271
"Remember That Calf, Aaron?!" — Verse 3 274
"Without the Camp" 277
"One shall slay her before his face" 279
Eleazar "Sprinkleth" — Verse 4 282
The Burning - Verse 5 284
"Red Stuff" — Verse 6 286
What Constitutes "Unclean?" — Verses 7 and 8 290
Blood and Water of Purification — Verses 9 and 10 291
Defining "Living" Water — Verse 17 294
Purified by Blood and Living Water — Verses 18 and 19 297

Part V – Heifer's Dramas and Types 301

15. Looking Again at The Gospel 303
Waiting For "The Living Water" 304
"You Want to Stay in Bethany?!" 306
"Maybe He IS Messiah!" 308

Jesus and "The Ineffable Name"..308
"At Evening, Before the Entire Congregation"..............................311
"What Time For The Burning?"..326
"Why Did The Temple Face Toward East?"..................................327
"Let Us Find A 'Clean' Man"..329
The "Casting" Director...334
Some Questions Concerning "A Clean Place"............................335
Were You There?..340
From Whence Cometh These Errors?..345

16. Ashes? Who Needs Them?...349
Other Pictures And Types..354
The Creation 354
    Joseph...357
    Jonah..357
    Isaac 357
    The Two He-Goats 358
    The Passover Lamb..361
    Born In A Manger...361
    Three Crosses at Calvary..361
    The Red Heifer..363
But, Why Do We Need Those Ashes Now?...............................363

17. Who is "Indiana Jones?"...367

18. What Happens After the Ashes are Recovered?...............371
Where Is The "Holy Place"?..378
Who Needs An Earthquake?!..380
    Praying for the Third Temple..390
    A "Clean" Building..393
    Washed And Purified — At Evening................................396
Standing-tall, but Bowing-low 401
"Worthy is The Heifer!"..403
References and Bibliography for: The Red Heifer......................407

Part VI – Hidden Gospel Mysteries...411

19. Secrets Hidden in The Passover..............................413
    Introduction..414
    Geometric Clues...416
    The Seder Table..421
    The Matzah...421
    Some Haggadic Themes..424
    The Father's Place Setting...428
    The Magen David..429
    The Afikoman..429
    After Breaking the Middle Matzah..................................434
    Closing Remarks...442
    References and Bibliography for: Secrets Hidden in the Passover.....458

20. Really "3 Days and 3 Nights?"..............................461
    It's "Only" A Question of "Time"......................................462
    When Did Jesus Arise?..463
    The Schedule of Events...470
    Could the "Last Supper" have been a "Seder"?..............474
    Which "Law"?..477
        Fulfilling The Law..478
        The "Jewish Rapture"..485
    Traditional "Days" and "Nights".....................................486
    "It must have been on a Wednesday!".........................487
    "Or, maybe it was a Thursday!"....................................493
    Three Jewish Days and Three Jewish Nights In The Tomb................493
    Summary & Conclusions...500
    References and Bibliography for: Really "3 days and 3 nights?"........507

21. God's Favorite Aroma..509

Part VII – Miracles, "Acts" and "The End"..............................511

22. A Miracle Overlooked...513

23. "The Acts" of The Apostles.......................................517
    The Temple..518
    Priests and "Signs"...520
    The Time(s) of Messiah(s)..521
    "Forty Years Before The Temple Was Destroyed"...............522
    The Ascension...523
    Shekhinah Withdrawal and Ascension into Heaven..........524
    Some Conclusions...525

24. Jewish Concept of the World to Come...................527
    Something to Think About...546

25. Go Tell It To the World..547
    A Messenger's Plea 547
    But...How Can We Be Sure?..549
    Questions For The Skeptics..550
    So, That's What "They" Want! 553
    What Should We Do to Tell this Story? 555
    Drawing Jews and Christians Closer Together"..............555

Appendices and Glossary..559

    Appendix A — Josephus Excerpt....................................561
    Appendix B — Midrash Excerpt......................................563
    Appendix C — Integrity of Josephus...............................571
    Appendix D — Ark of The Covenant................................573
    Appendix E — A Trilogy at the Mount of Olives................575

Appendix F — Translations from Greek and Aramaic.................583
Appendix G — Temple Site..593
Glossary..603

Indexes..621

Scripture References..623
Talmud References..639
Midrash References...643
Alphabetical Index..645

Illustration Index

1: Ark and Staves Behind Veil..8
2: Comparison of Ark Orientations..9
3: Old City of Jerusalem and Mt. of Olives..19
4: Threshingfloor..20
5: Dome of the Tablets..21
6: Chronology of Principal Events in This Work...33
7: Temple Mt. Viewed from Chapel of The Ascension..42
8: Could this be the Miphkad Altar Site?...47
9: Chapel of The Ascension..57
10: Church of Mary Magdalene (Russian Church)..59
11: Jewish Cemetery on the Mt. of Olives...76
12: Tomb of the Prophets..77
13: Temple Mt. "At the 9th hour"..79
14: Scenario of the End of Days..119
15: Plan of Second Temple (by Dr. A.S. Kaufman)...148
16: Isometric View of 2nd Temple..149
17: Detailed Elevation of 2nd Temple..150
18: Elevation Profile of Temple and Temple Mt...151
19: Elev. Profile: Temple Mt., Kidron VLY., Mt. Olivet....................................152
20: Jerusalem as it Appeared in 70 C.E..153
21: Detail of the 2nd Temple..154
22: The Sanctuary of the 2nd Temple...155
23: Mt. Olivet viewed from Temple on Crucifixion Day......................................156
24: Detail of "pit or cavity" in face of Mt. of Olives...................................157
25: Checklist for Locales of The Crucifixion..253
26: Temple Mt., Contoured Mt. of Olives...324
27: Clean Babes, Foundation, House..406
28: Round or Square Pointing Which Way?...417
29: Corruption of Seder Matzah Symbolism..444
30: Position: 1st (Lower) Matzah at Seder Table...445
31: Position: 2nd (Middle) Matzah at Seder Table..446

— x —

32: Position: 3rd (Upper) Matzah at Seder Table..447
33: Final Arrangement of Matzoth at Seder Start...448
34: Breaking Afikoman from 2nd Wafer..449
35: Equal Perforation Spacing = Triangular Pieces..450
36: Arrangement: Matzoth After Afikoman is Broken...451
37: Seder – 1st Day in Messianic Period in Israel..452
38: Seder – 2nd Day in Messianic Period in Israel...453
39: Seder – 3rd Day in Messianic Period in Israel..454
40: Seder Matzoth Show God, Holy Spirit, World...455
41: Seder Matzoth Show God Leading Israel..456
42: Seder Plate Arrangements: Various Haggadoth...457
43: Chronology of Passion Week..503
44: Days, Events for Feast of Unleavened Bread..504
45: Western & Jewish: 3 Days, 3 Nights in Tomb..505
46: Western & Jewish: 3 Days, 3 Nights...506
47: Scenario of Messiah's Arrival and Kingdom..545
48: Appendix G – Comparison of Ark Orientations...597
49: Appendix G – Diagram of Ark and Staves...598

Photos by author. Photo of Church of Mary Magdalene courtesy of the Jewish Virtual Library, www.jewishvirtuallibrary.org

Foreword by Professor Asher S. Kaufman

Racah Institute of Physics, Jerusalem 91904, Israel

A feature common to Jewish Rabbinic thought and scientific progress is to question. A question is asked and an answer is to be found. Robert Reiland asked the question: *"What happened to the Divine Presence (Shekhinah) after the destruction of the Temple in Jerusalem by the Romans in 70 C.E.?"* — This book provides his answer.

Mr. Reiland amazed me by his erudition in the ancient Jewish literary record. He seems to be as at home with *Midrash* (exposition of verses of the *Tanakh*) as with the New Testament.

My interest in his book stems from my research on the Temples of Jerusalem, especially their location on the Temple Mount. After asking the question concerning their location, I came up with the answer that the traditional site, the extant Islamic Dome of the Rock, is not where the Temple stood. The Holy of Holies of the Temple is marked today by a humble cupola, the Dome of the Tablets (or Dome of the Spirits), situated about 100 meters (330 feet) to the northwest of the Dome of the Rock.

The traditional site has been revered for hundreds of years, so it is not surprising that there should be vehement opposition to a new proposal. This does not worry me. I am completely convinced that my proposal is correct. Moreover, I am fortified by the thought that opposition to a new concept is not new in the physical sciences. Witness the early opposition to quantum theory which is now fully accepted. The first part of this book refers to the Second Temple of Jerusalem and it gave me great satisfaction to discover that Mr. Reiland supports my thesis about the location of the Temple.

A fair portion of the book is devoted to theology and I do not wish to be drawn and plunge into these deep waters. Mr. Reiland is not ambitiously seeking fame. He states: *"It is my hope that, if nothing else, this book will have stirred an interest in the Bible."* He brings ancient sources to show that the Divine Presence departed from the Second Temple. (See, for example, Appendix B). However, I am prepared to quote other references which contradict this statement. *"Rabbi Aha says: The Divine Presence (Shekhinah) never departs from the Western Wall"* (*Midrash Rabbah* Exodus 2:2). *"Decreed from Heaven that the Western Wall shall never be destroyed."* (*Midrash Rabbah* Lamentations 1:31).

The sages who made these pronouncements and similar ones lived in the first half of the 4th century C.E. This seems to indicate that the western wall of the Temple was seen standing and recognized as such at that time prior to the attempt to rebuild the Temple under the auspices of the Emperor Julian. This wall is not the outer western wall (also named the "Wailing Wall") of the Temple Mount. The wall referred to in these texts is in fact the peripheral western wall of the Temple visible in the form of the extant row of monumental stones at the foot of the northwestern staircase to the platform on which stands the Dome of the Rock*.

In conclusion, this is a book proclaiming the Word of God. *—Asher S. Kaufman*

*Identifying Stone Remains of the Western Wall of the Second Temple at Jerusalem, by Kaufman, Asher S. 2000 ASMOSIA 2000, VI international conference, Venice (abstract and poster presentation).

Preface

We must all remember this is not my story. This story belongs to Almighty God, the great "I AM." He lived it. This work became a book without my realization or intent. It began with the questions: What ever happened to the *Shekhinah*? What impact was felt by the Jewish people at the time of His departure from the Temple? When did this happen?

The answers to these questions came together during a long search that started even before the questions began to stimulate my curiosity. During this closing period of my life, I have become driven to a search for Christ as Messiah within Judaism. The pieces began accumulating and fitting together with a "snow-balling" effect. Before I knew it, this wonderful story emerged — one that no longer could be withheld from those who would be open to hearing it.

Acknowledgments

We are indebted to Beth, my now departed wife, for her wise counsel, for her strength, sacrifice, patience, love, and stenographic skills; and certainly to my present wife, Barbara, for her patience and understanding during many hours of neglect and absence on my part; to Dave and Harriet Sanford for their encouragement and many prayers; with eternal gratitude to Harriet for her contributions to this revision with her typing and computer skills; to my anonymous Jewish friend who translated critical Hebrew segments; to the late Professor Ernest Martin for exposing this Holy Event in his works; certainly to Asher Kaufman for his support and close scrutiny of the first three parts of my work in his disciplines of Biblical Archaeology and History; to my friend, Leon Wilson, for his thoughtful review and insightful critique that kept me from some embarrassing errors with his thorough understanding of Scripture and his heartfelt interest in this story; and to the unrivaled Temple Israel Library, and especially, librarians Elsie Leviton and the late Adele Sayles for their kindness and unflagging assistance during my search for Messiah through dozens of Judaica volumes.

This book might never have been written, except for the Lord having brought about a chance meeting between Mrs. Jo Lynn Contino and myself at an Evangelical seminary professor's meeting at a local Bible College. She had asked the renowned speaker to share any news of recent progress in recovering the ashes of the Red Heifer. This revered Hebrew Christian evangelist from a prestigious Mid-western seminary responded with a typical conservative Evangelical attitude as he answered that he knew nothing about the Red Heifer nor was he at all interested in it.

After his program I introduced myself to Jo Lynn and offered to fill her in on what I had known about the Red Heifer at that time. She thereupon challenged me to write down all of my comments I had made to her about the Red Heifer, later to be presented for her church group. As I proceeded to summarize my thoughts, she prayed that I would obtain my own private copy of the *Babylonian Talmud*. That prayer was answered swiftly! As I proceeded to study the *Talmud* for the Law concerning the Heifer, this story literally "snow-balled," eventually becoming the manuscript for the last four parts of this book.

Jo Lynn's query led to these parts, and we must all thank her. We also must certainly thank the Rabbis and scribes of the Jewish *Talmud* and *Midrash* for having left us such detailed accounts concerning this holy rite. Although, we can be certain that none of these writers and teachers was aware that he was relating these beautiful "pictures" of Christ and His Crucifixion and which appear so obviously and clearly to Christians through the Law statutes pertaining to the Red Heifer.

Forever we are indebted to my friend, Mr. Leon Wilson, for his scholarship, counsel and support. His task was to proofread the manuscript, not only to find typographical and compositional errors, but also and more importantly to discover breaks in thought, voids in logic and just plain incorrect statements! This task he tirelessly and cheerfully completed to my amazement and simultaneous humbling admiration for this man. Without Leon's dedication and hard work, this work would have been hopelessly without value as the serious theological study it is intended and deserves to be. Leon Wilson salvaged this work from failing that objective.

This project has been skillfully managed and produced by Marshall Masters and Janice Manning of *Your Own World Books, Inc.* The dedication and publishing skills of all these professionals have greatly contributed toward attempting to present fair treatment of some extremely sensitive material. Simply stated, I could never have done this work without their guidance, patience and skills.

I remark, with understatement, that the ONLY persons in The Universe who have EVER matched my devotion and passion to tell these marvelous stories are *Your Own World Books* publisher, Marshall Masters, and his rock-solid, dependable editor, Janice Manning. This is all the more remarkable, in that we all three come from diverse theological bases. I am the only person aware of the circumstances through which we *"three"* came to reach each other. It could only have been just another of those Marvelous Works of the Lord Himself. – It was NO "accident"!

We owe our thanks to several friends who read and critiqued the earliest manuscripts, giving many new thoughts, questions and comments to enrich our text. We are also grateful for the endurance and attention received from our earliest critical reviewers, who would obviously prefer to remain anonymous. These are of the conservative clergy, who regrettably are not yet able to recognize the significance of this Event.

Nevertheless, a few did not ignore me and actually supplied the arguments we have addressed. For this, we owe them our thanks and prayers, that they and all our readers will see the Glory of God in this story.

All of us, Jews and Christians, certainly owe our gratitude to Flavius Josephus and to the hundreds of Rabbi sages who witnessed, felt, and recorded for us the many beautiful and spiritual thoughts and facts which not only "made" this story, but which serve so stalwartly to make this an exciting and personal story of The Creator.

We are grateful for copyright permission granted from the following publishers for the works listed:

—*Biblical Archaeology Review, March/April 1983*—Copyright © BIBLICAL ARCHAEOLOGY SOCIETY. Reprinted by permission. Subscription inquiries should be mailed to: Biblical Archaeology Society, P. O. Box 7026, Red Oak IA 51591

—Scripture quotations marked (NEB) are from The New English Bible. Copyright © The Delegates of the OXFORD UNIVERSITY PRESS and The Syndics of the CAMBRIDGE UNIVERSITY PRESS, 1961, 1970. Reprinted by permission.

—Holy Bible—From the Ancient Eastern Text—George M. Lamsa's Translations from the Aramaic of the Peshitta— Copyright © HARPER & ROW, PUBLISHERS, INC. Reprinted by permission.

—The Works of Josephus—Copyright © HENDRICKSON PUBLISHERS. Reprinted by permission.

—Will The Real Jesus Please Stand?—Copyright © THE INSTITUTE OF JUDAIC-CHRISTIAN RESEARCH. Reprinted by permission.

—The Coming Prince—Copyright © KREGEL PUBLICATIONS, Division of Kregel, Inc. Reprinted by permission.

—Scripture quotations marked (NASB) are from the New American Standard Bible, © THE LOCKMAN FOUNDATION 1960, 1962, 1963, 1968, 1971, 1972, 1973, 1975, 1977. Used by permission.

—The Babylonian Talmud—THE SONCINO PRESS, LIMITED, Quincentenary Edition—1978. Used by permission.

—Midrash Rabbah—Third Edition—Copyright © THE SONCINO PRESS LIMITED. Reprinted by permission.

—THE JUDAIC CLASSICS LIBRARY CD-ROM, produced by DAVKA CORPORATION – CHICAGO, IL – contains digital presentation of THE SONCINO PRESS, LTD. Tanakh, Babylonian Talmud and Midrash Rabbah that is used extensively in referencing Judaic sources in this work.

—Scripture quotations marked (NIV) are from the Holy Bible, New International Version. Copyright © 1973, 1978, 1984 International Bible Society. Used by permission of ZONDERVAN BIBLE PUBLISHERS.

—Certain quotations are taken from Cruden's Complete Concordance, by Alexander Cruden. Copyright © 1949, 1953, 1955, 1968 by ZONDERVAN BIBLE PUBLISHERS. Used by permission.

—The Works of Josephus – New Updated Edition — Copyright © 1987 -- HENDRICKSON PUBLISHERS. Reprinted by permission.

—Encyclopedia Judaica — Copyright © 1972 — KETER PUBLISHING HOUSE JERUSALEM LT'D. Reprinted by permission.

--The Fire and the Cloud, Updated and Revised Edition – Copyright © 2003, XLIBRIS Corporation, Philadelphia PA – Reprinted by permission.

It would greatly burden my conscience if I were to neglect stating the immeasurable worth of what I refer to as my "Secret Weapons." They shall be "secret" no longer.

- *Online Bible is a CD-ROM containing countless notes, commentaries and library references in combination with literally dozens of Bible translations. It is available from: www.onlinebible.com*

- *Davka Judaic Classics Library is a CD-ROM containing both English and Hebrew renditions of the Jewish Tanakh (Jewish Scriptures), Babylonian Talmud and Midrash Rabbah. It is available from: www.davka.com*

Introduction

The World searches and hopes for ways to bring peace and stability soon to our planet. The vigil for this noble and comforting goal will be attained with the Arrival of Jesus as the Messiah – long-awaited by Jews and Christians – and perhaps Muslims as well. When He arrives, He will restore a Temple to be built on the Temple Mount in Jerusalem. It will be "The Third Temple" – Messiah's "Headquarters" for His rule of all the nations of the Earth. There He will rule for one thousand years until The Final Judgment. Consequently, all peoples from all nations will come to that Holy City to adore Him and to draw from His Infinite Love and Mercy.

This work closely documents the historical and Biblical events of past as well as those of the present. Together, they have laid the foundation for future events that will usher in the Glorious time of the Third Temple. A time when all of Earth will be restored to peace and will have been returned to that same condition that Earth enjoyed at The Creation. There will be no war, no crime, no disease, no disasters, no injustice – no suffering of any kind!

About This Book

Jesus and the Third Temple is divided into seven parts. The first three parts are devoted primarily to tracing from that first appearance of *Shekhinah* – The Divine Presence – who appeared to Moses and The Jewish People as a *"pillar of cloud by day"* and as a *"pillar of fire by night"* – to the miracles and Glorious Events in the Second Temple, and finally, a Glorious Departure of *Shekhinah* into Heaven.

> Part I – *Shekhinah* Departure Event
> Part II – Examining the Departure Event
> Part III – Rebutting Critics and Skeptics

The remaining four parts interpret the cryptic meanings of the Red Heifer ceremony, Judaism's most important Temple rite. Additionally, several other aspects of Judaism's Mosaic Law are discussed with regard to how it was fulfilled by Jesus as presented in the Gospel and within many of the Rabbinical interpretations of The Law.

> Part IV – The Red Heifer and The Law
> Part V – Heifer's Dramas and Types
> Part VI – Hidden Gospel Mysteries
> Part VII – Miracles, "Acts" and "The End"

In order to adequately cover the story, we begin with the earliest Appearance of God's Divine Presence – the Glory of the Lord – Israel's *Shekhinah* – to Moses and the Jewish People.

Parts I Through III

This book is about truth — the first three parts tell the truth about the withdrawal of the *Shekhinah* Glory from the Temple in Jerusalem. Whatever happened to the Glory of the Lord — His visible Divine Presence — the *Shekhinah* (or *Shechinah*) who dwelt in the Temple? Unless you are a really "deep" scholar, you may never have thought about this. Some may even be surprised to know the Glory was Almighty God in person. (The Great I AM who spoke to Moses from a "burning bush.")

The withdrawal of *Shekhinah* is, in my opinion, perhaps the most important Biblical event since the Holy Spirit was manifested as tongues of flame on the Day of Pentecost (*Shavuot*) after The Resurrection. Strangely, the *Shekhinah* withdrawal has gone virtually ignored for all this time, despite the fact that it has been documented by eyewitness accounts from four highly respected sources. Furthermore, since very few Christians, Jews or Muslims have ever heard it before, this story will cause a "shock" reaction from readers from all three faiths because it will show how the teachings of all three faiths were completely erroneous about this for 1900 years.

The author clearly understands that this would cause *Jesus and the Third Temple* to be a very controversial story. Readers who are inclined to regard only Biblical information taught from their own Sunday School, church or synagogue may have difficulty accepting this report. However, when we recover from the initial "shock" to our traditional "security blankets" and look at the evidence, Scriptural and secular, we see a very beautiful, God-glorifying story. But, above all, this story is true.

Jesus and the Third Temple is, as the title tells us, building toward the eventuality of Israel's Third Temple. So, we should point out that at least a few Christian scholars insist upon referring to the remodeled construction of the Second Temple by King Herod as "The Third Temple." We must therefore, in order to avoid potential of confusion spawned from such scholars, make clear that we are NOT identifying *that* Temple by Herod as "The Third Temple." Some of these scholars – so-called "Amillenialists" – are of the eschatological position that ALL of the prophetic Events preceding Jesus' Return already occurred at The Cross! – In that position, perhaps they must identify Herod's remodeled version as their "Third Temple." They may be "trapped" into that stance because Ezekiel 40 – 44 told of a Temple that was going to be for Jesus in His Kingdom.

There may be other scholars who call Herod's version a "Third Temple" just because it was in fact greatly more beautiful and magnificent than the Second Temple that was built during the reign of King Zerubbabel. Nevertheless, we are considering the "Third Temple" in this work to be that Temple which will be the NEXT Jewish Temple that will be consecrated to God and will be rebuilt on its Divinely and genuinely appointed position on the Temple Mount. It will be built atop the very *same* foundations of the First (Solomon's) and Second Temple. Nevertheless, however doubtful the prospect at present, even so – it *may* be built by the Jewish Rabbinate before Messiah arrives; OR – it *may* be built *"speedily"* in fact BY Messiah when He arrives! – MUCH more about these "alternatives" will be discussed in Parts Five and Six.

Of course the beliefs and hopes and prayers of both Judaism and Christianity will reach a mutual and Glorious fulfillment on that Magnificent Day! The Law and virtually all facets of this work are drawn to that Day of His Coming to claim His Kingdom. In preparing this work, the purpose and goal was based upon the belief that Christian Believers should need and should want to know of the Laws that Jesus fulfilled. In this way, Christians can come to a clearer understanding of the Gospel as well as the Mosaic Laws, by which The Savior conducted His life and taught His followers.

As you read, you will encounter several rather unfamiliar names, such as: "*Parah*," "*Yoma*," "*Middoth*," etc. These are Hebrew titles for "tractates" or divisions of the *Babylonian Talmud* that is so often referenced in this study. The *Talmud* was prepared by the Rabbis and sages as an interpretation of the Law that Moses had received from the Lord. The Law has of course been greatly "amplified" by the Rabbis having added many laborious details through centuries of Jewish tradition in application of the Law. Each tractate is comprised of a somewhat formal "*Mishnah*" (or ruling) in the Law. This is usually accompanied by a "*Gemara*" (or discussion) that is a less formal exchange of Rabbis' views in debate concerning the *Mishnah*.

The Hebrew *Midrash* is also referenced in this work. Written by several councils of Rabbis, *Midrash* is actually a commentary on the Hebrew Scriptures. The commentary covers all of the five books of Moses and five other books from what the Jewish people call: *The Holy Scriptures* or *Tanakh*. The *Tanakh* contains all of the books of the Old Testament used by Christianity, except that they are in a different sequence.

The **Tanakh** consists of:

Torah, which is comprised of Moses' first five books of the Bible and is the most sacred portion of the Hebrew Scriptures.

Prophets, consists of the books of the prophets from Old Testament Scripture.

Other Writings is comprised of the Song of Songs, plus the remainder of the books that make up the total of the Hebrew Scriptures – the *Tanakh* – or, what Christians have termed as the "Old Testament."

It is unfortunate that very few Believers have any awareness of the *Talmud* and *Midrash* or other *Judaica* writings. This lack is more saddening because Messiah is "hidden" in these writings throughout! He is hidden, however, *only* from the Jewish people. Christians led by the Holy Spirit can see Jesus Christ immediately in the Law and customs preserved for so many centuries in these ancient and revered Jewish writings.

We should explain that the Jewish views expressed by *Talmud* and *Midrash* are mostly in agreement with theology accepted by Orthodox Judaism. Whereas, Conservative, Reformed and Reconstructionist Judaism hold more liberal positions on these matters. Similarly, the Biblical outlook we have expressed fits mostly with the conservative, Evangelical form of Christianity. Nevertheless, in many cases some of our material would not be supported, and would in fact be vigorously opposed or completely ignored by some Christian groups.

During study of this work, readers may observe that *both* Orthodox Judaism and Evangelical Christianity adhere consistently to the principle that the Word of God is to be accepted "literally." – *It is as He has said!* – It must be noted, however, that although Evangelical Christians regard all books of Scripture to be the Word of God and are therefore of equal stature; the Orthodox Rabbis are consistent in their teaching that *Torah* has superior authority over the other books.

Another facet of Jewish belief that we should keep in mind as we proceed through this study is that Judaism's regard of Messiah varies within each of the three major denominations. Nevertheless, it is somewhat surprising to many Christians to learn that even the Orthodox branch believes that Messiah is a human being; although, they do not believe that He is Divine! The other branches have even weaker Messianic hopes. All this stands in contrast to the fervent Jewish pleading for Messiah to arrive! God has, for His Own Reasons, hidden Messiah from His People during these past "two days" (2000 years) of what Evangelicals have called: "The Church Age." God has proclaimed this Scripturally in the First Person through His prophet in Hosea 5:15 –

"I will go and return to My place, till they acknowledge their offence and seek My face: in their affliction they will seek Me early."

An accompanying chart presents the chronology of dates for the most significant events, personages, etc. in this study. Additionally, a map of Jerusalem's Old City is provided as a convenient reference to sites of the present day in the Holy City.

Parts IV Through VII

The major portion of the last four parts relates the story of Judaism's most important and yet least known and/or least understood rite of all the Temple offerings – the burning of the Red Heifer. According to Jewish tradition, even King Solomon, arguably one of the wisest of all mortals, humbly admitted he did not understand the meaning of the Red Heifer ceremony.

We shall attempt to make clear what was such a puzzlement to King Solomon. Significance and importance of this rite will be revealed here. Those factors will become increasingly apparent to Believers as the soon Return of our Lord Jesus approaches.

The remaining parts of the book comprise seven individual theses that demonstrate in their own way how the life, death and resurrection of Jesus was applied and had "kept" the rigid statutes of *Talmudic* Law. Part Seven of this work presents some of the Jewish teaching on eschatology; i.e., study of "The Last Days," heralding the Coming of Messiah, Son of David. The other parts also deal with that subject throughout, even if only with an indirect connection. The "Time of the End" in the Jewish context is a fascinating subject and cannot avoid blending with Christian eschatology.

Of course the beliefs and hopes and prayers of both Judaism and Christianity will reach a mutual and Glorious fulfillment on that Magnificent Day! The Law and virtually all facets of this work are drawn to that Day of His Coming to claim His Kingdom. In preparing this work, the purpose and goal was based upon the belief that Christian Believers should need and should want to know of the Laws that Jesus fulfilled. In this way, Christians can come to better understanding of the Gospel as well as the Mosaic Laws by which our Savior conducted His life and taught His followers.

Further importance for Christians exists in the fact that the Red Heifer ceremony is a beautiful "picture" of Jesus Christ. The details of this rite are revealed in the Jewish *Midrash* and *Babylonian Talmud* in a unique fashion and which few Jewish people or Christians have seen before. In addition, *Talmud* and other Judaica provide even more detailed information concerning how Jesus so Magnificently fulfilled the Law with His Sacrifice at The Crucifixion. This should come as no surprise, however, because Jesus was Commissioned by The Father to fulfill *all* of the Law, including the Law of the Red Heifer. We believe you will be spiritually inspired and blessed by what you see here for perhaps the first time.

Finally, unless otherwise noted, Biblical quotes are from the King James Version – KJV – translation of both the Old Testament and the New Testament. Most Jewish Scriptural quotes are taken from the English translation of the Greek *Masoretic Text* of the *Tanakh* or *Tanach*. A Scriptural Index, a *Talmud* Index, a *Midrash* Index and a General Index are contained in the last pages of this work. References and/or Bibliographies (listed as superscripts in the text) also are listed at the end of each major section of discussion.

In accommodation to modern scholarship and to avoid offending diverse religions, we have used the following abbreviations to denote historical dates; the meaning of each to be selected at the reader's preference :

B.C.E. – Before the Christian Era *OR* Before the Common Era

C.E. – Christian Era *OR* Common Era

The majority of events reported will have been seen here by the general public for the first time. The most dramatic and least reported Event is the departure of Israel's *Shekhinah* Glory (Divine Presence) from the Temple at Jerusalem. This is only one of several events that depart from traditional teaching on the incidents and the Truth of which has deluded most scholars for centuries. It follows that much of the material in the series will become controversial, especially to persons who prefer adhering to traditional lore in such matters. Most controversial are: The place of The Crucifixion, The Departure of *Shekhinah* and The Week of The Passion – Jesus' Final Week.

The Holy Scriptures are of course the Primary and Superior source for our presentation. The series includes, however, a great amount of material that is often termed "extra-Biblical;" nevertheless, having considerable reliability in an historical sense. Much of the analysis is augmented by entries from the *Babylonian Talmud* and *Midrash Rabbah*, along with intriguing and thought-provoking use of Biblical "typology" (symbolic comparisons of Biblical Events).

Recent discoveries of Biblical archaeological evidence influence greatly in the analysis. All sources for our information are well-known and easily available; although, not generally accessed or consulted by Christian clergy or laypersons. They are however, for the most part, documented in Judaic antiquity and are found in many synagogue libraries.

It is our prayer and hope that "open-eyed" Jews, Christians, and Muslims will read and evaluate this work. It is also my prayer and hope that, by considering Scripture and the simple facts, even those who do not yet "believe" will be able to "see" the Glory of the Lord through this story. I have been thrilled by what I have found and I fervently wish to share these blessings. I believe the reader will find at least a few surprise blessings. If you love the Lord, this book will make you cry; and it will also make you shout with joy.

As you read this, we are confident you will not only be edified by new learning, but also will even be entertained – because these Events and thoughts have *never* before been reported, other than to a few scholars. – They are, therefore – *NEWS* !

Part I - *Shekhinah* Departure Event

1

"His" Story

The "flaming" bush – "pillar of cloud" and "pillar of fire" lead Israelites from Egypt – Shekhinah in the Temple – Shekhinah speaks to His People – Ark of The Covenant

- *When did the Shekhinah Glory leave the Temple?*
- *What was the reaction of the Israelites to that event?*
- *How does this event link Judaism and Christianity?*

The answers to these provocative questions have been well documented and have been available for more than 1900 years. However, these things are not generally known or discussed except, perhaps among the most diligent and informed scholars. Neither are these answers directly available from Scripture, since only the prophet Ezekiel describes the departure of the Glory of the Lord, but without answering any of those questions listed.

Our purpose is to offer answers to these questions and to provide new insight through recent archaeological discoveries in Jerusalem.

This story tells what really happened to the Lord's Divine Presence (*Shekhinah*), who first appeared to Moses and later dwelt in the Temple. This story refutes the traditional lore we have been hearing for 1900 years. It presents Scriptural evidence and ancient documentation of this event in order to corroborate the real story.

Here we will see a personal side of God, whom we mostly seem to regard somewhat fearfully as a remote and intimidating Holy Authority. Although we certainly view Jesus as a person, as a "man;" we seldom consider Almighty God as having "human" traits. The Event we are reporting does show God with emotions just like man's emotions, except that God's emotions are Perfectly under His control. We believe therefore that God appears more "human" and more approachable and more loving in this account than most had previously contemplated.

Almighty God Himself dwelt among the Israelites in the Temple as a visible Presence, the *Shekhinah* Glory. Through eyewitness accounts, we shall "see" the events leading up to and including His dramatic withdrawal from the Temple, followed by the Ascension of *Shekhinah* from the Mount of Olives forty years after the Ascension of Jesus Christ from that same mountain.

Let us briefly review the history of the *Shekhinah* Glory as provided in the Old Testament:

1500 B.C.E.

- The Glory appeared first to Moses as a "burning bush." Moses' face shone from the "brightness" after confronting this light. (Exodus 3:2 and 34:29, 30)
- The Glory led the Israelites forty years throughout the *Sinai* as "...a pillar of cloud by day...and a pillar of fire by night..." (Exodus 13:21)
- The Israelites heard the Lord speaking to Moses from His great "fire" and from the "cloud." (Exodus 19:9)
- The Glory dwelt in the Tabernacle, in the Holy of Holies, over the Ark of the Covenant during the forty years of wandering in the *Sinai* and later in The Promised Land until the First Temple was built by King Solomon.

1000 B.C.E.

- In the First Temple, built by King Solomon, the Glory dwelt within the Holy of Holies, just as He did in the Tabernacle. He was seen only once each year, on *Yom Kippur* (Day of Atonement), albeit only by the High Priest within that chamber. (Leviticus 16:1 – 17 and 16:34)

586 B.C.E.

- It is not known what happened to the Glory after King Nebuchadnezzar destroyed the First Temple and during the subsequent Babylonian Captivity, 606 B.C.E.-536 B.C.E. Nevertheless, the Glory must have departed from the Temple before the first destruction. One of the Apocryphal Books (II Maccabees 2:4 – 8, see Appendix D) states that King Nebuchadnezzar gave the Ark of the Covenant to the Prophet Jeremiah for safekeeping. It was then sealed within a cave on Mount Nebo. (God alone knows.)

515 B.C.E.

- Zerubbabel completed the Second Temple. No Ark of the Covenant (not even a replica) was in the Holy of Holies. (Ref. Jeremiah 3:16, also *Middoth* 1:1-Note 11, Josephus Wars 5.5.5/219)

20 B.C.E.

- King Herod (the Great) began remodeling the Second Temple to achieve the grandeur it possessed at the time of Jesus.

30 C.E.-100 C.E.

- Two New Testament verses testify to the contemporary dwelling of *Shekhinah* in the Temple during Jesus' lifetime and afterward. The first is from the Gospel in Matthew 23:21:
- *"And he who swears by the temple, swears both by the temple and by Him who dwells within it."* (New American Standard Bible)
- The other is proclaimed by the Apostle Paul in Romans 9:4:
- *"They are Israelites: they were made God's sons; theirs is the splendour of the divine presence, theirs the covenants, the law, the temple worship, and the promises."* (New English Bible)

Thus, *Shekhinah* was in the Second Temple. Jesus declared it and so did Paul. Yet, most of the writers of the New Testament seem to have left this for granted, as if to say: "Of course *Shekhinah* dwells in the Temple! Everybody knows that! He is part of Israel! Where else would He be?!"

Such brief and "obscure" disclosures should not surprise us, since none of the New Testament writers would have been permitted to enter the Holy of Holies to stand before the Divine Presence. By the Law, only the High Priest was authorized for such a visit each year on the Day of Atonement (Leviticus 16:2, 11 – 15)

In addition to the Scriptural statements, considerable Rabbinical comment in *Midrash* and *Talmud* indicates *Shekhinah* was dwelling in the Second Temple. Although there is no mention of the specific return of *Shekhinah* to the Temple in the Old Testament, considering the tone, the emotion, and spirit conveyed through these verses, it would seem that the Lord could hardly reject the pleas from Nehemiah and the People asking for His Blessing and Presence. (See Nehemiah 8 – 12, especially 12:43.) One century earlier, Haggai was told to encourage Zerubbabel by Promising him: *"I will fill this house with Glory"* (Haggai 2:7). *Talmud* states that "forty years before the Temple was destroyed" (70 C.E. minus "forty" equals 30 C.E.!); that is to say, immediately following Christ's Crucifixion, strange "signs" in the Temple indicated that *Shekhinah* was going to depart. (See "SIGNS AND WONDERS," Chapter 7.)

At this point it should be mentioned that what our English Bibles refer to as "The Glory of the Lord" has been identified by several names: "The *Shekhinah* Glory," from the Hebrew "*Shekhinah*" meaning Presence or Dwelling, The Father of the Triune God: "I AM," "*Elohim*," "*Yahweh*," "*Jehovah*," and others. Occasionally, Scripture refers to the Divine Presence as: "*The Angel of the Lord*." The *Shekhinah* (or Divine Presence) is the visible form of Almighty God Himself, who appeared to the Jews in the *Sinai* and dwelt in the Tabernacle and in the Temple in the *Kodesh Ha-Kodashim* (Holy of Holies). And, as also regarding God's Holy Spirit, the *Shekhinah* or Glory should never be mentioned as "it" but as "He" since He is God, a personal being (not an inanimate object).

A cloud of doubt drifts into the minds of some Believers who will say, "But why do you refer to this *Shekhinah* as 'He'? Is this a person?" Many Christians who have studied the Bible only from a traditional teaching position do not realize that "I AM" was "*Yahweh*" or "*YHWH*" — Almighty God Himself. They don't comprehend, or maybe accept, that God actually spoke to Moses and to the "children of Israel" and was visible to them as a "fire" and as a "cloud." Furthermore, many are not aware that the same "fire" or "cloud" was actually in the Temple — including during the time of Jesus.

The Jewish *Talmud* (*Sotah* 5a) makes it clear that The Creator was the *Shekhinah* (Divine Presence) and was The One who abided in the flaming bush on the Mount. *Yoma* 9b describes it as "The Divine Voice." Most of us have received a large portion of our culture from the movies. We therefore are familiar with Hollywood sound-track versions depicting "the Voice of God" in many cinema epics. Such portrayals typically use an actor resonating the walls and even our seats with a rich, deep, masculine *basso profundo* . Such tone naturally commands attention and respect, sometimes sending chills down our spines.

However, another *Talmud* source (*Berakoth* 51b) describes this Divine Voice as "the daughter of a voice" (Hebrew *Bath Kol* — pronounced: "BAT-COAL") — actually a feminine voice. *Talmud* and *Midrash* describe many occasions in which a voice that had spoken to Israel was, in fact, a *Bath Kol*. (See Appendix B and/or Reference 13; pp.51) Jewish teachers often refer to the *Shekhinah* as "The Holy Spirit." Thus, we can conclude that God's Holy Spirit spoke to Israel, at least occasionally, with a feminine voice.

This feminine gender for the Lord Jehovah's voice is another indication that we are not to assume that worldly characteristics exist for the Lord or for our Eternal home in Heaven. We are reminded of the question posed to the Master by the *Sadducees* in Matthew 22:23 – 30, asking which wife a man would have in Heaven if he had more than one wife during his Earthly life. Jesus answered that in Heaven the angels neither "marry" (as men) nor are they "given in marriage" (as women). That is to say, the angels are neither masculine nor feminine. Angels do not propagate. — They do not reproduce their kind. Similarly, although we will not be "angels;" we will have glorified bodies that will have eternal life. Since we will never die, there will be no need for procreation.

Among other things, Jesus was telling the *Sadducees* that Heaven is not going to be a continuation of the worldly pleasures we have in this present life. This comparison tells us therefore not to be so worldly that we assume that God's voice sounds like that of an authoritarian male figure, as our culture has taught. (We might fail to recognize Him when He calls!)

The Lord in fact may have used the feminine touch in order to better gain their *full* attention! There is modern support for such a purpose as seen in audio systems employed for warnings on airplanes, locomotives, etc. In an airplane cockpit, for example, if the pilot is approaching a dangerously low altitude, low oil pressure, etc., a female voice announces the approaching peril. Psychologists have found that flight crews, especially among the masculine gender, are much more likely to be "awakened" from their concentration on routine tasks of flying the airplane if a soft feminine voice issues the warning. (It would seem God had known that all this time!)

Another indication of the feminine suggestion rendered by *Shekhinah* was brought by the staves used for carrying the Ark of the Covenant and in the way they were positioned in the Tabernacle and later in the First Temple. (We should note here that there was no Ark — not even a replica — in the Second Temple.) – Therefore no staves.

According to *Menahoth* 98a, the staves "pointed eastward and westward and protruded at right angles to the length of the Ark." It is further explained that the Ark was the only article in the Temple that was oriented with its longer axis extending parallel to "the breadth of the House," which was of course north-south. (See Illus. 1: Ark and Staves Behind Veil, Page 8 and Illus. 2: Comparison of Ark Orientations, Page 9.)

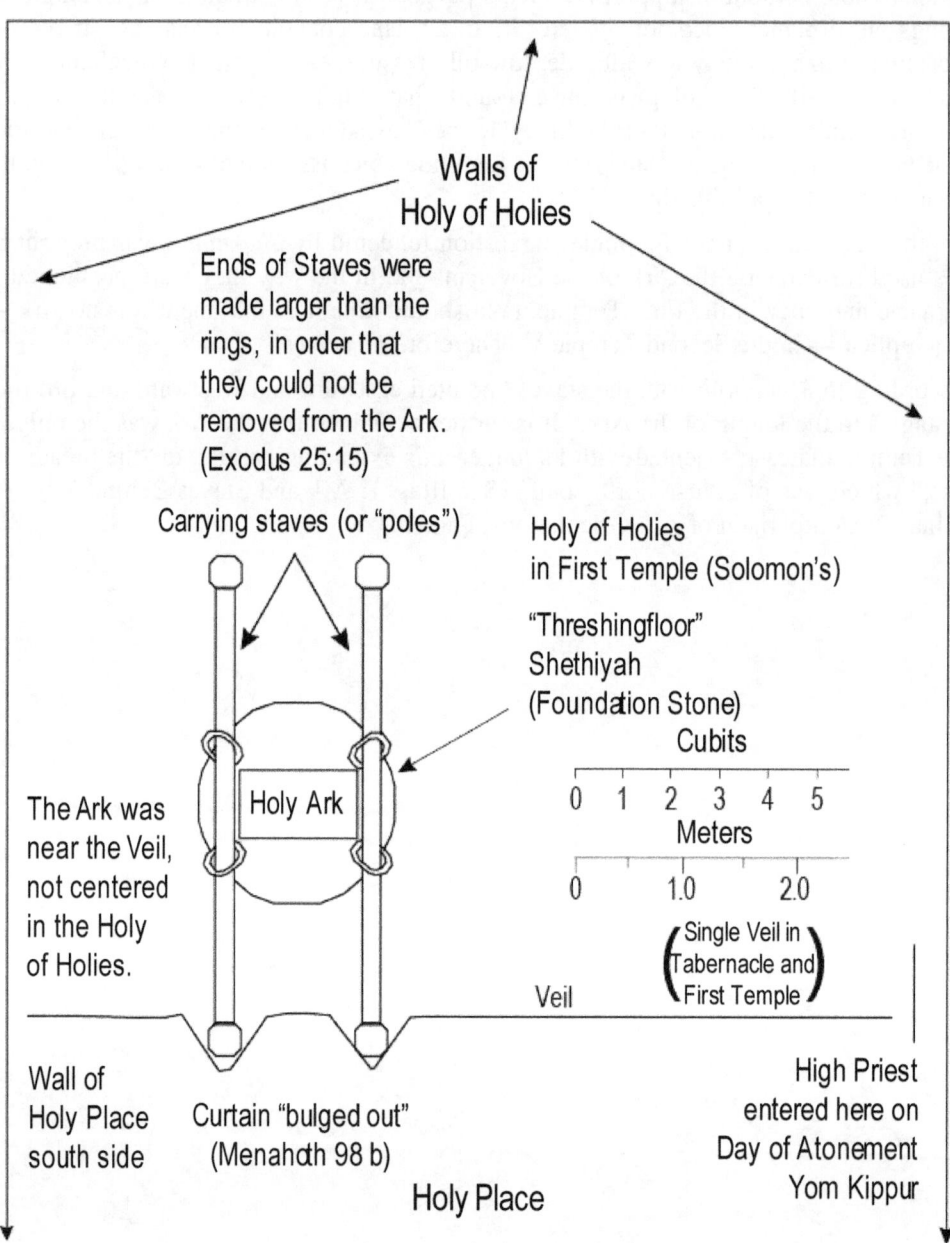

Illus. 1: Ark and Staves Behind Veil

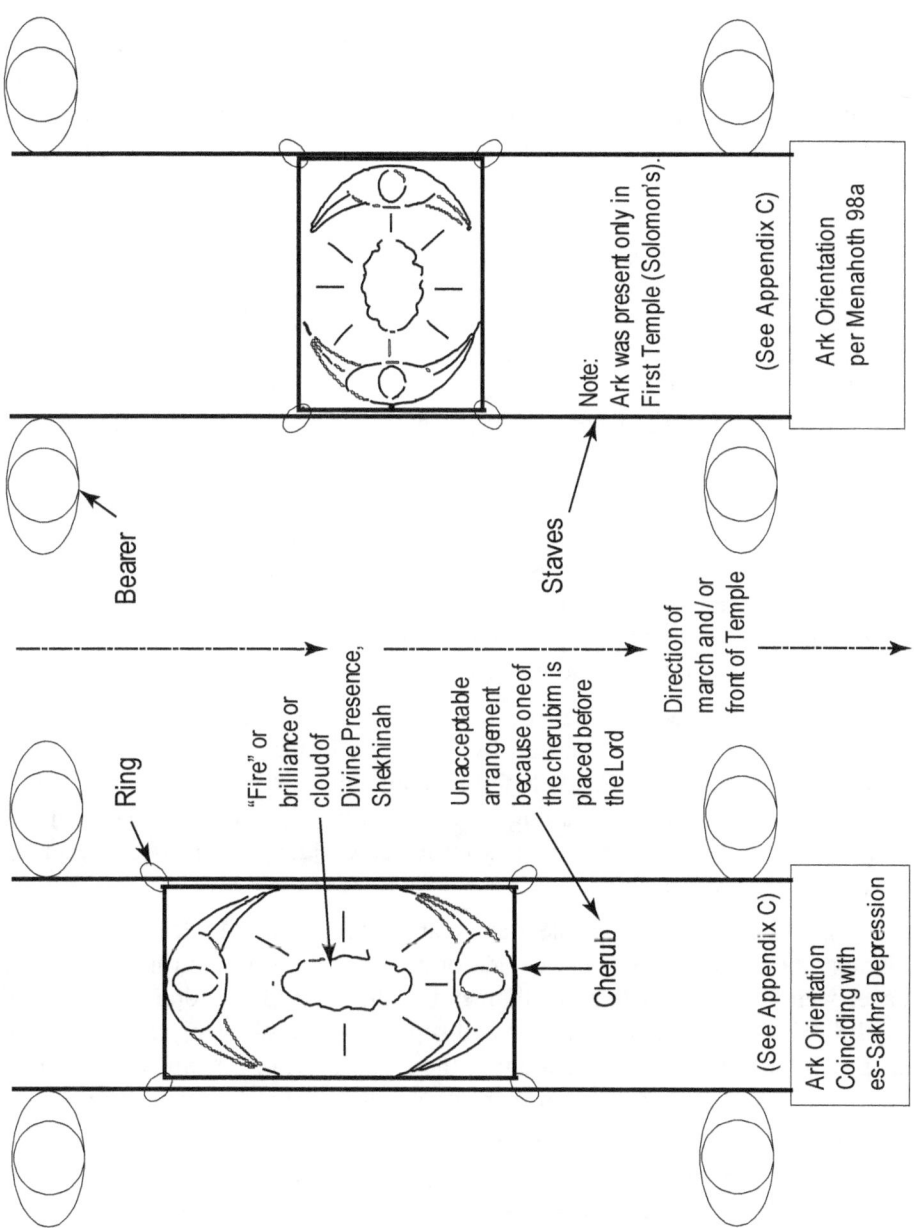

Illus. 2: Comparison of Ark Orientations

It is interesting to note the reason for the Ark's longer axis having been parallel to "the breadth of The House." Examining the diagram, it can be seen that the Lord's Divine Presence was located at the center of the Ark. It would have been forbidden as "profane" for the Divine Presence (*Shekhinah*) to have been "demeaned" by having one of the cherubim standing in front of the Lord, blocking His view, as it were. Moreover, this is a much more architecturally and aesthetically appealing arrangement of these three Holy figures.

Whereas, with the Ark oriented with the longer axis extended across the breadth of the *H'ekhal*, each of the cherubim would be stationed respectfully in attendance as an honored messenger at each side, without committing the "affront" of blocking the Lord's view toward the Holy Place within His House. Similarly, when the Lord's Ark was to be carried or transported by carrying on the staves with this same arrangement, His "view" was not to be interrupted, nor would the Lord be "preceded" by having a cherubim stationed in front of Him.

An interesting "engineering" feature of the arrangement of the staves for carrying the Ark is observed in the way the bearers are positioned relative to each other. Each of the bearers on the rear at each side during the march is at a "safe" distance behind the man in front of him. This distance reduces and actually eliminates the danger of the man at the rear stepping or "tripping' on the heels of the bearer in front of him. Such an accident would likely cause the tragic possibility of The Ark falling to the ground.

We may be assured, however, that the Lord would not tolerate man "rescuing" Himself from such an accident. This is witnessed by precedent in the tragic but supernatural event described in I Samuel 4:4-22. Tragedy befell Hophni and Phinehas, the sons of Eli – as they sought to "rescue" the Ark from falling to the ground. Nevertheless, the design as it is specified greatly reduces a "repeat" of possibility of accidents such as experienced in the tragedy with the "sons of Eli" incident.

Talmud Yoma 72a observes that the staves, about ten cubits (15 ft.) in length, could be moved through the carrying rings, but could not be removed from the rings because the ends of the staves were made larger than the diameter of the rings. Therefore, *Menahoth* 98b says that since the Ark was placed so near the Veil separating the two Holy chambers, the staves "pressed against the curtain and bulged out as the two breasts of a woman." Quoted with this is a verse from the Hebrew Scriptures in Song of Solomon 1:13, "My beloved is unto Me as a bag of myrrh, That lyeth between My breasts."

It must be kept in mind that, since there was NO Ark in the Second Temple, all these details about the Ark's orientation and the staves pertained only to the Tabernacle and to the First Temple. (See Illus. 1: Ark and Staves Behind Veil, Page 8) Nevertheless, again, it is apparent that God chose to demonstrate that He was dealing with mankind *both* as a masculine and as a feminine Presence. As we have seen, He did this with the feminine voice speaking to Moses and the children of Israel. Also, with the staves of the Holy Ark in His Residence in the Holy of Holies, He caused the curtain to "bulge," suggesting a womanly Presence in His Holy chamber. Truly, this circumstance causes us to regard again that verse which says: *"For now we see through a glass, darkly; but then face to face: Now I know in part; but then shall I know even as also I am known."* I Corinthians 13:12

Since very little interest exists in Christian teaching concerning *Shekhinah*, most preachers and Sunday school teachers never seem to talk about the fact that the Divine Presence actually dwelled among the Jews! But, not among the Gentiles! This is difficult for many Christians to swallow. (You mean God loved "them" more than us?! And after what "they" did?!)

Most Christian believers, including myself (until recently), have never even thought much about the Glory of the Temple. Most Jewish worshipers are probably resigned to the fact that the Temple is gone, the *Shekhinah* is gone, and they are now awaiting Messiah. Like the Gentiles, the Jewish people have not been told about this sad, remarkable, and Glorious event. Scholars have known of it for many centuries, but now with the advance of communications technology, clergy and laypersons throughout the world can hear this fascinating story plus some additional facts that emerge as a result of recent archaeological discoveries.

This event has important bearing on Biblical archaeology, Jewish evangelism, and even on the written Gospel of Jesus Christ. Much of the controversy arises because this story reveals certain facts and timing of events that are contrary to some of the "traditional" teaching in those areas.

Many believe that the Glory withdrew "sometime" before the time of Jesus or the Glory departed when "the veil was rent in twain." Others maintain that the Glory departed when Ezekiel "saw" Him withdraw from the First Temple and that He never resided in the Second Temple. But most ministers have never really thought about when or how this spectacular event occurred. As we will demonstrate, these traditional views are at great variance not only with Scripture and each other, but also with recorded history. All three traditional concepts are at variance with recorded details of the Second Temple and, in some ways, even contradict Holy Scripture, including the Gospel of Jesus Christ.

Christian scholars have ignored (?), overlooked (?), or misunderstood (?) the Event, especially since it is recorded by Jewish historians. They are "suspicious" of Jewish historians,...except of course those who recorded *all* the books of our Bible! Some Christian teachers suspect the credibility of the *Talmud* and *Midrash* because they are not Divinely inspired of the Holy Spirit. Of course not! But, that doesn't mean we should ignore such works. It would appear that very little, if any, of our most treasured secular literature was inspired by the Holy Spirit. We regard it as the works of man and separate the wheat from the chaff. – We don't ignore it!

The history, tradition, and "Law" of the *Talmud* and other Judaica have many beautiful "pictures" of Christ that are tragically unseen by some, but have rich blessings for those who have eyes *and heart* to see within these writings.

Christians who are uninformed concerning Jewish Law and tradition not only are missing a lot of rich blessings, but also are missing great opportunities to more fully understand and appreciate the Gospel of Jesus Christ. Jesus was the greatest Jew of all time. Many of His parables and teachings were drawn directly from Jewish tradition, the "Law" and Judaic teaching of that time. Should not we obtain more blessings by learning more about the base from which our Lord teaches us?

Jesus is the "bridge" between Jews and Gentiles as well as the bridge between God and man. Jesus, of course, was crucified for claiming to be that "bridge ." In discussing this story with friends, Jewish and Gentile, I have found that anyone who claims to understand and appreciate both Judaism and Christianity is apt to be misunderstood and condemned by many of both faiths. Paul was such a man.

Most of the Apostolic Fathers (all, save John) died horrible deaths as they tried to "bridge" both faiths. I certainly don't compare myself with any of those saints; however, I have already experienced a degree of "stress" from both sides as I attempt to point out the bridge revealed throughout this story. There are still a few Pharisees and *Sadducees* out there, even in our day, who absolutely close their minds (and hearts) to anything pertaining to the other faith — be it Judaism or Christianity.

Having reached the time of Jesus in reviewing the history of the *Shekhinah* Glory, we can end the suspense and get on with the story. But wait! What does the Bible say about this event?

The only Biblical description of the departure of the Glory from the Temple was given as a vision to the prophet Ezekiel about 591 B.C.E. Ezekiel saw the Glory leave the Temple and go to the Mount of Olives. (Ezekiel Chapters 10 and 11.)

Please keep in mind that Ezekiel was a prophet of the Babylonian captivity and therefore could not have seen the Glory "in person;" besides, Ezekiel describes it as a vision (Ezekiel 11:24). So, did the departure of the Divine Presence occur before or after Ezekiel's vision? Was it a report or a prophecy? Like many others, during my earliest Bible awareness, I had assumed the vision had reported this to Ezekiel and that he was the only man who saw the event. I had also supposed that the Glory just sort of faded away one night while nobody was watching. After all, the Israelites had become sinful and were acting as if the Lord didn't exist (much less that He dwelled in their Holy Temple!). So it was easy for me to assume God would just "pout" (as I would have done) and go out the back, slam the door, and not come back. So, there! (I'd show 'em!)

I had even imagined a little scenario in which I speculated about the shock, dismay, yes, heartbreak! felt by that one unfortunate High Priest the next *Yom Kippur* as he entered the Holy of Holies to plead before the Lord's Presence, offering atonement for Israel's sins, and: "*Oi*! He's gone! The *Shekhinah*...Where is He? Oh, NO! The Lord's Presence has deserted his Holy Abode in His Temple! This is terrible! What will I tell the King? How can I tell the people?"

But I was wrong — just not thinking. Because we know all prophecy in God's Word must be fulfilled. We also know (or should have known) God would not just "sneak out" in a "pouting" farewell. (Not HIS Style!) Also, it is not likely that the brilliant light ("fire") or cloud would depart through the corridors and along the walls of the Temple and over to the Mount of Olives without having been observed by priests, attendants, and guards. This is exactly how Ezekiel described each movement in Chapters 10 and 11.

Thinking back on this now, it seems almost ridiculous to suppose Ezekiel to have been the only person who witnessed the departure of Almighty God from His Earthly dwelling. Almighty God would not just "sneak" out of His Holy House! This Glorious Event had to have been seen by the entire populace, regardless of when it happened. Josephus in fact records that the occasion was "publicly declared" by the Jewish "men of learning." (See Appendix A). Therefore, since Ezekiel was captive in Babylon when he had this vision, he "saw" this as a prophetic vision of a future event. In fact, Ezekiel says *three* times that it was a *vision*.

So, we know Ezekiel's prophecy (God's Word) had to be fulfilled. We know there was no Temple after the Second Temple destruction in 70 C.E. Therefore, there can now be no question that *Shekhinah* departed, was seen "publicly" in fulfillment of Ezekiel's prophecy, and that it *had* to have occurred either when the First Temple was destroyed in 586 B.C.E. or when the Second Temple was destroyed in 70 A. D. Perhaps it was even fulfilled both times; although, we have only the 70 C.E. Event as documented history.

Since Ezekiel was very precise about dates, we know his prophetic vision was given 591 B.C.E., about five years before the First Temple was destroyed in 586 B.C.E. But this does not prove the fulfillment occurred only before the First Temple was destroyed. Plenty of prophecies have been (or will have been) fulfilled more than once, at least partially or "in type."

Since this was a "public" event, did no one record this in some patriarchal document? This event must have made a profound, if not frightful, impression on those who witnessed it. Why haven't we heard about this in churches or synagogues or from Jewish history? – (A *very* interesting question.)

Perhaps no one can answer this "why" question, but we can certainly see what has been recorded about the event and, as far as most of us are concerned, has been lying dormant "within Jewish History" for almost 2,000 years. It has certainly not been hidden — perhaps not even really suppressed — but certainly not "advertised" either. In the next chapter we shall discuss and describe this remarkable event as it actually happened.

2

The Event

Strange "signs" – Shekhinah Departs the Temple – "Sits" atop Mt. of Olives – Pleads with His People to repent – They refuse – He ascends into Heaven from Olivet. – A Master Cover-up by our "Shepherds"

The question regarding "when?" and curiosity concerning the Jewish reaction to the withdrawal of *Shekhinah* persistently came into my mind. For a few years, however, I was never able to locate any book on that subject in Christian, Jewish, or secular libraries. Then finally, in Professor Ernest L. Martin's scholarly and controversial book, *The Original Bible Restored*[1], I came across his brief, though comprehensive, reporting on this event.

There are four ancient documents that report the event, all of which are greatly respected and available. The renowned first century Jewish historian, Josephus, documented much of the story (See Appendix A), but omitted (or was unaware of) some interesting details. Also, the *Midrash* exegesis (a Hebrew Bible commentary — See Appendix B), and the *Babylonian Talmud*[21] (Jewish interpretation of The Law and Jewish tradition) provide a good description of most of the story, but omit some items reported by Josephus. This Holy Event is also reported by that highly regarded Christian church historian, Eusebius[26], so often credited as "the father of ecclesiastical history."

Thus, from the complementing statements of these four documents and supporting Scriptural statements, we can obtain a good accounting as to when *Shekhinah* withdrew and how it happened. Then, with the benefits of Dr. Kaufman's discovery of the Temple site and with some rudimentary surveying techniques, some interesting archaeological observations surfaced. These subjects are discussed in Chapter 4. (We should remember here at this same time, and indeed from 30 C.E. until 70 C.E., many other strange "signs" were reported by Josephus and by the *Talmud*. These events are discussed in Chapter 7.) The Jewish *Talmud* mentions the withdrawal, but does not provide as much detail as the other sources. The *Talmud* also takes what is considered a more "traditional" view, as we shall point out later.

Summarizing collectively and chronologically from Josephus, the *Talmud*, and the *Midrash*, the *Shekhinah* withdrawal occurred as follows:

1. About 3 A.M. on the 8th day of *Nisan* (approximately April), 66 C.E., as several (perhaps twenty or so) priests were preparing, spiritually and physically, for the Passover Feast, the Divine Presence came out from His position inside the Holy of Holies and went into the Holy Place and then to the threshold of the Temple. (Illus. 15: Plan of Second Temple (by Dr. A.S. Kaufman), Page 148.

2. Next, He moved back again into the Holy of Holies as if to bid farewell and to have just one last look before leaving.

3. Next, He passed over the Altar of Sacrifice to the East Gate, all within the space of about half an hour. (Illus. 16: Isometric View of 2nd Temple), Page 149

4. From the gateway He went to the roof of the Temple and remained until the Feast of Pentecost. (*Shavuot*)

5. On Pentecost (approximately June) He went back into the Temple just once more, weeping and speaking a saddened farewell, caressing His "Precious Vessel." Returning to "kiss" the walls and the Altar, He says: *"Good-bye, My Temple. Good-bye, My Precious Vessel. Good-bye!"*

6. From the Temple, the Divine Presence moved through the East Gate and across the Kidron Valley, weeping and calling out to the "city" below (with many voices), *"Let us remove hence."*

7. The Divine Presence next arrived at the summit of the Mount of Olives and remained for 3½ years, quoting from Scripture and pleading to the Israelites (as "naughty" children) to repent and "return to the Lord." But they would not.

8. Finally, toward the end of the year (approximately December), 69 C.E., perhaps ironically during *Chanukah* (or *Hanukkah*), the Festival of Lights, the Divine "Light" ascended into Heaven from the summit of the Mount of Olives saying: *"I will go back to My Place."* (Hosea 5:15)

References:

Josephus: Wars, 6.5.3/290 – 3000

Midrash Eichah, Lamentations, Part 25 (Proems)

Talmud, Tractate Rosh Hashanah 31a.

Eusebius: "The Proof of the Gospel" — Book VI, Chapter 18/288,

(Also see Appendix A and Appendix B.)

Just a few months later, spring 70 C.E., the Roman Army under Titus began that final siege of Jerusalem[5], which ended with destruction of the Temple and "scattering" of the Jewish people to "the four corners of the earth." (Isaiah 11:12)

Jewish tradition seems at first not to agree as to disposition of *Shekhinah*. *Talmud Rosh Hashanah* 31a says that after He departed the Mount of Olives, the *Shekhinah* "tarried for Israel in the wilderness six months in the hopes they would repent," but a lament is given over the fact they did not repent. Beloved first century Rabbi Yohanan ben Zakkai made this remark. Professor Asher Kaufman has stated in his Foreword that other Jewish opinions exist concerning the present location of Israel's *Shekhinah*.

Another source rationalizes, from *Midrash Rabbah* Exodus 23:5, that *Shekhinah* accompanied Israel into exile because He said: "...*I cannot abandon them.*" Still another source[35] proclaims, quite logically, that the Temple could never be destroyed so long as *Shekhinah* dwelled in it. *Midrash* here refers to Leviticus 26:44 to justify this comment. This source agrees, however, that the Divine Presence returned "to His original abode in Heaven" after withdrawing from the Temple and Jerusalem.

Reference 35, referring to several ancient Judaic texts, states: "...there are also authorities who maintain that the *Shekhinah* never left the Western Wall, as it is said: *Behold, He standeth behind our wall.*" (From the Song of Songs, or Song of Solomon 2:9) In his Foreword for this book, Prof. Kaufman has pointed to the Western Wall of the Temple as a location of *Shekhinah*. That same disposition is given in *Midrash Rabbah* Exodus 2:1 – 2. Another Rabbi in that same paragraph agrees that *Shekhinah* is now in Heaven since the Temple was destroyed. *Midrash Rabbah* Lamentations 1:54. states that *Shekhinah* accompanied Israel to exile in Greece.

Here, we must remind ourselves that God is Omnipresent. — He can be *anywhere* and/or *everywhere* at *any* moment. And, Jewish tradition certainly would emphatically agree with that principle. So, suffice it to say, *Talmud* and *Midrash* both agree that *Shekhinah* returned to "*His Place.*" We call attention also to the fact that *nobody* has reported having seen the Divine Fire or Cloud at *any* of these places since the Event reported between 66 – 70 C.E. Not at the Western Wall, not in Greece, not "in the wilderness."

It therefore appears that God's Divine Presence – *Shekhinah* – has, in fact, gone back to His Place. We can rely, nevertheless, on the prophecy from Ezekiel 43:1 – 7, that the Lord's *Shekhinah* surely *will* return to His Holy House "*on that day.*" And, we can also be certain that *this* prophecy refers *only* to His Third Temple. Our confidence in that declaration comes from the Word of God from Verse 7:

> "*...where I will dwell in the midst of the children of Israel for ever, and My Holy Name, shall the house of Israel no more defile...*"

It is certain that His Third and last Temple will never again be desecrated by *any* party, whatever! But that isn't the end of this story. As a result of modern archaeological discoveries, some interesting facts emerge.

For many centuries it was believed that the site of the Temple was beneath The Dome of the Rock, No. 10 on Illus. 3: Old City of Jerusalem and Mt. of Olives, Page 19. This created a difficult situation, because that mosque is the third most holy shrine for the religion of Islam (Muslim faith).

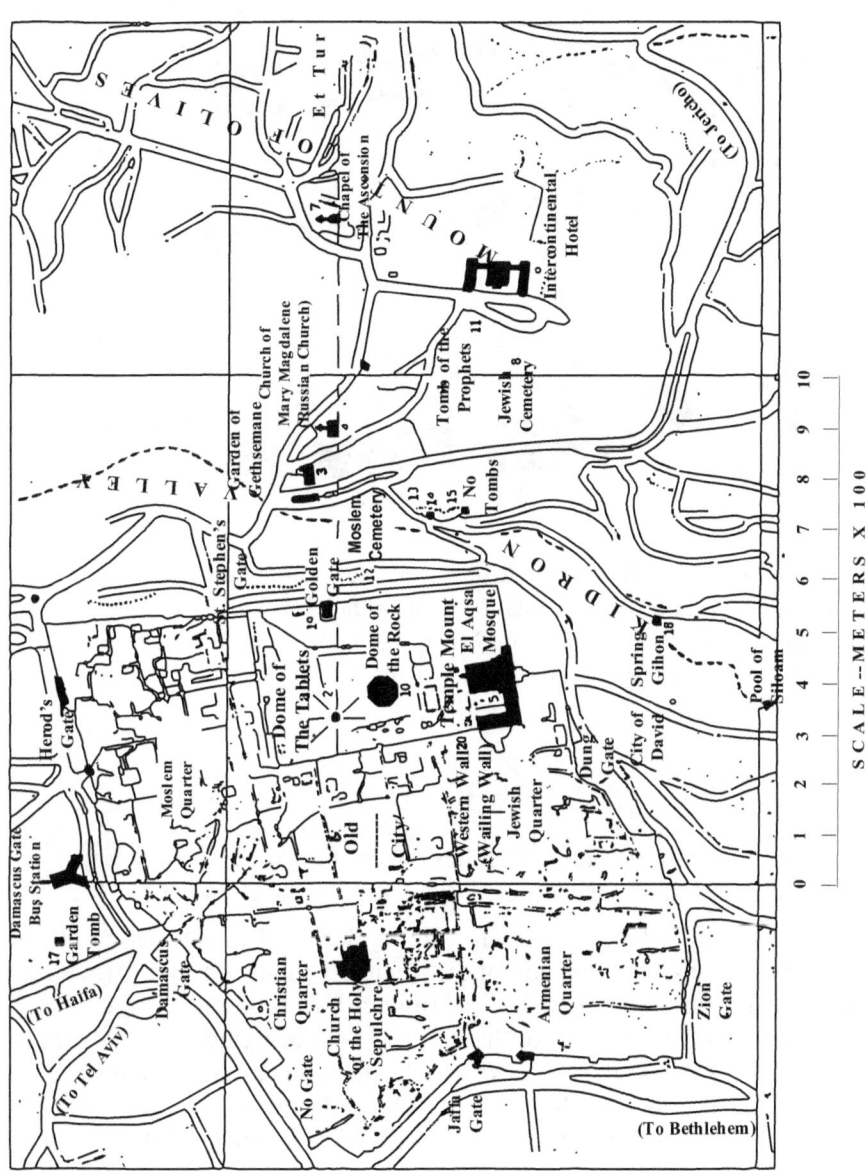

Illus. 3: Old City of Jerusalem and Mt. of Olives

Illus. 4: Threshingfloor

Then, in 1978, Dr. Asher Kaufman[7] discovered the Foundation Stone of the Temple, the bedrock on which the Ark of the Covenant rested in the Holy of Holies, the threshingfloor of Araunah (Ornan) the Jebusite. (II Samuel 24:21 – 25) The Temple site is now determined to be about 100 meters northwest of The Dome of the Rock. (See Photo Illus. 5: Dome of the Tablets, Page 21)

The Threshingfloor

The Foundation Stone in the Holy of Holies, where the Ark of the Covenant rested in the Temple. This flat, level limestone bedrock is sheltered by The Dome of the Tablets.

Dr. Kaufman has shown that the East Gate of the Second Temple was *exactly* due east of "The Dome of the Tablets," the position of the Temple Foundation Stone. (See Illus. 4, page 20. Also see Illus. 15: Plan of Second Temple (by Dr. A.S. Kaufman), Page 148.) The Dome of the Tablets, (or sometimes "Dome of the Spirits") has been plotted on Illus. 3: Old City of Jerusalem and Mt. of Olives, Page 19. Now, refer to the map and watch what happens. A straight line is extended from The Dome of the Tablets directly eastward to the summit of the Mount of Olives. This line indicates the reported farewell route of the *Shekhinah* Glory according to Ezekiel, the *Talmud*, and the *Midrash*, also as supported by the Temple orientation determined by Dr. Kaufman.

The Dome of the Tablets

Recently identified location of the Holy of Holies in the First Temple and in the Second Temple — identified by Dr. Asher Kaufman, 1978 (See Reference 7.)

Illus. 5: Dome of the Tablets

Precisely at the intersection of the extended line at the Mount of Olives Summit is The Chapel of The Ascension (No. 7 on Illus. 3: Old City of Jerusalem and Mt. of Olives, Page 19). Most of the local Jerusalem guides casually point to this site saying: "According to tradition, that is the place from which Jesus ascended into Heaven." But notice, the guides never mention that the *Shekhinah* Glory also ascended to Heaven from this summit. (They haven't heard this story yet!) Could both have ascended from the same location?

The line, thus oriented and extended from "The Dome of the Tablets," continues across the summit of the Mount of Olives and passes through the Arab village, *Et Tur* (The Mountain). Now, if this analysis is correct, and if you stood at The Chapel of The Ascension or if you walked through the village of *Et Tur* along the line shown on Illus. 3: Old City of Jerusalem and Mt. of Olives, Page 19, you might be treading on Holy Ground; for this is the area from which the Lord Jesus and *Shekhinah* both ascended into Heaven.

Well, we don't really know the exact spot location for either Ascension, but we can be almost certain it was along the line shown. Why? We have Scriptural confirmation of this because such a route is outlined in Ezekiel's prophecy of the withdrawal. Chapters 10 and 11 of Ezekiel's narration indicate: *"from the altar (of incense) to the threshold"* and *"from the threshold to the gate."* The Prophet continues with the departure route in Ezekiel 11:23, *"And the glory of the Lord went up from the midst of the city, and stood upon the mountain which is on the east side of the city."* — The "mountain" being the Mount of Olives, east of the Temple.

A path so described passes directly along the center-line of the Temple, or directly eastward, continues to the summit of the Mount of Olives, and passes through The Chapel of The Ascension (See Illus. 3: Old City of Jerusalem and Mt. of Olives, Page 19, Illus. 21: Detail of the 2nd Temple, Page 154, and Illus. 22: The Sanctuary of the 2nd Temple, Page 155.). The place of the Ascension of Jesus and for the Ascension of *Shekhinah* is most likely the same point from which Jesus wept over Jerusalem (Matthew 23:37) and the same point where Messiah's feet will stand (again) on that Great Day when He returns in Power and Glory. *"And His feet shall stand in that day upon the Mount of Olives..."* (Zechariah 14:4)

Now, after almost 2,000 years, we are able to more accurately locate this "Holy Ground," the last earthly position of our Lord and our God. That position is somewhere along this line, at most only a few meters from the "traditional" site of Jesus' Ascension. We cannot prove this is the location, but...the probability is overwhelming!

So, it is possible for each of us to climb to the summit of the Mount of Olives today and, if elevated sufficiently for an unobstructed view of The Temple Mount, to align oneself due east of The Dome of the Tablets with the aid of a compass. Once aligned, you would probably be standing at or very near the point where those Precious Feet will stand on that Great Day.

But, if you are at Jerusalem on that Great Day, be sure you don't stand at that spot or anywhere along the line shown. Because the prophet Zechariah says:

> *"...and the Mount of Olives shall cleave in the midst thereof toward the east and toward the west, and there shall be a great valley; and half of the mountain shall move toward the north and half of it toward the south." From Zechariah 14:4*

With access to the geologic fault line detail of Mt. *Olivet* and the Kidron Valley, it would be interesting to compare such data with the east-west line plotted on Illus. 3: Old City of Jerusalem and Mt. of Olives, Page 19 as the apparent departure route of the Divine Presence. (More about this in Chapter 4.)

There are some interesting thoughts we should now consider. From the timing involved, considering the Ascension of Jesus in 30 C.E. and Ascension of the Glory of the Lord in 69 C.E., it is evident that the Jews of the first century knew this point on the *Olivet* Summit was the same point from which followers of Jesus had claimed the risen Savior had ascended into Heaven in 30 C.E. These same disciples could not have preselected that spot. But lo-and-behold, about forty years later, in 69 C.E., the Divine Presence apparently ascended from that very same point! And everyone has kept pretty quiet about that fact all these years.

It is important, also, for us to remember this departure was not a secretive movement. The Lord didn't just "sneak" away, sulking into the night! He went, displaying His Glory in full public view, beginning with a large group of priests in the Temple that first night. Then, in even more public "style," He remained on the Mount of Olives for three and one-half years. He must have been seen and, yes, even heard by literally thousands of Jews, Christians, and Romans.

First century Jewish historian, Flavius Josephus recorded that this departure of the Glory of the Lord from the Temple was a publicly acknowledged event. It was "publicly declared" by the Temple priesthood ("men of learning") as described from Appendix A:

> *"But the men of learning understood it, that the security of their Holy House was dissolved of its own accord, and that the gate was opened for the advantage of their enemies. So these publicly declared, that the signal forshewed the desolation that was coming upon them."*

It was certainly not an occasion that they could keep secret; although, both our Jewish and our Christian "men of learning" have kept this secret for almost two millennia. – Surely, it can be said that to ignore history is folly, but to distort history is *criminal!*

At least two Biblical scholars contacted concerning the events reported in this book acknowledge that the Event is in fact authentic. Nevertheless, they will not speak or write of any acknowledgment concerning these things. They of course are understandably fearful of persecution and rejection by their peers. This calculated suppression, both by Rabbis *and* by Christian scholars, by withholding, denying or ignoring the reporting of this Event is certainly a Master Coverup of the so-called "Church Age."

A most appropriate quote is due here to describe the guilt attached to such silence – both from Christian scholars and from Jewish scholars:

> *"Truth is not only violated by falsehood; it may be outraged by silence."* – Henri Frederick Amiel[41], 1821-1881, Swiss writer

With some help from the late Professor Martin, just try to appreciate now the predicament of the Jewish people at the time of the Lord's Withdrawal from the Holy Temple. While in the *Sinai* wilderness they knew that when the "fire" moved from the Tabernacle, they were to move also (Exodus 40:36 – 38). So, here they had just recently completed the Temple (64 C.E.) and now the Glory moves out! They couldn't just move the Temple! – *"But, what shall we do?! – The Lord commanded us to move out when He moved His great fire or cloud. – What can we do?"*

To the serious-minded, this meant that God was abandoning His abode in Jerusalem and leaving it behind. He even had left the gate open, leaving the Temple as a "gift" to whomever wished to have it. The Temple was now just another building without a tenant — no more sacred than any other building. Meanwhile, as all of this is happening, the Romans are marshaling legions for that final brutal siege, which was to result in unspeakable cruelties on both sides. So, is it any wonder this story has been shunned for all these years? This is the kind of story where, especially in those times, it was customary to kill the messenger! (I pray to be spared.)

All of these events must have been most puzzling, especially to the Jews: "Could that young Rabbi, who was put to death, actually have been the Son of God? Now Jerusalem and the Temple are destroyed. Are we abandoned? Our troubles are just beginning! We don't have time to argue or discuss 'signs' — we must survive!"

And survive they did — Jews and Christians. The wisest Jews and Christians saw the departure of the Divine Presence from their midst as a signal from God that they should "move out of the camp." (Exodus 40:36–38). Actually, many of the "wisest" of Christians fled even a few years earlier after James, the "half"-brother of Jesus, was martyred by the *Sanhedrinists* in 62 C.E. – These wisest, therefore, "scattered" themselves away from Roman Judea where hundreds of thousands of Judeans, Jews and Christians (it mattered naught to the legions), would, in a few more months, be slaughtered without restraint.

Professor Martin explained that this warning was, to a large measure, responsible for preserving Christianity and Judaism for their coming ordeals through the Church Age. Since the Romans didn't discriminate between Jews and Christians in the post-siege slaughter of 70 C.E., those Judeans who recognized this event as a warning "got out of camp" before the slaughter. And, since they were evidently "serious" believers, they were presumably selected by God to preserve both faiths in the ages to come.

Satan, of course, would have destroyed both faiths at a single stroke (by the hand of Titus) but for the escape of these blessed "fruit," who were "harvested" via God's own warning. (See commentary Note **9** on *Midrash Eichah* Narrative, Appendix B.)

Another thought we must develop involves the relationship of Jesus to the Temple. It is obvious, from Matthew 23:21 and from the *Midrash* and Josephus, that the *Shekhinah* Glory dwelt in the Holy of Holies of the Second Temple during the time of Jesus. Please consider for a moment that the New Testament records about four or five occasions when Jesus entered the Temple. Knowing the Divine Presence resided in the Temple must have been a great wonder to the disciples, especially to Peter, James, and John, after having seen Jesus transformed bodily and illuminated by the Glory of God, The Father, at the Transfiguration; yet, they later were with Jesus when He entered the outer courts of the Temple where His Father's Presence also dwelt in the Holy of Holies! (Matthew 17:1 – 5, 23:21).

Also, can we just imagine for a moment the indignation of the Jews at the claims of this man, Jesus of Nazareth? The Divine Presence (the Father) dwelled within the Holy of Holies at that time; and here is this "man" who claims, "I and my Father are one." (John 10:30) Jews had then, and still have today, no concept of more than one "God" although, at times, they called Him "*Elohim*" — indeed, a plural name. (Or how about, "Let *us* remove hence"?)

Small wonder that unbelievers and legalists called Jesus a blasphemer. How could this "man" be God, while everyone knew God was in the Holy of Holies? In fact, God is everywhere! – Again! – How could this "man" be God? – He was not even a priest! – And, descended only from Galilean peasant stock. – A carpenter's son! – From Nazareth – of all places! – C'mon!

Christians have been smug in judging the Jewish people for missing/rejecting their Messiah. Awareness of some of the things discussed here could help us to be more understanding. How could this humble son of a carpenter be God? — Could he be that same

God who could strike a man dead for coming uninvited into His Presence, into the Holy of Holies? If you had been a Judean at that time, what would *you* have thought?

It just might be appropriate to think about this for a while next time we try to explain the Holy Trinity – especially to a Jewish person. Even the Disciples didn't understand the concept of The Trinity, until after Pentecost 30 C.E., at the earliest. Perhaps some did not even understand until after *Chanukah* 69 C.E. (More about this in Chapters 6 and 11.)

3

Impressions

Why has this Event not been reported to Jewish and Christian worshipers? – Possible reasons why Rabbis are silent – Christian "Shepherds" also silent – Messages for Jews and Christians from this Holy Event

The withdrawal of *Shekhinah* from the Temple may qualify as the most important Biblical event since Pentecost. It is of importance, if for no other reason, because it is a well documented fulfillment of Ezekiel's prophecy.

After learning of this event (1900 years late), one must ask: "Why aren't Bible believers informed about this story? Why has this story been ignored for nearly 2,000 years, even though the event has been thoroughly documented by at least four respected and authoritative historical sources during that same length of time?"

There are no simple answers to these questions. Many people do not *want* to hear of this event because they do not want it to be true! They do not *want* to know that God continued to show compassion, patience, and mercy toward the Jews forty years after The Crucifixion. "After what they did, how could He show mercy?" Judge not lest ye be judged!

Most modern Christians have been misled while being brought up on what Vendyl Jones describes[4] as "Replacement Theology" — i.e., "God is finished with the Jews. The Old Testament is just Jewish history. We need not concern ourselves with all those Jewish Laws and customs, etc. We (Christians) are His new and faithful Chosen People, etc., etc."

Such thinking might have originated during the Crusades. Nevertheless, many Christians today (especially since World War II) truly love God's Chosen People; but, unfortunately, many are just not interested in Judaism, Jewish history, tradition, archaeology, etc., unless it pertains directly to Jesus.

If we really study our Bibles, we will come to realize that some knowledge of Judaism is important to all Christians, because much of the symbolism in Jewish rites, feasts, traditions, etc., pertains to Messiah. Much of the Old Testament Law (*Torah*), all of the Feasts of Jehovah, and most prophecy is, of course, Christ-centered and is therefore important to all Christians and should not be ignored.

Many modern Jewish people have very weak hopes concerning their Messiah. (Just as many professed Christians do not believe Jesus is really going to come back to this earth.) Besides, the departure of the Lord's Presence from their midst just before desolation came upon them was just not a very positive occasion for the Jewish people. One can easily understand why they might not wish to call attention to the event — even if they knew about it.

Even more understandable is the Jewish resistance to anything "Christian." The *Shekhinah* Event was a Jewish event. How can we say it related to Christianity? Jewish scholars were well aware this happened after The Crucifixion and that it could be interpreted as a judgment against them. They were also aware of the obvious implications of the fact that Jesus and *Shekhinah* both ascended from *Olivet* summit. Traditional Jews do not want to hear this! Neither do the Jews want Christians to throw this in their faces to remind them of why it happened. So, they have not told this story.

Christian objection to the story is more complex and more difficult to understand. History provides partial explanation in the years following the shame of the Crusades. Pope Gregory IX decreed in 1239 that all copies of *Talmud* be seized and burned after denouncing *Talmud* as a distortion and blasphemy of the Bible. Other Jewish writings were attacked as well.

The "Church" — Catholic and Protestant — although perhaps restrained only short of "book-burning," has followed Gregory's example throughout Christianity ever since that time. Knowing these things, it is easier to understand the traditional suspicion against any "religious" information labeled as "extra-Biblical." Further, Christians then paradoxically ignore *any* Jewish information written after The Crucifixion. Still, they surely revere highly the New Testament, which definitely was written by Jews after The Crucifixion.

At least three different traditional versions of the *Shekhinah* departure have been taught within Christianity, because few, apparently, are willing to accept what Jewish historians (and Scripture!) have related. Neither are any of these groups willing to agree with any of the others, primarily because all of these theories are merely based on opinion. None of them has even one shred of evidence as a basis. But, as we know, tradition is a powerful force and is not easily set aside or overcome.

- The most popular conservative/fundamentalist/evangelical view has been that Ezekiel "saw" the Glory withdraw before the First Temple was destroyed by the Babylonians. They add that since the Lord was so displeased with the decadence of the Jews, He never returned His Divine Presence to reside in the Second Temple. Conservatives' doubts are further nourished by absence of Scripture describing a return of the Glory to the Second Temple, such as was given when the Glory entered the First Temple, per I Kings 8:10, when "...*the cloud filled the House of the Lord.*" Such critics therefore reason that since the first occupation by the Glory was described in Scripture, then if there was a second arrival, it also would be described in Scripture. Ignoring that Scripture (Zechariah 1:16) says He did reside, they base their argument on a claim that no known record exists. They assume, therefore, He did not return. This group further insists that God would never have "defiled" Himself by residing in "Herod's" Temple and that Jesus called it "a den of thieves."

- Liberal Christianity just never thought much about this. They appear to assume the *Shekhinah* maybe just sort of "drifted away" – and/or: "we need not concern ourselves about what is evidently merely Jewish history."
- Middle-of-the-road Christianity seems to hold to the belief that the Glory of the Lord left the Temple when "*the veil was rent in twain*" or takes the same views as stated for liberal Christianity.

There may be even a few more "theories" bouncing around out there. However, all three of these groups have formulated these concepts from their own imaginations, based on assumptions, without any attention to historical accounts, eyewitness descriptions, or literal statements from Scripture. Since this series is, even as labeled by its title, building toward the eventuality of Israel's Third Temple, we should point out that at least a few Christian scholars insist upon referring to the remodeled construction of Zerubbabel's Second Temple by King Herod as "The Third Temple." We must therefore, in order to avoid potential of confusion spawned from such scholars, make clear that we are NOT identifying *that* Temple that was remodeled by King Herod as "The Third Temple." Some of these scholars – so-called "Amillennialists" – are of the eschatological position that ALL of the prophetic Events preceding Jesus' Return already occurred at The Cross! – In that position, perhaps they must identify Herod's remodeled version as their "Third Temple." They may be "trapped" into that stance because Ezekiel Chapters 40 – 44 told of a Temple that was going to be for Messiah in His Kingdom.

There may be other scholars who call Herod's version a "Third Temple" just because it was in fact greatly more beautiful and magnificent than the Second Temple built during the reign of King Zerubbabel.

At present there are Jewish groups in Israel looking forward to "someday" building the "Third Temple." Some of such extremely zealous and religious groups are undeterred by the presence of a mosque adjacent to the Temple. Since these are Jewish groups, they are forgetting and/or do not regard the prophecy of the "abomination" of that Temple by the "man of sin" that is set to take place "in the midst of the week." (Daniel 9:27) Some Rabbis of course have taught that the "abomination" event has already occurred. Moreover, as Jews, they are unaware or are ignoring the "great earthquake" prophecy of Revelation 16:16 – 20:

"And he gathered them together into a place called in the Hebrew tongue Armageddon.

> *And the seventh angel poured out his vial into the air; and there came a great voice out of the temple of heaven, from the throne, saying, It is done.*
>
> *And there were voices, and thunders, and lightnings; and there was a **great earthquake**, such as was not since men were upon the earth, so mighty an earthquake, and so great.*
>
> *And the great city was divided into three parts, and the cities of the nations fell: and great Babylon came in remembrance before God, to give unto her the cup of the wine of the fierceness of his wrath.*
>
> *And every island fled away, and the mountains were not found.*
>
> *And there fell upon men a great hail out of heaven, every stone about the weight of a talent: and men blasphemed God because of the plague of the hail; for the plague thereof was exceeding great."*

From this we can see there will not be a wall left standing when Messiah arrives. If there is a *next* Temple, it will have a very brief time upon Earth. First, having been defiled by Antichrist, it will be no longer fit to accommodate the Returning King of Kings. Further, after the "great earthquake," it will likely not be left standing.

Especially for those reasons stated, in this work we are considering the "Third Temple" to be that Temple which will be rebuilt on its Divinely and genuinely appointed position on the Temple Mount and will be Sanctified and occupied by Messiah – Jesus! – It will be built atop the very *same* foundations of the First (Solomon's) and Second Temple. It is unreasonable to expect that it will be built by the Jewish Rabbinate before Messiah arrives; simply because Jesus will NOT occupy or honor a Temple that has been defiled by Antichrist.

Therefore, it is much more likely that it *may* be built *"speedily"* (supernaturally) by Messiah when He arrives! – MUCH more about these "alternatives" will be discussed in Parts IV and V. – Even so – *"For now we see through a glass, darkly;..."*

Scholars of Christian theology then, have virtually ignored the *Talmud* and *Midrash* and have formulated three completely different versions of the *Shekhinah* Withdrawal. All three versions are based on assumptions; none agrees in any way with any other version and none is supported by literal Scripture or by recorded history. The documented Jewish version is supported by both of these. It was written by "Jews" and the Jewish story says the Christian theologians are mistaken. Some Christians just don't want to hear this.

In summary, we see that Jews don't want to hear (even from Jewish historians) a story that says the Lord "scolded" them because they failed to recognize their Messiah. Christians don't want to hear a story (especially from Jewish historians) that says their Christian version is totally in error. Many conservative Christians are further disturbed by a story that says God (and Jesus) actually forgave the Jews, remaining in their Temple *after* The Crucifixion!

Both groups are, therefore, understandably embarrassed and have withheld and/or suppressed information about this beautiful and Holy Event from the grassroots laity of their "flocks." In modern times this might be called a "cover-up," but I do not believe modern Jewish or Christian scholars are intentionally suppressing this story. More likely it is that they have been hearing their own "traditional" versions for so many centuries that any "new" information just cannot penetrate that traditional prejudice.

This human appetite for tradition is just one of several manifestations of man's resistance to "change," which must always accompany acceptance of Truth. This attitude and tendency probably has been with us since man first walked this planet. Human adherence to traditional concepts is a very powerful and emotional trait. It must be respected even when we assail it in order to let truth prevail.

The renowned Roman poet of the first century, Ovid, has said:

"Nothing is stronger than custom (i.e., tradition)."

Tradition is still at least as strong as it was in Ovid's time; however, we moderns have much more accumulated information to evaluate in our quest for TRUTH than did those of earlier societies. The data presented in this work has not really been "hidden." We just haven't been looking for the truth. Instead, we have been content to take the easier course by "sticking" with the traditional Bible stories.

I realize I am getting into a perilous situation by challenging "Bible stories." However, I am challenging them on the foundation of what Scripture actually says, instead of what everybody has been telling us it says. Moreover, we shall present historical and physical (archaeological) evidence that agrees with Scripture, whereas the traditional stories cannot be supported either by Scripture or by the physical evidence. As you read this account, we pray that you will see what Brother Ovid failed to see — that Scripture and truth are stronger than tradition or custom. Our Lord wants us *never* to settle for less than the Truth.

Apparently the Lord just wasn't ready for us to know all of these things before now — (because we weren't ready!). But, now...who knows? Could it be that now He is preparing "Believers" among His people for His imminent arrival at the summit of the Mount of Olives?

"And in that day His feet will stand on the Mount of Olives..." Zechariah 14:4

"...they will look upon Me whom they have pierced and they will mourn for Him, as one mourns for an only son..." Zechariah 12:10

"And one will say to Him, 'What are these wounds in your hands?' Then He will say, 'Those with which I was wounded in the house of my friends.'" Zechariah 13:6

(Above verses quoted from NASB.)

Some skeptics and critics will say, "Well, this is all very interesting, but how do we know it's true?" Indeed, this is not just another "Indiana Jones" story. (But it would certainly be terrific for a movie!) My favorite answer to this criticism is provided by the Rabbis of the first and second century in the *Midrash* texts. These men were writing a commentary on the Book of Lamentations. Their lament was certainly appropriate in light of the fulfillment of Israel's tragic destiny as foretold by many of their prophets. (Illus. 25: Checklist for Locales of The Crucifixion is presented below, Page 253.) It is evident that the Rabbis recognized the tragedy of this event, not only for an unrepentant Israel, but also in the pathos seen and heard in the Lord's movements and in His voice(s).

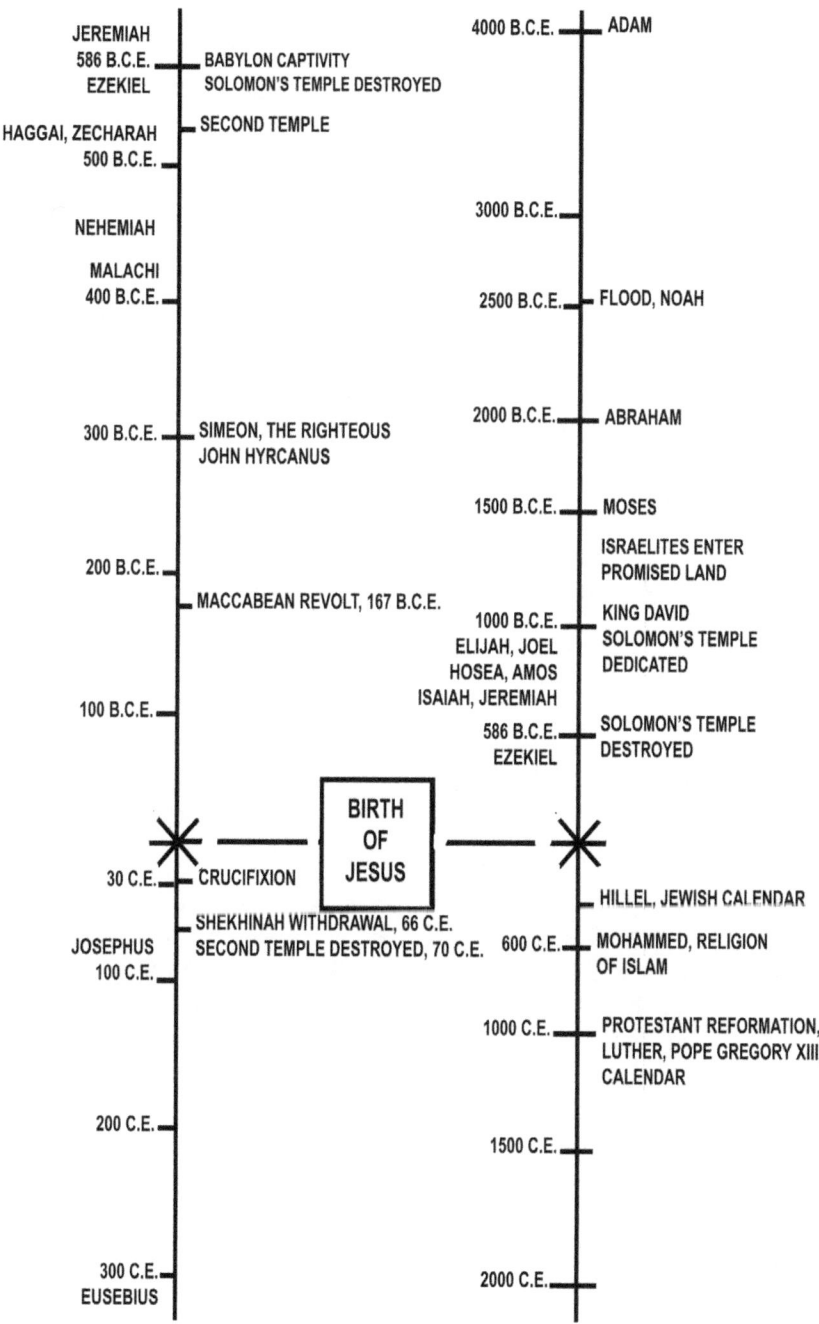

Illus. 6: Chronology of Principal Events in This Work

Part II – Examining the Departure Event

4

Archaeological Comments

Topography and Geometry of Temple Mount and Mt. of Olives – Astronomical and Architectural precision rules design of the temple – Red Heifer Laws demand that precision – The Veil – Significance in details of the Holy House and the Court – A Bulldozer "finds" the Temple!

As a somewhat seasoned engineer, Bible student, eschatology student, and Biblical archaeology "enthusiast," I was immediately inspired upon first reading of Dr. Kaufman's discovery of the Temple site.[7] Having recently been intrigued by Ezekiel's prophecy concerning the departure of the *Shekhinah* Glory, I plotted a line on my Jerusalem tourist map to see just where a line, passing due east from the Dome of the Tablets, would intersect at the summit of the Mount of Olives. I was excited, although not surprised, when this extended line passed straight through The Chapel of The Ascension at the summit of the Mount of Olives. Notably, however, we must surely be impressed by the fact that — after two millennia — this "traditional" position for Jesus' Ascension has remained intact.

Even so, a perplexing thought persistently entered my mind: "When, where, how, and what ever happened to the *Shekhinah* Glory?" The answers to those questions (although few persons know of it) are of course a matter of record as we have already discussed. But, there is much more — and the material and thoughts developed are of such detail that it was considered better to present these detailed discussions separately from the main story.

Additionally, there was the consideration that too much detail would dilute the main story — which, I believe, urgently needs to be heard by "the man on the street."

The quest for answers began first with The Holy Bible (and a concordance) and next, the library, for some searching through *Encyclopedia Judaica and The Universal Jewish Encyclopedia*, as well as the *Talmud* and other Judaica. Having become interested in the traditions of Jewish rites (weddings, purification, feasts, etc.), I also took note of anything along that line, especially the purification rites of the Red Heifer. This interest was stirred initially by reading about Reverend Vendyl Jones' search for the urn containing the Red Heifer ashes.

Meanwhile, for reasons known only to God, I finally decided to discipline myself to read a book[1] on entirely different subjects, which I had received months earlier as a gift from an evangelical scholar. My quest regarding the *Shekhinah* Glory then received a "quantum jump." Professor Martin opened the way for this whole story to fit together by revealing the documentation of the departure of the Glory of the Lord from the Second Temple. Here, we are presenting the details relating to Biblical archaeology, because this information provides important background to the overall discussion of the event.

Assumptions

The analysis made here concerning the line of travel for the departure of the Divine Presence from the Temple is based on the following assumptions. However, presented later in this discussion are some arguments regarding these assumptions and possible conclusions from the analysis. I hope that scholars will have a "field-day" in criticism of this discussion, although, I don't intend any conceit by flattering myself with such an expectation. I sincerely hope and pray that such scholars will improve the analysis of this unheralded but historic event. The assumptions are:

1. Facts based on Biblical references used in this analysis are reliable as the infallible Word of God.
2. The records provided by Flavius Josephus, the *Midrash*, and *Talmud* are reliable. (See Appendices A, B, and C.)
3. The locations of the Foundation Stone and the orientation of the Second Temple as discovered by Dr. Asher Kaufman are accurate.
4. The Divine Presence moved along a straight line extending from the Foundation Stone, along the center axis of the Temple, through the east gate of the Temple, and on to the summit of the Mount of Olives. (See Illus. 15: Plan of Second Temple (by Dr. A.S. Kaufman), Page 148, and Illus. 20: Jerusalem as it Appeared in 70 C.E.), Page 153
5. The surveyed map locations of the Dome of the Tablets and The Chapel of The Ascension are accurate.

The Open Gate

A remarkable event occurred during the few hours prior to actual departure of *Shekhinah* from the Temple. The description by Josephus[2] of the mysterious opening of the east Temple gate (Illus. 16: Isometric View of 2nd Temple, Page 149) has interesting areas for archaeological investigation as well as theological interest.

Josephus (Appendix A) explains: "at the sixth hour of the night" (about midnight) this gate "was seen to open of its own accord." He expresses a certain amount of wonder at this by describing, in some detail, the gate hinge structure and floor mounting and that it "had been with difficulty shut by twenty men." One of my friends, upon first hearing of this, immediately remarked, "Just like He rolled away the stone." (Read more about the miracle of this gate in Chapter 7.)

It would seem that theological interest could be addressed from some archaeological (and engineering) fact-finding. Specifically, it would be interesting to find:

a. Detailed sketches of this "brass" gate. Was it ornate? What figures or decor were present? What of its construction, thickness, dimensions, etc.? Such information should be stimulating to architectural, engineering and archaeological minds; especially with respect to this incident.

b. The description: "...rested upon a basis armed with iron, and had bolts fastened very deep into the firm floor, which was there made of one entire stone..." invites at least one archaeological search. Could those "very deep" (and likely, very large) bolt holes be visible even now in the bedrock of the Temple Mount somewhere on a line east of the Dome of the Tablets?

c. If such details are available from ancient Jewish or Roman writings and/or from archaeological study, a few engineering calculations for weight, size, friction, etc., would give better understanding as to why twenty men closed it "with difficulty."

Such data would provide means for investigating the "great noise of its turning hinges," which is reported in the *Talmud* (*Yoma* 39b). Since only a few measurements are available concerning the gates and the courts of the Second Temple (Illus. 21: Detail of the 2nd Temple, Page 154), it is not certain whether this "one entire stone" was bedrock or a large slab floor piece at this entrance. Without more detailed information, on the basis of sound engineering and construction practice I prefer the bedrock option. But this one will, of course, have to wait, because the present Muslim authorities, who have jurisdiction over the Temple Mount, would prohibit even a "peek" at that bedrock.

What "*City?*"

There was at first some confusion (at least for myself) regarding just what was considered to be the "city" mentioned by the prophets Ezekiel and Micah. (See comments in Appendix B.) Professor Martin explains[12] that because of crowding of Jerusalem's overnight accommodations during feast days, and in order to enable pilgrims to remain within the *Talmudic* travel laws on the Sabbath, the official city boundaries were extended "a Sabbath day's journey" (Acts 1:12), 2,000 cubits, or about 1/2 or 2/3 of a mile from the Temple, depending upon actual cubit measurement. (See "Oregano and Red Stuff.") There is perhaps a more definite answer to this query within the intricacies of *Talmudic* Law dissertations — and, therefore, it may or may not be applicable in this question.

Where was the "*Miphkad Altar?*"

According to an article in *The Jerusalem Post*,[11] Dr. Asher Kaufman stated that part of his search for the Temple site involved reasoning from Ezekiel 8:16, that the site of the Red Heifer ceremony (on the western slope of Mt. *Olivet*) might offer a clue toward locating the Temple. It didn't work out that way, because to this day the Red Heifer site (or *Miphkad Altar*) is known only in an approximate way. This most important ceremony was commanded in Numbers 19.

The only mention of the word "*Miphkad*" in our Bible is in Nehemiah 3:31, as "the gate *Miphkad*" — believed to be a gate on the east of the Temple and where the Red Heifer was led out for her journey to the Mount of Olives. The name "*Miphkad*" is the Hebrew word meaning an assembly or a group, but more specifically a "muster"; i.e., an "accounting." This particular definition of the term may be reflected in the Law that pertains to the ritual for burning of the Red Heifer.

Parah 3:10 requires the High Priest to hold up each of the three materials to be tossed into the fire and to ask the bystanders: "Is this cedarwood? — Is this cedarwood?" Each time the crowd replies, "Yea — Yea." The Priest then continues by asking, "Is this hyssop? — Is this hyssop?" And then: "Is this crimson wool? — Is this crimson wool?" The group replies again, "Yea — Yea." This series of *three* questions is addressed to the assemblage *three* times each, with *three* responses each time. In this way the materials that must be added to make the burning complete have been, as they say, "mustered." Hence, the name "*Miphkad.*"

Encyclopedia Judaica, under "Mount of Olives," estimates that this site was located "somewhere above Absalom's Pillar" (No. 14 on Illus. 3: Old City of Jerusalem and Mt. of Olives in the Kidron Valley, Page 19). It appears that a somewhat more specific location for this altar can be determined through application of some elementary geometric principles along with a detailed study of *Talmudic* Law and other ancient records. *Parah* 4:2 describes that area as a "pit or cavity" on the western slope of *Olivet*, suggesting a flat, shelf-like clearing such as if it were carved out of the face of the mountain. (See Illus. 24: Detail of "pit or cavity" in face of Mt. of Olives, Page 157, and Illus. 8: Could this be the Miphkad Altar Site?, Page 47)

Talmud Middoth 2:4, states that all the Temple walls were built high, except the eastern wall, which was lower than all the others so as not to obstruct the priest's view of the Sanctuary when burning the Red Heifer at the top of the Mount of Olives. The same observation is also recorded in the tractate *Yoma* 16a. Thus, location of the *Miphkad Altar* at

Olivet summit is verified to a large extent by application of Judaic Law plus the archaeological and geometric principles discussed in this study.

It can be seen from the map that the locale just described should be along the line extended from Dr. Kaufman's Temple site to the *Olivet* summit. The Red Heifer site, then, can perhaps be located by examining soil samples (see Oregano and Red Stuff) along the line described, if this can be done without desecrating graves. The aforementioned conclusion is, of course, right in line with Dr. Kaufman's Biblical observation. According to *Middoth* 2:4, the priest standing at the *Miphkad Altar* on *Olivet*, by "directing his gaze carefully," must be able to look across the Kidron Valley, over the City Wall, over the Beautiful Gate, and through the East Gate of the Sanctuary and see the doors of the *H'ekhal* as he sprinkles the heifer's blood "directly before the Tabernacle...seven times."

This implies that a rather small sight-picture required the priest to "direct his gaze carefully" in order to see the doors of the *H'ekhal* through the East Gate. The *Universal Jewish Encyclopedia*[9] and Josephus indicate that no lintel rested across the top of the Beautiful Gate and that it had no "doors." In other words, it was really just an opening in the outer wall of the Temple Courts, rather than a "gate," *per se*. Nevertheless, this problem did not emerge for the Eastern Gate in the City Wall because it was much lower than the Temple gates. (See [6] and Illus. 7: Temple Mt. Viewed from Chapel of The Ascension below.)

Illus. 7: Temple Mt. Viewed from Chapel of The Ascension

Temple Mt. Viewed from Chapel of The Ascension

The Dome of the Tablets stands to the right of the Dome of the Rock about one hundred meters. It is standing just in front of the four arches in the center of the picture. (See arrow.)

It should be noted that *Middoth* 2:4 neglected to mention the Veil, sometimes described as the thick "Babylonian curtain," that was drawn across the doors at the front of the *H'ekhal*. The priest, therefore, would actually be looking to see the Veil ("curtain"), and not actually the doors of the *H'ekhal*. This fact is supported by evidence from Josephus and *Talmud* and by Scripture in the Lamsa Bible[8], translated from the Gospel in the Aramaic language.

> *In Lamsa, Matthew 27:51 says:* "And immediately, the curtains at the door of the Temple were torn in two, from the top to the bottom;..."

> *Also in Lamsa's translation of Mark 15:38, it reads:* "And the curtains at the door of the Temple were torn in two, from the top to the bottom."

> *Again in Luke 23:45, Lamsa says:* "And the sun was darkened, and the curtains at the door of the Temple were torn in the center."

Contrast these verses with the texts in Western Bibles where they say only: "...and the Veil of the Temple was rent..." Many scholars, unaware of these details, have therefore assumed this was a "Veil" separating the Holy of Holies from the Holy Place inside the *H'ekhal*. However, there were actually two much thinner "Veils" hanging between the north and south walls of the *H'ekhal*, separating the Holy Place from the Holy of Holies. (See Illus. 18: Elevation Profile of Temple and Temple Mt., Page 151, Illus. 21: Detail of the 2nd Temple, Page 154, and Illus. 22: The Sanctuary of the 2nd Temple, Page 155) The priest, therefore, would not (under *normal* circumstances) be able to see the Veils inside the *H'ekhal*. Rather, he would instead be looking to see the thick "Babylonian curtain" (also called a "Veil") that covered the outer doors, as just described. Later in this work, we will demonstrate how the Centurion at The Cross *was* able to see that the Veils inside the Temple were torn as well. (Matthew 27:51 – 54) The priest, therefore, would actually be looking to see the Veil, not the doors, but the writers of the Gospels probably just presumed everyone already knew that!

We have observed from *Middoth* 2:4 that the High Priest must "direct his gaze carefully" to be able to see the front of the *H'ekhal* (and the Veil) as he stands at the *Miphkad Altar* "on the top of the Mount of Olives." All of this means that careful positioning is required for the High Priest during the Red Heifer ceremony in order that he will be able to see the Veil through a rather small viewing aperture. This "tight" aperture (or "sight picture") results because the view is directed through the open doors of Nicanor's Gate or East Gate. (See Illus. 16: Isometric View of 2nd Temple, Page 149, Illus. 17: Detailed Elevation of 2nd Temple, Page 150, Illus. 18: Elevation Profile of Temple and Temple Mt., Page 151, and Illus. 19: Elev. Profile: Temple Mt., Kidron VLY., Mt. Olivet, Page 152.)

Field of view is reduced because the viewer is at a much greater distance from the gate than the Veil is from the gate, at a ratio of approximately 14 to 1. (See Illus. 19: Elev. Profile: Temple Mt., Kidron VLY., Mt. Olivet, Page 152.) The Veil is about 30 feet wide and Nicanor's gate opening is about 38 feet wide. This means an observer at *Olivet* summit is viewing at a very small angle of vision through the gate. The priest must therefore be centered at a position where he can view the entire Veil with almost no room for movement to either side. With the relative distances involved, if the priest were to move or sway left or right but a few inches, the Veil would be off-center. *Talmud* teaches us that the Rabbis were not "sloppy" or so careless or "profane" as to permit the Veil to appear off center. The priest must therefore be standing where he will see the Veil centered *perfectly* within the gate opening. From this we can observe that the priest must not be pacing back and forth. We can now fully comprehend why he must stand in place in order to "direct his gaze carefully."

Further evidence from *Talmud*, *Middoth* 2:4 and *Zebahim* 40a, 93b, alludes to a requirement for strict precision on the part of the High Priest while standing at the *Miphkad Altar* at the burning. The priest is commanded to dip his finger in the heifer's blood and sprinkle the blood directly toward the Tabernacle. He is required to do this exactly seven times. If he forgets to dip his finger, if he loses count of the sprinkles, if he flinches or miscasts off to left or right, if he loses his balance, stumbles, falters, sneezes, or whatever, the whole ritual is "invalid." The whole deal is off! Back to square one! A new heifer — everything!

Considering the severity of the Law in this ceremony, it is to be expected that the priest must also have a perfect sight-picture of the Veil as he sprinkles, while he must "direct his gaze carefully to see the door of the *H'ekhal*." (*Middoth* 2:4) Remember, it says "directly before the Tabernacle" or it is back to square-one! Some type of error evidently occurred two times during about 1500 years of Temple worship. *Talmud Parah* 3:5 states that a total of nine heifers were slain, but only seven were "valid." Ironically, the two High Priests who erred in this Holy ceremony were Israel's two most beloved High Priests: Simeon the Righteous and John Hyrcanus.

Using dimensions of Nicanor's Gate and the Veil as provided in the *Talmud* and by Josephus, it might be feasible to survey the location of the *Miphkad Altar* within just a few meters. We have also explained that this may be very near the position of The Cross of Jesus.

So, again — knowing elevations of the intervening gates along the line-of-sight, using basic surveying methods, we could recreate the "sight-picture" that the priest would have had while facing the Temple and standing at the *Miphkad Altar* near *Olivet* summit. Since the burning took place "without the camp" (2,000 cubits), it had to be near *Olivet* summit. (See Illus. 19: Elev. Profile: Temple Mt., Kidron VLY., Mt. Olivet., Page 152) Such a sight-picture would result when viewed from *Olivet* just below the summit and directly above *Gethsemane*. Professor Martin[12] suggests that *Gethsemane* of 30 C.E. was much nearer that summit than the present olive grove bearing that name. If this conclusion is valid, some intriguing theological questions emerge; not the least of which is: WHY did Jesus pray at *Gethsemane*? When we answer this question, it appears even more likely that Prof. Martin's conclusion is correct. (See "Why *Gethsemane*?" in Chapter 5.)

Nevertheless, another Gospel question arises, which may provide additional insight concerning location of this important and holy rite. Since the Veil was several meters back under the overhanging Portico (porch) of the Temple, it would be difficult to see the Veil from *Olivet* summit during any hour at which the Veil would be in the shade. So, at what hour would the Red Heifer burning be planned in order that the High Priest could see the Veil as he sprinkled the heifer's blood "directly before the Tabernacle?"

Most tourists visiting Jerusalem are eager to get a snapshot (or a video) of the Old City before their luggage is even delivered to the room. However, those who are patient enough to wait for their tour guide to schedule that marvelous sight will find that he has wisely scheduled a trip to *Olivet* summit for the next morning — first thing! The reason is, of course, from that vantage at that time the Old City, the Dome of the Rock, the East Wall, etc., will be painted in bright, golden sunlight just as the sun rises over *Olivet* summit behind their backs.

In fact, the best "photo-opportunity" occurs at about 9 A.M. when the earliest and best light appears after burning off the early morning mountain haze. This is also about the only time when the priest would be able to see the Veil through the open East Gate with the glorious colors of the Veil fully illuminated by the sun. As we explained earlier, in saying that the High Priest must "direct his gaze carefully" to see the door of the *H'ekhal*, this implies that he is "sighting" through a rather small opening.

This implied situation, then, has been somewhat verified by our examination of gate details and topography of *Olivet* and the Temple Mount. The sun must not be too high or the Veil is shaded by the Portico above — too low and it becomes shaded by the lintel across the top of the East Gate in front. Ideally then, the sun should be up at about a 45 degree angle at 9 A.M., beaming into the court in front of the Temple and bathing the Veil with sunlight, revealing its brilliant, glorious hues of scarlet, purple and blue. (See Illus. 17: Detailed Elevation of 2nd Temple, Page 150, Illus. 18: Elevation Profile of Temple and Temple Mt., Page 151 and Illus. 19: Elev. Profile: Temple Mt., Kidron VLY., Mt. Olivet, Page 152.) It will become significant in later chapters to note that this time was named as "the third hour of the day" during Biblical times.

Further, he would need to select a time of year when the sun would be directly behind the Priest; i.e., due east. Since the Temple was oriented to face due east, this was necessary in order that he would have the sun's rays passing straight through the East Gate and against the Veil under the Portico. Otherwise, if he chose to conduct this rite in, say, December — the sun would be too far to the south; or in June — too far in the north. Thus, in either case, the Veil would be partially shaded on the right or left by the wall extending to the sides of the East Gate. Then yes, the sun must be directly behind him and in good weather — preferably in the Spring rather than in Autumn — actually at the time of the Vernal Equinox. This would of course occur in the first Jewish month, *Nisan*, when the moon is full — *at the time of Passover!*

All this alignment in order to avoid a shadow is not based upon any frivolous principle. It would have been considered "profane" to have sprinkled the blood while a shadow was being cast on the Veil or even across the steps approaching the *H'ekhal* entrance. (See Illus. 16: Isometric View of 2nd Temple, Page 149, Illus. 17: Detailed Elevation of 2nd Temple, Page 150, Illus. 18: Elevation Profile of Temple and Temple Mt., Page 151, and Illus. 19: Elev. Profile: Temple Mt., Kidron VLY., Mt. Olivet, Page 152.) Jewish tradition held that a shadow indicated presence of a demon. (*Yebamoth* 122a) There is much "hidden" in this picture that will be discussed in later chapters.

We can now observe, from all this precision, that the designers and architects who built the Second Temple followed the Law by very "religiously" adhering to the geometric/astronomical *Talmudic* requirements noted here. The prophet Ezekiel detailed many other specifications that were implemented in the Second Temple and will be discussed later in Chapter 6.

Additional information from *Talmud* further underlines the precise location, timing, and opportunity one must have had in order to see the Veil. The *Mishnah* of tractate *Shekalim* 8:4 details that each time a new Veil was woven (twice a year) it was displayed atop the Temple colonnade roof "so that the people might behold its fair workmanship." Here, "the people," so considered were: women and girls, underage lads, and of course, all lepers. These had limited opportunity to see this beautiful curtain, because none of these would ever be permitted to tread beyond Nicanor's Gate. They might be able to crane their necks and push through the crowds to "peek" at times when the gate was open, as it was on Sabbaths, New Moons, and Feasts. However, we know the Veil would be at least partially shaded unless one gained this opportunity at around 9 o'clock in the morning.

The *Miphkad Altar* was also "off limits" because it was "a clean place." All of these "people" had their only good opportunity to see this "fair workmanship" from almost any location on the western slope of the Mount of Olives, but only twice per year and not while the Veil was hanging in its rightful place before the Temple doors. This semiannual display also provided the only opportunity for "strangers" (Gentiles) to behold Israel's beautiful curtain.

From the analysis I have been able to perform to date with the present dimensional data, it appears that the priest would be able to see the full forty-cubit height of the Veil. According to analysis of the elevation profiles available, Illus. 17: Detailed Elevation of 2nd Temple, Page 150, Illus. 18: Elevation Profile of Temple and Temple Mt., Page 151, Illus. 19: Elev. Profile: Temple Mt., Kidron VLY., Mt. Olivet, Page 152, and Illus. 21: Detail of the 2nd Temple, Page 154, the full Veil would be visible through the gate and beneath the lintel across the top as viewed from *Olivet* summit at a range of about 2,000 cubits. However, more work is needed in this area before any conclusion can be formed concerning the priest's exact "sight picture" when viewed from the vantage point described.

During my last visit to Jerusalem, I performed a very cursory version of this procedure and using the most basic surveying techniques. The location resulting was "a pit or cavity" on the western slope of the Mount of Olives, just a few meters below the summit. (See Illus. 24: Detail of "pit or cavity" in face of Mt. of Olives, Page 157 and Photo below, Illus. 8: Could this be the Miphkad Altar Site?, Page 47) It is significant to note this occasion took place before I ever came across the description of the "pit" as described in *Parah* 4:2. I therefore was not searching for a locale of such description.

Archaeological Comments 47

Illus. 8: Could this be the Miphkad Altar Site?

Could this be the *Miphkad* Altar Site?

The flat, level clearing in the midst of rugged terrain and thick undergrowth was located using crude surveying techniques, just below *Olivet* summit and on-line with the Chapel of The Ascension and the Dome of the Tablets. The actual location of that sacred place must be at most only a few meters from this spot.

Professor Martin stated his conclusion, placing the Red Heifer site at the *Olivet* summit. Nevertheless, I would like to check it out via the "sight-picture" technique earlier described. If the elevations of the Temple walls and portals were known with infallible accuracy and detail relative to the Dome of the Tablets, it would be relatively simple to "sight-it-in" in much the same way as a survey instrument operator would do.

Who Shut Which Gate?

> *"Then the man brought me back to the outer gate of the sanctuary, the one facing east, and it was shut. It must not be opened: no one may enter through it. It is to remain shut because the Lord, the God of Israel, has entered through it. The prince himself is the only one who may sit inside the gateway to eat in the presence of the Lord. He is to enter by the portico of the gateway and go out the same way." Ezekiel 44:1 – 3 (New International Version)*

Some prophetic scholars, at least until James Fleming's discovery,[6] have pointed to the Turkish conqueror, Suleiman the Magnificent, as the one who (unwittingly) fulfilled one of Ezekiel's best known prophecies; because Suleiman ordered the eastern gate (Golden Gate) to the City mortared shut when he heard of the prophecy that the Jewish Messiah would enter through that gate.

Such teaching is seen to be incorrect, because of the Scriptural identification of the gate in the prophecy. The "gate" to be shut was the outer gate of the sanctuary. Obviously this was not the gate in the City Wall, but more likely it was Nicanor's Gate, the immense brass (or bronze) gate to the Temple (sanctuary) court. This gate was probably "shut" when the Roman soldiers razed the Temple, 70 C.E. (Read much more about this prophecy in Chapter 6.)

Dr. James Fleming miraculously discovered what appears to be the arch of a gate in an earlier wall, which is directly beneath Suleiman's Gate (Golden Gate) in the Outer Wall of the City. (In our discussion we shall refer to this as the "City Wall.") This magnificent gate apparently has been named for the sixteenth-century Islamic conqueror, Suleiman I, because he ordered the gate mortared shut in order to prevent the Jewish Messiah, "the Prince," from entering through it "by the way of the porch." (Ezekiel 44:3) However, as we shall demonstrate later, "the gate was shut" fifteen centuries before Suleiman arrived in Jerusalem.

Fleming's discovery resulted when the rain-softened soil gave way beneath his feet, dropping him a few meters down into a Muslim grave just outside of Suleiman's gate in the City Wall. It is likely that top remnants of Fleming's wall were actually used as the foundation for the present City Wall. (See Illus. 18: Elevation Profile of Temple and Temple Mt., Page 151.)

It is possible that some teachers may now speculate, albeit incorrectly, that Fleming's "Lower Gate" may be "the gate that was shut." Further confusion exists concerning which wall was built low, in order that the High Priest would have a clear view of the front of the *H'ekhal* as he sprinkled the Heifer's blood. The footnotes of *Middoth* 2:4 confirm that three walls stood between the Holy of Holies and the Mount of Olives: (1) the east wall of the Temple Court, (2) the east wall of the Court of Women, and (3) the City Wall. (See Illus. 19: Elev. Profile: Temple Mt., Kidron VLY., Mt. Olivet., Page 152) Since all these gates and walls are so closely related, and since they are important to this study, some clarification is necessary to eliminate or reduce the confusion.

First, since the prophecy said "the outer gate of the sanctuary" would be shut, this could not be the gate in the City Wall because that was not the outer wall of the sanctuary. Also, the reference would not be to the gate in the outer wall of the Temple courts, i.e., "The Beautiful Gate," because this was an opening into the Court of Women. According to Josephus, there were no "doors" in that gate and there was no "portico" above it. The prophecy must therefore refer to the East Gate of the Temple, which was also called Nicanor's Gate, as already stated.

Continuing, if James Fleming indeed saw the top portion of the first century City Wall, then the wall was already much too low to have caused any obstruction of the High Priest's view. Most scholars agree that even the present City Wall would have to be much taller to pose that kind of problem. However, this fact led at least one scholar, F. J. Hollis (referenced in the footnotes of *Middoth* 2:4), to conclude that the wall between the Court of Women and the Court of the Israelites was built lower to provide the view from *Olivet*.

However, that wall could not be a factor in this problem, because Nicanor's Gate in that wall would have been opened so the Priest could see the *H'ekhal*. The wall that was lower then, was the east wall of the Court of Women. This may also be the reason there were no "doors" and there was no lintel over the Beautiful Gate. (See Illus. 16: Isometric View of 2nd Temple, Page ,149 and Illus. 19: Elev. Profile: Temple Mt., Kidron VLY., Mt. Olivet, Page 152.)

In summary, perhaps the clearest settlement of this matter is found in the *Mishnah* of *Middoth* 2:4, where this lower wall is identified to be the east wall of the Court of Women, since that wall bounded the easternmost limits of the Temple. (See Illus. 15: Plan of Second Temple (by Dr. A.S. Kaufman), Page 148, Illus. 16: Isometric View of 2nd Temple, Page 149, Illus. 17: Detailed Elevation of 2nd Temple, Page 150, Illus. 18: Elevation Profile of Temple and Temple Mt., Page ,151 Illus. 19: Elev. Profile: Temple Mt., Kidron VLY., Mt. Olivet, Page 152, and Illus. 21: Detail of the 2nd Temple, Page 154.) This is the wall, portions of which were discovered by Asher Kaufman[7] as the key for his locating the Second Temple. Ironically, the wall was uncovered by a Muslim construction crew, having bulldozed the area to provide a water reservoir. These stones were then covered with asphalt, but not before an alert Israeli scholar photographed the site. Prof. Kaufman fortunately discovered the photos and the key to the Temple site location was revealed.

Christian scholars will recall Jesus' prophetical reference to the destiny of their Glorious Temple – from Mark 13:2:

"Seest thou these great buildings? – **There shall not be left one stone upon another that shall not be thrown down."**

Based upon that prophecy then, some of those same scholars will question Kaufman's claim that the stones exposed by the bulldozer's blade, saying those could not be Temple stones, because Jesus had said there would not be "one stone upon another." Nevertheless, this objection is nullified as we examine one important detail of this discovery. This great prophecy remains intact – because Jesus did not say the stones comprising the Temple foundation would be "dug up." – Kaufman's stones are claimed to be the foundation of the *Azarah* wall. – And, sure enough ! – There are **NO** stones remaining "*upon*" that foundation – Just as stated in Jesus' prophecy ! – Any fears of threatening reliability of Scripture in this claim therefore may easily be put to rest. – (In our work, one must learn to *think* like the Rabbis!)

Obviously, not all archaeologists and theologians agree with Prof. Kaufman's conclusions. Indeed, it is most difficult to persuade against the traditional belief that the Dome of the Rock (Arabic: *es-Sakhra* — "the rock") is the Temple site. This belief has been in place for at least thirteen centuries and persists even today among some of our most respected scholars, despite the facts revealed.

Although Kaufman's proposal cannot yet be proved incontrovertibly, it is in fact easy to disprove any claim for *es-Sakhra* as that Holy Place, based solely on the *Talmudic* laws pertaining to burning of the Red Heifer and considering simple geometric specifications for the Temple.

Briefly, the geometry of the Temple courts and gates, in concert with the Law and with the contour topography of *Olivet* and the Temple Mount, produce a profile criteria for this landscape that is undeniable. The priest at *Olivet* summit *must see the Veil* at the door of the Temple as he sprinkles the Heifer's blood. If the priest stood east of *es-Sakhra* at one Sabbath Limit from that rock, he would not be able to view the Veil, simply because he would be too far over the brow of the hill and behind *Olivet*. There is considerable geological evidence (tombs, etc.) indicating that this region of the *Olivet* profile has not been altered significantly during the past 1900 years. The geometry we see today is therefore essentially the same as it was during the first century.

Moreover, the probable Eastern Gate of the first century City Wall; i.e., Fleming's "Lower Arch," is several meters north of a Temple axis as proposed through *es-Sakhra*; whereas, Fleming's arch is very close to an east-west line extended from the Dome of the Tablets, the location of the Holy of Holies as proposed by Prof. Kaufman. With further excavation and examination, this could indicate a possibility that this arch was part of a City Wall from Second Temple times, or even from a wall during the time of the First Temple. Unfortunately, Muslim authorities at the Temple Mount (the *Waqf*) will not permit any study of that area.

We should at this time note, as an example of "accuracy" vs. "tradition," the difference in Prof. Kaufman's outline of the Second Temple (Illus. 15: Plan of Second Temple (by Dr. A.S. Kaufman), Page 148) in comparison with a popular illustration of the Second Temple shown in Illus. 21: Detail of the 2nd Temple, Page 154. In Illus. 15: Plan of Second Temple (by Dr. A.S. Kaufman), Page 148, the rear of the Temple (*H'ekhal*) has the shape of a trapezoid, or "boat tail." This description is supported by a discussion in *Middoth* 4:7, stating: "Thus the *H'ekhal* was narrow behind and broad in front, resembling a lion, as it says, '*ah, Ariel, Ariel, the City where David encamped.*' (From Isaiah 29:1) Just as a lion is narrow behind and broad in front, so the *H'ekhal* was narrow behind and broad in front."

Other differences may be noted through close examination of our illustrations. It is significant to observe, especially in Illus. 16: Isometric View of 2nd Temple, Page 149, and Illus. 21: Detail of the 2nd Temple, Page 154, how in the floor plans of the Women's Court and the *H'ekhal* itself, *both have the shape of The Cross!*

There are other factors in the category of common sense that indicate against *es-Sakhra* as the Holy of Holies. The most glaring of these is the fact that the Holy of Holies was in fact "a threshingfloor," (II Chronicles 3:1) and there is not a level place on *es-Sakhra* much larger than a man's hand.

At least one scholar has promoted *es-Sakhra* on the basis of a flat, rectangular depression in the rock and which is near the dimensions of the Holy Ark. However, *Yoma* 5:4 notes that the Foundation Stone, *Shethiyah*, was actually raised "three fingerbreadths" *above* the floor level. Furthermore, since the Foundation Stone was the actual resting place for the Holy Ark, it hardly seems likely that God would accept its being placed in a depression — actually below the ground surface.

Additional fault exists in that, according to *Menahoth* 98a, orientation of the longer axis of the Ark was at 90 degrees to the longer axis of the Temple, instead of being parallel to the Temple axis as proposed by that same scholar. Moreover, *Middoth* 2:5 and *Sanhedrin* 36b teach that the threshingfloor is circular in shape rather than rectangular.

In its present configuration, therefore, *es-Sakhra* could never be considered as "a threshingfloor." Contrastingly, however, the Dome of the Tablets stands over a circular, flat, level exposed portion of limestone bedrock of at least six feet in diameter. There can be no denying — in every way, it resembles "a threshingfloor!"

Now, from literal interpretation of Scripture, from archaeology, from Jewish historical data, from Temple Mount/*Olivet* topography, and from Jim Fleming's "fortunate accident," we confidently conclude that Suleiman's Gate is not the gate the prophet was writing about. And Suleiman didn't shut the gate — God shut it, centuries before Suleiman, "because the Lord had entered through it."

At this point we should reiterate that the "outer gate of the Sanctuary," as stated in Ezekiel 44:1-3, is known by at least two other names. It is sometimes called the "East Gate." In Jewish Rabbinical texts that same gate has been popularly named "Nicanor's Gate," after the wealthy Jewish Temple patron who funded its construction and its miraculous shipment from Alexandria. (See *Yoma* 38a)

Applying some elementary logic: The gate has been shut since 70 C.E.; therefore, the God of Israel (Messiah) must have "entered through it" before the gate was shut. It shouldn't take anybody very long to come up with a pretty good guess as to WHO that was and WHEN He "entered through it." The Lord Jesus of course "entered through it" — "by the portico of the gateway" when He came through Nicanor's Gate, bringing His sacrifices into the Court of the Israelites. (See Illus. 21: Detail of the 2nd Temple, Page 154)

Jesus would have done this many times as He followed all of the practices of Jewish Temple worship whenever He visited Jerusalem. It must be pointed out that Jesus, as just another one of the Israelites, after entering through Nicanor's Gate into the Court of the Israelites, would have presented His offering to the priests at the Slaughterhouse. Then, complying with Temple worship rules, He would have exited through the Gate of the Flame, instead of returning against the one-way traffic flow of worshipers and through the crowd to exit at Nicanor's Gate.

Then, later, the Lord as the Divine Presence, *Shekhinah*, was seen to "go out the same way" i.e.; through Nicanor's Gate, when *Shekhinah* withdrew from the Temple, Pentecost, 66 C.E. on His way to the summit of the Mount of Olives. Thus, Ezekiel's prophecy was fulfilled by two Personages of the Holy Trinity: the "Prince" — the Son of God, when He "entered through it" — and, 36 years later by the Holy Spirit — *Shekhinah*, as He "went out by the way of the same."

Although the Dome of the Tablets (Arabic: *Qubbat el-Alouah*) or Dome of the Spirits (Arabic: *Qubbat el-Arwah*) is a Muslim shrine of sorts, neither Muslim scholars nor anyone else can offer any historically verified or documented explanation to justify either of these names given to this tiny, unimposing and humble structure. However, recognizing the significance of this little monument in the light of Prof. Kaufman's proposal that it covers the spot where the Ark of the Covenant rested, offers at least two interesting speculations leading to its two names through t over the centuries.

1. Many Jewish people refer to *Shekhinah* as the Holy Spirit. In this work we have quoted several ancient documents that confirm the presence of Israel's *Shekhinah* in the Holy of Holies where the Ark rested. It follows then, that local tradition may have assigned the name "Dome of the Spirits" based upon the fact that *Shekhinah* was in the Temple which was formerly on the Temple Mount where the Dome of the Tablets is presently located.

2. It was also known, from II Chronicles 5:10, that Moses' two stone tablets bearing the Ten Commandments were contained within the Ark. It could therefore be considered that the name arose (again, from tradition) from knowing the Tablets had been contained in the Ark at that location on the Temple Mount.

Oregano and Red Stuff

"And the priest shall take cedar wood, and hyssop, and scarlet and cast it into the midst of the burning of the heifer." (Numbers 19:6)

Most laypersons can readily identify cedar, but what is "hyssop?" The dictionary, by several routes, will eventually tell us the hyssop is an oily herb and is related through various botanical "families" to oregano. The " oregano connection" is, in fact, revealed in the botanical Latin name for this ignominious weed: *"Origanum syriacum."*

It would be interesting to know more about this hyssop plant, which was (and perhaps is yet) indigenous to the *Sinai* wilderness and to Israel. (See Reference 16.) There must be some Biblical and/or practical reason for the command to use hyssop. More "Law" and detail is given regarding this lowly plant in the Red Heifer ceremony than is presented for any of the other materials used in that most important Holy rite of Judaism. In Jewish tradition, the "scroungy" hyssop is a symbol of humility and the stately Lebanon cedar is a symbol for power and strength, but occasionally it represents haughtiness.

The scarlet (or crimson) was red wool, apparently dyed or dipped in some sort of material that produced red smoke when incinerated; and this was evidently intended to represent blood. *Encyclopedia Judaica* refers to this material only as "red-stuff."

Recently, a joint Israeli/American team of archaeologists, Rev. Vendyl Jones et al, has located some red material, which Rabbinical authorities have verified to be the *Qetoret*; i.e., the actual incense used for the Altar of Incense in the Temple. Jones' team also located nearby a cask of oil that the same Jewish authorities have confirmed to be anointing oil (*Shemen Afarshimon*) that was used for anointing priests and Kings of Judah.

The reddish caste of the incense is largely due to the fact that eight varieties of cinnamon are present in the formulation. It has all the ingredients and characteristics needed for qualification as the "red stuff," *including the emission of red smoke when it is incinerated.* The Red Heifer itself — pure, unyoked, innocent, and "without blemish" — of course, is interpreted by many Christians to be representative of the Messiah, as is the Paschal lamb.

More study of *Encyclopedia Judaica* reveals that the Red Heifer ceremony resembled the purification of recovered lepers (Leviticus 14:1 – 4), because cedar, hyssop, and crimson "stuff " were also used for that rite. It is further stated that the red smoke "alludes to the power of blood to overcome death."

- *"For the life of the flesh is in the blood: and I have given it to you upon the Altar to make an atonement for your souls: for it is the blood that maketh an atonement for the soul."* Leviticus 17:11

It is worthwhile here also to note that these heifers were "purchased at a very high price" because the animal's coat had to be so near perfection, by *Talmudic* Law, that no more than two hairs of the entire coat could be other than red. (*Parah* 2:5) Any herdsman who owned a prize heifer that would meet the qualifications could expect, therefore, to receive a pleasant remuneration.

Talmud Parah 3:9, offers an interesting clue as an ash ingredient as well as reflecting a poignant "picture" in the Gospel of Jesus Christ. Along the roadway Jesus used on his Triumphal Entry, The Descent of the Mount of Olives, palm branches (or fronds) were strewn by the excited citizens of Jerusalem. This action "kindled" the wrath of the Jewish religious hierarchy. (John 12:13) Interestingly, dried palm fronds were used to kindle the blaze for burning the Red Heifer at the *Miphkad Altar* immediately along this same eastern approach to the Heifer's Gangway Bridge. (Illus. 18: Elevation Profile of Temple and Temple Mt., Page 151) This of course led to Jesus being slain as a "type" of the Red Heifer.

Now, as a challenge for archaeology, it would seem that cylindrical coring samples of soil from regions identified along the extended line-of-sight from the Temple site may yield the probable location of this burning. A few feet beneath the surface, there may be found in that soil, some trace ash residue from the animals, mixed with ash from palm fronds, cedar and hyssop and the other woods, plus wool and the ingredients of the scarlet material.

Parah 3:5 states that a total of seven heifers were burned. Depending upon known persistence of the materials involved, there may be some evidence remaining even after all this time. *Talmud*[21] offers us some very definite encouragement toward finding some of the Heifer's ash residue. In *Parah* 3:11 the *Mishnah* relates that if there were large chunks of charred remains, such as the skull, bones, etc. separated by the sifting, these materials were then "hammered" into powder. This granulated residue was then divided into three parts, equally distributed as follows: one part to the twenty-four orders of the priesthood; one part to the "ramparts" — i.e., a flat promenade or terrace within the Temple courts; *and one part to be deposited on the Mount of Olives!*

At any rate, with so many burnings, even after almost two thousand years, there may be one location along that line that shows trace residue of all ash products involved. Professor Martin makes an excellent case[12] for the location of this rite at a distance just slightly greater than 2,000 "cubits" from the Dome of the Tablets

Now, if we believe in the aforementioned line established and if we know the cubit size involved, we could survey to a position very close to the Red Heifer burning site, which Professor Martin identifies as the *Miphkad Altar*. Professor Kaufman determined the Second Temple cubit as 43.7 cm (17.204 in.); whereas, Professor Martin used a 21 inch cubit (53.34

cm). It is our conclusion that Prof. Kaufman's measurement is correct based upon Scriptural and *Talmudic* specifications. Prof. Kaufman's cubit size is supported by his measurements of ashlars on the Temple Mount,[7] as well as from agreement with the accurate translation of Ezekiel 40:5 in the Lamsa Bible[8] and with the cubit dimensions stated in *Kelim* 17:9.

Measuring from the Dome of the Tablets, then, 2,000 of Prof. Kaufman's cubits locates a position of 874 meters, somewhat below the summit; which may have been the 30 C.E. position of the olive grove called *Gethsemane*. Applying dimensions of Prof. Martin's cubit places the site well up on the *Olivet* summit at 1,067 meters (in the middle of the main road). Within these areas, using "high-tech" organic chemistry sleuthing, might be found ash from wool, "red stuff," pine, spruce, fig, palm fronds, with cedar and hyssop ash mixed with ash from incinerated heifer flesh, bone, horns, dung, hooves, and hide.

Please Stay Downwind

> *"While He (Jesus) was in Bethany, reclining at the table in the home of a man known as Simon the Leper..." Mark 14:3 (NIV)*

Professor Yadin[14] points out, from the *Midrash*, that during the Second Temple period it was believed leprosy was transmitted through the air as well as by bodily contact. Lepers who lived in the area of Jerusalem and leprous pilgrims who journeyed there to worship were therefore housed at Bethany, which is east of *Olivet* summit and about two miles east of Jerusalem. Yadin makes the point that Bethany was founded there because the prevailing winds (off the Mediterranean Sea) are from west to east and Bethany was therefore established as a "safe" place to quarter "the unclean." The Rabbis were so strict on this point, in fact, that it was forbidden to even walk or stand east of a leper! *Oi!* (*Midrash Rabbah* Leviticus 16:3)

On Holy feast days there would be a large influx of Jewish worshipers coming into Jerusalem. Therefore, in order to provide additional space for their accommodations, even in tents, the city limits of Jerusalem were extended a "Sabbath Day's journey" or 2,000 cubits. This measure also insured that these pilgrims would be able to adhere within the travel laws of the Sabbath.

But how about the lepers? At a distance of about two miles east, Bethany was located significantly greater than a Sabbath Day's journey from Jerusalem. You may have questioned (as I did) just how this would have eased the lepers' compliance with Sabbath travel laws. Professor Yadin offers no explanation; however, he deserves our sympathy because the maze of *Talmudic* travel laws would probably have challenged even the best of Pharisee "lawyers."

A partial explanation of at least one legal loophole is provided in the footnotes under tractate *Hallah* 1:8, as the "*Erub* of Cooked Foods." In a family or a group of persons, if each contributes to a supply of food, enough for up to two meals each may be placed in a container and cached in advance at a point that is a Sabbath limit from the intended destination. Then, on the Sabbath day they may travel *any* distance from home to arrive and consume that food which is each person's "legal domain" in the Law. Each person may then proceed a Sabbath Day's journey from where the food was stashed, thus "keeping" the Law. This was a very practical and accommodating provision; however, one wonders if the Lord saw this as a practical necessity or as legal "squirming."

Now, some interesting pictures develop:

    a. As Professor Yadin observed from Mark's understatement: Jesus didn't just visit overnight with Simon the Leper. Virtually the entire Bethany population were lepers!

    b. And yes, this also means that Lazarus, a "Bethanite," was probably a leper and complications from that ravaging disease may have caused that death from which Jesus raised him. No wonder his sister Martha said, "...Lord, by this time he stinketh..." (From John 11:39) Bad enough a leper! But in the tomb four days!

    c. When Jesus rode into Jerusalem, He probably passed right by the *Miphkad Altar* and He may have done something unseemly before the Pharisees that aroused their displeasure. In fact, Professor Martin[12] has proposed that incidents in this area of Mt. *Olivet*, including the Triumphal Entry, may have been used in prosecution of Jesus as a "criminal" against Judaism and, further, against Rome itself. (More about this in Chapter 5.)

Line of Departure

A more comprehensive depiction of first-century Jerusalem relative to subjects in this study is offered with the details of Illus. 18: Elevation Profile of Temple and Temple Mt., Page 151.

When approaching this investigation, I will freely admit there was initially a tendency (through my own ignorance or carelessness) to assume the line of departure made by the *Shekhinah* was to be established through the Dome of the Tablets and the Eastern Gate (Suleiman's Gate) in the City Wall. This assumption was clearly in error of course, because, from Dr. Kaufman's analysis, the Second Temple was not aligned with the gate in the present City Wall. Rather, the Temple axis was aligned 6.2 degrees southward of that line and facing due east.

In addition, we observe from Scripture (Ezekiel 10:19) that the prophecy refers to the east gate of "the Lord's House." (See Illus. 15: Plan of Second Temple (by Dr. A.S. Kaufman), Page 148.) Further, we know from Scripture (Ezekiel 8:16 and Numbers 3:38) that the Temple faced eastward. An even more direct statement from the New Testament "clinches" the fact that the Temple faced eastward.

"When He was sitting on the Mount of Olives facing the Temple..." (From Mark 13:3 NEB)

There can be no doubt that the Temple faced east. Nevertheless, an interesting archaeological question arises now concerning the location of the eastern (city) gate of the Second Temple period. James Fleming's discovery[6] of the "Lower Arch" may at first be assumed to be directly (center-for-center) beneath the corresponding arch of the ground-level observable Suleiman's Gate. But what if — for some strange reason — Fleming's Arch, being directly beneath Suleiman's south entry arch, is actually the north entry arch in the wall of the Second Temple period? Or there may even have been three arches in the City Wall of 70 C.E., as in the Huldah Gate. If there are two more "Lower Arches" south of Fleming's arch, the center arch would be approximately online with the center axis of the Temple as outlined by Dr. Kaufman, Illus. 15: Plan of Second Temple (by Dr. A.S. Kaufman), Page 148.

Elevation Profile of Temple Mount, Kidron Valley and Mt. *Olivet* presents the recent (1986) terrain contour of the profile extending due east from the Dome of the Tablets to *Olivet* summit at The Chapel of The Ascension. In the accompanying profile, the 70 C.E. contours have been estimated considering information from Fleming's Lower Arch and other features. Some "filling" of the Kidron basin has likely resulted from tumbling rubble produced by dozens of sieges and more than as many earthquakes and landslides during twenty centuries.

This is a question that needs answering, although it does not appear to have any obvious direct bearing on either the Second Temple location or this *Shekhinah* withdrawal story. However, remnants of the western end of the "Heifer's Gangway" bridge may presently be buried somewhere beneath Suleiman's Gate in the vicinity of Fleming's Lower Arch. (See Illus. 19: Elev. Profile: Temple Mt., Kidron VLY., Mt. Olivet, Page 152, and Illus. 20: Jerusalem as it Appeared in 70 C.E., Page 153) We have assumed this bridge extended due east and parallel to the Temple axis rather than perpendicular relative to the City Wall. This assumption is founded upon orientation of walls of the Temple Courts as analyzed from Prof. Kaufman's data showing that the Second Temple was oriented to face due east. The bridge evidently was built during the time of the Second Temple. It appears logical therefore that its axis would have coincided with the axis of the Second Temple. Importance of this bridge is discussed under "Signs and Wonders," Chapter 7. Nevertheless, this question will have to wait for an answer, because Muslim authorities will not presently permit excavation to investigate the Lower Arch (or "arches").

The line of departure for the *Shekhinah* then, is presently established by a line extended due east of the Dome of the Tablets. This determination is based on Dr. Kaufman's location of the *Kodesh Ha-Kodashim* at the Dome of the Tablets. However, a more definitive basis for this line could be claimed if just one more authenticating point could be located, rather than depending solely upon a surveyed due easterly location.

Location of such a point not only would establish the line of departure, but also would provide a secondary verification of sorts for the Temple site. As discussed previously, the *Miphkad Altar* site is perhaps the best candidate for such a point. Some slight encouragement for the accuracy of Dr. Kaufman's analysis is already provided by the very accurate alignment of the extended easterly line from "The Dome of the Tablets" to the "traditional" site at The Chapel of The Ascension. (See Photo below and Illus. 18: Elevation Profile of Temple and Temple Mt., Page 151). However, it is understood here that The Chapel of The Ascension can hardly be considered as a verified archaeological site.

Archaeological Comments 57

Illus. 9: Chapel of The Ascension

Chapel of The Ascension

This contested Christian/Muslim site is marked by the small minaret and dome (indicated by arrow) just to the right of the lofty spire of the Russian Tower, dominating the skyline of the Mount of Olives. The view is taken from the Dome of the Tablets.

I certainly don't mean to suggest it is significant whether the Chapel of The Ascension is at the exact location of Jesus' Ascension. Rather, it appears to be much more important that Dr. Kaufman's location of the Temple site appears to be substantiated, at least to some extent, by establishing a line that can be extended to pass very closely to the traditional site of Jesus' Ascension in 30 C.E. Jesus probably ascended from somewhere along that line (we do not know where), but most likely at a point on or very near the *Olivet* summit. We have attempted to show that this is also likely the same location from which the *Shekhinah* Glory ascended in 69 C.E. Finding the *Miphkad Altar* would just about "close-the-book" for most scholars concerning the location of the line of departure and the Temple site.

Where the "*Fault*" Lies

"...and the Mount of Olives shall cleave in the midst thereof toward the east and toward the west, and there shall be a very great valley; and half of the mountain shall remove toward the north and half of it toward the south." (Zechariah 14:4)

In other words, on that Great Day, there is going to be a terrific earthquake, splitting the Mount of Olives to produce "a very great valley." Some geologists were reported to have been surprised when they located a seismic fault line that passed through the Mount of Olives, extending from east to west. (Imagine that!)

Geologists[22] indicate the landslides at the midst of *Olivet* reveal a fault that has existed since the time of King Uzziah. (Zechariah 14:5) Increased soil porosity produced by repetitive landslides enhances growth of trees, shrubs, and weeds, especially in an arid climate. *Olivet*'s western slope exhibits an obvious proliferation of growth, especially "in the midst thereof" and heading directly toward the Temple Mount platform area. Evidence of such dense vegetation is visible in the Photo below.

Church of Mary Magdalene (Russian Church)

This is one of the most beautiful landmarks on the Mount of Olives. The thick-forested growth at the center of the mountain attests in some measure to the seismic fault-line found in this area. "On *that* Day...the Mount of Olives shall cleave in the midst thereof." (From Zechariah 14:4)

Illus. 10: Church of Mary Magdalene (Russian Church)

(Church of Mary Magdalene – Russian Church – image courtesy of the Jewish Virtual Library, www.jewishvirtuallibrary.org)

But, there is much more to the geological/seismic quest that pertains to this Holy ground. Please read what Ezekiel and Zechariah say about that "very great valley." In Ezekiel 47:1 – 10 you will see that a "very great" river of "living waters" will run right past the south side of the Temple. In fact, the Kidron Valley will apparently become a large lake or inland sea. The river will extend from Jerusalem to the Mediterranean, also to the Dead Sea, and then southward to the Red Sea. (Zechariah 14:8) The desert village of *En Gedi* will become a prosperous fishing village(?)! You *can* believe it! (More about this river in "The Truth about Watergate!")

This brings us to another interesting prophetic observation from Revelation 11:2.

"But the court which is without the temple leave out, and measure it not: for it is given unto the Gentiles: and the Holy City shall they tread under foot forty and two months."

During the time of the first and second Temples, the Court of the Gentiles was needed as a barrier to keep Gentiles from entering, thereby defiling the Temple grounds. We should mention here, again, that some people refer to that *next* Temple to be erected in Jerusalem as the "Third Temple." It is *possible* that a genuine "Temple" will be rebuilt under the auspices and sponsorship of Antichrist at the start of his tenure. This is predicted to occur seven years before arrival of Messiah. Three and one half years later, however, Antichrist will "defile" that "temple" – or whatever type of Jewish worship facility has been sponsored by Antichrist. Maybe a Tabernacle, for example.

Moreover, he will cause the "oblations and the sacrifices" to be "cut off." – Our option would therefore decline from referring to that "temple" as authorized by Antichrist as a "Third Temple." This option is preferred primarily because that temple will not have been properly consecrated by the Lord's Presence – and will in fact be "made desolate." And, since "the time of the Gentiles" will not have been "complete" during those years, it will still be necessary to border *that* "temple" with a "Court of the Gentiles."

Only a few years later, however, a sobering prospect for Jerusalem is announced by the prophet, Zechariah 12:2.

"Behold, I will make Jerusalem a cup of trembling unto all the people round about, when they shall be in the siege both against Judah and against Jerusalem."

Such actually will be what is known by its popular title of: "The Battle of Armageddon." The nations will "gather" at the Valley of Meggido and "come against Jerusalem." There, they will be vanquished as, from Revelation 19:15 – 16:

"And out of his mouth goeth a sharp sword, that with it he should smite the nations: and he shall rule them with a rod of iron: and he treadeth the winepress of the fierceness and wrath of Almighty God.

And he hath on his vesture and on his thigh a name written, KING OF KINGS, AND LORD OF LORDS."

Thus, Messiah, Son of David will have returned and defeated Israel's enemies to claim His Kingdom.

It can be seen, therefore, that during the Millennial reign of Messiah on Earth, such a "barrier" at this THIRD Temple would indeed be superfluous. It can be reasoned that *all* nations and peoples will at that time be *required* to worship and honor Him at His Temple (the "Millennial Temple") at Jerusalem on the Feast of Tabernacles. (Zechariah 14:16):

"And it shall come to pass that every one that is left of all the nations which came against Jerusalem shall even go up from year to year to worship the King, the Lord of hosts, and to keep the Feast of Tabernacles."

Therefore, no longer will it be necessary or appropriate that there should be any "Court of the Gentiles." In that day "the time of the Gentiles will be fulfilled." At that time all inhabitants of Earth shall worship the Lord together, united as one Church.

So, our Lord told John not to bother measuring that part of the Temple Mount, because it isn't going to be there after the Gentiles "tread" there for that last 3½ years, "until the time of the Gentiles be fulfilled." The Gentiles' part of the Temple Mount is just going to be "river-bottom" after our Lord returns to reign from that Mount with His Kingdom.

(We really need to examine those fault lines.)

The Truth about Watergate

> *"...and behold, waters issued out from under the threshold of the House eastward...and the waters came down from under the right side of the House, at the right side of the Altar." From Ezekiel 47:1*

Readers will no doubt be relieved to know the "Watergate" incident discussed here has not the slightest connection with the deplorable political scandal bearing that name. An archaeological detail exists concerning the "Water Gate" of the Temple, which has bearing on this seismic prophecy. (See Illus. 21: Detail of the 2nd Temple, Page 154.)

Talmud, Shekalim 6:3 asks, "...and the water gate. Wherefore was its name?" Rabbi Eleazer ben Jacob offers: "...because through it the waters trickled forth and in the hereafter they will issue out from under the threshold of the House..." *Talmud* refers to Ezekiel 47:1 – 2 concerning this statement.

We see that Holy Scripture supports this statement from Rabbi Eleazer. It is also exciting to note that in the last few years some evidence of an active aquifer exists in this very region under the Temple Mount. This aquifer happens to be on the south side, away from the Dome of the Tablets (on the "right side" of the House.)

Several years ago, Muslim authorities began accusing Israeli archaeologists of having undermined the *El Aqsa* mosque by diverting aqueducts to erode supports beneath the foundation. The *El Aqsa* mosque is located at the extreme south end of the Temple Mount platform above the Western Wall or "Wailing" Wall. (See Illus. 3: Old City of Jerusalem and Mt. of Olives, Page 19, and Illus. 18: Elevation Profile of Temple and Temple Mt., Page 151.)

At the same time, Jewish Orthodox scholars complained that Muslim custodians of the Temple Mount platform had diverted drainage circuits so as to cause water intrusion into those revered Jewish study areas deep underground, beneath *El Aqsa* mosque and beneath the Western Wall.

As accusations grew sharper and louder, tempers and patience shortened until Jerusalem civil officials stepped in to investigate. Hydrologists were engaged to determine the cause of this flooding, because each side swore to innocence. The hydrologists found an active aquifer in that region, having a very substantial source of water supplying it from "somewhere."

Some Obvious Arguments

Even with all the analyses discussed here, there is of course still neither proof nor obvious conclusion to be reached. There are, however, at least two obvious arguments that deserve some thought.

First, some could say that the first-century Christians claimed the "traditional" site of Jesus' Ascension after *Shekhinah* had Ascended. Remember, Jesus' Ascension in 30 C.E. was witnessed by only a small number of (perhaps eleven) disciples (Mark 16:14 and Acts

1:13), whereas the Temple Withdrawal and Ascension of the Glory of the Lord was certainly a very public event.

However, Jesus' Ascension was recorded as having occurred (30 C.E.) at the summit of the Mount of Olives (near Bethany) by at least one New Testament writer, during the first century, and a number of years prior to 69 C.E. (Luke 24:50, Acts 1:11 and 12). Also, it is significant here to note the Book of Acts must have been written no later than 63 C.E. This is evident because Luke (the apparent writer) was very close personally to Paul the Apostle and the book closes with Paul still imprisoned in Rome in 63 C.E. Luke would most certainly have reported Paul's death had he been writing after Paul's execution, which was 66 or 67 C.E.

Certain atheistic and agnostic, and even some sincere Christian teachers' criticisms of the Bible, have charged that many or all New Testament books were written after 70 C.E. That criticism is rendered impotent with the evidence of two significant historical events:

1. Public awareness that *Shekhinah* had withdrawn from the Temple and Jerusalem 66 – 70 C.E.

2. Destruction of the Temple and Jerusalem in the siege of 70 C.E.

Not one of the New Testament writers mentioned either of these spectacular, and what would seem, unforgettable events. As we have shown, the *Shekhinah* Event was recorded and "hidden" and now cannot be forgotten. Nevertheless, it is difficult for the logical mind to believe those writers would have skipped two such opportunities to criticize Judaism's hierarchy, to demonstrate to them that they had put their Messiah to death on that Cross. Eagerly, they would have shown that *Shekhinah* had resided and pleaded for Israel's repentance at the same spot from which the resurrected Jesus had been crucified and had ascended to the Father forty years earlier, 30 C.E.

The enthusiasm for those writers would certainly have been fueled by the fact that *both* events were forecast by Biblical Prophecies, as we have shown. Jesus had accurately foretold of the coming destruction of the Temple and Jerusalem. Three of the four Gospel Apostles quote the Temple prophecy from The Master's own lips after He had been asked about His impression of their beautiful Temple. Matthew 24:2, Mark 13:2 and Luke 21:6 quote in unison, saying: "...*There shall not be left here one stone upon another, that shall not be thrown down.*" — Do you think any of these faithful zealots, who suffered horrible deaths after refusing to recant their faith, would have passed up either of such opportunities? — I don't think so!

The Apostle Paul was of course himself put to death about 66 C.E. and likely before *Shekhinah*'s departure from the Temple, explaining why neither occasion is described in Paul's epistles.

The Revelation is totally an exception of course, and did not need to discuss either event, because that book is a vision that relates future events, exclusively. It was revealed to John, the Apostle, *circa* 96 C.E.

It is therefore obvious that the Gospels and other New Testament books were written *before* these events occurred, 66 – 70 C.E.

Demonstrative evidence that *Shekhinah* resided in the Temple immediately following The Crucifixion and for a total of at least thirty-six years afterward is shown in the actions of Jesus' followers after Jesus had ascended into Heaven. The Twelve, as well as the other Jews who had joined them in their faith, continued Jewish worship daily in the Temple until they were driven out of Judea at the time of the martyrdom of James, the brother of Jesus, 62 C.E. It is certain that these faithful would never have continued Temple worship at that time if *Shekhinah* were no longer residing. This would have been an abomination! Under similar reasoning, it is clear that, IF *Shekhinah* had already departed, these Jewish writers of the New Testament would not have omitted reporting that *Shekhinah* was departed, and for that reason, they could no longer have worshiped in the Temple.

The earliest indication of their continued Temple worship is found in the Gospel of Luke 24:51 – 53:

"And it came to pass, while He blessed them, He was parted from them, and carried up into Heaven. And they worshiped Him, and returned to Jerusalem with great joy: And were continually in the Temple, praising and blessing God. Amen."

There would have been no purpose in their worship at the Temple if God (*Shekhinah*) were not present. It would have been a sacrilege and a waste of time!

Further evidence appears in Acts 2:46 as it details how they were

"...continuing daily with one accord in the Temple,..." Acts 3:1 states that *"...Peter and John went up together into the Temple at the hour of prayer,..."* Later, after Paul had traveled from Caesarea to Jerusalem, Acts 21:26 states: *"Then Paul took the men, and the next day purifying himself with them entered into the Temple,..."* Other verses describing similar Temple activity by Jesus' followers are: Acts 3:8, 5:17 – 21, 25, 42, 22:17, 24:12, 18, 26:21.

Again, — it is obvious that Jesus' followers continued *Jewish* worship in the Temple as *Jews* for many years after Jesus had departed from them. Although ALL were written AFTER The Crucifixion, NONE of the New Testament books mentions anything about departure of *Shekhinah* from the Temple. Nor does ANY of those books even mention the Romans' destruction of Jerusalem and the Temple – *and which Jesus had actually prophesied!* (Mark 13:2) Moreover, Jesus' disciples continued worship in the Temple at least until Jewish Christians were driven out of Judea after James was martyred in 62 C.E.

All these facts lead to the following conclusions:

- *Shekhinah* indeed *was* dwelling in the Temple until 66 C.E.

- All of the New Testament books, except Revelation, were written before 66 C.E.

- With all this evidence, if persons still do not believe the Divine Presence occupied the Second Temple during the 1st century, it is probably because they just do not *want* to believe it.

Some critics might cater to skeptics by charging that Jesus' Disciples claimed Jesus' Ascension from *Olivet* summit only *after* the *Shekhinah* ascension. This, they might claim, was done in order to be able to say: *"See!* — We told you so!" There are good reasons why such a claim would fail. —

1. The Disciples had already departed Judea after James' martyrdom, 62 C.E. They were not in Jerusalem or even Judea when *Shekhinah* withdrew from the Temple, 8 *Nisan* 66 C.E.

2. To have made such a claim falsely would have been a great blasphemy. The Disciples would have been executed immediately in Jerusalem and history would have recorded it. Actually, very little is documented verifiably regarding the eventual destinies of those saints. For the most part, only traditional legends exist on that subject.

3. Good evidence was presented earlier to indicate that the book of Acts was written before 63 C.E. This is because the writer, Luke, a close friend of Paul, does not mention Paul's trial that occurred at that date.

We know from the Gospel of Luke and from Acts that Jesus ascended from *Olivet* about 30 C.E. One must then ask the question, "Isn't it strange how everyone knows that Jesus ascended from *Olivet* summit, but why do we never hear about the ascent of the *Shekhinah* Glory?"

There is some understandable doubt concerning the "exact" location of the Ascension(s) because the Bible does not say Jesus ascended from *Olivet* summit, but implies that it was from the vicinity of Bethany — which was very near the *Olivet* summit. But then the narration terminates by saying that after His Ascension (Acts 1:12): *"Then returned they unto Jerusalem from the mount called Olivet, which is from Jerusalem a sabbath day's journey."* Now, we know that "a Sabbath Day's journey" is 2,000 cubits or about 900 – 1,000 yards from the Holy of Holies; actually on or very near *Olivet* summit (See Illus. 19: Elev. Profile: Temple Mt., Kidron VLY., Mt. Olivet, Page 152.) The group may then have applied the *erub* of cooked foods, described earlier, in order to be obedient to the Law and still be able to travel from Bethany all the way to Jerusalem on a Sabbath day.

Many respected Bible teachers often say: "Let Scripture be interpreted by Scripture!" In this case we can gain new insight to this question by letting Scripture interpret itself.

The two angels of Acts 1:10 – 11 told Jesus' disciples: *"...(He) shall come in like manner as ye have seen Him go into Heaven."*

We know from Zechariah 14:4 that His feet shall stand on the Mount of Olives upon His Glorious Return. Also, we know that all of Jerusalem will see Him and look upon Him whom they had pierced. In order to be seen by all, He must therefore descend to *Olivet* summit — *not* down in the Kidron Valley and *not* over the hill behind the summit.

Then, if He is going to return "in like manner," this means He ascended at that same place. We confirm this easterly position from Zechariah 14:4, because the prophet says the Mount of Olives shall cleave *in the midst thereof* toward the *east* and toward the *west*. The departure route we have shown for *Shekhinah* is an east-west line, passing through "the midst thereof" on *Olivet* and directly through the Chapel of The Ascension. Jesus therefore must have ascended from *Olivet* summit and on an easterly line extended directly from the Temple. We can know this because He will return "in like manner" as He ascended. (Literally, a "literal" interpretation of literal Scripture.)

As stated earlier, I believe that "exact" location (wherever it is) to be the same location where His feet will stand on that Great Day. I think God just does things that way.

These are obvious arguments, but still we have no proof. That will have to wait. However, most scholars would agree that on that Great Day:

Messiah's feet will stand on the Mount of Olives. (Zechariah 14:4):

People will look upon Him whom we all have pierced. (Zechariah 12:10)

Then, someone will ask Him, "What are these wounds in your hands?" (Zechariah 13:6) And He will say, "Those I received in the house of my friends." (Zechariah 13:6)

5

Some Updated Bible Stories

Where was "Golgotha"? – Why that name? – Who "organized" The Crucifixion? – It was THE day! Rending of the Veil – If you had been there – Traditional errors exposed – What would YOU have done?

It is perhaps only natural that an engineer with an enthusiastic interest in the Holy Word, especially concerning eschatology, archaeology, and Judaic customs, feasts, etc., relating to Messianic Promise, would want to "analyze" this fascinating event. Adding further intrigue to this analysis, several thoughts surfaced, concerning prophecy, Gospel writings, and "signs" appearing to the Judeans of the Second Temple period. I wish to share those thoughts with others, without diluting the "main story," which has been already too long neglected. There are meaningful aspects of the story that can enrich the hearts of those who hear of them. (These things are not taught in Sunday school!)

The story and implications surrounding this event bring about some revisions and "improved" blessings from several familiar Bible stories. Some of these are presented here. Maybe you will even think of some additional stories that should be "updated" as a result of this event and its meaning to Scripture.

Why *Gethsemane*?

This question, in light of what is found in this study concerning the *Miphkad Altar* — the Red Heifer burning site — brings out a few other questions:

- Did that agonizing hour of discourse at *Gethsemane* between Jesus and the Father (Luke 22:39 – 44) require some proximity with the *Miphkad Altar*? That important but little known Jewish purification rite; i.e., the Red Heifer ceremony, was certainly also representative of "cleansing" through that Greater Sacrifice of another Innocent being who was also "without blemish."
- Why this proximity with the *Miphkad Altar*?
- Would Jesus have deliberately irked the priests by treading on that sacred ground? (Maybe He would!)

As observed in Chapter 4, there is very likely some relationship between the *Miphkad Altar* and Jesus' Triumphal Entry into Jerusalem. This likelihood is based on the fact that the *Miphkad Altar* had to be on the line shown on the map and was therefore along His route into the Temple. (See Illus. 18: Elevation Profile of Temple and Temple Mt., Page 151.) Although there is no reference to the possibility in any of the Gospels, it is interesting to explore the speculative thought that Jesus may have provoked the wrath of the *Sanhedrin* in other ways, in addition to letting His followers proclaim him as a king, and later, by driving the moneychangers from His Father's House.

One can now speculate with some rationale that He may have performed some unacceptable act or made some remark concerning that Holy Ground (*Miphkad Altar*), which was later reported to the *Sanhedrin* as a blasphemous act. Remember, just a few days before, the Pharisee became irritated with Jesus because the Lord hadn't washed His hands before coming to the table...tsk! tsk! (Luke 11:36 – 38). Or, even more likely, perhaps some of the lying "witnesses" fabricated some action or utterance that they falsely attributed to Jesus and used this to prosecute this "blasphemer" at His trial before Caiaphas.

Jesus had said (Luke 6:5) that He was Lord over the Sabbath and also announced that He was sovereign over the Law. The "lawyers" were understandably incensed at such claims from this Galilean, especially when He repeatedly demonstrated this claim by healing many on the Sabbath. Now, what if Jesus had declined ritual cleansing after His exposure to lepers as a further demonstration of His sovereignty over the Law? Then He comes into the City and even the Temple!

Our imagination can extend to the Pharisee's reaction if He remarked about the significance of His blood. Jesus said (John 4:10) that He was the source of "Living Water." This is a much-used expression in Jewish purification rites, especially in the Water of Purification mixed with the Red Heifer ashes. What if Jesus had dropped such "hints" as He sat astride that donkey crossing the Heifer's Gangway Bridge? That bridge was used in order to avoid the uncleanness of the burial sites on the Mount of Olives. And here He is, this impostor, using this clean bridge after He has visited and even stayed overnight in the homes of lepers!!!

Regardless, it seems altogether reasonable that the *Miphkad Altar* must have had some connection with His false trial and innocent death. After all, any believer (Jewish or Christian) should recognize the "unblemished" innocent heifer as certainly a "type" of the Messiah, whose blood washes away all uncleanness. In Jewish tradition it is said that, despite all his wisdom, King Solomon humbly admitted he did not understand the meaning of the Red Heifer ceremony. (*Midrash Rabbah* Numbers 19:3) — So, maybe it is not so obvious to some, even though they "believe."

For example, although King Solomon was a devout Jew, He could not have known the symbolic reasoning for using dried palm branches to kindle the blaze at the burning of the Red Heifer.

(*Talmud, Parah* 3:9) Palm branches on the Mount of Olives, "kindling the blaze" beneath *our* Red Heifer, Jesus! Of course! That dramatic and Triumphal Entry into the Holy City struck the spark that "kindled" the wrath of the Jewish religious "establishment" and incited them to plot the death of Jesus.

Christians today can see the significance immediately, but it is doubtful those excited Judeans were aware of this symbolism as they spread palm fronds along the Descent of the Mount of Olives and shouted:

"Hosanna! Blessed is the King of Israel that cometh in the name of the Lord!" John 12:13

The name "*Golgotha*" (or Place of the Skull) has held a mystery of sorts concerning The Crucifixion because there seems to be no historical record of such a "place." This happens even in our modern society. Some names of persons, places, and things just never reach a status of acceptance into lasting folklore. Some streets and byways in your area, for example, have nicknames that are not on the map, yet they possess great contemporary popularity, especially among the "locals." Here in Palm Beach County we have State Road 710. Still, all of us call it "The Bee-Line" — nobody calls it Highway 710, not even local news writers. Much the same type of semantic acrobatics may be involved with the meaning of *Golgotha*.

In this way a popular label may have arisen for the area of the Crucifixion, from the fact that when an animal is burnt, at least one part of its skeleton survives the blaze in recognizable form — the skull. With this reasoning in mind, it may be that "place of the skull" or *Golgotha* was the local nickname for the *Miphkad Altar*. A convincing discussion from *Talmud* Rabbis (*Yoma* 68b, *Zebahim* 106a) indicates that the sin offerings of the bullocks and goats were *also* burned here. Earlier we had suggested taking soil samples. We should find an abundance of skulls and skull fragments. After one thousand years of *daily* sacrifices and burnings, that place would have been strewn with literally thousands of animal skulls. And, *Talmud* says it was a place that is sloping and "where the ashes naturally pour down." (*Yoma* 68b and *Zebahim* 106a) Knowing these facts, it is easy to see why *Olivet* summit might be called "place of the skull." (See Illus. 23: Mt. Olivet viewed from Temple on Crucifixion Day, Page 156, and Illus. 24: Detail of "pit or cavity" in face of Mt. of Olives, Page 157.)

Earlier we noted that Roman law required a crucifixion to be conducted at the scene of the crime and/or the place of arrest. We know from Gospel Scripture that Jesus was pointed out by Judas in a garden called "*Gethsemane*" and was then arrested by the Temple guards. (Matthew 26:36 – 50) Also, we discussed the possibility that *Gethsemane* was likely much nearer *Olivet* summit than the present traditional Garden of *Gethsemane*. The summit location would have been at or very near the *Miphkad Altar*.

Now, we are getting some strong hints about why Jesus chose to pray at *Gethsemane* that grim night. It wasn't just because it was a pleasant setting with picturesque olive trees. And, it wasn't because Jesus had told Judas He would be there waiting for His betrayal. Well, maybe *Gethsemane* was just a nice quiet place where Jesus could speak in private with His Father. C'mon! — Jesus didn't have to come to *Gethsemane* for prayer. He could pray anywhere! Jesus was the greatest "pray-er" who ever lived!

Well, then why did Jesus choose to pray at *Gethsemane*? Maybe it was just a coincidence. He had to pray somewhere, didn't He?

Remember? Jesus came to fulfill the Law. Part of that assignment was to fulfill all of the Law concerning the Red Heifer. Strangely, although we hardly ever hear a word about it, the Red Heifer burning is the most important of all the Jewish rites, although it was not actually a "sacrifice." None of the sacrifices, nor the priests — not even the Temple — can be valid without "cleansing" from Red Heifer ashes mixed with "living water."

Jesus knew exactly what He was doing. He knew all the precepts of Roman law and Herodian "puppet" statutes and certainly knew the Jewish Levitical Law. (His Father was the author!) Jesus, therefore, selected the vicinity of the *Miphkad Altar* as the place of His own Crucifixion by deliberately arranging to be arrested at that precise location. After all, Jesus is God! Would God just leave it to Pilate or Caiaphas or Judas or some centurion to choose where His Supreme Sacrifice would be given?

It is interesting to note that in Jewish tradition the palm leaf is a symbol for victory! Jesus was our Red Heifer! Our burnt offering. Jesus had His Victory! Kindled by palm branches on *Olivet*.

Luke informs us in Luke 19:37 – 39 that this procession began at *Olivet* summit on a road called "The Descent of the Mount of Olives." This was a major thoroughfare that coursed downward from the summit to the eastern end of the Heifer's Gangway Bridge. The beginning of that road at *Olivet* summit was (and is today) at or very near the Chapel of The Ascension, which we have shown is very near the place of Jesus' Crucifixion. Then, according to Luke 19:38, this is in fact the very locale where Jesus was proclaimed as a "king" — an act of sedition against Caesar. It was here that "the whole multitude of the disciples" said: *"Blessed be the King that cometh in the name of the Lord!"* This "act" would then have been sufficient to qualify this place as appropriate for execution of such a "criminal" under Roman law.

Still, we do not know for certain why Jesus was arrested at *Gethsemane* or what specific "charge" was issued to warrant His capture. Jesus must have said or done something here (or was falsely accused of such). But what??? Some day we will know. One possible "affront" that can be postulated concerns the bridge that extended during the Second Temple period from the East Gate across the Kidron Valley to the Mount of Olives.

Talmud Shekalim 4:2 and *Parah* 3:6 describe the bridge ("viaduct" or "causeway") that has become known as the "Heifer's Gangway." (See Illus. 19: Elev. Profile: Temple Mt., Kidron VLY., Mt. Olivet, Page 152, and Illus. 20: Jerusalem as it Appeared in 70 C.E.., Page 153) The eastern end of the bridge was just down the slope from the Heifer's burning site. The priest would carry the ashes across this bridge to the Temple.

In Jewish tradition and the Law, one becomes "unclean" if he touches or even walks across the grave of a dead person. It is then reasoned that one avoids defilement by being separated from the graves by dead air space or a "vault." (*Talmud Parah* 3:6) The double-vaulted bridge then was designed to provide a "clean" passage to the Temple from the Mount of Olives. The graves of thousands of Jewish dead in the valley below had to be "insulated" from the bridge traffic by those air-filled vaults.

These consecrated ashes, to be used later for "purifying" those who were "unclean" from having touched a leprous person or the dead (or even a grave), could then be carried across the Kidron Valley above the Jerusalem cemetery burial sites without the slightest exposure to that "uncleanness."

Another "act" that may have stirred anger among His prosecutors was the overnight accommodation Jesus apparently accepted in the home of Simon, the Leper — and in Bethany, the local leper colony! (See Chapter 4, "Please Stay Downwind.") If Jesus ignored the man-made "laws" about such a contact with "uncleanness," this would have added more fuel to the fire. Some of the locals interpreted the Law very strictly, it seems.

To illustrate, an amusing and exasperating story was related by Professor Yadin[14] pertaining to the strict adherences of the Essene sect. The Essenes of that day would not defecate on the Sabbath and for this reason one of the Western Gates of the City was sometimes called the " Essene Gate." This was so named because these pious "hold outs" would come racing out of the Temple, "hastening" through that gate as soon as the Sabbath had ceased, since the latrines were outside the gates and northwest of the City. So, we can easily agree that some extreme "legalism" existed during the time of Jesus.

Lest we begin judging the Jews for their seemingly almost "paranoid" attitude toward "cleanness," we might reflect upon one of our own popular folk-sayings: "Cleanliness is next to Godliness." (I wonder who said that?) Well, it *may* have been Ben Franklin, but if he did originate that pearl of wisdom in our WASP-culture, he borrowed it from the Jewish *Talmud*!

Tractate *Zabim* ("they that suffer a flux") explains in the introduction that cleanliness in Judaism is regarded not only as next to Godliness, but as Godliness itself. Neglect of a person's health is regarded as a serious offense against the Lord, in whose image we are shaped. (Remember? Your body is, after all, a Temple to the Lord.) We should keep this tradition in mind as we consider our own personal health and the Jewish legalism that we will encounter in this study.

Now, What about this "*Jesus?*"

Very likely, this legalism was distorted by the priests (and by Pilate) in order to justify capital punishment of this innocent Nazarene. Let us examine, from the Jewish point of view, the incidents occurring just before, during, and after that Triumphal Entry into Jerusalem by this strange, gentle peasant.

The night before, He was a guest at the home of His friend, Lazarus, in Bethany — the local leper colony! (John 12:1 – 13)

Next morning, He instructs His followers to place Him on a burro colt to ride into Jerusalem as "mock-fulfillment" of Zechariah's prophecy. (Zechariah 9:9, John 12:14 – 15)

Many of His followers are proclaiming that He is Messiah, Son of David, whom the prophet Daniel had said would arrive at Jerusalem on this very day. They refer to the fact that the date, in accordance with the prophecy, is exactly "69 weeks of years" (69 x 7 = 483 years) since Persian King Artaxerxes had proclaimed the Jewish people should return to their Land and had authorized Nehemiah to rebuild their Holy City. (Daniel 9:24 – 25; Nehemiah 2:1 – 10). Indeed, for years they had been marking their calendars, eagerly anticipating this day.

He begins His "royal" procession down the road called "The Descent of the Mount of Olives" and the jubilant demonstrators throw down palm fronds – and even their cloaks – for Him to tread on His path into The Holy City. They believe He has come to claim His Kingdom and that He will thereupon promptly eject their Roman oppressors from Eretz Israel FOREVER ! – Stirring the ire of the Jewish hierarchy, He nevertheless abstains from cautioning the adoring crowd against their enthusiastic and worshipful proclaiming: "Blessed is He who comes in the name of the Lord," a well-known implication that He was Messiah. (Such audacious blasphemy!) (Psalms 118:26 and Matthew 21:9–11)

Then, with even more "arrogance," after some local church officials admonished Him for neglecting to discourage the adulation and Hosannas from the throng, He "boasts": "...I tell you, if my disciples keep silence, the stones will shout aloud." (Luke 19:40, NEB)

He probably..."strutted" directly past the Miphkad Altar. We don't know what – "blasphemous" – act He may have committed at this sacred shrine. He had said many times before that He was "sovereign" over the Law. (Another "offense"!)

He continues His approach via The Heifer's Gangway, the two-tiered bridge over which the two he-goats, brought for the Day of Atonement offering, are marched into the Temple for the casting of lots. (Also see "Signs and Wonders.") Now, if Jesus didn't bother to have His "impurity"...ritually cleansed after having spent the night in the leper colony, this would have been considered an offense, a defilement of this Holy bridge, which was built to avoid "uncleanness" as described earlier.

Only "Very Important People" (VIP's) were privileged to use this sacred bridge; another act of "presumption" and "mockery" on the part of this "pretender." (He probably didn't ask to use it.) The Gospels do not actually say Jesus used the Heifer's Gangway Bridge, nor do they even mention it. But, a person entering the Temple as a King, would certainly have crossed that bridge with His procession.

He enters the Temple and His anger "burns" at the bartering by the "businessmen" selling animals to religious pilgrims for their burnt offerings. He overturns their tables and literally runs them out of the Temple, actually calling the Temple, "a den of thieves."

Upon leaving the Temple, He declares that one day it will all be torn down, "...not one stone upon another." (Matthew 24:2) Later, He was reported by witnesses to have claimed that He could destroy and then rebuild the Temple in three days! (Matthew 26:60 – 61)

To the utter consternation of everyone, all during the week He insists on spending each night in that "leper-haven" up on the hill. He stays at the home of this Simon fellow and has expensive perfumed oil poured on His head. Only a few nights earlier, a sister of Lazarus (that "phony"!) washed His feet with the stuff! — Who does He think He is? (John 12:3)

As if all this weren't enough, at His trial (facing death), this trouble-maker, with un-blushing temerity, still refuses to deny that He actually claims to be a king. (John 18:37)

Now, when we look at this Gospel narrative from the aspect of first century Judaic and Roman Law, the Gospel of Jesus Christ takes on new "light." After all, in order to obtain full appreciation for the Gospel, Christians need at least rudimentary knowledge of "the Law," because Jesus came to fulfill the Law (Matthew 5:17). Christians, therefore, can neither recognize these fulfillments nor experience the joy of such unless we know these "legal" details, even though we (Gentiles) are certainly not bound by the Law. Continuing, watch what happens.

What Judeans and Romans were Thinking

The Triumphal Entry on the burro colt was a "mockery" to some, but to many this was a genuine and expected fulfillment. Why "expected"? Then (just as now), but especially then, Israel was *expecting* Messiah. The prophet Daniel had said Messiah, The Anointed One (the "Christ"), would appear exactly 483 years (seven plus sixty-two "weeks," each "week" of seven years) after *"the commandment to go forth and rebuild the street and the wall."* (Daniel 9:25 – 26) This commandment was indeed proclaimed to Nehemiah by the Persian King Artaxerxes exactly 483 years earlier. (Nehemiah 2:1 – 8)

They all knew "it was the time." But their Rabbis had taught a more "popular" theme in which he was to be a conquering Messiah — not a suffering, down-trodden...loser. The people had been taught traditionally that Israel was the "suffering" Messiah. So, they were expecting the "conquering" Messiah rather than a "suffering" Messiah — i.e., a radical, but meek Galilean carpenter's apprentice. Of course, with our 20/20 hindsight, it is very easy for us to see what most first-century (and modern-day) Jewish people were "blinded" from seeing. (Blinded by "traditional" teaching, not necessarily by disbelief.)

Each time we review this scenario of Jesus being rejected by most of the people, we should apply some self-introspection before we judge those people of Jerusalem during those days. We must ask, within our souls, "Would I have stood up for Jesus when the Rabbis accused Him? – Would I have assented to His Crucifixion along with the crowd when Pilate asked whether Barabbas or Jesus should be released? – Which one of us would have stood with Jesus at The Cross? – What would I have done?" – The honest answer to those questions are painful for each of us to face.

The priests and Pharisees were, of course, furious that this rabble-rouser would disrupt the commercialism being practiced in the Temple and then call it a "den of thieves." This larcenous operation was actually conducted by relatives of the High Priest, Caiaphas, as a family business! (Just imagine what would happen if you acted similarly by going up against the elders and "hierarchy" in some of our local churches.) And referring to the Temple as "a den of thieves" was certainly a major offense against the Holy House.

Both the priests and Pilate distorted the laws of the land at the "trial" in more than one way. But the claim of being a "king" was falsified, yet vital, to the cases of both prosecutions. So, they both distorted and twisted the testimony of Jesus and witnesses in order to make the case that Jesus had claimed to be King — an act of sedition against Rome. Jesus never claimed to be King of Judea, but the priests cleverly coaxed Pilate into making this charge, because to claim to be a King (of any sort) within Caesar's empire was an act of treason against Caesar and punishable only by death. In this way the priests twisted Jesus' admission that He possessed a kingdom "not of this world" — (John 18:36) as a capital offense against Rome in order to "push" a reluctant Pilate into ordering the crucifixion of a man whom he knew to be absolutely innocent.

Remember, at the time of His arrest at *Gethsemane*, Jesus had not yet been charged under any Roman civil statute. (They did not even read Him His "rights" from a Miranda card!) He was picked up by the Temple guards. Herod's trivial civil authority was not even being invoked against this "criminal."

So, the priests actually goaded Pilate into finally bringing a grave civil charge (sedition) against this man. (Luke 23:1 – 2) Also satisfying the priestly conspiracy, the charge of sedition against Caesar called for the death penalty under Roman law. Thus Jesus very likely made a point of announcing His "Kingdom" publicly at the precise location that He selected for The Crucifixion, because Jesus knew all about their laws and statutes and customs. He also had foreknowledge of exactly what, where, when and how they would accomplish His entire Sacrifice. (Nothing was left to chance. Jesus was in control.)

Then Pilate, in order to "make it look good" legally (back home), ordered a sign to be placed on the Cross saying: "King of the Jews." (John 19:19 – 22) Over the priestly protests at this abomination, Pilate stood his ground (this one time) and insisted: "What I have written, I have written." It was Roman custom to write the offense on the cross and to crucify the offender "at the scene of the crime." The "crime" and the execution therefore took place, as Professor Martin[12] has so brilliantly shown, at the *Miphkad Altar* or very close to that location, somewhere near *Olivet* summit.

Now, seeing all these events from the Jewish viewpoint, is it any wonder that Jesus was put to death? (It was all part of His Perfect Plan!) The Jews didn't kill Jesus. The Romans didn't kill Jesus. It's just that none of us prevented it! We couldn't have! It was planned an eternity earlier and by none other than the Lord himself!

Where was The Crucifixion?

Earlier in this chapter you probably jumped right up out of your chair at even the "suggestion" of The Crucifixion having taken place on the Mount of Olives! Rubbish! Why, everybody knows it was either at the Church of the Holy Sepulchre or somewhere over near the Garden Tomb...or...somewhere! ("Gee! I wonder which it really was!")

We should point out, as gently as possible, that no evidence has yet been found that would indicate either of those treasured and traditional tourist "attractions" as the actual location. Hallowed and precious as those sites are to millions of Christians, they both hold their "verification" based only on centuries of tradition. Sorry, no facts. However, we will present just some of the evidence here that backs up the untraditional location "on the other side of town."

Before any of you think I have just gone "off the edge" in my excitement, we can begin by presenting verification of the *Olivet* Crucifixion with just three passages from Scripture.

> *Ezekiel 8:16* "...with their backs toward the Temple of the Lord, and their faces toward the east..."

Therefore, the Temple (and the "veil") faced toward the east. There can be no doubt!

> *Mark 13:3* "And as He sat upon the Mount of Olives facing the Temple..."

Therefore, Jesus faced the Temple (and the "veil") "as He sat upon the Mount of Olives." There can be no doubt!

> *Matthew 27:51 – 54* "...the veil of the Temple was rent in twain...the earth did quake ...and the rocks rent...and the graves were opened...Now the centurion, and they that were with him, watching Jesus, saw the earthquake, and those things that were done..."

Therefore, the centurion and the others *saw* the "veil" rent-in-twain. In fact, they *saw* all "those things" from the top of the Mount of Olives. That is the only place from which they could have seen "those things." There can be no doubt!

As Professor Martin emphasized, the Centurion and the others who witnessed this tearing of the Veil at the instant of Jesus' death could only have seen the veils (and/or Glory Brilliance) from a point directly east of the Temple and high on the western slope of Mt. *Olivet*. In Chapter 4 we showed that the High Priest at the heifer burning "must direct his gaze carefully" in order to see the Veil through the aperture of the East Gate. Would not the centurion have to do likewise in order to see the Veil? He simply could not possibly have seen any of these things either from the Church of the Holy Sepulchre or from the vicinity of the Garden Tomb (Gordon's Calvary) near the Damascus Gate bust station, both of which are west of the Temple site. (See Illus. 18: Elevation Profile of Temple and Temple Mt., Page 151, Illus. 19: Elev. Profile: Temple Mt., Kidron VLY., Mt. Olivet, Page 152, and Illus. 20: Jerusalem as it Appeared in 70 C.E., Page 153.)

Further circumstantial evidence in favor of the Mount of Olives as The Crucifixion site is found in the traditions and Law surrounding the Jerusalem cemetery at that location. There are now, and have been for many centuries, literally a multitude of Jewish dead buried in that ground on the west slope of *Olivet*. (See Cemetery Photo below) This included many Old Testament Prophets and sages, some of whose tombs were opened when the centurion "saw those things." (See Tomb Photo below; also Matthew 27:52 – 53)

The Jewish Cemetery on the Mount of Olives

Multitudes of Jewish dead rest here awaiting Messiah, for: "...*His feet shall stand in that day upon the Mount of Olives...*" (Zechariah 14:4)

Illus. 11: Jewish Cemetery on the Mt. of Olives

Tomb of the Prophets

This well-known tourist stop is the traditional place of entombment for the prophets: Haggai, Malachi, and Zechariah, who also await Messiah at the summit of the Mount of Olives!

Illus. 12: Tomb of the Prophets

Jewish tradition (*Kethuboth* 111b) says: Many Jewish faithful from all over the world are buried at that cemetery because they look forward to *The Resurrection* when Messiah arrives at *Olivet* to rescue Israel from her enemies. They wish, therefore, to meet Him on the

Glorious Day at that point and they don't want to burrow through the Earth in order to greet Him! (Sounds ridiculous?) Not to me. I rejoice that they want to greet Him!

Another Scriptural verification of the Mount of Olives site is drawn from John 19:36 – 37 as John speaks as an eyewitness to events during The Crucifixion. John says:

"For these things were done that the Scripture might be fulfilled, 'A bone of Him shall not be broken.' And again, another Scripture saith, 'They shall look upon Him whom they have pierced.'"

Then, it is almost as if John had been saying: "And there we were at *Olivet* summit, seeing the prophecies of Zechariah fulfilled before our very eyes!" Recalling, we know that Zechariah said: *"They shall look upon Me whom they have pierced."* (From Zechariah 12:10) and *"His feet shall stand in that day upon the Mount of Olives."* (From Zechariah 14:4)

Another point of law concerns the distance of an execution from the Holy of Holies. Yep! You guessed it! A "Sabbath Day's journey." Both traditional Crucifixion sites are located much less than two thousand cubits from the Dome of the Tablets. The Romans also did their best to conduct such punishment where it would be seen by all — as an example, to keep the populace thinking about "staying in line." The summit of the Mount of Olives can be seen from almost anywhere in The Old City or the Temple Mount. Keep in mind, also, the fact that the populace, the citizens, looking up at the Mount of Olives, would not have to squint into the sun at the time Jesus died, "the ninth hour" — 3 P.M. (See Photo below; also Illus. 19: Elev. Profile: Temple Mt., Kidron VLY., Mt. Olivet, Page 152, and Illus. 20: Jerusalem as it Appeared in 70 C.E., Page 153)

Illus. 13: Temple Mt. "At the 9th hour"

Temple Mount "At the 9th Hour"

This telephoto view is from the estimated vicinity of the *Miphkad Altar* as seen at *"the ninth hour of the day;"* i.e. 3 P.M., and near the time of the Passover. Notice the darkly shaded City Wall. (Do you think the centurion — without a telescopic lens! — could have seen that the Veil of the Temple was torn under just these circumstances alone?)

Such detail would certainly be obscured since, at the time of Jesus' death (approximately 3 P.M.), the Veil, on the east side of the *H'ekhal*, would surely have been darkened by the shade of the Portico. (Illus. 16: Isometric View of 2nd Temple, Page 149.) Also, while you were squinting into the 3 P.M. sun, the Veil would be especially difficult to see.

Another "new" thought develops in the Gospel when we contemplate that Sunday morning "foot race" between John and Peter. (John 20:4) If they raced from Jerusalem to a burial site on the near slope of *Olivet*, they ran indeed up a steep incline and it is a credit to the athletic prowess and eagerness of both young men that morning. Otherwise, it would have been just a little jog through the streets to the present "traditional" site at the Church of the Holy Sepulchre or the Garden Tomb.

Tradition has overlooked another obvious factor that should apply the "*coup de grace*" to any thought for The Crucifixion taking place anywhere west of the Temple. All of the sacrifices took place in front (east) of the Temple. It just seems very unlikely that God would choose to offer His only Son for a burnt offering at just some "random" location behind the Temple! (He must surely get a good chuckle at some of "our ways.")

The prospect of Jesus' burial at *Olivet* and not in the Garden Tomb will be a "bitter pill" to many who have romanticized that beautiful site. However, when we look at the evidence truthfully, we may have to redirect our thinking and our "romance" to a different locale.

BAR Magazine published an article[15] in which Mr. Barkay presents good evidence that dates the Garden Tomb to the eighth century B.C.E. The tombs found in that area of Jerusalem today would have been far outside the Jerusalem City walls of the eighth century B.C.E., perhaps even in the environs of a neighboring village — a suburb of sorts. Thus, although the possibility is disappointing to many Christians (including myself), the evidence from Scripture, the Law, history, and logic just doesn't seem to add-up for either the Garden Tomb or the Church of the Holy Sepulchre as the burial site of the Lord Jesus.

But, you say: "If they buried the dead west of the City in the eighth century B.C.E., why do you think they changed the cemetery location to the east during the time of Jesus? Perhaps that's only what you have called 'modern tradition'!"

Zechariah's prophecy was the primary reason for moving the Jerusalem cemetery to the east side, although the proximity of the northwest latrines may also have had some influence on this decision. Zechariah's prophecy concerning the Glorious descent from the Heavens to the Mt. of Olives was pronounced about 516 B.C.E. — a couple of centuries after the period of burials in the Garden Tomb area. Thus, by the time of Jesus, 500 years later, the "rush" to be interred at the Mt. of Olives Cemetery was well established into the tradition of the Jews of the Second Temple. I am confident, therefore, that Joseph (of Arimathea), a very devout Jew and a member of the *Sanhedrin*, surely purchased the family crypt in one of the "choicest" locales on Mt. *Olivet*. It had to be the very BEST of tombs to be the resting place for the broken body of The Lamb of God.

Scriptural evidence proves that The Crucifixion took place on the Mount of Olives. There is also a preponderance of evidence available from historical and archaeological sources that agrees with the Scriptural conclusion. As we proceed through the chapters to follow, much additional evidence, though certainly not all, will be presented.

Professor Martin published a more recent book[25] detailing a much more comprehensive and scholarly analysis of The Crucifixion site. His analysis is supported by many ancient documents, including early Christian historians such as Eusebius of the fourth century. (See Reference 26, Book VI, Chapter 18) Professor Martin's work outlines several of the factors put forth in this discussion as well as several other items of evidence. In any case, these works display an overwhelming preponderance of evidence that indicates *Olivet* summit as the place of The Crucifixion.

Again, may we be reminded, not one strand of evidence, Scriptural or otherwise, has been found that would support even one of the traditional locations for The Crucifixion. I realize

1900 years of traditional teaching by learned, respected, and well-intentioned scholars is difficult to "shake" — but, there it is — for all the world to see.

Evidence in The Temple

The tearing of the outer Veil (curtain) of the Temple at the instant when Jesus "gave up the ghost" has been the subject of some speculation. Scholarly evidence from Temple details, however, can improve our analysis of this subject.

Specifically, there were actually three veils (or curtains) in the Second Temple — not just the thick outer Veil that the centurion is reported to have seen "rent-in-twain." (More about that later.) *Talmud*, (*Yoma* 51) describes in some detail the two inner veils that separated the Holy Place from the Holy of Holies. These two inner curtains replaced the two cedar partitions, which provided the separation of these two holy chambers in the First Temple as discussed in I Kings 6:16.

Moreover, we know from Ezekiel 8:16 and Mark 13:3 that the Temple faced eastward toward *Olivet*, and we also know it was placed high on top of the Temple Mount. The centurion at the Cross, then, would have to be well up the western slope of *Olivet* in order to "see" the Veil at the entrance of the Temple. He could not have seen it from below the City Wall at the floor of the Kidron Valley. (See Illus. 19: Elev. Profile: Temple Mt., Kidron VLY., Mt. Olivet, Page 152)

Even casual familiarity with Temple details would indicate that the massive East Gate of the Sanctuary (Nicanor's Gate) would have to be open in order for the centurion (or anyone) to see the Veil from outside the Temple court. (Illus. 16: Isometric View of 2nd Temple, Page 149, Illus. 17: Detailed Elevation of 2nd Temple, Page 150, Illus. 18: Elevation Profile of Temple and Temple Mt., Page 151, and Illus. 19: Elev. Profile: Temple Mt., Kidron VLY., Mt. Olivet, Page 152.)

No centurion or any other Gentile would be permitted even in the Court of the Women. The centurion therefore had to be standing near the Mount of Olives summit "when he saw those things that were done."

The East Gate provides even more drama to the occasion when we consider that it had to have been open. This massive and beautiful, bright golden bronze gate was opened for all Sabbaths, New Moons, and on Holy Days (feasts). (See Ezekiel 46:1 and *Talmud*, *Sukkah* 53b.) This gate, also known as "Nicanor's Gate," produced "a great noise" because of friction on its "turning hinges" according to *Talmud*, *Yoma* 39b.

On the eve of a Sabbath and the Passover, as when Jesus was crucified, this gate would have been opened with its "great noise" being accompanied by no less than forty-eight trumpet blasts from the ram's horn or *shofar*. (*Sukkah* 53b) Details covering the exact hour of the gate opening schedule on the eve of Passover are unclear from *Talmud* research at this time. Nevertheless, there can be no denying that, on the eve of Passover as The Crucifixion was taking place, "the great noise" of the gate and mixed staccato and squeals of the trumpet calls would certainly have added to the "spooky" conditions leading up to the eclipse, the earthquake, the opened graves, the tearing of the Veil, etc.

We just don't know for certain whether the gate was being opened at the "ninth hour," (3 P.M.) or if it had already been opened at the "third hour" (9 A.M.) as Jesus was being "lifted up." Or maybe it even had "opened of its own accord," as it was to do forty years later. My own preference in this speculative question is that the third hour (9 A,M.) may have been the customary time for opening on the eve of the Sabbath.

The gate opening at 9 A.M. certainly would have been more in keeping with Jesus' fulfillment of the Law concerning the "sprinkling" of His blood "directly before the Tabernacle." We recall that the priest had to see the Veil at the doors of the *H'ekhal* as he sprinkled the heifer's blood seven times. The Veil of course would need to be bathed in sunlight in order that the Priest could see it from a distance of almost one kilometer. We have shown that "the third hour" — 9 A.M. — would be the only time for that opportunity. Otherwise, the curtain and its magnificent coloring could not be viewed, because it would be shaded by the Portico at other times of the day.

It would seem that if the gate had swung open mysteriously by itself at that moment, then the New Testament writers would have noted it. Such a miracle would seem to have been noted as one of "those things that were done." But this is not mentioned. We have already seen that those otherwise marvelous reporters seem to have omitted many details that now appear significant as we behold them with our 20/20 hindsight.

So, we can make all sorts of speculations as to exactly when it was opened or how it was opened, but it had to have been opened on the eve of the Sabbath and it must have been open if the Veil was visible — and it was — because Scripture says "he saw" the Veil rent. We can say for certain that gate was open when "he saw those things." From our detailed study of that gate "aperture" in Chapter 4 we also know the centurion had to be standing at precisely the same location where the High Priest stood when he "directed his gaze carefully" to see the Veil. Nevertheless, we shall need to explain later in our discussion how some spectacular Event and circumstances enabled the centurion to discern that the Veil was torn when Jesus gave up the ghost at the ninth hour, even when the Veil was fully shaded from the 3 P.M. sun.

Not your ordinary "Veil"

We should point out here that we are not attempting to "update" Scripture by changing it even in the slightest manner. Rather, we are endeavoring to enrich Scripture by filling in pertinent and Glorifying details that are provided by secular historians of that same date and locale. Of course, I do concede that some of my own imagination has been sprinkled in here and there. However, again we are attempting to bring more appreciation for Scripture with local information on the events and details discussed.

Understandably, there has been a lot of attention directed toward the Veil of the Temple in this entire work. The Veil that receives most of this attention, is, of course, the thick Babylonian curtain that covered the front doors of the *H'ekhal*, the Holy House itself. We also know this is the veil which was "rent in twain" and is one of "those things" seen by those at The Cross at the moment Jesus died. We can have a bit more appreciation for the

Biblical accounts concerning the Veil if we are better informed about Jewish tradition and the Law regarding the Veil.

Earlier in Chapter 4 we mentioned that the Veil was replaced two times each year with a new one exactly like the previous curtain. We also pointed out that it was customary to display the new Veil each time "so that the people might behold its fair workmanship" as they stood atop the Mount of Olives. But there is much more.

The Veil needed to be replaced at this interval because it would lose its beautiful colors after a time as a result of a number of factors. The blood of the sin bullocks (Leviticus 4:6, 17) was sprinkled *"seven times before the Lord, before the vail of the sanctuary."* Also, it had to be immersed occasionally for cleansing if defiled by anything "unclean." They did not have very many so-called fast color dyes in those times.

Moreover, it was exposed to sunlight and some amount of mountain weather and dust despite its position under the Portico. But, perhaps the strongest reason was because its great weight would cause the Veil to "creep" and to sag non-uniformly, thereby losing its majestic form and symmetry. The Jews were rightly proud of their Veil.

The Veil was not produced by "workman"-ship so much as by young "ladyship!" *Talmud, Shekalim* 8:5 informs us that it was braided by "eighty-two young damsels" using seventy-four cords of twenty-two threads each. This task probably kept these lasses occupied steadily all during those six months intervals because of the size of the task. The Veil was over three inches thick, about thirty feet wide and about sixty feet high. Three hundred priests were required to lift it for its immersion for purification. We detail this in order that a more realistic picture is available when considering the "rending." This was not just your ordinary religious drapery!

Its striking beauty came from its colors, which, according to Exodus 26:36, were blue, purple, and "scarlet." Can you just picture how it would appear to the High Priest as he "directed his gaze carefully" to view the Veil in the sunlight through the open East Gate?

If You Had Been There

It would be interesting now to place oneself in the position of that centurion at The Crucifixion. On the mount called *Olivet*, you and your men have been detailed to crucify, with two other criminals, a Judean who claims to be a king! You are to nail them to three crosses at a place the Judeans call "*Golgotha*" — their word for skull. *Olivet* in that area is piled deep in ashes and skull remnants from burned carcasses of bulls, rams, goats, lambs, etc. from what the Judeans call their "sin offerings." The place is a hideous and depressing scene and has an overpowering stench because they have been dumping *all* of their ashes, skulls, bones and charred remains from *all* their animal sacrifices at this place for about 1000 years. (See Illus. 23: Mt. Olivet viewed from Temple on Crucifixion Day, Page 156, and Illus. 24: Detail of "pit or cavity" in face of Mt. of Olives., Page 157)

This is the place where their "Holy Book" tells them the ashes must be "poured out" (Leviticus 4:12) and where their "nitpicky" Rabbis have further interpreted that this means the ashes must "naturally pour down from a place that is sloping." (*Talmud Zebahim* 106a)

And, this place certainly is sloping; although, we actually are standing back from that spot and in a kind of shelf or pit that has been cut into the western slope. (See *Parah* 4:2, Illus. 24: Detail of "pit or cavity" in face of Mt. of Olives, Page ,157 and Illus. 8: Could this be the Miphkad Altar Site?, Page 47)

The Judean "king's" cross stands centered between the other two and at the exact spot where witnesses have claimed He committed some sort of "abomination." This also is the same spot where their chief Rabbi stands when they burn one of those red cows up here. You look across the valley and see their Temple as the sun behind you bathes the huge curtain at the entrance, rending an explosion of blue, purple and red — a wondrous sight. But you don't know just why all this is happening. You cannot get involved in religion or politics. You just have to do your job as you have been ordered.

Having arrived on the slope of Mt. *Olivet* at about "the third hour," (9 A.M. — Mark 15:25) you heard those weird calls of the Temple priest's trumpet and then that bone-chilling, ominous tone that was building up as the Temple guards opened that huge bronze gate in front of their Temple across the valley. All this happened just as you were "lifting up" this wretched Judean to be crucified for sedition against Caesar — something about claiming to be "King of the Jews"...HA!

It is now about "the ninth hour" (3 P.M. — Mark 15:34) and light of day has returned — after the sun had been mysteriously darkened since "the sixth hour." (12 o'clock, noon — Mark 15:33) Presently, this Judean "crackpot" astoundingly shouts a couple of sentences in His native Aramaic — and "in a loud voice." (Mark 15:37) You are justifiably impressed at this, because you saw this fellow beaten nearly to death during the scourging at your barracks. And now, barely able to take a breath after hanging on that Cross for six hours, still He has strength and mental presence to actually shout two or three complete sentences. Unreal! You have seen many men, "bigger" and "tougher" than He, who didn't have the strength or breath to beg even for water after being suspended during crucifixion for that time.

All "those things" that you "saw," — i.e., the earthquake, the rocks rent, the Veil torn, the graves opened, of course took place very rapidly and at about the same time that this man suddenly died, after His display of inhuman strength and endurance. He just "up-and-died!" (Matthew 27:50) Even in their usual weakened state, some crucifixion victims suffer on that miserable "wiggot" for as long as seven days before finally "giving up the ghost." But this man, who earlier seemed to be doing much better than His two "companions," now dies suddenly and resolutely almost as if He had willed His own death — as if He were in control!

Now, some would think all this had "terrified" you and your men, convincing you at this point that this person was, as He had claimed, the Son of God. Well, not quite. He was evidently not an "ordinary" man. He did have some impressive strengths, including a perfect physique. He didn't even let out so much as a whimper while He was literally stripped of His hide by that flagellum. Neither did He wince or blink His eyes when you drove those quarter inch diameter spikes into His wrists and feet. He just looked at you. And those eyes! All knowing, yet loving and forgiving, as you put Him to death for a crime that nobody had committed. An unusual man, yes — but, maybe not a God.

Next, you feel a little earthquake and there is now light-of-day after the darkness that set in from about noonday until this time. The quake opens some of the graves around you there on the front slope of the mount called *Olivet* and some believe it was "those things" that frightened you and your men and caused you to think perhaps this fellow was a God. That just doesn't figure though, because you and your troops are hardened Roman foot soldiers, well accustomed to seeing "things" like earthquakes, dead bodies, graves, all kinds of unspeakable, unprintable gore, death, sieges, and disasters.

Then, some will say you were terrified when you saw the Veil tear from top to bottom. (Heavy and thick as that curtain was, it is difficult for me to understand why Roman infantrymen would be "terrified" by that.) The Bible goes on to say that not only were you terrified but also you, a Roman centurion — an officer in Caesar's army — said, *"Surely, this man was the Son of God."* Now that is especially hard to swallow. I can have no doubt that you were suddenly convinced of the Divinity of this Galilean, because Holy Scripture says it is so. But, it should take more than just "those things" as described in Scripture to bring you to terror and to this conclusion. What is missing? The Bible has intentionally omitted something subtle in this Event, which we have overlooked in our analysis.

You can see the Temple Veil is torn now. Or can you? Or would you even notice it is torn? It seems unlikely you would notice that kind of damage from that distance (800 to 1,000 yards) across the Kidron Valley.

After all, there had just been an earthquake. The shock must have caused the great weight of the curtain to produce a rip from top to bottom. This shock also may have caused collapse of the Temple doors behind the outer Veil and collapsed the lintels supporting the veils or in some way caused all three veils to part simultaneously, at least for several moments. In this way, a view was provided from the Mount of Olives straight into the Holy of Holies. You would have been looking straight into the Earthly dwelling of the Divine Presence of Almighty God Himself! What a glorious sight that must have been! It also had to be very frightening as that brilliant "fire" — brighter than the sun! — lighted up the man on The Cross above you.

It would seem that the Lord had intended the sun to be in the centurion eyes as he saw this flash. He knew it wasn't just a reflection from some soldier's burnished shield or helmet. It came from under that deeply shaded "front porch" of the Judeans' Temple — almost in the dark. Yet, although the sun was now shining brightly again, this light was even much brighter than the sun — and coming from inside the Temple — and through the torn curtain. Now, with that brilliant light beaming through the rip, we understand how you were able to see that the Veil was torn. What a sight to behold! Almighty God Himself "glowing" proudly yet painfully as He watched His Son, Jesus, lay down His Victorious Payment before the World!

Now I see why you and your squad were so terrified and were moved to believe at once as you did: *"Truly, this man was the Son of God!"* (See Chapter 9, "The Rending of the Veil.") But, I still don't understand why the Bible didn't tell us all "those things."

In any case, the centurion would have reason to be impressed because, even in daylight, a brilliant light from the Judean's Temple has just illuminated the man on the Cross above him

— like a spotlight or perhaps even lighting up the entire mountainside! This sight would understandably have "terrified" the centurion and his execution detail squad.

"Then, when the centurion and those with him who were guarding Jesus saw the earthquake...and all that had happened, they were terrified, and exclaimed, "Surely he was the Son of God." Matthew 27:54 (NIV)

Keeping His Schedule

We should not miss the opportunity to observe how the Glory of God is magnified in these events by His Precise Timing. Earlier we showed how the Lord "set up" His own sacrifice and fulfillment of the Law by arranging to be "lifted up" at "the third hour." This timing was necessary in order to fulfill the Law pertaining to the sprinkling of the Red Heifer's blood, which also was done at the "third hour."

Leading up to His offering upon The Cross, Jesus had to complete a little-known statute from the Law; nevertheless, it was a very important statute. Under *Pesachim* 96a, as directed by Exodus 12:3, *"...In the tenth day of this month (Nisan) they shall take to them every man a lamb,...a lamb for a house."* And, in Exodus 12:6 they are commanded: *"And ye shall keep it up until the fourteenth day of the same month; and the whole assembly of the congregation of Israel shall kill it in the evening."*

The "little-known statute" is manifested by two footnotes in *Pesachim* 96a which point out that the lamb was selected on the tenth day and "examined every day until the fourteenth" to insure there was no blemish on this Holy offering. Jesus fulfilled this somewhat obscure statute as the Rabbis selected Him for death when He entered the City triumphantly on the tenth of *Nisan*. He "kindled" their wrath as the excited throng shouted Hosannahs and adoringly placed palm fronds across His path. The Rabbis then questioned and *watched Jesus every day until the fourteenth of Nisan.* During those four days, NOBODY — not even Pilate — could find any "blemish" or "spot" on the Lord's Passover Lamb.

Jesus also exercised His own will, of course, in controlling His death on The Cross "at the ninth hour." It was not a coincidence and that hour was not at the discretion of the centurion The Lord died at that hour in order to maintain His Schedule.

He had to die as the Paschal Lamb of God on the Passover because, according to the Law of Exodus 12:6, on the fourteenth day of the month, *"...the whole assembly of the congregation of Israel shall kill it in the evening."* In ancient cultures, "evening" began at about 3 P.M. That was also the precise hour at which the priests began slaying the Paschal lambs in accordance with the Law, in compliance with Exodus 12:6 and *Aboth* 5:6, *Pesachim* 61a. Josephus 2 Wars 6.9.3/423 states that the sacrifices began at 3 P.M., continuing until 5 P.M.

In this way Jesus fulfilled the Passover. The next feast to be fulfilled was the Feast of Unleavened Bread. He therefore had to be off The Cross and in The Tomb before the next day began (at sunset) because the bread must be "eaten" with the Lamb. Jesus had to begin "baking" as our Unleavened Bread of Life in The Tomb. (Perhaps you knew that the name of

His birthplace, little Bethlehem, is from the Hebrew: "*beth*" (house) and "*lehem*" (bread); i.e., "House of Bread.")

It was necessary for Jesus to die at 3 P.M. on the eve of the Sabbath, in order that the East Gate of the Temple (Nicanor's Gate) would be open at that precise moment for the centurion to be able to confront the Divine Presence of Almighty God when the Veil was rent in twain from top to bottom. Perfect Timing! It had to be! The Law must be fulfilled — every "jot" and "tittle."

We would be remiss here to neglect another fulfillment of the Law if we did not mention His avoidance of the breaking of the legs, as suffered by the two thieves. (John 19:31 – 37) In order to hasten the death of crucifixion victims, sometimes their legs were broken in order that they would not be able to lift themselves to relieve their cramped, agonized, breathless position. In doing so, they actually prolonged their agony as well as the entire ordeal. And so it was on this day, as Passover was approaching. Everybody wished to "get it over with" and go home. However, when they came to Jesus to break His legs, the soldiers passed Him by because He was already dead. In this way, Jesus fulfilled His service to the Law of the Passover Lamb in Exodus 12:46.

"...neither shall ye break a bone thereof."

This was also a fulfillment of the prophecy in Psalms 34:20,

"He keepeth all His bones; not one of them is broken."

Of course, the "Divine Schedule" proceeded from there to fulfill all the other feasts and Law, which we cannot take time to discuss here. However, all was fulfilled on Schedule. Who but the Lord Himself could have written, produced, directed, and starred in any drama even approaching this for message, plot, staging, and just plain class?

Caiaphas; Should we "judge" him?

There is a natural inclination, especially for those of western cultural origin, to assign "good-guy" or "bad-guy" connotations to characters we meet. It occurred to me as I was writing this, that we have been guilty of "judging" Israel's High Priest, Caiaphas, by tabbing him as arch-villain in our Passion drama.

But, since we know that the Divine Presence was indeed dwelling in the Temple after The Crucifixion, let us just pause to consider a "tradition-shaking" implication. This means God actually *accepted* Caiaphas as High Priest!

On the next Day of Atonement, after a few months following The Crucifixion, Caiaphas was required to appear as Israel's High Priest before the Lord (in His form as *Shekhinah*) in the Holy of Holies to plead atonement by confessing and requesting forgiveness of his own sins as well as those of Israel. (See *Talmud Mishnah* quoted under "The Crimson Strap," Chapter 7.)

If the Lord did not accept Caiaphas after his vile actions at the "trial," He could have struck Caiaphas dead. He certainly wouldn't have to permit Caiaphas to come before Himself at the Divine Presence. There, especially, He would have had "just" reason to strike Caiaphas dead, to show all of Israel His displeasure with their High Priest.

Talmud, *Yoma* 9a, records that the period of the Second Temple was rife with corruption in that high and Holy office. Further, tractate *Pesachim* 57a reveals that often men who once became High Priest would retain that lofty title and continue to hold great prestige even after being deposed! At times there were often several men who held such power and intimidation just through the title of the position. Reading between-the-lines of the Gospel, we see some of this intrigue and injustice in the nepotism and blatant criminal blasphemy of Caiaphas and his father-in-law, Annas. More of this shameful history will be presented in Chapter 7.

But the Lord chose not to deal with Caiaphas and Israel in the way that perhaps you or I would have preferred. Everyone knows the "bad-guy" always gets his just "reward" eventually. (The Lord forgave all of us at The Cross.) If Caiaphas repented after he saw all those weird signals "forty years before the Temple was destroyed," he may have even received salvation. We cannot judge Caiaphas.

If the Lord can forgive King David and Paul (and you and me) and King Nebuchadnezzar (Daniel 4:34 – 37) and lots of other "bad-guys," then maybe — just maybe — He can also forgive Caiaphas. Let us not hate Caiaphas by judging him; even though we must certainly detest his actions when he was confronted by the Lord Jesus.

Historians[5] record that Caiaphas was deposed from his office as High Priest after The Crucifixion, 36 C.E. We can only wonder now — did he see these things as they began to happen during those "forty years before the Temple was destroyed?" Of course he did. He had to have seen those signs. He was the High Priest. This happened during his "watch."

Did Caiaphas perhaps have second thoughts about that resolute carpenter who would not deny that He was Messiah? After all, didn't these signs begin to appear immediately after that "wretched impostor and blasphemer" was put to death? We recall that Gamaliel, Paul's mentor and a Pharisee "lawyer" of high reputation, had cautioned the *Sanhedrin* that they might be in grave error by persecuting the followers of Jesus. (Acts 5:34 – 39) Was Caiaphas relieved as High Priest perhaps because all these incidents caused him to soften his position against this "Galilean apostasy," which was now gaining strength in Jerusalem, and in all Judea, and in Samaria, etc.? Who can know?

The Character of God

This story of *Shekhinah* illustrates the character of God. We see Him saddened by the disobedience of His children. We share His sorrow as we hear Him weep and rebuke them as He withdraws from His earthly palace. The Lord is saddened at leaving and, with "human" emotions, He returns for one-last-look before leaving His house. He is depressed, but at the same time He is firm and resolved to correct these "naughty children." Yet, He is also patient and caring in that He doesn't just condemn them and rush off. He stays to rebuke and to plead with them for 3 ½ years — trying to keep them from certain disaster.

Finally, however, after giving them adequate time to repent, He departs using a subtle gesture involving locale (*Olivet* Summit) to show them that He will return for them after He goes "back to His Place." This single incident shows the "human" qualities of the Lord, which are often seen in the Scriptures, but which we seldom have seen from any other historical source.

Truly, this is a love story, another like so many stories in the Bible, that demonstrates God's love for His People and for the rest of us. It all begins with our response to His "courting" of our favors, our acceptance and use of his "gifts," but at first without our commitment to a "betrothal." Then, our fickle hearts turn away from Him after being attracted to other "lovers." This rejection does not deter Him, however; for He continues to "pursue" us (His "bride") and forgives our perfidy. Finally — a happy ending! We surrender to Him "unconditionally" and are reunited with Him.

Jesus said it best, when Phillip asked about God's character:

"...he that hath seen Me hath seen the Father..." (From John 14:9)

6

Prophecies Seen in This Event

Ezekiel shows need for Heifers – How Feast of Trumpets will be fulfilled – A "HIGH" Sabbath – Seven years of Tribulation – "Timing" in the Last Days – They will know "the Day"

Several popular and Scripturally sound teachings of prophecy are impacted by the *Shekhinah* event and other related facts in this story. This discussion addresses some new thoughts that should be considered. Again, you are invited (encouraged!) to think of other prophetical relevance that we have not discussed.

More Heifers for the Unclean

Much of this story has touched upon the Ashes of the Red Heifer and the *Miphkad Altar* because of archaeological interests and other factors that are fundamental to the *Shekhinah* Withdrawal Event, as well as being of great importance relative to The Crucifixion. These facts also are of vital importance in prophecy and should be included in this segment of our study.

A key prophecy relating to the "Last Days" is given in Daniel 9:27.

The "prince that shall come" (Antichrist) "shall cause the sacrifice and the oblation to cease" exactly three and one half years (one half "week") before Messiah arrives. It is obvious then, Israel surely must resume the Temple sacrifices at some time before the sacrifices are halted.

BUT — The sacrifices cannot be offered unless and until the ashes of the Red Heifer are recovered. The Law requires that the Temple, the priests, and all articles used in those offerings must be purified by sprinkling of those ashes from the burnt Red Heifer mixed with "living water." (Numbers 19)

Furthermore, the ashes of that first heifer, burnt by Moses and Eleazar in the *Sinai*, mixed with the ashes from all heifers offered since that time are the only ashes that are acceptable under the Law. A commandment from the Lord (Numbers 19:10) and from the Law (*Talmud*, *Parah* 3:1 and 3:5) instructs that those first ashes are "for a statute forever." In other words, they cannot just burn a new heifer. The original ashes as mixed with all the others must be found and recovered and used "as a purification for sin."

For all of the reasons stated in Scripture and in the Law then, the burning of the Red Heifer is the single most important rite of all the Jewish Temple rituals, without question. No ashes, no priests, no Tabernacle, no Temple, no sacrifices! — no fulfillment of prophecy! We know *that* cannot be! So then, "It's not to worry!" Those ashes *will* be found! There can be *no* doubt!

Rabbinical authorities consider the Law regarding the Red Heifer ceremony to be a classic example of a *hukkah*. That is, a statute for which Jewish teachers can *presently* derive no logical explanation, and yet, it is of such Divinely commanded stature that it must be rigidly followed in every detail. One source, Reference 36, under Numbers Chapter 19, referencing a most respected 11th - 12th century French/Jewish Rabbinical sage, Rashi, says it means, in so many words, that the Lord is saying: "It is a decree from before Me, and *you are not at liberty to cavil at My decrees.*" A major rationale for such firmness is that "the evil inclination" (Satan) as well as hostile Gentile detractors would use such disobedience to accuse Israel of being lax or careless in their faith.

It is a tragic irony that the Red Heifer is the least known and the least understood of all the Jewish rituals while it is without question the most important. So, is anybody trying to find these ashes? Again, it's not-to-worry! A joint Jewish and Christian archaeological team is close to recovering the ashes after an exciting search of about forty years at this date, 2007 C.E.

Through a "stroke-of-luck" (more like a miracle!) directions and detailed instructions for locating the ashes were found in 1952. One search team, headed by Texan minister/archaeologist Vendyl M. Jones and formerly the late Chief Rabbi of Israel, Shlomo Goren, is expected to reach the precious urn (*Kalal*) containing the ashes sometime in the very near future. Then we can get on with the remaining fulfillments of all prophecies leading up to the return of the Lord Jesus! However, we must take note here that the ashes and fulfillments of prophecies discussed here have absolutely nothing to do with the next fulfillment; i.e., the taking away or "rapture" of The Church.

Another reason for urgency toward finding the Red Heifer ashes (and *Miphkad Altar*) is that the Jews are almost certain to run out of ashes unless they burn at least one new Red Heifer during the coming seven years of The Tribulation. Many scholars of prophecy teach that the battle of *Gog* and *Magog*, the Russian invasion of Israel, will occur early during the Tribulation and perhaps soon after Antichrist is revealed. (This is not the battle of Armageddon.)

The key to this subtlety concerning an early need for more ashes is given by the prophet Ezekiel. Briefly, the armies of *Gog* will be so badly mauled that only one sixth of their number will survive in defeat *"upon the mountains of Israel"* (Ezekiel 39:2). Then comes the cause for nearing depletion of the ashes. *"Yea, all the people of the Land (Israel) shall bury them."* (Ezekiel 39:11 – 13)

Yes! There will be so many dead among the invaders from Russia and her allies that seven months will be required for the Israelites to bury the dead in order *"that they may cleanse the Land."* (Ezekiel 39:12) This means all those Jews who bury the dead must be purified afterwards by those ashes if they are to return to "cleanness" under the Law. Over one million Israelis burying dead enemy soldiers is going to require an awesome quantity of ashes. According to the prophecy then, all or most of Israel will have returned to living under the Law at that time. A tendency towards that condition can be seen today in Israel's political strata.

An interesting clue concerning timing of this invasion by *Gog* and *Magog* is given by the phrases saying it shall require Israel seven months to *"cleanse the Land."* The Land (Israel), including each and every house, must be purified for the Passover. Then, if it is going to require seven months prior to Passover, the burying of that multitude will begin before *Yom Kippur*, Day of Atonement. Israelis would then be disposing of all those dead bodies during the coming seven months. Demonstrating for readers who are unfamiliar with the Jewish calendar months, we cover seven Jewish months as we begin with *Yom Kippur* in the month of *Tishri*, followed by *Cheshvan*, *Kislev*, *Tebeth*, *Shebat*, *Adar* and extending until the Passover, which is in the month of *Nisan*. This might be at the same time when Antichrist will be revealed; i.e., when he makes that seven year covenant with Israel. (Daniel 9:27)

Antichrist may, in fact, be elevated to power by having taken credit for the "miraculous" destruction of *Gog*'s forces *"upon the mountains of Israel"* — i.e., Lebanon. (Ezekiel 39:4) From what we have read about him, it would be not at all surprising that "the man of sin" would lie greatly, seeking to derive glory for himself by claiming to have done what God in Truth had done.

Ancient Judaism was not so blind concerning Ezekiel's prophecy (Ezekiel 38 and 39) of the invasion of Israel when this great army from the North comes *"to take a spoil"* in the latter days. Rodkinson's *Talmud*,[24] in *Pesachim* tractate, records a statement written in about 200 C.E. by Rabbi Johanan ben Nappaha, in which he says the time of that war will be just before the coming of Messiah and "will be the worst period for the Israelites to pass through." (Also *Pesachim* 118a in Reference 21)

Worse than the Holocaust? Sadly, yes. Jesus says the Earth will be in such turmoil, if He were to delay beyond His timely arrival, there would be nobody remaining to greet Him.

"And except that the Lord had shortened these days, no flesh should be saved; but for the elect's sake, whom He hath chosen, He hath shortened the days." Mark 13:20

His "elect" will survive that "time of Jacob's trouble," having been "elected" to greet Him at His coming and to *"look upon Me whom they have pierced."*

It is interesting that the Jewish tradition of the *Talmud Sukkah* 2a, referring to Isaiah 4:6, discloses that Judaism considers the Messianic age as that same time which Evangelical Christians call the Kingdom Age or the Millennium, etc.

Along this same trend, "at the end of days" another *Talmudic* commentary reveals a traditional view of things "of the future world." Tractate *Berakoth* 17a says the future world is not like this world. In the next world there will be no eating, no drinking, no propagation, no business, no jealousy, no hatred, no competition. But, the righteous will sit with their crowns on their heads feasting on the brightness of the Divine Presence. This observation is taken concerning Exodus 24:11.

So, we see that in some ways the Jewish Believers are not so far different from Christians in some of their interpretations of Scripture. Surely the basic difference exists only in the *Personal* identity of that *One* whose (pierced) feet shall stand that Day on the Mount of Olives.

Closed Door Policy

One of the key archaeological interests in this study has been the immense Eastern Gate (Nicanor's Gate). Its halting expanse of gleaming, golden-hued bronze dominated the front of the Temple complex and shielded the front of the *H'ekhal* from direct view. This same gate is very prominent in prophecies of "the End Times" as well:

> *"Then He brought me back by the way of the gate of the outward sanctuary which looketh toward the east; and it was shut.*
>
> *Then said the Lord unto me; 'This gate shall be shut, it shall not be opened, and no man shall enter in by it; because the Lord, the God of Israel, hath entered in by it, therefore it shall be shut.*
>
> *It is for the Prince; the Prince, He shall sit in it to eat bread before the Lord; He shall enter by way of the porch of that gate, and shall go out by the way of the same.'"* Ezekiel 44:1 – 3

We encounter a curious situation here concerning Jewish interpretation of this prophecy of the gate that "shall be shut." That is, "the gate of the outward sanctuary which looketh toward the east." Almost anyone would reason that Ezekiel is referring to the mammoth east gate (Nicanor's Gate) because everything he has been describing (measuring) during the previous two chapters and beyond this passage has been "outside the House" — in the courts and walls. Moreover, he has referred to the intricate arrangement of folding doors, located behind the Veil at the entrance, as "doors" and not as "gates." (Ezekiel 41:2) *Middoth* 4:1 describes these as two *"folding doors,"* having one pair of *"hinged leaves"* on the south side of the *H'ekhal* entrance and another pair of leaves on the north side.

Ezekiel was given these measurements in "*the five and twentieth year of our captivity;*" several years before the Second Temple was built by Zerubbabel. The Jews were following the measurements and "ordinances" directed through that prophet as they rebuilt the Temple. The Rabbis did not consider any difference between the "Millennial Temple" and this rebuilt (Second) Temple. They thought they were building the Temple for Messiah, the Prince. – **They even *knew* the date of His Coming! – as they had read from Daniel 9:25-26.**

They expected this to be the Temple from which "living waters" would flow from the "Water Gate" on the "right side" of the House. (Ezekiel 47:1 – 2) They followed all the cubit measurements for the House, the courts, the chambers, the gates. All of the Lord's "ordinances" for the priests and the sacrifices were instituted "to the letter." And yes, they "shut the gate" as they believed the Lord had instructed — but they shut the wrong gate at the wrong time!

The Jews of the first century were expecting the Messiah to come and rest His feet on *Olivet* and bring victory over Israel's oppressors and enemies. They expected *Olivet* to "*cleave in the midst thereof*" and the *living waters* would cause the little desert village of *En Gedi*, on the shores of the Dead Sea, to be a prosperous commercial fishing center! (Ezekiel 47:10) If you have ever been to *En Gedi*, it may be difficult to believe it could ever become a fishing center. But the Lord says it *shall be*!

They were expecting a victorious, conquering Messiah to sit in that Gate. They were not looking for — nor did they welcome — this Nazarene carpenter who surrounded Himself with the likes of commercial fishermen, tax collectors, prostitutes...lepers!

Nevertheless, imagine now the frustrating, puzzling, "pained!" choice the Rabbinical "lawyers" faced. Some of the vision of the Temple was instruction for building the Second Temple and some of it was prophecy of things that were to happen to the rebuilt (Second) Temple and even to the Millennial or Third Temple in days to come. Close inspection of this Scripture while following the Temple descriptions recorded by Josephus, *Talmud*, etc., reveals that the Jews were "religiously" dedicated to compliance with Ezekiel's specifications. Nevertheless, the Jews of the Second Temple encountered considerable difficulty in separating "instruction" from "prophecy" in Ezekiel's message. Put yourself in their position.

Their reasoning must have been something like this:

- If this is prophecy that has been fulfilled sometime in the past, then it means if the Lord had already "entered through it," just when could He have done that? — The Second Temple had not yet been built when Ezekiel wrote in the "five and twentieth year" of our captivity.

- Or, if this is a prophecy not yet fulfilled, then He will shut the gate whenever He does "enter through it."

- But, on the other hand, if He is instructing us to keep Nicanor's Gate shut, how can we do that? In the words of the Prophet himself, that gate must be opened on the eve of each Sabbath, on each new moon, and on each Feast Day. (Ezekiel 46:1) The High Priest must "carefully direct his gaze" through that gate from

Olivet summit when he sprinkles the heifer's blood "*directly before the Tabernacle seven times.*" He must be saying the "*folding doors*" at the front of the *H'ekhal* must remain closed. Yea! That's it!

- The opposing "lawyers" counter: "Rubbish! We cannot close the entrance to the *H'ekhal*! — that the doors '*shall not be opened.*' The High Priest must enter there to plead for our atonement on the day of *Yom Kippur*. He must enter through those doors and walk along the north wall of the Holy Place carrying the Censer and the Blood into the Holy of Holies. How can the doors remain shut?!"

- Then, one attorney who was well-practiced in the delicate jurisprudence of compromise, offered a brilliant codicil to the parties favoring closing the folding doors at only one side of the *H'ekhal* entrance. He suggested, "Let us keep the folding doors on the south closed in perpetuity; in accordance with the Scripture: 'that they shall not be opened.' However, we shall grant easement to the High Priest for entry on *Yom Kippur* on the appointed day through the folding doors on the north. In this way, we will remain in compliance with the principal overgoverning statute by maintaining closed doors in keeping with the 'incontestarium' statute from the Lord's solemn instruction; which at the same time, will satisfy all of the pursuant clauses in participle with the aforementioned ancillary statutes; namely, the incinerated Offering of the Red Heifer attendant with and pertaining to the ministrations stipulated in adherence by the High Priest on *Yom Kippur*."

This is how they seem to have settled the matter. The southern doors ("gates") were shut, but the priest was permitted entry through the north doors on the Day of Atonement. This way everybody was happy — everybody except the Lord, that is. The Rabbis did not want to accept this idea that the Lord would shut Nicanor's Gate as punishment for their iniquities and transgressions.

The Lord Jesus "entered in" by Nicanor's Gate to make his sacrifices, thus fulfilling that portion of prophecy. And we *now* know for certain this was a prophecy and not an instruction. Forty years later the "closure" was fulfilled, when Nicanor's magnificent doors were crushed, burned, and melted by rampaging Roman soldiers.

Now, at this point some may argue, as no doubt some Rabbis countered, "But Ezekiel 43:4 says the Divine Presence *entered* the Temple by that gate 'whose prospect is toward the east' and the prophecy was thereby fulfilled when He 'entered in.' So, we must see that it remains shut. — It is a commandment from the Lord thy God."

Others would amend that by saying Ezekiel 43:4 refers to the return of the Glory to the Millennial or Third Temple and/or possibly even the "New Jerusalem" and the prophecy of Ezekiel 44:2 was therefore fulfilled when Jesus "entered in." With these latter scholars I must agree, because the Temple Ezekiel discussed here has "waters" rushing from under the "right" side of the threshold. We must pause here to consider again the fact that the Jewish planners of what we call "the Second Temple" sincerely believed they were building that Temple for the Glorious arrival of Messiah, Son of David – to claim His Kingdom. In effect, therefore, they were building to the same "PLAN" that will be implemented for what we – in this series – are calling the "Third Temple." – For this reason, you can observe the Plan of the TRUE Third Temple by viewing Illus. 15: Plan of Second Temple (by Dr. A.S. Kaufman), Page 148.[7, 40]

How do we know Ezekiel is speaking of a much later Temple? Just a few verses later, Ezekiel 43:7, the Lord says:

"...where I will dwell in the midst of the children of Israel forever..."

That latter Promise has not yet reached fulfillment, because Israel has not yet reached the Messianic Age.

We maintain therefore that Jesus fulfilled the "entering in" portion of Ezekiel 44:2. Then, the return of the Glory to the Millennial Temple or possibly the New Jerusalem (Heaven) will (someday) satisfy Ezekiel 43:4.

Yes, it is complex and difficult to follow. Although, it is much easier if one has 20/20 hindsight. The Rabbis could not figure out how the Lord was going to "pull this off." Sadly then, the Rabbis interpreted the Scripture into a "Law" to make this a "statute" instead of recognizing that it was a prophecy.

The prophecy continues by saying in Ezekiel 44:2 that *"The Lord, the God of Israel hath entered in by it"*; and in verse 3, *"...He shall enter by the way of the porch of that gate, and shall go out by the way of the same."* Here is a very subtle legal problem. By the Law, every person who entered the Temple was required to exit at a gate other than the gate through which he had entered. (Ezekiel 46:8 – 9 and *Berakoth* 62b) And NOBODY, not even Jesus, was permitted to leave the Temple by exiting through the East Gate; because in so doing, one would turn his back on the Holy House. Remember in Ezekiel's vision (Ezekiel 8:16 – 17) how the Lord considered it an "abomination" that those priests worshiped the sun with their backs to the Temple? It *was* an abomination! There was only *One* who could turn His back on the Holy House while deliberately ignoring and departing from His former dwelling. He certainly was seen to do just that as His Divine Presence – the *Shekhinah* – departed through the East Gate on the Feast of Pentecost, 66 C.E. — See Appendix B.

Jesus entered by "the porch" of Nicanor's Gate, with all other devout Jews, to bring ritual sacrifice for a burnt offering on the Altar in the Court of Israelites. As an obedient and "ordinary" citizen, Jesus exited the court at either the south or west gate just like the other Israelites had done for fifteen centuries — ever since the Tabernacle.

In 66 C.E. on the Feast Day of Weeks, the Pentecost, the East Gate was opened in keeping with the Law, and the Lord, the God of Israel (as *Shekhinah*), "went out by way of the same" gate that He (as Jesus) had entered in about thirty-six years earlier, in 30 C.E. The prophecy was fulfilled, exactly as Ezekiel had foretold. Ezekiel omitted one important detail. The Lord entered through the East Gate traveling incognito as a Galilean carpenter come to present His burnt offering before God. Most would agree that it would have been difficult for first-century Judaism to have understood this.

And so, the Gate was shut. Not by Suleiman in the sixteenth century, but by the Roman soldiers as they burned and sacked Jerusalem and the Temple after the siege in 70 C.E. So, it was written; and so it came to pass.

Fulfilling the Feasts

Many scholars and teachers of end-time prophecy have taught (and not with casual reasoning) that Jesus has fulfilled the first four of the seven Feasts of Jehovah so far, with each in its chronological order and on the exact day of each feast. The last feast fulfilled is considered to have been *Shavuot* (Pentecost) and — most believe — the next to be fulfilled will be the Feast of Trumpets (*Rosh Hashanah*.)

It would seem that the departure of the Divine Presence from the Temple on Pentecost in 66 C.E. would be another major fulfillment. There also may be prophetic significance in the fact that this occurred exactly thirty-six years (6 × 6) after Pentecost 30 C.E., which we recognize as the beginning of the Church Age. (Later in this chapter we shall explain some of the significance of the number "six.")

Although *Chanukah* is not one of the seven Feasts of Jehovah, the likelihood of the *Shekhinah* Ascension occurring during that season may also figure into this puzzle in some way. But this sequence certainly is disruptive to the order that has been taught (and accepted) with such popularity. Perhaps an explanation is needed, but presently I do not have any explanation to offer.

Before discussing fulfillment of these feasts, strictly a Christian interpretation, we should identify the significance of each feast from the traditional Judaic perspective.

Pesach (Passover)

Celebrating the sparing of Israel's firstborn in Egypt when the blood of the Passover Lamb was smeared on the doorposts to turn away the Angel of Death. The lamb is to be selected, unblemished, on the 10th day of *Nisan* (Exodus 12:3 – 5) and is to be slain on the evening of the fourteenth day of the month, *Nisan*. As it says in Exodus 12:6 –

> "And ye shall keep it up until the fourteenth day of the same month; and the whole assembly of the congregation of Israel shall kill it in the evening."

Hag Hamatzah (Unleavened Bread)

In memory of the haste in departure of the children of Israel from Pharaoh's tyranny. – They could not wait for their bread to rise. The Lamb having been slain on "the evening" of the fourteenth; then the Passover meal is served *that night*, which is *after* sundown and therefore is conducted actually on 15 *Nisan*. Again, as it says in Exodus 12:8 –

> "And they shall eat the flesh in that night, roast with fire, and unleavened bread; and with bitter herbs shall they eat it."

After sunset, as the fifteenth of *Nisan* begins, the Passover Lamb is eaten at the meal (*Seder*). *Talmud* (*Pesachim* 119b) instructs that one who eats the *Seder* must finish the meal with the taste of the Paschal Lamb and the unleavened bread in his mouth. Since fermentation is ritually "unclean," no yeast or leavened bread is permitted for seven days. The day of 15 *Nisan* is always a "Sabbath" — regardless of which day of the week it falls upon.

First Fruits

Thanking the Lord for the first harvest of Spring, especially the barley harvest. This feast begins on the 16th of *Nisan*. In compliance with Leviticus 23:11, this would be *"the morrow after the Sabbath,"* wherein the "Sabbath" is the day following Passover; i.e., the 15th day of *Nisan*. The 15th is a "Sabbath" regardless of whether it arrives following sunset on a "Friday" night. That is, it is not *necessarily* on the weekly Sabbath. That day is a Sabbath because, as it says in Leviticus 23:7 —

> *"...ye shall have an holy convocation: ye shall do no servile work therein."*

For many centuries and continuing even in these times, there has been great disagreement among Biblical scholars as to whether First Fruits occurs on the day after the weekly Sabbath or if 15 *Nisan* is actually a "Sabbath" as it says: "a holy convocation and permitting no servile work." A respected Judaica source, Reference 36, notes under Leviticus 23:11 that the *Sadducees* held to the interpretation that the "Sabbath" reference was indicating the weekly Sabbath. First Fruits then would, under that ruling, occur on the first day of the week (Sunday) following the Passover. The Pharisees, nevertheless, adhered to the literal interpretation which called for that Passover Sabbath to be 15 *Nisan*, and which of course could occur on any day of the week. It is interesting no note that this often bitter controversy is not confined to Rabbinical scholars. Some Christian teachers are allied to either of these positions as well.

Through "Divine Coincidence" as it happens, Jesus was resurrected on 16 *Nisan* and which also fell on the first day of the week (Mark 16:9) and which was not only "the morrow after the Sabbath" ruled under Leviticus 23:7, but also followed a regular weekly Sabbath Day, the seventh day of the week. By fulfilling the Law of First Fruits in this way, Jesus left neither side any opportunity for complaint.

In Jewish tradition, when 15 *Nisan* falls on the weekly Sabbath, such an occurrence is called a "High Sabbath" and is termed "a more Holy feast" in the Passover *Haggadah* (instructions) when those Sabbaths coincide in the manner just described. The occasion of Jesus, the Lamb of God, being risen as the Lord's First Fruit of The Resurrection was indeed appropriately *"on the morrow"* following a *High* Sabbath. (See John 19:31)

We must take note here that, during Biblical times, the waving of the first Spring harvest on 16 *Nisan* — the *omer*, or sheaf of barley, was the most holy and therefore the most important of the "first fruit" offerings. There were similar offerings for all of the other crops that were harvested later; although, historians are clear that the *omer* feast day was done with "considerable ceremony," as reported in Reference 37. It is further explained that this was done "in order to emphasize dissent" against the *Sadducees* in the argument concerning interpretation of *"the morrow after the Sabbath"* just described.

Emphasis and holiness of the *omer* ceremony is demonstrated by the details of the procedure. The procedure is described thoroughly in Reference 37 and in *Menahoth* 6:3.

The ceremony began just at sunset on the first day of unleavened bread, which would be as 15 *Nisan* was ending, on the *next* evening following the evening of the Passover meal, the *Seder*. Remembering, 15 *Nisan* is a "Sabbath" because no work is permitted on *that* day. A huge throng of people came to Jerusalem from all nearby villages to witness the occasion. Just as darkness fell, as 16 *Nisan* arrived, the priest who was to "harvest" the *omer* asked the assemblage: "Has the sun set? — Has the sun set?" The people answered, "Yea. — Yea." Twice more he repeated the question and twice they replied, "Yea. — Yea." Continuing, the priest asked: "Is this the sickle? — Is this the sickle?" "Yea. — Yea." And, twice more the question was repeated and twice answered. Then, "Is this the basket? — Is this the basket?" And they replied, "Yea. — Yea.", etc.

If the 16th of *Nisan* was a weekly Sabbath day (Saturday), the more Orthodox Pharisees had a specially contrived ritual arranged so as to "rub it in" for the unruly *Sadducees* by adding: "Is this the Sabbath day?! — Is this the Sabbath Day?!" And gaining the familiar response — "Yea. — Yea." At no other time was it lawful to "work" (harvest with sickles) on a Sabbath; however, in the Pharisees' interpretation, such "work" was an actual requirement during a weekly Sabbath falling on that date, in order to be in compliance with Leviticus 23:11. They could not harvest the *omer* during 15 *Nisan* because that Sabbath was more Holy than the weekly Sabbath, according to Leviticus 23:7. Therefore it was ordered that the harvest would be done on 16 *Nisan* — *"the morrow after the Sabbath"* — even if 16 *Nisan* was a weekly Sabbath. Hence, they really made an issue of this in order to ridicule the *Sadducees*. The priest then asked: "Shall I harvest? — Shall I harvest?" This was answered by, "Do harvest, — Do harvest." — and twice more the entire routine was repeated.

Obviously, the questioning in the procedure is very similar to the queries at the Red Heifer ceremony: "Is this cedarwood?,"

"Is this hyssop?," etc., etc., described earlier. The sheaf was then "waved" before the Temple and the grain was made into two loaves of "the bread of the first fruits." (From Leviticus 23:16 – 17) The loaves were to be *exactly alike*. No meal offering could be brought to the Temple until these two loaves had been offered up on the Feast of *Shavuot*, seven weeks later. In this we see reflected some of the same "pictures" that came with the Atonement Goat and the Scapegoat, to be discussed in a later chapter.

Significantly, the Lord's Holy number — three — is emphatically present in this ritual. Three men were assigned as "harvesters," and there were three *seahs* (totaling about one bushel) of sheaves and *three* sickles and *three* baskets. Each of the questioning sequences was pronounced *three* times. Such a procedure led to a lengthy and complicated ceremony, thereby underlining its importance. Sadly, the ceremony has been greatly diminished in content and importance since destruction of the Temple and since the children of Israel have been "scattered to the nations."

In fact, in modern Judaism, more "practical" application of the Law has ruled that First Fruits shall be more than a month later — on 6 *Sivan* (which is actually *Shavuot*; i.e., Pentecost or Weeks) — to occasion *all* of the harvests at one holiday or "feast." (See References 9 and 37, also *Menahoth* 9:1) It is evident, therefore, that modern Judaism is not observing the Feast of First Fruits on 16 *Nisan* as commanded by the Lord in Leviticus 23:10 – 12.

Although I have so far found no documentation to support such a speculation, it may be that Judaism is avoiding celebration of First Fruits on 16 *Nisan* as a result of Christian "pressure." It is highly probable that many Christians over the centuries have pointed out to Jewish brethren that the Lord Jesus was raised alive from death as The First Fruit of The Resurrection on that *very* same day.

Then, with Passover and First Fruits both arriving at about the same time as Easter, the most Holy of Christian observances, this may have produced pressures that the Jewish people preferred to avoid. This persistent confrontation, in combination with the *pogroms* and other persecutions, may have convinced the Rabbis to make this change in their worship.

There is very early evidence of similar Jewish response to such pressure, which surprisingly is even reported in a Jewish publication[39]. It is stated that the earliest 1st century Christians in Jerusalem immediately recognized that the three *matzahs* in the Passover *Seder* represented the Holy Trinity: Father, Son and Holy Spirit. Those bold zealots further insisted that the broken middle piece — the *afikoman* — of course was emblematic of the broken body of The Lamb of God — Jesus of Nazareth, Who was crucified as a blasphemer or impostor of Messiah, Son of David.

When confronted with this identity postulated by these earliest followers of that "Jesus," Rabbi Gamaliel (Paul's mentor) ordered that the Passover *Seder* would therefore in the future be arranged to assure that participants understand and adhere to the "traditional" identity of the three wafers. Whereas beforehand the *matzahs* had always been identified later during the meal, Gamaliel thereupon decreed that the pieces would be announced *at the beginning of the Seder* as: Cohen, Levi and *Y'israel*. Not surprisingly, this order continues today.

Another example of Jewish resistance to Christian symbolism is seen in these same *matzahs*. *The Universal Jewish Encyclopedia*[9] reports that the earliest *matzahs* were often triangular in shape until the Middle Ages. During the Middle Ages, especially in Europe, Christians informed the Rabbis that the three *equal* sides and three *equal* angles of the triangles "obviously" indicated the three *Equal* Personages of the Triune God. Countering, the Rabbis therefore ordered that henceforth all *matzahs* could have any form — *except triangular!*

It may be that similar other incidents goaded the Rabbis into avoiding other such confrontations with Christians or the other problems we have suggested. They had enough of trouble. — They had to survive!

It is further a possibility that a strictly Jewish concern brought about this change in observation of the Feasts. We have already discussed the uproar between the Pharisees and the *Sadducees* regarding the Feast of First Fruits. The Rabbis may have rationalized this departure from the Law in order to avoid the division and strife caused by the disagreement concerning the Sabbath, etc. For just such reasons, they may have preferred just to avoid the entire question as a step toward improved unity among the "warring" Jewish factions. After the *Diaspora* and their "scattering" among the Gentiles, it was going to be difficult enough to survive even as a unified faith, but much less so if they were to be in such bitter turmoil.

It is possible that any one or a combination of these problems (or *none* of these!) may have precipitated such an abandonment of this Holy Feast. Actually, in fairness to Judaism, Jewish people probably still feel as though they are honoring that feast as they observe *Shavuot*; although, they are not observing it "technically" in the same way as the Lord had directed in

Leviticus 23:10 – 12. Another reason for sympathy toward their posture on this exists in the fact that the Holy Temple is no longer available for waving the sheaf of the *omer*.

Regardless of our sympathy or the reasoning behind this deviation from the Law, it is with somewhat bitter irony that we should notice that now instead of *seven* Holy Feasts as commanded by the Lord, modern Judaism observes only *six* of the Feasts. The irony is wrought in that *seven* is God's number for Perfection; whereas, *six* is God's number for "imperfect" man. (See References 17 & 33) These assignments of numbers are demonstrated throughout Scripture as follows:

Man was created on the sixth "day" of The Creation.

God's Universe was created (for man) in six "days" and the Lord rested on the seventh "day" after His creation was Perfect.

- Jesus suffered (for man) six hours on The Cross.
- The sun was darkened at the sixth hour as Jesus suffered.
- Man practices his worldly pursuits during six days in the week, but the seventh day is the Lord's Day and which brings His week to completion; i.e., Perfection.
- Man's sinful dominion on Earth will endure but six "days" = 6000 years, but the Seventh "Day" will usher in the Lord's Kingdom Age of 1000 years of Perfect Peace on Earth.
- When the False Prophet of The Revelation 13:15 – 18 makes the image of the "Beast," it is significant that "the number of his name" shall be "666." Men will be at that time, as many in this World are at present, seeking to "deify" man and to refute all claims concerning Deity of The Son of Man. Truly, the symbol for man is "six" and which sadly reaches short of being Seven; i.e., Perfection.

Shavuot (Weeks or Pentecost)

Celebrates the spectacular events that occurred at Mount *Sinai*, when Moses was given the Law, by observing those forty-nine days as "counting the *omer*" (a measure of grain). This period connects between the barley harvest (First Fruits) and the beginning of the wheat harvest, *Shavuot*, on the fiftieth day after First Fruits. (Leviticus 23:15 – 16)

Rosh Hashanah (New Year)

Jewish interpretations of *Rosh Hashanah* are varied and numerous. Brief discussion would hardly be adequate to describe some of the deep (and hidden) meanings involved. Briefly, however, according to *Rosh Hashanah* tractate, the teaching concerns:

The Feast Day, *Rosh Hashanah*, which is the first day of the seventh month, *Tishri*, and the beginning of the Jewish New Year.

- The beginning of Creation.
- Coronation of the King of Kings

- The first of ten days of repentance.
- A reminder of the destruction of the Temple.
- Sounding of the *shofar* makes one tremble before God.
- A recalling of fear of the coming Day of Judgment.
- To awaken a yearning for the future gathering of Israel's dispersed returning to the Land — as we shall verify from Scriptural prophecies.
- To recall faith in the future resurrection of the dead.

During the Second Temple period and since that time, Jewish teaching is mixed on the concept of life after death. Nevertheless, those who do teach of a resurrection seem to have looked forward only to life in Messiah's Kingdom on Earth during the Messianic Age to come. Some say those who go to punishment in *Gehenna* (Hell) will suffer eternally, but others teach that punishment of the wicked will be for a limited time (maybe twelve months). Still another opinion offers that "the intermediates" will descend to Hell (*Gehinnom*) and "squeal" and then rise totally "healed." (See *Shabbath* 33b, *Rosh Hashanah* 17a and then see Daniel 12:2.) The Lord says that "*some will go to everlasting shame and contempt.*" (His Words.)

The ten days between *Rosh Hashanah* and *Yom Kippur* constitute the most Holy season of Jewish observance. The thirty days preceding *Rosh Hashanah* and extending to *Yom Kippur* are known as "the Days of Awe." This entire forty day season is known also as the season of *Tshuvah*, meaning a return to the Lord and / or repentance. (The Hebrew word *tshuvah*, which means "repent," also means "return.")

Yom Kippur (Day of Atonement)

This most Holy of all Jewish festivals occurs on the 10th day of *Tishri* and is a day of deep introspection, prayer and repentance by observant, worshipful Jews. Rabbis caution that repentance can atone only for offenses against God. Trespasses against a fellow human must be atoned by reconciliation with the person who has been wronged. (Leviticus 23:27 – 32 and *Yoma* 85b.)

During this Holy season, Jewish people seek the objective of being at peace with their fellow men. They do this in order to be "inscribed" in the "Book of Life."

Sukkoth (Booths) Feast of Tabernacles

A commemoration of the Israelite's life in the *Sinai* desert *en route* to their Promised Land. (They dwelled in huts or "booths.") This is also a celebration of the Autumn harvest — sort of a Jewish Thanksgiving. (Leviticus 23:34 – 36) *Sukkoth* has the most direct association with the nations of any of the other feasts. Seventy bulls were offered in the Temple, looking forward to this as a symbol of all the nations of the world, united forever to Honor God in Jerusalem at the Third Temple. The offering was intended to bring God's Blessings to ALL nations.

It is poignant to observe that the same Rabbi mentioned earlier regarding the doubts and anxiety at *Yom Kippur*, made an accurate observation about that Day when the nations unite at Jerusalem. He noted that this period will only arrive after the war that will gather all those nations coming together against Jerusalem. It is to his credit, that despite these foreboding prophecies, as a faithful and worshipful Jew, he also is nevertheless looking forward to rebuilding the Temple pursuant to that period. Considering Antichrist and his horrible roles in this drama, Christians have to think: "How much easier it would be if the Jewish People would just accept Him and Honor Him *before* He Comes !"

Christian Interpretation of Jewish Feasts

Christian interpretation of the Jewish feasts is of course in the Messianic context and is therefore understandably greatly different from the Jewish view. We should note here that *all* of the first four feasts have been fulfilled under five common criteria as follows:

- Fulfilled *only* by Jesus of Nazareth — Messiah, Son of David
- Fulfilled *only* to Jewish people.
- Fulfilled *only* in Jerusalem.
- Fulfilled each feast on its *exact* day as prescribed in the Law.
- Fulfilled each feast in its *exact* order, beginning with Passover in the first month, *Nisan*, as prescribed in the Law.

We shall now discuss each of the first four feasts as they were fulfilled on the exact day and in the exact order as they were commanded to Moses. Jesus fulfilled these feasts *only* to Jewish people, and always at Jerusalem, and always within a Jewish context in The Law, as follows:

Passover

Celebrates the sparing of Israel's first born. The Crucifixion — (The Lamb of God, His "Firstborn" and *only* Son, was slain to defeat the angel of death.)

Unleavened Bread

No leaven. The body of Jesus lay in the tomb. (The sinless, "unleavened" body rests.) No fermentation or any type of ritually "unclean dough," representing impurity or sin, is permitted in the Jewish home during the coming seven days. (See *Pesachim* 1:1 and introduction to *Pesachim* tractate.)

First Fruits

Celebrating the first fruits of the spring harvest. The Resurrection — (Jesus was the First of those to be resurrected from The dead. He now lives in a resurrected, incorruptible, eternal body. That first "harvest.")

Pentecost

Celebrating Moses' receiving the Ten Commandments.

Jesus sent the "comforter;" i.e., The Holy Spirit, as tongues of Flame, descended to the disciples. They received their commandments." (John 14:16, 14:26; 15:26; 16:7)

Feasts of Jehovah remaining to be fulfilled will continue in the following order and on the occasions described. The remaining feasts will continue to be fulfilled *only* by Jesus Christ *only* to Jewish people and *only* in Jerusalem and *only* within the Jewish context of The Law. (Note: *Purim* and *Chanukah* are not Feasts of Jehovah; i.e., they are not commanded for observance under the Law.)

Trumpets (Rosh Hashanah)

Celebrates the New Year. The *"great trumpet will sound"* and Jesus will command that all Jewish people will be *"gathered up"* to Jerusalem to prepare for their "New Year" with the Lord, the inauguration of the Messianic Age. (Isaiah 43:5, 6; Matthew 24:30 – 31)

Atonement (Yom Kippur)

All Jews and the nation atone for the sins of the past year. Messiah will arrive at *Olivet* summit. Jews will be atoning when *"they look upon Me whom they have pierced."* (Zechariah 12:10 and 14:4)

Tabernacles (Sukkoth)

Celebrates Israel's exodus wherein they shared their Tabernacle with their Lord. Messiah will begin His reign over His Promised Kingdom as Son of David. All nations will come to "Tabernacle" with the Lord at Jerusalem (Zechariah 14:16 – 17) in The *Third* Temple

It is important to note, however, that the first Christians were Jews and that no Gentile Christians were yet "in the fold" with Jesus' disciples at the time of the Crucifixion and the Resurrection. Neither were any Gentiles present fifty days later at Pentecost. This "no-Gentiles" policy is even more specifically reflected in Exodus 12:48 in the Lord's commandment that no "uncircumcised person" (Gentile) shall eat at the Passover meal (*Seder*).

For these reasons a theory is formulated to suggest that the next feast to be fulfilled, *Rosh Hashanah* (Feast of Trumpets), also will be fulfilled to the Jews. This concept is in opposition to a popular concept that Feast of Trumpets will be fulfilled when Gentile Christians are "gathered up" at the Rapture of the Church. This concept is obviously inspired by the words "the trump of God" in I Thessalonians 4:16, describing Believers being "gathered up."

The theory we propose, however, would continue with the prophetic indication that all Jewish people remaining alive on Earth at the end of the Tribulation will be translated bodily to Jerusalem *"from the four corners of the Earth"* when *"the great trumpet sounds."*

This theory is based on a Promise from God to Israel in Isaiah 43:5, 6, (KJV):

> *"Fear not: for I am with thee: I will bring thy seed from the east, and gather thee from the west; I will say to the north, Give up, and to the south, Keep not back: Bring my sons from afar and my daughters from the ends of the earth.*

Also, the prophet Jeremiah has delivered this same Promise:

> *"And I will gather the remnant of my flock out of all countries whither I have driven them, and will bring them again to their folds, and they shall be fruitful and increase.*
>
> *And I will set up shepherds over them which shall feed them: and they shall fear no more, nor be dismayed, neither shall they be lacking, saith the Lord. Jeremiah 23:3, 4 (KJV)*

Now, listen again to the Word from our messenger, Isaiah:

> *And it will come about in that day, that the Lord will start His threshing from the flowing stream of the Euphrates to the brook of Egypt; and you will be gathered up one by one, O sons of Israel.*
>
> *It will come about also in that day that a great trumpet will be blown; and those who were perishing in the land of Assyria and who were scattered in the land of Egypt will come and worship the Lord in the holy mountain at Jerusalem. Isaiah 27:12 – 13 (NASB)*

The "*great trumpet*" will sound "*that day*" and "*those scattered*" will be "*gathered up*" and brought to Jerusalem "one by one."

The references to "Assyria" and "Egypt" are not to be interpreted literally, simply because "that day" was far in the future and may still be. "Assyria" and "Egypt" instead were used here to denote far and distant lands in terms of the known world of Isaiah's time.

At this point some prophecy students will say: "But Israel has already returned to The Land — in 1948. Is he saying they are going to return again?" — Not at all. — The miraculous rebirth of the *nation of Israel* in 1948 was a *partial* fulfillment of the prophecy in Ezekiel 37; whereas, *complete* fulfillment will occur upon return of all *people of Israel* to The Land. Arrival of that event is yet future and will include *all Jews*, living or dead. Yes, the Lord has said He will "*gather them up out of their graves,*" one-by-one, on that Day — Rosh Hashanah — Judgment Day. This is *not* The Great White Throne Judgment. That final judgment is to occur about one thousand years later.

That great prophet, Ezekiel, gave thorough coverage of the return of Jews to The Land in Ezekiel 37:13-14:

> *"And ye shall know that I am the Lord, when I have opened your graves, O My People, and brought you up out of your graves,*
>
> *And shall put My Spirit in you, and ye shall live, and I shall place you in your own Land; then shall ye know that I, the Lord, hath spoken it, and performed it, saith the Lord."*

This is another of those prophecies that heralds the coming of The People to the Mount of Olives to greet their Messiah on that Day of Judgment. Many thousands of Jewish people have rested for centuries in their graves at the cemetery on that Blessed Mount of Olives, faithfully and hopefully awaiting that Day. (See Illus. 11: Jewish Cemetery on the Mt. of Olives, Page 76)

The prophet Daniel also describes this exciting deliverance of his people, Israel:

And at that time shall Michael stand up, the great prince which standeth for the children of thy people: and there shall be a time of trouble, such as never was since there was a nation even to that same time: and at that time thy people shall be delivered, every one that shall be written in the book.

And many of them that sleep in the dust of the earth shall awake, some to everlasting life, and some to shame and everlasting contempt. Daniel 12:1 – 2

Michael is the name that certain occult religions have assigned to Jesus. Perhaps they were influenced by this verse. However, Michael is the angel who protects Israel and he will especially protect Israel during this *"time of trouble."* Nevertheless, he is *not* Messiah and he is not Jesus. — Michael is an angel.

Some Christian theologians have even taught that Michael the "protector" is he who will also deliver Israel. Again, Michael will only *protect* until Messiah, Son of David — *The Deliverer* — arrives at *Olivet* summit. But ten days before that — on *Rosh Hashanah* — many of them that sleep, and who are written in The Book of Life shall awaken to *everlasting* life. And some, from "that other book," will awaken to *everlasting* shame and contempt. This is why the "intermediates" need to repent and pray toward having their names entered into the right "book." This is also why those who are already *delivered* need to pray and give thanks that they are already in the right "book." That is what we call "Blessed Assurance!" The choice is ours: To be "In The Book" or to have "an unlisted number."

Christians who agree that Believers will be *"gathered up"* before the Event described here takes place, can see that it is obvious from Jesus' own words that these are a *Jewish* Elect, chosen to greet Him upon His arrival at *Olivet*. Jesus declared in Matthew 24:31:

"And He shall send His angels with a great sound of a trumpet, and they shall gather together His Elect from the four winds, from one end of Heaven to the other."

Some Christians will insist (because they have been taught in error) that Jesus is speaking here about the Rapture, the "trump of God," the "gathering up" of Believers to meet Christ *"in the air"* as described in I Thessalonians 4:17. The fact that these are Jewish Elect, and not the Christian "Elect" at the Rapture, is further confirmed by considering the text preceding Verse 31. Clearly, Jesus is describing Events toward the end of the Great Tribulation, occurring just before He arrives *"with power and great Glory"* at the Mount of Olives. According to Luke 21:36 and Revelation 3:10, Believers already will have been *"gathered up"* seven years earlier. Jesus warns in Matthew 24:21 —

"For then shall be great tribulation, such as was not since the beginning of the world to this time, no, nor ever shall be."

And again, Jesus advises in Matthew 24:22:

> *"And except those days should be shortened, there should no flesh be saved: but for the Elect's sake those days shall be shortened."*

In other words, conditions will be so frightful on Earth at that time, that if He were to delay any longer, there would be no survivors to meet Him — Jewish or Gentile.

All of this will occur ten days *before* that reunion at *Olivet* summit, which they have been awaiting so eagerly (and poignantly) for all these centuries. Messiah wants them to be prepared and waiting for Him across the valley in The Old City of *Yerushalayim* when He alights on the Mount of Olives. He will not wait to "roust" them out of their graves on *Yom Kippur* because that mountain is going to "*cleave in the midst thereof.*" It would not be a very gentle or appropriate way to awaken His Elect, many of whom have "slept" on that Holy Mountain for centuries, just so they can be there to behold Him and greet Him when Messiah comes at last.

This "gathering" obviously has not yet been fulfilled because, for example, today there are still more Jewish people in the United States than there are in Israel. This Promise, in fact, is given about two dozen times in the Old Testament. Does anybody think the Lord was making this Promise to people other than His Chosen? He said: "*O sons of Israel.*"

The prophet Joel, in his graphic and dramatic descriptions of "that great and terrible Day of the Lord," adds another Promise concerning this remnant body of Jewish survivors, in Joel 3:5:

> *"And it shall come to pass, that whosoever shall call on the name of the Lord shall be delivered; for in Mount Zion and in Jerusalem there shall be those that escape, as the Lord has said and among the remnant those whom the Lord shall call."*

> * — *In Christian Bibles, Joel 2:32 is equivalent to the Jewish Scriptures Joel 3:5.*

Close scrutiny of Joel 3:5 in the Jewish Scriptures reveals subtle indications that *two* distinct Jewish groups will be at Jerusalem to greet Messiah. This is derived from the phrase shortly following "those that escape," where it says: "And among (that) remnant;" i.e., among "those that escape." Those two groups are:

> *"those that escape"* are Jewish survivors, the *"remnant"* that will be preserved through the seven years of the Tribulation under Antichrist, and who will be *"gathered up"* to Jerusalem.

> *"those elect whom the Lord shall call"* from the four winds are the Jewish righteous dead who will be resurrected and *"translated"* to Jerusalem.

This latter group consists of those whom Daniel 12:2 states "shall awaken to everlasting life." They will be "delivered" because "they called upon the name of the Lord" as was Promised them in Joel 3:5. *Both* Jewish groups will be present to greet Messiah; and as the Scripture has said:

> ▪ the Elect will be *among* the remnant at Jerusalem on *that* Day.

- And yes, ALL of them *will* see their "pierced" Messiah and ALL will mourn for Him greatly because they had not recognized Him *"in the time of their visitation."*
- All Christian "Saints" will accompany Messiah Jesus to arrive with Him at the Mount of Olives to be united with our Jewish brethren. (I Thessalonians 3:13)

Prophecy reveals that on *Rosh Hashanah*, the "Feast of Trumpets" (1 *Tishri*, the first day of the seventh Jewish month, *Tishri*), 1,250 days after Antichrist halts the sacrifices by committing "the abomination of desolation" in the "Holy Place," *all* Jewish survivors of that seven terrible years of tribulation will be carried supernaturally to Jerusalem; just as Phillip was "caught-up" unto Azotus (Acts 8:39 – 40).

It will probably take the next ten days for them to "get-their-feet-on-the-ground," so to speak, after their fantastic "ride" to Jerusalem from Johannesburg, Poughkeepsie, Buenos Aires, Munich, Sydney, or wherever they might be among *"the four corners of the Earth"* on That Day. They will then be alert, anxious, and ready for the next ten days, discussing and encouraging each other for what is about to happen on 10 *Tishri*.

There they will be *"encompassed by armies"* from all nations of the world. Nevertheless, in faith they will "minister" to each other, prepared to make atonement as they *"look upon Me whom they have pierced"* on the Day of Atonement, *Yom Kippur* (10 *Tishri*). He will then arrive at *Olivet* summit *with Shekhinah*, *"in Power and great Glory"* on the clouds, to rescue Israel's surviving remnant from the armies of "the world." (Ezekiel 43:2; Matthew 24:30; – 21)

Then, They Will See Their Conquering, Pierced Messiah!

Still not convinced?—Well, the Lord Jesus said:

"But in those days, after that tribulation, the sun shall be darkened, and the moon shall not give her light, and the stars of Heaven shall fall and the powers that are in Heaven shall be shaken.

And then they shall see the Son of Man coming in clouds with great power and glory.

And then shall He send his angels, and shall gather together His elect from the four winds, from the uttermost part of the earth to the uttermost part of Heaven." Mark 13:24 – 27

Some scholars from the "Post Tribulation" eschatology position, by applying what has been called "Replacement Theology," would insist that Jesus was speaking of His Church as His "elect." These mistakenly reason that this is the Resurrection and gathering of Believers from "the four winds" at the end of the seven year Tribulation. However, it is emphatic that this is referring to Jewish people because of the way the event is described multiple times by Old Testament prophets. Even more to the point, again from Isaiah 27:12 – 13, He says: *"...you will be gathered up one by one, O sons of Israel...when the great trumpet sounds."* Clearly, He is not talking about the rapture of Believers when He says, "O sons of Israel."

Perceivably, some Jewish readers might take exception to these words of doom since they are quoted from the New Testament — a wholly Christian source. However, as is frequently the case throughout the New Testament, Jesus is quoting *all* of these prophecies from the *Jewish Bible*, the *Tanakh* or what Christian Gentiles call the Old Testament. These can be summarized in detail as follows:

New Testament Reference – Old Testament Sources

Mark 13:24 – Joel 2:10 and 3:15, Isaiah 13:10

Mark 13:25 – Isaiah 34:4

Mark 13:26 – Daniel 7:13

Mark 13:27 – Deuteronomy 30:3, Zechariah 2:6

If we examine each of these Scriptures, we find that Mark was surely quoting from the *Tanakh* — the Old Testament. Primarily, we offer this comparison to demonstrate that most of the New Testament prophecies of End Time events (as well as the life stories of Jesus) have their origins from Old Testament prophecies. Indeed, if all Bible prophecies were detailed in this manner, they would comprise a fair sized book. Here, Jesus has described the days of the Tribulation, "The Time of Jacob's Trouble." *Talmudic* Rabbis and conservative Christians agree that it will be the most terrible period in Earth's history — the worst that *ever* has been or *ever* will be. These things will "come to pass" immediately before the arrival of Messiah (Son of David) to rescue a then beleaguered Israel from destruction. Jewish agreement with this interpretation of prophecy is stated in *Talmud, Sanhedrin* 97a.

Thus, it appears that the Earth is going to be in great turmoil on "that day" and everyone on Earth will be in a state of panic and desperation (They will think "the world" is-coming-to-an-end...and it IS!). That is, the world as we know it will be ending. They will behold an amazing spectacle of "lights" in the heavens surrounding this one "Super-Light."

Finally, near the end of this seven year period of Tribulation, on *Rosh Hashanah* (Feast of Trumpets), every Jewish man, woman, and child on Earth will be gathered up and translated to Jerusalem for protection from a world gone mad. These are the Jewish people "elected" to survive the Tribulation as well as the Jewish dead "elect," all of whom will be "gathered" to Jerusalem to greet Him when He arrives at the Mount of Olives on *Yom Kippur* (Day of Atonement).

But Jesus is going to make the world "sweat it out" for about ten days before He arrives at the Mount of Olives, accompanied by whom??

Why, it's the Glory, the Divine Presence, *Shekhinah*. (And, oh yes! — the Church, will also arrive with Him). That "Super-Light" is really comprised of three "lights," remember?

1. The Father (as *Shekhinah*, His visible Presence)
2. The Son, Jesus (the Bridegroom)
3. The Holy Spirit, which at this time will be "lighting-up" all Saints (the Bride) like a *Chanukah* bush! — because He dwells in us.

The whole world will be watching, terrified and in wonder at what is happening. During those ten days the world will go absolutely mad. There will be *"gnashing of teeth"* and *"men's-hearts-will-be-failing-them-for-fear."* (Matthew 25:30; Luke 21:26) They will be able to observe the "light-show" very well because the sun will be blotted out at that time.

During those ten days the last armies of the Age will be marshaled and readied in the valley of *Megiddo*. (Zechariah 12:11) There they shall prepare for their own grisly destiny in the Valley of Jehoshaphat at the east wall of the City of God, Jerusalem, on *Yom Kippur* — 10 *Tishri*. His feet will then stand on *Olivet*. Yes, on this Day of Atonement, this feast will be fulfilled and atonement will be made as Jewish people will at last see their Messiah as *"they will look upon Me whom they have pierced, and they shall mourn for Him as one mourneth for his only son, and shall be in bitterness for Him, as one is in bitterness for his firstborn."* (From Zechariah 12:10)

Five days later the Kingdom Age will begin when all will come to "tabernacle" (gather) with the Lord in Jerusalem on the Feast of Tabernacles (Booths) on 15 *Tishri*. Thereupon, all seven Feasts of Jehovah will have been fulfilled — fulfilled to the Jews — in a Jewish context. These fulfillments have not been made to Gentiles, except as we, "the Church," are identified within our relationship to Messiah and the Jews.

Daniel 9:27 predicts the desolation of the Temple by the Antichrist. Since the Evil One will defile the Temple 1,260 days before the Lord returns, then, counting back from 10 *Tishri*, that date becomes near 14 *Nisan* (Passover) if some Jewish calendar "leapmonths" are included within those 3½ years. Still, I do not have any explanation to offer as to what fulfillment the *Shekhinah* Event may have presented other than for Ezekiel's prophecy.

Many sincere and learned prophecy scholars have taught that the next feast, *Rosh Hashanah* or the Feast of Trumpets, will be fulfilled when Jesus comes to "gather up" all believers at what is known as "the rapture of the Church." Nevertheless, since all of the first four feasts were fulfilled only to Jews, I believe the remaining three will also be fulfilled exclusively to the Jews. Another reason for eliminating *Rosh Hashanah* as a time for the rapture is that Jesus said He will come at such time that *"ye think not."* (Luke 12:40, Matthew 24:44) In other words, the rapture will come as a *"thief in the night"* — a surprise. He wants Christians to be expectant and alert for His coming, but does not want all of us to be standing over at the Mount of Olives on each *Rosh Hashanah* waiting for Him to arrive. Jesus wants Christians to live every day in such a way that they would be prepared and expect that He might arrive to take them unto Himself at any time.

Finally, it is my belief that all Bible-believing Jewish people who survive until seven years later, at the end of the "Great Tribulation," will know the exact date of His Coming at *Olivet*. They will know the exact date because by that time they will have become convinced that the New Testament and the Old Testament are both speaking of the same One who will stand at the Mount of Olives. Both of these Scriptural works state, in several places, that Messiah shall arrive three and one-half years after the Evil One defiles the Holy Place and proclaims himself as God. They will believe and know He will arrive exactly 1,260 days (or 42 months or 3½ years) after Antichrist commits this "abomination of desolation." They will know when He is coming and they will be ready. (Daniel. 9:27; Revelation 11:2 – 3)

Jewish tradition has always observed those ten days between *Rosh Hashanah* and the Day of Atonement (the High Holy Days) as a time of preparation, a time to alert themselves to a consciousness of their behavior toward other men and their relationships with God. Since *Rosh Hashanah* is regarded as "The Day of Judgment," a time for repentance and renewal prayers is in order. The High Holy Days are sometimes specified as "the Days of Awe" (*Yamim Nora'im*) being from thirty days prior to *Rosh Hashanah* and continuing until *Yom Kippur*. Awe is inspired in the fact that men will be judged on *Rosh Hashanah* and their "doom is sealed" on the Day of Atonement.

A deeper and more spiritual background for the High Holy Days is stated in tractate *Rosh Hashanah* 16b. The narrator, Rabbi Kruspedai, says that three books are opened in Heaven each New Year: one for the thoroughly righteous, one for the wicked, and one for the "intermediate." He continues by saying that names of those in each category are inscribed in either the Book of Life or the Book of Death, as appropriate to one's behavior — *except the "intermediate!"* The doom of the intermediate (*Beinonim*: "in the middle") is "suspended" during those ten days from *Rosh Hashanah* until *Yom Kippur*

A comment from a beloved Rabbi typically identifies that source of sadness that Christians feel for Jewish people during those "Days of Awe." The Rabbi laments that so much doubt and anxiety passes through a person's mind as *Yom Kippur* draws to completion. – "Will the Lord know my repentance is sincere?" – "Will The Holy One accept my repentance?" – "Have I really been sealed for a favorable meeting with Him?"

During those days, then, if one is not quite confident as to which "book" will have his name inscribed, he is advised to pray and repent earnestly during the time. Many modern Jews of the most conservative observant groups continue this practice today. In Reference 38, Pg. 567, Rabbi Telushkin points out that modern Jewish tradition recommends that all Jewish people consider themselves *Beinonim*. This is as if to say "You can't be too sure! – So, just in case..." –Contrastingly, those who already have found Messiah do have that *Blessed Assurance* that their names are even *sealed* in the Book of Life For Ever! – AMEN !

All during the forty days approaching *Yom Kippur*, the prescribed Jewish greeting becomes, "*Le-Shanah Tova Teekataivu*" — "May you be inscribed (in the Book of Life) for a good year." This introspection then prepares them for their atonement on the Day. In the same way, those Jews who will be translated to Jerusalem when "the great trumpet" sounds will have the same interval in which they will contemplate the imminent arrival of Messiah on the Day of Atonement.

During the Kingdom Age that follows, Messiah Jesus will rule the World from Jerusalem. (Revelation 19:14 and 20:6) All true believers will return with Him to the Mount of Olives. (I Thessalonians 3:13, Revelation 19:7 – 9, 14 and 15)

So, there we are with the Prince of Peace in our glorified bodies ready for one thousand years of Perfect Peace on Earth. It would hardly seem that He would not have us work during this period. He certainly does not need man's puny, insignificant efforts to assist Him, but He has always wanted us to work. Of course, it does not matter to us because men will cheerfully do Jesus' bidding.

Jeremiah gave a hint about this work in Chapter 23, verse 4: *"And I will set up shepherds over them (Israel) which shall feed them..."* Yes, we saints of the Lord's Purpose will be assigned as shepherds, to teach ("feed") the survivors of the Tribulation. We will teach them like no Sunday School teachers they ever saw. By that time Jesus will have trained us to teach His flock what they would not (or could not) hear from Him *"at the time of their visitation."*

Thus, we begin to understand now why it is important for people to love and respect and learn about how Jesus can be seen in Judaic tradition and in the Old Testament.

When did those *"Two Days"* Start?

Another popular concept in prophecy relates to the "two days" of "smiting" against Israel after the Lord said, *"I will go back to My place."* (Hosea 5:15 and 6:1 – 3) A question emerges concerning the Lord's return after the "two days." Popular teaching has been: "Of course, the 'two days' is to be counted from when the Lord Jesus returned 'to His Place' in 30 C.E." Now, we must also ask the question: "But, what about the Lord's returning to His Place in 69 C.E.?"

Some believers, nevertheless, are somewhat justifiably excited by this; although, we should not try setting up a "time-schedule" for the Lord's return based on this or any other prophecy.

The prophecy that brings this focus is as follows:

"Come, let us return to the Lord.

He has torn us to pieces, but he will heal us;

He has injured us

But he will bind up our wounds.

After two days he will revive us;

On the third day he will restore us,

That we may live in his presence.

Let us acknowledge the Lord;

Let us press on to acknowledge him.

As surely as the sun rises, he will appear;

He will come to us like the winter rains,

Like the spring rains that water the earth." Hosea 6:1 – 3 (NIV)

It is understandable at the present time in history why this specific prophecy should be exciting for all who believe. The Lord has said He will punish "naughty" Israel, but He will heal them, raise them up after "two days"; i.e., after He goes back to His place. After the two days (two thousand years, prophetically) they (Israel) will live in His presence during the Kingdom Age, in His 1,000 year earthly reign. As surely as the sun rises, Messiah will come after the Tribulation, that final seven years of Israel's *"refining as silver"* during *"the time of Jacob's trouble,"* the "week" of temptation, etc. (See Zechariah 13:9 and Jeremiah 30:7)

In fact, immediately prior to arrival of Messiah, the sun will be *seven* times brighter than normal. From Isaiah 30:26 *"...the light of the moon shall be as the light of the sun, and the light of the sun shall be sevenfold,..."* — Yes! It will be possible to get a "moonburn" during "those days." Men will be hiding under anything they can find to shield themselves from those broiling rays. His arrival and subsequent restoration of this parched planet at that time will certainly be welcome as *"the winter rains."*

It is interesting to note another interpretation of prophecy that is derived not so much from Scripture as it is taken from what should be called "tradition." It is therefore not to be taken very seriously; although, this prophecy may have been "inspired" by Hosea's prophecy of the "two days."

The so-called Apostolic Father, Barnabas, is credited with having written an "epistle" or letter that included this prophetical observation. It should be pointed out that Barnabas was certainly not a valid Apostle nor was any of his work Canonized as Scripture. Nevertheless, he was a righteous man despite some human failings and was well known as a companion of the Apostle Paul.

Barnabas noted the following "time table" concerning prophecies of "The Time of the End":

- There were two thousand years or two "days" from the time of Adam until the time of Abraham.
- There were two thousand more years (two more "days") from the time of Abraham until the time of Jesus Christ.
- There will be two thousand more years (two more "days") from the time of Jesus' first visitation until the time of His return.

This prophetic vein continues (although not from Barnabas) with the observation that six "days" are given unto man on Earth. "Six" is the number of "man" in the context of Scriptural numerology. Man was created on the sixth day, etc., etc. Then, the seventh "day" shall be the Lord's Day, a day of rest and peace, which is of course the one thousand year Millennial reign of Christ on Earth. (Revelation 20:4)

Barnabas may have been influenced by Jewish traditional interpretation in having made this somewhat profound observation. The thoughts expressed can be traced back to Jewish tradition on this subject as recorded in *Talmud, Rosh Hashanah* 31a. Here it is stated that the world is to last six thousand years. Then, at this point the Rabbis seem to be confused about how many "days" are to follow those six. One Rabbi says the world shall be "desolate" for one thousand years. Another says it will be desolate for two thousand, as he then refers to the verses from Hosea, which we have discussed.

Now, we with our 20/20 hindsight, would say the latter Rabbinical interpretation is the more accurate, although, the "desolation" has been determined upon Israel rather than to the world. This same Rabbi evidently had been reading the "Fine Print" in his *Tanakh* also; because he goes on to quote: "...as it says, *'After two days He will revive us.'*"

A tragic Rabbinical note is recorded in tractate *Sanhedrin* 97a, which also teaches that the world is to last six thousand years. In the first two thousand there was "desolation;" i.e., there was no *Torah*. In the second two thousand years the *Torah* is said to have "flourished." Then it is stated that the third period of two thousand years was the Messianic Era — meaning Messiah, Son of David, *was* to have arrived at the *beginning* of that interval, at the dawn of what we call "the first century." Some call that time C.E. ("Common Era") and others call that time A.D. (*Anno Domini*). But...no matter. — It was THE time!!!

Then, in remorse, the narrator says the delay "is due to our sins." (They *were* expecting Him then, as now!) Another Rabbi states in *Talmud Sanhedrin* 97b, "all the predestined dates (for redemption; i.e., through Messiah, Son of David) have passed." He is telling Jewish people that God had announced through the Prophet (Daniel 9:24 – 26) the *exact* date when their Redeemer would come. And, since God is not a liar and since that date has passed, there can be only one conclusion — He *was* already here! However, as we have shown from Hosea 6:2, after "two days" He will revive them and they will live in His sight forever. We shall present much more about this tradition in Chapter 10.

It should be clear to all of us at this point that none of us can agree on what these prophecies reveal as to the "day" of His coming. Despite our "20/20 hindsight" advantage, it appears that Christians cannot reach agreement on this concept of prophecy much more than our Jewish brethren at this time. We shall all agree later, but we certainly cannot agree right now about when "later" is to be.

Temptation to "calculate" dates for these Events is of course a trait of "human nature" — albeit futile as it is. Nevertheless, it appears that some credibility can be established at least for the beginning and ending of these Events, spanning the seven years of the Tribulation, in accordance with the Feast Days on the Jewish calendar.

Earlier, we gave speculation through application of logic to chronological sequence, that the remaining unfulfilled feasts will be fulfilled in their proper Biblical order and exactly on the proper Jewish calendar dates. The next feast to be fulfilled is, of course, the Feast of Trumpets, when the Jewish "Elect" will be "*gathered up*" to meet Messiah. Following that will be Day of Atonement when ten days later Messiah arrives at the Mount of Olives, when *"they shall look upon Me whom they have pierced."*

Since we know the seven years of Tribulation will begin when the Antichrist establishes the seven year covenant with Israel, and since we know the Tribulation will begin exactly seven years previous to arrival of Messiah, we can "calculate" that Antichrist will be revealed on the Day of Atonement, *Yom Kippur*. As we calculate, we must remember to count in *Jewish* years, consisting of 12 months of 30 days each. Since the "abomination of desolation" will occur three and one half years after Antichrist is revealed (Daniel 9:27), that date will be at the time of Passover. We know this because Passover is six months (1/2 year) before (or after) the Day of Atonement.

Earlier we noted the possibility that the "two days" may have started at the time when the Lord's *Shekhinah* "returned to His Place;" (from Hosea 5:15); i.e., about 69–70 C.E. We have interpreted that application of the "two days" is a fulfillment of the prophecy in Hosea 6:2:

> *"After two days will He revive us:*
>
> *In the third day He will raise us up,*
>
> *And we shall live in His sight."*

Counting 2000 years (two "days") from 69 or 70 C.E. would then bring us to about 2069–2070 C.E. for Jesus to return in Glory to the Mount of Olives and seven years earlier the Tribulation would begin at about 2062–2063 C.E.

The preceding calculation uses what we shall call "astronomical years" — consisting of 365.25 days each. However, oftentimes, Biblical prophecy counts years as in the Jewish calendar years of 12 x 30 = 360 days instead of the astronomical years. From this we can convert the "two days" in terms of "Jewish years" back to equivalent "astronomical years" as follows:

2000 x 360/365.25 = 1971 "Jewish prophetic" astronomical years.

Then, IF 69–70 C.E. at the *Shekhinah* departure began the "two days" from Hosea 6:2, the "calculated" date for Jesus' arrival at *Olivet* summit using "Jewish years" can be derived as follows:

1971 + 69 = 2040 C.E. (or 2041 C.E. if counting from 70 C.E.)

Seven "Jewish" years before this time would be about 2033 C.E., when the Tribulation would begin and when Antichrist would be revealed.

There is excellent credibility for applying the Jewish calendar year (360 days) because Scripture states that the Israelites will be hidden from Antichrist for 1260 days (Revelation 12:6). That is 42 months (Revelation 11:2); or three and one half years described poetically as "times and time and half a time" (Daniel 12:7 and Revelation 12:14). It is evident, therefore, in these prophecies that 30 days comprise a month, because 1260 days is exactly 42 months or 3½ years when using 30 days = 1 month. Further credibility is evidenced by the work of Sir Robert Anderson.[3] Using this same relationship with Jewish years, Anderson has shown that Jesus was crucified *exactly* 483 Jewish years after King Artaxerxes issued the commandment to restore Jerusalem as a Perfect fulfillment of Daniel 9:26.

At this point it is interesting to question whether those "two days" may have begun at the time when Jesus went back to "His Place." That would have been 30 C.E. according to our Gregorian calendar. In line with that calendar, Jesus' Birth was about 4 B.C.E. That would be in agreement with many Biblical scholars' determination that Jesus was at age 33 years at His death. The date of 30 C.E. is verified to a great extent by the Rabbis of *Talmud* who frequently bemoan a period they refer to as: *"forty years before the Temple was destroyed."* The dramatic importance of that time in Israel's history will be detailed in the next chapter. The date of 30 C.E. is further verified by the fact that most historians consider 70 C.E. an accurate date for destruction of the Temple.

Nevertheless, we are moved to issue a sort of "disclaimer" against our having calculated precise "dating" of these years – say, within a year or two. There are certain "reasonable" doubts that scholars express concerning accuracy of the Gregorian calendar as far back as the first century. Such errors can therefore logically diminish accuracy of our "calculation."

Counting 2000 Jewish prophetic years from 30 C.E. would bring us again to 1971 + 30 = 2001 C.E. for Jesus to arrive at the Mount of Olives. BUT, *where* is (was!) that seven years of the Tribulation? — Where is Antichrist? — Where are all the other events that accompany and *precede* His Coming? Since none of these questions can be answered, and because we already have arrived at 2001, this "calculation" is eliminated as invalid.

Therefore, maybe — in God's eyes — the Earth is just not yet sinful enough to be judged. (HARD to believe!) Besides, the Lord is not willing that any men should perish, but that all would come to repentance and everlasting life. (From II Peter 3:9) His Holy Spirit may just need more time to harvest more souls for Him.

We pointed out earlier that those persons who are alive during the middle of the Tribulation *will* know that Jesus will arrive at the Mount of Olives exactly 1260 days after Antichrist commits the "abomination of desolation" (at the Passover season). We estimate the Passover date because that Feast occurs six months after *Yom Kippur*, which we estimate as the day for the arrival of Messiah. In this way, the six-month difference fits into the three and one-half year period. The Passover date therefore falls exactly at the midpoint of the seven years. Survivors *will* be able to "calculate" that date of Messiah's arrival — from what Scripture has said. At the beginning of those perilous seven years, they will also be able to calculate the exact date when Antichrist will desecrate the "Holy Place" *exactly* 1260 days after he makes that seven year "covenant" with Israel. Nevertheless, we cannot at this time "calculate" the time of His Coming. There are too many unknown factors.

This concept does not, however, conflict with Jesus' statement because Jesus spoke *only* of the Rapture of Believers, the gathering up of the TRUE Christians, when He said, in Matthew 24:36:

"But of that day and hour knoweth no man, no, not the angels of Heaven, but My Father only."

Although we are certain the time is near — because we have been "watching" — we must point out that NOBODY can now or ever will be able to "calculate" the time of the Rapture or "calling out" of Believers. Jesus also cautioned in Matthew 25:13,

"Watch therefore, for ye know neither the day nor the hour wherein the Son of man cometh."

That Glorious Event can occur at ANY TIME! — Believers today are therefore cautioned to be watching, waiting and always ready — in Luke 21:36 —

"Watch ye therefore, and pray always, that ye may be accounted worthy to escape all these things that shall come to pass, and to stand before the Son of man."

This is just one of several verses declaring that Believers will "escape" the wrath during the Tribulation.

In this discussion we have shown some prophetic significance in the departure of *Shekhinah* returning to His Place. Nevertheless, we have NO credible means for "calculating" the date when these events will begin to unfold. We don't even have a calendar that is reliable covering the past 2000 years. Based on that fact alone, besides relying upon the Words of Jesus, an accurate date prediction of His Coming cannot be made by anyone. I am certainly not taking a dogmatic position on this "calculation;" although, I do wish to offer it as a possibility — something to think about. And finally, it goes without saying, that many scholars would certainly question even the scenario we have described.

If nothing else, these kinds of observations should be another gentle cautioning against our temptation, at the present time, to "set dates" for the Lord to arrive at the Mount of Olives. My favorite anecdote on this sort of temptation is based on something the distinguished novelist, Mr. Alex Haley, once commented upon. In the closing epilogue of the ABC television epic, "Roots," Mr. Haley recalled his grandmother's feelings concerning the slaves' impatient hopes for freedom as she rocked with him on their old porch swing. "De Lawd don' always do things jess 'wen folks thinks He should, but He always dooze 'em RIGHT ON TIME."

Prophecies Seen in This Event

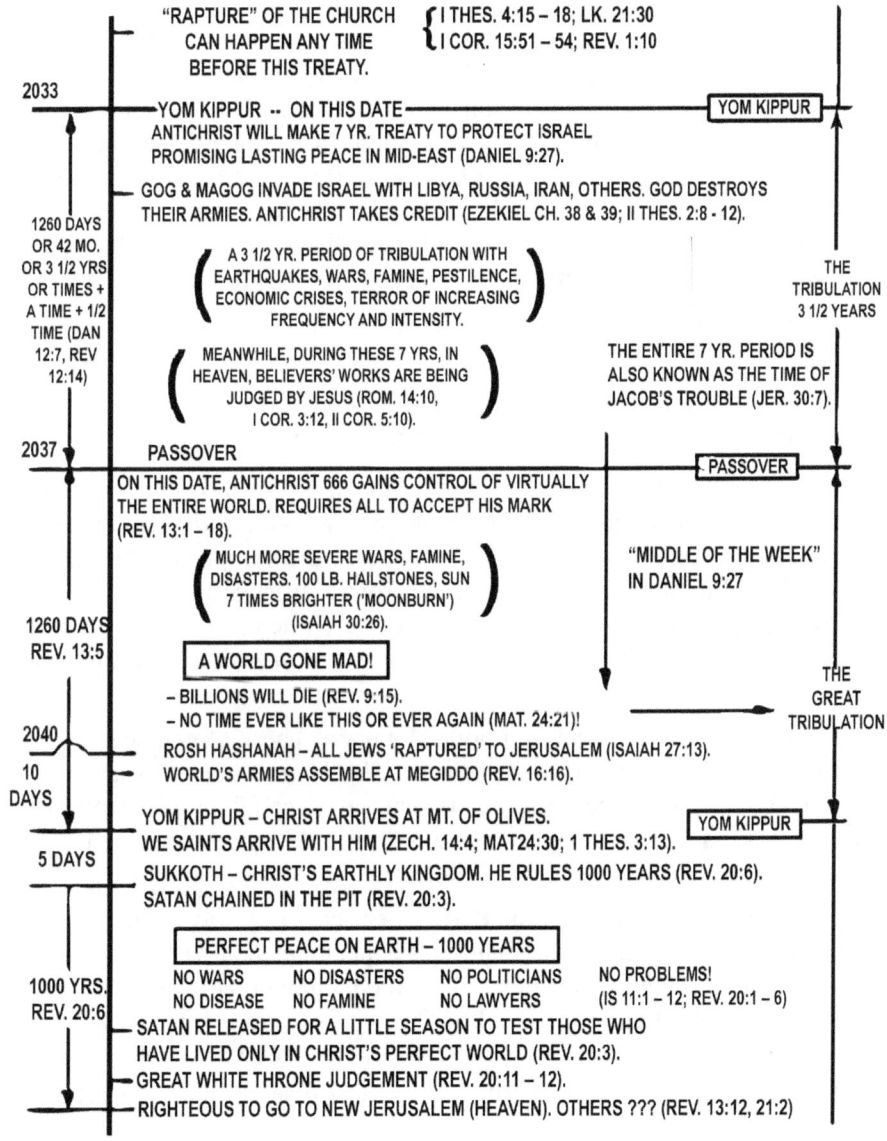

Illus. 14: Scenario of the End of Days

Olivet, a Holy Mountain

A prophecy observation of my own inspiration may be of interest here, especially since it is nearly certain that Jesus was crucified on the Mount of Olives.[12, 25] In fact, the Mount of Olives should probably be considered one of the most Holy places on Earth; perhaps second only to the *Kodesh Ha-Kodashim* (Holy of Holies) on Mount *Zion* at the Temple site. Mount *Zion* is, of course, frequently called Mount *Moriah*. In fact, II Chronicles 3:1 refers to the Temple Mount as *Moriah*, thereby leading us moderns to assume that to be the place where Isaac was offered. The *Moriah*-connection (if you will) then, is carried back to a traditional belief that Abraham's obedient approach to the sacrifice of Isaac was on Mount *Zion* as "Mount *Moriah*." As we have seen, traditional "thought" is extremely difficult to dissuade from our minds, especially after hundreds of years of such "thinking."

However, the popular name of that particular mountain is of man's choice, not from God, necessarily. From Genesis 22:2,

> "...get thee into the land of Moriah; and offer him (his son, Isaac) there for a burnt offering upon one of the mountains which I will tell thee of."

God didn't tell us which mountain. He told Abraham. We have a subtle clue, however, because in verses 3 and 4 we are told that Abraham "*went unto that place*" and that "*he saw the place even from afar off!*" — "Afar off?" — Yes, the Mount of Olives can be seen even from "afar off," but Mount *Zion* cannot be seen from a distance because *Olivet* looks down upon *Zion*! In fact, *Zion* is the lowest peak in the area, whereas *Olivet* is by far the highest peak. In fact, the Mount of Olives can be seen even from *Masada*, at a distance of about forty miles, "*even from "afar off."*

Two additional events rate *Olivet* as a holy Mountain. These of course are The Ascension of our Lord Jesus (30 C.E.); and the Ascension of *Shekhinah* forty years later (70 C.E.). One obscure Judaica source, Reference 35, reports that the voice (*Bath Kol*) from the *Shekhinah* pleaded three times daily to the People, saying to them: "I will go back to My place, till they acknowledge their guilt and seek My face." Reference is made to Hosea 5:15.

We demonstrated in Chapter 5 that the Red Heifer ceremony was the most important of all the Jewish rituals. Considering all the important happenings that have occurred and will yet occur on the Mount of Olives, this is most likely the mountain on which Isaac, as a "type" of Christ and of the Red Heifer, was offered. (Why, Isaac may even have had red hair!) That offering of Isaac may even have taken place at the site of the *Miphkad Altar*, which may also have been the place of that greatest sacrifice, ever! (Also see Professor Martin's analysis.[12, 25])

But, of course the story doesn't end here, because in Genesis 22:7 – 8 Isaac asked:

> "...'but, where is the lamb for a burnt offering?' And Abraham said, 'My son, God will provide Himself a lamb for a burnt offering'..."

Since the ancient Hebrew script had no punctuation, as we know it, can it be that this last sentence has a very profound meaning, which is lost by the absences of subtly intended Hebrew punctuation? It may be that this sentence should read:

"My son, God will provide Himself, a lamb for a burnt offering..."

For that is exactly what God, the Father, did at that same mountain about 2,000 years later. God provided His own and only Son, our Lord Jesus, as a *"lamb for a burnt offering."* Thus, when we place that last phrase in apposition, the meaning is profound indeed. The Lord did not merely supply the sacrifice "Himself;" rather, He supplied "Himself" as the sacrifice.

Punctuation does not appear in *any* manuscripts before the ninth century, and those earliest punctuations are found only in Latin manuscripts. It is significant to note, therefore, that all translations from Greek, Hebrew, and Aramaic, where punctuation produces an influence on the meaning of the text, have interpretations based merely on *human* authority. The commas we have added to this verse then give it a different meaning, although we possess no greater and no lesser "authority" than that of the King James translators. It is left to our readers to decide for themselves which version they prefer.

Further detailed study of Scripture, however, provides a clearer identification of "Mount *Moriah*." Genesis 22:13, 14 says that Abraham looked behind himself and saw a ram caught by its horns in a thicket. Abraham may then have gone westward across the Kidron Valley to take the ram and offer it there on what later became the Temple Mount. Verse 14 says Abraham built an altar, named the spot, and that the place is still known as Mount *Moriah*, to this day. Notice, the ram was sacrificed at Mount *Moriah*, but the lamb that God provided (Himself) was offered at the Mount of Olives — the same place where Isaac was offered.

Yes, the Temple Mount is also the place where, one thousand years later, rams and goats were offered at the Temple Altar and it is still known as Mount *Moriah* to this day. But, that place cannot be seen *"afar off,"* whereas, we know from Verse 4 that the place where Isaac was offered had to be higher than the surrounding peaks. The topographic features and placements of the Temple Mount (*Moriah*) and the Mount of Olives are consistent with Scripture as well as *Talmudic* Law and tradition concerning the Temple sacrifices and the Red Heifer ceremony. There were distinct and separate locations for the "ordinary" sacrifices at the Temple — on the Temple Mount (*Moriah*) — and for the most Holy "burned" offerings *"outside the camp"* at *Olivet* summit; e.g., the Red Heifer, the Atonement Goat, the sin offerings and a few other most sacred offerings.

As a result of studies involved with this work, I am moved to make the following speculations:

I believe the offering of Isaac, the burning of the Red Heifers, as well as all the other burnt offerings, and the Crucifixion of Jesus of Nazareth *all* took place at (or near) the *Miphkad Altar* site on the Mount of Olives. The Lord provided Himself as a lamb for a burnt offering. He sacrificed His son in our stead and withheld the "blade" of judgment.

I further speculate that *three* Holy Events: the Ascension of Jesus of Nazareth, the Ascension of the Divine Presence (*Shekhinah*), and the return of *Shekhinah* with Jesus Christ as King of Kings will all have taken place at a single location on the summit of the Mount of Olives.

The Master of the Universe places considerable importance with the number "three." One cannot prove these speculations, but they nevertheless are interesting.

The Divine Number

Notice in both sequences just discussed that there are three fulfillments. There seems to be a somewhat obvious prophetic pattern here, which punctuates the authority and the Glory of the Trinity. With some help from Mr. Clarence Larkin's priceless storehouse of truth,[17] we see the importance of the pattern described:

- Three is the "Divine Number" because it appears so often in connection with Holy personages, events or things.
- Father, Son, and Holy Spirit (The Trinity of God.)
- Body, Soul, Spirit (The Trinity of man).
- God appeared on Earth in three forms: as "fire," as "cloud," and as man.
- The three great feasts: Passover, Pentecost, Tabernacles. (All Jewish men are commanded to participate)
- Three pieces of *matzah* are served at the *Seder* (Passover meal).
- Israel has been brought back to The Land three times.
- The three temptations of Jesus.
- Peter's three denials of the Lord.
- Jesus asked three times: "Lovest thou me, Peter?"
- Jesus commanded three times: "Feed my lambs (Sheep)."
- Jesus was anointed three times with perfumed oil.
- Three crosses at Calvary.
- Three "days" are associated with the restoration of Israel and with the Resurrection of Jesus and with Jonah's deliverance. ("Three" different personages raised on "three" different occasions.)
- God "parted the waters" of the Jordan River three times. (Joshua 3:15 – 17, II Kings 2:8, 2:14)
- Three "veils" in the Temple.
- Man, woman, child (The trinity of marriage, birth, family.)
- Day, month, year (The trinity of time).
- Land, sea, sky (The trinity of Earth).
- Red, blue, yellow (The trinity of color).

- Solid, liquid, gas (The trinity of matter).
- Animal, vegetable, mineral (The trinity of Creation).

Also, there is the trinity of dimension: length, width, height. One might ask, "What about the fourth dimension, relativity, the speed-of-light, etc.?"

It is my view that there will be no fourth dimension under the control of man; i.e., where man would actually control "time." Time is a part of Creation. — Creation and Eternity belong only to God.

Another Divine Number

In case you did not notice in the earlier discussion, **OLIVET, A HOLY MOUNTAIN**, there were a total of SEVEN events that are considered to have occurred or will at some future time occur at that *same* spot on the summit of the Mount of Olives. –

There were, of course the *two* groups of *three* "fulfillments" each that took place on *Olivet* summit, but when we count individual events occurring at that Holy peak, there were again – SEVEN – separate events or functions that of course underline that Divine Number of Perfection – SEVEN! – These are:

- The "offering" of Isaac.
- The burning of the Red Heifers.
- The "Burnt Offerings" – such as the daily Sin Offerings and the Atonement Goat.
- The Crucifixion of The Son of God as The ULTIMATE "Offering" to pay for the sins of ALL men.
- The Ascension of Jesus of Nazareth after His Resurrection from The Tomb.
- The Ascension of the Divine Presence, Israel's *Shekhinah* forty years after The Ascension of Jesus.
- The Return of Jesus AND *Shekhinah* to that same Mount when He Returns to claim His Kingdom as *King of Kings* and *Lord of Lords!*.

And, yet Another Divine Number

As if that preceding series were not enough to convince us, The Lord scheduled again, SEVEN, Events in which His Divine Presence or *Holy Fire* was witnessed by men on "public" occasions; i.e., not in the Temple or the Tabernacle. We can observe the following seven Events, in chronological order, on these occasions:

- Moses saw *"the burning bush"* that was not aflame.
- The People saw a *"pillar of cloud"* by day; and a *"pillar of fire"* by night, as they journeyed from Egypt to The Promised Land.

- The centurion and his men at The Cross saw the Lord's Mighty "Fire" when the Veil was rent – and *"they feared greatly."*
- Forty days after The Resurrection, on the Day of Pentecost ("Weeks"), The Divine Presence manifested His Presence in the form of flames to "deliver" His Holy Spirit to Jesus' Disciples by *"baptizing them with The Holy Ghost"* before their embarking on their ministries to *"Jerusalem, and in all Judea, and in Samaria, and unto the uttermost part of The Earth."*
- The Divine Presence (*Shekhinah*) removed from His Holy Abode and "sat" atop the portico of the Temple forty days.
- The Divine Presence departed across the Valley Kidron, and again, "sat" at the summit of the Mount of Olives for three and one half years; pleading with the People to *"Return unto Me."*
- *Shekhinah* departed Jerusalem, ascending into Heaven, saying, *"I will go back to My Place."*

Again, God UNDERLINES, MAGNIFIES, "SPOTLIGHTS" His Glory and Magnificent Power with keen precision in the World of man by demonstrating His Holiness with such Events in the view of men on Earth.

What if Israel had Repented?

Before closing our subject of prophecy, we should address an important eschatological question: "What would have happened if Israel had repented and returned to the Lord in 69 C.E.?" We can only speculate on the events to follow, but we know for certain that all prophecy would have been fulfilled. Somehow, God would have brought on the Antichrist, the wars, the famines, etc., and would have "refined" Israel. Then, they would have been purified to accept "the one whom they had pierced" when He arrived in power and glory at the Mount of Olives. The "Church Age" would have been of very brief duration and the Kingdom Age would have had a much earlier beginning than we shall witness. Nevertheless, it would ALL have "come to pass" at that time, had Israel returned unto Him who had Promised that He would then return unto them.

But, we modern Gentile Christians would never have been born. Our potential ancestors would have been annihilated in the final wars. Without The Crucifixion and later failure of first-century Judaism to recognize their Messiah, it would all have ended right then and there.

However, Jesus came to save that which was lost. Yes! That included not only "the lost sheep of the house of Israel," but also the Gentiles! We had no way to come to the Lord except as proselytes through Judaism. The Lord wants all of humanity to be heirs in His Kingdom. (John 10:16) He had a far better plan for reaching Gentiles and washing away their sins — by offering His Son as "the lamb for a burnt offering" — on one of the mountains "*in the land of Moriah.*"

The Lord permitted the "blindness" of the Jewish people in order that we might "see!" Both faiths wait for the same One to touch His feet on that Holy Mountain, *Olivet*.

Tucked-away obscurely in the Index of *The Works of Josephus* under "prophecy" is the following note:

"Prophecies could not agree to the events, if the world were governed by chance."

7

"Signs and Wonders"

"Signs" of Woe – That ONE <u>crucial</u> date – Some Judeans recognized the "signs" — The Rabbis lament that crucial date – The "Voice" of God (not like we thought) – Was our "9/11" a sign? – Holy Spirit now withdrawing from Earth.

I never cease to wonder at the fact that Israelites always have expected the Lord to "give them a sign." And God has been very responsive and accommodating to His Chosen People in that regard. No other people in history have ever been given so many "signs," including the ultimate sign — God Himself dwelling in their midst — as "fire" — as "cloud" — and as man. God may sometimes ask, "What do I have to do for these people?" Well, He does know what to do, and He will do it, in His time.

It is interesting to observe that no other nation (or people) have ever had personal visitations from Almighty God Himself. – Only Israel. – He appeared to them as a "fire" and as a "cloud" during the Exodus. He dwelt in the Temple as this same "fire" or "cloud," to which they refer as *Shekhinah* (or Divine Presence). A Muslim friend, after reading this book, expressed surprise that *any* man had ever *seen* God. He accepted the explanation that they in fact actually *saw* only God's Divine Presence – as He chose to appear to His People.

Nobody said it better than the Lord Himself in Deuteronomy 4 (NASB):

4:7 for what great nation is there that has a god so near to it as the Lord our God whenever we call on Him?

4:33 Has any people heard the voice of God speaking from the midst of the fire, as you have heard it, and survived?

4:34 Or has a god tried to go to take for himself a nation from within another nation by trials, by signs and wonders and by war and by a mighty hand and by an outstretched arm and by great terrors, as the Lord did for you in Egypt before your eyes?

4:35 To you it was shown that you might know that the Lord He is God; there is no other besides Him.

4:36 Out of the heavens He let you hear His voice to discipline you; and on earth He let you see His great fire, and you heard His words from the midst of the fire.

4:37 Because He loved your fathers, therefore He chose their descendants after them. And He personally brought you from Egypt by His great power,

4:38 driving out from before you nations greater and mightier than you, to bring you in and give you their land for an inheritance, as it is today.

4:39 Know therefore today, and take it to your heart, that the Lord, He is God in Heaven above and on earth below; there is no other.

After hearing these pronouncements of His great love for this People, how can anyone say the Lord has not maintained His Promises to Israel today? And, as He says, has He shown His great fire to any other nation? Or has Almighty God Himself ever spoken in person to any other nation?

Signs of the Jewels

Among the many little known or seldom discussed "signs" is one that Josephus[2] describes, *Antiquities* 3.8.9/214–218, which was given to Israel via the jewels that adorned the shoulders of the robe worn by the High Priest. The accounts given by Josephus, as well as the accompanying commentary by the translator, are quite detailed and I hesitate to repeat all of them here. Briefly, therefore, one of the jewels, a sardonyx on the priest's right shoulder, shone when God was present at one of their sacrifices. Brilliant rays darted from this gem and could be seen even at a great distance.

A concealed and delicate "picture" is suggested in this sign of the sardonyx. But, just what is a "sardonyx"? The sardonyx is a translucent, quartz-like gem having a reddish brown hue. So, what is so "delicate" or subtle about a reddish brown jewel?

The Red Heifer certainly had a reddish brown coat (and with no more than two odd-colored hairs). Many Christians would agree that the Red Heifer is a "type" or "picture" of Jesus, pure and "without spot or blemish" and offered *"for a purification for sin."*

What is not so obvious is a remote document from Roman antiquity which records that Jesus had hair and a beard "the color of wine" or what might be called reddish brown or auburn in color. This description, although unauthenticated, is presented[27] as having been recovered from a document supposedly written by an acquaintance of Pontius Pilate.

It may also be noted that King David, the earthly ancestor of Jesus, is mentioned in Scripture (I Samuel 16:12 and 17:42) as being "ruddy and of a fair countenance," which is to say "reddish" in his coloring — perhaps hair, skin, or both. So, there may be some "genetic" background in this connection as well as a spiritual picture.

Now that we have seen Jesus reflected in the Red Heifer, could He also have been represented in the sign of the sardonyx? This really appears to have too much credence to be just a coincidence. It was a "sign" to the Jews, but to Christians it is a "picture" of the One who was giving the signs. One wonders if modern Christians can continue to ignore these Jewish "signs."

Josephus indicates another sign from this source, "...still more wonderful than this..." took place before Israel was to go into battle. Here God declared prior to the battle whether Israel would be victorious; causing all twelve of the stones, known as the *Urim and Thummim*," which were inserted into the High Priest's breastplate, to give off a "super-brilliance" such that all of Israel's army could see this encouraging sign.

The commentary by Mr. Whiston is quite interesting. He states that apparently King Saul was the first to become slack in consulting this "oracle," but that King David consulted this sign frequently and complied with God's recommendations with appreciation. (So, why shouldn't we be impressed by David's military victories?) But *none* of David's successors ever consulted God through this Divine Revelation.

Then, after the return from Babylon, this "sign" returned, was consulted by "some" of the kings over the years, until the death of one of the most beloved of all High Priests, John Hyrcanus. (See Reference 12.) Josephus says this sign ceased to come forth about 200 years before his writing, perhaps about 100 B.C.E. Further comment hardly seems necessary.

Signs Above the City

Josephus was really "into signs." Again, just before the departure of the Glory from the Temple, he describes: "Thus, there was a star resembling a sword, which stood over the City, and a comet, that continued a whole year." (See Appendix A.)

Now, what does a sword resemble, especially when the blade is in a vertical position with the hand-guard at the uppermost? Of course this description also resembles a cross, a *patibulum* fastened to a tree, a "sign" that, a few centuries later, became one of the best known emblems of the Christian faith.

Josephus doesn't stop here. Just a few days after the Glory of the Lord departed from the Holy of Holies, another strange "sign" appeared over Jerusalem: "On the 21st of *Iyar*, just before sunset, chariots and troops of soldiers in their armour were seen running among the clouds, and surrounding of cities." Many similar incidents were reported during the 1967 "Six Day" Arab/Israeli War.

A Sign to be Seen, but not Heard

Earlier, in Chapter 4, we discussed the mysterious opening of the huge brass (or bronze) gate, Nicanor's Gate, east of the sanctuary. This miracle was described in detail that is typical of the reporting expertise of Flavius Josephus. However, Josephus either neglected to inform us or was unaware of the most spectacular facet of this miracle of the gate.

Talmud, Yoma 39b, observes that whenever this mammoth gate was opened or closed, the noise of its "turning hinges" could be heard at a distance of eight Sabbath "limits." A "limit" is the distance a person may travel on the Sabbath, as permissible under the Law, a Sabbath Day's Journey, or two thousand cubits and being almost 1000 meters. Thus, at a total of nearly 8,000 meters, the gate noise could be heard from a distance of more than four miles.

This gate must have been bronze rather than brass as described by Josephus[2] since brass had been invented by the Romans only a few years earlier in 15 B.C.E. and bronze had been in use since about 3500 B.C.E. *Talmud, Yoma* 38a, describes Nicanor's gates as Corinthian bronze, a more refined bronze having a brilliant golden hue, as opposed to the duller ordinary bronze. Nevertheless, both of these metals have good resonance properties and would have high friction coefficients against the iron hinge supports. These qualities would have contributed strongly toward creating the vibration or "hummmm" tone that could be heard at a distance of eight Sabbath limits — almost as far as Bethlehem, six miles to the south of Jerusalem.

The noise was apparently produced by resonant vibration of the heavy brass gate structure caused by friction of its "turning hinges." They did not have effective lubricants in those days. Josephus says twenty men were needed to open or close this gate "with difficulty." The sound of its opening on the eves of Sabbaths, on New Moons, and on the Holy days would herald such occasions to much of surrounding Judea.

The fact the gate opened "of its own accord" would seem to be of sufficient stature alone to rate as a "miracle." The Lord, however, was only content to open it so quietly that the guards had to run upstairs and TELL their captain the gate had opened. Under "normal" conditions, the captain and all of Jerusalem would have been shaken out-of-the-sack at midnight by its great noise. (And they wanted a sign!!)

Since the gate was finished in brilliant Corinthian bronze, it shone with a dazzling, blinding reflection in the early morning sun. As the sun rose above the Mount of Olives, the magnificent splendor of the Temple blazed forth with an unforgettable scene. This golden bronze gate, the white marble buildings, and walls gave the Temple a glory unmatched by any other architectural marvel before or since that time. (Other mysteries concerning Nicanor's Gate are described in the *Talmud*.)

A Time of the Signs

I am certainly no authority on Josephus. I must, however, respect these declarations from this marvelous reporter because he was there on the scene! It appears that many strange events were taking place just prior to and during this first century Divine Judgment on

Jerusalem. Josephus (and many others) were apparently impressed sufficiently that they documented these events in considerable detail — to be noticed later by those who would look. At least one noted and brilliant scholar, Joseph Scaliger, had the highest praise for Josephus as an historian. (See Appendix C.)

As mentioned earlier in the main story of this work, my own speculation is that the departure of the Divine Presence from the Mount of Olives summit may have taken place during *Chanukah*, which is, ironically, the Festival of Lights. This event occurred forty years after Jesus, the Light of the World, was "put out."

This speculation that the departure occurred at *Chanukah* should not, however, appear to be purely a guess. The estimation is based on extending 3½ years beyond Pentecost, the time of the *Shekhinah* withdrawal from the Temple, until the time when *Midrash* says *Shekhinah* ascended to Heaven. Since Pentecost is generally near June, 3½ years later would be near December, which is the season for *Chanukah*. It does seem peculiar, however, that the *Midrash* commentary makes no mention of the date or that feast. With a better understanding of the first century Jewish calendar, leap years, leap months, etc., perhaps some scholar will elaborate or improve our understanding of the date for that final ascent from *Olivet* summit.

A Woe in the Darkness

At the Crucifixion it is well known that the sun was darkened from the sixth hour until the ninth hour when Jesus gave up the Ghost. (Luke 23:44) Whether this was truly caused by a solar eclipse or by dense cloud cover cannot be determined conclusively from Scripture alone. Some recent scholars of the twentieth century have proposed that a solar eclipse did in fact occur at Jerusalem in 30 C.E. on the 14th day of *Nisan* (Passover eve) from about 12 noon until 3 P.M. These conclusions are based on analyses performed by "back-calculating" from astronomical data, using modern computer technology to solve the complex orbital mechanics problem that must be addressed.

Some of those same orbital analyses add that a lunar eclipse also was experienced at that same Passover in Jerusalem. This dual eclipse must have been regarded by Judeans as a "sign." Scripture makes mention only of darkening the sun between noon and the hour of His death. However, the Jewish tradition and culture of that day considered an eclipse of the sun or the moon as a harbinger of doom.

Talmud, *Sukkah* 29a, notes that an eclipse of the sun is a bad omen for the world. Further detailed disclosure states if the sun is eclipsed in the east, a bad omen is seen for the nations to the east. If the sun is in the west during the darkening, it bodes ill future for nations to the west. But, if the sun is darkened while it is "in the midst of heaven" (i.e., at midday), the woe will befall the entire world. Matthew 27:45 says there was "darkness over all the land" from the sixth to the ninth hour; i.e., noon to 3 P.M., while the sun was "in the midst of heaven."

Even more depth of meaning is seen in Jewish superstition regarding a lunar eclipse, which was taken as an extremely ill omen for Israel. Among the reasons believed to cause Israel to deserve such an omen are:

- On account of "those who perpetrate forgeries" — as in the case of the "forged" charge of sedition, the claim of "kingship," etc., against Jesus.
- On account of "those who give false witness" — as for those lying witnesses at the "trials" of Jesus.
- On account of "those who cut down good trees, even though they are their own" — as was "The Branch" who was cut down by His own who received Him not!
- On account of "cutting down a fruit tree" (even if He was their own) — as Jesus was the First Fruit of The Resurrection.

The *Gemara* of *Sukkah* 29a goes on to add that when Israel fulfills the Lord's will, they need not fear all these omens. Reference is made to Jeremiah 10:2:

"Thus saith the Lord; learn not the way of the heathen, and be not dismayed at the signs of heaven, for the heathen are dismayed at them."

The idolaters and heathen of the nations will be dismayed by such signs, but Israel will not be dismayed, *Talmud* says. How sad it is that Israel was dismayed by these omens, because she did not remain in the Lord's will, failing to see His victory at the empty Tomb three days after these "signs ."

If a dual eclipse did occur, just picture yourself as a Judean on that day. The City drew mysteriously dark at midday, without a cloud in the sky (presumably). This dark "hour" occurred as the Romans were crucifying, along with two thieves, the gentle Galilean teacher, so beloved by many of the common folk and who caused such a stir as He rode into the City astride a donkey the other day. Several of the Pharisees were very distraught, because many of the people had proclaimed Him Messiah, the Lord's Anointed. Some of the Rabbis had said that was the day foretold by Daniel the prophet for the Coming of Messiah, Son of David. (Daniel 9:24) The Pharisees were openly hostile to Him, but who would have thought it would come to this? They have crucified Him! And now the City and all around is in darkness. I wonder...has there been a terrible mistake?

That was bad enough to warn the populace of the Lord's displeasure, but then that night they were expecting their usual and astronomically prompt full moon of the Passover. On the Jewish calendar, received from the Great "I AM," the fourteenth day of the month was a full moon. They were all expecting that full moon to rise, glistening, over the top of the Mount of Olives. But all that came up was darkness. Nothing! Empty! So, now this! No moon on the Passover! Something is wrong! ("Do you suppose He was Messiah?!" they whisper, "Is this another sign?!")

Those at Jerusalem on that Passover had to be frightened, regardless of whether they believed Jesus was Messiah. Seeing these signs had to be a moving experience. What would you have thought? What would you have felt?

It would appear that the Lord tried to speak to Israel through "the sons of Aaron" for a full generation by giving "signs" through Jesus, the Temple, and sacrifices. Then, having been spurned by the priesthood, it seems He "took His case to the People" by speaking to them in Person from the "fire" and the "cloud" on the Mount of Olives for 3½ years; perhaps the same duration as Jesus' ministry.

Some observations can be made here on the subject of dates and "years" used in this historical study:

1. It is not clear, after two millennia, what type of "year" was being used by any given historian at any given time.
2. The intricacies of the Judaic calendar, leap-years, leap-months, etc., are extremely difficult to apply with dates prior to the calendar revisions by Hillel II, about the fourth century C.E.
3. Synchronizing dates between the presently revised Judaic calendar and the Gregorian (sixteenth century) calendar leaves room for an amount of error that could be of significance. The revision by Pope Gregory XIII in 1582 was, after all, a fairly "recent" date in comparison with the time of the first four centuries.

It has already been shown by the late Professor Martin and others that the birth of Jesus was probably on *Rosh Hashanah* about 3 or 4 B.C.E. relative to our Gregorian calendar. (See Reference 27.) Thus, it is hoped that more precise dating for the *Shekhinah* Event can be established by more informed and talented scholars using application of astronomy, orbital mechanics and/or more precise historical documentation.

"*Sign*" of the Disappearing Signs

Several wondrous supernatural events, that are reported by *Talmud, Yoma* 39, occurred in the Temple during the forty years in which Simeon The Righteous served as High Priest, about 300 B.C.E. These events occurred regularly during that period. Then, after his death, these signs would only appear occasionally and, when they did show, a "good omen" was interpreted.

This strange sequence would seem to indicate the Lord was "speaking" to Israel through all this and saying there was something admirable in this man. Removal of the constancy of these events after Simeon's passing told the Jews they were doing something wrong, because the priest who followed Simeon (John Hyrcanus) was also apparently in the Lord's praise.

This man, Simeon The Righteous, lived around the time of Alexander the Great and was respected and proclaimed throughout the civilized world of that day. Jewish historians record (*Talmud, Yoma* 69a) that during a Jewish revolt, upon meeting Simeon at Antipatris, Alexander dismounted from his carriage and bowed before this beloved sage in deep respect. Judging by the supernatural signs beginning in the Temple during his time, Simeon must certainly have been high in the Lord's favor as well.

So far, no definite evidence has surfaced to explain why these signs appeared during the tenure of Simeon. It would be interesting to study that era of Judaism to find why the Lord might have given Israel this "reward." The giving of these signs from the Lord would seem almost as if He were commending them. It would be interesting also to find whether there is any correlation of the later sporadic signs with any particular merit on the part of Israel or her priests at those times when the signs did occasionally appear after Simeon's time.

History is somewhat obscure regarding early (350–300 B.C.E.) Greek rule of Palestine. However, the Gentile conquerors of that period seemed to delegate actual administration and civil control of the Jewish citizenry to the High Priest and the Council of Elders. Their oppressors comprehended and appreciated the benefits of ruling a disciplined society already conformed to a rigid system of law, likely even more effective than their own. Then, reading between the lines, it appears that some of these periods were more pleasing to the Lord than other periods, depending to a large extent upon the integrity and obedience of the High Priest.

This period began a decline in Jewish tradition and obedience under the worldly influences of the "advanced" Grecian society and under leadership of some corrupt "shepherds." Israel's failures under these decadent High Priests can be understood through a maxim that is reputedly quoted from a Prussian general:

"A regiment can be only as good as its sergeants; but it will always be as bad as its colonel."

This principle applies also to nations, free or servile, just as it applies to Judaism or the Church. Through these signs, the Lord may have been trying to encourage Israel when they had chosen a good "colonel" and to chastise them when they had a poor one.

The so-called minor prophets relate some of Jewish history up until about 400 B.C.E. (Malachi). No Biblical entries were given between 400 B.C.E. and 164 B.C.E. Then, our awareness of Jewish history is again restored in the Apocrypha as we reach the time of the Maccabean Revolt, 164 B.C.E. Grecian Hellenistic rule under Antiochus III brought a tighter rein on the Judeans than previous masters had drawn. When his heir and successor, Antiochus IV Epiphanes, humiliated and oppressed the Jews (and the Temple) to a new low, they had finally had enough, and once more, they called upon their Lord. During the revolt that followed, the Lord answered them by the "Miracle of Lights," which has inspired the season of *Chanukah*, and was definitely a positive indication from *Shekhinah* that "*YHWH*" was pleased with their resolve and renewed faith.

From the history we have sketched for the High Priests, it can be seen that Judaism had again reached a despicable state by the time of Jesus. But, the Lord still did not give up on His "naughty children." He didn't give up on them then and He didn't give up on them in 70 C.E. — Even though we Christians have treated Jews as if He had rejected them. But, He did "go back to His place" for a time.

An obscure passage in *Yoma* 9a indicates that Simeon The Righteous was High Priest for forty years and was succeeded by John Hyrcanus who remained for eighty years. These two most beloved sages had by far the longest tenures of all the priests in that office during the times of both Temples. The discussion continues by pointing out that the First Temple had a total of eighteen High Priests in a period of four hundred and ten years. In comparison, over three hundred High Priests served during the four hundred and twenty years of the Second Temple. Other than Simeon and John Hyrcanus, all but two of them served less than one year. At the last, including the time of Caiaphas, the office was purchased from Roman officials.

After The Crucifixion, these supernatural signs *never* again appeared in the Temple. (They were "no more forever," as He says in Exodus 14:13). The Rabbis and *Talmud* lament this loss as they describe each sign as it appeared under Simeon, then occasionally appeared, then completely voided during the "forty years before the Temple was destroyed." One thought that may have been going through Jewish minds at that time was: "Titus destroyed the Temple 70 C.E. Seventy minus forty! Hey! 30 C.E...That Nazarene! Could he have been Messiah?"

However, some of the Judeans at that time perhaps also recognized, through absence of these signs, that something was wrong. Examine these signs now as we describe their detail and possible meanings to Judeans after 30 C.E.

"Drawing the Lots"

On the Day of Atonement, two unblemished male goats ("he-goats") were brought into the Temple from across The Heifer's Gangway. Then, both goats were brought before the High Priest, one goat on his left and one to his right. Two "lots" were placed in a golden urn (*kalpei*), *Yoma* 4:1. According to some sources, they were black and white "pebbles," but they could be made of any material (*Yoma* 37a). One of these lots bore the inscription: "For the Lord;" on the other was written: "For *Azazel*;" i.e., "scapegoat." (It is interesting here to note that the ritual of the "blackball," a rejecting vote as cast against a prospective member of a fraternal organization, has very ancient "roots.")

The urn was then shaken and the High Priest would reach into the urn, grasping one of the lot pieces in each hand. Closing his fists to hold one lot piece in each hand, the Priest then would lift his hands from the urn and open his fists to see which lot applied to which goat, to his left or right. Then came a supernatural "sign."

During the time of Simeon The Righteous (about 300 B.C.E.), the lot "For the Lord" *always* came up in the High Priest's right hand. However, after that time the lot "For the Lord" would come up "now in the left hand or now in the right," purely at random. If the Lord's lot came up in the right hand, this was considered "a good omen."

Then, of course, the goat on the side facing the priest's hand holding the lot "For the Lord" was slain and given as the burnt offering for the atonement of Israel's sin. But the other goat, the *Azazel* or "scapegoat," was set free to roam in the wilderness after being led out of the City across the *Azazel* Bridge (Scapegoat's Gangway — Illus. 20: Jerusalem as it Appeared in 70 C.E., Page 153). A priest was selected to follow this spared goat, representing a renewed and now penitent Israel, to see that no harm came to him and that he adjusted to his new environment and freedom.

From this we find that the term "scapegoat" is used incorrectly as a figure of speech to denote someone who has been punished, in a sacrificial way, for having committed a crime that was also committed by others who are not being punished. In this ancient Jewish ritual, from which the term is borrowed, quite the opposite is true.

After the Crucifixion, 30 C.E., the Rabbis of the *Talmud* refer lamentably to that period of time only as: *"forty years before the Temple was destroyed." Talmud* records that, during those times, the lot piece "For the Lord" *never* came up in the priest's right hand. The Rabbis noted that the absence of that sign was indication of a very bad omen for Israel.

"The Crimson Strap"

Another supernatural sign concerning the *Azazel* was perhaps the most spectacular of all of these that we shall discuss. Each end of a "strap" (or strip) of crimson cloth was tied to the scapegoat's horns, thus hanging under his throat, to represent symbolically the severed throat of the Lord's goat, which was to be slain and its blood to be sprinkled on the Altar of Sacrifice. The situation is discussed in the *Gemara* of *Yoma* 39a.

The importance of this sign existed in the fact that Jewish "tradition" said (although, God never said this) Israel's sins were turned from "*scarlet*" to "*snow-white*" only when the *Azazel* goat reached the wilderness. During the time of Simeon, that crimson strap was tied to one of the Temple doors when *Azazel* was led out. (*Yoma* 68b) Consistently, the strap then turned snowy white and after a few hours it was determined, that, yes, Israel's sins had been washed, as promised. (They simply would not trust Him. They still had to have a "sign.")

Then after Simeon, when this sign was no longer "reliable," they devised an elaborate system to determine when the promise was manifest, just in case the strap did not turn white that time. Guards were stationed with "towels" (probably white) along the *Azazel* departure route (Illus. 20: Jerusalem as it Appeared in 70 C.E., Page 153) at distances where each guard could be seen by each other guard at the stations before and after his own station. In this way, when the Scapegoat reached the wilderness, they relayed a signal back to the Temple by waving the white "towels." Then they considered their sins had been forgiven by the Holy One.

Again, after The Crucifixion, the crimson strap *never* turned white as in previous years. Truly a startling supernatural "sign" to the priests. This was very disturbing to the Jews because from the *Talmud* it is said, "If it became white, it signified that the Holy One, blessed be He, had forgiven Israel's sin," and referring to Isaiah 1:18. This verse has a profound meaning here where it says "*...though your sins be as scarlet, they shall be as white as snow...*" But, they still didn't make any connection of this "sign" with that fateful day at Passover "forty years before the Temple was destroyed."

Further drama of this occasion is drawn from the *Mishnah* of this text, describing some of the movements and speech of the High Priest on the Day of Atonement. Again, from *Yoma* 4:2:

> MISHNAH. *He bound a thread of crimson wool on the head of the he-goat which was to be sent away. And (meantime) he placed it (at the gate) whence it was to be sent away; and the he-goat that was to be slaughtered, at the place of the slaughtering. He came to his bullock a second time, pressed his two hands upon it and made confession. And thus he would say: "O Lord, I have dealt wrongfully, I have transgressed, I have sinned before thee, I and my house, and the children of Aaron, thy Holy people. O Lord, pray forgive the wrong doings, the transgressions and the sins, which I have committed, transgressed and sinned before thee, I and my house, and the children of Aaron, thy Holy people. As it is written in the Torah of Moses, thy servant: "For on this day atonement be made for you; from all thy sins shall be clean before the Lord." And they responded: "Blessed be the name of His glorious Kingdom for ever and ever."*

One must not scoff or ridicule this Jewish ritual. How unlike His "ways" are man's ways. Men, Jewish or Christian, still have much difficulty in the discernment of "works" from "Faith." The Lord accomplished all the "work" that was needed for cleansing our sins, "forty years before the Temple was destroyed." All we need is Faith to believe He will do as He promised.

The Two "He-Goats"

The connection of the Atonement goats with the sacrificial death of Jesus does not end here, however. The Roman Procurator, Pontius Pilate, actually took a "type" role of the High Priest as he had Jesus and Barabbas before him. An obscure note from Reference 33 under Luke 23:18 reveals that both men had the Hebrew given name "*Y'shua*." This fascinating information is recorded in the works of Origen, the Alexandrian theologian, scholar and martyr of the 2nd and 3rd centuries.

The name "Barabbas," as stated in the New Testament, was actually derived from the Aramaic form of this young man's name. His "full" Hebrew name was *Y'shua ben Abbah*, meaning "*Y'shua*, Son of the High Father." But the New Testament translators used an Anglicized version of the Aramaic form of this name, which was "*Jesu bar Abbas*." The translators may also have wisely called him "Barabbas" and dropped the given name (Jesus) in order to avoid confusion of his name with that of Jesus of Nazareth.

Whereas, the other young man, whose Hebrew name was *Y'shua ben Yusef*, was of course the true "Son of the High Father," JESUS of Nazareth. Thus, Pilate "drew the lot" by leaving the choice to the assembled crowd as to which "*Y'shua*" would be spared as the Scapegoat? (All say, "Barabbas!"); and which "*Y'shua*" would be "For the Lord?" (Jesus.) Knowing all these things, and knowing how thoroughly Jesus fulfilled the Law, we can develop the following speculations:

— Both Jesus and Barabbas were probably brought into Jerusalem by way of "The Heifer's Gangway" Bridge, which was near the place of His betrayal and "capture," *Gethsemane*. (See Illus. 20: Jerusalem as it Appeared in 70 C.E., Page 153)

— Jesus of Nazareth was probably standing on Pilate's right and Barabbas on his left when Pilate asked the crowd to decide the "lot" of each man.

— Barabbas was probably adorned in some way with a "crimson" sash, neckerchief, hat, or other article as he was released.

— Barabbas was probably escorted out of the City via the *Azazel* Bridge ("Scapegoat Gangway").

— Barabbas probably left that same scarlet (or crimson) article tied to a Temple door or gate after being released to be led out of the City and into the "wilderness." It later turned mysteriously white after a few hours,"...because the Holy One, Blessed be He, had forgiven (all) sin."

— Somebody probably was sent to keep Barabbas under surveillance for a few days to insure that he behaved himself; at least until all the "fuss" about this Nazarene "troublemaker" blew over.

Thus, an interesting picture of "types" appears relative to the Atonement goats, very closely paralleling the Jewish Laws and the rituals concerning that Holy Day. We saw a similar picture earlier with the two loaves that are exactly alike in the "Bread of the First Fruits" (Leviticus 23:17). In these ways, Jesus fulfilled the Law concerning *Yom Kippur*, the Day of Atonement. All must be fulfilled!

An appropriate but poignant footnote is given in *Yoma* 63b concerning the he-goat to be sacrificed "For the Lord." The Rabbis had ruled that casting of lots was necessary because the lot determines what is "fit for the Lord"; i.e., whose time has come. How tragic it is that the Jews did not recognize their Atonement "he-goat" who was truly "For the Lord"; though surely, His time had come!

"The Westernmost Candle"

A very meaningful sign appeared during the time of Simeon concerning the candlestick (*Menorah*) in the Holy Place. The seven candles were positioned along the south wall of the Holy Place; the western-most candle being nearest the Holy of Holies and the *Shekhinah* dwelling therein. (See Illus. 22: The Sanctuary of the 2nd Temple, Page 155.) All seven candles were cleaned each evening and filled to the same level with oil. The westernmost candle was lighted first and the other six were lighted from the flame of the western candle. And yet, during Simeon's priesthood, the westernmost candle always was still burning each evening after all six remaining candles had long been consumed!

Then, after Simeon's passing, the western candle would sometimes continue burning after the others — and sometimes not. Finally, during the "forty years before the Temple was destroyed," the western candle *never* outlasted the others. Was the Lord trying to tell them something?

Talmud states (*Shabbath* 22b) this miracle was taken as a sign that *Shekhinah* rested over Israel. Thus, it was well understood that when that miracle ceased, this was recognized as a warning that *Shekhinah* was going to depart. As we have shown, about forty years later (69 C.E.) the Lord did indeed depart into Heaven from *Olivet* summit.

"The Logs for The Altar"

By the "Law," only two logs were used for the burnt offerings on the Altar of Sacrifice. The fire was ignited in the morning and could not be rekindled until the next morning and no more logs could be added during the day's burning. During Simeon's time the two logs were sufficient to last for a full day of Temple sacrifices. However, the *Talmud* is clear that after 30 C.E., this miracle also ceased to be manifested at the Temple.

"The Breads"

Talmud describes this miracle in somewhat cryptic fashion and only the main theme of this story is clear. It is stated as follows: "...an '*omer*,' the two breads and the shewbread. Each priest got a piece the size of an olive, ate it, and was satisfied, some leaving something over. There was a curse on the breads 'from that time on' so that each priest received a piece the size of a bean." The implication is that after "that time" the priests were no longer satisfied from having eaten a piece the size of an olive. The discussion of the "curse," etc., is not clear at this writing.

"The *H'ekhal* doors"

It is also stated that during this same "forty years before the Temple was destroyed," doors of the *H'ekhal* would open by themselves. It can be observed in the Temple plan details, Illus. 21: Detail of the 2nd Temple, Page ,154 there were many "chambers" and "gates" within the walls of the *H'ekhal*, which had doors to contribute to some occasions that must have been a little "spooky" for the Temple custodians, guards, and priests.

How Jews Regarded the Signs

Never do *Talmud* Rabbis note the obvious connection of that period which they so mournfully bemoan as: "*forty years before the Temple was destroyed*" with The Crucifixion of Jesus of Nazareth, 30 C.E.

As we now look back on the tragic disappearance of all these Temple signs, it's almost as if the Lord were saying: "You have ignored the meaning of all the 'signs' I have given to you; including the 'burnt offering' of My only Son here on this Holy mountain, *Olivet*. Now, I give you one last 'sign' as I speak to you in Person on the mountain. If you still will not heed this sign, repent, and return to Me, I will go back to My Place." But, they did not.

Jewish people, as well as the rest of us, have ignored and/or have been shielded from this story. Nevertheless, it would be interesting to hear what worshipful Jews would find from this Event as a meaning for their people.

This occurred at a terrible time for Judeans. They were intent upon survival and most of these events happened very rapidly, during much pressure from the Romans. Maybe they were so confused, frightened, and harassed, they didn't know what to do, think, or feel. However, we know from the historians and from Scripture that the siege of Jerusalem and burning of the Temple left them with wounded hearts that can be healed only by Messiah.

It is a bitter irony that they wait for Messiah, and yet, He waits also for them.

> "*Behold, I stand at the door, and knock: If any man hear My voice, and open the door, I will come in to him, and will sup with him, and he with Me.*" Revelation 3:20

For Christians, there are some deep meanings that can be derived from some Jewish impressions received at this time. First, a summary statement in *Yoma* 39b, which yields some of the pathos and alarm felt through all of this.

> *Our Rabbis taught: During the last forty years before the destruction of the Temple, the lot ("For the Lord") did not come up in the right hand; nor did the crimson color strap become white; nor did the western-most light shine; and the doors of the H'ekhal would open by themselves until Rabbi Johanan ben Zakkai rebuked them, saying: "H'ekhal, H'ekhal, why wilt thou be alarmer thyself?" (i.e., Predict thine own destruction.) "I know about thee that thou will be destroyed for Zechariah ben Ido has already prophesied concerning thee." (i.e., concerning this significant omen of the destruction of the Temple.) "Open thy doors, O Lebanon, that the fire may devour thy cedars." (Zechariah 11:1)*

According to Judaic historians, Rabbi Johanan ben Zakkai was the most honored and prestigious Jewish sage of the first century. Thus, the Temple priests knew desolation of the Temple was imminent. They must have prepared replicas and then secreted the most precious Temple articles to desert caves. An exciting archaeological search is currently seeking these items.

Talmud presents some interesting history relative to the *Sanhedrin* during that period: "forty years before the Temple was destroyed." We have noted that period began immediately following The Crucifixion. It is stated in *Shabbath* 15a that when the miracles such as the Westernmost Candle, etc. had ceased, the *Sanhedrin* "went into exile," moving their gatherings to the "trade halls" (*Hannuth*) on the Temple Mount. Previous to that period the *Sanhedrin* had always convened in the Chamber of Hewn Stone in the Temple Court of the Israelites. (See Illus. 21: Detail of the 2nd Temple, Page 154) Later they moved into Jerusalem and then to a series of a few towns, eventually residing in Tiberias on the Sea of Galilee around 70 A. D. *Rosh Hashanah* 31b says that here the *Sanhedrin* had finally dropped to its lowest point in authority. This failure is somewhat difficult to understand because at that time Tiberias was the home of beloved patriarch, R. Yohanan ben Zakkai.

The Judeans of the First century, as well as twentieth century Jewish people, have been taught that *Shekhinah* has accompanied Israel into exile. From *Midrash Rabbah*, Exodus 23:5, "Whence do we know that the *Shekhinah* accompanied Israel in exile? Because it says, 'For your sake I was sent to Babylon.'...and Moses said: (Leviticus 26:44) '*and yet for all that, when they are in the land of their enemies, I will not reject them.*'" Again from *Midrash* Leviticus 26:44: "*I cannot abandon them, for I am the Lord their God.*"

Encyclopedia Judaica points out that although the presence of God is everywhere, the *Shekhinah* rests permanently on Israel rather than on the Gentiles, because Israel is a people chosen and sanctified by God to be carriers of His will to the world. (See Exodus 33:16.) *Judaica* also mentions concerning *Shekhinah*: "...which dwelt in the Temple, and was seen by the prophets in their visions, and which disappeared with the destruction of the Temple..."

Earlier, in Chapter 2, we referenced yet another traditional Jewish view on *Shekhinah's* movements from tractate *Rosh Hashanah* 31a. Here it is said: "The Divine Presence tarried for Israel in the wilderness six months in the hope that they would repent. When [it saw that] they did not repent, it said, let their soul expire, as it says, 'But the eyes of the wicked shall fail and they shall have no way to flee and their hope shall be the expiry of the soul.'" (From Job 11:20) We quoted another *Judaica* source[35], claiming *Shekhinah* is behind the remnant of the western wall of the Temple.

In his Foreword to this book, Professor Asher S. Kaufman brought out that a few other opinions have been recorded to discuss Jewish thought on *Shekhinah*. Some of those references are listed in Chapter 2 with brief comment. Nevertheless, at this point we need to examine the Jewish emotion that leads to such diverse opinion.

From these comments, it appears that Jewish authorities are mixed in their opinions, as to the present disposition of *Shekhinah*. We can note, however, Hosea said that He (God) was going to "return to His Place" and the *Midrash* has documented that *Shekhinah* did depart into Heaven indeed, saying those very words, likely during *Chanukah*, 69 C.E.

It is abundantly clear that *Shekhinah* has *never* been reported as having appeared *anywhere* to *anybody* since 66–70 C.E. However, many Jewish people would prefer to think that *Shekhinah* is still among them. It is certain that God has preserved His Chosen People through about 3500 years of persecution, scorn, exile and holocaust to survive into this 21st century. He has returned them to their Land, *Eretz Israel*, with their language and customs intact. NO other nation or people has *ever* done that!

It is my opinion that, if Jewish people want to believe that *Shekhinah* — God — is *still* with them, our compassion should compel us to accept this attitude. In fact, this "hope" they display in this fashion demonstrates a Jewish faith that God has *not* abandoned them — *and which He has not!*

Rabbi Akiba (first century) wept as he expressed his grief at the departure of *Shekhinah* from the Temple. His lament is recorded in the *Talmud, Sanhedrin* 65b: "...he who fasts that the pure spirit [the Divine Presence] may rest upon him — how much more should his desire be fulfilled! But alas! Our sins have driven it away from us, as it is written,

"But your iniquities have separated between you and your God..." (from Isaiah 59:2)

Thus it is seen again that deep grief and mourning accompanied this Event as the most devout Jews looked back and contemplated the Scriptures, the circumstances and the signs given to them just prior to this period. It is significant that Rabbi Akiba is credited as the most published of the *Talmudic* writers of the first century. He wrote at a time when all these events were still fresh in memory of those on the scene at this tragic sequence of events.

Reference 35 directs comment from several Rabbinical sources discussing this most critical period in Jewish history. It is said that the Temple could never have been destroyed as long as *Shekhinah* dwelled in the Temple. However, when *Shekhinah* gradually withdrew from His Place above the Ark of the Covenant, the Temple and the Holy City were then left unprotected. This same fateful conclusion was stated in the journal of Flavius Josephus, as appears in Appendix A. Josephus, we must recall, a most prolific and reliable historian of the first century, was on the scene at Jerusalem as these events were unfolding. We can therefore be confident of his accuracy in this matter.

Josephus testifies regarding those terrible days in Jerusalem just before the siege by Titus. In *Wars* 5.1.3/19 — he mourns concerning the impending doom for the Temple and Jerusalem: "...For thou couldst be no longer a fit place for God..." And in *Wars* 5.9.4/412 — Josephus sounds familiarly like the prophet Jeremiah (Jeremiah 21) as he chastises the Judeans for their sedition against Rome, saying their subjugation under Rome is, after all, God's instrument of their punishment from the Lord. Josephus declares: "Wherefore I cannot but suppose that God is fled out of His sanctuary, and stands on the side of those against whom you fight."

We should pause to note here that many of those first-century Christians were of the Priests and Pharisees. Many perhaps came to know Jesus as their Lord and Savior as a result of being closely involved with the Temple and having seen these signs. Acts 6:7 states: "*...a great company of the priests were obedient to the faith.*" These fortunate and wise saints "made the connection." During those "forty years" they saw these things happen, recognized the error that had been made, told their friends, and...the "Church" was on its way to Glory!

So, we have reviewed here just a few of the "signs" given to the first-century Jews immediately following their rejection of and the Gentiles' indifference to the most endearing "sign" God has yet sent to man. Jesus declared (Luke 11:29) that these were a "wicked generation," continually asking for "signs." We can see that they had been given what should have been more than enough signs, but many of them still didn't "see" their Messiah because they were blinded by their disbelief, by "tradition," and/or were being misled by their Rabbis.

Hear now, as the Lord admonished young King Solomon about what would happen to Israel if they did not continue keeping their part of the Covenant, from I Kings 9:6 – 9 (NASB):

> *9:6 But if you or your sons shall indeed turnaway from following Me, and shall not keep My commandments and My statutes which I have set before you and shall go and serve other gods and worship them.*

> *9:7 Then I will cut off Israel from the land which I have given them, and the house which I have consecrated for My name, I will cast out of My sight. So Israel will become a proverb and a byword among all peoples.*

> *9:8 And this house will become a heap of ruins; everyone who passes by will be astonished and hiss and say, "Why has the Lord done thus to this land and to this house?"*

> *9:9 And they will say, "Because they forsook the Lord their God, who brought their fathers out of the land of Egypt and adopted other gods and worshiped them and served them, therefore the Lord has brought all this adversity on them."*

The Lord certainly held His children to this warning and twice the Holy House *was* "a heap of ruins." Moreover, in order to emphasize His displeasure and to leave those disasters as a lasting memory to the People, He "underlined" this date on Israel's calendar. Both the First Temple and the Second Temple were destroyed on the 9th Day of the Jewish Month, *Av*. The day is known as *Tisha B'Av*, the saddest day on the Jewish calendar.

As a furthering of their misery, England banished all Jews from that country on this date in the year 1290. During the Inquisition, Spain expelled all Jews on the same date in 1492. The Nazi concentration camps tauntingly offered Jews extra wholesome food on the two fasting days of *Yom Kippur* and *Tisha B'Av* as a further torment during the Holocaust.

Talmud declares (*Ta'anith* 29a) that *both* times the Temple was destroyed on the first day of the week (Sunday) and during a year that followed a Sabbatical year. Any significance of such a sequence is not apparent at this time; although, we can be assured that the Lord had embedded some kind of message and, this was *not* by "coincidence."

Modern synagogue congregations observe this day, occurring in July or August, with fasting and reading of the scroll of Lamentations. *Baba Bathra* 60b requires that Jewish people should, observe this mournful time by reducing pleasures during those days. Orthodox Jews pray three times each day for restoration of the Temple and the sacrifices.

Again, Biblical numerology shows a message, since *Tisha B'Av* occurs on the ninth day of the eleventh Jewish Secular or Civil month. Nine is the product of Divine Completeness = 3 x 3. God's number for Finality of Judgment is nine. Twelve is His number for Governmental Perfection. God's number for disorder, chaos or disorganization is eleven. God deemed it appropriate that eleven, being one short of twelve, marks the month for the complete collapse and destruction of Israel as a nation. He further marked it as a day of Divine Judgment by ordaining it to occur on the ninth day. — I believe God made His Point.

The Lord would say (again) to Israel today:

Deuteronomy 4:7, 8, 27 – 40

I Kings 9:3 – 9

Ezekiel 37

Hosea 5:15 and 6:1–3

John the Apostle was very accurate in John 12:40, as he sadly referred to grim prediction from Isaiah 6:10 –

- *"He has blinded their eyes*
- *and deadened their hearts,*
- *so they can neither see with their eyes,*
- *nor understand with their hearts,*
- *nor turn — and I would heal them."*

This "stiff-necked" attitude of Israel was portrayed eloquently by the farmer, Tevyeh, in one of the early scenes of the musical, *Fiddler on the Roof*. In his description of the Jewish "position," he proudly said it was...TRADITION!

God has certainly held up His Chosen People as a "learning" example to us Gentiles as "a proverb and a byword." The same destiny falls to our "kings" and peoples, as has befallen the Jewish rulers and people, when we go astray and/or turn our backs on the Lord.

Even as I write this, the United States may have been issued a judgment as well as a warning on a day that we Americans, and perhaps the World, will never forget. The eleventh day of September, 2001 marked the terrorist attack that destroyed the World Trade Center in New York City and demolished a huge section of the Pentagon in Washington D.C. That was the so-called "9/11 Attack." The United States may have seen a Judgment on the eleventh day of our Julian calendar's ninth month. Israel has experienced multiple national catastrophes and mourning on the ninth day of their Jewish calendar's eleventh month. One might say those were Israel's "11/9" Judgments.

- Regarding our homeland, the United States, it can be questioned as to how long in time will our Just and Holy God withhold His Judgment from a nation that:
- purveys poison (tobacco) to poor nations to whom the U.S.A. could and should instead send food.
- Permits and even sponsors legislatively the murdering of babies in their mothers' wombs.
- Permits and even promotes "tolerance" of homosexuality, adultery, pornography and other types of fornication in its society, touting these measures as rights of "freedom."

Do we just assume it was mere "coincidence" that our "9/11" Wake-up Call occurred with destruction of one of our Worldly "Temples" of our World Prominence? – The eleventh day of our ninth month may have been indeed a warning judgment for the United States of America from an angry Creator. Here we should further recall that God chose "heathen" nations to bring His Judgment against Israel: Babylon, Rome, England, Spain and Germany.

Is *"The World"* Learning?

Just as Israel was given "signs," the World today, not just the U.S.A., is also being given "signs." The World is being given "Latter Day signs."

The World and yes, even many Christians and Jewish folks, are of the opinion that storms, floods, earthquakes, etc. – "natural disasters" – are, as we say, "Acts of God." –RUBBISH ! – After Adam's "fall" the Lord's Earth was defiled and no longer a fit place for a PERFECT God. The Lord therefore *"letteth"* Satan have control of the atmosphere, the Earth's crust, the seas, the weather, lightning strikes, wars, death and destruction. That power in Satan, whom the Rabbis call *"The Evil Inclination,"* explains why he also has the name: *"The Prince of the Air."* Those "natural disasters" that destroy human life and property are NOT "acts of God" ! – Although, we mortals cannot understand – nor must we "judge" God's choice to *"letteth"* Satan commit these horrible acts, *God then **uses** the results of those acts to achieve His Own Holy Purpose !* – (Strangely – Satan has not caught onto this fact yet!)

Probably one of the most dramatic and yet one of the most horrible occasions under which the Lord used Satan's evil works to fulfill God's Holy Purpose was the Holocaust. Yes! – God used this most heinous deed to bring The People back to The Land – *Eretz Israel*! – Again – We cannot understand how God could justify granting permission to *"letteth"* Satan conduct such an evil scheme. – "Couldn't He have done it some other way?! – Why would a "loving God" do such a thing to us?" – None of us can chastise the Jewish People for having such a human reaction, even though none of us is "justified" to question any of God's motives or actions. – These are among the thousands of His mysteries that He shall probably explain to us when we are with Him in the Glory to come!

Similarly, the diseases, birth defects, deformities, etc. assuredly are NOT of God's Holy Works. They are the "works" of Satan's demon hordes – against whom we wage an ever frustrating and evermore severe conflict. – BOTTOM LINE: – God did NOT invent sin! – And, God does NOT create misery for mankind – although, even the most righteous among us are surely deserving of His wrath at times. Given man's puny efforts against Satan and his "Principalities and Powers," the ONLY restraint against Evil is The Holy Spirit. In recent times, we can accurately observe that the Holy Spirit now *"letteth"* more and more.

Even as I write, God is withdrawing His Holy Spirit from the Earth – at least in part. He NEVER withdraws from man's domain entirely – ALWAYS preserving a "remnant." During this, the "Church Age," Believer's are indwelt by His Holy Spirit. We are presently then His "Remnant" until we are taken up at the "Rapture" to be forever with Him.

Nevertheless, we are at present fighting a "delaying action" against the Evil Inclination. The Lord is presently in the process of conducting – in military terms – a "strategic withdrawal" from Earth. His departure is so subtle as to be almost imperceptible, especially to the cynical and unbelieving secular world. However, during the seven years of Iniquity under the yoke of Antichrist, there will be a "passive resistance" to his evil practice. The resistance will be driven by the Holy Spirit through newly confirmed Christians AFTER The Rapture of the Church. Many, many of these new Believers will be reached by those 144,000 "Jewish" Witnesses that we hear so much about. (Revelation 7:5 – 8)

The increased strife, multitudinous wars, incredulous crimes, mindless terror, suicides, famine, pestilences, "natural" disasters, etc. are on the increase during these times, This is BECAUSE God's Holy Spirit surely is removing "for a time" as we approach those seven years of Judgment on the Earth. Jesus referred to those days as *"the beginnings of sorrows."* (Mark 13:8) Then later, as the final months of those seven years are tallied, the Earth will be "almost" completely under Satanic rule – but for that tiny Remnant of God's servants. There are even right now, plenty of "signs," but...

— Is the World ignoring the "sign" of tremendously increased occurrences of major earthquakes and volcanic eruptions? Major quakes occur all over the world *"in diverse places."* (See Matthew 24:7)

— Is the World ignoring the "signs" from the recent increase in devastating famines...starving literally millions of people? (See Mark 13:8)

— Is the World also unaware of the "sign," showing many times more wars, rebellions, military aggression, riots of all sorts than have ever occurred simultaneously during all the history of the Earth? Our newest "high-tech" news-media can't even keep up with all the "wars" and "rumors of wars." (See Matthew 24:6) And now, we are faced by world-wide terrorist attacks even in the United States, killing thousands.

— Is the World ignoring the "sign" given to all mankind by the recent strange and alarming (not to mention "deadly") increase of incurable, highly contagious diseases and viruses? New disease ("pestilences") such as AIDS, Herpes Simplex, "Mad Cow Disease" and Anthrax outbreaks are appearing in greater numbers than ever before. (See Luke 21:11)

— Is the World ignoring the "sign" consisting of Earth's relentless temperature increase ("global warming") which is producing "weird" weather, raising sea levels, causing the increased drought, depletion of rainforests, etc.? The world's leading scientists admit they are powerless to halt, retard, or reverse this trend which, if it continues, will produce the "greenhouse effect" which sheltered man from the sun before The Great Flood. (This vapor shield protected men from the sun's radiation; perhaps explaining why men at that time lived to be about 1000 years old.) You CAN believe it ! – We are having Global Warming and we will continue to have it. That is a condition that will exist at "The End of Days." This is a condition which existed before the Great Flood and which will exist again on Earth during Christ's Millennial reign. – How far can we be from "that day?" (Isaiah 65:20, 22) — In these times especially, we should take note of Jesus' words from the unique translation given for Luke 21:9 – 11 in the Lamsa Bible[8] Among the signs He describes as appearing during the years preceding His return are: *"wars and revolutions," "great earthquakes in different places," "famines and plagues,"* and with a phrase that has been omitted from our western Bible translations He says, *"the winters will be severe."* And, He was not referring to winters in Siberia, Spitzbergen or even Minneapolis. Jesus was describing winters in the region we now call the Mideast. In recent years there have been paralyzing snowstorms in Jerusalem, Damascus in Syria and Amman in Jordan. Praise the Lord...Perhaps the Lord is saying, "Signs? You want signs? Children, I'm giving you signs!"

Emergence of these signs are what Jesus described as *"the beginning of sorrows,"* to occur just prior to the seven years of the Tribulation. (Matthew 24:8)

> *"Indeed God speaks once, or twice, yet no one notices it." Job 33:14 (NASB)*

But, He is giving us lots of "signs" in the meantime (especially for those of us who are just a bit "near-sighted"). Not to "scare" us, though. For He said, *"...when you see these things, you will know that your redemption draweth nigh."* (From Luke 21:28) We are instructed, also: *"...wherefore comfort ye one another with these words."* (From I Thessalonians 4:18)

Those who are not familiar with the Promises of God may ask: "How can you say 'comfort' when all those horrible times are going to come upon the Earth? What kind of 'redemption' is that?"

The "*Good News*" is:

The Lord wishes that all men should fear not. The Lord says if you will truly repent of your sins and if you will accept eternal salvation, paid for by the life blood of the Lord Jesus Christ, and offered as a free gift through His Grace (You do not EARN it), then you will not be on this Earth *"when those things come to pass."* You will be taken up *"in the twinkling of an eye"* to be forever with the Lord, before these things "come to pass."

If you believe that Jesus is your only "burnt offering" and believe that He conquered death by rising alive after three days in The Tomb, then, you have a "confirmed reservation" to dwell forever with Him.

Don't take my word for it. Please read:

Luke 21:36

I Corinthians 15:51 – 57

I Thessalonians 4:16 – 18

Revelation 3:10

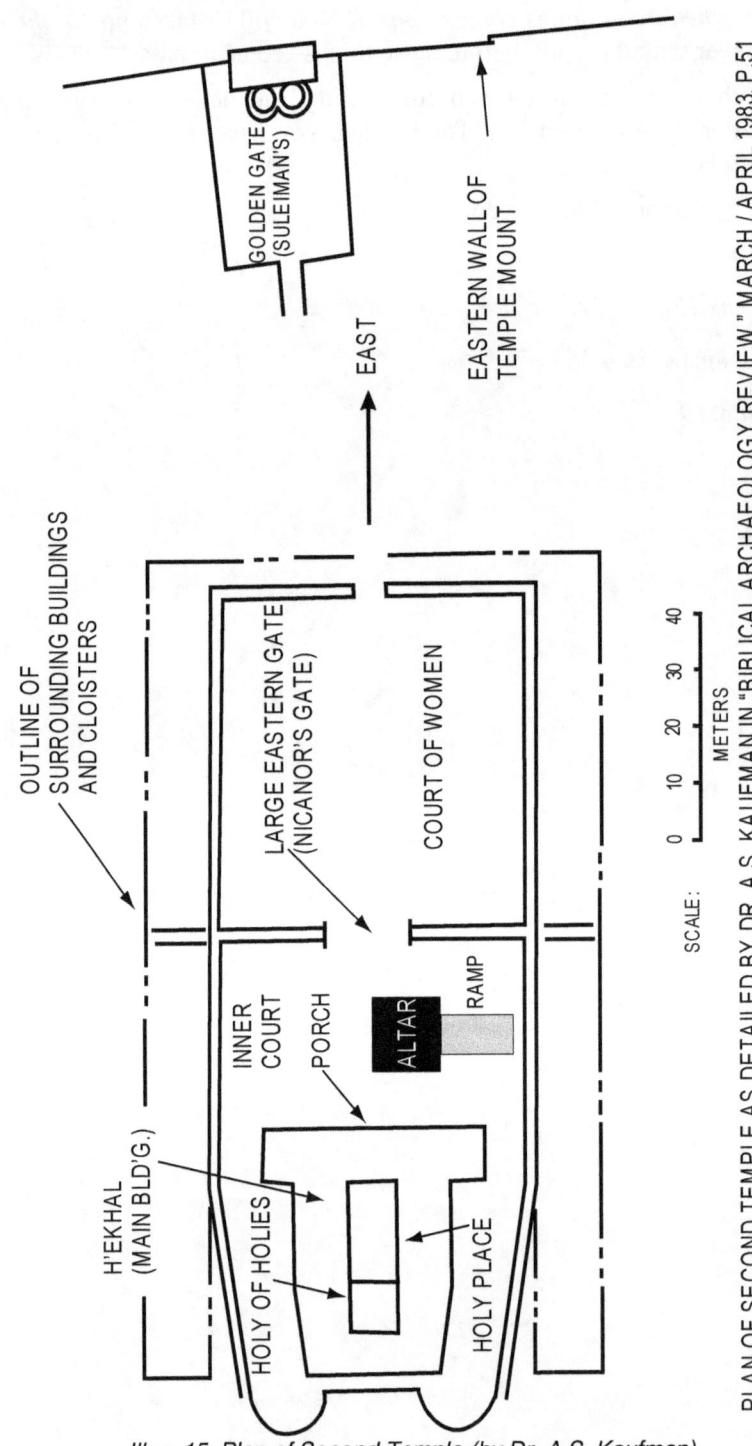

Illus. 15: Plan of Second Temple (by Dr. A.S. Kaufman)

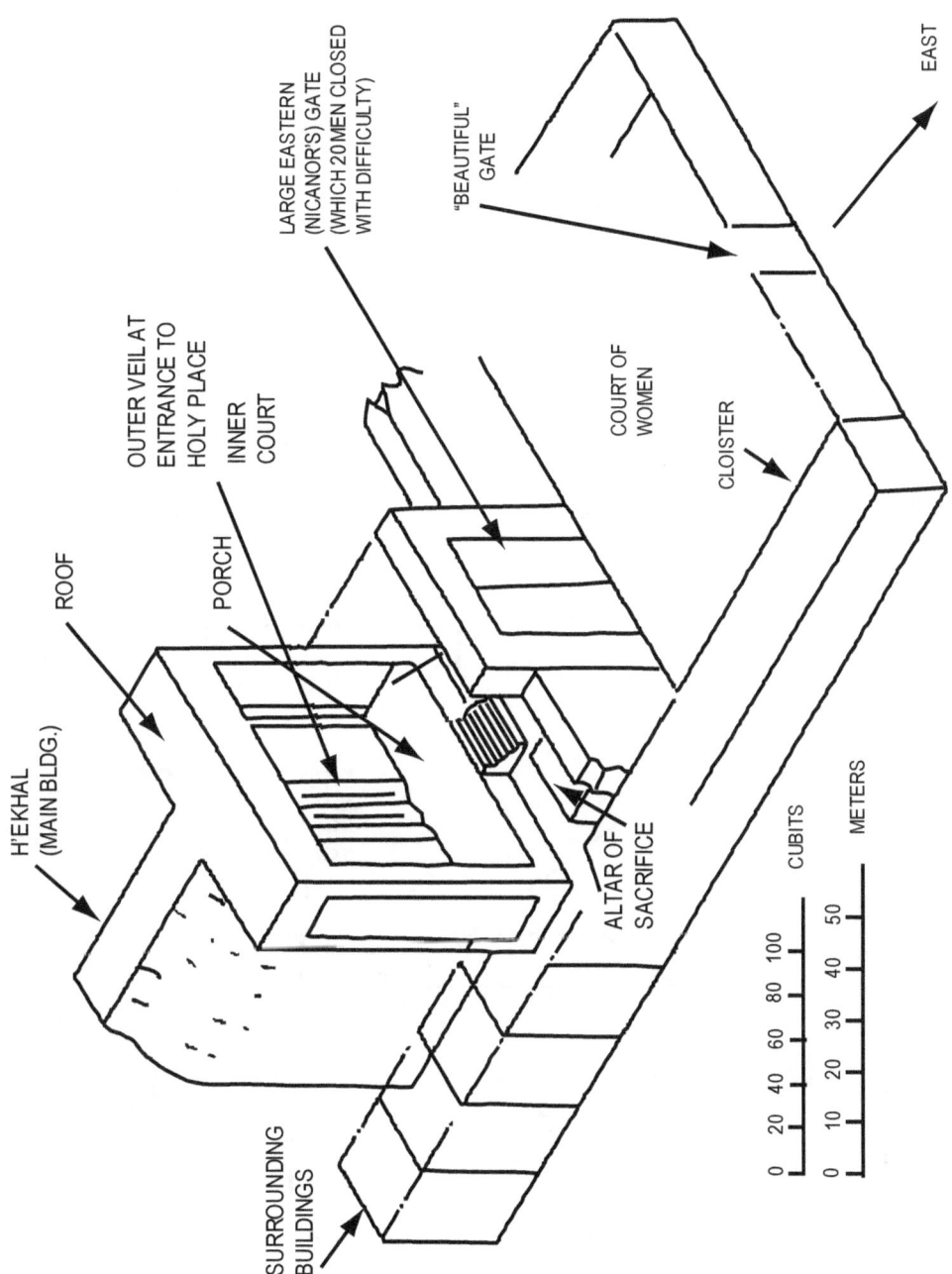

Illus. 16: Isometric View of 2nd Temple

150 Jesus and the Third Temple

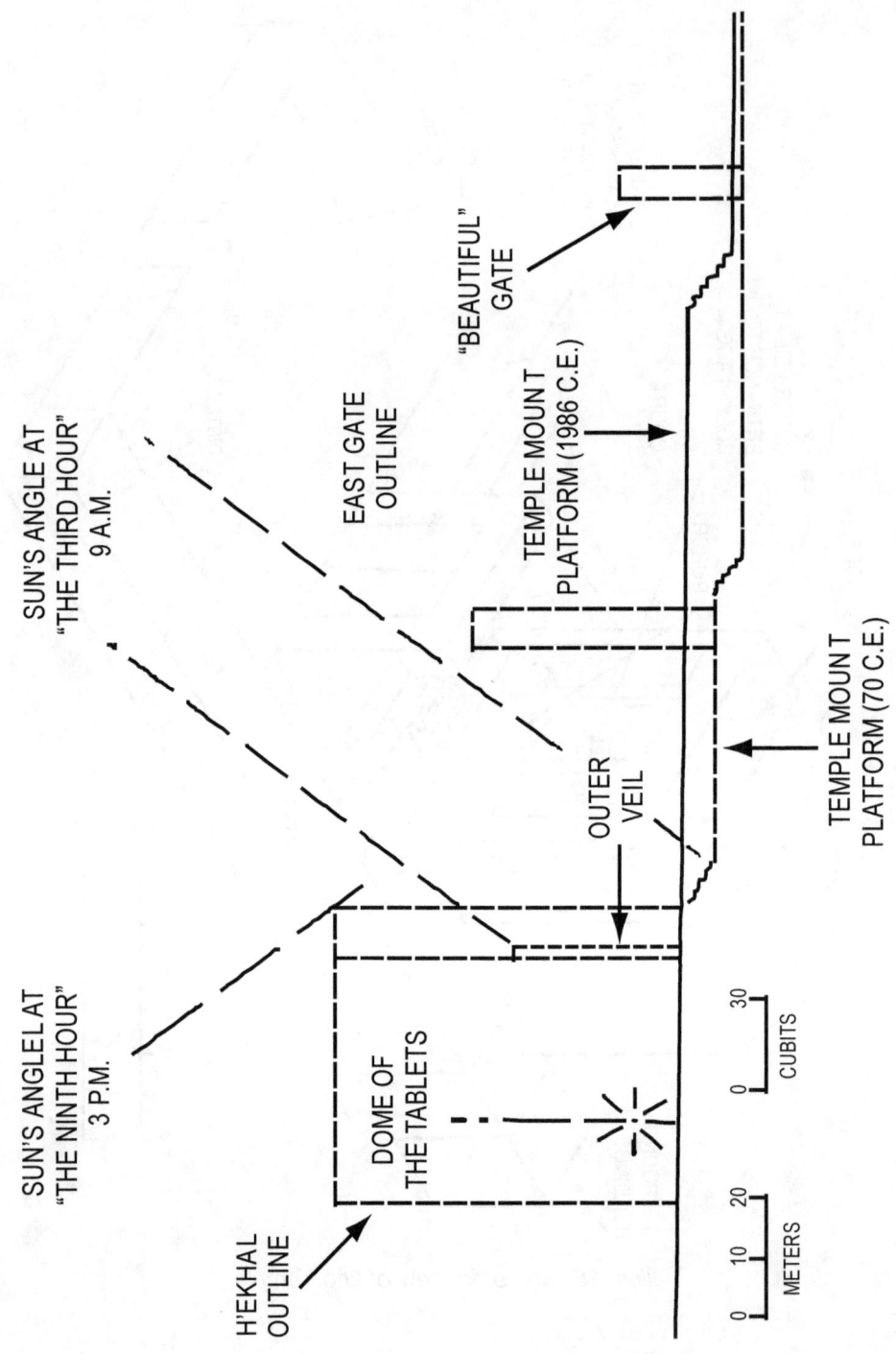

Illus. 17: Detailed Elevation of 2nd Temple

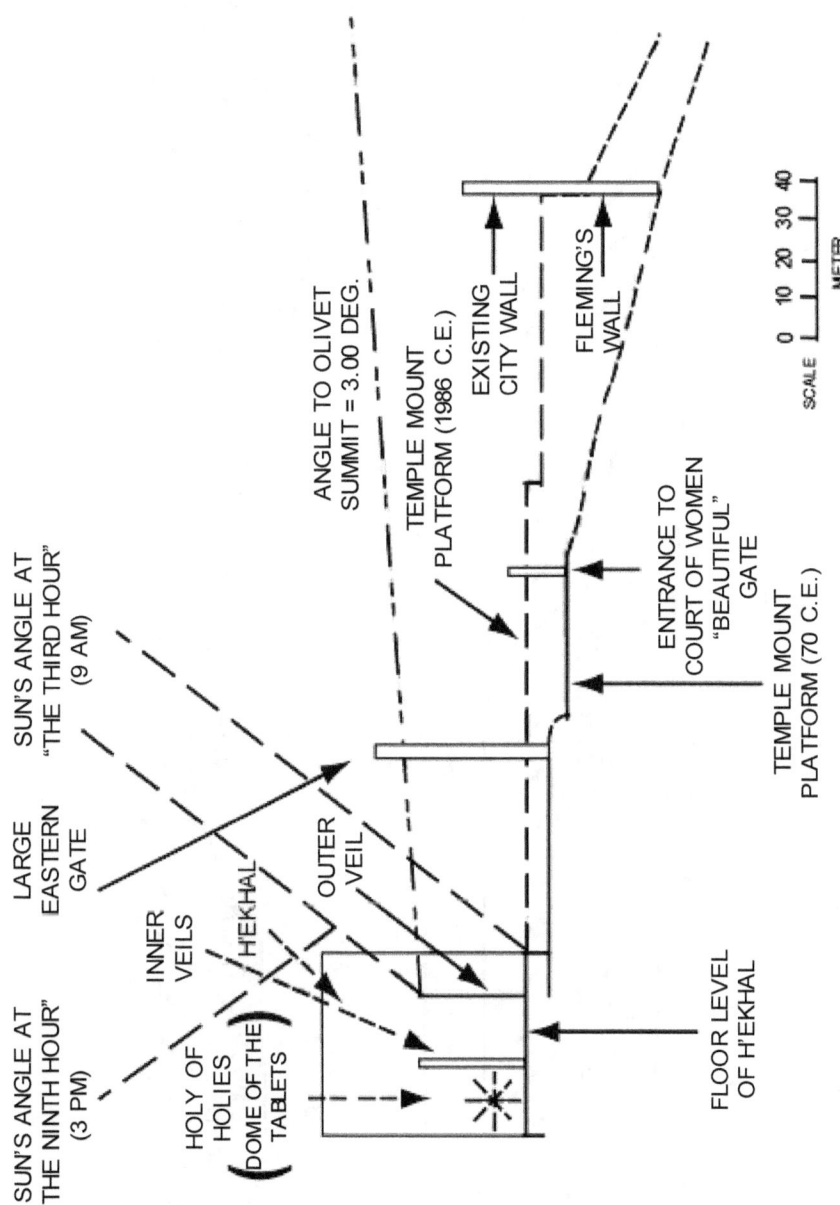

Illus. 18: Elevation Profile of Temple and Temple Mt.

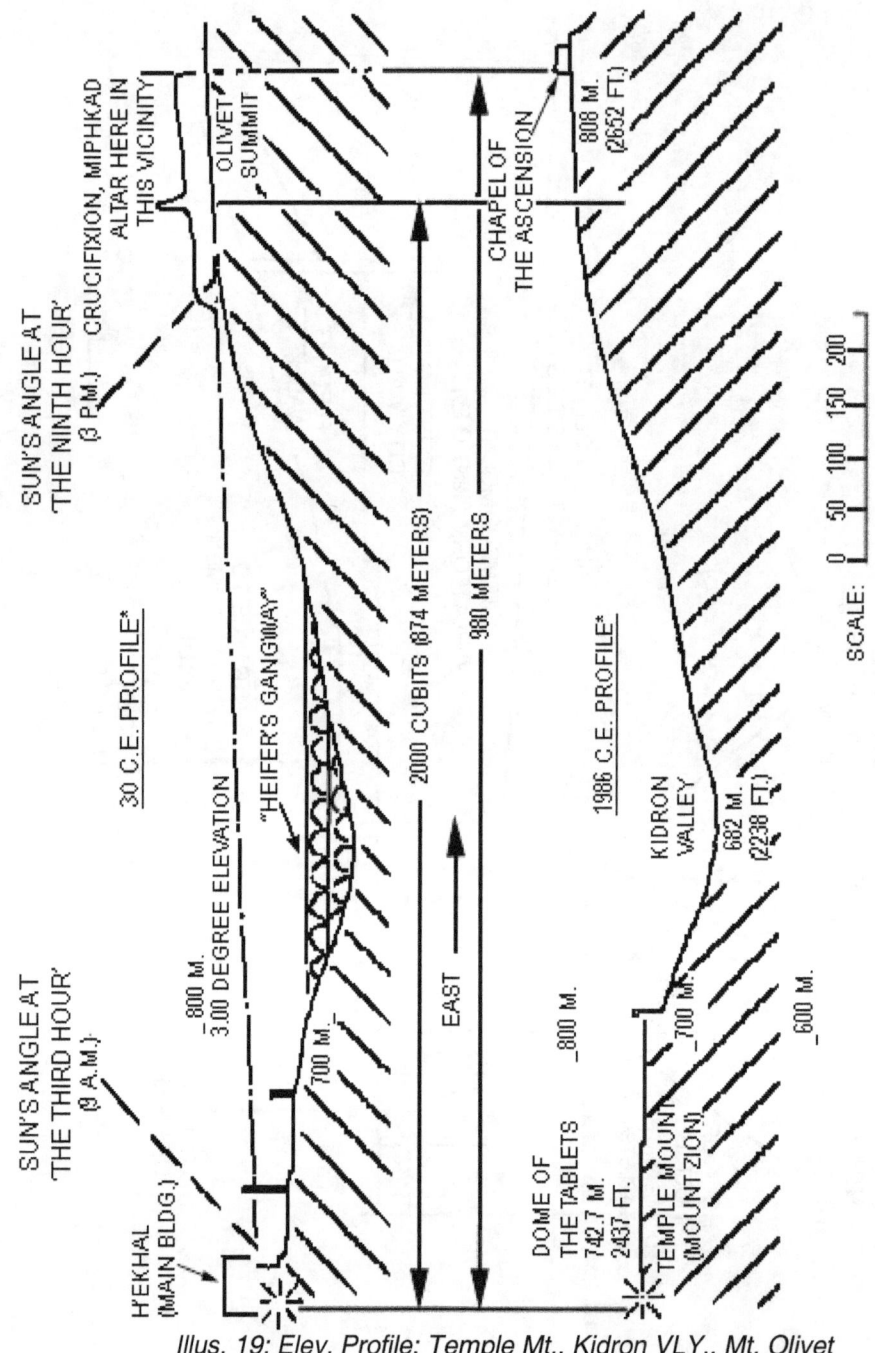

Illus. 19: Elev. Profile: Temple Mt., Kidron VLY., Mt. Olivet

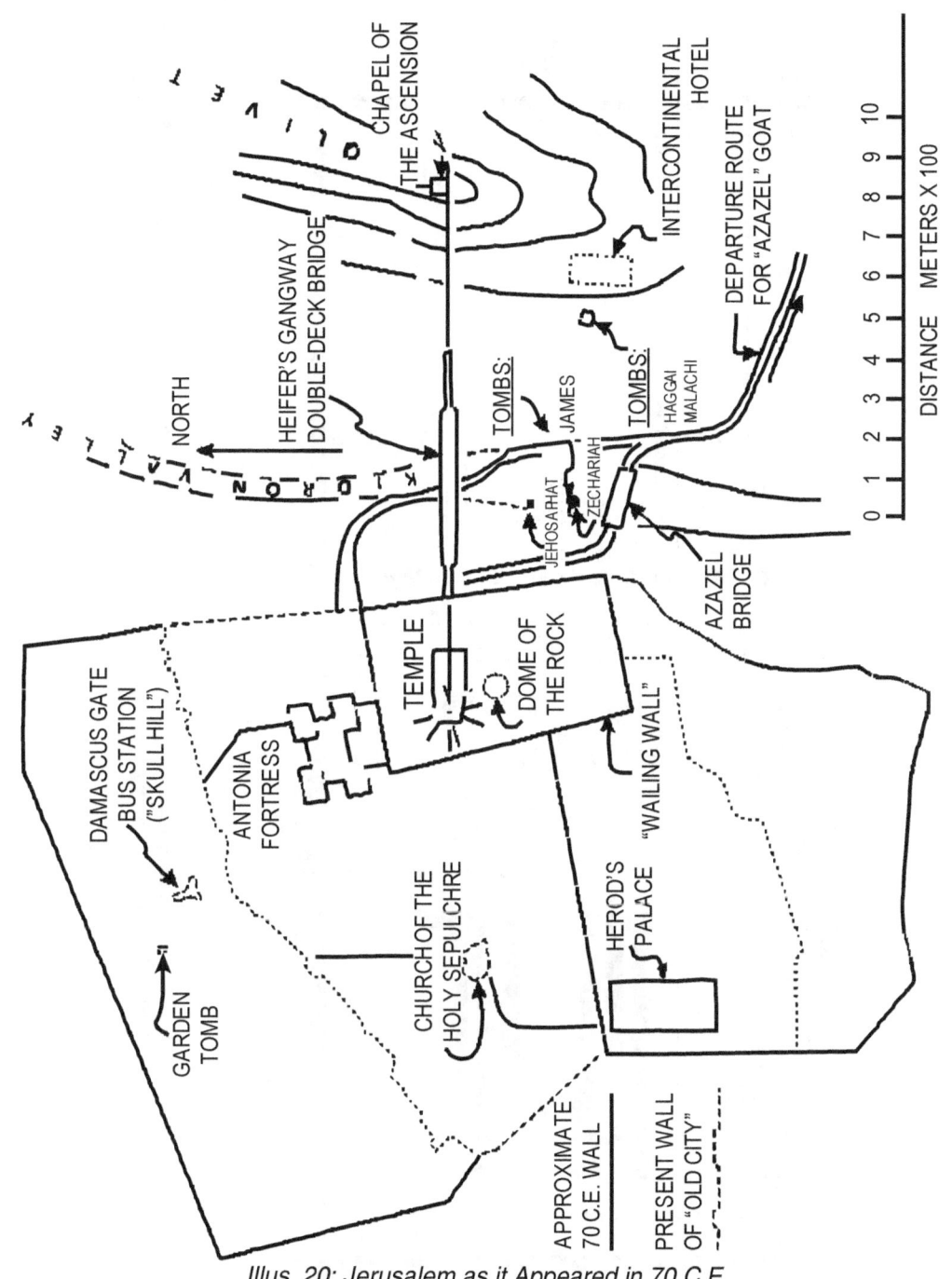

Illus. 20: Jerusalem as it Appeared in 70 C.E.

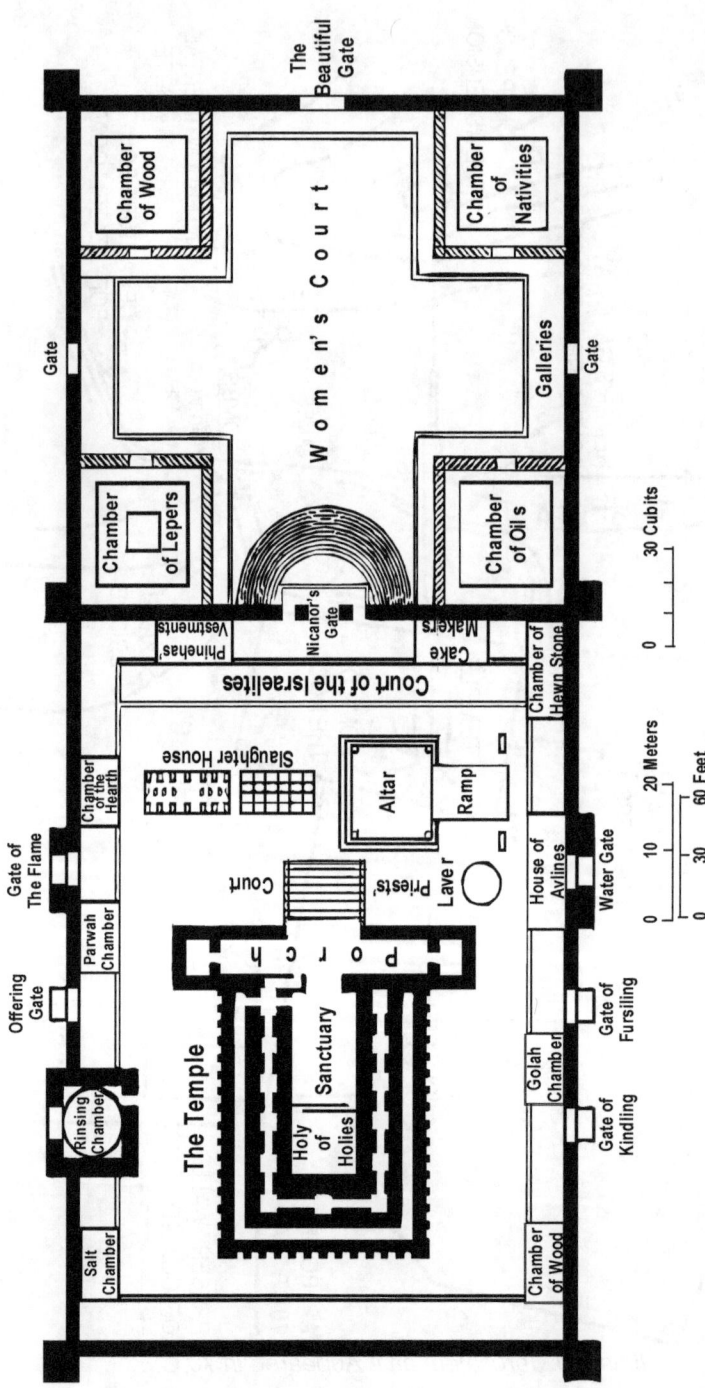

Illus. 21: Detail of the 2nd Temple

"Signs and Wonders" **155**

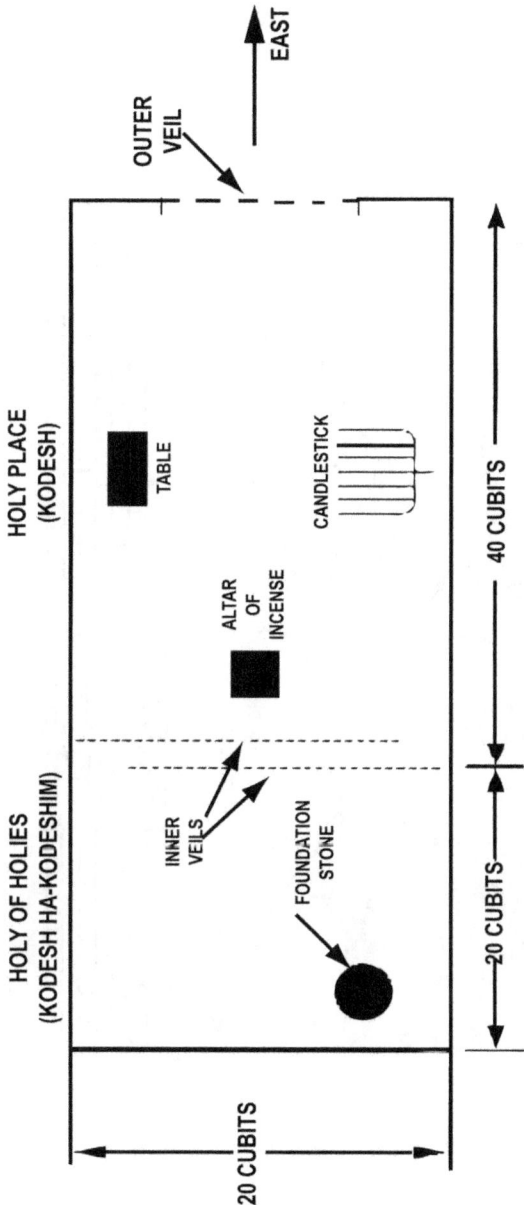

Illus. 22: The Sanctuary of the 2nd Temple

156 Jesus and the Third Temple

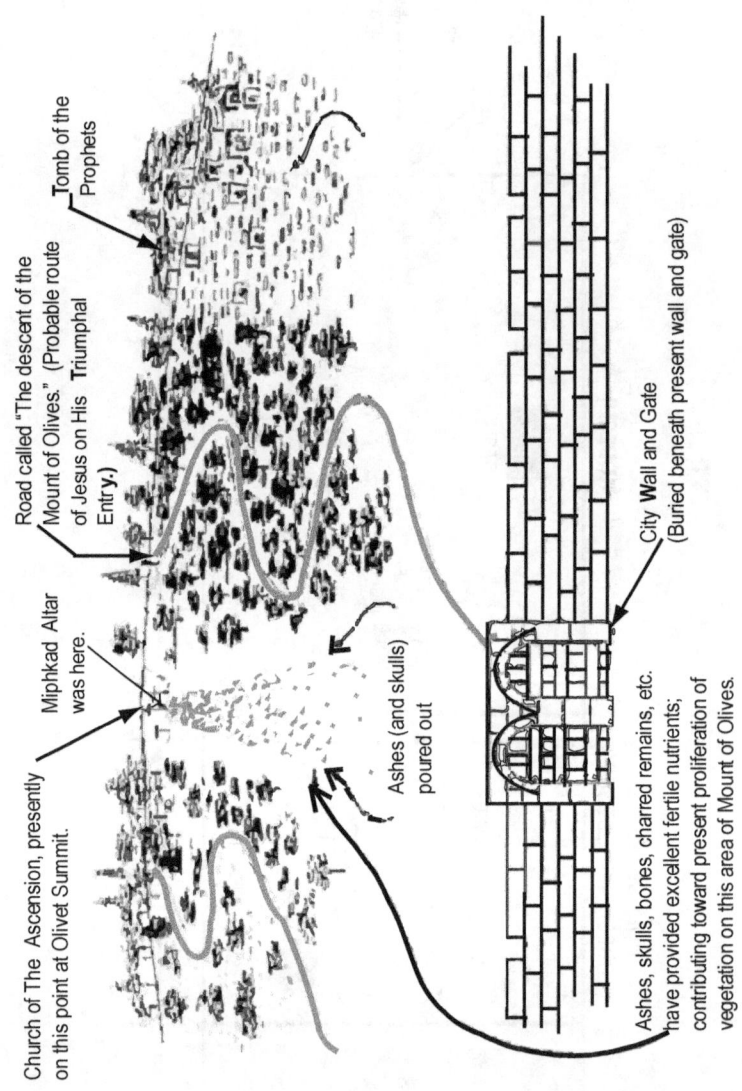

Illus. 23: Mt. Olivet viewed from Temple on Crucifixion Day

"Signs and Wonders" 157

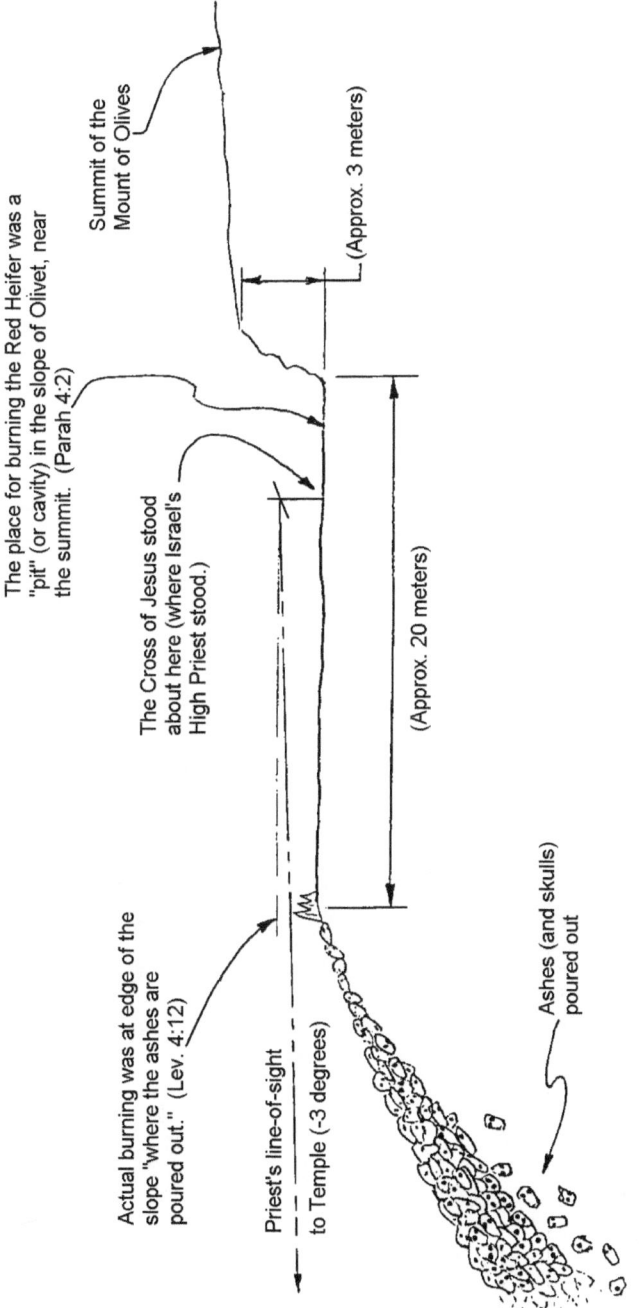

Illus. 24: Detail of "pit or cavity" in face of Mt. of Olives

Part III – Rebutting Critics and Skeptics

8

The Controversy

Debating the critics – Subtle Anti-Judaism – Doubters & "Squirmers" – Scripture and documented evidence stands strong against critics.

Telling this story to Jewish friends and to fellow Christians, I have occasionally met some obvious lack of enthusiasm from each side. In fact, I have encountered indifference, resistance, ridicule, suspicion, doubt, and yes, even hostility. My experience in this has been very much like that of Prof. Asher Kaufman, such as he described in the Foreword of this book. Both of us have been subjected to the most cruel, and yet the most impotent treatment in that we are ignored by our detractors. They will not even come out to debate with us on these matters. Could it be that they know they cannot refute The Truth?!

But, especially in my case, this is to be expected when an "unknown" person tries to bring out hard evidence in the face of almost 2000 years of prejudice and suspicion between Judaism and Christianity. This task becomes even more difficult because these negative views are backed up by some very "stiff-necked" teaching from some of the most beloved and well-intentioned "patriarchs" of both faiths. Then, of course there is also that most awesome ally of The Evil One and the enemy of Truth – TRADITION! – All of these opponents are powerful, cunning and deeply ensconced in the teachings of our "shepherds."

Many readers understandably will feel some of the same skepticism, fears, doubts and accusations. We must therefore identify these factors to prepare the foundation for debate of these points and in order to stimulate thinking on both sides. Those who would support this account need to be aware of these points as well.

The Accusations

For most people, never having heard of this event before, I know one doubting thought they must have:

"If this story is really genuine, why have we never heard of this before now in any Christian or Jewish teaching? Why are we hearing it only now?"

I do not know why we have not been told this story. Nevertheless, I have only uncovered a lot of hitherto "unknown" facts that have been chronicled by ancient historians (presented in Appendices A and B) and have been sitting in our libraries, more or less ignored by our scholars for all these years. It has turned out to be certainly a very beautiful and yet a very sad story.

Neither can we explain why competent scholars have not reported this Event. As we have indicated, Jewish scholars understandably are not eager to point out this story; because it can obviously be interpreted as a judgment from God. Moreover, for that reason alone, it is truly remarkable that the Rabbis have reported this to exquisite detail in their ancient documents such as *Talmud* and *Midrash*. Conservative Christian theologians have either ignored it or possibly overlooked it, probably because they have convinced themselves that Ezekiel "saw" the Divine Presence depart before the Second Temple was built. We offer powerful Scriptural evidence showing they are mistaken in that conviction. Another facet of their objection is their immediate rejection of any material written by the Rabbis of antiquity.

Another charge we have received is:

If well qualified and prestigious scholars from the past several centuries have not brought forth this story to a public exposure, why then should we accept it from this retired engineer fellow from Florida?!

Coming out in opposition to traditional teaching and prestigious scholars without myself having any formal credentials as a theologian or even as an archaeologist does make the preceding question a fair charge. I can offer only my years of study, well-documented secular records and the Biblical Authority and Truths we have presented as my "credentials." We ask therefore that readers will examine the evidence presented and that they will please disregard society ordained authority and "credentials" in establishing the integrity behind this story.

One local Rabbi said: "It is all a mistake. The *Midrash* translation is in gross error." This was especially amusing because, unknown to the Rabbi, this translation was given by a member of his own congregation who speaks, reads, and writes Hebrew with much greater skill than this Rabbi himself. (The Rabbi was "squirming.") Those who will take time to read this passage from a published English translation of the *Midrash*[13] will soon discover that my Jewish friend's version is almost verbatim with the published English text and is, in fact, a much more beautiful and a much more heart-appealing translation.

The Soncino[13] English translation, however, has one particular variation that we should discuss. That source translates the Hebrew word "*shalom*" as "peace" instead of "good-bye" or "farewell." This oversight or variation overlooks (whether intentionally or not) the principal theme or essence of the occasion. Of course, most Gentiles already know "*shalom*" means "peace" or "good-bye" or even a friendly greeting. The word *"shalom"* can have a few different meanings, depending on its context in usage. Its use here within the context of this occasion as a farewell or an expression of sorrow at parting should be obvious.

Nevertheless, reading from the Hebrew *Midrash*, my translator felt the emotion, pathos, and drama of this Holy Event. He translated *"shalom"* as "good-bye" (my precious vessel) "goodbye" (my Temple), etc. The quotation from Rabbi Akha (Appendix B) makes it obvious the Divine Presence was leaving His "palace," His "precious vessel," etc. — making "good-bye" most appropriate in this drama. Somehow, "O' the peace of my precious home," etc., just does not come across with what the Lord should be feeling and is feeling about His People and His Temple.

Some critics and skeptics would challenge the claim that the *Shekhinah* who dwelt in the Temple was the same "fire" that Moses saw in the flaming bush. Critics would then lodge a counter-claim that the *Shekhinah* was really only an "angel" and that God Himself was not actually in the Temple. Such criticism may arise from words in Exodus 3:2 saying "the Angel of the Lord" appeared to Moses. Many Christian commentaries agree that the Angel of the Lord spoken of here was not an "angel" — but was, in fact, the Lord Jehovah Himself. Verse 4 should remove any doubt as to "Who" was speaking from the flames, as it says:

"...God called to him out of the midst of the bush, and said, 'Moses, Moses.' And he said, 'Here am I.'"

A discussion in *Sotah* 5a declares that the Great "I AM" humbled Himself greatly by "causing His *Shekhinah* to abide in a bush." (The Rabbis point out that God *could have* chosen a tall and magnificent Cedar!) As if all this were not enough to convince the skeptics, further Scriptural confirmation of the Lord's identity comes from Deuteronomy 33:16, where the Lord is described as: *"...Him that dwelt in the bush:..."*

Finally, in the Words of Jesus Himself, we read in Mark 12:26, "...have ye not read in the book of Moses, how *in the bush God spake unto him,* saying, 'I am the God of Abraham, and the God of Isaac, and the God of Jacob?'"

The indifferent make no accusation. It's much worse! They just say: "So what? What does this mean to me as a Christian? I see no salvation message here — nor any life-application of the Gospel of Jesus. That's just Jewish theology. It doesn't strengthen *my* faith. The Jews are lost. Sorry, but this story just doesn't do anything for me...etc., etc."

This is usually the same reaction I get from those same Christians when I try to share with them Biblical archaeology discoveries or End Time events showing in the world today. These I pity most of all. They are just not excited by this sort of news. They do not realize that even though such is surely not needed for their salvation, there are many unsaved who may be reached if only they could learn these things. Many of us are like Thomas, needing to "see the print of the nails" and to "put our hand in His side" in order to believe.

Some Christians simply do not *want* to believe this story. Such especially applies to some who have attended so-called conservative seminaries. These have been instructed that the Glory of the Lord was never present in the Second Temple. This conclusion apparently is founded solely on the assumption that He did not reside because Scripture includes no description of an arrival of the Glory, fire or cloud, as was supplied for the First Temple in II Chronicles 5:14.

Such "reasoning" completely ignores the literal quotations we have noted from Scripture. These seminary-trained resisters defend their position by accusing that we are "stretching" our interpretation in claiming these verses indicate that *Shekhinah* was in the Second Temple. We have shown verses that prophesied His Presence in the Second Temple. We have presented verses saying, literally, that He *was* in the Second Temple at the time those verses were spoken and/or written.

With these kinds of Scriptural evidence, even without Judaica and secular sources, their resistance appears to persist only because these persons clearly do not *want* to believe this Event. And, as we have noted earlier, they do not want to believe because it is different from what they have been taught by their teachers, who in turn were taught by their teachers, etc. Traditional belief is extremely difficult to dislodge from the human mind — even in the presence of Truth and logic.

One question we might ask in order to examine their "hearts" is: "Well, OK, but don't you agree that this would have been just a really Glorious and Holy Event, IF indeed the withdrawal of God from His Temple *had* happened as we have described?" If the answer is in the negative, we would have cause to wonder what is in the heart of this person.

One pastor I spoke with had the impression that the *Midrash* had occult contents. The *Midrash* is certainly not canonized as Scripture, and I will certainly agree that there is some material in those writings that could be challenged. Nevertheless, it seems unfair to reject all *Midrashic* text on the principle that some portions are undesirable. Further, one could expect the Rabbinical authorities made fairly stringent review of *Midrashic* text before it was accepted and passed down through all these centuries.

Unless we find contradicting Scripture, I am prepared therefore to give the *Midrash* Rabbis benefit of the doubt as far as this story is concerned. We certainly should hold no doubt, since a major prophet (Ezekiel) said this was going to happen. Another source also recorded the event (Josephus) and the Gospel of Jesus Christ (Matthew) declares literally that *Shekhinah* (the Father, "I AM") was present in the Second Temple. Eusebius[26] wrote of this event as further corroboration of the accounts from the Rabbis and Josephus. One simply cannot discount all of the *Midrash*, even if there may be some occult influence in other portions of that text.

Some clergymen say all this is merely "extra-Biblical-trivia" and is of no spiritual importance. It seems to me that this story can hardly be dismissed as trivia, if for no other reason than the fact it is a well-documented eyewitness account of the last Public Appearance and Farewell from Almighty God as He left His Temple, His Holy People and this Earth. Further, a documented Event marking fulfillment of Ezekiel's prophecy should without question rank as a significant Biblical Event. This story is "extra-Biblical" only because it happened after the last New Testament books had been written. Indeed, one of the most "popular" accusations has been that no record of this Event is stated in Scripture. Again, not only is there Scripture that says it was *going* to happen (Ezekiel 8 – 11), and that *Shekhinah* would dwell in the Second Temple (Zechariah 1:16 and Haggai 2:3 – 9), but also there is

Gospel and a statement from the Apostle Paul that literally says *Shekhinah* (Divine Presence) was there at the time. (Matthew 23:21 and Romans 9:4)

The actual Withdrawal Event is not mentioned in the New Testament simply because the last books (except The Revelation) were written just before 66 C.E. — before the event. It is likely those writers only knew of the Withdrawal afterward, since none of them remained in Judea after James ("the Just"), brother of Jesus, was martyred (62 C.E.). They were obedient in fulfilling their commission to preach the Gospel *"unto the uttermost part of the earth."* John's Revelation, although admittedly written much later (96 C.E.), dealt only with future events.

We cannot know why God chose to withhold this truth from His Word. Nevertheless, we can no longer ignore such a Glorious Event just because we are embarrassed to find out about it at this late date or only because some just do not want to hear it!

Also, we have plenty of other non-Scriptural Judean eyewitness whom one would expect to be the very last persons to admit (and even record) this incident. I believe such "circumstantial" evidence would certainly bring a "conviction" in a fair court!

We must not forget to list the understandable but unjustified Jewish accusation that Josephus was a traitor to the Jewish cause at the siege. Those who would so accuse should read the speech (more like a sermon) Josephus delivered at the Jerusalem wall to plead with his countrymen to surrender. (Reference 2, *Wars* 5.9.1/348–419) Titus, the Roman commander, did not want all the bloodshed and certain destruction of that beautiful City that a siege would surely bring about.

For this reason mostly, I suppose, even modern Jewish people do not hold Josephus in esteem as a "Jew," although perhaps they recognize him as an historian. Those who object to the position of Josephus at that wall should read his speech and then read the messages delivered by Jeremiah some six hundred years earlier. (Jeremiah 7 and 21) They have very similar themes. Josephus must have read and believed *The Works of Jeremiah*. Read more about a scholar's evaluation of Josephus in Appendix C.

One "accusation" is that Ezekiel "saw" the Glory withdraw in 586 B.C.E. This is absurd, since Ezekiel clearly states (Ezekiel 8:1 – 3) he was given this *"in the visions of God"* while he was physically in Babylon, sitting in his house, with a group of the elders of Judah seated before him. In fact, Ezekiel states *three times* that he had seen a *vision*.(Again, more "squirming.")

Some critics then claim that Ezekiel was "raptured" to Jerusalem. More than one Judaica commentary is in agreement that Ezekiel was not "raptured" or "translated" to Jerusalem in order to actually witness this occasion of the Lord's withdrawal from the Holy Temple. Under Ezekiel 8:3 in Reference 34, it is noted that Ezekiel was "transported to Jerusalem only in spirit." Some opposing critics claim support for their "rapture" theory in Ezekiel 8:3, saying that he was taken up "by a lock of mine head." Reference 34 is emphatic that this was only a figure-of-speech. Further comment supporting this conclusion is given under Ezekiel 11:24 as the Prophet closes this narration saying: *"...So, the vision that I had seen went up from me."*

A seemingly legitimate criticism might contend that if the Glory had been in the Temple as late as 167 B.C.E., Antiochus Epiphanes would have been struck dead before he could have sacrificed a sow on the altar. This argument is of course based on "assumed" entry of Antiochus into the *Kodesh Ha-Kodashim*. However, since the Altar of Sacrifice was outside the *H'ekhal*, it was not necessary for Antiochus to have actually confronted *Shekhinah* and he therefore was spared.

Roman conqueror Pompey even entered the Holy of Holies about 62 C.E., but was spared, perhaps, because he was respectful of the Temple and because he immediately urged the Israelites to resume their religious practices. The Romans did not admire "backsliders," even within the religions of vanquished nations. Titus entered the forbidden chamber in 70 C.E., but of course, the Presence had withdrawn from the Temple just three and one-half years earlier.

Another accusation persists when some people are confronted with any sort of "Biblical" information. In defense, they instantly dig in their heels by saying: "But how do we know that's true? There are so many 'interpretations,' so many language changes over the years, so many 'contradictions,' etc., etc." (And so many excuses for disbelief!)

The Resistance

The second category of criticism is so-named because, although most of these are sincere Believers, they do not want to believe this story. Why not? I can only surmise it is because they have been brought up on what has lately been termed "Replacement Theology."[4] This is the popular Christian concept that Christians are now God's Chosen and He is, for now at least, finished with those "naughty disobedient" Jews. The fact that this story (let alone the Bible and recorded history!) says the Glory was in the Temple at the time of Jesus and forty years afterward really disturbs some Christians. Although they would never wish to be accused as being "Anti-Semitic," some are distressed because the story seems to be saying exactly what God said as He hung, dying on The Cross: "*...Father, forgive them; for they know not what they do.*" (From Luke 23:34)

Ironically, however, most Jewish people also "resist" because it is obvious from this story that *Shekhinah* had some sort of "connection" with Jesus of Nazareth. So, here we have a story that is documented by Jewish records, but which the Jewish people "must" resist. The Jews therefore have preferred to keep it quiet. Then, also it is resisted by Christians because they have overlooked, ignored, or doubted this event and have all along been taught something entirely different. Now, neither group seems to want to hear the real story.

— Jewish people are embarrassed to be shown, from their historians (and from Scripture!) that...YES!!! Jesus "probably" is Messiah.

— Christians are embarrassed to be shown, again from Jewish historians, that we have been either ignoring or teaching in error concerning the visible Divine Presence during the time of Jesus. And yes, God did "forgive them for they knew not what they did."

So, it is no wonder that I have been getting "flack" from both sides. Most people will turn away when we try to tell them something they do not *want* to hear or know about! What we have here is some very human behavior.

But why cannot Christians, at least, overcome their human "phobia?" This story certainly underlines the fact that Jesus is Messiah and that "I and My Father are One." It takes nothing away from Jesus; in fact, it brings new meaning to the Gospel in addition to documenting the fulfillment of Ezekiel's prophecy. How could believing Christians resist, doubt, ignore, or delay such a beautiful story about our Lord, which demonstrates (historically) the close relationship of the Son to the Father?

Much as I dislike stereotyped "labels," my own religious position label would fit most closely as a conservative/fundamental/evangelical, "born-again" Christian. The most bitter and "stiffnecked" criticism of this story has come from "traditionalist" brethren of that same label. Liberal Christian contacts have been inclined more to politely doubt my claim, smile and simply say, "No thank you."

Conservatives have given more of a "hardball" type of response. Most have just totally ignored any request for review, examination, or discussion. They respond with deafening silence. That is the most cruel, most humiliating, most insulting, and yet most impotent of arguments. Some of my more compassionate conservative brothers use an accusation borrowed from the Gospel and from Paul's epistles. These accuse me of "straining at a gnat" and some caution me against becoming "puffed up with knowledge." (I Corinthians 4:6)

Jesus scolded the *Talmudic* scholars (lawyers) against "straining at a gnat" (Matthew 23:24), but it is obvious to any who would examine the *Talmud* that His advice went unheeded.

Rigid laws pertaining to the Sabbath, food preparation and burial of the dead are but a few examples of how *Talmudic* "lawyers" have piously embellished God's Law, causing it to become so desperately impossible to maintain. This story, although quite intricate in many ways, has been shown to be that complex by the Lord's own design — not entirely by man's choice. He went to a lot of trouble to make this Event happen as it did, as indicated by Scripture, by the Law, and by historical records. It is an affront to the Lord to belittle or ignore this Event. Those who would dismiss this as "gnat-straining" or "puffing-up" need to be wary and watch for the truth. Jesus said He would fulfill "every jot and tittle." He also Promised that the truth would make us free, but not if we remain complacently mired down in the quicksand of tradition.

Some "resisters" say they don't accept Josephus and the *Midrash* as reliable sources. This is mindful of that well-known resistance put up by unbelievers who say they don't believe the Bible, but admit they have never read it.

But the chief resistance gets back to the problem some Christians have with the thought of God's Presence remaining in despicable Herod's Temple after Jesus had said it would be "desolate" and even called it a "den of thieves." They take this to be a claim that God then accepted both Christ-rejecting Judaism and Christ-glorifying Christianity by remaining "under the same roof with those devils after what they did." They just cannot accept the fact that God gave the Jews another full generation of years to repent and return unto Himself.

After all, the first "Christians" were Jews who came to know and accept Jesus as Messiah during those forty years after The Crucifixion. And, as reported earlier, many of those early Believers were priests (Acts 6:7) who had seen those strange "signs" in the Temple and had witnessed this Holy Event. God did not just go out through the torn Veil and slam-the-door on the Jews when Jesus gave up the ghost. We have been assuming such and it is difficult to change, but the real story is far more beautiful, far more Christ-glorifying, and far more God-glorifying.

Some preachers who have refused to accept this story are so bound by their past traditional teaching that they are just too embarrassed to change their positions — even for that of the Truth! One such critic has been teaching for decades that Gordon's Calvary, near the Garden Tomb, is the Place of The Cross. Each year he takes a couple of large groups to tour the Holy Land and visits these sites. Now, he just cannot take a different position. In his desperation to defend against the Truth, he has taken a thoroughly ridiculous position by claiming that the Centurion saw the Veil from one of Antonia's Towers. The nearest tower was the southeast tower, about two-hundred meters to the side (north) and almost even with the rear of the *H'ekhal*! (See Illus. 20: Jerusalem as it Appeared in 70 C.E., Page 153)

Much of anti-Semitism and what I call patronizing of Judaism stems from the Gentiles' "gut-reaction," which faults the Jews for the Crucifixion. Condemnation of the Jewish people for the death of Jesus Christ makes about as much sense as blaming the citizens of Dallas, Texas for the assassination of President John F. Kennedy. They did not cause it to happen. They simply did not prevent it. They could not have prevented it!

One type of "squirming" is the frequent use of Bible verses to prove "assumptions." Keep in mind that the latest writings of the New Testament, except The Revelation, were written about 66 C.E. in places far from Jerusalem and just prior to this tragic event. Some enjoy a particular "zeal" in quoting verses that were written a few years previous to this event, a thousand miles distant, and are obviously being taken out of context concerning *Shekhinah*. And yet, these "resisters" stand with unblushing ignorance and disbelief, attempting to discredit historical records from those on the scene, at the time. One critic said, expressing doubt about this story: "Don't you know that the Glory of God is reflected in the face of Jesus Christ?!" — referring to II Corinthians 4:6. Here Paul writes from Ephesus, circa 57 C.E.:

> *"...knowledge of the glory of God in the face of Jesus Christ."*

This is certainly speaking of the Glory of God, and which certainly is shown in the face of Jesus Christ, but it is certainly not speaking of the "cloud" — the "fire" — the *Shekhinah*. *Shekhinah* was an extraordinary visible Presence of the "I AM." But, He appeared only to the Israelites — perhaps only to the High Priest, after 970 B.C.E. when the First Temple was completed — and until He departed the Temple and "removed hence" to *Olivet* summit in 66 C.E. This remains a fact that is very difficult for some Gentiles to accept; nevertheless, it was His Promise to the Jews in Deuteronomy 4:33 (NASB):

> *"Has any people heard the voice of God speaking from the midst of the fire, as you have heard it, and survived?"*

But the Jews (and Gentiles) seem to have forgotten or ignored these words. They also have overlooked verse 30:

"When you are in distress and all these things have come upon you, in the latter days, you will return to the Lord your God and listen to His voice."

Finally, some Christians who resist this story are apparently disturbed, albeit mistakenly, by anything that might be construed as overshadowing The Resurrection of Jesus Christ. Heaven forbid! Rather, The Resurrection and Ascension of the Lord Jesus Christ is Punctuated — Magnified — "Spotlighted" — Glorified — even more greatly by this event on the part of the Father, "I AM." Let us not forget, either, that the Father IS first and sovereign within the Trinity. Jesus always prayed to His Father before He did anything. Jesus also always gave His Father the Glory and credit for anything He (Jesus) did.

We should therefore take delight from and see glory in the action of the Father in having ascended from that same locale (*Olivet* Summit) forty years after His Son, Jesus. I surely don't believe Jesus would have "pouted" because His Father had the last "Word" — nor should we.

Scriptural/Historical/Archaeological Evidence

Prophecies indicate that *Shekhinah* would occupy the Second Temple:

Ezra 6:12 (*Lamsa Bible*) — *"And the God whose name we have found to be here, there shall He dwell."*

Haggai 2:4 – 9 (KJV) — *"Yet now be strong, O Zerubbabel, saith the Lord,...and work, for I am with you, saith the Lord of hosts,...and I will fill this house with Glory, saith the Lord of hosts."*

Zechariah 1:16 (KJV) — *"...I am returned to Jerusalem with mercies: My house shall be built in it, saith the Lord of hosts,..."*

Scripture says *Shekhinah* was in the Second Temple during and after Jesus' time: Matthew 23:21 (KJV) — *"And whoso shall swear by the Temple, sweareth by it and by Him that dwelleth therein."* Luke 24:52 – 53 (KJV) — *"(Disciples) were continually in the Temple, praising and blessing God."* John 2:16 (KJV) — *"... make not My Father's house an house of merchandise."* Romans 9:4 (New English Bible) — *"...theirs is the Divine Presence..."*

Prophecies of the withdrawal of *Shekhinah* from the Temple:

Ezekiel 9 – 11, Ezekiel 11:23 (KJV) — *"And the Glory of the Lord went up from the midst of the city, and stood upon the mountain which is on the east side of the city."*

Hosea 5:15 (KJV) — *"I will go back to My Place..."*

Historians' accounts of *Shekhinah* Withdrawal, 66–70 C.E.:

Josephus, *"Wars of the Jews"* 6.5.3/290–300

Eusebius, *"Proof of the Gospel"* Chapter XVIII

Midrash Rabbah – Eichah, Lamentations, Part 25 (Proems)

Babylonian Talmud-*Rosh Hashanah 31b*

Archaeological Evidence:

Dome of the Tablets identified as Holy of Holies (Dr. A.S. Kaufman) *Shekhinah* departure path (due-east) leads directly to traditional site of Jesus' Ascension at summit of Mount of Olives. (See Illus. 3: Old City of Jerusalem and Mt. of Olives, Page 19, and Illus. 20: Jerusalem as it Appeared in 70 C.E., Page 153)

Some Missing Pieces

An "accusation" or doubt that deserves answer is the absence of certain details from Scripture or even from the usually detailed reporting by Flavius Josephus. Such answer can be provided only by speculation based on "assumptions," a little imagination, and simple logic using available history and of course, Scripture. Realizing I have shown scant mercy toward traditional criticism for having founded its stand principally on "assumption," I will likely feel a merciless response from "traditionalists." We cannot know why these pieces of this puzzle have been kept from us; however, if we are moved to try, then we must start somewhere.

Typical of these kinds of missing pieces are:

Why didn't Josephus and the Rabbis of the Midrash report the "great noise" of Nicanor's Gate?

Why didn't Josephus or the Rabbis report that this gate opened silently, if that were the case?

Why did the guards need to tell their captain the gate had opened, if it did not open silently — "of its own accord?"

My only certain answer to these questions is simply, "I don't know." However, there are several things for which we have some confidence as "fact" because they seem to be supported by Scripture, by the writings of Josephus and/or by plausible reasoning:

— Each bronze "door" of Nicanor's Gate was about 60 ft. high by 23 ft. wide.

— The gate must have been very heavy and had great friction, because it "had been with difficulty shut by twenty men" and effective lubricants were not available to ease its friction.

— The conditions described would, from an engineering sense, indicate a possibility that such a gate would make a "great noise" when pivoted on "its turning hinges."

— The noise was sufficiently "great" to be heard at a distance of more than four miles — almost as far as Bethlehem.

— Both Scripture and the Rabbinical reporters of *Talmud* verify that this gate was normally opened only on the eve of each Sabbath, on New Moons (first day of the month), and on Feast Days.

On the basis of the information listed then, it has been assumed that the gate opened *silently* "at about the sixth hour of the night." Reasoning for the assumption follows:

— Midnight was not the normal time for opening the gate.

— Midnight was not the Sabbath eve, even if that day had been on a Sabbath, because for the Jews each day begins at sundown.

— The date was the eighth day of the month (*Nisan*) and not a New Moon, which occurs on the first day, and not a Feast day until the fourteenth of *Nisan* which is Passover.

— For the aforementioned reasons, nobody was expecting to hear the gate being opened, especially the captain who was probably asleep in his quarters. He had forty guards under his command. He did not remain awake throughout all three watches. This was delegated to lower ranking officers of the guards who commanded each shift or "watch."

Yet, for all the reasoning and data outlined here, it has been assumed that the gate must have opened silently at this Holy occasion because the guards ran to *tell* their captain the gate had opened. Under normal conditions, the captain would have been awakened by the "great noise of its turning hinges" and he would have jumped out of his bunk and raced out shouting something like, "Why in blazes are they opening the East Gate?! What's going on out there?!" But, no. The guards instead ran to *tell* their captain they had seen the gate open.

It has been assumed then, nobody heard the gate — not even the townsfolk in Jerusalem a few hundred meters west of the gate. It is assumed again, Josephus would perhaps have included the midnight rousing of The City, if they had heard this. I cannot explain these voids of explanation. Perhaps some scholar can provide these answers from other records.

Another question, even more obvious, concerns the omission of the details of that sight, which was beheld by the centurion and his squad at The Cross. Here we need to remember that all of those "stalwarts of the Faith" (the twelve) scattered like flushed quail even before Jesus was "lifted-up" — even at His capture and arrest. Mark literally "barely" escaped! (Mark 14:50 – 52) Yes, all except one! John was the only one of "the twelve" who is known to have been at The Cross.

Some might say that since John was the only disciple at The Cross, and since he did not say the centurion had seen the torn Veil, then it must have been the earthquake that "terrified" the soldiers. None of the other three Gospel writers is known to have been at The Cross, yet all three wrote of the torn Veil. Why didn't John write of this, especially since apparently he was the only one of the disciples at *Golgotha*? — He didn't even mention the earthquake.

We just don't have all these answers; nevertheless, examining carefully and literally the words of the Apostle, in John 19:27 we find:

> *"Then saith He (Jesus) to the disciple, "Behold thy mother!" And from that hour that disciple took her unto his own home."*

This verse is given early in John's narrative of The Crucifixion. Then, continuing, in verse 28:

"After this, Jesus knowing that all things were now accomplished, that the Scripture might be fulfilled, saith, 'I thirst.'"

Then, in verse 29, they gave Him the "spunge." Summarizing then, while John was at The Cross, they gave Jesus the sponge just before the ninth hour when He departed, just after he had instructed "the disciple whom Jesus loved" to take their mother home. John, a sensitive and compassionate man, probably saw a nod or eye-cast from Jesus that expressed silently: "John, if you are the one whom I love, please take 'our' mother away from this. I prefer that she not be here at the end."

Jesus had foreknowledge to know the gory events that were to follow His death. He therefore wished to spare His mother from that final trauma. After Jesus *"gave up the ghost"* (John 19:30), we can speculate that John obediently and immediately *"from that hour"* may have removed gently to take Mary away from the scene. He may have escorted Mary to a friendly home nearby, perhaps even as far as Bethany. That absence would explain why John did not mention the earthquake, the rending of the veil, etc. The tremor of the earthquake may have been very localized to the vicinity of The Cross so that he might not have noticed it while walking some distance away. On more than one occasion, I have been walking about during a minor earthquake, including the fifth floor of a hotel, but unaware of an earthquake. Although I was in the near vicinity, I had no knowledge of the tremor until I heard about it on TV moments later or read about it the next day in the news.

Moreover, Scripture seems to imply that a time interval spanned between Jesus' death and when the Romans began breaking the legs of the two thieves. (John 19:32) It is especially reasonable that a significant length of time would have been required, if only for the typical noisy and enthusiastic "haggling" and argument from the Jewish religious "lawyers" that would have confronted the soldiers, rushing them to complete their task.

Even more plausible is the almost certain requirement in the military chain-of-command that the centurion would have needed to send a messenger to Pilate, seeking his permission to deviate from the original execution orders. There would then be even more time consumed for the messenger to return with the Procurator's authorization to dispatch the condemned Judeans early in order to accommodate the Jewish Law. (See Deuteronomy 21:23) Such an interlude would certainly have allowed sufficient time for John even to stride "over the hill" to Bethany and return. We do know that John himself saw that scene wherein the soldiers broke the legs, indicating that he must have returned alone to The Cross after caring for Mary. In this scenario, John may not have been actually present at The Cross to witness the earthquake, rending of the Veil and the centurion's exclamation. (Matthew 27:51 – 54)

We just do not have all the details of that occasion to be able to rationalize precise timing and sequence of events at The Cross. It appears that John reported only what he actually saw. We do know, however, from John 19:35, that John saw the soldier thrust the spear into Jesus' side. This final and "gory" event very likely occurred at a significant time interval after Jesus' death and as the crowd and the soldiers hastened "to-get-it-over-with" — so they could all return to their homes before the Sabbath and to partake in their Passover meal.

The other three Gospel writers didn't see this final scene, but all three say the centurion SAW "those things." Somebody perhaps told them about the centurion's witness, but maybe they did not know the centurion saw Almighty God. Although, neither do they tell us of any other event that was so terrifying that tough Roman foot-soldiers *"feared greatly"* (Matthew 27:54) and that might inspire this sudden Roman evangelical response. (Maybe they thought nobody would believe their story!)

Nevertheless, we know the time of day (3 P.M.) and that the soldiers were facing the Temple. Common sense then reveals that they could only discern that the Veil was torn by the fact that they could see a brilliant light coming from behind the Veil and inside the Temple.

It may be significant that Mark and Luke reported *only* the torn Veil, with no mention of the quakes, the graves, or any other of "those things." This can be taken to imply that the other *"things that were done"* were less important. So, what was so important about the Veil being *"rent in twain from the top to the bottom?"* Mark says this was sufficiently impressive that the centurion said, *"Truly, this man was the Son of God."* Yet, neither Luke nor Mark says anything about the centurion being "terrified." (Only Matthew.) They just say the Veil was torn and this convinced the centurion that Jesus was the Son of God. But, we know that He saw the *Shekhinah's* fire gleaming through the parted Veils and *that* is why the centurion was so impressed, even though Mark did not present any rationale for the centurion's remark. (See Matthew 27:51 – 54; Mark 15:38 – 39; Luke 23:45 – 47, and John 19:30 – 36.)

I don't know why the writers of the Gospel omitted such details, but those historical and Scriptural details that are available provide the answers we have offered. Although some of the pieces of these puzzles are missing, we can see the picture assembled, except for a few details that the Lord has preferred to cloak in mystery for a time. Notice: "Three" writers reported that the centurion saw the torn Veil.

It has been said that Jews search Scripture to discover "why?"; while Christians search Scripture to discover "how?" Those philosophical positions remain intact considering everything we have encountered in this story.

You Shall Know The Truth

Extracting the truth by unfastening all the buttons, buckles, zippers, snaps, etc., holding in place the cloak of prim, comfortable, convenient, respectable, "traditional" teaching can be compared to dealing with constipation. It may require taking some unpleasant medicine, perhaps even an enema — may cause some discomfort (struggling, even!) — may even take some time — and we may have some awkward moments as we "hasten" to unfasten all those zippers, buttons, etc., when we finally begin to realize and accept the TRUTH. But, when we finally release all that "blockage" of tradition that has been holding back the "freedom" that accompanies the truth, we are going to feel a lot better. And, as the Essenes of that West Gate discovered, despite our holding back, we will eventually have to "come forth" — perhaps not without some pain and embarrassment.

Again, the Bible provides added meaning (and rich blessings) when we know the *Shekhinah* still resided in the Temple during the time of Jesus and when we accept literally those things described by the New Testament writers, instead of just accepting "traditional" teaching without question. As Professor Martin noted, the local Jewish "tourist-guides" of the fourth century really "did a number on us" when they showed Helena, Emperor Constantine's mother, several alleged Christian "Holy Places," which were actually revered Jewish sites, tombs, etc., or nothing at all. Many of our most popular sites were identified to Helena by those ancient "rip off artists" and some actually by Constantine himself, through his idolatrous divinations and "visions."[25]

For reasons we might never know, Christian scholars at that time must have overlooked Chapter 27 of Matthew, or else they could never have been so completely hoaxed. And after all, who was going to argue with this brand-new Christian, Emperor Constantine? Even Bishop Eusebius[26] eventually had to bow to this concept from his Emperor's "Divine Revelation." And so, for all these years, we have followed the tradition associated with this Roman Catholic shrine; although, more recently a more "modern" and more "accurate" and more "Protestant" location has been proclaimed by Britain's hero of Khartoum, General Charles Gordon.

One year before his death at Khartoum, the distinguished general toured Jerusalem, observing what appeared to be the image of a skull on a cliff of clay northwest of the Old City, near the present Damascus Gate Bus Station. Gordon fondly but blindly concluded, "This must be Calvary!" Although General Gordon was not an archaeologist, he *was* a treasured national hero, even before Khartoum — and, it is very unwise to contradict war heroes (or *any* generals *or* emperors for that matter!) concerning religion or warfare or anything else!

Understandably, General Gordon could not have known that area had been the site of the city latrines during the first century. Sadly also, the general did not possess thorough Biblical awareness of the centurion's line-of-sight to The Veil, as related by Matthew. No evidence has surfaced to indicate that Gordon was misled by "tourist guides." Just as many of us might be tempted to do, he evidently misled himself by eagerly and fondly seeking what he *wanted* to see, rather than by seeking the Truth.

A few decades later, some Christians discovered an empty tomb a short distance from "Gordon's Calvary," perhaps having been similarly inspired by romantic but blind enthusiasm. This popular and revered Christian pilgrim stop has been named "The Garden Tomb." In these fashions, Christians tragically for many years have been misled concerning authenticity of these Holy sites. Nevertheless, they continue to cling to these traditional spots with a most tenacious romantic fervor that surely will not easily give way to the Truth, no matter the facts. Tradition is powerfully seducing, sedating, soothing, and addictive, as well as being a poison to Truth.

Even so, lest we be derelict in this effort, we still need to determine why the Jewish survivors at Jerusalem would seek deliberately to deceive Christian pilgrims. They demonstrated what is perhaps the ultimate *chutzpah* by doing this in the face of the mighty Emperor, Constantine!

The answer to this query appears obvious when we stop to consider the fact that the Jews of the third and fourth centuries were even then eagerly awaiting their Messiah and the restoration of their Temple. (We must never forget that this situation exists with many Jewish Faithful today as well.) When and if the Temple were restored and the burnt offerings, the Red Heifer burnings, etc., were resumed, *the Jews would certainly not have wanted Christians or anybody else erecting shrines, conducting tours, gawking around, and tramping over the graves in the vicinity of their Miphkad Altar at Olivet summit!* So, the Jews grasped these naive, wide-eyed Christians by the nose and led them precisely in the opposite direction from the true location — to the west side of The City, rather than eastward to *Olivet*.

It well may be also that this is one of the reasons why the Lord has permitted delay of publication of this book for several years. Consider this: If Christians were suddenly to awaken to the fact that The Crucifixion occurred at *Olivet* summit, and if the Jews were to resume use of the *Miphkad Altar* and begin dumping ashes from Temple sacrifices on the western slope of *Olivet*, just imagine what would be the reaction of Judaism and Islam. To say the least, it would be an "explosive" situation.

All this should at least in part explain why we and our theologians and scholars have been so inaccurate during all these centuries in our location of the place of The Crucifixion. (After all, God has "permitted" our ignorance for His Holy Purpose.) From what we have developed in our study, the evidence points undeniably to *Olivet* summit for that most Holy site.

This was a piece of very cleverly contrived "disinformation" that was perhaps originally intended as a cruel joke on some very powerful but very gullible Christian Gentiles. (They were telling them what they wanted to hear!) And so, for many generations afterward we have continued to be "duped" by those rascals — partly because we have followed traditional teaching instead of studying and believing the literal wording of the Scriptures to obtain and verify the truth.

Nevertheless, we must agree from the findings of this study that tradition has been very accurate in its disclosure of the Place of The Ascension. As always, Satan again has managed to delude and confuse us by "salting" his lies with just a "dash" of truth. That Prince of Darkness surely knows how eagerly we mortals are willing to reach out and grasp those things we want to hear.

It is apparent that Gospel writers omitted (and/or were not "commissioned" to reveal) several details of the Law that are very important and relevant toward more thorough understanding of certain contexts in the Gospel. It seems the Lord inspired them to write their stories and to just drop these details, as if to say, "Why, everyone knows that!"

Typical of such a void in our Judaic awareness is our Biblical misunderstanding concerning "the veil." The Bible (Exodus 26:31 – 35) instructs only that a veil of blue and purple and scarlet of "fine linen" shall separate the Holy of Holies from the Holy Place and that "*...with cherubim shall it be made.*" Then, in verse 36 it says, "*...thou shall make an hanging for the door of the tent, of blue, and purple, and scarlet...*"

We have demonstrated thoroughly the importance of this majestic and beautiful Temple article. Despite that importance, we hardly ever hear mention of the Veil in our teachings and literature other than in those well-known verses taking place at The Cross. I was moved to learn more of appearance details for the Veil, since we seem to have less information about it than for any other Temple article or feature. One reason for this "secrecy" is that it would be "an abomination" if anyone were to create a copy or replica for display anywhere other than the Holy Temple.

After a long search, including attempting contact with Temple authorities in Jerusalem, I finally located an excellent description from Josephus;[2] although his dimensions of the Veil appear to be in error in comparison with *Shekalim* 8:5. The description of the Temple in *Wars* 5.5.4212–214 details: "It was a Babylonian curtain, embroidered with blue, and fine linen, and scarlet, and purple, and of a contexture that was truly wonderful." Josephus continues, saying the Veil's mixture of colors was not "without its mystical interpretation of colors, but was a kind of image of the universe."

He observes that the scarlet seemed to represent fire and the earth was signified by "fine flax" — i.e., fine linen. The blue represents "the air" (sky) and purple denotes the sea. Josephus recorded, in *Antiquities* 3.7.7 (183), that the fine linen signifies earth because it grows from the earth's soil. Purple represents the sea because its dye came from a sea shell. A gland from certain species of the spiny Murex shell (family *Muricidae*) secretes a yellowish fluid which turns purple when exposed to sunlight. Such dye, obviously very expensive, has long been used to color the purple robes of royalty.

His narrative continues with a somewhat cryptic dialog in Josephus' ancient prose, describing: "The foundation of this resemblance, but the fine flax and the purple have their own origin for that foundation." He notes that the curtain had "embroidered upon it all that was mystical in the heavens" and then some undecipherable phrase about "twelve signs" and "living creatures" (angels).

Nevertheless, it would be interesting to see more detail, not only about the "curtain" or "hanging" at the *H'ekhal* entry, but also concerning the two veils dividing the inner chambers. The people who are preparing for the rebuilt temple, The Temple Institute, must eventually possess this information; although, they may presently be required to guard it because of the unfortunate potential for copies or replicas.

Confusion for us Gentiles arises from the fact that the Jews deviated a bit from the Biblical instructions pertaining to The Tabernacle given in Exodus. the First Temple had two cedar partitions separating the two Holy chambers of the *H'ekhal* and had a veil before the outer partition and "an hanging" covering the Temple entrance doors. In the Second Temple, however, the cedar partitions were replaced by two veils. And, as in the Tabernacle and in the First Temple, they provided "an hanging, of blue, and purple, and scarlet" covering the doors at the entrance to the *H'ekhal*.

Then, adding to our confusion, they called this outer "hanging" a veil, also. (Thus, three "veils," OK?) Josephus referred to this outer veil as a huge Babylonian curtain. Since he never mentioned them in his descriptions, this outstanding historian apparently was unaware that two veils divided the *H'ekhal*. Now, since the Gospel writers were Jewish, they also referred to this outer curtain as a veil or our translators used the word "veil" to describe that "hanging" or "curtain." After all, in ancient languages such as Hebrew and Aramaic, which have far less vocabulary choice for words than is available in, say, English; the words "veil" and "curtain" or "hanging" can have virtually the same meaning.

Evidence of this multiplicity of terms concerning "the veil" can be cited in the *Talmud*. Tractate *Hullin* 90b describes the "curtain" that graced the entrance to the Temple. This passage further states that the curtain was one handbreadth thick, woven twice each year, and had to be immersed by three hundred priests, etc. Tractate *Shekalim* 8:4–5 describes the "veil" as one handbreadth thick, woven twice each year, etc. Both tractates mention the eighty-two damsels who braided a new veil twice each year.

It is appropriate at this point to observe the New Testament translation from the Greek word for "Veil." It is *katapetasmah*, meaning "that which spreads outward and downward." The Lamsa New Testament is of course translated from the original manuscripts in Aramaic and derives the word "curtain" instead of "Veil."

The translators of the New Testament from Greek manuscripts then used the word "veil" when they described "the rending of the veil." The centurion could have seen the outer "curtain," under the proper conditions, but he could not have seen either of the two veils inside the Temple because, as a Gentile, he would be forbidden inside the Temple or even its outer courts.

Nevertheless, once again it has been shown that what some would call Biblical "confusion" or "contradiction" is not the result of error or failure in the Scriptures. Rather, it is because of man's failure to "do his homework!" We have cut ourselves off from Jewish Law and tradition and anything "Jewish" in order to avoid having our Christianity become "corrupted" by Judaism. Ironically, however, this persistence in ignorance has hidden much of the "beauty" of Christ that is cast throughout The *Talmud* and *Midrash*.

Now, having encountered a few such details from the *Talmud* in this work, the following thought comes to mind: Any Jewish scholar who is knowledgeable in Judaic Law and tradition must sometimes regard parts of our Christian teaching with a certain amount of humor. He might be justified to have that thought when he observes how misinformed and how uniformed we are about the very roots of our faith. (We have not done our "homework!")

At the same time, we Christians are so smug with our 20/ 20 hindsight, as we observe the Jewish people sympathetically, but impatiently, "How could Jews have been so blind?" Jews must also be saying, "How can Christians be so naive?!"

So much of our "traditional" teaching has overlooked these details of Judaic Law and history, which are so important to Christian knowledge. Gentiles descended from Ham and Japheth are supposed to *"dwell in the tents of Shem;"* i.e., "learn" about God from Shem (Genesis 9:27). Shem was the eldest of Noah's sons and is the ancestor of all "Semitic" peoples, including the Israelites. God's Word is further glorified by these "jewels" from its Judaic roots.

9

The Debate

Ezekiel's prophecy misunderstood – Traditionalists cannot face Truth, even from literal Scripture – What the centurion "SAW" – The centurion and his men were terrified and KNEW Jesus!

Now that we have discussed most of the doubts and "fears" that cause the critics to "accuse" and/or "resist," these issues can be debated.

Ezekiel's Prophecy: The Glory Withdrawal

Scholars calculate that Ezekiel was carried off to Babylon about 597 B.C.E. and was given this particular vision about 591 B.C.E. — about five years before the First Temple was destroyed. Some critics of this account would therefore insist that Ezekiel "saw" the Glory of the Lord withdraw from the Temple before the Babylonian destruction (586 B.C.E.). This point is then used to counter any claim that the Glory was ever residing in the Second Temple. These have assumed *Shekhinah* never returned. This is the first of two popular, traditional "myths" concerning the *Shekhinah* that we shall disprove.

This position proposes that Ezekiel was translated or "raptured" to Jerusalem from Babylon to witness the departure of the *Shekhinah* Glory. Even if the prophet had been translated to Jerusalem, it is not reasonable to suppose that he was the sole observer of this Glorious Event. If, in fact, he "saw" the departure, why did no others see it? Why is there no 586 B.C.E. record of that remarkable, dramatic occasion? Supporters of this theory have no plausible explanation for these voids. They are simply teaching as they have been taught, by tradition!

These would suggest that blinding "fire" or that imposing "cloud" would have just passed over all the Temple guards, priests, townspeople, etc., and would have just moved over to *Olivet* without even a soul present to behold this scene. We are left to believe nobody in Jerusalem even looked up to see their Lord. They all just went on about their business. When one stops to think about such a suggestion, it is ludicrous.

These should be reminded that Ezekiel was very specific about times and places of his visions — and this was a vision; although some of our most beloved and knowledgeable teachers insist Ezekiel was translated to Jerusalem. Ezekiel clearly states, beginning in Ezekiel 8:3, this entire dissertation was a "vision ." He also indicates he was not physically in Jerusalem when he "saw" these events, "*in the visions of God,*" but that he was in his house in Babylon seated before a group of elders (Ezekiel 8:1 – 4). True, he does say he was taken up "*by a lock of mine head,*" but that he was brought to Jerusalem "*in the visions of God.*"

Reference 34 explains that the term "*taken by a lock of mine head*" (from verse 3) is a Hebrew figure of speech denoting that this was a vision and that Ezekiel was taken up "only in spirit" — actually "as a sign of displeasure." It is explained that an angry master might treat a laggard servant in this way; whereas, in the vision that heralded Israel's redemption, he is carried gently to Jerusalem. This can be understood to mean that Ezekiel did not really *want* to see *this* vision. So, the Lord "grabbed" him and took him "as if by a lock of his hair."

Many Christian commentaries and subsequent teachings believe Ezekiel was translated or "raptured" to Jerusalem. Their error and misunderstanding results from favoring traditional interpretation over the literal Word of God and a refusal to consult Judaica sources in order to become aware of the Hebrew idiom described.

Ezekiel even says his vision of the rebuilt Temple (Ezekiel 43:3) was given in the same way (Ezekiel 9:5) as this vision. As mentioned, this prophet was meticulous about dates. He records that the vision, which extends from Chapter 8 through Chapter 11, was given "*in the sixth year of our captivity.*" The date he records for his vision "*given in the same way*" for the future Temple, to be rebuilt upon Israel's return to The Land, is "*the five and twentieth year of our captivity*" — about fifty-two years before Zerubbabel began construction. Definitely a vision of the future.

Then, closing in verse 11:24, he explains: "*...So the vision that I had seen went up from me.*" The literal Word of God says there was no "rapture." Ezekiel saw this only as a *vision*.

Clearly, any insistence that Ezekiel was raptured, or even physically on the scene when *Shekhinah* withdrew, is based "purely" on assumptions, which contradict literal translations of Scripture and are boldly opposed to documented historians' dating and timing of the event. Josephus notes the date as "before the Jews' rebellion," i.e., 66 C.E. *Talmud, Rosh Hashanah* 31a, dates departure of *Shekhinah* as before the destruction of the Temple. Josephus is even more specific in documenting this Event by <u>recording the exact date and hour</u> of its occurrence; i.e., the 8th day of *Nisan*, at the ninth hour of the night." (3 A.M.) — See Appendix A.

Some sympathy can be offered toward the misunderstanding, which results by assuming Ezekiel "reported" this event rather than "predicted" it. This prophecy is yet another example of the "prophetic-perfect-tense" that is frequently used by the Prophets to emphasize importance of certain prophecies. In this style they actually wrote in the past tense in order to emphasize that the prophecy was so certain that it could already be considered to have happened! Ezekiel's prophecy of the *Shekhinah* departure is just such a prophecy. The prophet stated his vision in past tense; although, it was most definitely an event scheduled for the future. Let us not be confused and therefore miss the truth and the importance of this Glorious event.

Some would say that no Scripture ever described the Glory withdrawing from the Second Temple and that only Ezekiel describes it (before the First Temple was destroyed — 586 B.C.E.) and therefore that prophecy applies only to the First Temple.

Ezekiel did not indicate when the prophecy was to be fulfilled. Claiming this applies only to the First Temple, just because the vision was given before the First Temple was destroyed *(ignoring that it was stated in the past tense!)* is simply another unfounded assumption. This assumption, even if it were correct, includes the implied proviso that a prophecy can be fulfilled only once. Most beginner Bible students soon learn that many prophecies have been or will have been fulfilled more than once.

Some examples of multiple fulfillments are listed as follows:

1. Israel has been brought back to The Land two times since about 585 B.C.E., when Ezekiel issued the prophecy (Chapter 37) of their eventual return. They subsequently returned about 483 B.C.E. and again about 1945 C.E., after having been *"scattered among the nations"* since 70 C.E. The *complete* fulfillment of that prophecy, however, has not yet occurred. *Complete* fulfillment will be manifested when God will cause Israel *"to come up out of your graves and bring you into the Land of Israel."* (Ezekiel 37:13) That event will occur just a few days prior to arrival of Messiah at the Mount of Olives. We shall discuss that future event in a later chapter.

2. Antiochus Epiphanes IV sacrificed a pig upon the Altar, as a "type" fulfillment of the "Abomination of Desolation" from Daniel 12:11. A repetition of that same "type" occurred when Titus "defiled" the Temple by entering the Holy of Holies when Jerusalem surrendered in 70 C.E.. *Complete* fulfillment will occur when Antichrist stands *"in the holy place"* as foretold in Mat. 24:15. We don't know what "type" of abomination he will commit.

3. John 19:37 proclaimed the events at The Cross as fulfillments of Zechariah 12:10; although, *complete* fulfillment is yet future, and will of course occur when Jesus returns in Glory to the Mount of Olives.

Literally, Ezekiel's vision says only that the Glory would (someday) withdraw from the Temple and stand upon the mountain east of the City (Jerusalem) and would (someday) return to the Temple from the mountain (Ezekiel 43:2). Strangely, Ezekiel made no announcement that *Shekhinah* would "sit" on the mountain for three and one-half years and would appear and speak to His People. Neither did Ezekiel announce that He would ascend into Heaven from that point, as was described by the Rabbis in the *Midrash*. Hosea 5:15 declares that God will "go back to His Place." The *Midrash* Rabbis confirmed that He did in fact do just that — because "they" would not repent, despite the fact that Scripture does not fill in all the details concerning His delay at the Mount of Olives and His Ascension afterward.

The favorite evasion of some "squirmers" seems to be an insistence that all prophecy and Biblical knowledge must be verified by Scripture — no secular records accepted. There are scores of prophecies that have been, and are today being fulfilled without Scriptural "verification." Many of these do not appear in Scripture simply because they were fulfilled after the last books of the Bible had been written. Some prophecies, however, have even been fulfilled during the Biblical period and still are not documented by Scripture. Let's take just one example as an illustration Ezekiel 26:14 said Tyre would be *"like the top of a rock."* And it is — Alexander (The Great) saw to it. The Bible doesn't need to say it happened! All Believers could rest assured it would happen — some day. (Not when or how it would happen.) Jesus alluded to that fulfillment in Matthew 11:21 and Luke 10:13, but He did not describe those *"mighty works which were done"* in Tyre. And they were done and yet, this is documented and described only in secular records *circa* 300 B.C.E., and by what we see of ancient Tyre today.

A more recent example of non-Scriptural fulfillment documentation is the rebirth of the nation, Israel. Ezekiel 37 issued the Lord's Promise 2,500 years ago that He would *"make them one nation"* (Ezekiel 37:22). Although no documentation of Israel's rebirth appears in Scripture, you can see for yourself that He has made them "one nation" as Promised — beginning as of May 1948. (How many times had we heard that old spiritual ballad about "dem dry bones?" And we didn't even know that was from Ezekiel's prophecy!)

However, the best example is Jesus' prophecy that the Temple would be destroyed,"...*There shall not be left here one stone upon another,...*" (Matthew 24:2). Since the last books of the New Testament were certainly written *before* the destruction, no Scripture reports that fulfillment. And yet, the world surely believes the Temple *was* destroyed and in the manner and on the date as described by Josephus and the Rabbis of *Talmud* and *Midrash* — the *same* historians who recorded the *Shekhinah* Withdrawal.

Whose "*House?*"

Another form of Scriptural opposition claims *Shekhinah* could not have returned to the Second Temple because Scripture does not describe such an event (as was given for the First Temple,II Chron. 5:13 – 14).

We do not witness prophetic fulfillment by what the Bible doesn't say about these events. We have just shown that the Bible doesn't tell everything. Just because the Bible does not say *Shekhinah* returned doesn't mean He didn't return. The remote Aramaic *Lamsa Bible* includes a Promise that has been omitted from our more popular ("conventional") Western Bibles. Lamsa[8] translates Ezra 6:12 *"And the God whose name we have found there, there shall he dwell,"* in describing the Lord's dwelling in His rebuilt Temple after the return from Babylon.

Scripture makes no mention of the return of the "cloud" to the Second Temple. However, as we read Nehemiah 8, 9, and 10, it is difficult to believe our Merciful and Loving Father would continue to punish and "turn His face away" from these worshipers after they had repented, confessed, rejoiced, and praised and covenanted with Him so fervently and sincerely on that occasion. Nehemiah 12:43 says their rejoicing at Jerusalem *"was heard even afar off."* (How could He resist?)

Additional Scriptural evidence of this return through the Promise of prophecy exists in God's message through the prophet Haggai. In Haggai 1:4 (paraphrasing): Upon their return from Babylon, He tells Haggai to ask Zerubbabel and the People: *"Is it right for you to build houses for yourselves, but then to permit My House to remain as a heap of rubble?"* Then, in verse 8 the Lord declares: *"Go up to Mt. Zion and bring wood and build My House and I will take pleasure in it and I will be glorified."*

Next, in Chapter 2, verses 3 and 4, the Lord says: *"Even though this House you have been building is not nearly as magnificent as was My first House, be strong! For I am with you!"*; and in verse 7 He says, *"... 'the desire of all nations' shall come and I will fill this House with glory,"* and in verse 9 He says: *"The glory of this latter House shall eventually be greater than that of My former House..."*

More of the emotion and empathy toward His People can be seen from God's Word as translated from the Hebrew Scriptures (*Tanakh*) in rendition of Haggai 2:3 – 5 following:

2:3 Which among you of the remnant saw this Temple in its first glory? And what do you see (as the Temple) now? Is it not almost as if it were nothing in your eyes?

2:4 Yet now be strong, O Zerubbabel, said the Lord, be strong, O Joshua ben-Jehotzadak the High Priest; be strong all ye people of the land, said the Lord, and serve (to build) because I am with you, said the Lord of Hosts.

2:5 That covenant which I made with you when you left Egypt and My Spirit stands in your midst, do not fear.

The foregoing verses seem to convey the Lord's unconditional Promise to Zerubbabel and the People concerning the Second Temple:

Be strong!

Build My House!

I am with you!

My Spirit stands in your midst!

Fear not!

Many would agree that the Lord makes it sound as though He intends to occupy this House as soon as it is built.

Now does anyone believe that the Lord would so exhort and encourage the Israelites to build that "latter House," which would be greater than the first House, and which He will "fill with Glory," and that He would then rescind His Promise to them? Moreover, at this point we must point out that when the word "spirit" is used in the Hebrew Scriptures as in this case: "My Spirit," it is actually referring to His Divine Presence, the *Shekhinah*. Jewish people usually refer to the *Shekhinah* as the Holy Spirit. The Lord therefore was saying My *Shekhinah* "*stands in your midst.*"

Some scholars have claimed that five things from the First (Solomon's) Temple were missing from the Second Temple, and that one of these was *Shekhinah*. This belief was probably inspired by an entry in *Yoma* 21b, in which Rabbi Samuel ben Inia said that the First Temple differed from the Second Temple in five things. He was apparently defending against critics who were questioning the Lord's Promise in Haggai 1:8, in which God said He would "*take pleasure in it (the Temple) and be glorified.*" Opposing critics, as they so often "rush" to do, miss the true context of statements during their search for opposing evidence. They "stop" reading at the point where they read what they WANT to believe. As we read further in this passage, we find the concluding remarks from R. ben Inia do not support the opponents' enthusiastic and premature conclusion.

Referring to those startling supernatural signs in the Temple, the Rabbi concludes by saying: "I tell you. — They *were* present, but they were not as helpful as before." He is emphatic in saying *Shekhinah* was in the Second Temple, but He *was* not as "helpful" as before. For example, the "Fire" no longer came down to light the logs on the Altar as it had done in the First Temple. (II Chronicles 7:1) There were several other such miracles from the First Temple that were not as "helpful" in the Second Temple.

Those miracles such as the Westernmost Candle, the Crimson Strap, etc., appeared *only* in the Second Temple, beginning about 300 B.C.E. with the tenure of Simeon the Righteous as High Priest. These signs clearly were recognized by the Rabbis as a sign that *Shekhinah* certainly *was* dwelling in the Second Temple, regardless that some of the signs from the First Temple were absent.

The Rabbis have reported lamentably and mournfully that the signs in the Second Temple disappeared *completely* "*forty years before the Temple was destroyed.*" *Talmud* points out that the Rabbis *knew* that when those signs were removed, *Shekhinah* was preparing to depart the Temple. That ominous conclusion was in fact emphasized by the Rabbis when the Westernmost Candle "failed" completely, never to appear again, during those grievous "forty years." – They *had* to know, therefore, they had made a mistake.

Critical opponents of this account will no doubt point to my enthusiasm for the Withdrawal as being inconsistent with my apparent reticence concerning the claimed return of *Shekhinah* to the Second Temple. "Why did nobody witness and 'document' that occasion? Was it not Glorious enough? Did the Lord 'sneak' back into the Temple?"

Okay — You got me on that one. I do not know why we have no Scriptural description of His return such as we were given when the Glory "cloud" filled the Sanctuary at the dedication of the First Temple. (I Kings 8:10) Nevertheless, it should be agreed that His Glorious Withdrawal from the Temple was a much more dramatic event than His apparent return to residence after Babylon. Maybe the Divine Presence did not return until the time of Simeon the Righteous, as evidenced by appearance of the signs discussed in Chapter 7 earlier. That period, 300 B.C.E., was after His Promise to Zerubbabel and after the last book of the Old Testament; i.e., Malachi in 400 B.C.E.

However, as discussed earlier, it is difficult to understand why the Lord would not have responded to the fervent prayers and rejoicing described in Nehemiah 12:43. As the prophet said: "*...for God had made them rejoice with great joy so that the joy of Jerusalem was heard even afar off.*" Nehemiah's description of that jubilant occasion indicates a new-found sincerity and praise among the returned nation after the captivity. (Still, no mention of *Shekhinah*.)

True, we don't know when His glory returned. But it must have been some time before "*The Desire of All Nations*" (Messiah) arrived because, as we shall soon demonstrate, "The The Desire of All Nations" Himself declared that His Father indeed dwelled in that House during His time on this Earth.

Some critics may counter this interpretation of Haggai 2:9 by claiming that the reference is to the return of our Lord and His glory to the Millennial or Third Temple ("latter" house). Such a claim will not stand, however, because the Lord clearly states that *this* House will be filled with His glory. Yes, He will also fill that Millennial "*latter House*" with His glory, but identification as a "present" House is further verified in that He is encouraging Zerubbabel to take heart and to continue building this (present) house. The New International Version emphasizes this by the translation of Haggai 2:9 as "*...this present house...*" instead of "*this latter house.*"

The Father (*Shekhinah*) filled that House with His physical (?), visible Presence and Jesus filled it figuratively with His Glory as Messiah. It was the Lord's Promise to Zerubbabel that it would be filled with Glory. How can we deny that which the Lord had Promised?

Did you notice? This is another of those Messianic prophecies that we can lovingly and gently point out to Jewish friends to indicate that Messiah must surely have been in the Second Temple. Haggai 2:7 says: "*...the desire of all nations shall come and I will fill this House with glory...*" As suggested earlier, maybe His Glory returned to the Holy House during the time of Simeon the Righteous. Then Jesus, The The Desire of All Nations, did surely come and, as we have shown in this story, His Father (*Shekhinah*) filled that House literally with His Glory up until Pentecost of 66 C.E.

Some would "spiritualize" this verse, claiming Jesus fulfilled that prophecy when He filled that House with His Glory. First of all, "the House" is the *H'ekhal*, the main building of the Temple, the dwelling place of God (as the Divine Presence). Some teachers, including perhaps some New Testament translators, frequently gloss over references to "the Temple" as anything within the Temple court complex. Entering the "Temple" does not necessarily include entering the "Holy House," the *H'ekhal*. Jesus, son of David from the tribe of Judah and not a Levite, was not a priest. Only priests were permitted to enter the Holy House. Jesus, in fact, would not have been permitted to pass beyond the Court of the Israelites as He came to bring His sacrificial offering.

Please let us not be careless with the facts by treating such details as trivial. They were important to the Jews. God gave them these details. Jesus was a Jew. He thought they were important, also. Jesus didn't need to enter the *H'ekhal* to display His Glory. Besides, He would never have violated His Father's Law by doing so. Jesus displayed His Glory by His healings, teaching, forgiveness, and ultimately by His Glorious death and Resurrection and Ascension.

Continuing in Chapter 2 of Haggai, the statements about "shaking" the nations, heavens, earth, etc., in verses 6 and 7 may be both figurative and literal. The appearance of Jesus, as "The Desire of All Nations," has caused considerable "shaking." Then of course there will be literal shaking (earthquakes) before He returns to build His Temple in the Kingdom. So, there may be a dual fulfillment of these prophecies, although they may not be stated chronologically in Haggai's text.

But hear now this convincing prophecy from Zechariah 1:16,

"Therefore thus saith the Lord; I am returned to Jerusalem with mercies: My house shall be built in it, saith the Lord of hosts..."

Nevertheless, although it is clear here that the Lord had Promised He would return to His House, it is strange that no prophet seems to have recorded the actual return of *Shekhinah*. Similarly, it is strange, too, that we have no Scriptural witness of the adolescent and young manhood years of the Lord Jesus. God, in His Infinite Wisdom, has seen fit to withhold such mystery from us — at least during the Church Age.

In fairness to all theories and positions discussed here, we should focus attention on the prophecy of Ezekiel 43:2,

"And, behold, the Glory of the God of Israel came by the way of the east..."

Critics who claim that Ezekiel saw the Glory withdraw in Ezekiel 8 – 11 need to answer an obvious question: If Ezekiel actually saw the Glory depart in that earlier vision, then in light of Ezekiel 43:2 – 3, why do they claim the Glory never returned? Ezekiel says again, he saw the Glory of God return to the Temple as He "came by the way of the east." Their position is especially strange in this case because the prophet declares in Verse 3 that these "*...visions were like the vision that I saw when I came to destroy the city;*" and that vision is the one that "saw" *Shekhinah* withdraw.

So, was Ezekiel translated to Jerusalem again to see this? Certainly not — because of the reasons just stated and because this vision was given only fourteen years after the First Temple was destroyed. (See Ezekiel 40:1.) This return of *Shekhinah* is going to take place in the future when Messiah arrives. An obvious question — with an obvious answer.

Fourteen years after its destruction by King Nebuchadnezzar, "*in the five and twentieth year of our captivity,*" the Temple had not yet been rebuilt. For this reason, nobody saw the Glory return — because only Ezekiel "saw" it — "*in the visions of God.*" However, I must concede that to date I have found no historical record to say anybody saw the return of the Glory to the Second Temple. Record of His Glorious Withdrawal, nevertheless, is available in ample measure, as we have demonstrated.

In Chapter 6 of this work, we pointed to Ezekiel's prophecy of the gate *"which shall be shut"* as having been fulfilled by the Lord Jesus, who *"entered in by it,"* and by the Lord's Divine Presence, *Shekhinah*, who went *"out by the way of the same."* (Ezekiel 44:3) The prophet relates, in the remainder of that chapter, the ordinances that the priests are to follow in the Second Temple. How do we know he is speaking of the rebuilt, Second Temple?

Verses 6 and 13 give the Levites (priests) a good "chewing out" for their behavior and "*they shall bear their iniquity...their shame...and their abominations which they committed.*" And yet, in verses 14 through 16 and despite their disobedience: "*But I will make them keepers of the charge of the House...and they shall stand before Me to offer unto Me the fat and the blood, saith the Lord God.*" (Yes, even Caiaphas!)

Very simply, this cannot be referring to the period of the Levites' ministrations in the First Temple, because it had been destroyed thirteen years before this vision was given. Neither can Ezekiel be referring to the Millennial or Third Temple, because the Levites will not be committing any abominations in that Temple. So, this passage is specifying the ordinances they were to follow in the Second Temple, including standing before Him. (*Shekhinah*).

Jewish sages from the Second Temple period give a subtle testimony, saying the Jews considered that "He" resided in the Holy House. The Rabbis' testimony relates a beautiful, yet tragic comforting that mourners and excommunicates could receive from the Divine Presence. *Middoth* 2:2 says to mourners: "May He who dwells in this House comfort thee." And to excommunicates: "May He who dwells in this House inspire them ("thy colleagues") to befriend thee again." And finally, a third comfort and urging: "May He who dwells in this House inspire thee to listen to the words of thy colleagues that they may befriend thee again."

This last advice is accompanied by an explanation in a footnote. It is noted that excommunication was usually inflicted upon an elder "who would not conform to the majority." The Jews may have had some men who had difficulty matching tradition with what they had read in Scripture and in history and, yes, with the truth.

To insist that the Divine Presence was not dwelling in the Lord's Temple (not Herod's!) during the lifetime of Jesus is inconceivable when Scripture said He was going to return to the Second Temple. (Haggai 2:7, Zechariah 1:16), Scripture never said *Shekhinah* had actually departed, only giving Ezekiel's *vision* of a future departure. Neither has Scripture said that He did *not* dwell in the Second Temple. Secular witnesses in fact say they saw Him "remove hence" in 66 C.E. Just because the Bible does not describe the actual return of the Glory to the Temple, no "proof" is rendered that He did not return. We have just shown His Promises saying that He would return. Moreover, we have presented eyewitness accounts of His later Withdrawal, fulfilling Ezekiel's prophecy.

As we study the New Testament we need to remember those writings were not composed by WASP Baptist or Presbyterian or Methodist preachers from Middle America, or even from the green and brown countryside of the British Isles. They were written by Jews! It would never have occurred to a Jewish writer to make a finite statement about the Divine Presence being in the Temple! "Of course He is there! Everybody knows that!" That would be like, say, A New York author telling everybody the Statue of Liberty is in New York Harbor. "He must be kidding! Everybody knows that!" (Don't they?)

Notwithstanding their nonchalance concerning the detail of *Shekhinah*'s dwelling, not one Jewish Scriptural writer ever said *Shekhinah* was not in the Temple. Still, they stated in two verses of the New Testament that He was in the Temple. Otherwise, they wrote as if to say: "Everybody knows that!" (But do we?) Now do you begin to see what "tradition" has done to our teaching?

Possibly the Divine Presence remained with the Ark of the Covenant when it was removed from the Temple. One of the Apocryphal Books (II Maccabees 2:4 – 8, see Appendix D) states that King Nebuchadnezzar gave the Ark to Jeremiah the Prophet for safekeeping. After all, the Temple was only "shut-down" for a little more than seventy years — hardly even a "jitter" of the sweep-second hand on God's Eternal Timepiece! Besides, the king had heard what happened to the Philistines who captured the Israelites' "golden box." He didn't want any hemorrhoids in *his* secret parts! (I Samuel 5:9)

Again, there are no witnessed records of a 586 B.C.E. withdrawal (if there was an actual "withdrawal"). It is not "in character" for Almighty God to "sneak" away, "slinking" out the back door, sulking into the night. When He withdrew in 66 – 69 C.E., He left in a manner that all could see. We actually "obscure" the Glory of God by ignoring this story. He went out with what we moderns would call: Real Class!

There is a definite "mind-set" among some traditional Christian teachers saying the Glory of the Lord (*Shekhinah*) was not in the Temple during the ministry of Jesus. This "mind-set" is apparently based primarily on the negativism discussed in the preceding debate article. There is "noisy" opposition to any suggestion that the Lord would dwell in "Herod's Temple" built by that disgusting puppet. "The Lord would never permit Himself to be defiled by honoring such a place with His Presence, etc., etc."

Another similar objection points out that Jesus referred to the Temple as "a den of thieves," and said it had become "desolate." The claim is that Jesus would never have referred to the Holy House of the Lord in such terms if the Divine Presence had been dwelling within at that time.

The key evidence, so long overlooked by all of us, is a single verse spoken by the Lord Jesus Himself in Matthew 23:21 (NASB):

> "And he who swears by the temple, swears both by the temple and by Him who dwells within it."

That's right, He said "...*by Him who dwells within it.*" Definitely, present tense is used and certainly nobody else dwells within; indicating clearly, once and for all — The Divine Presence was in the Temple during the time of Jesus. Jesus declared it.

Most Gentiles actually have scant knowledge concerning the Jews' Holy Temple. Truly, *nobody* else dwelt in the Temple. Many Christians have the mistaken impression that the Temple was just some sort of "Central" Synagogue, located in Jerusalem. They probably receive this impression from hearing modern Jewish people talking about "going to *Temple*" — and synagogue names such as: *Temple* Israel, *Temple* Emmanuel, *Temple* Beth David, etc., etc.

Only God dwelt in The Temple, His residence in Jerusalem among His People. Only men from the tribe of Levi were permitted in the Temple sanctuary, the *H'ekhal*. Only the Chief Priest was permitted entry into God's "Private" Chamber, the Holy of Holies — and that only on *Yom Kippur* once each year.

Again — Nobody else "dwelt therein" — *Only Shekhinah*, the Divine Presence of Almighty God.

There is at least one more Scriptural verse that declares the Glory of the Lord still dwelled in the Temple after Jesus was crucified. Listen carefully now, as the Apostle Paul is expressing his grief that his kinsmen, the Israelites, have not accepted their Messiah. Then, he goes on to say, from Romans 9:4 (NEB):

".They are Israelites: they were made God's sons; theirs is the splendour of the divine presence, theirs the covenants, the law, the temple worship, and the promises."

Paul said: *"theirs is the splendour of the Divine Presence"* — not "was" (as we have been taught). Some other translations say "Glory" or "Presence," but in almost all versions, the present tense is used; i.e., "the Glory (or Presence) is theirs."

One skeptic charged that Matthew 23:21 is a "weak" claim for *Shekhinah* having been in the Temple. — Do they think Jesus was just using a figure of speech?! Luke 24:53 says the Disciples *"were continually in the Temple, praising and blessing God..."* In fact, there are numerous additional references to Apostles Peter, John and Paul, as well as many others of Jesus' followers worshiping in the Temple *after* Jesus had ascended. (See Acts 2:46, 3:1, 3, 8, 5:17 – 20, 25, 42, 21:26 – 27, 22:17, 24:12, 18, 26:21)

Now (after The Cross) does anyone really believe these would praise and bless God in the Temple if God (*Shekhinah*) were *not* present?! Do they think the Disciples were just going through the motions in worship as a matter of tradition (as Jews!) after what Jesus had taught them about His Father?

So, if the "squirmers" still want to squirm or if the "doubters" still want to doubt, they will need to "explain away" the Scriptural references offered here. It is my belief that one should assume that God's Word is first to be taken literally. That is, He says what He means and He means what He says! Several Scriptural verses say He (*Shekhinah*) was in the Temple right up until the withdrawal as described by the Rabbis and by Josephus. Again, these are: Haggai 2:7 — Zechariah 1:16 — Mathew 23:21 — Romans 9:4

Have you noticed how thoroughly God establishes this fact through His Word in each of our three divisions of Scripture?

But, there is more. The NASB translation of Matthew 23:38 yields:

"Behold, your house <u>is being left</u> to you desolate."

And the little-known and seldom-quoted Lamsa Bible[8] presents this verse as translated directly from the Aramaic of the *Peshitta*:

"Behold, your house <u>will be left</u> to you desolate."

If the NASB and the *Lamsa Bible* are actually providing more precise translations, this verse has a much deeper meaning than previously noticed. In saying it is (in-the-process-of being) or (will be) "left to you desolate," Jesus may have alluded to those strange goings-on in the Temple that would begin a few days later and continue for "forty years" until the Temple was destroyed. The Rabbis of the *Talmud* recognized this later when they said these "signs" meant *Shekhinah* was going to withdraw. However, by that time perhaps few or none of them recalled or knew that Jesus had said this was going to occur. However, Josephus has said: "So these publicly declared, that this signal foreshewed the desolation that was coming upon them." (See Appendix A.)

Answering those critics who say the Lord would never have occupied "Herod's Temple," I believe the Lord would take exception to calling His Holy House, "Herod's Temple." Besides, there were numbers of Kings of Judah who were far more despicable than Herod; and despite their idolatry, sin and disobedience, the Divine Presence remained faithfully in the Holy of Holies right up until the situation was absolutely hopeless — as at *Chanukah* Season, 69 C.E.

But, what about the "den-of-thieves" remark? Again, the clear answer is in the words of Jesus Himself:

"...*make not my Father's House a house of merchandise.*" *(John 2:16)*

Did you get that?! Jesus thought of the Temple as, "His Father's House." (*Note: Jesus did not call it "Herod's Temple!"*) Again, the Temple on Jerusalem's Temple Mount was not just a big synagogue or in any way like a mere "church" building. If His Father were *not* dwelling in His House, it would be just another building, with no reason for Jesus to object to the moneychangers.

Also, in Luke 19:47, just after He had called it "*a den of thieves*" in verse 46, Jesus taught daily in the Temple. Now, why was it OK for Jesus to be in this "den of thieves," but not OK for His Father, the Divine Presence, the Great "I AM?"

Even after all this, historical record from Josephus has stated, regarding the Temple after the *Shekhinah* Event: "For thou couldst be no longer a fit place for God." (Reference 2, *Wars*, 5.1.3/19)

We believe it has been shown conclusively, through Scripture and by documented historical records, *Shekhinah* was at Jerusalem until 69 C.E. But, some people are difficult to convince. Some just don't *want* to believe this story, regardless of any evidence. It is my prayer and hope that my readers will examine the evidence and judge for themselves.

Rending of The Veil

Traditional teaching says the significance of the rending of the Veil exists in that the Temple was then opened to all men. Because of the sin offering of our Savior, man was no longer separated from God. This romantic position is based on the premise that the "Veil" was all that had been separating men from God. Part of this same teaching is sometimes augmented by claiming the Glory of God withdrew from the Temple at that same instant, when Jesus "*gave up the Ghost.*"

But, "There they go, again!" This is another example of Romantic symbolism that certain Christian teachers have conceived as a result of a lack of understanding (and acceptance!) that God had a residence among the Jewish people. We might say it was sort of the Lord's Holy Condominium" here on Earth. God's Divine Presence, *Shekhinah*, actually dwelt in that most Holy chamber, the Holy of Holies. This was definitely not just a synagogue.

Those who might believe they could have just strolled into that Holy Chamber after they describe it as "then opened to all men," would have met tragic endings as they opened the curtains. Only the High Priest was allowed to enter on *Yom Kippur*. Otherwise, a few workmen (carpenters, roofers, masons, etc.) would be given special dispensation by the Rabbinate in order to enter for maintenance and repairs.

I fully agree that the Temple was then opened for man, brought about as a "sign" at the death of Jesus, because He now is our Intercessor at the Throne of God, the Father. Nevertheless, the traditional version leads to a very "romantic" doctrine, but it is just not in line with the facts as recorded by historians and Judaic Law, and finally even by the Bible itself. By contrast, when we become aware of these facts, this event becomes even more spectacular, even more glorifying of our Lord Jesus Christ and of His Father than the Gospels ever revealed to us when taken just by themselves.

There were actually three veils; not just the large, thick, braided curtain at the entrance to the Temple main building (*H'ekhal*). Two additional veils, presumably much thinner, separated the Holy Place from the Holy of Holies. These two were placed in lieu of the two cedar partitions that similarly divided the *H'ekhal* in the First Temple (I Kings 6:16). *Talmud Yoma* 52a explains this was necessary in order that the High Priest would avoid an "affront" to the Lord by approaching Him directly, just striding into His Holy Chamber as maybe one would walk into his neighbor's living room, for example.

These two veils were placed one cubit apart (about 18 inches), so the High Priest, on the Day of Atonement, would be required to "sidle" along carrying the ash censer between the veils with a sort of sideways "scissor-step." He approached the veils (see Illus. 22: The Sanctuary of the 2nd Temple, Page 155) by first traversing along the north wall of the Holy Place, so as to avoid walking past the candlestick (*Menorah*). He did this so that his immaculate priestly robe would not be "sooted" by the candles.

Next he turned to pass southward across the chamber and behind the Altar of Incense to eventually reach the entrance opening between the veils at the south wall. Now, as described before, he continued by "scissoring" between the veils to finally enter the Holy of Holies at the north wall. He then came before the Divine Presence to plead atonement for Israel's sins.

Thus, we find this romantic notion about the "veil" being "rent in twain" and ending man's separation from God is faulted because of casual knowledge concerning details of the Temple. This is also paradoxical in that most of these same critics who say God was not in the Holy of Holies at the time of Jesus are the same ones who tell us this "veil" separated man from God in a symbolic way.

The traditional story of course suggests that the "Veil" that was rent was a single curtain separating the Holy of Holies from the Holy Place; whereas, *Talmud* states there were two veils. (See Illus. 22: The Sanctuary of the 2nd Temple, Page 155) Most commentaries refer to "the Veil of the Temple" as separating those same chambers. However, the *Lamsa Bible* confirms, in all three Gospels of Matthew, Mark and Luke, that "the curtains *at the door of the Temple* were torn in two, from the top to the bottom."

Traditional teaching has been unaware that there were in fact two veils separating the two chambers and that the huge, thick "Babylonian curtain" covered the entrance to the *H'ekhal*.

This void of knowledge is evidenced even in popularly acclaimed models of the Second Temple as renovated by King Herod. The huge 30 ft. x 60 ft. curtain was arguably the most glorious of all the Temple furnishings, robust in its coloring with hues of red, blue and purple. It must have been a magnificent sight for those who could position themselves to view it as the sun was beaming through Nicanor's Gate, directly illuminating the Veil with all those colors.

But, even with the Veil at the entrance torn apart, how could the centurion see into the Temple through the entrance doors located just behind the Veil?

One could not just peer into the *H'ekhal* as if the Veil were like a drapery across an open doorway or portal, for example. More detailed information about the Temple reveals to us from Josephus and the *Talmud* (*Middoth* 4:1) that a complex arrangement of four folding doors ("gates") stood just behind the Veil (or curtain) at the entrance. From Chapter 7 we may recall that *Yoma* 39b told of the doors in the *H'ekhal* having opened by themselves during those "spooky" forty years. So, maybe all of the doors opened at this time...by themselves!

Then to be able to "peer" into the *H'ekhal*, these doors would have to either be collapsed as a result of the earthquake or because they were opened at the time. In Chapter 6 it was noted that only the northern half of these folding doors was opened and then only on certain occasions. However, even the north doorway would leave an opening only about seven or eight feet wide on that side for the centurion or anyone else at The Cross to be able to see the inside of the House of God after the Veil was torn. Such a narrow opening would have appeared almost as a slit when observed from *Olivet* summit.

And what about the Holy of Holies? Do they believe God's Divine Presence in the Temple was just arrayed out in the middle of the Temple floor? Or that the Temple was merely "symbolic" of God's Presence? We Gentiles just sometimes have difficulty in accepting that the Jews are God's Chosen People and that He did indeed dwell in their midst, visibly, in a "House" built for Him by those Special People.

But there is much more to this "veil" story. We are going to stand at the Precious feet of our Lord on that Cross, next to the centurion; and we shall "see" as "when he 'saw' all these things that had happened." (Matthew 27:50 – 54) As we have shown from Scripture, since the Temple faced eastward, (Ezekiel 8:16) and since the Jerusalem cemetery of the Second Temple period was, and is today, east of the City, the only way the centurion and his squad could have "seen" these things was if they had been standing east of the Temple on the western slope of *Olivet*. They could not have seen the Veil rent nor the graves opened from any position west of the Temple, such as the Church of the Holy Sepulchre or The Garden Tomb vicinity. (Not unless they had searchlights, mirrors, and binoculars!)

We have shown some evidence in Chapter 5 indicating why the Judeans of the Second Temple period chose *Olivet* for their cemetery. Further justification for that site exists in Judaic Law. The Jews would just never have buried their dead on the west side of the City, next to the latrines, as Professor Yadin[14] has shown were northwest of the City.

Nevertheless, regardless of the Law and tradition, it should be difficult for any Believer to agree that God the Father would sacrifice His only son just someplace out beyond the "back door" of the Temple! Outrageous thought! They should also have to consider that *all* of the Jewish sacrifices (which certainly do point to Jesus!) were offered in front (east) of the Temple. In fact that most important Jewish rite, the burning of the Red Heifer, was offered at a point due east and about a Sabbath Day's journey from the Holy of Holies. Now, it just appears logical that God would also *"provide Himself, a Lamb for a burnt offering,"* as that most important of *all* offerings...East of the Temple! Of course, it is not easy to abolish twenty centuries of traditional belief — even when hard facts are presented to refute those beliefs.

Painful and disappointing as it is to find that some of our most revered Holyland sites are not authentic, some of this "romantic" tradition (and "tourist" tradition) just does not hold up in the face of truth. And our Lord teaches us always to seek and defend the truth, in all things. This just means we have to "unstiffen" some of our past teaching and look a little deeper.

This happens in the fields of science and engineering all the time. The more we test, the more we learn about "perfecting" theory in order eventually to get theory and test to agree — eventually reaching the truth. We cannot afford to assume we are doing things right just because:

- We've always done it that way.
- We must be doing something right. – Look at our achievements.
- You can't argue with success.

Truth finally caught up with NASA management on 28 January 1986. We must look more deeply and do our best continually to correlate Scripture and secular records as they complement each other. (Rightly dividing the Word of God.) We must strive to do as Daniel the Prophet said man would do in the "last days" (Daniel 12:4). We must *"run to and fro"* through the Scriptures and we will have *"increased knowledge"* of end-time prophecies as we look at history, science, etc., and compare with fulfilled and unfulfilled prophecy. We who live in the "last days" have a better opportunity to have "increased knowledge" concerning "the end of days." We moderns have the advantage of 20/20 hindsight, as we are able to look back at Scripture, science, history, and archaeology over all those centuries. Thus, we draw ever closer to THE TRUTH.

But, before X-teen millions of my fellow Believers jump all over me — I am certainly not saying the Bible needs to be tested. The TRUTH needs to be tested. We must never close our minds to secular facts, especially when these facts bring new "light" to Scripture; (even though it may show our traditional interpretation of Scripture to have been in error.)

A Lesson for Us: The Jewish people overlooked their Redeemer because this gentle Galilean didn't fit their traditional interpretations of Messianic prophecy. They were (and still are) taught that Israel was the suffering Messiah. They had been (and still are) expecting the conquering Messiah, not this peasant "misfit!" They have surely been blinded by tradition. So have some of us Gentiles.

What, then, did the Centurion See?

He saw the earthquake open the graves of many Old Testament Saints who were buried on that western *Olivet* slope. Several tombs of those Blessed are, at least "traditionally," located there even to this day. (See Illus. 20: Jerusalem as it Appeared in 70 C.E., Page 153.) The tombs of Zechariah, Haggai, and Malachi for example, are well-known tourist sites at the present time.

And yes — he saw the Veil *"rent-in-twain."* But, how could he determine if the Veil was parted at 3 P.M., *"the ninth hour,"* as he would be squinting into the newly undarkened sun, which was above and behind the Temple? Scripture does not tell us how he was able to see this. Nevertheless, we know for certain that he did see it, because God says he saw it. That is truth. However, common sense tells us that, since the Temple faced eastward, he could not possibly have seen this from any position west of the Temple.

Sound logic also reveals that under normal conditions, he could not have seen that the outer Veil was torn, because it was either in the shade of the *H'ekhal* portico (150 feet high) or because the sun was possibly still darkened. (See Matthew 27:45 and Luke 23:44) In either case, *under ordinary conditions* (sun or no sun), it would have been impossible to see the Veil even from the Mount of Olives at that time. (See Illus. 13: Temple Mt. "At the 9th hour", Page 79)

Further illustration pertaining to visibility of Veil details from the Mount of Olives is provided in *Talmud, Shekalim* 8:4. It is stated that the Veil, the thick (over three inches) braided curtain across the Temple doorway, was spread out on the roof of the colonnade each time a new Veil was produced. This was done twice each year. The Veil was displayed in this manner "so that the people might behold its fair workmanship" from the summit of the Mount of Olives. Otherwise, only the menfolk could see the Veil when they brought their sacrifices into the Court of the Israelites. Remember, the women and girls, underage boys, and of course all lepers were not permitted beyond the Court of Women. This biannual exhibition was likely their only opportunity to see and admire this magnificent Temple furnishing.

At this point some traditionalists have actually come out with the defense:

Well, the Bible doesn't say they saw the Veil. It only says they saw the earthquake. Maybe somebody told the soldiers afterward about the Veil having been torn.

One traditionalist was so desperate to wriggle from the Truth here that he seriously proposed that *other* Roman soldiers observed the rending of the Veil from atop Antonia Fortress' southeast tower. That tower, according to Josephus, *Wars* 5.5.8/242 – 244, was erected adjacent to the north wall of the Temple and was much taller than the other three towers. In this way, the activities of Jews in the Temple courts below could be monitored for formation of plots and rebellions, just by noting "who" was talking to "whom," "when," etc. (See Illus. 20: Jerusalem as it Appeared in 70 C.E., Page 153) In his wriggling, this doubter was never able to explain how an observer above and even somewhat west of the Temple portico (porch) would be able to view the Veil. The Veil was *recessed* into the face of the Temple wall and was underneath the portico. It therefore could not be viewed even from the side of the Temple (See Illus. 16: Isometric View of 2nd Temple, Page 149) Neither could he explain why Matthew says the *centurion* at The Cross *saw* it, and not some other soldier in Antonia Tower.

Now, come on! Next, I suppose if they can wriggle away from this one, they will want us to believe "maybe" the Roman soldiers went over later that evening after "chow" to inspect the damage at the Temple and *that* is when they saw the torn Veil. Stop squirming! Scripture says: *"They saw the earthquake and those things that were done."*

How was the centurion able to see this? And, what was terrifying about an earthquake? A torn curtain? A few open graves? (Those saints appeared in Jerusalem only after The Resurrection.) Roman soldiers terrified by such as this?

The earthquake possibly caused collapse of lintels or other structures supporting all three veils, causing them to part for perhaps just a moment. However, some theologians, both from Judaism and from Christianity, in fact believe the Veil was torn by supernatural means, rather than merely as a result of "gravity" causing the rip. It was noted earlier that the doors at the front of the *H'ekhal* also would have to be opened or collapsed by this tremor, as maybe they were. And, oh yes, this now opened the Holy of Holies for man to approach God, but only through His Son.

And there was perhaps something truly breathtaking about that "moment." The centurion saw something very spectacular (yes, frightening and terrifying!), which glorifies Jesus and Almighty God as One in a flash! And that was a flash of brilliant light!

The "Fire:" the Glory of The Lord!

Beaming straight through the parted veils from the Holy of Holies! Brighter than the sun, a brilliant shaft of light from the Judeans' Temple across the Kidron now illuminated this Galilean who had just before cried out with a loud voice, *"It is finished!"* (From Mark 15:37 and John 19:30) and now was suspended in death on The Cross above the centurion.

What a sight that must have been! Now we understand how the centurion "saw" that the Veil was torn. The Brilliance of the Glory of the Lord — the *Shekhinah* — burst through the opening of the parted Veil. What a dramatic event. How much more dynamic and glorifying than the "traditional" scenario. Of course the centurion was terrified. He had just encountered Almighty God face-to-face — the Fire — the *Shekhinah* — in Person!

Furthermore — and this is most important, as we have shown in our detailed study of the "sight picture" of the Veil through the open gate — the centurion would have to be standing at the same spot from which the High Priest must "direct his gaze carefully." Just like the priest, the centurion would not be able to see the Veil even from a few meters away from that precise location on the summit of the Mount of Olives.

Now, we don't know whether any of the other Gospel writers were at *Golgotha* or not. Nevertheless, even if Matthew, Mark, and some of the others had been "hiding out" somewhere else on *Olivet*, they could not have seen the Veil. The only ones who could have seen it were standing at The Cross and "directing their gaze carefully" through the East Gate at "the ninth hour." This is just simply a matter of geometry. (Illus. 17: Detailed Elevation of

2nd Temple, Page 150, Illus. 18: Elevation Profile of Temple and Temple Mt., Page 151, and Illus. 19: Elev. Profile: Temple Mt., Kidron VLY., Mt. Olivet, Page 152)

Earlier we demonstrated that Jesus willed His own death at the *"ninth hour"* because He had to maintain His Holy Schedule of fulfilling the Law. There may also be another reason for this timing. The Lord knew where the sun would be at 3 P.M. and He used this condition to enhance the drama of the occasion to those standing at The Cross where they were to see *"those things."* Jesus wanted those Roman "GI's" to be startled and terrified by that blinding flash coming through the parted veils. The flash had to be much more prominent (and terrifying) coming from the darkened face of the Temple in the afternoon than it would have been had the Veil been in bright sunlight. Therefore, "the ninth hour" was "scheduled" by the Lord in order to achieve this dramatic effect on His executioners and to still permit honoring the Sabbath and fulfilling of the Feasts.

Notice now the beautiful "picture" that has developed:

- Three veils represent the Father, Son, and Holy Spirit.
- Entrance to the Temple (representing Heaven) can be achieved only through the now "torn" outer Veil.
- The torn Veil represents the "broken" body of the Son, Jesus.
- *"...He hath consecrated for us, through the Veil, that is to say, His flesh;"* — (From Hebrews 10:20)
- The other two veils were also parted to reveal the Glory of God to be seen by men at the instant of His "payment" for their sins.
- A similar picture is portrayed at the Passover meal (*Seder*) when the second *matzah* (*Afikoman*) is broken and "hidden away" for a time and later revealed ("found") and enjoyed by all present.

Some traditional teaching contends the Glory of God withdrew from the Temple at the moment Jesus *"gave up the ghost"* when the *"veil was rent in twain."* Again, for all this time we have been accepting a very convenient, simplistic, romantic interpretation; but based on assumption — not fact, Biblical or secular; completely ignoring the documented history of the Event. Thus, such assumption results in gross inaccuracy and therefore misses the truth and the blessings that come with it.

This assumption completely ignores the requirement for fulfillment of Ezekiel's prophecy of the *Shekhinah* withdrawal. But, the traditional teaching gets around that problem by very conveniently assuming, again, that Ezekiel Chapters 10 and 11 were fulfilled only before the First Temple was destroyed. Although there is no record of such an event concerning the First Temple, there is ample record of His withdrawal from the Second Temple forty years after Jesus was crucified.

10

Will the Real "Chosen People" Please Stand?

God forgave righteous Jewish people at The Cross – Debunking "Replacement Theology" – The Lord deals with Jewish people differently – Messiah "hidden" — We Christians can "see" because Jewish people are "blinded."

Now, we must address another very fundamental debate question: If, as we have been taught all these years (centuries), God was finished with the Jews after they rejected Jesus, then why did His Divine Presence remain in the Temple for another forty years?

Here we have a real "hard-point" for many Christian teachers (who have, in turn, been taught by their teachers), when we challenge the traditional stories we have all been taught. Since we have been taught that the Jews stand in rejection from God because they rejected Jesus as Messiah, the answer to the aforementioned question becomes very perplexing. This is really "the bottom line" for why traditional teaching has such difficulty in accepting a story that claims the Divine Presence remained with Israel until 69 C.E.

Since I am neither a theologian nor a minister, I hesitate to debate on this point with seminary-educated ministers. However, I do wish to surface this argument for all to see. It has been closeted far too long. I wish then, to ask all who are knowledgeable of the

Scriptures (pastors, Christian laity, Jewish worshipers, Rabbis) to examine facts and Scripture and to answer this question in the light of truth — tradition cast aside.

It is appropriate here that we examine this number "forty" because it must bear significance concerning those Jewish people who were touched in *any* way by Jesus' ministry. What Holy Purpose might God have held to warrant His remaining with His Holy people Israel forty years after they had rejected the Son of God?

In Biblical numerology, forty is God's number for testing or probation. The testing ordeal of The Great Flood was of the duration of "forty days and forty nights." Jesus was tempted forty days in the wilderness. Nineveh was granted forty days to repent. Moses spent forty years of exile in *Midian* as probation. The children of Israel were tested forty years in the *Sinai* wilderness to reckon those who were fit to enter the Promised Land.

It is reasoned therefore that God sought to test His Chosen through those forty years after The Crucifixion. He accomplished this by showing signs in the Temple. Those of His children who recognized that a huge mistake had occurred at Passover, 30 C.E. became the core of Christ's Church. God tested all of those who had been on the scene during Jesus' ministry and then He closed their Temple and cut off their worship. Since the destruction of the Temple, He has dealt with the Jewish people in His own way. God would seem to hold those who were in Judea during Jesus' time to a different standard than for those who never saw Him. Jesus will judge all those Jewish people of the past many centuries when He arrives for them to look upon Him whom they have pierced.

It seems that God did forgive them ("for they knew not") at The Cross. But then, through "signs" in the Temple and through the Disciples via the Holy Spirit, He ministered to Israel for a full generation (forty years) after The Crucifixion. During those forty years many Jews did come to find Jesus as their Messiah, including some of those from the Aaronic priestly orders. Acts 6:7 states that "...*a great company of the priests were obedient to the faith.*" (We seem often to forget or ignore the fact that the first "Christians" were "Jews.")

But then, after those forty years, for those who still refused to repent and return to Him, it seems He said:

"I will go back to My Place.

Your sacrifices are for naught and your House is desolate.

I am going to punish you — for two days.

I will refine you (in the fire) as silver.

But in "the third day" I will return for you and you will look upon Me whom you pierced and you will mourn for Him as for an only Son.

Then we will spend eternity together in peace and all of your iniquities and transgressions will be removed and forgotten forever and ever."

Jews cannot be saved under the Law unless they repent of their sins. The Law cannot save them from judgment and death for their sins, but it can lead them to repentance if they come to realize that they cannot, by their works, "keep" the Law.

Christians have a similar problem. They cannot be saved from their sins unless they repent — Law or no Law. But, all Christians have that "Blessed Assurance" that if we repent, our sins have been already forgiven because we accept Messiah's payment for our sins. Jews must take a similar route to salvation, but can have no assurance of being acceptable. They can only hope they have pleased Him. Nevertheless, if they love the Lord, they will regret and repent of having offended Him in even the smallest way. Would any deny the same is true for all who would claim to be of Christ's church?

A poignant note on Jewish apprehension concerning their salvation is seen from *Talmud, Berakoth* 28b, a statement attributed to Rabbi Yohanan ben Zakkai, noted and beloved patriarch discussed in Chapter 7. He is lamenting his fear of death, even though he was considered a very righteous man.

When this beloved sage was on his deathbed, he began to weep as some of his followers gathered to visit. Listen now to his humility and trembling at "meeting his Maker."

> *They asked, "Lamp of Israel, pillar of the right hand, mighty hammer, wherefore weepest thou?" He replied: "If I were being taken before a human king who is here today and tomorrow in the grave, whose anger with me would not last forever, who would not imprison me forever and who would not put me to an everlasting death, and whom I could persuade with words or could bribe with money, even so I would weep. But, now I am going before the Supreme King of Kings, the Holy One, Blessed be He, who lives and endures forever and ever, whose anger is everlasting, who may imprison me forever and ever, who may put me into an everlasting death, and whom I cannot persuade with words or bribe with money. Nay! When there are two ways before me, one leading to Paradise and the other to Gehinnom (Hell), and I do not know to which I will be taken, shall I not weep?"*

Although he was a very righteous man, beloved by the Rabbinate and by the people, Rav ben Zakkai still was not confident that the "Supreme King of Kings" would accept him and take him to Paradise. Although ben Zakkai knew he was a sinner, sadly he did not know of "The Good News" saying that his sins — no matter how manifold or foul — would be washed "white as snow" by the blood of his Redeemer, Jesus. All of us could learn something from Rav ben Zakkai about humility concerning our own "goodness" and "works" in this world.

We must note here, however, the contrast with the Apostle Paul, who referred to himself with what could be marked as restrained boastfulness, as the Lord's "prisoner." Even as Paul contemplated and awaited the headsman's inevitable sword, from his prison cell he wrote: "It's not to worry!" As comforting to his helper Timothy and to the church they had founded at Philippi, he said in Philippians 1:21, "...*to live is Christ, and to die is gain.*"

How different and how ecstatic it is for all of us "prisoners of the Lord" to contemplate our being "imprisoned forever," with Him who will give us everlasting life; and who has already forgotten His anger at our transgressions; and who perpetually must persuade us to share His infinite riches without asking or expecting even the tiniest insignificant gift or offering from us. We only weep for joy and we know where we are going because we have that Blessed

Assurance — merely because we have accepted His most precious gift — Messiah, the Son of God.

Penitent Jewish people who live with righteous intentions and who love the Lord may be "sealed" for Heaven, but — as with Rabbi Yohanan ben Zakkai — they cannot know if they have pleased Him.

Nor can you or I know whether they have pleased Him; just as you or I cannot know whether another is really "saved" or "born again." Only you and God know whether you have really accepted Messiah.

Indeed, Christians can truthfully shout that expression cultivated by the Jewish mamas:

It's Not to Worry!

None of us is qualified to say whether Jewish people, even after 70 C.E., stand in rejection from God. He said He would provoke them to jealousy (Romans 11:11), but I cannot agree that He has rejected them. After all, He has resurrected them as the nation Israel.

In our large "family" of nations, Israel (the Jewish people) may be compared to that one favorite child in some large families. The picture that develops is interesting:

- That one special child is usually somewhat spoiled because he knows he is the father's favorite.
- The father is often more severe in punishment when his favorite disappoints him, even though he seems to let the favorite "get away with more" before he finally administers punishment.
- The father is sometimes more strict with his "laws" for this favorite because he loves this child just a little bit more in a very special way and wants more for him and expects more from him.
- This entire situation is often exasperating to the other children, but they are not jealous and they love that favorite child also (sometimes even contributing to spoiling him) because they love their father and they know also how much their father loves that special child.
- The other children know also that their father loves each of them very much as well, but that one special child is still their father's favorite. (The "apple of his eye," etc.)
- He is chosen. They accept this and they love him because they love their father.

Still, some Christians will insist: "But, we are chosen! Don't you believe what Paul says in II Thessalonians 2:13?" Yes, of course, we are chosen, but the Jewish people are "*chosen above all the nations.*" (Deuteronomy 14:2) We must accept this. — It is the Word of God.

Something to Think About!

During the past 2000 years the Jewish people have taken quite a "shellacking" from Christian Gentiles. When the subject of "anti-Judaism" (or anti-Semitism) arises, we have a few thoughts that we Gentiles should consider before we do any more "shellacking" of our Jewish neighbors on this planet.

James, the Just – "half" brother of Jesus – was considered by many of his contemporaries to have been the "second most righteous" man who ever lived. James was Bishop of the 1st century Church at Jerusalem. He was martyred at the "Pinnacle of the Temple," from where Satan tried to tempt Jesus to leap. [See Josephus[2] *Antiq*. 20.9.1 (200)].

Now, just think for a moment. – Would you condemn or ridicule or debase any man such as this "James" ? He truly was, after all, a Jew. Although James certainly was what we would consider a Christian – "Christians" had not yet been invented. He was also a "brother" of Jesus; although, James – just as many others – did not at first recognize that his elder brother is Messiah.

Knowing all these things, it is difficult to believe that true Christians would persecute or malign a man such as James. Then, the thought arrives to confront us that perhaps James married and had descendants. After all, Peter (Simon) was also high in the early Church authority, but he was surely married. (Mark 1:30) It is possible also that Jesus' other siblings had descendants as well.

Today then, there are surely descendants of the family of Jesus among us – some perhaps still worshiping as Jews – but, some perhaps now worshiping as Christian Gentiles!

It would be well for all of us to recall these possibilities before we are inclined to discriminate, harass or persecute Jewish people – IN ANY WAY ! – They actually might be distant relatives of *You-Know-Who!* – Moreover – and closer-to-home – and, especially if there is *any* Jewish background in your ancestry – Just T H I N K of it! – YOU and I might even be descendants from *any* of that privileged family and *unknowingly* therefore a distant "blood" relative of Jesus as well as His Spiritual descendants! – Definitely something worth thinking about!

Can a "*Jew*" Love The Lord?

Over the years, many well-meaning Christian teachers have sincerely put forth the concept that we Christians (not the Jews) are now God's Chosen People. This concept is what Rev. Vendyl Jones[4] has labeled as "Replacement Theology." There is some indication, though not necessarily a dramatic thrust, from this story of *Shekhinah* that says the Jews are still God's Chosen People and that His everlasting covenant with them is still in effect.

This "replacement" philosophy may have originated from a misunderstanding or misinterpretation of the New Covenant principle introduced by Jeremiah 31:31 – 34 and as quoted by Paul in his epistle to the Hebrews. Some theologians have taught therefore along the following lines:

- Jeremiah 31:31 says the Lord will make a New Covenant with the Jews.
- That New Covenant is salvation for sinners paid for by the blood of Jesus Christ.
- In rejecting Christ, therefore, they rejected the New Covenant.
- The first covenant is now obsolete and is no longer valid. (Here they refer to Hebrews 8:13.)
- The Jews, like all others who reject Christ, are therefore lost. There is no more to be said. The Jews are lost.

Please take a closer look now at this idea through the Scripture used as its base, beginning with Jeremiah 31:31,

"Behold, the days come, saith the Lord, that I will make a new covenant with the house of Israel, and with the house of Judah."

Then, verses 33 and 34,

"But this shall be the covenant that I will make with the house of Israel; After those days, saith the Lord I will put My Law in their inward parts, and write it in their hearts; and will be their God, and they shall be My people.

And they (Israel) shall teach no more every man his neighbor, and every man his brother, saying. "Know the Lord!": for they shall all know Me, from the least of them unto the greater of them, saith the Lord: for I will forgive their iniquity, and I will remember their sin no more."

Then, just after Paul quotes this passage, he says in Hebrews 8:13 (NASB),

"When He said "a new covenant," He has made the first (covenant) obsolete. But whatever is becoming obsolete and growing old is ready to disappear."

It is clear today that God has not yet put His Law *"in their inward parts;"* nor has He yet written it *"in their hearts."* Today we know also that *"every man his brother"* does not yet know Him. The key phrase here is *"after those days."* After what "days?" This is to say, after some time He will write His Law in their hearts — some time. He obviously has not done this yet for the Jews; although, he has most certainly done it for Christians, because Christians have already received the New Covenant. We have His Law placed *"in our inward parts"* and His Law is *"written in our hearts."* Yes, and He "remembers our sins no more!" We have Blessed Assurance. And remember — the first "Christians" were Jews. But not all. God said all Jewish people shall know Him when they reach His New Covenant — but not yet.

What about Paul saying the first covenant is obsolete, old, dying? Paul didn't say that, Paul said the first covenant was "becoming" obsolete, and it was "ready to disappear." Here, we need to remember that Paul, as well as all the other New Testament writers, was *certain* that Jesus was going to return in his lifetime. This point is extremely important. (Barnabas must have come up with this "two-day/two-thousand year theory" much later, after they had become aware that He had "delayed" His return.)

Paul just didn't have access to the Lord's time-table (and neither do we!). He didn't realize that "those days" were going to be about two thousand years of what Christians have called "The Church Age." Paul thought the New Covenant was going to begin imminently — as soon as Jesus returned! Paul and the others were expecting Jesus to return at any moment! This is why we read such an urgency — almost panic — in Paul's message to his Jewish brethren, especially. Paul truly believed that first covenant was *"becoming obsolete"* and *"was ready to disappear."* And that is true today as well. Time is short. We just don't know what "time" it is.

When Messiah arrives at *Olivet* summit *"after those days,"* the New Covenant will then begin for all Jews and for all who live on Earth. Then, the first covenant will disappear. The New Covenant then will be *"in their inward parts"* and will then be *"written in their hearts."* It is a Promise!

For us, Gentiles, to claim we are His Chosen, must be quite repugnant to even an agnostic Jewish person. It causes one to wonder how many Jewish people we may have turned away from recognizing that Jesus is their Messiah because of our insistence on such a cruel, judgmental, and erroneous concept through all these centuries of the Church Age. (Our Lord may judge us as presumptuous "impostors.")

The Lord has used Israel's blindness as an example lesson for Christian Gentiles. We see so clearly and vividly what Israel fails to see. We have persecuted and murdered and tortured and reviled and cursed the very ones who, although they are "blind," are responsible for providing *our* clear vision in beholding Messiah. Through their "blindness" we are made to "see."

Gentiles can be cleansed of sin (become righteous before God) only by approaching Him through their "burnt offering," Jesus. But there are some indications that Jews before and after Jesus can and have come to righteousness, through Messiah, by observing the Law. We must surely all agree that multitudes of Jews became so-called Old testament saints under the Law before the time of Jesus. How could they have achieved "sainthood?" Only by believing that Messiah is their Redeemer and by sincerely attempting to keep the Law and by loving the Lord their God with all their heart and with all their soul and with all their might and by loving their neighbors as themselves.

Only God can judge whether or not Jews truly love the Lord and are "keeping-the-Law" in their hearts — which is the only place that matters. Of course, since destruction of the Temple, Jews cannot keep the sacrifices as that part of the Law — except as they may sincerely yearn and mourn for such in their hearts. And, after all, we know each of the sacrifices is a representative "picture" of the Lamb of God — Messiah, Jesus of Nazareth.

We are driven now to wonder why modern Jewish scholars have not solved this mystery of recognizing their Messiah. This is especially difficult for "modern" Christians to fathom because of all the recent public discussion, books, movies, etc., relating better understanding of eschatology (study of "end times").

Indeed, Jewish scholars are forbidden, under threat of a curse, to study such things. They are *commanded* NOT to study to *"calculate the end."* That edict is pronounced in *Sanhedrin* 97b, saying: "Blasted be the bones of those who calculate the end." The Rabbis somehow derived this severe interpretation from Habakkuk 2:3 (in the Hebrew Scriptures); wherein it is stated: *"For the vision is yet for the appointed time, and it declareth of the end, and doth not lie..."* Following, it is stated that some will say that "since the predetermined time (for Messiah) has arrived, and yet He has not come, then He will never come." Shortly following is an admirable admonition from another group of Rabbis, however, to say: "But, even so, wait for Him, as it is written:"

'Though He tarry, wait for Him' (From Habakkuk 2:3)

We must then admire also the Rabbis' comments continuing: "If someone says that we look forward to His Coming, but He does not (come); Scripture saith:" (From Isaiah 30:18)

"And therefore will the Lord saith, that He may be gracious to you, and therefore will be exalted, that He may have mercy upon you."

Continuing, they inquire: "But since we look forward to His Coming and He does likewise, what delays His Coming?'" — The Rabbis answer that He delays because we are not yet worthy of it. But, they say we will be rewarded because, as it is written (again, from Isaiah 30:18):

"Blessed are all they that wait for Him."

Then, if they do earnestly yearn for and await Messiah hopefully (as we yearn for His return), Jews yearn for the same One the Church awaits. They just missed Him when he was in their midst. He might forgive them for failing to recognize or comprehend that He really was their Messiah, but He will not forgive those who do not love Him.

One of the best sources for answering this question concerning the Jewish approach to salvation can be derived from perhaps the third most famous Jew who ever lived, Paul of Tarsus. (Third after Jesus and Moses.)

But Paul said: "I am a man which am a Jew from Tarsus" Acts 21:39.

Yes, Paul introduced himself as "a Jew," and yet he was certainly what we would call a "Christian." How could a Jew be a Christian? Well, for one thing, the term "Christian" had not yet been created. Furthermore, his statement demonstrates clearly that Paul considered himself to be a Jew. He did not give up all his "Jewishness" in order to accept Jesus as Messiah. He didn't need to give it up. He was proud to be Jewish.

So many conservative Christian teachers insist that one can no longer be Jewish after accepting Jesus as Messiah. They point so often to a single verse from Paul, in Galatians 3:28, in order to establish this claim, by saying:

There is neither Jew nor Greek...for ye are all one in Christ Jesus.

They omit the middle portion because they really aim to paraphrase this to say: "There is neither Jew nor Gentile because we are all Christians who believe in Christ." The middle portion, which they have omitted, reveals the true context or meaning, however, because it says,

"...there is neither bond nor free, there is neither male nor female: for ye are all one in Jesus Christ."

Of course we are united in Christ, but we cannot change our worldly status as bonded or free, male or female, and yes, Jew or Gentile. If you were born Jewish you *are* a Jew. And from what we have shown in this study, if you love the Lord your God, you should be proud to be Jewish! (And, if you love Him and if you read and study and believe His Word, you should now understand that Jesus of Nazareth is also Lord!)

Nobody recognized this more than Paul did in his ministry to Jews and Gentiles. Please listen now as Pastor Paul describes his evangelizing technique in I Corinthians 9:20 – 21 (NEB).

"To Jews I became as a Jew, to win Jews; as they are subject to the Law of Moses, I put myself under the Law to win them, although I am not myself subject to it.

To win Gentiles, who are outside the Law. I made myself as one of them, although I am not in truth outside God's law, being under the law of Christ."

Thus, Paul considered that Jews and Gentiles were "different" as people, but both are under God's Law. Similarly he noted, slaves could not change their worldly status as slaves, nor could men or women (then or now!) change their sex, although they were "all one in Christ Jesus." And, notice — Paul says "I am a Jew" — (not "was a Jew") — but not under the Law of Moses — because now he has that "Blessed Assurance!"

Paul also said God looks only for what is in the heart as he writes in Romans 2:29:

"But he is a Jew, which is one inwardly, and circumcision is that of the heart, in the spirit, and not in the letter; whose praise is not of men, but of God."

He expresses a somewhat nonsectarian view in Hebrews 11:6 (NASB) as he describes in the most simple terms how man must come to God.

"And without faith it is impossible to please Him, for He who comes to God must believe that He is, and that He is a rewarder of those who seek Him."

Paul told the "Hebrews" (his brethren) and Gentiles that the Lord is open to any who seek Him and believe Him — have faith in Him. Moreover, Paul seems to have "said-it-all" in Romans 10:12:

"For there is no difference between the Jew and the Greek: for the same Lord over all is rich unto all that call upon Him."

Father, Forgive Us!

Those Jewish people who do attempt to come to God through the Law are really "doing it the hard way." Famous evangelist Hal Lindsey has referred to these choices as Plan "A" and Plan "B." Plan "A" entails coming to God through the Law given to Moses. — A difficult — make that *impossible*(!) — route for any mere man to follow on his own merit. The Law coming from a Perfect God is Perfect and must be obeyed Perfectly or it becomes meaningless. Man is imperfect and cannot therefore follow God's Perfect Law Perfectly. Therefore, "salvation" or communion with God is impossible for man via the Law. However,

God *may* be merciful to believing Jews who have repented and have earnestly striven to obey God through attempting to keep the Law. God will judge ALL of us by what is in our hearts.

Plan "B" is of course the "easy" way, through Jesus Messiah. Those Jews who have come to Jesus and accepted Him as their "burnt offering" have the Law fulfilled (kept) Perfectly through Jesus. They have that "Blessed Assurance."

Some conservative Christians express righteous indignation at any idea of Jews being acceptable to God without first accepting Jesus as Messiah: "That is like saying Jesus died in vain!" Of course not! Jesus died for all. The Jewish problem is that they just haven't identified or recognized Jesus, yet. Many Jews have already "accepted" Messiah in their hearts, but they still don't know He is actually Jesus of Nazareth. If they are truly still waiting for Messiah and "keeping" the Law, *in their hearts,* they may have reached salvation — (*But,* no assurance!) They are just going to be really surprised when they "look upon" and recognize Him who was "pierced" and with those wounds in His hands, standing up there on the Mount of Olives on That Day. We cannot understand His logic, but this is the way God has chosen to deal with His Chosen People.

Nevertheless, it seems that the Lord has permitted Jews to come unto Himself through the sacrifices, which we Christians recognize as representing The Lamb of God — Messiah — Jesus. "Why can't they see this?" we ask, impatiently. With even more impatience, we frequently quote from Jesus' words through another famed Jewish writer in John 14:6:

"I am the way, the truth, and the life: no man cometh unto the Father, but by me."

With this we demonstrate unequivocally that Jews (or anyone) can only approach God through Jesus. And this has certainly not been rescinded. The tragedy is that Jewish people are approaching the Lord through Jesus IF they have the Law and repentance for their sins and the love for their Lord in their hearts. They just don't see Jesus reflected in all this, but He is there.

This same Jewish writer gives some light in this direction in one of his epistles, written somewhat later — after he had been preaching the Gospel of Jesus Christ to Jews — in Judea and Samaria.

"Whoever believes that Jesus is the Christ is born of God; and whoever loves the Father loves the child born of Him." (I John 5:1)

If one truly loves God, the Father, that person also loves all men, who certainly are "born of Him." It then becomes obvious that he also loves the Son, Jesus, because Jesus IS God. Jesus said, *"I and My Father are One."* (John 10:30) And, remember that Greatest Commandment:

"Thou shalt love the Lord thy God with all thy heart, and with all thy soul, and with all thy mind. And, thou shalt love thy neighbor as thyself." (Matthew 22:37 – 39)

The Temple sacrifices and even Jewish worship today honors their Messiah (Jesus). Many Jewish people unknowingly love Jesus because they "love the Lord their God" and they hopefully await their Redeemer — Messiah, Son of David. (They just do not yet realize WHO He is.)

So, there is no ambiguity here. We still must come to God through Jesus. The Jewish sacrifices mean nothing without Jesus. They never did; because they only formed a "picture" of Him as He *"provided Himself — a lamb for a burnt offering."*

The Jewish "picture" of this situation is dramatized beautifully at the Passover meal (*Seder*), although its meaning is hidden from the Jews. The second piece of the three pieces of *matzah*, the *Afikoman*, is "broken" and then "hidden away for a time" until after the meal has been consumed. Then, the "broken" piece is searched for and then "found" and eaten as the third cup of wine is taken. The Cup of Redemption! This is the cup that Jesus declined at the Last Supper, saying, *"...until that day that I drink it new in the Kingdom of God."* (Mark 14:25)

Most Christians can immediately see that the broken piece, the second Person of the Triune God, represents Jesus. Following this logic, we also can see this with the third cup of wine taken; i.e., "Redemption" is delivered with the recovered (found) broken piece after two "days!" Each previous cup represents passage of one "day" or one thousand years. Remember? — God said:

"After two days He will revive us: In the third day He will raise us up, And we shall live in His sight." (Hosea 6:2)

Messiah is in the *Seder*. Jewish worshipers just have not seen Him...yet! Sadly, they are still waiting for "Elijah" (who appeared in "type" as John the Baptist) and they are still looking for their *Afikoman*. The "two days," pictured in the *Seder* as two cups of wine, are nearing completion now as we approach 2000 years after God "went back to His Place." — Time is short.

Christians who study "typology" are aware that the *Afikoman* as well as the Jewish people themselves are actually "types" of Messiah. Like Messiah and the broken *Afikoman* wafer, Israel was "broken" and scattered — "hidden" — among the nations for two-thousand years — two "days." At the end of the Church Age, when Messiah arrives, the nations will "find" Israel AND Messiah and their final TRUE Purpose in God's Plan. At that time, Israel will be "eaten" — (enjoyed) — by all nations and will reach her Glorious Destiny. This is truly a reflection of the "broken" *Afikoman*, hiding it for *"two days"* symbolically at the *Seder* meal, then to be found and eaten and enjoyed by all participants.

One prominent Protestant body has adopted a resolution[23] acknowledging that Judaism has not been replaced by Christianity and that God has not rejected the Jewish people nor has He withdrawn or transferred His covenant. The story of the *Shekhinah* withdrawal appears to reinforce that position. Unfortunately for those Jews who have been persecuted, murdered, and scorned over the years, this story and the Church's resolution arrived 1,900 years late!

Consider the facts presented by this account as well as the resolution mentioned, excerpted as follows:

"This historical denial by the church has led to outright rejection of the Jewish people and to frequent violence. We pray for Divine grace that will enable us, more firmly than ever before, to turn from this path of rejection and persecution to affirm that Judaism has not been superseded by Christianity; that Christianity is not to be understood as the suc-

cessor religion to Judaism; God's covenant with the Jewish people has not been abrogated. God has not rejected the Jewish people, God is faithful in keeping covenant..."

Then, for those who *still* are not convinced that the Lord has not cast away His Chosen People, we lead them to these verses written by the Prophet Jeremiah 31:31 – 35, 36 and 37.

"Thus saith the Lord, which giveth the sun for a light by day, and the ordinances of the moon and of the stars for a light by night, which divideth the sea when the waves thereof roar; the Lord of hosts is His name.

If those ordinances depart from before Me, saith the Lord, then the seed of Israel also shall cease from being a nation before Me for ever.

Thus saith the Lord; if heaven above can be measured, and the foundations of the earth searched out beneath, I will also cast off all the seed of Israel for all that they have done, saith the Lord."

The Lord is emphatic in these words as He has said, *if* the sun, moon, and stars disappear, *then* Israel will cease forever to be a nation. And, *if* someone can measure Heaven, *then* He will "cast off " *all* of "naughty" Israel — "saith the Lord," AMEN. (Gentiles! Are you listening?!)

Yes, there is *"neither Jew nor Greek"* as a requirement to receive and accept the Lord's salvation through His Grace. And yes, both can only approach the Lord through His Son (the Lord) Messiah. Jewish Believers wait for Messiah to arrive. — Christian Believers wait for Messiah to return. The Father will not reject those who *still* are awaiting Him — if *in their hearts* they truly are waiting for Him.

Messiah, Son of Joseph – and a Carpenter!

An intriguing entry is noted in *Talmud, Sukkah* 52a, referring to the Scripture in Zechariah 12:12:

"And the land shall mourn, every family apart, the family of the house of David apart, and their wives apart..."

The narration asks about the cause of this mourning. A second century Rabbi Dosa replies that the reason is the slaying of "Messiah the son of Joseph." (Did you catch that? The "son of Joseph" was slain!) The text justifies such mourning through reference to Zechariah 12:10, as quoted from the Jewish *Tanakh:*

"...and they shall look upon Me because they have thrust Him through, and they shall mourn for Him as one mourneth for his only son..."

A detailed discussion follows concerning the time at which Messiah destroys Satan while the righteous weep and behold Satan, "the Evil Inclination," and ask how they were able to "overcome such a towering hill." Contrastingly, the wicked weep and behold this same "Evil Inclination" and ask why they were not able to "conquer this hair thread." (See also Isaiah 14:15 – 17.)

A single reference is made to Messiah the son of David which is certainly acknowledged as the Scriptural genealogy of Messiah. In fact, *Talmud* gives vent to an emotional outburst as the Rabbi pleads, "May He (Messiah) the son of David reveal Himself speedily in our days!" Christians should be enthusiastic knowing these very same words appear frequently throughout Jewish worship liturgy. Notably this includes the weekly Sabbath services in most synagogues and, especially, in the words spoken during the *Seder* Feast at the Passover.

The Promise of the Son descended from King David is given through several of the prophets, but nowhere is it stated so clearly as from Isaiah 9:6 – 7:

> *"...and His name shall be called Wonderful, Counselor, The Mighty God, The Everlasting Father, The Prince of Peace. Of the increase of His government and peace there shall be no end, upon the throne of David, and upon His kingdom, to order it, and to establish it with judgment and with justice from henceforth even for ever..."*

Later we shall attempt explanation as to how this "son of Joseph" tradition originated. The conclusion is not obvious, because there is no apparent direct Scriptural reference to such a person. This Messianic view has been handled down through Judaism from the distant past. Notice that Rabbi Dosa is from the second century. Jewish tradition relates that Messiah "the son of Joseph" is to be the "precursor" (forerunner) of Messiah the son of David, who will usher in the Messianic (Kingdom) Age after a period of great devastation on Earth.

Christianity, of course, teaches that Messiah is both "son of Joseph" and "son of David;" although the former is not of the tribe of Joseph, but actually the "adopted" son of Joseph of Nazareth — a mere carpenter! Christians also teach that John the Baptist, as a "type" of Elijah, was the precursor of Jesus. Furthermore Jesus, as "son of Joseph," was the "precursor" of His own appearance as a humble Rabbi from Nazareth. He will be glorified as "son of David" later upon His return to begin the Jewish Messianic Age, which is also the beginning of His Kingdom Age, bringing Glory and Peace on Earth to all men.

Again, Jewish people are just going to be really surprised to see that He is the same One whom they had *"thrust Him through."* We should also recall, in Zechariah 13:6:

> *"And one shall say unto Him, 'What are these wounds between thy hands?' Then He shall answer, 'Those with which I was wounded in the house of My friends.'"*

It is interesting to observe that this verse is quoted from The Holy Scriptures, the Jewish *Tanakh*, which Gentiles call "The Old Testament." The words differ slightly from that of the King James Version, but render the same thought. Now, watch what happens next.

Rodkinson's *Talmud*[28] states (*Sukkah* 52 in *Soncino Talmud*[21]) that Jewish tradition considered two Messiahs: one to be "son of Joseph," i.e., from the tribe of Joseph, and the other to be "son of David." Jesus of Nazareth was in fact a "son of David" by virtue of His earthly parentage, both with Joseph and with Mary, but He was most definitely not from the tribe of Joseph. So, now we begin to reach more understanding of Jewish "confusion" concerning Jesus, son of Joseph of Nazareth.

Further confusion is revealed as Rodkinson's states that both, Messiah son of David and Messiah son of Joseph, were to be carpenters! There was this "son of Joseph" who was a carpenter from Nazareth — born in Bethlehem — and who was also a "son of David!" Could

He actually have been the "precursor" for Himself? Modern Bibles say "craftsmen" or "smiths," but "carpenters" is much more exciting!

Earlier, in Chapter 6, we learned that early *Talmudic* scholars in *Sanhedrin* 97a taught that Messiah, son of David, originally had been expected to appear as Israel's Deliverer at the beginning of the third two-thousand year period after the birth of Adam. This would have been at the start of what we call the first century. — YES! — At the time of Jesus' birth! — After putting all of this together then, at this time one must surely inquire concerning *who* the Rabbis believe to have been "the other Messiah" — the son of Joseph. You know — the One who was slain. The obvious question is: "*Who* was He?" They never say who He was — just that He was slain.

The *Talmud* reference to "carpenters" is taken from Zechariah 1:20 in the King James translation or from Zech. 2:3 in the Hebrew Scriptures.

"And the Lord shewed me four carpenters."

Rabbi Hanah ben Bizna (third to fourth centuries) explains that these four carpenters are to be identified as: Messiah son of Joseph, Messiah son of David, Elijah, and "The Righteous Priest" — Melchizedek (or Cohen Zedek). Can you see what is derived now when we realize that two of these four carpenters are actually One person? There are really *three* "carpenters" in this picture! And yes, "son of Joseph" was slain. (And we still refer to Zechariah as one of the "minor" prophets!)

Did everybody notice how "They" (*Elohim*) said: "...they shall look upon *Me* because they have thrust *Him* through, and they shall mourn for *Him*..."? ("Me"?..."Him"?) This is another indication of the plurality *and* "Oneness" of The Almighty, "I AM," "WE ARE."

Any confusion Jewish people have had concerning their Messiah will end dramatically on that Day. They will remember all those rituals of breaking the *matzah* at the Passover, cutting the sacrificed lambs, sheep, goats, the Red Heifer ashes, the letting of blood, the burnings at *Olivet* summit, the sprinklings — all of the Temple worship liturgy and the Law. They will then recognize that all of those were "pictures" of Messiah (Jesus) dying, giving His life for their sins and ours. Yes, they will mourn for Him. — Oh! How they will mourn for Him!

One might ask *why*, *how*, and by *whom* were these *Talmudic* traditions originated within Judaism, since many of these items are omitted from Scripture. One could perhaps reason that this tradition concerning Messiah, "son of Joseph," for example, may have been given through one of the earlier unpublished prophets. The Jews then may have assumed this meant this "precursory" Messiah was to be from the tribe of Joseph; whereas, we can see now that He was actually the "legally" firstborn son of a man named Joseph and a "son of David" as a bloodline descendant, through Mary, of that favored King. (See Matthew 1:1 – 16 and Luke 3:23 – 28)

There were of course many prophets whose words and visions were derived through The Holy One, although some of these were never recorded by the scribes of that day into the Scriptures. As we examine Judaism through the *Talmud* and *Midrash*, we can see often the workings of His Holy Spirit in the Law and traditions passed down through ages of Rabbinical thought and custom. Also, as we have seen many times in this work, we will find

Messiah "concealed" within the Law and Jewish tradition by using our Christian 20/20 hindsight.

Many times during my study, I have pondered this question concerning how Jewish teaching has derived this "son of Joseph" Messianic figure. The answer comes from an obscure passage in *Midrash Rabbah* Numbers 14:1.

The discussion turns to what is presented as a quote from Psalms 80:3, (Psalms 80:2 in Christian Bibles) saying: "Ephraim is the defense of my head." The text then states that this verse "alludes to the Messiah anointed for war, who will be descended from Ephraim,..." A footnote explains that the son of Joseph will precede the son of David and will lead a war against Israel's enemies, symbolically identified as *Gog* and *Magog*. Another footnote refreshes our knowledge of Jewish tribal genealogy, saying the verse refers to the tribe of Joseph since Ephraim was Joseph's son. The *Midrash* quote from Psalms 80:3 is apparently from an ancient translation, because it differs significantly from that derived from the *Masoretic Text* and other more recent translations.

The Jewish teaching that son of Joseph is "anointed for war" and will lead a war against *Gog* and *Magog* generates an intriguing speculation. We have stated, under the observation of eschatological prophecies, that Antichrist will likely claim fraudulent credit for defeating *Gog* and *Magog*. It may be that Jewish teaching about Messiah, son of Joseph, will then bolster Antichrist in a claim that he is Messiah, son of Joseph. This would be a necessary step in deceiving Jewish people of his stature and his ascendancy to power.

Later, three-and-one-half years actually, Antichrist will have become completely possessed by Satan. At that time he will claim to be Messiah, son of David (God) and will desecrate Jewish Temple worship by committing the "Abomination of Desolation." (Daniel 9:27, Daniel 11:31, Matthew 24:15) Again, this is speculation. Nevertheless, it is based upon a connection between Scriptural prediction of future events and Jewish interpretation of Messianic identity.

The Jewish concern about the coming of Messiah is poignantly illustrated by a quote from *Sanhedrin* 97b. Having been asked why Messiah has delayed His coming, the Rabbi answers: "All the predestined dates for redemption (by Messiah) have passed, and the matter now depends only on repentance and good deeds." This is followed by a lengthy *Gemara* arguing about whether Israel *must* repent in order to be redeemed. There is a huge preponderance of rationale and Scripture pointing out that — Yes! — Israel *must* and *will* repent before Messiah comes. The Jewish Elect surely will repent as they "...*mourn for Him as one mourneth for His only Son.*" (From Zechariah 12:10)

But, now we must pause to consider something that should be very obvious. If all the "predestined dates" already have passed, then somebody is just not thinking. Foremost — God is *not* a liar. — God gave us these "predestined dates" in Scripture. (See Daniel 9:24–27)

Daniel delivered the most truly amazing prophecy in all of the Bible. This prophecy declared the actual date for the coming of Messiah, "The Anointed." It was to be 69 "weeks" of years = 69 x 7 = 483 years after the commandment to restore Jerusalem after the Babylonian captivity. This "commandment" was issued by Persian King Artaxerxes in 453 B.C.E.

On that day when Jesus rode into the City astride the donkey, the citizens of Jerusalem knew of that prophecy and they had "done the math!" — They knew that was the day — 10 *Nisan*,

C.E. 30 — 453 B.C.E. + 30 C.E. = 483 years — That is why they threw down those palm branches along His path. That was The Day! — and that is why they proclaimed Him as a King (as the Son of David), and shouting, from Matthew 21:9 —

> *"Hosheannah to the Son of David; Blessed is He that cometh in the Name of the Lord; Hosheannah in the highest!"*

God does not lie! If God said Messiah, Son of David, would be there at a specific time, and if that date is already passed, *then it is obvious that Messiah has already been here!* Jewish worshipers must now ask: "If Messiah has already arrived, then when did He come to us? — Who saw Him? — Who was He? — Where and when did He appear? — Why did we not know Him? — WHY has nobody told us about this? — Do our Rabbis know this? HOW can we find out about this?! Surely the Truth is beautiful when stripped to its nakedness; but, an uncovered lie is an abomination.

After a Christian once becomes aware of these Jewish "pictures," which the Lord has played out in bittersweet dramas, he can have a much better understanding of the Gospels. He will also develop a more sympathetic understanding of the Jewish vigil for their Deliverer.

I, for one, would like to hear what the scholars have to say after evaluating the secular and Biblical historical account we have presented. We have shown clear evidence that the Glory of the Lord (*Shekhinah*) did in fact withdraw from the Temple forty years after The Crucifixion of Jesus Christ. I leave it to the scholars then to decide what this event really means to Jews and to Christians. It must not be ignored any longer. This event has to have some significance. God Himself wept at this occasion. How can we not want to know about this event and feel what He felt?

11

The Debate Continues

WHY would the Rabbis have "invented" this Event ? – (NO answer so far !) – Skeptics do not WANT to believe – Event exhibits Divine Judgment for disobedience, but Glorifies BOTH The Father AND The Son, Jesus of Nazareth, as if in one breath.

There are a few remaining debate items that emerge with a unique relevance to Jewish perspectives. It is important that Christians should TRY to understand and be sympathetic concerning some of the confusion, doubt, suspicion, and resistance that has caused so many Jewish people to overlook their Deliverer.

So, who Believes in Signs?

One major criticism of this story by "conservative-traditional" Christian teaching is that God would not honor the Temple with His Divine Presence because King Herod was so wicked. That teaching also "assumes" God would not honor Christ-rejecting Judaism by residing in their Temple after The Crucifixion. I intend here to show through the most elementary logic that *Shekhinah* did remain in the Temple for a time after The Crucifixion. I offer this just in case there are still those who doubt or do not understand the meaning of Jesus' own words in Matthew 23:21.

We know from the New Testament that the Judeans (Israelites) were still conducting animal sacrifices during the ministry of the Lord Jesus. God had long ago Promised the sins of Israel would be purified under the Law by the blood of these "burnt offerings." But immediately following the death of Jesus (by "strange coincidence?") several strange and alarming "signs" occurred in the Temple. More specifically, the signs that had previously assured them of God's approval disappeared entirely; i.e., the westernmost candle, crimson strap, etc. In place of these comforting signs, they were faced with the doors of the *H'ekhal* opening by themselves, the eclipses, the sword over the City, etc.

The priests and the *Sanhedrin* knew something they had done at that time had drawn the Lord's disapproval. *Talmud Yoma* 39b describes and dates these events as "forty years before the Temple was destroyed." Of course, there is no mention of the timing with The Crucifixion of that "pretender" in 30 C.E. Neither did the scribes mention Messiah, son of Joseph, who was slain.

Talmud mentions at least one of these "signs" was taken to mean *Shekhinah* was going to depart imminently. The Rabbis must have had some sort of records of similar events ("signs") having occurred just before the Temple Destruction in 586 B.C.E. Otherwise, how would they have known such a meaning existed when these signs appeared in 30 C.E. — 70 C.E.? Then, by elementary logic, this information from the *Talmud* also indicates that the Rabbis who authored that text were saying *Shekhinah* then dwelled in the Temple; otherwise how could these signs have indicated that he was going to depart?

Of course, you and I now know what happened "forty years before," but the Rabbis apparently never made the connection with their rejected Messiah. Sadly enough, they still haven't made this connection. This is just another of the many reasons why this story must be told.

Yes, *Shekhinah* had been in the Temple probably for about 500 years before Jesus, even though the Temple had certainly been "polluted" many times before and by kings who were far more corrupt than Herod. This is further demonstration of God's Eternal and Infinite Love, Patience, Understanding, and Forgiveness of "this stiff-necked people." As discussed earlier, He apparently regards them somewhat like a spoiled-rotten, but favorite child in our large family of nations. We therefore must not be belligerent toward our Father nor resentful toward that favored "spoiled-brat" whom He loves so much.

Now, realizing the *Shekhinah* Glory did reside in the Holy of Holies, we can all the more appreciate the indignation (yes, wrath!) of our Lord Jesus when He referred to "His Father's House" as a "den of thieves." I am certain this was not the first nor the last time the Holy House was defiled by such vermin, and yet *Shekhinah* remained right up until their situation was desperate and "desolate" both times. The Lord Jesus Christ made good on His Promise that their house would be "left desolate" and that *"there shall not be left here one stone upon another,"* but cessation of His recognition of that House did not take place until 66 C.E.

It seems we patronize our Jewish friends when we say:

Of course we love the Jews.

Some of my best friends are Jews.

But they are lost without Jesus.

We must convert them to be "Christians!"

But then we say they are not really God's Chosen people anymore. And next we say Jesus will purify them when He returns and then we will all be Christians. No, we won't — because *they will still be Jews* — fulfilled Jews! And, yes, still His Chosen People!

How can we be so certain "they will still be Jews!" A very simple prophecy is given by Zechariah concerning Jewish/Gentile relations during "those days" when Messiah rules His Kingdom on Earth.

"Thus saith the Lord of hosts; In those days it shall come to pass, that ten men shall take hold out of all languages of the nations, even shall take hold of the skirt of him that is a Jew, saying, 'We will go with you: for we have heard that God is with you.'" Zechariah 8:23

During "those days" there will be Jews. And they will know their Lord (Jesus) and all Gentiles ("the nations") will also know Him and all will know that He is Jewish!

Some might try to "spiritualize" this verse by saying this is speaking of the present Church Age. (Have you seen anybody following Jews to worship because they have seen that God is with them?) This has not yet happened, but it will happen during "those days." In fact, the entire eighth chapter of Zechariah gives a view of a better world "in those days" when Jews and Gentiles will all worship together under One Lord. Israel will be "a blessing" (verse 13) to all nations "in those days" in Jerusalem as all nations worship One Lord Jesus, who was "pierced" for all nations.

Now the Lord knows that I certainly don't know how to "convert" Jewish people, but I pray this story may help some Jews to find their Messiah.

Presence of *Shekhinah* in the Temple does certainly not indicate God's approval of the Jews' failure to recognize their Messiah. (He forgave them on The Cross *"for they knew not what they did."*) (From Luke 23:34) But he most certainly did condemn their disobedience and pleaded: *"Return unto Me and I will return unto you."* (From Malachi 3:7) Then, sadly with the *Midrash* Rabbis' own humble and lamenting admission, "...but they did not."

So, by the most elementary logic, again: WHY would anybody suggest that those Rabbis would "hatch" such a story that shows God departing from their midst? It certainly wasn't a proud moment in Jewish history. I am just baffled that they even bothered to record it at all. The Rabbis' reporting of this is all the more baffling in that the event described actually Glorifies Jesus of Nazareth. Jesus is Glorified in that *Shekhinah* is reported to have ascended into Heaven from the *same* locale from which Jesus had ascended into Heaven forty years earlier. The fact that Jewish teachers have kept this quiet all these years actually provides credence and affirmation of this story. It has to be *true,* because it makes no sense for them to record a fabrication of that sort.

"The" Unanswered Question

There are a few more thoughts I wish to offer concerning that critical unanswered question as to WHY those Rabbis would have fabricated a false story of this event. What possible motive could they have had? What "gain" for Judaism (or for themselves) could they promote or achieve? How can anyone believe the Jews would conspire to conceive this story as a lie? So far at least, not one critic or doubter of this story has been able to offer even a feeble answer to that burning question.

A few serious, sincere "conservative-fundamental-evangelical" ministers have actually labeled this story as ridiculous — this despite the fact that it was documented by two respectable Jewish authorities who were "on the scene" in Jerusalem at that time. One of these sources, the Rabbis, could be expected to be openly hostile to any connection of this story with Jesus. Those Rabbis of the first century surely had not forgotten about that incident forty years earlier. The other source, Flavius Josephus, is openly sympathetic to Jesus, saying: "He was [the] Christ..." and "...he appeared to them alive again the third day..." (Josephus, *Antiquities* 18.3.3/63 – 64)

Both of these ideologically opposite Jewish sources tell virtually the same story. Yet, the sympathetic source certainly had nothing to gain by "inventing" such a story. Josephus was a Jew, although considered by many modern Jewish people as somewhat of a self-serving "lackey" or even a traitor for the Romans. However, Josephus recorded many wonderful things and many beautiful thoughts about the Lord. (Detailed in Chapter 12) Do we, therefore, select as truthful only those incidents that happen to agree with our Latter Day tradition?

And how about the *Midrash* Rabbis? Does anybody really believe they would fabricate a phony story that would actually glorify Jesus Christ forty years after they had rejected Him? They had not forgotten the incident, but they just didn't make the "connection" of this incident with the fact that His radical followers claimed Jesus had ascended from *Olivet* forty years earlier. Therefore, they had no reason to lie.

The fact that this event began just prior to the Feast of Unleavened Bread, as the priests were preparing the Temple for that Holy Season, has important bearing on verification of this story. The "ministrations" of the priests on such occasions were performed by the full body of the twenty-four orders of Aaronic priesthood.

Professor Martin pointed out that God surely arranged that His withdrawal should be witnessed by this full body of priests in order that they would know for certain this was a "sign" from God.1 (He knew they were always looking for yet another sign!) Jewish tradition held that when a momentous change in their political or religious system was imminent, this called for a "clear sign" from the Lord. Thus, there was no higher authority in the world to witness the occasion and it was a "clear sign" to all Judeans that this supernatural event did in fact occur. The priests made a public announcement of this fact. (See Appendix A.)

We know this is true also because it was a fulfillment of a prophecy. It had to happen. And it did happen. There is no report of this Event having occurred at any other time. The *Midrash* Rabbis were fervently proclaiming this event as fulfillment of Ezekiel's prophecy.

This was not a prophecy they looked forward to witnessing. This was an act on the part of the Lord to show His displeasure with their disobedience. (Hasn't anyone noticed that this commentary is in the "Lamentations" portion of the *Midrash*?)

They were "lamenting" this fulfillment — this event. They didn't enjoy writing this. It certainly doesn't glorify Judaism. There was certainly no reason for them to "make-up" such a story, one which clearly is pointing to their disobedience while at the same time glorifying the Nazarene whom they had caused to be put to death forty years earlier. How does it glorify Jesus? It glorifies Jesus and "I AM" by showing that they both ascended into Heaven from the same point — a dramatic demonstration to those present concerning two of the Divine Personages of the Triune God.

Understanding the Cohens and The Trinity

By demonstrating the close relationship of the "I AM" to Jesus, this story may help some Jewish people overcome one of their chief obstacles to accepting the Divinity of Jesus — the concept of the Trinity. They are taught: "*...the Lord your God is one God...*" Yes, He is one God, but He is also "*Elohim*." During The Creation (Gen. 1:26) "*Elohim*" said: "Let **us** make man in **our** image, after **our** likeness..." (Notice, The Creator(s) affirm this plurality of The Creator three times in this single sentence.) This statement, in God's own Words, means "us" and "our" refer to beings of God's same form — after "our" likeness, like "us" — and not like angels, for example. This also means that we humans are like God — except for the present we have been created to be "*a little lower than the angels.*" (Psalms 8:5)

The Lord ("*YHWH*" or "I AM") is also two other Divine Personages. One is Messiah, His Son (as Himself), and the other is His Holy Spirit (also Himself) who ministered to Israel through the Prophets, delivering His Word to ALL of us through Israel.

Try it this way. Let us say there is the Cohen family, consisting of the father Isaac, the wife Edith, and the children: David, Laurie, Michael, and Elizabeth. They are all equal. They are all one flesh. They are all Cohens. And yet they are each different and separate.

But if one Cohen is grieved, for any reason, ALL of the Cohens are grieved. Likewise, when one has joy — again, for any reason — ALL are joyous. When one is absent, ALL are lonely. If someone offends or insults one Cohen — *any* Cohen — ALL are offended.

If you say you love only Mr. Cohen, he cannot accept this unless you also love his son(s). The Cohens are a very "close" family. One cannot just love one Cohen. You must love them all — because they are One. If you are friendly only to one, you are the friend of none.

Nevertheless, even though the Cohens are One, the father (Isaac) is first — first in everything, above all others. The father is responsible for everything. He pays for everything, even if it is paid "through" his son(s). He "rules the roost." He even has his own private area in his "house," usually a special chair — perhaps even a "room" — a den, or workshop, but private.

But they are still One family. Together they are One. But the father is first. Should you have any doubt about this, his son(s) will be the first to tell you that he is first.

Mr. Cohen would be disappointed in someone who claims to be his friend but refuses to love, accept, and obey his son, even after the son paid the "debt" owed his father by this "friend." But, maybe the friend just didn't realize that was Mr. Cohen's son. Mr. Cohen earlier had told this friend about his son; i.e., how to recognize him, when and where he would "appear," etc.

But, maybe the friend still just did not recognize the son when they met. After all, he was just an "ordinary guy" who walked in off the street one day. He was dressed like a laborer — a "carpenter!" and he said he was from some little "hick" town. Nobody here even knew him! The friend had naturally "assumed" of course the son would be rather an imposing, aristocratic, powerful figure — more like his father, Mr. Cohen.

Well, you and I *now* understand that "ordinary guy" was Mr. Cohen's beloved son, but only Mr. Cohen can judge whether this friend actually made an honest mistake or if he committed an intentional "snub" to the entire Cohen "family." After all, the son has said, *"Forgive them, Father, for they know not what they do."*

How Many "*Gods*" did You Say?

Just as Jewish people have difficulty with the concept of more than one entity as "one" God, some Christians (especially very "young" Christians) may have trouble with the question: "Yes, I know about the Father, Son, and Holy Spirit; but now, who is this '*Shekhinah?*' Is he saying there are four persons in the Godhead?"

To avoid confusion on this point it is necessary to remind ourselves that God is omnipresent. He is everywhere. But the *Shekhinah* is a visible presence of God, the Father ("I AM," *Yahweh*, Jehovah, and other identities). So, *Shekhinah* is the Divine Presence of God, the Father — the ONE who spoke to Moses — not a "fourth" deity of any sort. This story should, however, demonstrate more than ever the "Oneness" between The Father and The Son, Jesus. That "Oneness" is demonstrated by the fact that the Father (as *Shekhinah*) punctuated the Ascension of Jesus by ascending from the same point on the Mount of Olives forty years after "the stone was rejected by the builders."

References and Bibliography for: *Shekhinah* Departure

1. Martin, Ernest L., *The Original Bible Restored*, 1984 – Associates for Scriptural Knowledge (A.S.K.) – P.O. Box 25000, Portland, OR 97298–0990
2. Flavius Josephus, (Translated by William Whiston, A.M.); *The Works of Josephus*, 1987 – New Updated Edition, Hendrickson Publishers, Peabody, MA 01961–3473
3. Anderson, Sir Robert, *The Coming Prince*, pp. 129, 1983 – (Reprint, 10th Ed.), Kregel Publications, Grand Rapids, MI., 49501
4. Jones, Vendyl M., *Will The Real Jesus Please Stand?*, 1983 – Institute of Judaic-Christian Research, Box 120366, Arlington, TX 76012-0366
5. Keller, Werner (Translated by William Neil), *The Bible as History*, 1956 – William Morrow and Company, New York
6. Fleming, James, "The Undiscovered Gate Beneath Jerusalem's Golden Gate," Biblical Archaeology Review, 4710–41st Street NW, Washington, D.C. 20016, Jan/Feb-1983
7. Kaufman, Asher S., "Where the Ancient Temple of Jerusalem Stood," Biblical Archaeology Review, 4710 41st Street NW, Washington, D.C. 20016, Mar/Apr-1983
8. Lamsa, George M., *Holy Bible-From the Ancient Eastern Text*, 1984 – translated from the Aramaic of the *Peshitta*, Harper & Row, Publishers, San Francisco, CA
9. *Universal Jewish Encyclopedia*, 1939 – Publisher: Universal Jewish Encyclopedia, New York, NY
10. *Encyclopedia Judaica*, 1972 – Keter, Inc., 440 Park Avenue South, New York, NY 10016
11. The Jerusalem Post, International Edition, 6 April 1980
12. Martin, Ernest L., *The Place of Christ's Crucifixion*, 1984 – Associates for Scriptural Knowledge (A.S.K.) – P.O. Box 25000, Portland, OR 97298–0990
13. *Midrash Rabbah*, Third Edition – 1983 – Lamentations (*Proems*) XXV, pp. 51 – Translated by Rev. Dr. A. Cohen, M.A., Ph.D. – The Soncino Press, Limited, 123 Ditmas Avenue, Brooklyn, NY 11218
14. Yadin, Yigael, "The Temple Scroll," Biblical Archaeology Review, 4710–41st St. NW, Washington, D.C. 20016, Sep/ Oct-1984
15. Barkay, Gabriel, "The Garden Tomb-Was Jesus Buried There?" Biblical Archaeology Review, 4710–41st Street NW, Washington, D.C. 20016, Mar/Apr-1986

16. Frenkley, Helen, "The Search for Roots-Israel's Biblical Landscape Reserve," Biblical Archaeology Review, 4710–41st Street NW, Washington, D.C. 20016, Sep/Oct-1986

17. Larkin, Clarence, *Dispensational Truth*, 1920 – Rev. Clarence Larkin Estate, P.O. Box 334, Glenside, PA 19038

18. Berry, George R., *The Interlinear Greek-English New Testament*, 1976 – Zondervan Publishing House, Grand Rapids, MI 49506

19. Berry, George R., *The Interlinear Hebrew-English Old Testament*, 1974 – Kregel Publications, Grand Rapids, MI 49501

20. Cruden, Alexander, *Cruden's Complete Concordance*, 1975 – Zondervan Publishing House, Grand Rapids, MI 49506

21. *The Babylonian Talmud*, Quincentenary Edition, 1978 – The Soncino Press, Limited, 123 Ditmas Avenue, Brooklyn, NY 11218

22. Levitte, Dov, and Wachs, Daniel, "Earthquakes in Jerusalem and the Mount of Olives Landslide," Israel-Land and Nature, Vol. 9, No 3-Spring 1984

23. "Sixteenth General Synod of the United Church of Christ," Associated Press Release, 1 July 1987

24. Rodkinson, Michael L., *New Edition of the Babylonian Talmud*, 1918 – Volume III, pg. 251, The *Talmud* Society, Boston, MA

25. Martin, Ernest L., *Secrets of Golgotha*, 1988 – Associates for Scriptural Knowledge (A.S.K.) – P.O. Box 25000, Portland, OR 97298–0990

26. Eusebius (Edited and translated by W.J. Ferrar) "The Proof of the Gospel," book VI, Chapter 18, 1981 – Baker Book House, Grand Rapids, MI 49506

27. *Halley's Bible Handbook*, 1976 – Twenty-Fourth Edition, p. 532, Zondervan Publishing House, Grand Rapids, MI 49506

28. Rodkinson, Michael L., *New Edition of the Babylonian Talmud*, 1918 – Volume IV, pp. 79–82, The *Talmud* Society, Boston, MA

29. *New American Standard Bible* (NASB), 1973 – A.J. Holman Company, Division J.B. Lippincott Co., Philadelphia and New York

30. *The New English Bible* (NEB), 1970 – Oxford University Press and Cambridge University Press

31. *New International Version of the Holy Bible* (NIV), 1978 – Zondervan Bible Publishers, Grand Rapids, MI

32. *The Encyclopedia Americana*, 1955 – Published by Americana Corporation, New York, NY

33. *The Companion Bible* (KJV), 1990 – Kregel Publications, Grand Rapids MI 49501

34. *Ezekiel – Hebrew Text & English Translation With An Introduction and Commentary* – pp. 41 – Rabbi D.S. Fisch, M.A. – 1978 – The Soncino Press, New York, London, Jerusalem

35. *The Legends of the Jews*, Vol. 6, pp. 392–393 – Louis Ginsberg – The Jewish Publication Society of America – Philadelphia PA – 1946

36. *The Pentateuch and Haftorahs*, Second Edition, 1965 – Edited by Dr. J.H. Hertz, C.H. – The Soncino Press, Limited, 123 Ditmas Avenue, Brooklyn NY 11218

37. *The Jewish Encyclopedia*, Volume V – Isidore Singer, Ph. D., Managing Editor – Funk and Wagnalls Company – New York and London – 1910

38. *Jewish Literacy* – Rabbi Joseph Telushkin – William Morrow & Co. – New York – 1991

39. *A Passover Haggadah* – Herbert Bronstein – Central Conference of American Rabbis – New York – 1975

40. *The Temple Mount – Where is the Holy of Holies?* – Asher S. Kaufmann – Har Ye`ra'eh Press – Jerusalem 96269, Israel – 2004

41. Henri Frederick Amiel in Webster's Electronic Quotebase – Ed. Keith Mohler – 1994

Part IV – The Red Heifer and The Law

12

Do Christians Need The Law?

Christians not bound by The Law of Moses — Christians should be curious about The Law — Where and by Whom was "The Law" written? Do modern Jewish persons keep The Law?

- *Why are Christians not bound by the Law of Moses?*
- *Why should Christians be curious about the Law?*
- *Where, how and by whom was "the Law" written?*
- *Do modern Jewish persons "keep" the Law?*

We find a profound acclamation for study of The Law (*Torah*) from the *Chumash*[16] and with reference to Proverbs 6:23:

"For the commandment is a lamp; and The Law is light; ... and reproofs of instruction are the way of life."

The narration goes on to declare that it is easy to understand why the commandment to study *Torah* is of a higher order than the other commandments. This is justified, it says, because of the "exalted nature and ineffable essence" of *Torah*. Referring to the Scripture from Proverbs, it is suggested to consider the difference between a lamp and a light. The lamp consists of the jar, the oil and the wick that provide the light.

- Without the lamp there would of course be no light.
- However, a lamp without light is but cold and of no use.

In a similar comparison, *Torah's* wisdom is involved with worldly objects, such as *matzahs*, money, measurements. God's Wisdom insists that man should attain higher spiritual appreciation by obeying the commandments of *Torah* regarding those worldly items – just as a lamp produces light.

- Man's highest opportunity and achievement is in study of *Torah,* acquiring The Light.
- That Light, actually enables man to join in the thought and wisdom of God Himself.

With this encouragement and *"lamp,"* then we proceed with our study of The Law of *Torah*; i.e., Judaism – to obtain God's *"light"* for us, as derived from a wholly Christian perspective and with the Ultimate Fulfillment of Christianity through Christ Jesus in mind.

Next, we must define the word: "LAW." – From Scripture as well as from Jewish sources[8,9,10] we find that occasionally the term "the Law" is used to refer to the entire Old Testament; i.e., the Jewish *Tenakh* or Holy Scriptures. An example is found in John 15:25, where the verse refers to the Law, – quoting a phrase from Psalms 35:19,

"But this cometh to pass, that the Word might be fulfilled that is written in their Law: They hated Me without a cause."

Here is an obvious reference that Jesus was and still is "hated without a cause." He had broken no Law. He had never injured any individual nor had He damaged his country or His people in any way. He never said anything evil about any person. Still, sinners hate Him despite His seeking their Salvation to escape eternal death. He persistently forgives their hostility and pursues them, asking them to repent and return unto Him. Sinners ignore His pleas and go their own way to certain destruction. But, He remains steadfast to the end. No person in all of History has been more hated, despised, rejected and ignored. Yet, no person has given more Love to Mankind. – He came to us and died for us in order that we may come to Him without the impossible fulfillment of the Law through our own incapable efforts. Why do they hate Him? – And, as it is said: *"Without a cause."*

Most Christians are actually "taught" or are certainly "encouraged" to ignore Judaism and "all that Law stuff. – Who wants to know about *erubs* and *seders* and heifers and *matzah*?!" Some sincere Believers say: "But, what difference does it make if it was Sunday or Monday? – or the 10th or the 23rd of the month? – All that Law detail has no bearing on our Salvation. All those nit-picky details are just Jewish Rabbis' baloney! – Who needs it?!

Why should we have to study how Jesus fulfilled "all that Jewish stuff" about God's Law? – It should be obvious to every Believer that Jesus Glorifies The Father EVERY time He fulfills or "completes" even one tiny "jot or tittle" of The Law. In turn, we Believers Glorify both The Father and Jesus when we observe, study and honor every act that Jesus performed in achieving those fulfillments. And ultimately, therefore, Believers continue by Glorifying and Honoring The Father, Jesus (The Son) and the Holy Spirit when we "edify" –share – announce those fulfillments to other Believers, to the Jewish people, especially – and, to The World. – Can there be ANY valid argument in opposition to such a work?

It must be said that the *most* revealing way to see Jesus as Messiah is to observe how – in countless incidents and occasions – Jesus observed and even fulfilled The Law. We shall encounter and observe many of those incidents and occasions in this work.

Consider how God, The Author, feels about treatment He receives from His Loved Ones. Clearly, one of the most hurtful actions *any* "author" receives is to be ignored, ridiculed, doubted and belittled by his friends and loved ones. Constructive criticism, however, is – or always should be – gratefully accepted. Perhaps Jesus expressed the painful relationship of being ignored and/or ridiculed by those who are close to us with this quote from Mark 6:4:

> *"A prophet is not without honour, but in his own country, and among his own kin, and in his own house."*

Of course we are in no position to offer ANY kind of criticism toward God or His authoring of His Word. However, before we ignore, ridicule, doubt or belittle ANY of God's authored Works – that *includes* The Law – consider how painful such rejection is for Him to receive this treatment from His Loved Ones. – THAT'S US !

Haven't you ever wondered about that word *"selah"*? – An example of "willful ignorance" is shown in how many Christian teachers answer that question:

> *"What is meant by the word 'selah' that we so often see in the Psalms?*

Typically we receive the reply that:

> *"Oh, it has something to do with the music or the way the Psalms were sung."*

...or something like that, because most Christian teachers choose (and have been taught by their teachers!) to ignore most Jewish sources. This is a passive form of anti-Semitism – *but*, anti-Semitism, nevertheless.

The term: *"selah"* is found explained by the Rabbis as having been derived from Psalms 48:9 (Psalms 48:8 in Christian Bibles) along with some other terms in *Talmud Erubin* 54a, which is paraphrased as follows:

- Wherever the expressions: nezah, selah or wa'ed occur, the process to which it refers never ceases.
- 'Nezah'? Because it is written: "For I will not contend for ever, neither will I be always wroth."
- '*Selah*'? Because it is written: "As we have heard, so have we seen in the city of the Lord of hosts, in the city of our God — God establish it for ever. — *Selah*.'
- '*Wa'ed*'? – Because it is written: *"The Lord shall reign for ever and ever.'"*
- So, now we know that the expression *"selah"* means: "God establish it for ever."

We also know that the Rabbis had derived the phrase from Psalms 48, and that an explanation is offered in *Talmud Erubin* 54a. We intend no harshness toward our Christian "shepherds" in this rather typical example showing Christian indifference to Jewish "roots" of our Faith. It is sad that they do not see the Blessings they are missing! We should pray that more Christian teachers would seek to find the *roots* of the Faith they are teaching. They mostly just do not even know where to search for such information, nor do they have the resources to do so. We hope in this series to demonstrate that much of such "roots" may be found in Jewish writings of the sages and Rabbis of old.

A local pastor frequently cautions his congregation about the tragic spiritual loss to Believers who "squander spiritual opportunities and privileges." By this he means we must not neglect finding new and beautiful insights in God's Word. This can best be achieved, he says, by study of scholars and/or listening to messages from fellow Believers. It is with irony, however, that it must be said that pastor refuses to review or even discuss the work of this book. Could be that even he is "squandering" a spiritual privilege.

In this section, we hope to stir an interest for Christians – and, for "open" Jewish worshipers – on *how* Jesus of Nazareth fulfilled The Law. Of course, while we are demonstrating His acts in this, we must describe the specific statutes involved. Most Christians read through the New Testament, having no knowledge – and, therefore, no appreciation for the fact that a principle of The Law is involved in that event or situation being discussed. This is particularly applicable in study of most of the parables in the Gospel. Consequently, the readers' hearts are cold to the beauty of the "Jewishness" in Jesus' life – because they have not been taught the meanings of His Works in fulfillment of The Law.

Nevertheless, in this discussion, we are addressing more specifically the Mosaic Law known as the code as written in the "Book of the Law of Moses." The foundational principle of Mosaic Law is that it is "theocratic." That is to say, it is of Divine Authority rather than having been devised by men. The "Law" we are studying refers to Commandments from God as the foundation for all human activity. However, it will become apparent that the Rabbis and scribes took that foundational criteria to great extremes, often rendering it impossible for mere mortals to obey.

It is a vast understatement to say that men do not fully understand The Law. For example, haven't you ever wondered why Jewish people are forbidden to cook (*"seethe"*) any kind of meat with milk? The more Orthodox cultures within Judaism do not permit even storing or refrigerating meat and dairy products together. – Hence, TWO refrigerators in those Jewish homes! That commandment is stated in fact *three* times in Scripture: – Exodus 23:19; 34:26 and Deuteronomy 14:21. The Rabbis reason that, since meat represents death and milk sustains life, God has ruled it is therefore "profane" to *"seethe a kid in his mother's milk."*

Similarly, what Jesus represents – in fact, IS – Life. And, Satan represents death, simply because he represents sin – which IS death. Jesus fulfilled the Law about the meat and the milk by refusing to compromise (join) with Satan's offers in His Temptation. It certainly would have been "profane" for Jesus ("Life") to intermingle or "negotiate" with Satan ("death"). This is why I believe Satan contrived that famous "compromising" expression to excuse some action that is done with the acknowledgment that it is "somewhat" an injustice. We say, then: "*It was for the greater good.*" – A "profane" purpose was achieved!

The Rabbis have outlined and explained the Law in several volumes that are frequently used for reference in this book: *The Babylonian Talmud* and *The Midrash Rabbah*. We must remember that Hebrew writings in *Talmud* and *Midrash* are certainly not of any Divine Inspiration. They are merely the works of men and must be viewed only for what is said by these writers. Students of these Judaica sources will observe some entries that are highly suspect and even objectionable. Still, we shall demonstrate thoroughly that there are also many entries that are greatly enriching to our knowledge and our growth as Christians and that are Glorifying of God, The Father and of Jesus Christ. The Rabbis certainly are not speaking for the Lord; although, in some of their discussions and laws we can see the Hand of God (although sadly it is unseen by the Rabbis!) as we view these ancient records *in the Light of Scripture.*

Frequently in the Gospels, Jesus addresses the "lawyers" and admonishes them for their often pious, hypocritical interpretations and applications of the Law. It is intended to demonstrate here that Jesus applied the most detailed and precise adherence to obedience of those statutes in His completion of the Law. The most broad and yet the most rigid of these statutes appear as demonstrations showing Jesus' fulfillment of the Law as it applies in the Red Heifer ceremony.

As one studies *Talmud*, it appears that the Rabbis actually compete with each other to determine who can be the most detailed and most stringent (and thereby most pious) in their rulings. What may be typical of such pious "striving" is seen in the ruling on the Rabbis' most "accurate" measurement of a Sabbath Limit. The Sabbath Limit is the prescribed distance that Jewish people are authorized to travel during Sabbath. It is based upon the distance from the farthest corners of "the Camp" to the Tabernacle, which was their place of worship during the Exodus from slavery in Egypt. That distance is "nominally" two thousand cubits, or about one thousand yards. A most highly respected French Rabbi, Rashi, judged that the surveyors themselves err in their measurements and their error is carried over to citizens who unwittingly then violate the Sabbath Limit. This error resulted because what they record as two thousand cubits is actually only one thousand-nine hundred and eighty-five cubits. This is determined from *Erubin* 52b as follows:

Sabbath Limits are surveyed using a rope that is fifty cubits in length (*Erubin* 59b). One Sabbath Limit then would equal 2000/50 = 40 lengths of ropes. However, since the rope was held by two men, one at either end – covering in his grip a portion of the rope to the extent of one handbreadth plus one half a fingerbreadth. Then, it follows that each length of rope actually represented 50 minus 2 handbreadths and one fingerbreadth. With 40 rope lengths, the deficit amounted to 2 x 40 = 80 handbreadths plus 40 x 1 = 40 fingerbreadths. Then, with four fingerbreadths being equal to one handbreadth and six handbreadths equal to one cubit, the total deficit amounts to 80 + 40/4 = 90 handbreadths; 90/6 = 15 cubits.

Such laborious detail is not only challenging to our arithmetical skills, but it also results in a shorter allowable distance that one may travel on a Sabbath day. The more "correct" Sabbath Limit is therefore diminished by 15 cubits to a more "stingy" 1985 cubits. This, by some interpretations, would be considered therefore "more pious;" as if to say: "See how we take even less than the Lord hath given us!" (Oh! – How "magnificently" we suffer!)

An obscure footnote in *Erubin* 3b states a fundamental of the Rabbis' philosophy that can be observed throughout their interpretation of the Law. In cases where more than one application is eligible in a statute, it generally follows that the most "rigorous" application of the Law is to be applied. For example, there are at least three different cubit lengths. In measuring a Sabbath Limit (1985 cubits), the shortest (Moses) cubit applies. In this case then, travel on the Sabbath is limited to a lesser distance than if one of the longer cubits were specified.

This approach would at first appear to be brought from a motive of vain piety, as if to say: "See how we endeavor to sacrifice convenience and comfort in our obedience to our Lord!" On the other hand, the *Talmud* Rabbis at times actually exhibit "practical" compassion for the people who must "keep" these rulings through everyday life, toils, travels, etc. Here they sometimes appear to rule less on the side of piety, and more toward a way to "reason" with the Law. We might even call it a type of "chiseling" or finagling.

One such "compassionate ruling" is the *"erub of cooked foods."* This statute will be explained in greater detail in later parts of this book. Briefly, the ruling permits a family or group to "cache" some prepared food on the day prior to the Sabbath at a place that is within one Sabbath Limit of a destination planned for that Sabbath day. A journey to the Temple, for example, otherwise might be more than a Sabbath Limit from their home. This would then make it possible for them to travel from that longer distance from their home to where their food is waiting. Then, they travel a "legal' Sabbath Limit from that place to their place of worship ON THE SABBATH DAY, although still within the Law..

The ruling is rationalized on basis that prepared food is actually a part of the "home" domain for that group. It is considered as though they were still at home when they partake of this food that was deposited at this "strategic" location the day before! – CLEVER! – But, this does in fact show an ironically different Rabbinical approach compared with the previous example on measuring the length of the Sabbath Limit. These two examples embrace much of the type of philosophy that went into these laws.

It is fitting that before we discuss the Mosaic Law, we should answer some of the questions listed at the beginning of our discussion of the Law. This is particularly appropriate since very few Christians (and few Jewish people as well!) have much knowledge of the Law and as to how it has been interpreted by the Rabbis over so many centuries.

Since it is assumed that most of our readers will be of the Christian Faith, it is appropriate at this point that we should recognize the demanding precepts of the Law as compared with the principle of Grace. Jewish worshipers strive through obeying or "observing" or "keeping" the Law in order to achieve sufficient righteousness that they "hope" will derive acceptance by their Lord God.

A Jewish person who diligently and faithfully tries to "keep" the Law might inquire of God: "Okay, Lord – I have done my very best to obey your statutes as instructed by the

Rabbis. I have tried to be a decent human being in this life. Now, you have Promised that, if I am worthy, my name will be written in your Book of Life. – So, okay. – Did I make it?"

Christians are of course justified through the Grace of Salvation from Christ Jesus. I sincerely pray not to offend any with this discussion; although, it is certain that we are entering a very challenging theological debate in these two "closely opposing" principles of these two closely opposing Faiths.

The Law and Grace differ fundamentally in that Law condemns sinners; whereas, Grace absolves them, but empowers them to overcome and to resist temptation. Jewish worshipers "hope" to have pleased God, knowing themselves that they have failed Him even in small ways by not always "keeping" the Law. Jewish people "hope" that their names are written in the Book of Life. (Daniel 12:1). Contrastingly, Christians KNOW they have been already accepted by God, having been "washed" of their sins as a result of Jesus having died for their punishment. Christians point to this knowledge as: Blessed Assurance.

The Law requires perfection in "the-letter-of-the-Law." Throughout this book, we shall discuss many examples of statutes from strict *Talmudic* interpretations under the Law. The Rabbis have taught within the pages of *Talmud* how detailed situations should be treated in order to "keep" the Law "Perfectly" (according to the Rabbis, that is!). For example, this strict interpretation of His Father's Law was one of Jesus' most frequent "jabs" at the scribes and Pharisees. These men were devout Jews and were sincerely "observant" of the Law. These stalwarts trusted that they were serving the Lord in the very best way by directing the people to adhere to these rigid statutes *that were not actually specified in the Law received by Moses!* Although the Rabbis founded these rulings on Scriptural verses, they derived sometimes by s-t-r-e-t-c-h-i-n-g and ordering severe "interpretations" of the Law. Again, the Rabbis often appear to actually "compete" for the highest degree of piety.

An example of this "rigidity" is their repetitive criticism that Jesus was healing people and therefore violating the Law (according to the Rabbis) by "working" on the Sabbath. Jesus very patiently, nevertheless, usually demonstrated to these men that "compassionate" statutes also existed and which would permit one to remove suffering from even an animal of "the flock" on a Sabbath. The Rabbis were bound up in that very human trait which causes us to become distracted by our pride and so intent upon achieving a self-glorifying "goal" that we forget the True and final objective, from Deuteronomy 6:5 –

"And thou shalt love the LORD thy God with all thine heart, and with all thy soul, and with all thy might."

Grace accepts grateful and child-like obedience. Nevertheless, we will occasionally fail, but if we truly love God, we will grieve at having offended Him even in the smallest ways and will repent of our deeds. We need not fear damnation, because He has Promised our Salvation from His rightful wrath, as a result of the Ransom for our souls having been accepted by God, having been purchased by the Atoning blood of The Son of God, Jesus Christ. Our only Judgment will be at His Judgment Seat in Heaven when He judges our works. (Revelation 20:12 – 13)

Let us be cautioned against "judging" the Rabbis who have led the Jewish people to hold up their faith through all these centuries, and all that time under vicious persecution. Already mentioned, Rashi (1040-1105 C.E.) was one of the most beloved of Jewish teachers. His well-known surname is actually an acronym from his given name: Rabbi Shlomo ben Isaac. Born in Troyes, France, Rashi is known indisputably as the outstanding Biblical commentator of the Middle Ages. Rashi is quoted at more than 3400 places in *Talmud*. Perhaps under Divine shielding, he survived the massacres of the first Crusade in Europe. Rashi devoted his life to explaining every word of the *Tanakh*, and doing so using as few of his own words as possible. He is worthy of our admiration, not only for his teachings of the Law to all of us, but also for his unbending dedication to the Word of God – the *Tanakh*.

One reason for our ignorance of the Law is of course because we and our teachers (and their teachers and their teachers before them, etc.) have been indifferent toward that "Jewish" portion of Jesus' ministry. Throughout the Gospel are stories relating how Jesus obeyed, taught and fulfilled the Judaic Laws – in Marvelous detail. We have not taken much initiative to go and seek for ourselves, that which, according to the Gospel, was very important to Jesus and the Disciples.

A second reason for this tragic void is that we have been taught, through Christian "tradition," that we are exempt from the Law and: "That's just Jewish stuff – and so why bother!" (Here is seen a subtle though sinister form of anti-Semitism.) And, again along that line of argument, a frequent excuse or accusation from conservative Christianity against other Christians and especially scholars such as myself, having any interest in details of Jewish worship, goes something like: *"Well, we aren't bound to the Law! The Lord Jesus completed the Law for everyone. – So why study all that extra-Biblical Jewish stuff?!"*

Answering, they certainly are correct in that Christians are not bound to the Mosaic Law. Paul having said in Romans 6:14 –

> *"For sin shall not have dominion over you: For ye are not under the law, but under grace."*

A summary of the difference between Judaism and Christianity "keeping" or "meeting" the Law can be stated as follows:

- Paul does not release Christians from the moral Law.
- Christians are not justified to Salvation through the "legal" Law.
- Jewish people seek justification through obedience to the "legal" Law.
- Jesus justifies Salvation for *any* who believe and accept His payment for their sins.
- Some Jewish people prayerfully await their Redeemer and "eventually" will recognize and accept Jesus and will be saved.
- Christians already have believed and accepted Jesus, and therefore are *presently* and *Forever* saved.

Since Jesus saved us from condemnation under the Law, we should at least be interested in just H O W He did it! Perhaps one of the most unique facets of our witness to Jewish people is our claim to righteousness, but without our keeping the Laws of *Torah*. Jewish teaching[5], in fact, holds Gentiles to a standard known as the *Noahide Laws*, with Jewish teachers considering Noah as having been the most righteous of Gentiles. – Yes, Noah was in fact, "technically" a Gentile, because he lived before the Jewish tribes were born through the sons of Jacob (Israel). Many people are surprised as well to learn that Abraham and Isaac were not Jews! They certainly were "Hebrews;" although, actually and "technically," they were nevertheless Gentiles! – Because they were *before* Jacob, aka *Israel*. This fact comes as a great surprise to many people, and some even will be offended by such an observation!

Consulting Reference 1 and *Sanhedrin* 56a, these *Noahide Laws* are as follows:

- Not to deny God. (as in idolatry)
- Not to blaspheme God.
- Not to murder. – (Just as in the 6th Commandment –Notice, it does not say "we shall not kill")
- Not to engage in incestuous, adulterous, bestial or homosexual relationships.
- Not to steal.
- Not to eat a limb torn from a living animal. (Sounds reasonable!)
- To set up courts to ensure obedience to the other six laws.

An in-depth discussion justifying Christian study of *Talmud* quotes several Christian theologians from the 19th and early 20th centuries in *Rodkinson's Talmud*[9]. These statements are too numerous and lengthy for quotation here, but we shall present just a few of them to forward this thought in our work. Following are excerpts from such statements:

Christian theology and Jewish theology having really followed two parallel paths, the history of either cannot be understood without the history of the other.

The Talmud, then, is the written form of that which, in the time of Jesus, was called the Traditions of the Elders, and to which He makes frequent allusions.

What light the Talmud may shed on the words of Jesus and Paul to know the modes of thought which were (for) such a perfect world in their time!

To treat the Talmud with scorn because of its oddness, on account of much that it contains that does not conform to our more mature modes of thinking, because of its evident errors and misconceptions – errors from ignorance or errors from copying – to throw it overboard, as it were, as useless ballast, would be to insult history, to deprive it of one of its strongest limbs, to dismember it.

Those who have not in some degree accomplished the extremely difficult task of reading this work for themselves, will hardly be able to form a clear idea of this polynomial colossus.

> *The absurdity (of considering Talmud as worthless) is too obvious to require another word from me. Such, however, is the continual treatment the Talmud receives at both the hands of its friends and its enemies. Both will find it easy to quote in behalf of their preconceived notions, but the earnest student will rather try to weigh the matter impartially, retain the good he can find even in the Talmud, and reject what will not stand the test of God's Word.*

A seemingly legitimate reason for Gentiles casting contempt against *Talmud* and the Law is Jesus' frequent disdain for "the lawyers." These were the scribes and Pharisees, whom we, in our ignorance, have so unfairly identified as "heavies" or villains in the Gospel drama. After all, the Pharisaic sect were "the religious right" of Judaism; although they were certainly somewhat to the "left" of extremist groups such as the Essenes. We are prone not to recognize the fact that the *first* Christians were probably Pharisees – as were Joseph of Arimathaea and Nicodemus, for example, and Paul as well. The Pharisees believed the Word of God; although – just as with many of us today – through their own pride and ignorance –at times they somewhat dogmatically and harshly misinterpreted His Word.

Even before His birth, Jesus' Earthly progenitors were under the Law, because of course they were Jews. One question in this regard emerges in that: "How many of Jesus' ancestors were Gentiles?" – "Were any of those Gentiles women?" – The reason for the latter question is the Rabbinical ruling that a person is not a Jew unless the mother is Jewish. This is rationalized on the basis that "Man is born of woman." An important interpretation of this law considers that a child born of a Jewish mother is Jewish – *even if the mother conceived him while she was a "heathen"!* Considerable detail of that possibility and others within this statute are discussed in: *Yebamoth* 45b; *Kiddushin* 68b; *Baba Metzia* 73b; *Sanhedrin* 58a.

All of this comes into question because one of Jesus' "mortal" ancestors was the heathen harlot heroine of Jericho, Rahab (or Rachab). (Matthew 1:5) It is evident that Rahab (a Gentile) at some time before the birth of Boaz became proselytized to Judaism – because it is firm that Boaz certainly was a Jew. Whereas, had he been born of a "heathen" mother, Boaz would not have been Jewish. This is of importance in establishing that Jesus was Jewish – even within the Law constraints of having had a Gentile Great-great-great, etc. Grandmother – aka: Rahab!

Moreover, from the very beginning of His childhood, possibly even as He was in Mary's womb, Jesus was directly involved with the Mosaic and *Talmudic* Law. For example, under the Law from *Niddah* 43b, a boy infant one day old is subject to all of the Law, including inheritance of his father's estate. In fact, the *Mishnah* of *Niddah* 43b states: "... and he counts to his father, to his mother and to all his relatives as a fully grown man."

It is clear from the narrative of Matthew 1:24 – 25, that even before the birth of Jesus, Joseph had "adopted" Him at the urging and instruction from the angel. *Sanhedrin* 19b gives several Biblical examples wherein a son had been "begat" by one individual; although, he takes the name of a different person who had raised him and/or taught him. In the Law of *Baba Bathra* 127b, if a man says the words: "he is believed," he claims the son as his own. Moreover, *Baba Bathra* 55a states inheritance rights of a firstborn son, which Jesus was.

The adoption status of Jesus under the Law is further demonstrated in the comments from *Midrash Rabbah* Exodus 46:5. Here the narration quotes Isaiah 63:16:

"*...he who brings up children is called the father, and not he that gives birth, as it says, 'for thou art our Father, for Abraham knew us not'.*"

This makes the point that a man truly is a "father" by the act of raising, teaching, leading a child through adolescence into life as an adult. Certainly, Joseph was Jesus' father under the Law taken from this concept of Jewish thought and teaching.

As the adopted son of Joseph, Jesus was then "legally" in the Royal line to David's throne by having as His Earthly father, Joseph, a descendant of King David and his son, King Solomon. (Matthew 1:7 and 16) – Jesus' is an heir to that throne in fulfillment of Isaiah 9:7. It was a legal line to royalty even despite that Joseph was descended through King Jeconiah. However, if Jesus had been a "blood" descendant of Joseph, He would have been disqualified to occupy the throne of David. None of Jeconiah's "blood" descendants ever ascended to the throne; although, "legally," the line of Royalty did pass through them. They were banished from ever becoming kings, Jechoniah's family having been disgraced upon the death of his father, King Jehoiakim (Jeremiah 22:19). This had been prophesied in Jeremiah 36:30 – 32.

Mary, on the other hand, was indeed a "blood" descendant of King David through David's son, Nathan (Luke 3:23 – 38) – although not through the "Royal" son, King Solomon. Jesus nevertheless received His bloodline to King David through Mary. Jesus therefore was in line completely – legally and by bloodline from birth – for ascendancy to the thrones of David and Solomon, exactly as prophesied in I Kings 2:45 –

"*And King Solomon shall be blessed, and the throne of David shall be established before the Lord for ever.*"

And, from the famous quote in Isaiah 9:7 –

"*Of the increase of His government and peace there shall be no end, upon the throne of David, and upon His Kingdom to order it, and to establish it with judgment and with justice from henceforth even for ever...*"

It has been shown, then, that the Lord "covered all the bases" – as He always does! – by having made His Son not only a blood descendant of His highly favored King David, but a "legal" Heir to David's throne as well – by having applied and fulfilled His Law to the Jewish people. – INCREDIBLE!!!

The Biblical and legal complexity of Jesus' genealogy and birthright is very complex. There are several other facets involved in this situation that have been explored and debated by generations of scholars. For example, typical of these questions is what at first glance appears to be a "Biblical discrepancy" between the genealogies of Matthew and Luke. Matthew 1:16 states that Jacob, the son of Matthan, begat Joseph, the husband of Mary. However, Luke 3:23 claims that Joseph was *the son of Heli*, who was the son of Matthat.

The similar spelling of the names: *Matthan* and *Matthat* obviously adds to the potential for confusion; although, these are two separate persons. Confidently, the alleged "discrepancy" is voided when we learn that Joseph was actually *the son-in-law of Heli*. This seemingly inaccurate listing was nevertheless intentional because during Biblical times it was customary to list only the men in Jewish family genealogies. That practice in fact was in those times traditional in nearly all, if not all, cultures of Abrahamic origin. Nevertheless, despite all of the "technical" details, Scripture affirms that Jesus is heir to the throne of David and Solomon, both legally and by bloodline.

It is appropriate, as we discuss the beginning of Jesus' Earthly Life, to briefly study the Name of Jesus, which in the Hebrew was *Yeshua* or *Y'shua*. Matthew 1:21 states that Joseph was instructed by an angel of the Lord in a dream, that he was to give the name *Y'shua* to the son in Mary's womb. The Hebrew etymology pertaining to this name would be derived as a "contraction" of the name *Y'hoshua* (Anglicized as: Joshua), and which has the literal meaning: "*YHVH* IS SALVATION." – His Name therefore could not be more appropriate, for The Son of God who came to be the Savior of The World! – This reference to The Tetragrammaton: "*YHVH*" – is a Holy and most reverent acclamation, and well recognized as such throughout all of Jewish culture. The *"Y"* is an abbreviation of sorts, and profoundly necessary because – except for only a few of Israel's High Priests – it was blasphemous to pronounce the Name of the Lord. The Anglicized version of this is usually *YHWH* in our Western Bibles.

We are shown from the second chapter in the Gospel of Luke, how Jesus was involved in the Law of Leviticus 12:2 – 8. He was circumcised on His eighth day of life, as required by that statute. After his mother, Mary, had accomplished *"the days of her purification"* for thirty-three days – again in compliance with the Law (Leviticus 12:4), as the "firstborn" son of Mary and Joseph, he was dedicated to the Lord even while He was an infant. In Exodus 13:2, the Law decrees:

"*Sanctify unto Me all the firstborn, ...*"

And, in Verse 12:

"*...the males shall be the Lord's.*"

As mandated through Leviticus 12:6, and since Mary and Joseph were not among the "affluent" in the society of that day, presumably they were not able to afford both a *"lamb of the first year for a burnt offering* **and** *a young pigeon or a turtledove for a sin offering."* Under the provisions of Leviticus 12:8, they instead were permitted to bring *two turtledoves* **or** *two pigeons*, one of which was to be for a burnt offering and the other for a sin offering.

A subtle difference can be noted here between the translations rendered from the original language of the Scriptures versus Western Christian theologians' more popular and so-called *"Authorized Version."* That difference is, between the King James Version (KJV) and two other more closely "ethnic" versions that are *equally*, if not *more* "authorized." The KJV says, in Verse 8, "two *turtles*;" whereas, both the Jewish Scriptures from the *Masoretic Text* and the Lamsa translation[3] from the Aramaic of the *Peshitta* (or *Syriac*), translate this again as two "turtle *doves*," as was prescribed earlier in Leviticus 12:6. It is pleasing to note that most of our modern translations have corrected this error.

This may appear to some as "insignificant Jewish trivia" or "nit-picking" or "gnat-straining." Before expressing such negative thoughts, persons need to consider: EVERYTHING that God is or does or directs any man to do is IMPORTANT and for His Purpose and Glory! Even though God did intend that *only* the Jewish people were bound by these Laws, the detail and precision is *commanded* by the Lord. We Gentiles cannot therefore just shrug and say: "All this Jewish stuff is too complicated – and besides – it's just for Jews."

The Law is very specific about details that were commanded by the Lord or inspired by the Holy Spirit and are not to be trivialized and/or held up for ridicule – especially by Gentiles. We should observe and be cautioned here to study more broadly in our examination of Scripture, especially regarding the Old Testament, as it is impacted by the Gospel. Jesus was, after all, an Old Testament "congregant," notwithstanding His frequent confrontations regarding Judaic legal principles with the Pharisees, etc.

Further insight in these passages is provided from a Jewish source[4] that provides interesting details about these laws. The Rabbinical Law, as interpreted in *Talmud – Shabbath* 132a, decrees that the circumcision *must* be performed on the eighth day, even if it be the Sabbath; and it must be done during the daytime – not at night

There is obviously good reasoning for the timing specified in this ruling, in that this "delicate" procedure should be performed with good lighting! – More "Scripturally," however, the daytime ruling is derived from the wording of Leviticus 12:3 –

"And in the eighth _day_ the flesh of his foreskin shall be circumcised."

Continuing, the Jewish source narrative instructs that the sin offering is usually stated first; however, here it is merely for *"purgation;"* i.e., uncleanness where no sin had been committed. The burnt offering symbolizes a re-dedication to the Lord following the mother's restriction from the Sanctuary. Then, since she was a woman and not a man, Mary was permitted to bring the offerings only as far as the door of the Eastern Gate, to *"make atonement"* which now permits her to return to the Sanctuary after her period of banishment because of her "uncleanness" caused by her body fluids during that time. This appears to be difficult for Gentiles or even Jewish people to understand, but it is a Commandment from God, nevertheless.

These precepts of the Law of course were completed with Jesus having been taken to the Temple, It is impressive that, even at that early occasion in His life, the infant Jesus was recognized as Messiah and to be blessed by a hopeful and watchful Simeon. (Luke 2:25 – 32)

The Law of *Chagigah* 2 illustrates a *Talmudic* requirement that is not readily apparent in what has been a familiar Bible story. Luke 2:41 – 52 relates the incident where Jesus, at age twelve years, has accompanied His parents to Jerusalem during the Passover. He became separated from Joseph and Mary, who anxiously searched for and later found Jesus "teaching" the Rabbis at the Temple!

Many of us Westerners would just assume that: "Oh, yes. – Jesus was there with His folks on a little vacation trip to Jerusalem to visit relatives, sightseeing, etc." Actually, this visit was a requirement under the Law. Each year as specified in Deuteronomy 16:16, all Jewish males are required to make Pilgrimages to Jerusalem at the festivals of: Passover, Pentecost and Tabernacles.

One group of very strict Rabbis in *Chagigah* 2 further specifies that this statute applies to any male child who is able to sit up on his father's shoulders to be transported up to the Temple Mount. Another less stringent Rabbinical authority tempers that ruling by stating that it applies only to those boys who are able to hold their father's hand as they walk up to the Temple Mount.

At any rate, it is clear from *Talmud* that this was not just a little recreational excursion for the family to visit the Holy City. Jesus was there because He was fulfilling His obligation to obedience of the Law.

Another incident of the Gospel dealing with male recognition under the Law appears in John 9:23 where the parents of a man who had been blind from birth, and whom Jesus miraculously had enabled to see. When astonished and skeptical Pharisees queried about their son's newly received sight, the parents replied: *"He is of age. Ask him."* In the Law, being "of age" was considered as more than twenty years of age. This ruling derives from *Talmud* as well as a few other references and particularly from Scripture in Numbers 1:3 and 1:18. Scripture identifies the age of twenty for men to go into battle for Israel and to be "numbered" in polling of the tribes, determining the numbers of "men."

Yebamoth 39 states: "until a minor becomes of age...he is not to be listened to." The parents therefore were announcing to the Pharisees that their son was to be recognized under the Law to make his own declarations with credibility under his status of manhood.

We may be reminded that this twenty years of age for credibility was applied by the Lord when the children of Israel came into their Promised Land. Numbers 26:65 and 32:11 relate that those Jewish refugees from slavery, who were "twenty years and upward" when they left Egypt, would not see The Land.

They all would in fact die in the desert. This, the Lord declared was because *"they have not wholly followed Me."* No doubt He referred to many disgraceful incidents, such as the Golden Calf affair and the "murmuring" led by Miriam. And, especially, the Lord was wrathful towards their weak faith when the "spies" returned with lies, saying that The Land was inhabited by "giants." (Numbers 13:31 – 33) Joshua and Caleb were honest spies, who had been loyal to Moses and the Lord during those forty years in the desert, and were of course exempted from that Judgment.

It is of interest to regard the Judaic Law that was applied for Jesus to begin His ministry. The *Mishnah* of *Aboth* 8:21 brings out that Jewish men are "at full strength" at the age of thirty years. That is, they are "at the prime of life" at that age. This ruling appears to be reasoned not so much from Scripture, but more likely it seems from tradition. It is noted that Joseph was placed in charge of Pharaoh's wealth at the age of thirty. Also, David was made King of Israel at age thirty. Jesus then apparently held to the "traditional" age of "strength in maturity" when He began to preach in the synagogue at Capernaum. (Luke 4:17 – 21) Most scholars assume that Jesus was thirty years of age at that time, and that He continued in ministry until He was 33 1/2 years of age at His "Death."

Do Christians Need The Law?   **239**

At the very beginning of Jesus' ministry, He was chosen from among the men of the congregation to read a portion of Scripture, Isaiah 61, before the public presence in the synagogue of His hometown, Nazareth. (Luke 4:16 – 21) Since the day was a Sabbath, one man of the congregation is asked upon such occasions to read what is known as the *HafTorah*. The Scripture selected is to be from the Prophets and is a reflection upon the Word read first as a portion (*Sedrah*) from the *Torah* on that specific Sabbath or Feast Day, as appropriate. Chapter III of *Megillah* tractate details the protocol and procedures for reading these portions of the *Torah*; this practice continues in synagogues today as well.

The *HafTorah* is to be chanted immediately after the reading of the *Torah* portion for that week. The Rabbis reason that, because Moses received those words directly from the Lord, the *Torah* then has precedence over the books of the prophets, as well as all other portions of the Scriptures. The *HafTorah*, with but few exceptions, has a relationship to that *Torah* portion that had just been concluded in the reading.

An example illustrating the relationship that is interpreted to exist between the *Sedrah* and its accompanying *HafTorah* is shown for Numbers 18 as follows:

A comparison is made through similarity of the plights of Moses (in the *Sedrah*) and Samuel in the *HafTorah*, which for that day is I Samuel 11:1 – 11 through I Samuel 12:22. Reference 4 reports that the People had "murmured" unjustly at the leadership of Moses. Samuel encountered the same type of disgruntled populace as he attempted to build the nation as the last of Israel's Judges; whereas, the people wanted instead to be led by a "King" (Saul). Prophets and sages expected a King to be a shepherd of his people, whose authority would maintain peace, liberty, compassion and righteousness – such as God would do!

Too bad it NEVER works out that way. There is a lesson for all of us here, in that, if the Children of Israel had not departed from having YHWH as their "King," they would never have had any of their later scatterings and sufferings. Their "Kings" provided for them exactly what they deserved. – Just as we other nations ALL do the same! – Has anybody ever noticed that Israel is the ONLY nation that has laboriously and persistently recorded for history (from its Prophets) ALL of its grievous errors, disobedience and punishment for ALL the World to behold?!

One of my favorite Judaism sources[5] observes that to be assigned the public reading of the *HafTorah* at the synagogue is a great honor. The assignment further augments the honor in that it identifies the reader as a Jew who has reached a significant level in Jewish knowledge, such as a graduate from a *Yeshiva*. The reader must be able to read Hebrew fluently and to chant the words exactly to the musical notes in the intonation and rhythm as prescribed. – No doubt can exist that Jesus could do this Perfectly! – The Nazareth congregation could *never* have made a better selection for the *HafTorah* reading – *especially on that Day!*

It is stated[4] that even at times when the *HafTorah* does not have a direct reference to the *Sedrah* for that day, still it is intended to reinforce the teaching of the weekly reading on the minds of worshipers *by a prophetic message of Consolation and Hope!* That is precisely the kind of message Jesus delivered to his assembled "peers." He was effectively informing His neighbors and friends from His growing years in Nazareth that their long awaited Redeemer was standing in their midst that very day! – as He read His assigned portion from Isaiah 61 and beginning at Verse 1, as it is quoted in Luke 4:18 – 19,

> *"The Spirit of the Lord is upon Me, because He hath anointed Me to preach the Gospel to the poor; He hath sent Me to heal the broken-hearted, to preach deliverance to the captives, and recovering the sight to the blind, to set at liberty them that are bruised. To preach the acceptable year of the Lord..."*

And at that point in the Scripture, Jesus halted before completing Isaiah 61:2 and the verses following, and instead rolled up the scroll and concluding by saying, from Luke 4:21,

> *"...This day is this Scripture fulfilled in your ears."*

We, of course, cannot imagine the shock and perplexity that His declaration brought to those in attendance at that synagogue service!

The remainder of this *HafTorah* would have included Verses 2 through 11 of the Isaiah portion, to complete the chapter. Jesus omitted those remaining verses of course because they are not to be fulfilled until after Jesus returns to Redeem Israel and to establish His Kingdom when He arrives at the Mount of Olives "on that Day." Later the neighbors and peers accused this son of Joseph, the carpenter, of blasphemy and attempted to throw Him to His death from a cliff – which, by-the-way, still stands today at the outskirts of the worldly Communist city of Nazareth in Galilee. (Luke 4:22 – 30)

One Jewish source[13] presents the *HafTorah* of Isaiah 61 to be read as a message of consolation on the Sabbath prior to *Rosh Hashanah*. The notation says this passage ties in with that season of Holy days and with the *Sedrah* that challenges Israel "to make a choice for life and for God." This note further points out, poignantly from Isaiah 62:5, this relationship declares: "as a bridegroom rejoices over his bride, so will God rejoice over you."

It is interesting in our modern times to observe that this *HafTorah* reading that Jesus brought to His congregation, has been reduced[4] by Jewish teachers to include only the verses 10 and 11 from Isaiah's Chapter 61. It would seem that the Rabbis have read Luke 4:18-19 and prefer to avoid any reference to someone once having "fulfilled this Scripture in their ears"!.—We must concede that it is not at all certain that Jesus had read this *HafTorah* from Isaiah 61 on the Sabbath preceding *Rosh Hashanah*. During the fourth century Rabbi Hillel II, last President of the *Sanhedrin*, made some rather obscure and untraceable changes to the Jewish calendar and order of worship. Nevertheless, it is strongly implied just from the context of these verses that a relationship to the New Year exists.

Further confirmation that the date was at or near *Rosh Hashanah* is suggested from the opinion of many Christian scholars that the Earthly Ministry of Jesus lasted three-and one-half years. From this we confirm a calendar difference of six-months between starting and completion of His ministry as a "Mortal." We reason this on basis that Jesus completed His Work as a "Mortal" on The Passover. He therefore must have started it three and one half years earlier on *Rosh Hashanah*, since those two Feast holidays are separated by six months on the Jewish calendar.

Several Gospel stories are directly associated with the Law, but Christians may not be aware of that fact, nor have they been encouraged even to be interested. An example of such narratives tugs at the heart of any person and thoroughly illustrates the compassion of Jesus. The woman with *"an issue of blood"* (a *"zab"*) had struggled through a crowd in order just to touch His "garment" (Matthew 9:20) in the hope that she might be healed. We are told in David Stern's excellent *Jewish New Testament Commentary*[14] that the "garment" she touched probably was a *tzitzit* (tassel) of His *talith* (prayer shawl). As a VERY "observant" Jewish male, Jesus would surely have worn a *talith* in obedience under the Law.

Only if we incise the Law on this point of the *zab* can we truly understand the pain and desperation of this faithful woman. Under the restrictions of *Pesahim* 81a, she was considered so "unclean" that any place where she had been sitting was to be considered "unclean." This of course had cut her off from her family, from much of society, the synagogue and from the Temple for a time as long as twelve years. One could say that under this Law this wretched woman was treated as poorly as a leper would be regarded.

Another example from the Law is from Matthew 12:10 – 13, in which Jesus was chastised by some Pharisees because He had healed a man's withered hand on a Sabbath day. Jesus pointed out that each one of these critics would have rescued his sheep, if one had fallen into a pit on the Sabbath. The man, Jesus declared, was surely superior to a sheep. This is of course substantiated in *Talmudic* Law under *Shabbath* 117b. An example is stated, wherein on the Sabbath, if a keg of wine on the roof of the house is leaking, it is acceptable to place a vessel to catch the liquid flowing off from the roof. Jesus was saying only that if that example is "acceptable" then, too, it is acceptable to care for an injured sheep or to heal a man's injured hand. The critics knew this – and Jesus *knew* that they knew it!

Another Sabbath healing criticism was leveled at Jesus after He had healed the man at the Pool of Bethesda. (John 5:1 – 18) In His consistent humility, Jesus reminded His critics that not He, but "The Father" had cured the man of his infirmity. In Verse 17 Jesus instructed them that: *"My Father worketh hitherto, and I work."* This incident illustrates that early in His ministry the Jewish Rabbinate was working to have Jesus killed, especially upon hearing Him announce that God was His "Father." His adversaries interpreted this remark as saying that He was "equal with God." And, we of course understand that to be the Truth!

Shabbath 117b-120a, deriving through the *Mishnas* of 16:4 and 16:5, teaches in elaborate and boring detail how it is "legal" on the Sabbath to "rescue" one's clothing and food from fire and flood. – OKAY! – Jesus was therefore asking these "lawyers" to explain, then why is it NOT also "legal" to rescue the souls of men on the Sabbath?! After all, are not men and women worthy of being rescued from the "fire and flood" of Eternal Damnation?! Finally, in *Shabbath* 132a it is determined that it is permissible for a person to save another person's life on the Sabbath. Jesus was within the Law by saving a person's Eternal Life! – Jesus had beaten them at their own game! – As ALWAYS !

We see that Jesus often quoted *Talmudic* thought, reasoning and teaching in His Words that we see in the Holy Gospel. His teaching to the Disciples in Matthew 18:20 urged them to pray together:

"For where two or three are gathered in My Name, there am I in the midst of them."

A very similar passage appears in the *Mishnah* of *Aboth* 3:2 and in *Berakoth* 6a, saying, "...if two are sitting and studying the *Torah* together, the Divine Presence is with them." Similar *Talmudic* language comparisons with Biblical dialogue can be made throughout the New Testament, especially with some of the wording used in the Lord's Prayer.

The story of the Samaritan "woman at the well" (John 4:27) comes to mind as we compare the Gospel stories through the Law. The Disciples express dismay at the fact that Jesus is actually *talking with a woman!* – and, a Samaritan woman, at that! The Law, *Berakoth* 43b, directs that, among the six things that are "unbecoming" for a scholar is *"to converse with a woman on the street."* It is further explained that this measure is to include his avoiding conversing on the street with his wife or his daughter or even his sister. It is further explained that, after all, not everyone out in public knows who are his female relatives! – (Might give a bad impression regarding the scholar!)

In this story we therefore receive a lesson that would be overlooked without our knowing this ruling from the Law. Jesus is actually flaunting this ruling about a scholar "consorting" with a woman. He is demonstrating the fact that showing the Samaritan woman the error of her lifestyle and saving her soul is much more important than the vain and petty "propriety" that is attempted to portray in the ruling.

The fact that Jesus marched into the Temple and stirred the wrath of the moneychangers on the 10th day of *Nisan*, later to be put to death on the 14th of *Nisan* dramatizes His fulfillment of the Law pertaining to the Paschal Lamb. The Lamb was selected as Perfect and without blemish and then was required to be watched four days to make certain that it did not become ill or suffer a cut or scarring from an injury, etc. *The Jewish Book of Why* has a description of that sequence of events and is taken from Exodus 12:3 – 6 and from *Talmud* in *Pesahim* 96a.

Jesus confronted the Pharisees with their own Law in John 8:17, as He reminded them:

"It is also written in your law, that the testimony of two men is true."

Jesus was of course referring to Scripture from Deuteronomy 19:15 –

"One witness shall not rise up against a man for any iniquity, or for any sin, in any sin that he sins; by the mouth of two witnesses, or by the mouth of three witnesses, shall the matter be established."

This is yet again an example of Jesus demonstrating to the "lawyers" His knowledge and commitment to the Laws of Judaism.

The betrayal of Jesus for *"thirty pieces of silver"* brings us to an issue in the Law from *Pesahim* 90a, and referring to Deuteronomy 23:19 in the Hebrew Scriptures. (The equivalent of this verse as quoted appears as Deuteronomy 23:18 in our Christian texts.)

"You shall not bring the hire of a harlot, or the price of a dog, into the house of the Lord your God for any vow; for these are both abomination to the Lord your God."

Many commentaries, referring to Exodus 21:32, indicate that thirty pieces of silver was the "blood price" to be paid to an owner if a slave was accidentally killed. Justly then, such a comparison for the "blood price" paid to Judas by the *Sanhedrin* for the Betrayal of Jesus is certainly valid.

However, another possible and albeit fitting application of the Law exists in that some historians have said *"the hire of a harlot"* at that time was also thirty pieces of silver. We can view this as an accusation that Judas "prostituted" himself to the *Sanhedrin* for "the going price" to procure his "harlotry" service. (Matthew 26:15)

Further irony comes from Judas having thrown the silver *shekels* onto the floor of the Temple as he regretted his perfidious deed. The priests then purchased a "potter's field" with this filthy loot – because they could not bring this "abomination into the House of the Lord" under the Law of Deuteronomy 23:19. This latter measure; i.e., avoidance of an "abomination" would therefore appear to substantiate more in favor of the price for a harlot rather than as a "blood price."

Without argument, *either* comparison surely is appropriate. And so again, Jesus arranged the betrayal such that it would fit *either* the "harlot price" or the "slave price." These matters should be considered during review of Matthew 26:15, 27:3 – 5 and 6 – 10. That entire betrayal episode, by the way, was a dramatized fulfillment of the prophecy from Zechariah 11:12 – 13 –

"And I said unto them, If ye think good, give me my price; and if not, forbear.

So they weighed for my price thirty pieces of silver.

And the Lord said unto me, Cast it unto the potter: a goodly price that I was prised at of them. And I took the thirty pieces of silver, and cast them to the potter in the house of the Lord."

Matthew 27:9 refers only to a prophecy having been inspired through the Prophet Jeremiah. The narration from Zechariah, however, is much more direct as well as more dramatic toward portrayal of the entire betrayal scenario than is that from Jeremiah. In summary, it can be said that Judas sold himself for the price of a harlot. Whereas, Jesus was sold as the "blood price" for all of us, who are after all, merely slaves.

It is obvious and Glorifying to God to observe that He ordered these principles into His Holy Word hundreds of years before Jesus was born. The Father instituted this policy concerning these "prices" that later would be applied at the Betrayal of His only Son, Jesus, in accordance with the Law that He gave His People. When we really stop to think about this, and how the Lord planned and accomplished all this in such PERFECT detail and order, it is truly overwhelmingly Remarkable! – Actually, mere words cannot even express the Wonderment of such feats! – As we continue this study, we shall see more and more such evidence of predetermined Events in the Earthly Life of Jesus.

In Para. Seven of this book we have presented fascinating details of the Law concerning the two "he-goats" on the Day of Atonement being reflected in the drama of Jesus' appearance before Pontius Pilate. Reading of that account in the Gospel without having familiarity in the Law, the reader would miss the beautiful story that is "hidden" in that drama. The Red Heifer ceremony in Part Four is an even larger and more complicated example of the same type of hidden drama.

Many Gospel criticisms, especially from Jewish scholars, accuse that inconsistency and violation of Judaic Law "taints" credibility of the Synoptic Gospels' accounts of The Trial. Detailed and thorough study of these subjects invalidates that accusation.

The claim of inconsistency is rooted in the critics' accusation that Matthew and Mark say The Trial before the *Sanhedrin* was at night (which would be a violation of the Law). The confusion may arise from some of the verses that discuss events immediately following the arrest of Jesus in the garden. To some, these sound like the "FULL" *Sanhedrin* was in session; although, such may not be the case.

Luke stated that the elders, scribes, and chief priests *"came together and led Him into their council."* This was conducted *"as soon as it was day"*, after Jesus' arrest. Later in their narratives, both Matthew 27:1 and Mark 15:1 are in agreement with Luke 22:66. All three are consistent in stating that *"when the morning was come,"* Jesus was brought to trial before "all the chief priests and elders" and that they *"took counsel against Jesus to put Him to death."* Those earlier meetings during the wee hours of morning were perhaps "arraignments" or "interrogations" or "investigations" in terms from modern law enforcement agency jargon.

A second accusation points to *Sanhedrin* 35a, which rules that a trial for a capital offense must not be conducted on the eve of a Feast Day or a Sabbath. This ruling is based upon the fact that the offender, if so convicted, must be executed no later than the daylight hours following the trial. Therefore, if the judgment is pronounced late in the day on the eve of a Sabbath, the execution cannot be delayed such that it then would occur on the Sabbath, a forbidden time. Neither can the deed be delayed until the first day of the week, *Sanhedrin* states, because by that time the judges "might have forgotten their reasons."

Nevertheless, this argument is rendered moot by virtue of the fact that, during the first century, and during many previous decades, the sovereignty of the Israelites had been superseded by Rome. *The Sanhedrin had NO authority to condemn anyone to capital punishment.* However, the *Sanhedrin* could recommend a death penalty and deliver the offender to the sovereign Roman authority. And, so they did *"deliver Him to Pontius Pilate."* (Matthew 27:2)

We have shown, therefore, that the Gospels are in fact consistent in this matter. Also, we have shown that, although *Sanhedrin* 34b does require the trial before the *Sanhedrin* must be conducted during daylight, all three Gospels affirm that the statute had been upheld. Moreover, we have shown compliance with *Sanhedrin* 35a in that it was NOT a Jewish court, but it was the Roman official (Pilate) who "sentenced" Jesus to crucifixion and Roman soldiers carried out the execution. The Law, as ALWAYS, was kept to **PERFECTION!**

Any treatise purporting to analyze the Law within Judaism would rightly be expected to excise specific statutes from *Talmud* concerning Jewish courts, trials, sentences and executions of criminals for capital offenses. Such a discussion would obviously offer, via comparison, fascinating insight into the court, trial, sentencing and execution reported in the

Gospels. We have elected to forgo a detailed investigation which that subject certainly deserves. The reasons for this decision are as follows:

1. The amount of documentation of the Law in *Talmud* is rather voluminous, extremely technical and detailed, comprising seven-hundred-eighty-one pages in *Sanhedrin* tractate, alone.

2. We do not possess the legal background and expertise required to review these statutes and to competently interpret comparison to the Gospel case.

3. Most readers likely would not be able to fully comprehend a fully "qualified" legal presentation, based upon the same reasons stated in 1 and 2, above.

Nevertheless, a summary listing the theme and scope of the *Talmud* teaching therefore is in order for this book, proposed as an acceptable minimum toward a very challenging and technically forbidding subject. The summary shall consist of listing the subjects discussed under the Introduction and each of the eleven chapters of the *Sanhedrin* tractate. It is intended that readers, just through hearing which items are discussed, will gain improved insight regarding that renowned judicial body of Judaism. As in all *Talmud* texts, ample Scriptural references are given to substantiate rulings and/or philosophies.

Introduction – The tractate is not claimed to have the "fullness or precision" that could be desired. Although the discussion pertains chiefly to the rulings of "The Great *Sanhedrin*," comprised of 71 members, there were several of "The Lesser (or Small) *Sanhedrin*" – each comprised of 23 members. Some coverage of those bodies is presented as well. The Lesser *Sanhedrins* could try even capital cases; although, The Great *Sanhedrin* maintained its authority as the Supreme Court in appellant actions. The discussion states that the Rabbis were and are today well aware of Christian interest (and criticisms) of Jewish Law as it relates to the arrest, trial, sentence and execution of Jesus of Nazareth. For example, to illustrate the popularity of this tractate it is noted that when Johannes Reuchlin, 15th century Catholic scholar, searched Europe to find a *Talmud*, the only tractate he could obtain was *Sanhedrin*.

Chapter 1 – *Composition of the courts, with cases in civil, criminal, religious or political trials. Attitude of judges toward litigants, settlements, compromises, incompetent judges. A large portion is devoted to intercalation of the Jewish calendar. Authority of the Urim and Thummim and qualifications and city of origin for members of the Sanhedrin.*

Chapter 2 – *Privileges of High Priests and Kings in various court proceedings. Sanctity of a first marriage and evils of divorce.*

Chapter 3 – *Rights of parties to reject or choose judges and witnesses. Omissions permissible in documents. Grounds for disqualifying judges or witnesses. Rules of evidence, negotiations for selecting place of trial.*

Chapter 4 – *Differentiating between civil and criminal cases. Historic stories, especially concerning the Creation of man and disputations with heretics.*

Chapter 5 – Presents rules governing cross-examination of witnesses, referring to cases where witnesses were rendered subject to retaliation. Procedures for dealing with discrepancies or contradiction in evidences. Mode of procedure for judges in voting and at implementing a sentence.

Chapter 6 – Describes how the condemned was to be led to the place of execution, and how he was given a last opportunity for revocation of the sentence. Prior announcement of the pending execution to be announced by a herald. Procedures for avoiding abhorrent shame to females in executions. Burial of the condemned, sometimes in special cemeteries. Details on how an accused may justify self-defense.

Chapter 7 – Deals with the four modes of execution practiced in ancient Israel: stoning, burning, decapitation and strangulation, with descriptions of each mode.

Chapter 8 – Treats the case of the stubborn and rebellious son and states age limits and conditions that justify the "supreme penalty." Self-defense provisions judged in right to kill a house-breaker. Those who may be killed to prevent them from sinning. Age for possible childbirth, insidious dangers of strong drink, nature of the forbidden "tree of knowledge" in the Garden of Eden.

Chapter 9 – More on executions: burning for incest; crimes deserving decapitation. Interesting statute about flagellation before execution, capital crimes that seldom resulted in execution.

Chapter 10 – Strangulation and the crimes where it was applied. Nature of disputes between two major divisions of thought in Sanhedrin explained. Trial of a false prophet.

Elaboration on Biblical narrative about the sacrifice of Isaac.

Chapter 11 – All Israel to have a portion in "The World to Come." Identification of those who will not receive a portion. Stories of sieges by Sennacherib and Nebuchadnezzar. Description of the times preceding arrival of Messiah and Israel's Redemption.

It can be seen from the foregoing summary that *Sanhedrin* tractate promises fascinating study for Christian scholars of the Law. This would be especially true regarding The Crucifixion. It must be remembered, however, that at the time of The Crucifixion, the Law concerning executions as well as many other cases had long been corrupted and/or superseded by Roman sovereignty in Judea. This latter situation is another reason why these subjects are better left to be discussed by "real" lawyers.

Scholars familiar with The Crucifixion are frequently confronted by the statement that Jesus was put to death "nigh to the City" – i.e., near, but outside of Jerusalem. (John 19:20) In the Law, *Sanhedrin* 42b, a criminal – and, *especially* a blasphemer! – *must* not be executed within the Holy City. In fact, the offender must be dispatched at least at the distance of a Sabbath Limit from the Holy of Holies in the Temple; i.e., "outside the camp." (Leviticus 24:14) A Sabbath Limit, from *Erubin* 21a, is two thousand cubits (about 1000 meters) and is the distance from his home that a Jewish worshiper may travel on a Sabbath day. (More on this in Chapter 15.)

This requirement of the Law then can be used to challenge any claim of authenticity for The Crucifixion having been conducted at the traditional and popularly "touristed" site at the Church of the Holy Sepulchre or even the other popular site at "Gordon's Calvary." It is obvious that both of those sites are actually within only a short distance from the Temple Mount, where the Temple was located, and therefore would be disqualified under the principle of the Law just defined. Defenders of the traditional sites are quick to respond to this criticism by pointing out that Judaic authorities at the time of Jesus had corrupted many statutes of the Law and that this one was probably corrupted as well. Later in this work, we shall illustrate that Jesus fulfilled ALL of the Law PERFECTLY and there was NO! "corruption" involved with ANY of His fulfillments.

Josephus[2] describes the death of James, the brother of Jesus, as a martyr having taken place at the base of the "Pinnacle of the Temple." That location is at the southeastern corner of the wall that surrounds the Temple Mount and is definitely much nearer than a Sabbath Limit from the Temple. It can be said, then, that by the time of that event (C.E. 62), this Law had been virtually abandoned. Moreover, James was not fulfilling any prophetic event and it therefore was not required that his ordeal should be Perfect under the Law. The martyring of Stephen just outside the northeastern wall is another similar case.

At The Cross, a grim principle of the Law was fulfilled after obviously having been ordained by the Father, who directed Moses 1200 years earlier to incorporate this Law. In Deuteronomy 21:22 – 23, the Children of Israel were instructed that it is unlawful to leave the corpse from an execution upon a tree overnight. The plea to Pilate then, was to remove the three bodies before nightfall under that statute of the Law. (John 19:31) Before the beginning of Time, God of course had Planned the timing of this Event and He had ordained that Jesus' battered but Perfect Body would suffer *"no corruption."* (Psalms 16:10) God, then, actually "designed" this Law to serve in getting His Son's broken Body into The Tomb before it could suffer putrefaction – "corruption."

Even within modern Judaism this same statute of the Law is applied. The Code of Jewish Law[10], the *Kitzur Schulchan Aruch*, outlines this instruction in Volume IV, Chapter CXCVIII:3. Here it is also stated that if the body must be left overnight, as was the case being pleaded by Joseph of Arimathaea needing to observe the Sabbath, it is permissible to delay burial. Nevertheless, it is cautioned that the delay "must not lead to contempt of the dead." The delay for Jesus' burial extending through the Sabbath was then acceptable under the Law, just as all the other facets of His life met the Law PERFECTLY!

Chapter CXCVII:1 of *Kitzur Schulchan Aruch*[10] specifies that the body is to be wrapped in a shroud "of fine white linen." If The Shroud of Turin is in fact the burial cloth of Jesus, then He surely met the Law again for this statute. Also, Chapter CXCIX:2 of that same source presents detail for the position of the body in burial. It is to be "laid upon its back, with face upward." This again, is evidenced by the negative photo image from the Shroud of Turin. We will also learn that the *Afikoman* at the Passover *Seder* is placed on the napkin exactly in the same manner as the man was placed on The Shroud. The *Afikoman* napkin is folded over the "broken " *matzah* in exactly the same manner as The Shroud was folded over the man on the cloth. (Too much for "coincidence"? – I think so, too!)

In Chapter 20 we shall demonstrate how Jesus fulfilled a somewhat obscure but very important detail of the Law regarding the actual amount of time His Body was in The Tomb. But for this technical detail of the Law, the Gospel would be in contradiction with other portions of Scripture. *We know that can never be the case!* – And so, the Law provides the True solution for the problem that we shall address and explain.

Because we are listing items from the Law relating to Jesus and the Gospel, we must consider the Holy Temple. The Lord specified the basic layout of the Tabernacle to Moses and the children of Israel in the Law from *Torah* in Exodus Chapters 25 - 40. Solomon's Temple and the Second Temple later employed that same basic layout, depicted in Illus. 22: The Sanctuary of the 2nd Temple, Page 155.

Examining the illustration, we see that the positioning of the Altar of Incense, the Table of Shewbread and the Candlestick (*Menorah*) form the shape of the letter "T." The Cross of Jesus was in fact just such a shape as well; although, that is contrary to what traditionally has been shown in most artists' depictions of The Crucifixion.

Further presence of the Cross form in the temple is evident in Illus. 15: Plan of Second Temple (by Dr. A.S. Kaufman), Page 148, Illus. 16: Isometric View of 2nd Temple, Page 149, and Illus. 21: Detail of the 2nd Temple, Page 154. The *H'ekhal*, i.e., "The Holy House" or "The Sanctuary" exhibits that "T" shape in all three of these sketches. That shape was correctly provided for The Cross in the recent Mel Gibson film, *The Passion of The Christ*. The Cross was accurately configured by a beam, identified by its Latin name: *patibulum*, designed to support the victim's outstretched arms. After fastening the arms to the *patibulum*, the victim and the beam were "lifted up" and the beam rested in a groove on the top of a vertical post, which then was embedded into the ground.

We would be remiss if we neglected to point out that the cross shape in the form of a "T" consists of three ends or "points." This is a dramatically important feature, in that "three" is God's Number of Biblical Numerology signifying Holiness. More details on this symbol will be presented in later sections.

The Temple priests and the Rabbis may never have noticed this shape of The Cross appearing so prominently and yet with such subtlety in the Temple design. This is especially dramatic in that, by its very shape, it Glorifies Jesus Christ. It truly came about by this Glorious "coincidence" that I am certain was ordained by Almighty God to also provide Glory to Himself on that same Holy Occasion. We have shown, therefore, that His Cross was a required feature to be implemented into the design of the Temple. It cannot be denied, or avoided or ignored.

Perhaps the very last occasion upon which Jesus fulfilled a portion of the Law was just prior to His Ascension from the summit of the Mount of Olives. That was an application of the Law of *Hallah* 1:8, called "the *erub* of cooked foods." The occasion is from Luke 24:50 and includes application of *Erubin* 23a. In Chapter 15 the remarkable intricacy of these Laws in their importance to the Gospel is explained in detail.

There is a host of other situations in the Gospel that are taken directly from the Law. These incidents, as we have demonstrated, extend through Jesus' entire Earthly life, actually from-cradle-to-grave. Perhaps even from "Conception" to grave! In this way, Jesus "fulfilled" the Law, by actually "living" and even "dying" and continuing after He was in The Tomb as He enacted these statutes to the Jewish people as well as to the World. Without such a comprehensive study of the Law, Christians would never be able to receive the Blessings that come through understanding the contributions of Jesus to the Gospel stories in this way.

It is sad to observe that many Gentiles are critical of Judaism simply because of a poor example so often shown by Jewish people in their lack of enthusiasm for their own faith. By this I mean that Gentiles have been quick to notice that a large percentage of Jewish people never attend synagogue worship services. Most modern and so-called "Traditional" Jews do not observe the strict dietary laws requiring *kosher* restrictions concerning prohibition of pork, shellfish, etc. Intermarriage of Jewish people with Gentiles also has taken a heavy toll upon Jewish observance of the Law.

Some respected Jewish sources readily concede that Jewish practices are not wholly inspired from Scripture; although, God's Word is certainly primary and central in *Talmud*, *Midrash*, etc. It is declared that Jewish Law and tradition has never been static. The generations of Judaism have adapted to their individual locales and circumstances. Considering that the Jewish people have been *"scattered among the nations,"* great diversity in Jewish tradition is to be expected. A notable exception to such diversity, however, is the uniformity of custom in the *Seder*, the Passover meal. That precious and Holy ceremony has endured for the most part intact through all of the generations and in all of "the nations" and with almost no diversity. The *Seder* in Yemen or Libya is pretty much the same as it is in Brooklyn!

A successful deterrent to diversity has come through availability and authority provided in the *Shulchan Aruch*[10] (Code of Law) prepared by 16th century scholar, Joseph Caro. The *Shulchan Aruch* is in full acceptance and application within Judaism today. Its chief attribute is that it has an orderly format and condenses into a single volume what *Talmud* comprises in eighteen volumes pertaining to everyday applications of the Law.

Since their "scattering," Jewish practices have always been influenced by local customs of "the nations" – that is, Gentiles. Such influence, however, is typically in a negative sense. *Shulchan Aruch* (*Yoreh Deah* 178,1) cautions Jewish people not to "follow the ways of the heathen." An example of "negative" influence is the *yarmulke* (Hebrew: *kippah*) – the small skullcap worn by Jewish men. The Jewish people in Europe and Russia felt revulsion at the sight of Gentiles' worshiping with heads uncovered. Accordingly, therefore, the Rabbis have ordered that Jewish men should always worship with the head covered. Of course, the more liberal and modern Jewish denominations do not always wear the *yarmulke* unfailingly.

Sad to say, many Jewish people are not at all religious. These are sometimes called "Traditional Jews," in that they proudly claim their "Jewishness," but they do not observe the Jewish Law. Maybe they do not even attend synagogue. Some "Traditional Jews" merely observe the two most Holy Feast days, if at all; i.e., Passover and Day of Atonement, *Yom Kippur*.

It is equally sad of course that the same can certainly be stated regarding many Christians who display little "enthusiasm" for their faith. Yes, – we have observed so-called "C&E" Christians on Christmas and Easter, which might be the only time they attend worship services all year. And, you can bet with confidence that Jewish people, as well as others outside the Christian faith, are quick to take note and share with their friends when we Christians display actions (or inactions) that our Faith condemns.

ALL Jewish men are required to observe the Law stated by Deuteronomy 16:16:

"Three times in a year shall all thy males appear before the Lord thy God in the place which He shall choose; on the feast of unleavened bread, the feast of weeks, and on the feast of tabernacles; and they shall not appear before the Lord empty; every man shall give as he is able, according to the blessing of the Lord thy God which He hath given thee."

God requires that *every* Jewish male shall attend these three feasts at Jerusalem during *every* year of his life. Now, why do you suppose the Lord commanded such prestige for these three feasts? My belief is that it is because each of these holidays relates most significantly to Messiah, especially in the life and in fulfillment of the Law by Jesus of Nazareth.

Pesach – (Passover) His Sacrifice as the Holy Lamb of God was on this day.

Shavuoth – (Pentecost or Weeks) His Holy Spirit was delivered to the Church on this day, which was about one week after His Ascension.

Sukkoth – (Feast of Tabernacles or Booths) Upon Jesus' Return, He will reign over His Kingdom on Earth for one thousand years, beginning on this day.

Now, some might offer an excuse for modern day Jewish people that, since the Temple is not presently available for them to "*appear before the Lord thy God,*" they really cannot be held to this statute. – Not to worry! – The text immediately following instructs that it can be "*in the place which the Lord shall choose.*" This demonstrates that the Lord, obviously "thinking ahead," KNEW that His Chosen would have this stumbling block. The Lord thy God therefore chose His Words accordingly; meaning nowadays it can be "wherever" He might choose for each Jewish man. As we have shown in the life of Jesus, observance of the festival is what is important to the Lord. It must be in the heart. But, for most Jewish people this practice has fallen by the wayside.

A Jewish friend and co-worker made a fitting observation on this subject about the absence of Jewish worshipers from their synagogues on those three most Holy days:

"Notwithstanding the fact that this observance is a Commandment from the Lord; if for no other reason, we should observe these days in honor of those millions of Jews who died to preserve our heritage and tradition. – We owe them that much."

In this work it has been easy to understand another and very practical reason for our lack of scholarship in study of Judaism's "rules." *Talmud* and *Midrash*, as well as other ancient Judaica works, only in the last century have been translated into English editions. Moreover, those editions comprise many volumes, much of which is of doubtful spiritual worth and some of which is even suspect as having been derived from "The Evil Inclination," himself!

The Tamudic Rabbis were of course only men. Upon study of such Judaic works it is painfully obvious that some of these were corrupt and even hateful. Some critics of this book have been quick to point out these failings. And, in that way, they rationalize their action of "throwing out the baby with the bath water!"

Some critics from the more conservative corners among Christian theologians, brand this study of Judaica as undesirable because it is "extra-Biblical." – (Their word.) Here they proudly and piously claim *sola scriptura* (only Scripture) has any authority. They would ignore and reject any historical documentation even when it confirms Scripture! – Their disdain continues with stating that the writers of this material were "Jews" – as they actually spew that word. Even Flavius Josephus is shunned for being a Jew, except for those portions of his work that are strictly secular. This form of anti-Semitism (which they vehemently deny!) launched against Josephus and the Rabbis becomes even more painful as even Jewish people reject their teachers as well as that most respected of 1st century historians – because he "cast-his-lot" with the Romans.

Readers will notice that preparation of this work has frequently referenced statements from *The Jewish Book of Why*.[6,7] Jewish people naturally are curious regarding the complex and frequently puzzling aspects of their traditions. This is why Alfred *Kolatch*'s wondrous books are so valuable. But, it should also be valuable to Christians who have "heart" as well as "curiosity" toward Judaism and the Jewish people. Having made extensive study of *Talmud*, *Midrash* and other Judaica, as well as Jewish traditional practices, there can now be a basis for a *Christian Book of "How"*! – The thoughts and facts brought forth in all parts of this book dramatize some of the Christian "*How*" questions that should emerge, if only through curiosity.

In this book, therefore, we have made effort to explain "How" Jesus actually "lived" fulfillment of Jewish everyday Law principles. This required a detailed study of literal Scripture in concert with some Jewish works. Until modern publishing/media output has become available to ALL faiths, such works have been somewhat remote from Christian scholars. In order to extract worthwhile material from Judaica, Christian scholars must be willing and driven to search diligently through Jewish "extra-Biblical" material for connections to the Gospel.

Some critics are quick to point out the less appealing and even repulsive portions contained in *Talmud*. Well, of course there are some things in *Talmud* that are offensive to Christians, but that makes no excuse for ignoring such a source of Beautiful Gospel reflections. Again – *"Don't throw out the baby with the bath water!"*

The "purging" of Judaica can be traced back at least to Pope Innocent III early during the 13th century. The Pope decreed that all Jews be required to wear a distinctive garment or a badge of some sort to identify them as Jews. (Does this sound familiar?!) Their markings caused Jewish people to necessarily hide or to avoid being seen in public, for fear of beatings, chasing, jeering, etc. At that same time, an attack on Jewish writings was launched by churchmen all over Europe.

A few years later in 1239 C.E., Pope Gregory IX declared the *Talmud* as a distortion of Scripture and blasphemous against God and Jesus Christ. Gregory directed that all copies of *Talmud* should be seized and burned. His orders were carried out through all of Europe. Earlier, we referred to Johannes Reuchlin, who searched Europe during the 15th century to find a *Talmud*. The only tractate he could obtain was that of *Sanhedrin*. After that purge of *Talmudic* writings, obtaining such material remained difficult until the most recent century.

Do Christians Need The Law?   253

+ Qualified by Scripture, the Law or Historians
  Not qualified by Scripture, the Law or Historians

		Church of Holy Sepulchre	Vicinity of Garden Tomb	Olivet Summit
Temple faced eastward	Exodus 38:13 - 15	+	+	+
Temple faced the Mount of Olives	Mk. 13:3, Illus. 19, 20	+	+	+
Centurion saw the Veil and Jewish graves	Matthew 27:51 - 54			+
Jewish graves on Olivet since 500 B.C.E.	Zechariah 14:4			+
Latrines were on NW side of Jerusalem. (Graves would not be next to latrines)	*The Temple Scroll* Prof. Y. Yadin	+		+
John says Jesus fulfilled Zech. 12 - 14. (i.e., he stood on the Mount of Olives)	John 19:37 Zechariah 14:4			+ +
Jesus fulfilled Law of the Red Heifer:	Matthew 5:17			

Heifers were slain at Olivet Summit
   Priest saw Veil as he sprinkled blood
   Sprinkled at 3rd hour toward Veil
	Talmud, Middoth 2:4
	Talmud, Middoth 2:4
	Illus. 17, 18, 19
				+
				+
				+

And His Tomb must be a clean Place:	Numbers 19:9			
Must be an unused hewn stone chamber Must have air space beneath the corpse	Luke 23:53 *Parah* 3:2, 3:6	+	+	+ +
Eusebius says Cross and Tomb on Olivet	*Proof of the Gospel*			+
All sacrifices were east of the Temple.	Illus. 15, 16, 18, 21			+
Holiest sacrifice burnt "outside camp" i.e., about 1000 yards east of Temple at the summit of the Mount of Olives	Illus. 19, 20, 26 *Talmud, Yoma* 68a *Zebahim* 106a			+ + +
Names Golgotha -- Calvary -- Skull Hill arose when thousands of skulls remained after burning these animals atop the Mount of Olives.	Matthew 5:17			+
Jesus fulfilled Law of:				

Atonement Goats
   Atonement Bullocks
   Bullocks of Daily Sin Offerings
   Bullocks of Individual Sin Offerings
	Leviticus 16:27
	Leviticus 16:27
	Exodus 29:14
	Leviticus 411
				+
				+
				+
				+

Jesus fulfilled Law of Passover Lamb, which was killed outside the camp; i.e., 1000 yards from the Temple	Matthew 5:17 Exodus 12:6 Illus. 19, 20, 26			+ + +
Criminals executed outside the camp	Numbers 15:30 - 36			+

Illus. 25: Checklist for Locales of The Crucifixion

Checklist Summary for Locales of The Crucifixion

Temple faced eastward.

Temple faced the Mount of Olives.

Centurion saw the Veil and Jewish graves.

Jewish graves on *Olivet* since 500 B.C.E.

Latrines were on NW side of Jerusalem.

(Graves would not be next to latrines.)

Jesus fulfilled Zechariah 12 – 14, including that He stood on the Mount of Olives.

Jesus fulfilled Law of the Red Heifer: — Heifers were slain at *Olivet* summit — Priest saw Veil as he sprinkled blood — Sprinkled at 3rd hour toward Veil And, His Tomb must be "a clean Place": — Must be an unused hewn stone chamber — Must have air space beneath corpse Eusebius says Cross & Tomb on *Olivet*. All sacrifices were east of the Temple. Holiest sacrifices burnt "outside camp" about 1000 yards east of Temple at the summit of the Mount of Olives . Names, "*Golgotha* " – "Calvary" from "Place of the Skull," where thousands of skulls lay after burning these animals atop the Mount of Olives . Jesus fulfilled Law of:

— Atonement Goats

— Atonement Bullocks

— Bullocks for daily Sin Offerings.

— Bullocks for individual Sin Offerings.

Jesus fulfilled Law of Passover Lamb, which was killed "outside the camp"; i.e., 1000 yards from the Temple.

Criminals executed "outside the camp".

Thus, can anyone seriously believers those Rabbis "invented" this tragic drama just as "entertainment" for future Jewish generations to "enjoy?" Does anyone seriously suggest that the Rabbis of 100 – 200 C.E. would intentionally select, for the Ascent of the *Shekhinah*, that very same site which had already been recorded in New Testament writings for the Ascension of Jesus of Nazareth?

Rather, it seems surprising they recorded this event at all. One might think they would have preferred to forget all about it. But how could they possibly "just forget about it?" You've got to be kidding! Added to this is their dedication to detail — right down to each and every movement of the Divine Presence as well as His pleadings and farewell remarks. (They *couldn't* forget it.)

There was always, of course, a reviewing and regulatory authority to determine what was accepted for such documents as the *Midrash*, *Talmud*, etc. If the story was not true, witnessed by several other Rabbis and/or persons of integrity, this material would have been rejected and those Rabbis contributing such a "fish story" would have been discredited, dishonored, or possibly even "defrocked." It is no small wonder that modern Judaism has avoided/ignored this story; both in their own synagogues and in general publication. However, it surely must have been intended to be related to all of us, eventually, as a "lesson" from the Lord.

It is my opinion that this story shows two basic lessons from God to be noticed and studied by *both* Christians and Jews:

Christians: God did indeed forgive the Jews (and the rest of us) at The Cross. He did not terminate His Everlasting Covenant with His Chosen People. Rather, He fulfilled another Promise to them; which most of them failed to recognize and accept, because to a large extent they were (and are) "blinded" by tradition. Perhaps the Lord may forgive Jews for failing to recognize Jesus as Messiah. But, He will not forgive their sins unless they repent of their sins, yearn earnestly for Messiah and observe the Law that surely points to His sacrificial death and blood offering for their sins.

Jews: The Lord gave another "sign" in the fact that His Divine Presence ascended from the same place at which the earliest Jewish followers of *Y'shua ben Yusef* of Nazareth witnessed His Ascension forty years earlier. He did not cut you off from Himself at the death of His Innocent, as many Christians have been saying for centuries in order to justify their persecution of your people. But, He did "go back to His Place" (Hosea 5:15) and He has smitten and scattered you for almost "two days"; (Hosea 6:1 – 2); but not before He spoke to you again, just as He did through the "fire" and the "cloud" during the Exodus from Egypt.

We must especially take notice of the importance of this event to Jews and Christians, in that the most faithful and obedient of both faiths were warned by this startling Event to "get out of camp" before the destruction of Jerusalem and the Temple. Both groups of serious Believers were obedient to God's Word in the command given in Exodus 40:36 – 38, knowing that when the "fire" or the "cloud" withdrew from the Tabernacle, they were to move "the camp." This warning did much to preserve those who deserved to survive the slaughter to follow in 70 C.E. as well as guide both "flocks" through the Church Age.

Indeed, we see a tragic irony in that some of both groups knew, at that time, that the *Shekhinah* Withdrawal had a personal meaning for each of them. Bittersweet irony emerges in this day as neither group wants to hear this story. Both sides need to know these truths. It is becoming increasingly important that Jews and Christians draw closer together against the untruthful traditions of men and the worldly onslaughts of Satanism, anti-Judaism, Humanism and a general decline of so-called Judeo-Christian ethics.

Truly, this story brings about a convergence of Judaism and Christianity "at a point;" yes, both figuratively and literally (on the Mount of Olives). But it should cause us to question ourselves once more: "WHY does God even bother with us? WHY does He go to so much trouble to get through to us? He doesn't need us. We need Him! Why should He weep and lament over leaving His earthly abode?" Again, why should God even concern Himself over us?

Part of the answer is, of course, that God not only has Infinite Power and Infinite Riches: He also has Infinite Patience, Infinite Wisdom, and Infinite Time. He gives Infinite Love and Infinite Mercy. He gives all this to us, asking nothing from us but our love for Him and for each other. He gives all things to us despite our persistent inclination and surrender to every kind of sin. In fact, God can do no less than "infinity" in anything. God is ALL!

Persisting to this day and age, a continuing tendency among many Christian teachers, from liberal to conservative factions, exists to somewhat ignore even the Old Testament. An example of this is the practice of some Christian groups that distribute New Testaments to prospective Believer "candidates." This almost appears to be as if to say the Old Testament has been made obsolete by the New Testament and: "The Old Testament is just Jewish history." etc., etc. That type of thinking extends to what has been called "Replacement Theology;" which claims: "Oh, the Lord has banished the Jews. – We (Christians) are now His Chosen People." – Regrettably, such practice at times seems to smack of some subtle form of anti-Semitism.

This "Replacement" philosophy can be refuted easily by looking at the Jewish people today. One needs only to look at how God has "bruised" and "smitten" Israel during the past two millennia; and yet – He has miraculously preserved them as a people – and even as a nation. – Israel is truly a Miracle Nation! Contrastingly, does anybody know the present status of the nations of: the "Girgasites"? – the "Philistines"? – the "Edomites"? – etc., etc.

I am convinced that Christians have the best of intentions about leading persons to Salvation through the Word of God. And, maybe the "candidates" would be discouraged by the sheer size of the volume, if they were given the complete Bible. Since many people whom we might approach about accepting Faith have never had any contact with or had any knowledge of the Bible, it is obvious that the New Testament is "better than nothing" and at least it does present the Gospel of Jesus Christ. Nevertheless, at some point in a Believer's growth, that person needs to be shown and encouraged to study toward understanding the importance of the Old Testament.

Moreover, in leading Jewish people to Salvation through Messiah *Y'shua* of Nazareth (Jesus), Evangelical Christians can expect much more rapport with Jewish "candidates" if they bring them to recognize Jesus in their own *Tenakh* (Old Testament). Similarly, persons of Islamic faith also are familiar with the *Pentateuch*, and may be more easily reached if they see Jesus through those first five books of the Old Testament. And, a final recommendation: **Other than our righteous Christian "Walk," there is no stronger tool for evangelizing than having a thorough knowledge of both Old Testament and New Testament Scriptures.**

Many Christians would agree that:

"The Old Testament makes no sense without the New Testament.

And, the New Testament makes no sense without the Old Testament."

Finally, some Christian scholars issue the excuse that the Jewish people themselves are "hiding" their ancient works from outsiders and prefer that Gentiles should not enter the

Jews' domain in this way. Most any Christian scholar will find very soon that he is not only welcome to study at Judaica libraries; he is even encouraged! Jewish friends are pleasantly impressed by the efforts of *any* Christian who studies Judaism in even the most mundane facets of that Faith. A similar positive relationship develops when an American makes even a minimal attempt at the language in a foreign land. It is a sign of deep respect and is appreciated accordingly by the "host."

Finally, some Christian scholars issue the excuse that the Jewish people themselves are "hiding" their ancient works from outsiders and prefer that Gentiles should not enter the Jews' domain in this way. Most any Christian scholar will find very soon that he is not only welcome to study at Judaica libraries; he is even encouraged! What better way to reach Jewish people with the Gospel of Jesus as Messiah than to show them how He appears throughout their *Mishnaic* statutes, and even in "every jot and tittle" of their painfully strict and detailed Rabbinic traditions. These volumes are available in many libraries of universities, synagogues and private collections throughout the world. Yes! – and now these works are even available on computers. – There is no longer *any* excuse.

A rather cynical appraisal of *The Babylonian Talmud* from *The Encyclopedia Americana* (paraphrased) goes something like this:

Since Talmud reflects the fullness of life through many centuries of Judaism, it contains as many contradictions as life itself. A person can find in it whatever he seeks. Talmud has been not only a source of inspiration to Jews, but it has also provided critical argument for detractors of Judaism. Categories of logic as seen by the Talmudic thinkers who prepared the texts are so different from modern logic so as to appear almost ludicrous to an outsider.

A certain amount of truth is borne in these statements. However, it is not exactly true that one "can find in it whatever he seeks." As we continue through this book, readers will find some of these *Talmudic* statements strike right to the heart of Christianity and are not "contradicted" anywhere else in *Talmud*. The Red Heifer ceremony is a classic example of this claim. That most sacred rite is a Perfect "Picture" of the blood Offering and Cleansing provided through The Crucifixion of Jesus of Nazareth.

One remark is especially treasured from the author of that somewhat cynical *Encyclopedia Americana* appraisal, a professor of Jewish History, Literature and Institutions at a major university. He states that only a scholar who has "spent a lifetime" exploring *Talmud*, and whose mind has been conformed to think in "*Talmudic* idioms" is competent to discuss statements from *Talmud* "with impunity." As readers follow our work and considering the amount of study and background we have put into it, we hope that impunity will be granted to us upon those criteria. It is further our hope and prayer that persons who read this book will come to realize that, without some knowledge of the Law and Jewish tradition, they are missing a great amount of precious insight into the Gospel of Jesus Christ. Such would be the case for Christians, especially.

In closing this discussion of Judaic Law, it is heartening to learn, from *Baba Kama* 38a and from *Sanhedrin* 59a, Jewish Rabbinical teaching states that *"even a heathen* (Gentile) *who studies Torah is equal in status to a High Priest!"* A footnote adds that "studying" also includes "observing" the *Torah*.

References and Bibliography for: Do Christians Need the Law?

(References are noted as superscripts in the text)

1. *The Babylonian Talmud*, Quincentenary Edition, The Soncino Press, Lt'd., Brooklyn NY – 1978
2. *The Works of Josephus*, New Updated Edition, (Translated by Wm. Whiston, A.M.), Hendrickson Publishers – Peabody MA – 1987
3. *Holy Bible—From the Ancient Eastern Text*, George M. Lamsa, Harper San Francisco – 1968
4. *The Pentateuch and HafTorahs*, 2nd Edition, Dr. J. H. Hertz, (Ed.), Soncino Press, London – 1965
5. *Jewish Literacy*, Rabbi Joseph Telushkin, William. Morrow and Company, Inc., New York – 1991
6. *The Jewish Book of Why*, Alfred J. *Kolatch*, Johnathan David Publishers, Inc., Middle Village, NY – 1997
7. *The Second Jewish Book of Why*, Alfred J. *Kolatch*, Johnathan David Publishers, Inc., Middle Village NY – 1996
8. *Easton's Revised Bible Dictionary*, from The Online Bible CD-ROM (See Reference 15.)
9. *New Edition of The Babylonian Talmud*, Book 10; Volume II; Pgs. 70-79, Michael L. Rodkinson, The *Talmud* Society – Boston MA – 1918
10. 10. *Kitzur Shulchan Aruch* – Code of Jewish Law, R. Solomon Ganzfried, Transl. By Hyman Goldin, L.L.B. – Hebrew Publishing Co. – 77-79 Delancey St. – Brooklyn NY –1927
11. *The Soncino Talmud* CD-ROM* – *Davka* Corporation – Chicago IL – 2002
12. *The Soncino Midrash* CD-ROM* – *Davka* Corporation – Chicago IL – 2002
13. *The Torah, A Modern Commentary* – Union of American Hebrew Congregations – New York –1981
14. *Jewish New Testament Commentary* – David Stern – Jewish New Testament Publications, Inc. – P.O. Box 615 – Clarksville MD 21029 – 1996
15. *The Online Bible* CD-ROM* Cross Country Software – Niagara Falls NY – 2003
16. *The Chumash – The Stone Edition* – Sixth Edition – Compiling Ed. Rabbi Nosson Scherman – Mesorah Publications, Lt'd. – Brooklyn NY – 1996

13

The Forgotten Sacrifice

Judaism's most important, most sacred rite – Ashes of the "Red Heifer" evaded Solomon's wisdom — Unknown to Jews or Christians – Bodes Coming of Messiah –Hidden for centuries – Obvious "picture" of Jesus

The story of the Red Heifer burning, the most important of the ancient Jewish Temple rites. The ashes of this young, unblemished "Red Cow" — perfect in every detail — were mixed with water and used to purify all things "unclean."

Unravelling the mystery that overwhelmed even the supreme wisdom of King Solomon.

Meanings and messages for the Jewish people and "pictures" of Christ are revealed for Christians from Scripture for this rite and from the Hebrew Talmud and Midrash.

These sacred ashes soon will be recovered after being hidden for 1900 years, opening the way for prophecy fulfillments leading to appearance of the Jewish people's long awaited Messiah and their Hope for restoring the Third Temple.

Recovery of those ashes brings Christians ever closer to their Blessed Hope of Jesus Coming again to claim His Kingdom.

Several surprises revealed about The Crucifixion. — Some "NEW" Gospel stories – Several Biblical facts that you never heard before.

An intriguing story is unfolding in Israel's Dead Sea region and which very soon will herald an event of exceptional historical/religious/geo-political significance. This story is presently known to only a small band of Believers who are mostly supporters of literally only a handful of Evangelical prophetic ministries.

The story of which I write concerns the search for the Ashes of The Red Heifer. The Red Heifer (Hebrew: *Parah adumah*) was a burnt offering of a red "cow" as commanded by the Lord to the Children of Israel in Chapter 19 of the Book of Numbers. "*Parah*" appears frequently in this text as the title for the *Talmud* tractate of the Law for this ritual; and is actually the Hebrew word for a young cow or heifer.

The ashes remaining from the burning are then mixed with "living water" and sprinkled in order to purify persons or things that are "unclean" under the Law. It is the single most important and the most Holy of all the Jewish Temple ordinances and yet it is the least known and perhaps the least understood. It is the most important because none of the other offerings or sacrifices, nor the priests, not even the Temple, can be acceptable to God without being purified by the ashes from this burnt offering.

We should begin our discussion by referring to The Book of Numbers 19, Verses 1 — 6.

"*And the Lord spake unto Moses and unto Aaron, saying,*

This is the ordinance of the law which the Lord hath commanded, saying, Speak unto the children of Israel, that they bring thee a red heifer without spot, wherein is no blemish, and upon which never came yoke:

And ye shall give her unto Eleazar the Priest, that he may bring her forth without the camp, and one shall slay her before his face:

And Eleazar the priest shall take of her blood with his finger, and sprinkle of her blood directly before the Tabernacle of the congregation seven times:

And one shall burn the heifer in his sight; her skin, and her flesh, and her blood, with her dung, shall he burn:

And the priest shall take cedarwood, and hyssop and scarlet, and cast it into the midst of the burning of the heifer."

If the foregoing Old Testament Scripture is puzzling to you, please don't feel inadequate or intimidated. Jewish scholars have pondered over this rite from the time of Moses and continuing today. Some of the mystery is dramatized in a quote from *Midrash Rabbah* Numbers 19:2 from the Gaon of Wilna in *Adereth Eliyahu*, authored by a noted Russian *Talmudist* Elijah ben Solomon (1720 – 1797). This scholar "calculated" that the Biblical section dealing with the Red Heifer contains seven mentions of seven things; namely, seven mentions of a heifer, seven of burning, seven of sprinkling, seven of washing, seven of uncleanness, seven of cleanness, and seven of priests.

The scholar's calculations were evidently inspired by a passage at the beginning of *Midrash Rabbah* Numbers, which states that a Rabbi Hanan ben Pazzi declared that Psalms 12:7 (Psalms 12:6 in KJV) refers to the Red Heifer –

"The words of the Lord are pure words, As silver tried in a crucible on the earth, Refined seven times."

It is to be commented, however, that these "calculations" must have been from ancient Aramaic or Hebrew Scriptures. Applying such calculations from the relatively modern *Masoretic Text*[25] in the English translation of the Hebrew Scriptures does not reflect these same counts for these seven words. Still, these kinds of remarks from the scholars are fascinating and interesting to observe and investigate. Commentary concerning traceability of language origins in ancient Scriptural manuscripts is presented in Appendix F of this book.

According to Jewish tradition, even King Solomon, arguably one of the wisest of all mortals, humbly admitted he did not understand the meaning of the Red Heifer ceremony. This tradition is recorded in the commentary of *Midrash Rabbah* Ecclesiastes 7:36. King Solomon is quoted in a footnote, saying of the Red Heifer: *"Concerning all these ordinances (of the Torah), I have stood and investigated (their meaning), but the chapter of the Red Heifer I have been unable to fathom. When I labored therein and searched deeply into it, I said: '...I will get wisdom; but it was far from me.' "* In other words, Solomon was saying: "For certain, I am no dummy and I did try, but this one is beyond me."

Many Jewish Scriptural commentaries agree concerning the uncertainty of meaning in this rite. One source[26] has said the procedures for the Red Heifer ceremony are "often called the most mysterious laws of the *Torah*." It has been said that the Rabbis have long sought in vain to "plumb the rationale" of these laws and have finally concluded that the Lord set forth these ordinances to test the obedience of the Children of Israel. And, after having devoted many years to that study, this happens to be our conclusion as well. Another source[34] offers a declaration carrying wisdom reminiscent of Solomon to those who would question the Lord's intent in this ceremony:

"...an essential component of wisdom is the knowledge that man's failure to understand truth does not make it untrue."

It comes as no surprise, therefore, that the noted and brilliant Jewish historian, Flavius Josephus[4], made only the slightest mention of the Red Heifer ceremony (*Antiq.* 4.4.6) in his otherwise thorough coverage of Judaism. It would seem that Josephus did not wish to take up an intellectual challenge that baffled even King Solomon!

Then, you ask, "If King Solomon's wisdom could not unravel the mysteries of the Heifer, how can we Twenty-first Century Gentiles ever hope to comprehend this Jewish riddle?" You *must* inquire, also – "And, how do you, a retired engineer even without any seminary background, consider that – *you* – can explain what even King Solomon could not fathom?" -- It must be conceded to all that anyone – and most especially a Gentile layman (!) – must have more than an abundant supply of *chutzpah* (brass), impertinence, etc., to claim an understanding of this Jewish "puzzle."

Those are excellent questions and justifiable concerns. — Nevertheless, and intending no conceit, the simplest answer is that we now are blessed with "20/20 hindsight," since we are regarding this Jewish rite *after* Messiah. After all, King Solomon was the "24th Great" Grandfather of Jesus. Solomon could not have seen the picture that we are enabled to see of his "24th Great" **Grand-Son!**

However, knowing as we do, almost any Christian *should* see immediately the parallels of this ritual with the Gospel of Jesus Christ. Also, we now have libraries full of writings from the sages where many, although certainly not all, answers can be found, if one is interested and knows where and how to seek them. If we are familiar with the Gospel of Jesus Christ and if we have His Message in our hearts, we will see His Gospel all through this most Holy of Jewish sacrifices. The Gospel helps us to see clearly what even King Solomon was unable to decipher.

And, besides – King Solomon issued a challenge that he himself should have taken up against this daunting question:

> "It is the glory of God to conceal a thing: but the honour of kings is to search out a matter." – Proverbs 25:2

Watch now as the story unfolds.

Since we are going to show that the Red Heifer ceremony is a "picture" of The Crucifixion, Resurrection and Ascension of Jesus Christ, it is not surprising to note another indicator of its importance. That is, The Crucifixion, Resurrection and Ascension of Jesus Christ are, without argument, the most important Events in all of human history. From the evidence we have gathered here, it should be abundantly clear that the Red Heifer rite reflects Jesus' Crucifixion, Resurrection and Ascension accurately and thoroughly; thereby reflecting that importance.

To our surprise, we have encountered recognition of this picture of Christ even in one Jewish text[26], where a quote from the African priest/scholar, Augustine (C.E. 354-430), is offered. Augustine explained that the perfection of the Heifer and her death outside-the-camp portrays the ministry of Jesus as: Red denotes the color of the Blood of The Passion – Cedar suggests Hope – Hyssop as Faith – Scarlet as Charity. It is further noted that the dead who render men unclean are of man's dead works.

Notwithstanding this importance, both Christianity and Judaism nevertheless have ignored the Red Heifer ceremony for the past 1900 years. Seldom is this burnt offering even mentioned from Christian pulpits and with only brief and detached mention in the synagogue. This latter failing is especially difficult to fathom, considering the fact that it is the single most Holy and most important of all Jewish Temple rites. Our purpose here is to describe and explain that Holiness and importance and to show why in these "latter days" its importance is dramatically increased.

The Red Heifer ceremony actually is a burnt offering rather than a sacrifice *per se*. This is because, technically, the "sacrifices" are eaten by the Priests; whereas, the burnt offerings are more Holy and the entire animal carcasses are burned at the summit of the Mount of Olives at a particular location. At this point it is appropriate that we point out the fact that the word *"holocaust"* essentially means: "burnt offering." The word comes from the Greek *holocaustos* and/or the Latin *holocaustum*, meaning burnt whole – as in the burnt offering we discuss here. It is certain that God wept as His Chosen People were being "sent up" as a "burnt offering" from the World during 1940-1945.

The Red Heifer ceremony is important to the Jewish people because, with the imminent arrival of their Messianic Age, Jewish Temple worship will resume in fulfillment of the prophets' declarations for "the Day of the Lord." For Christians, the Red Heifer is of equal importance because the resumption of Temple worship is one of those signs that announce the Coming of Messiah. (See Daniel 9:27)

A note under the *HafTorah*[25] for the Sabbath and New Moon explains that the purpose for the Temple was to lead mankind to "reverence and uprightness." The sacrifices, it is stated, were instituted in order to help worshipers repel evil thoughts and desires from their hearts by representing them as burnt offerings upon the Altar.

The return to these practices of course then precedes the Glorious return of Jesus to stand victorious atop the Mount of Olives to begin His Kingdom Age. It is ironic that both of these ages will begin for both of these closely "distant" faiths (Judaism and Christianity) on that same "Day." Nevertheless, very few of either group are aware that the ashes of the Red Heifer are the "keystone" of the events that will lead up to the arrival of Jesus Christ as Messiah at the Mount of Olives to begin His reign in His Earthly Kingdom for 1000 years.

Just prior to destruction of the Temple in C.E. 70, Judean zealots, probably of the ultra-conservative Essene sect, hid the precious ashes of the Heifers in the desert region presently called *Qumran*, located near the Dead Sea. An anxious, tedious and often frustrating search to locate and recover the ashes has been under way since 1968. The team of archaeologists engaged in this search and excavation now expect to reach the ashes very soon. With this background, we wish to present a discussion to learn as much as possible about this important and timely venture.

The Red Heifer Ceremony is the most important, the most mysterious, the least known, the most unique and the least understood of all Jewish rites in Scripture.

- It is the most important because none of the Temple articles, the Priests or even the Temple itself would be acceptable for "cleanness" without purification from the ashes of the Red Heifer. Importance of the Red Heifer Ceremony is detailed in *Midrash Rabbah* Exodus 19:2, where Scripture is quoted from Psalms 119:80 – *"Let my heart be undivided in Thy statutes,"*

- This refers to the fact that the statute of the Red Heifer is similar to the Passover statute. A footnote explains that "statutes" means there are at least two statutes. The Rabbis conclude that the Scripture refers to the statutes of Passover (Exodus 12); and the statutes of the Red Heifer Ceremony (Numbers 19). Moreover, the

Rabbis point out, – "*Who is to say which statute is greater than the other?*" It is explained that; "*...those who would eat the Passover must be purified by the ashes of the Red Heifer; therefore implying equal importance and requirements.*" Certainly, and contrary to the Rabbinical conclusion, it is logical that the Red Heifer is definitely a higher requirement because the Passover participants are *first* required to be purified by the ashes of the Heifer.

- The most mysterious rite because its purpose is to purify the impure, and yet, their participation defiles and renders unclean *all* of those persons who participate in any of the purifying procedures in this Holy ritual. – Yea! It purifies the impure, while at the same time it defiles the pure.

- The most unique because:

    1. The Red Heifer is the *only* offering that requires an animal of a specific color.

    2. The Red Heifer is the *only* Jewish rite in which *all* procedures are to be carried out beyond the Temple courts, specifically one Sabbath Limit distance from the Holy of Holies – "*outside the camp.*"

    3. The Red Heifer is the *only* procedure in which the entire carcass of the animal is burned; i.e., "*...her skin, and her flesh, and her blood, with her dung, shall be burnt.*" In contrast, the daily Sin Offerings and the Atonement Goats were slain in the Temple and their entrails were burnt upon the Altar of Sacrifice in the Temple Court. Although, the remainder of those carcasses were burned upon the *Miphkad* Altar atop the Mount of Olives; same as the Red Heifer, the Atonement Goat and the daily Sin Bullocks.

    4. The Red Heifer ceremony is the *only* rite in Temple worship that renders *all* of those who participate as unclean. The High Priest wore only four white garments during this ritual, just as would any ordinary "*kohen*" (priest) serving in the Temple, instead of a High Priest's usual attire in the "golden vestments."

    5. The Red Heifer's blood is the *only* blood application; i.e., "sprinkling" that is performed outside the Temple Courts; again, at one Sabbath Limit.

    6. The ashes of the Red Heifer were the *only* "burnt remains" that were actually used for any purpose *after burning*. The Heifer's ashes were of course retained in a vessel (*kalal*), later to be mixed with ("living") water and were used to "sprinkle," thereby purifying "the unclean." *All* other ashes from *all* of the other animal sacrifices were taken from the Altar and were "*poured out*" at the same location where the Heifer, the Atonement Goat and the Sin Offerings were burned; i.e., at the *Miphkad* Altar atop the Mount of Olives.

- The Red Heifer ceremony is the least known of Jewish rites because this Holy rite is seldom ever discussed in Jewish or Christian or Islamic worship. This is to be expected, of course, because Temple worship, the sacrifices, etc. are far from modern Jewish cognizance because the Temple does not presently stand at

Jerusalem. A notable exception to that silence is observed, however, in that this portion of Scripture (Numbers, Chap. 19) is read every year in the synagogues as a part of the purification during preparation for the Passover. (To be discussed later)

- Only during recent years has the Red Heifer become recognized and acknowledged in any Evangelical Christian study; albeit in very minimal terms. The principal motivation for this belated interest being restricted to but a handful of Evangelicals is in their anticipation of events indicating the nearness of the Return of Jesus Christ. His arrival will be preceded by a Jewish resumption of Temple worship, sacrifices, etc. (Daniel 9:27) The articles to be used for the sacrifices, although perhaps even in a renewed Tabernacle rather than a rebuilt Temple, *must* first be purified by the ashes of the Red Heifer.

During centuries of studies by both Jewish and Christian theologians and scholars, there have been many attempts at explanation of this mysterious and puzzling Jewish liturgy. Much of this has been derived through symbolism and metaphors. For example, Pride is said to be represented by the mighty cedar; whereas, Humility is portrayed by the lowly hyssop. Reference 25 suggests a profound meaning from a Jewish perspective as a powerful lesson for all people who profess faith in God; i.e., a Holy God can be served *only* by a Holy People.

A Christian explanation is perhaps best derived from symbolism in a "picture" of Christ as follows:

A single, living being, Perfect in every way,

having no blemish or earthly taint, is slain.

Its blood is then used to wash other beings –

ALL of whom are imperfect in every way.

Could there ever be a more obvious "picture" of Jesus Christ?! – Although some of our most beloved and respected conservative Christian Evangelical teachers disagree, this picture of Christ *should* be obvious to almost anyone. Jesus Christ *was* Perfect and *living* as a "man," but without *any* blemish and with *no* worldly taint or sin. His Blood became the Burnt Offering for cleansing ALL men – ALL of whom are imperfect, and whose sins His Blood washed away for ever! – Again! – Could there *ever* be a more obvious picture?

But ask almost anyone: "What do you know about the Red Heifer Ashes?" and the answer probably will be: "The what??!" — Until very recently, few Christians and only the most observant Jews, ever heard of the Red Heifer..."What about it?...What ashes?" In hardly any Bible dictionaries, or books on Biblical customs or Biblical history, etc., will you find the Red Heifer listed or even mentioned. Some Christian commentaries discuss it; although, usually in a very casual and/or even negative context. Typically, these commentaries completely ignore and/or deny any picture of Jesus Christ in this most Holy offering. It is extremely rare that you ever will hear of the Red Heifer from your pastor.

We should point out, however, that some of the more traditional Jewish synagogue congregations take notice of the Red Heifer at the Passover season. As explained earlier, traditional synagogues read the chapter about the "Red Cow;" i.e., Numbers Chapter 19, on one of the Sabbaths prior to Passover.

In Paragraph 12 of this book we described the "portions" or *Sedrim* that are read from the *Torah* and a corresponding or "reflecting" reading from the Prophets is read for each as the *HafTorah* on each Sabbath in the synagogue. However, on certain Sabbaths, readings in addition to the standard reading for that Sabbath date also are read. *Talmud Megillah* 4:5 and 30a is specific in that two "additional" readings will be given before *Purim* and two will be given after that Feast Holiday as well. The instruction further details that the "Red Cow" reading takes place on the first Sabbath following *Purim*.

On that next Sabbath after the Feast of *Purim*, the additional reading (*Sedrah*) from the *Torah* is Numbers 19:1 – 22. The reading includes, from Numbers 19:19:

"...and the clean person shall sprinkle upon the unclean on the third day..."

The *HafTorah* corresponding to the *Sedrah* from Numbers is Ezekiel 36:16 – 38, which includes Verse 25, saying:

"And I will sprinkle clean water upon you, and ye shall be clean, from all your uncleannesses, and from all your idols, will I cleanse you."

The objective here is of course to commemorate the need for purification preparatory to observing that approaching sacred Holiday Feast (Passover) and that they shall enter it in a state of purity. The reflection of similar thoughts between the *Torah* and the Prophet would seem to be obvious in this case. From this it can be seen that Jewish worshipers are not ignoring the Red Heifer; although, perceivably they are puzzled as to its real meaning, other than its role as a purification ritual. Moreover, these congregations are following this procedure more by rote than from having any real connection as to the meaning behind these readings.

Even if Gentile Christians or Muslims or Jewish worshipers have heard of the ashes, they might not know of the vital importance of this somewhat obscure rite of Judaism, especially during these "Latter Days." Even fewer persons are aware of why, if, where or whatever became of the Ashes. Many just don't care anything about this subject, but maybe they would care if they knew this story and why it is so important and exciting for faithful Jews and Christians that those Ashes be recovered *soon*!

Very briefly, the Red Heifer Ashes were kept for ritual "cleansing" of the priests, buildings and persons and objects who became "unclean" as a result of having touched a corpse or a bone or blood. Most significant to Christians is the symbolism portrayed by the slaying of one unblemished, innocent life and mixing its ashes (blood) with "living water" in order to wash-away the sins of many others who are not innocent. (John 4:10) This "picture" or "type" of Jesus Christ has several profound meanings for all of us. The Passover Lamb, the Atonement He-Goat and all the Temple sacrifices of lambs, bulls, goats, doves, etc. represent a similar picture or type of our "burnt offering" - Jesus.

Think of it! – The Christian faith is the *only* belief founded on the concept that *one* death of *one* Perfect person, who *never* sinned, can pay – redeem – wipe out *all* sins of *all* who have sinned. – And, ALL *have* sinned! – INCREDIBLE! It is no wonder that one must permit the Holy Spirit to lead him to believe and accept such a concept. Man could never grasp such a tenet through his own wisdom and rationalization. (People would think he is insane!)

However, in His Mercy, God permitted His Chosen People to make atonement (Leviticus 1:4) for their sins in the system of Mosaic Law with the sacrifices outlined, with the addition of the Red Heifer. But there are some exclusive features of this Holy rite that set it apart from the others and give it a Christ-like resemblance not shared by any other Jewish sacrifice or offering. Savor these now as we examine Scripture and Jewish tradition to behold Jesus and The Gospel within these pictures.

14

"Pictures" from the Red Heifer

Verses interpreted – "Perfect" Heifer – "Legal" details – Outside the Camp – "Uncleanness" – A "Perfect" Ceremony – "Types" teach meaning – Temple design precision – Cinnamon Delight – A most important "weed"—Sacred Evenings – Raising "Clean" children

Verse-by-verse, let us examine God's Word in this event. As I was led to write this, I prayed and believed the Holy Spirit would guide me in these interpretations, some of which you may even oppose. But, please pray that He will open *your* eyes to newer pictures which will further edify and which may be even more beautiful than these.

Referring to Numbers, Chapter 19, remember that all of this was spoken personally by the Lord to Moses and Aaron when the Lord appeared to them as the "fire" or the "cloud" in the Tabernacle.

"Practically Perfect" — Verse 2

> "...Speak unto the children of Israel, that they bring thee a red heifer without spot, wherein is no blemish, and upon which never came yoke..."

Why should the animal have a red coat? The first reason most likely is for a representation of blood, although there may be a more subtle and more appropriate reason. Authenticated physical descriptions are rare; however, at least one unverified account[1] describes Jesus as having "hair the color of wine" — reddish-brown or what we might call "auburn" hair. This hue is very similar to the color of some coats found within several breeds of cattle. The Lord may have a far more lofty reason for that choice; nevertheless, these are offered as a best guess as drawn from the available information.

Another reason for such coloring might be that auburn is more exclusive and yet, it can be associated in an indirect fashion with brown, black or blond or even with carrot-red hair. Still, none of those four can, in any way, be associated directly with any of the other three. But, what about white hair? – White denotes purity and only God deserves that tone as His raiment. In this way, the auburn color may be God's way of telling us that this offering points symbolically to everyone and anyone; while at the same time it also points to His Anointed One – Messiah, Son of David.

So, why a heifer? It seems that a heifer would indicate gentleness and innocence. The difference in aggressive behavior comparing little boys vs. little girls can also be observed even among the young in the Animal Kingdom. Therefore, perhaps this submissive trait points to the innocence, reticence and passive side of Jesus. Most would agree that a young bull just would not bring across an image of submission or "low-key" behavior. (More about selection of the feminine gender under Verse 3.)

Other than the specifications from "*YHWH*" ("*Yahweh*" or "I AM") to Moses, there are many other constraints that were placed by the Rabbis on the selection of the Heifer. As the Rabbinate interpreted and formulated the Mosaic Law via *Talmud* and *Midrash*, they set forth some very stringent requirements. We shall examine those as well in our discussion.

Midrash Rabbah[3], Numbers 19:7 instructs that the Heifer (*Parah adumah*; Hebrew: a young cow) must be at least two years old. *Talmud*[2], in the *Mishnah* 1:1 and 2:5 of *Parah* tractate, presents considerable argument concerning the Heifer's age, ranging from one to five years. No reason or logic is stated; although, we can agree that such an age for a heifer suggests an individual that is youthful but mature — definitely not a calf, but neither shall she be an old cow!

Again, this reflects His youthful status during Jesus' Earthly ministry. He was at the richest years of young manhood, having just a few years earlier reached the legal Judaic age of maturity at thirty years. Thus, Jesus was youthful and mature, as was the Red Heifer.

A heifer without "spot" or "blemish" would seem to connote purity. No argument there. She must not have any scars, growths, chafes, abrasions, bare—spots, no white spots or black spots, cuts, infections, discharges, bites, lameness, deformities, broken horns or hoof cracks...NO defects...Period!

The prize Heifer had to be PERFECT. – Well, *almost* perfect. It appears that the Rabbis applied some leniency in the interest of practicality pertaining to the animal's red coat. For now, as always involves *Talmudic* Law, we get into a very "hairy" area. (Sorry!...No pun intended!)

Midrash Rabbah Numbers 19:8 and *Talmud, Parah* 2:5 decree that no more than one hair of the animal's coat may be other than red. (Honest!) However, *Parah* 1:1 argues that the Heifer can be five years old, but she can have no black hairs, but then *Parah* 2:5 counters by permitting maybe just a little "plucking" of the odd-color strands. It's no wonder that even Jesus had short patience with "the lawyers."

This passage of *Talmud* typifies the dodging, "cut-backs", twisting – yes, "weaseling" – of the Rabbinical "lawyers" as they interpret and try to apply practical(?) limits to the God—given Law. The more they try to "twist" and "pack" and "bend" and "dodge" God's Law to make it "practical," the more *impractical* it becomes. The more we study *Talmud* and *Midrash*, the easier it is to understand the Gospel descriptions of Jesus' confrontations with these "lawyers." These "legalizers" were versed in *"The Traditions of the Elders"* (Mark 7:5) and were equivalent of what today we would call "Theologian" scholars. Jesus and these lawyers were constantly at odds because the Rabbis continually made the Law more complex; whereas, Jesus continually simplified the Law — the way God intended.

Continuing in Verse 2, this Heifer must never have "felt the yoke;" i.e., never used as a work animal or for "work" of any sort. The most direct interpretation for reasoning here exists in a "cosmetic" objection to any presence of calluses, chafes, etc. from harness and wooden yokes. Such work animals in the rocky fields of the Middle East likely would also have damaged hooves and lower leg areas.

Talmudic laws are very strict on this point concerning the Heifer's "work" history. The Heifer must not have been delivered by Cesarean birth. The herdsman must swear an oath that nobody ever rode on her or even so much as threw a cloak across her back. But, she is still acceptable if a bird had landed on her back. (After all, we must be reasonable about this!) There are also some really complex statutes relative to barnyard mating antics that a heifer might encounter and which could be construed as "work."

But, perhaps the requirement for "no yoke" has a more important reference to separation from "worldly" environment. True, Jesus "worked," did manual labor, "sweated" as a carpenter, but He probably was never involved with any "worldly" business role in that trade. Joseph however, as head of the household, probably handled all of the buying, negotiating, dealing, "haggling," customer-relations, etc. that must be tended in running any business. Yes, Joseph surely "felt the yoke."

Moreover, as the first-born son in His family, under Mosaic Law (Numbers 18:15) Jesus would have been dedicated to the Lord as an infant. Remember Simeon? (Luke 2:22 – 34) In this case He perhaps would have served in the family carpenter shop only for a brief period as a teenager and then would have attended a *Yeshiva* to learn and become a Rabbi. Thus, the Red Heifer's exclusion from worldly pursuits probably does fit a parallel with Jesus.

It is seen that the Red Heifer had to be almost PERFECT. It was so difficult to breed and rear an animal meeting these specifications that it would indeed be so "precious" as to be valued well above the market value for just ordinary heifers.

Midrash Rabbah Deuteronomy 1:15 describes an incident in which a farmer sold a Red Heifer to the Temple sages. (*Talmud – Kiddushin* 31a, *Shebuoth* 11b and *Abodah Zerah* 23b relate slight variations on this same story.) In the story, the farmer was a "heathen" named Dama. Some sages came to Dama, who also operated a jewelry brokerage in Askelon. The sages asked to buy a jewel to replace one that had become lost from the High Priest's *Ephod*. The sages offered a price that would have given Dama a profit of one thousand gold pieces. However, the key to the jewel storage chest was under his father's pillow. Rather than dishonor his father by awakening him, Dama regrettably told the sages that he could not make the sale.

Thinking Dama was "playing-hard-to-get" to pressure them for a higher price, the sages desperately offered him a price that would render a profit of ten thousand gold pieces. Shortly, Dama's father awakened and he was then able to deliver the jewel. When the sages tendered 10,000 gold pieces as what they had assumed was the negotiated greatly increased price, Dama refused, saying, "I cannot make a profit from my father's honor." The price was therefore adjusted to the original price of one thousand gold pieces that had been offered while his father was asleep.

The following year, The Holy One, Blessed be He, gave Dama his reward. A Red Heifer was born to a cow in his herd. When the sages came to purchase the perfect heifer from him, Dama replied: "I know you, that even if I asked you for all the money in the world, you would pay me. But I ask of you only the money which I lost through my father's honor." Apparently in admiration and gratitude, the Temple priests purchased Dama's Red Heifer for 600,000 gold denarii – equivalent to a few million dollars at modern gold prices!

This incident illustrates that a tremendous price was paid for this purification under the Law. Similarly, Jesus paid the Ultimate (read: INFINITE!!!) price through His Innocent and Infinite suffering as His freely offered payment for our sins in order to win our "purification" before God. This again would fit the "picture" of Jesus as our "Red Heifer," in that He also was traded at "a very high price" for our salvation. Persons who have viewed Mr. Mel Gibson's controversial film *"The Passion of The Christ"* would surely echo that sentiment.

"Remember That Calf, Aaron?!" — Verse 3

> *"And ye shall give her unto Eleazar the priest, that he may bring her forth without the camp, and one shall slay her before his face:"*

Now, why Eleazar? – Why not Aaron? – Wasn't Aaron the High Priest? And yet, God specifically instructs Moses and Aaron to appoint Aaron's son Eleazar, to perform this rite. What goes on here?

Again, the ancient Hebrew commentary of the *Midrash Rabbah* – Numbers 19:8, provides an interesting though speculative answer to this curious move. *Midrash* states:

> *"Why are all the communal sacrifices male and this one a female? R. Aibu replied:*
>
> *This may be illustrated by a parable. A handmaiden's boy polluted the king's palace.*

The king said: 'Let his mother come and clear away the filth.' In the same way the Holy One, blessed be He, said: 'Let the Heifer come and atone for the incident of the calf!'"

This would seem to infer that the Lord had decreed this choice because He was intent on "squaring" things after the defilement and pollution resulting from the Golden Calf episode. (Exodus 32) The Lord was disappointed in Aaron for this sacrilege and would not permit him to "taint" this Holy cleansing rite with his impurity. The Lord therefore instructed that Eleazar should *"bring her forth without the camp."*

Josephus[4] describes the ceremony in much the same manner as we have detailed. He adds that: "Moses purified the People after this manner." Josephus affirms that this first burning of a Red Heifer was directed for purification after the death of Moses' sister, Miriam. Josephus states: *"They then made a public funeral for her, at a great expense."* As we have just discussed, a "great expense" would surely have resulted if they had to purchase a "perfect" Red Heifer.

Here, we should recall that Moses probably had great love and admiration for his elder sister, Miriam, and had forgiven her disloyalty and "murmurings" (Numbers 12:1 – 16) Moses would have gratefully remembered that it was Miriam who had schemed and guided the "rescue" of her infant brother by Pharaoh's daughter at the river's edge. (Exodus 2:4 – 10)

If we have assumed correctly that the Book of Numbers is narrated chronologically, it is apparent or implied from Scripture that Aaron died shortly after Miriam's death. According to Scripture (Numbers 19:4) Aaron's son, Eleazar, burned that first Heifer. Nevertheless, Aaron was not actually deposed from his position as High Priest until as described in Numbers 20:23 – 29. Aaron apparently had been deposed because of his idolatry concerning the Golden Calf. Further, and even more recently, Aaron had offended the Lord because he had not restrained the people from this horrible act and in fact Aaron even had participated with his brother when Moses "smote" the rock instead of obeying the Lord's Commandment that he should *speak* to the rock to bring forth its water for his "murmuring" People. (Numbers 20:1 – 13)

Since the Red Heifer burning is to be performed by the High Priest, Eleazar may have performed this rite after Miriam's death and it may be speculated that it was following the prescribed thirty days interlude of mourning. After all, it would take a while to search the herds to find an almost *perfect* Red Heifer; especially, to inspect her coat so tediously as to verify that no more than one odd-color hair was present. (They did not have magnifying glasses in those days!)

It is therefore determined from Scripture that Eleazar became High Priest immediately before Aaron's death, even as Aaron was stripped of his priestly garments at Mount Horeb. (Numbers 20:24 – 29) In this incident we are reminded of the Lord's later instructions that Solomon, and not David, would build His Temple, because King David had become "tainted" by so much killing (and other worldly behavior).

At this point let us take note of a later requirement that was put into practice after King Solomon replaced the Tabernacle by building the Temple. *Parah* 3:1 instructs that the High Priest must reside in the "Hewn Stone Chamber" of the Temple for seven days prior to the burning and here he must always face the northeast corner of the Temple. (See Illus. 21: Detail of the 2nd Temple, Page 154) Presumably, the reason for this is that once he is cleansed ritually and by "scrubbing" as well, he must remain isolated from the sinful world outside (even from his wife!) in order to avoid becoming "soiled." If he is to be purified and *remain* purified for those seven days before conducting this Holy rite, he must not mingle with the congregation, not even with his family.

In Judaic law, stone that has not been touched by iron tools is ritually "clean." All Temple masonry (with one small, but "necessary" exception) was held to that requirement, founded upon Exodus 20:22.

> "And if thou make Me an altar of stone, thou shalt not build it of hewn stones; for if thou lift up thy tool upon it, thou hast profaned it."

In *Middoth* 3:4 it is explained that iron was created to shorten men's days – as by the sword; whereas, the Altar was created to prolong the days of men. A comment by the revered French Rabbi, Rashi, recommends that proper justice is not met therefore if "*that which shortens should be lifted up against that which prolongs.*" The passage in *Middoth* 3:4 goes on to say that the plaster was not applied with an iron trowel, because that would risk touching and thereby disqualifying the stone beneath the surface.

Sotah 44b and *Gittin* 68a both state that neither a hammer – an axe – nor **any** tool of iron was heard "in the House" while it was being built. Moreover, it was forbidden to write upon any Temple stone with ink "*because it was like the engravings of a signet.*" That is, as with "engraving," part of the stone's material would be cut away as dust, and therefore, unacceptable. Mystical to those of us who are "strangers" is the secret process of how Temple stones were cut to shape and size "*without **any** part of the stones being cut away.*" *Sotah* 48a states, in *Talmudic* cryptic fashion, "*Through the action of The Shamir, the stones are split open along written lines* (although **not** with ink) *without any part of the stones being cut away.*"

Precise identity of "*The Shamir*" is a large part of the mystery of cutting the stones. It has been described as a miracle manifested by "*a greenish stone*" that has the quality of being able to "*split diamonds at a glance.*" Another legend has it that the "splitting" is accomplished by a *mythical* spirit creature. Another foists the idea that it is a worm that cuts the stone. Judging from these diverse and "wild" tales, it is apparent that this is a very closely held **secret** process.

For all of the reasons stated, implements of iron have no place in the Temple of God. The Lord is Glorified in a statement from a source[25] that explains: "*the stones must be of unhewn natural rock, with the stamp of God's handiwork alone.*" An interesting footnote in another valuable Judaica source, The *Chumash*[34], adds under Exodus 20:22 that the Hebrew word for sword: *cherev*, is derived from the word: *churban* (destruction) because swords bring destruction to the world.

Then, we must inquire, "How can the Temple tolerate this Chamber of 'Hewn' stone?" A painfully detailed reply to such a query is contained in the *Gemara* of *Yoma* 25b. Summarizing the content briefly, it comes down to the fact that this chamber is actually necessary in order to comply with the Commandment that ONLY kings of the House of David are permitted to sit in the House of the Lord and which stood in partial fulfillment when King David entered into the Temple and sat before the Lord. (See Deuteronomy 18:5 and II Samuel 7:18)

This brought about a problem in that the *Sanhedrin* met in that chamber and not all of those men were in the Kingly Line that was descended from King David. What were those *other* members to do? – Must they indeed *stand* during all their sessions? Similarly, for purposes of our discussion about this priest – was he to stand during all those seven days?

Attempting to limit the detail of this segment out of mercy for our readers, we shall say that the chamber floor was constructed so that half of it was on "Holy Ground;" i.e., from stone cut without iron tools. The other half was constructed so as to be "profane:" i.e., its stones were therefore *intentionally* cut (hewn) with iron implements. – Hence, the name: "Chamber of Hewn Stone."

In this way, only the Holy Ground portion qualified for use by any who were sons of David as a true part of the Holy House because they in fact were required to "*sit before the Lord*" in that House. Whereas, on the other hand, the adjacent "profane" portion was "necessary" in order to be available for seating those members who, by their birth, were prohibited from "sitting before the Lord" in His Holy House. Nevertheless, the problem was solved since *both* groups could then be "counted" together as in one assemblage for their required attendance in that esteemed council.

This location for the Hewn Stone Chamber at the southeast corner of the *Court of the Israelites* was probably considered to be the "cleanest" chamber for the Priest to occupy. There are several *Talmudic* principles that could be applied in speculating as to just why this might be the "cleanest" place. However, these principles are too remote, too complex and too vague for our discussion and purpose here. Nevertheless, we can be certain that all of Judaism was resolved to insure that their High Priest was doing his best to stay within the Law.

This sort of *minutiae* is typical of so much of the Rabbinical "logic" of the *Talmud*. As we study *Talmud* and *Midrash* it appears that the Rabbis are actually competing with one another in order to determine which of them can produce the most rigid and extreme (and, therefore the most pious!) interpretation of God's Law. It often is so severe, and yet there is a poignant quality in the "painful" way these pious competitors tried so earnestly to "please" God.

"Without the Camp"

This phrase has a deeper meaning than the words alone convey. The "man-made" *Talmudic* Laws of Judaism decree that, except for the daily sacrifices upon the Altar, no slaughter (or execution) shall take place within "a Sabbath Day's journey" from the Holy

House. (*Sanhedrin* 42b) More specifically, this distance is to be measured from the Holy of Holies, God's Earthly Residence in the Temple. A Sabbath Day's journey is a distance of two thousand cubits, or approximately six tenths of a mile, about one thousand yards (and measured as-the-crow-flies).

The place of the offering – the burning – was at the *Miphkad* Altar on the western slope of the Mount of Olives near the summit. There exists very convincing evidence[5, 9] to indicate this as the place of The Crucifixion instead of the two "popular" traditional sites: either the Church of The Holy Sepulchre or "Skull Hill" (Gordon's Calvary) behind the Damascus Gate bus station. The Law required that executions, especially for "blasphemers," must be conducted "outside the camp." (Leviticus 24:14, *Sanhedrin* 42b) The distance from either of these two popular Crucifixion sites from the recently located position of the Holy of Holies at the Dome of the Tablets, or even from the "traditional" Temple site at the Dome of the Rock, is far less than a Sabbath Day journey. This is only one of many reasons why *Olivet* summit is therefore a more realistic candidate for The Crucifixion site than either of these popularized and well-touristed locations.

Certain critics of this work have pointed to the fact that Scripture verifies that there were some killings within the City Walls. The murder of Zacharias as a martyr (II Chronicles 24:20 – 22 and Luke 11:51) in the court of the Temple is an example they cite early in any discussion. There can be no question that James, the "half"-brother of Jesus, was put to death within a short distance from the Temple. Another suggestion has been the martyring of Stephen; although, the location of that death is based solely on tradition.

Critics also have made the counter-claim that Stephen was martyred less than a Sabbath Limit from the Temple, at a point just outside the City Wall. Today there is a spot just outside the Wall at the northeastern quarter of the Temple Mount platform where it is currently "traditionally" claimed that Stephen was stoned to death. In fact, the earliest traditional claim for locating Stephen's stoning was reported to have been just outside the Damascus Gate – i.e., on the opposite side of the City! – leaving considerable doubt relative to the true site. We must remind ourselves that although both locations are less than a Sabbath Limit from the probable location of the Holy of Holies, there is NO archaeological or Scriptural evidence pointing to either of the locations for Stephen's martyring as authentic.

Nevertheless, we must concede that in fact James, the brother of Jesus, was martyred just outside the City Wall beyond the southeast corner and directly beneath what is known as The Pinnacle of the Temple. That locale is definitely within a Sabbath Limit from the Temple Mount. However, when this event occurred in C.E. 62, it can be reasoned that by that time much of Judaism had been corrupted by the priesthood and by the Rabbinate. Historians show that in fact the office of the High Priest was at that time actually purchased from Roman officials.

There may have been other deaths within those forbidden limits as well. Nevertheless, those killings were done in violation of the Law; especially this is true in the death of James. He was killed by a Jewish mob, but only Rome had authority to actually conduct executions. Whereas, Jesus – although Innocent – was executed "Legally" under Roman Law as a criminal convicted of sedition against Caesar. Similarly, having been "convicted" by the priests as a blasphemer, He was further executed "Legally" by being put to death under *Talmudic* Law "outside the camp." (*Sanhedrin* 42b)

However, it must be emphasized that the sentencing and execution of Jesus was ALL done within the most strict adherence to the Law, as we have labored to demonstrate throughout this work. It is important to observe that it is ironic and conversely true that the "Trial" and the conviction of Jesus were *completely* outside the Law. This of course had to be! – WHY??? – Because Jesus was Innocent of ANY and ALL crimes His enemies could bring forth, using false witnesses and whatever. And so, they necessarily had to accuse and convict Him under bogus charges.

"One shall slay her before his face"

Each of the three "types" of characters in this "picture" story is mentioned in this single phrase from Verse 3:

- The "one" (priest) who shall do the slaying.
- The Heifer who is slain.
- The priest who is watching the slaying "*before his face.*"

The Heifer was taken from the Temple by the High Priest and led across a two-tiered or double-vaulted bridge eastward to the *Miphkad* Altar, the place of the burning on the Mount of Olives. This bridge was known as the *Heifer's Gangway Bridge*. (Illus. 19: Elev. Profile: Temple Mt., Kidron VLY., Mt. Olivet, Page 152, and Illus. 20: Jerusalem as it Appeared in 70 C.E., Page 153) Its double-vaulted design fulfilled the Law of *Parah* 3:6 by isolating, with dead air spaces, any bridge travelers from defilement by the graves in the Jewish Cemetery below. A multitude of Jewish dead have rested there during many centuries in that *Olivet* cemetery awaiting their Messiah and The Resurrection. (Zechariah 14:4)

Thus, since the Heifer's ashes are to be used in purification rites, both the Heifer and the High Priest must avoid contact with any putrefaction. In fact, *Talmudic* law is so stringent on this point that, if a person even steps on a grave, knowingly or not, the person becomes "unclean." Suppose there are unmarked, unknown graves of prehistoric men or tribesmen, etc. buried beneath the ground where a person might walk at most any place. There is, after all, no way to avoid such defilement unless it is known that no graves exist below the ground that is walked. How would a person even know graves are there?! – It makes no difference! – There are NO excuses! – If any Jewish person has walked across ground where it is unknown whether any graves are beneath his path, that person becomes "unclean"!

Then, how could *any* Jewish person avoid becoming "unclean"? Could they avoid such graves? — No! — The picture lesson for us here is obvious. Just as we cannot completely avoid sin, certainly no Jewish people could avoid such "uncleanness" from unmarked, unknown ancient graves. It is not possible for us to "walk" *completely* without sin. We inherited our sinful natures from Adam. Regardless of where we "walk," we walk in sin.

From these thoughts, some will inquire: "Why all this morbid and elaborate concern over dead bodies and graves?" It would seem that God attached the utmost importance to this ritual. This "picture lesson" is a reminder, to the Jewish people as well as Gentiles, that the ultimate payment for sin is death. We need therefore to be purified, washed and cleansed from our sins, by the shed blood of our Red Heifer, Jesus, in order to defeat the sin (death) in our lives. The reason for the cleansing therefore comes about because every one of us, knowingly or not, at some time commits a sin – thus becoming "unclean."

The *Heifer's Gangway Bridge* was constructed at this site in order to provide a "clean" route for the Heifer and her procession from the Temple to the *Miphkad* Altar. The Heifer was escorted from the Temple, through the East Gate (*Middoth* 1:3) and continuing to the bridge. Even the Temple courts are "safe" from any such uncleanness. *Middoth* 3:3 explains that an air cavity exists beneath the courts. Asher Kaufman[47] further explains that these cavities are actually cisterns. According to the Law, the vaults of air space beneath the walkway of the bridge also serve to "insulate" the Heifer from any "uncleanness" as she proceeds to her destiny at the *Miphkad* Altar. The Temple and Jerusalem (the "camp") represent a "type" of Heaven. No defilement (sin) can take place therein. Hence, the Heifer is taken out to the World; i.e., "outside the camp."

When all three players in this drama are finally in place for the burning, the High Priest, the Red Heifer and the priest who slays and burns her are at the *Miphkad* Altar up near *Olivet* summit and due east of the Temple. — Why due east? – As we shall discuss later, the Rabbis reason from Verse 4 that the Priest must see ALL of the Veil as he sprinkles the blood toward the door of the Temple. We must remember that the Temple faced due east and the only way the High Priest could look over to see the Veil at the front of the Temple and sprinkle the Heifer's blood *directly* toward the Holy of Holies was to sight over the Beautiful Gate and through the open East Gate. — A rather limited field of view, especially at the legal distance of one "Sabbath Limit" — about 1000 yards.

Both the High Priest and the *Miphkad* Altar must be aligned on that east-west line coming from the Temple and through its center in order to have unobstructed view to the entrance of the Holy House itself through the opened gate. The *Mishnah* of *Middoth* 2:4 records that the east wall of the Temple was built lower than the other walls in order that the High Priest would be able to see the front of the Temple as he stood "at the top of the Mount of Olives" and sprinkled the Red Heifer's blood toward the Temple. (Illus. 16: Isometric View of 2nd Temple, Page 149, Illus. 17: Detailed Elevation of 2nd Temple, Page 150, and Illus. 18: Elevation Profile of Temple and Temple Mt., Page 151)

The High Priest then leads the Heifer to the *Miphkad* Altar and watches as the other priest does the killing "before his face." Next, the priest draws some of the Heifer's blood into a vessel from which the High Priest then dips his finger into the blood and then "sprinkles" the blood toward the Holy House. He must do this dipping and sprinkling seven times, without interruption, without *any* type of faltering or any missed count.

One interpretation may say these three players portray a symbolic drama that is a picture of God the Father, the "World" and Messiah. The High Priest could be the "type" of God. The other priest is a type of the ungrateful World as he slays and burns God's precious, innocent, Perfect gift, given for Salvation of the World. (Remember? Eleazar was to bring her "without the camp;" i.e., from Heaven to the World.) The Red Heifer, of course, is the gift and her blood is used for removing uncleanness (sin) from others despite the fact that she herself is pure, innocent and without spot or blemish.

But, here we must inquire: "If the High Priest is the type of God, how can the priest be '*unclean until even?*' (Numbers 19:7) – And how could Almighty God ever be considered '*unclean?*' " Here also we might say that perhaps God still feels loss and grief over having to "officiate" at the sacrifice of the Son of Man. Please consider the heart-crushing emotion God must have felt as He "letteth" Jesus suffer; albeit, knowing He had the Power to stop it! This loss could be reflected in this ritual as "uncleanness" for the priest. Even in the later Glorious Victory over the grave, The Father certainly must have felt for His Son such pain and grief that it reached incomprehensible bounds in comparison to that of our human compassion and understanding. Such "Supernatural" pain cannot even be comprehended by mere men.

This had to be felt as pain of immense proportions, even for a God who owns and controls all things in the Universe. Otherwise, if there had been no pain or grief even for Him, this would not have been of any sacrifice for Almighty God and certainly therefore would not have qualified as even a partial payment for our manifold sins *and which were redeemed at the very highest price!* – Satan justifiably would have scoffed at any payment requiring less than this! – Yes, God paid *The Price.* – And, as with everything God does, He paid with *Infinite* pain and He felt *Infinite* grief. God can do *nothing* short of Infinity in *anything* He does. — *God IS Infinity!*

The "camp" is the Temple Court, representing Heaven in the Law. (See *Pesahim* 92a) A significant clue suggests the High Priest as God since he returns to the camp (Heaven) even though he is still "unclean." However, the other priest (the World) must not return until evening, when he then becomes clean. (Numbers 19:8 and Deuteronomy 23:10 – 11) God, although He is in Heaven, does now grieve (feels "unclean") over the sufferings felt by all people, Jewish and Gentile. Later we shall discuss the significance of "evening."

For the slaying, the Heifer's legs are bound with rope of "bast" (similar to hemp) and which is woven from strands of the *meqeg* reed, because any other kind of rope is "unclean." (*Erubin* 58a and *Parah* 3~9) She is to lie with her head to the south and she is to be facing the Holy of Holies. This *same* position is ordered in the *Mishnah* of *Yoma* 3:5 for the burning of the Atonement Goat at that *same* location. Imagination tells us that a similar picture may have taken place as the spikes were driven through the flesh of Jesus at that *same* location. He was "probably" bound with "rope of bast" and lay with His head to the south and with His precious face turned toward His Father in the Holy of Holies, as He was about to be "lifted up" for our sins.

Sadly, this burning of the Red Heifer was a "picture" from God to the Jewish people showing them how one pure, innocent, "spotless" life could surrender its blood to be used for washing sinners so *they*, too, could be "*without spot.*" Only an infinitely merciful and loving Father could devise such a touching irony for reaching His "little ones."

Eleazar "Sprinkleth" — Verse 4

"And Eleazar the priest shall take of her blood with his finger, and sprinkle of her blood directly before the Tabernacle of the congregation seven times:"

The High Priest now stands just up the slope a short distance above the Heifer, such that he could face both the Temple and the Heifer as the other priest kills her and draws the blood into a bowl "before his face." He then dips his finger seven times into the bowl and sprinkles each time some of the Heifer's blood from his finger toward the Temple.

Talmudic ruling on this point is so rigid (*Parah* 4:2) that if the priest forgets to dip his finger, loses count of the sprinkles or if he flinches or if he mis-casts off-target to left or right — if he loses his balance, stumbles, falters,...sneezes! — if a passing cloud casts a shadow across the door of the Temple or even the Courts and stairway...or whatever, the entire ritual is "invalid." The whole deal is off!...A new Heifer must be found,...everything!...Back to "square one!" But, is this "pious or extreme?" Remember, God said: the Heifer's blood is to be sprinkled "*directly* before the Tabernacle."

Historical note is taken in *Parah* 3:5, where it is stated that a total of nine Red Heifers were slain over the years; *although, only seven were valid*. Two of Judaism's most beloved and respected High Priests, Simeon the Righteous and Johanan Hyrcanus, are each said to have erred sufficiently during this ritual that one of his Heifers was rendered "invalid." Perhaps they flinched or mis-counted the sprinkles, or committed some other regrettable blunder. Or, maybe a cloud passed across the scene, rendering it "profane." It is obvious as it is Glorious that there were seven "valid" Heifers, holding to God's Number of Perfection!

It is noteworthy to observe that these two highly revered Jewish patriarchs lived during the 4th century B.C.E., which certainly had to have been during a high point in Jewish history. This is evidenced by the spectacular and Glorious miracles that had occurred in the Temple during the tenure of Simeon as High Priest and with the miracle of *Chanukah* just two centuries later. (See *Yoma* 39a and Part III, Para. 7) These "signs" apparently were the Lord's way of showing approval of Jewish resistance at that time to the worldly encroachment of Greek (Hellenistic) Gentile teaching and lifestyle. With the removal of these signs "*forty years before the Temple was destroyed,*" the Rabbis lament that God registered His disapproval of their shepherding of His People. Since the Temple was destroyed in C.E. 70, the "forty years" places the time at 30 C.E. — The Time of The Cross. Tragically, they did not realize and still do not understand that God actually was chastising them for having rejected the One whom they had so long awaited and had yearned for. That is – their Messiah, Son of David, who of course was Jesus of Nazareth.

Another interesting historical note is found regarding the number of Heifers that were burned during the times before the Second Temple vs. the number burned during the Second Temple period. *Parah* 3:5 observes that one Heifer was of course the very first and which was burned by Eleazar, the son of Aaron. The second Heifer was burned by Ezra, which would have been about 515 B.C.E., upon his return from Babylon and during the restoration to build the Second Temple.

There was only one Heifer (Eleazar's) burned during about 400 or so years of Temple or Tabernacle worship from Moses' time (1000 B.C.E.) until 586 B.C.E. – subtracting 70 years to account for the captivity in Babylon. In contrast, there were then six "valid" Red Heifers burned during the period of the Second Temple – from 515 B.C.E. until C.E. 70. – almost 600 years. There was noticeably then a much more rapid rate of using the ashes during the time of the Second Temple. There may be an explanation for this difference; although, we have so far not located any history or obscure feature of Judaism that may have caused this disparity.

An interesting application of Biblical numerology is found from a *Talmudic* tradition stating that nine Red Heifers have been offered and the tenth Heifer will be sacrificed at the time of Messiah. It is more accurate to say there have been nine Heifers "killed," rather than "offered" because two of those killed were not "valid." They could not therefore be offered, presumably due to an error or some sort of disruption in what is required to be a Perfect Celebration. Ten is the Biblical number for "Worldly Completion." When Messiah comes, if a Red Heifer is offered at that time, it will be the tenth that was slain. It follows that in a World devoid of sin, there will be no need for purification with a new Red Heifer. And so, – Yes – The fact that ten will have been slain meets the Biblical numeric claim of "Worldly Completion."

Nevertheless, we have shown that "seven" is a highly regarded number because seven represents Perfection. Since we have shown that only seven of the nine Heifers slain were valid, then only seven were actually "offered." The next valid Red Heifer will be actually then the eighth *valid* Heifer. Eight is the Biblical Number of New Beginnings. It seems logical and therefore Spiritually appropriate that the Heifer of New Beginnings will be offered at the time of Messiah, which will be the beginning of what Jewish worshipers call the "Messianic Age" and what Christians refer to as the "Kingdom Age" or "Millennial Age" – a one thousand year Earthly Reign of Jesus at Jerusalem! At any rate, most should agree that it will surely be a Time of New Beginnings!

It would be expected of "Human Nature" at this juncture to comment that this discussion is so very complex as to almost "blow-the-circuits" in many of our brains! Even so, let us remember that God set forth these statutes to His Chosen People. He never said anything He ever gave them or expected from them would be simple! Indeed, it can be said that the more that mere men can comprehend from His complex Works, the more Glory their understanding brings to God! – If for no more than that reason, we *must* and we *will* continue this work!

It is true that the *Talmud* Rabbis did indeed add to that complexity often in their pious, but unwarranted zeal toward pleasing The Holy One. Nevertheless, if we remain patient and just WATCH for His Works and His Glory through all this, we will receive Blessings that are otherwise unattainable for Christians. Because God is **IN** the Law! Christians can see the Law in a much clearer and more meaningful way than can Jewish people because the Law, in its ENTIRETY !, is fulfilled ONLY by Messiah, whom Christians know, but sadly, Jewish people do not YET ! know Him! – By knowing the Law, Christians therefore are privileged to know Jesus even BETTER!

However, I must humbly concede, along with King Solomon, that I do not profess to understand all of the symbolism the Lord has presented in this part of the picture. We do understand that, in all Judaic sacrifices, the Lord instructed that the blood should be "poured out" during the slaughtering of these innocents. We believe now, with our "remarkable" Christian 20/20 hindsight, that the Lord did this to show Jewish people that He insists on payment for their sins, but not with their blood! – PRAISE GOD!

"But...Lord,...how could the blood of just one 'man' be poured out to pay for all of our sins?! – Sins too horrible to contemplate. How could a mere man ever pay for ALL of our many sins as a burnt offering?" In order to answer that question, we must remember that Jesus is NOT just a mere man!...INCREDIBLE! Neither the Rabbis nor the Pharisees understood this. (Many people today cannot accept this, either.)

The prophets, even before Jesus was born, had urged Israel to watch for their "Redeemer." Nevertheless, the "shepherds" of that day (C.E. 30) had taught (and had been taught by their "shepherds"), albeit in gross and tragic misunderstanding, that the Law ("works"), the ritual sacrifices of heifers, bulls, lambs, goats, doves, etc. "cleansed" them before the Holy One of Israel. Similarly, some Christian folks today occasionally lapse into convincing themselves that doctrinal rituals, "crosses", liturgical water, sprinkling or dunking, soggy grocery store bread or little crackers (salted or not), wine or grape juice, incense, ashes, etc. (snakes, even!) also bring them a certain "holiness."

At the same time, we sometimes point to our *fellow Christians* who do not perform their rituals exactly as we ourselves practice, and then we say: "*They* are idolaters! Pagans! *They* are lost!," etc. The Lord seems to be saying in this Temple rite, as well as in all of the others:

"My beloved ones!...Only ONE ritual cleanses you in My sight.

Only blood and only the blood of My Innocent, My Anointed,

the Desire of All Nations, Messiah, can wash you to be 'without spot."

The Burning - Verse 5

"And one shall burn the heifer in his sight; her skin, and her flesh, and her blood, with her dung, shall he burn:"

The High Priest, still standing just uphill from the *Miphkad* Altar, is now looking directly toward the Holy of Holies – over The Beautiful Gate and through the open Eastern Gate of the sanctuary (the latter also known as Nicanor's Gate). At the same time, he sees the other priest light the fire just in front of him and beneath the animal's lifeless form. At Jerusalem, I have aligned this line-of-sight to the Temple Mount and to Prof. Asher Kaufman's newly discovered Temple site at the Dome of the Tablets, extending due westward from the upper reaches of the near slope of the Mount of Olives. Even at a distance of two thousand cubits (approximately 1000 yds.), one would have a clear view of the front of the Temple over the City Wall and through the open East Gate of the Temple, if it were in place. (See Illus. 18:

Elevation Profile of Temple and Temple Mt., Page 151, and Illus. 19: Elev. Profile: Temple Mt., Kidron VLY., Mt. Olivet, Page 152)

Notice the subtle difference in phraseology used in these Scriptural instructions. The animal is slain "before his face," but the burning is in his peripheral vision ("in his sight") while the priest is actually looking across the Valley of Jehosophat (Kidron Valley) at the front of the Temple. *Talmud* (*Yoma* 42a) notes, during a lengthy dissertation, this means that "he must not divert his attention from it." The discussion then continues, explaining that strict attention is required *"because the burning is the central part of the ceremony!"* – (We must rejoice that they recognize this!)

We should pause here to question: "Why the burning?" – The flesh of the Red Heifer is not eaten; whereas, nearly all the Temple sacrifices were eaten by the Temple priests. Foremost, it is commanded in Verse 5 that the entire Heifer is to be burned – "...*her skin, and her flesh, and her blood, with her dung, shall he burn;*" — Yes! — It is HOLY. — It is CONSUMED!...nothing left but a heap of ashes.

Since the Red Heifer's flesh is not eaten, it is not actually or "technically" a sacrifice. However, there are a few of the Temple sacrifices in which the animal is burned. These are the burnings of the skin, flesh, and dung of the bullocks of the sin offering; also, the he-goat offerings on the Day of Atonement, *Yom Kippur*. The procedures in these offerings differ from the Red Heifer ritual in that, even though they are in fact burned at the *Miphkad* Altar, these animals are slain at the Temple and their blood is sprinkled and/or "poured out" at the Altar of Sacrifice in the Temple Court.

Nevertheless, each of these is seen to represent Jesus, Messiah, and each parallels His death and Glorious Resurrection. — Yes! — That is why the burning IS *"the central part of the ceremony!"* The burning in each case appears to picture His Resurrection, as with *"Non Corpus Delecti!"*...No body!...Only an empty tomb! There is nothing remaining that could even identify the Heifer as a living being — just a skull, a few bones and some ashes from a bonfire, later to be pulverized and scattered. This residue may be a picture of the grave cloths that remained in The Tomb (John 20:5 – 7); even though the cloths themselves still held no physical representation of Jesus' body, other than the bloodstains.

Before Secondo Pia's startling photo negatives were revealed in 1898, we knew only that the Shroud of Turin had what appeared to be bloodstains and dark patches forming what seemed to resemble the image of a man on the cloth. Pia's photo negative, in fact, dramatically announced that the cloth indeed had a photographic "negative" image of a man – most probably that of the crucified Jesus of Nazareth!

But, perhaps a more meaningful interpretation of the ashes is that they represent the Word of God pertaining to the Gospel testimony ("ashes") of the blood of Jesus as our burnt offering, because He also was "consumed" for us. Further, we must exercise faith ("living water") with that testimony in order to have salvation ("cleansing") from sin. (More on this thought later, when we discuss Verse 17.)

The firewood consisted of cedar, pine, spruce and "the wood of smooth fig trees" – because these produce "suitable ashes." (*Parah* 3:8) An interesting side note for Christians appears in *Talmud* concerning the fire for the burning. The fire is to be kindled with dried palm branches (fronds). — OF COURSE!! The burning took place nearby that very same path where Jesus passed during His Triumphal Entry into Jerusalem...Of course!...Get it?!...Palm branches!...On the Mount of Olives! The palm branches and *Hosannahs* from the throng "kindled" the wrath of His accusers...for One Innocent who is without spot or blemish...to be offered as cleansing for all others, who do have "spots" and "blemishes!"... – AMEN! – Oh! If only His Chosen could see this! — (They will see it all one day.)

We should pause here to observe that this day, the 10th of *Nisan*, saw the fulfillment of Daniel 9:24-26. In this, what has to be the most astounding prophecy in the Bible, Messiah was to arrive at Jerusalem *exactly* 483 years *to the day* (69 "weeks" (of seven years) after the Persian King Artaxerxes' commandment to Nehemiah (Nehemiah 2:1) to rebuild Jerusalem. That commandment *must* have been ordered on the 10th day of *Nisan*, because Jesus arrived on that day. *Expectant and worshipful Jewish faithful were anxiously and eagerly awaiting Messiah, Son of David to arrive victoriously on that day!*

It is certainly easy to understand why the people were so enthusiastic. This WAS the day! During all the centuries of Jewish worship leading up to this time, the Jewish people were hopefully and anxiously counting those days based upon Daniel's prophecy. – And, nobody before or since that day, other than Jesus of Nazareth, had ever done anything that could warrant his being called Messiah on that day. They had to believe Jesus was Messiah. – That *was* The Day'!

"Red Stuff" — Verse 6

> *"And the priest shall take cedarwood, and hyssop, and scarlet, and cast it into the midst of the burning of the heifer."*

The High Priest next walks downhill a few paces to the Heifer's pyre at the *Miphkad* Altar. He is commanded now to toss those three named materials "into the midst of the burning" as soon as the Heifer "bursts." Let us examine this verse for its message to Believers. There is symbolism here that is subtly concealed within Jewish tradition and folklore, but which also has some Biblical foundation.

The "crimson" (or "scarlet") is of course representing blood. In fact, literature on Jewish tradition[8] states that the red smoke alludes to the power of blood to overcome death. (Interesting thought, yes?!) Crimson wool is used, according to *Parah* 3:10. The wool is apparently dyed or coated with some material that emits red smoke when it is incinerated. Precise identity of this material requires challenging research. *Encyclopedia Judaica* refers to it only as "red stuff."

One Israeli scholar was reported in *The Jerusalem Post* as having identified the "scarlet" material. The article stated only that it is made from a "Crimson Worm." However fascinating, this limited information appears to have little credibility. The most convincing evidence concerning just what is this "red stuff" at the present time has been discovered by Rev. Vendyl Jones. His excavation team found a mysterious red substance at a location that

Jones and his associates have named: *The Cave of the Column*. Here Jones hopes soon to recover the *Kalal (urn)* containing the ashes of the Red Heifer. Jewish Rabbinical authorities in Israel have affirmed to Rev. Jones that the reddish brown material is the incense, *Qetoret*, that was used in the Altar of Incense in the Second Temple. By means of chemical analysis, eleven ingredients of this "red stuff" have been identified at this writing.

Talmud — *Kerithoth* 6a and *Encyclopedia Judaica*[8] list fifteen substances in all. It is said that these substances comprise the incense that was burned at the Altar of Incense. This fact has been confirmed by scientists at *Bar Ilan University* in Israel via the chemical analysis mentioned.

Exodus 30:34 lists only four specific ingredients for the incense; although, twice repeating "sweet spices." *Talmud* says that the incense must be made with "things whose smoke arises and fragrance spreads." Rabbinical tradition from *Shebuoth* 10b and *Kerithoth* 6a-b lists ingredients and their proportions. *Talmud* explains that eleven ingredients were specified to Moses at *Sinai*, but the increase to fifteen is derived by "homiletical interpretation" of Exodus 30:34. Following is a listing of the incense ingredients, along with some noteworthy sidelights:

Stacte* — A balm or oil of Balsam.

Onycha* — Powdered from a sweet smelling shell of the Red Sea region.

Galbanum* — An aromatic gum resin used in perfumes.

Frankincense* — An aromatic gum resin used in perfumes.

Myrrh* — An aromatic gum resin used in perfumes.

Cassia* (Cassia Cinnamon) — A cinnamon from India and the Far East.

* – These ingredients were used also for making the Holy Anointing Oil.

Spikenard — A perfume made from a plant from the Himalayas.

Saffron — An aromatic bulb of the Crocus family.

Costus — An oily herb from Kashmir.

Kiddah Cinnamon — (Similar to Cassia Cinnamon)

Cinnamon Bark — (From any qualifying cinnamon wood.)

Lye — Made from the leek, an onion-like bulb.

Cyprus Wine — (No details available at this time.)

Ma' Aleh' Ashan — "That which makes the smoke ascend" – was added to all of these materials in a small amount. This material contains *kippat ha-yarden*, which is believed to be from the Cyclamen bulb plant. But! — the most exciting(!) ingredient yet described is from the plant, *Leptadenia pyrotechnica*, which contains traces of nitric acid among its several constituents.

Nitric acid is used as the oxidizer in some rocket propellants. Combustion of nitric acid then releases nitrogen oxides, which are seen as red smoke! The mysterious "red stuff" that *Encyclopedia Judaica* mentions and that Vendyl has discovered is in fact the Altar Incense that was burned in the Temple, as substantiated through chemical analyses and by Jewish Rabbinical authorities. It is probably also the same "red stuff" or "crimson" or "scarlet" that was used at the burning of the Red Heifer. The "scarlet wool" used at the burning most likely was saturated with this incense in order to make it burn to emit red smoke. (Again, alluding to the power of blood to overcome death.) We must also note that cinnamon would surely cause a pleasant aroma to arise from the blaze. We should further recall that cinnamon has a reddish-brown caste, remarkably similar to the color of a Red Cow or *"hair the color of wine."*

The Rabbis in *Talmud — Yoma* 19b tell a glorious story that illustrates just how robust and appealing must have been the aroma from the burning of the incense at the Temple. *Talmud* says the goats in Jericho, about 15 miles to the east of Jerusalem, would sneeze at the odor of the incense. The smoke was carried eastward from Jerusalem to Jericho by the prevailing westerly breezes rolling in off the Mediterranean Sea. It is said that the women of Jericho did not need to perfume themselves because they were clothed in this sweet fragrance of cinnamon and frankincense sweeping into their city from the Temple. Of course, the brides in Jerusalem in those days are also described as having had no need for the usual perfumes, etc. to prepare themselves for their bridegrooms.

Imagine, if you enjoy the sweet savor of cinnamon rolls, cinnamon toast or raisin bread, how delicious this mixture of cinnamon, perfume and spices must have smelled. (The Lord surely must love cinnamon as much as we do!)

It may not be a coincidence that Vendyl Jones first discovered a stack of cedarwood over the place where the incense was found. — It would now almost appear that all we need are those ashes and some hyssop. Nevertheless, many learned persons need to study all these things before we jump to any conclusions just yet. After all, at the least we have shown that this purification must be PERFECT!

In Jewish lore the tall, stately cedar is a symbol of haughtiness and the lowly, ordinary looking hyssop weed is the symbol for humility and submissiveness. We noticed earlier that Jesus probably was bound to The Cross with "rope of bast" as the spikes were driven through His hands and feet. Could it be that Jesus' Cross also was of cedarwood?! And too, the hyssop weed had to have some emblematic role at The Cross. But perhaps it is seen only reflected in Jesus as the humble, submissive, obedient Lamb of God as He bore our punishment and did not even cry out. We do in fact recall that a "reed" of hyssop was used to give Jesus the "spunge" at The Cross. (John 19:29)

Hyssop, derived[38] through the Greek: $\upsilon\sigma\sigma\omega\pi o\xi$ (or *ussopoz*) from the Hebrew equivalent: *ezob*, is by far the "lowliest" of all materials represented in this account. However, this rite gives far more attention to that weed than is given to either cedarwood or "scarlet." Hyssop is one of the least interesting, dullest, most common, least useful, unattractive, ordinary weed plants on Earth. Even dried out prairie grass is more attractive.

Still, despite its lowly station, more is said about this humble vine than any of the other materials serving in the ceremony.

There is a great amount of controversy concerning exactly which of the dozens of botanical varieties of hyssop was the Scriptural variety. A convincing case is made[38] for the *Origanum maru* as the most likely candidate. It is described as having a square stem, slender leaves, no thorns, with a cluster of buds. This is proposed to be ideally suited to be gathered into a bunch for the purpose of sprinkling. The author suggests that no other plant in the Mideast is so well suited to this purpose. All hyssop varieties, however, typically grow in dry, rocky habitat, from cracks and on walls. But the Lord finds a very moving usefulness for this humble plant in His "picture" stories to His People. — Just watch.

The lowly hyssop has the most interesting "pictures" and associated sidelights of these three materials we are discussing. *Parah* 11:7 specifies that the hyssop used in this ritual must be a variety that bears no special name. Again dramatizing humility, it must be one of the most common, most "un—" special of the many varieties of hyssop plants. No "Greek" hyssop, no "Roman", no "Stibium" hyssop or... whatever...Just hyssop...Just *plain* hyssop!

Also, we must address the obvious question: "OK — Then, what is the meaning of the cedarwood in this drama? — Are you saying that Jesus or God is portrayed as 'haughty'?!" — It is my guess that the cedar did not represent haughtiness, unless it pictured the haughtiness of The World, which assuredly would be a credible claim. The cedar could perhaps represent Power and Strength, which certainly are traits of God, the Father — a "star" participant in this drama. Nevertheless, these are merely speculations and we may just have to join King Solomon on this question by saying: "We just don't know what it means."

As in the case of hyssop, much has been written regarding the true identity of the botanical variety of the "cedarwood." The same source[38] researched for hyssop presents a great amount of detail about this identity as well.

Before the High Priest tosses the three materials into the blaze, he holds up each material so that all the bystanders can see. He then asks the crowd: "Is this cedarwood?" They reply, "Yea, Yea." The Priest repeats: "Is this cedarwood?" Again, they reply, "Yea, Yea." A third time the Priest inquires of the bystanders: "Is this cedarwood?" And, a third time they answer: "Yea, Yea," And so, this little dialogue continues as he inquires: "Is this hyssop?" and repeats, twice more, etc.; and "Is this scarlet wool?" repeating, etc. Thus, everyone is assured they have all "the right stuff" before he tosses the bundle into the blaze. (*Talmud, Parah* 3:10)

Have you been wondering about the origin of the name "*Miphkad*?" What is the literal meaning of this word, etc.? It may be the meaning is derived from the ritual just described, because the Hebrew "*miphkad*" has the literal meaning: "muster." This alludes to a gathering and accounting similar to that of a military muster or "roll call" formation in which members of a unit are announced as: "All present and accounted for, sir!"

At the burning then, the High Priest held up each of the three ingredients and asked three times that the assembled onlookers "muster" each material by witnessing its presence at the ritual. (He even asked them three times for each one to make *absolutely* sure. In that way the cedar, hyssop and scarlet were verified as: "All present and accounted for."...(Sir!)

What Constitutes "Unclean?" — Verses 7 and 8

"Then the priest shall wash his clothes, and he shall bathe his flesh in water, and afterward he shall come into the camp, and the priest shall be unclean until the even.

And he that burneth her shall wash his clothes in water, bathe his flesh in water, and shall be unclean until the even."

These verses seem to portray two pictures. First, we see another Scriptural testimony that says ritual bathing, such as baptism for example, does not cleanse sin. This is shown in the fact that both priests remain "unclean" *even after they have bathed*. These priests will not be "clean" until "evening." There is deep symbolism in this ritual. We ask for the readers' patience and concentration through this drama.

Here each of these priests has bathed and washed his garments after being at the scene of death for this Heifer, but both are still "unclean!" — What goes on here?! — In this high drama, the High Priest (as God) returns to the camp (Heaven) and is clean at evening. The other priest (the World) is banished from the camp until evening, when he also becomes clean again. The obvious clue here is that *both are clean at evening*. Here we must ask whether "evening" has some critical significance here.

Before man's addiction to television violence and "disco—debauchery," evening was a time of peace and solitude. A man would look forward to returning from the fields or his flocks to dwell "at evening" with his loved ones in a quiet setting at his home. Thus, the Biblical reference to evening may be symbolic of the "Evening of the Age" when in His Heavenly Kingdom our Heavenly Father will be at Home to dwell with all His kindred in peace and comfort...forever.

The emotion and significance of "evening" in man's Earthly journey is beautifully immortalized in the classic painting – *Angelus* – by Jean Francois Millet – 1859. The painting seems almost to "speak" the feeling of gentle elegance and rest among loved ones after a hard day's work in the fields. It portrays all of those same emotions and rest and relief that men have welcomed for all of humanity's history when their daily toil was at end – at "evening." It appears that a picture having theme and heart and emotion similar to that of *Angelus* is written by the Lord into this Jewish rite.

Earlier, we noted that the Red Heifer ceremony is the most "mysterious" of the Temple rites, primarily because the purpose is to cleanse the unclean; and yet, all those who perform the ceremony are rendered unclean in the process – until "Evening." The picture here is, of course, the cleansing that Jesus performed for us; and yet He was rendered "unclean" as He took upon Himself our sins! – A clear picture it seems.

Consequently, when all Believers enter the Kingdom, "at the Evening of the Age," we will all be "clean" On that Glorious Day, we shall be in our Glorified bodies and will stand before the Lord, Purified by the Blood of The Lamb, Jesus. But, until that Day, we are all still "unclean," even though all our sins are presently and Eternally forgiven, because we remain "tainted" or "stained" so long as we live in this sinful World. Only *living water* (faith) and *blood* (ashes) from that ONE who is The Unblemished, Innocent Being, *Jesus*, can wash away our uncleanness. Believers will reach that state only when He comes to take us Home — "*at evening.*"

The second portrayal in this drama, then, is the arrival of the Kingdom. As Messiah gathers His subjects at that time (i.e., the "evening" of Earth's course of life), all in the Kingdom will be fulfilled; i.e., "clean." Believers, as the resurrected saints, will then be "clean" because we will be without sin and no longer will be in "the World." God, the Father, and Messiah, the Son, will also be fulfilled ("clean") because His Kingdom will have arrived at last! All sin will be cast out of the World and ALL will then be "clean"...at "evening." -A beautiful picture of that beautiful occasion.

Blood and Water of Purification — Verses 9 and 10

"And a man that is clean shall gather up the ashes of the heifer, and lay them up without the camp in a clean place, and it shall be kept for the congregation of the children of Israel for a water of separation: it is a purification for sin.

And he that gathereth the ashes of the heifer shall wash his clothes, and be unclean until the even: and it shall be unto the children of Israel, and unto the stranger that sojourneth among them, for a statute forever."

Parah 3:11 states that the ashes are to be ground to a fine powder using stone hammers and then sifted using stone sieves. Remember? Stone that is hewn without iron tools is ritually clean. It is further noted that any leftover chunks of bone or charred solid remains are also to be hammered into powder and then divided equally three ways as follows: One third to be deposited on the Mount of Olives; one third to be deposited on the "ramparts" (walls) of the Temple; and one third to be divided among the twenty—four orders of the Temple priests. Nothing is to be just left idly to a fate of chance. These remains are precious and Holy and are not just to be tossed into the wind.

If the ashes do represent the Word, we are reminded of a few Scriptural verses in this same reflection.

"So shall My word be that goeth forth out of My mouth: it shall not return unto me void, but it shall accomplish that which I please, and it shall prosper in the thing whereto I sent it." (Isaiah 55:11)

The Lord says that His Word shall not be wasted or futile. Again, in the New Testament, we see another image of Jesus as the Word, just as the Ashes of the Red Heifer represent the Word.

"And the Word was made flesh, and dwelt among us..." (From John 1:14)

Another similar message can be derived from Ephesians 5:26 as it pictures His Word (ashes) mixed with the Living Water –

"That He might sanctify and cleanse it with the washing of water by The Word."

Jesus IS the Word. This picture seems more and more to indicate those ashes are pictured as The Word.

The picture portrayed by Verse 9 may be that the man who is "clean" is the Church. The Church "lifts up" the blood of Christ as the Word (ashes) and distributes (lays up) this concept (the Gospel) before the World (outside the camp). The Church, as the Body of Christ, performs its Holy commission from a position of "cleanness" (righteousness); although, individuals of the Church (you and I) truly are "unclean;" i.e., sinful. We therefore must dwell presently in the World (outside-the-camp) "until the even" (the "end of days") when we shall return as "clean" to the Camp! (Heaven) purified by our Red Heifer's ashes – (Jesus). – Lots of "picture" here!

Some Christians are puzzled and disturbed by this typology that says, even though we are "in Christ" we are "unclean!" – Here, we must remind ourselves that we Christians are not yet in His Kingdom. We have The Promise of being in that Kingdom when He takes us unto Himself at His coming – as described in I Thessalonians 4:17 –

*"Then we which are alive and remain shall be caught up together with them in the clouds, to meet the Lord in the air: and **so shall we ever be with the Lord**."*

Nevertheless, while we are still in this World – until *"evening"* – we are "unclean" just like the man who **was** clean before he came in contact with the ashes.

Another similar picture emerges where, although the Church is ritually "clean" (baptized), we are still sinful (unclean) in this world and *must* repent in order to have the faith (living water) and the blood of Jesus Christ *"as a purification for sin."*

Notice that this is under a Commandment from the Lord *"for a statute forever."* This means that even some of the ashes from that very *first* Red Heifer, burned by Eleazar during the Exodus, must be included in the mixture of ashes to be used for any purification. So, as the Israelites used the ashes over those fifteen centuries afterward, why didn't they run out of ashes?

Obviously, at least every few hundred years they would need to replenish the supply of ashes. *Parah* 3:5 says a total of seven "valid" Red Heifers were burned during those years when this rite was performed while they were in The Land.

Nevertheless they are required by this "statute" *always* to retain some of those first ashes from Eleazar's Heifer. They do this by always making certain to burn a new Red Heifer before their supply is entirely depleted. In fact, they actually place the remaining ashes on the fire with the new Heifer. In that way, they retain remnants of the original Red Heifer as well as portions from all Red Heifers that were burned subsequent to that time; i.e., since 1500 B.C.E. According to *Yoma* 3b, a reserve supply of ashes was always maintained in the Sanctuary. These were probably stored in the Chamber of Hewn Stone because, as we reasoned earlier, it was the "cleanest" location available.

With all the conquests and "scatterings" the Jewish people have suffered through the centuries, you may wonder at this point how they have been able to retain any of those original ashes for all this time. Obviously, they had to hide them away for safe keeping until each time after being "scattered," they later returned to The Land. Always, the Temple authorities were able to perceive impending trouble before disaster struck. They hid away the precious ashes before King Nebuchadnezzar destroyed the Holy City in 586 B.C.E. Then, when they returned to rebuild the Temple, they had to recover the ashes in order to be able to purify the Second Temple, the priests, etc.

Midrash Rabbah Numbers 9:15 states that the Lord granted Abraham a reward because, after he pleaded that *Sodom* and *Gomorrah* be spared from His wrath, he had humbled himself before God, having said: "*I am but dust and ashes.*" (Genesis 18:27) The reward: Abraham's children, Israel, were to receive two ordinances:

1. The *ashes* of the Red Heifer, and
2. The *dust* for testing the unfaithful wife. (Numbers 5:17 – 31)

A footnote points out that, in the case of the Red Heifer, purification is effected; whereas, with the suspected unfaithful wife, her chastity is tested.

Rabbinical commentaries are almost unanimous about one observation in the opening paragraphs concerning the Red Heifer. The Rabbis consistently remark in several references[25, 26, 34] that the Red Heifer offering is "beyond human understanding" or "the most mysterious Laws of the *Torah*" or "the most mysterious rite in Scripture."

Moreover, remember that this ceremony is detailed to the Jewish people as a "statute." A footnote in a highly acknowledged Judaic source[25] at Numbers 19:2 announces that the word "statute" is used in connection with any law or ordinance "*whose reason is not disclosed to us.*" This source goes on to say the Hebrew word used here implies:

"*It is a decree from before Me, and you are not at liberty to cavil at My decrees.*"

It is safe to say the Jewish people have kept to this philosophy in all of their worship.

"*We don't know why we do it, except that the Lord our God says do it. – So, we do it!*"

Immediately following The Crucifixion, many strange and wonderful "signs" which had previously appeared in the Temple disappeared. The Rabbis of the *Talmud* refer to that period with lamenting as: "*forty years before the Temple was destroyed.*" – (They neglect to mention that those forty years began after The Crucifixion, Resurrection and Ascension of Jesus of Nazareth!) – Yes! From C.E. 30 until C.E. 70 was forty years! – Also, as the rebellion against Rome began in C.E. 66, the *Shekhinah* Glory departed from the Second Temple and later ascended to Heaven from *Olivet* summit, at or very near the place where Jesus ascended. These things occurred just prior to the destruction by the Roman legions in C.E. 70. – See Parts I - V; also *Josephus, Wars*: 6/290 — 300; *Midrash Rabbah* (Eichah) Lamentations, Part 25 (*Proems*); and *The Babylonian Talmud*, tractates *Rosh Hashanah* 31a and *Yoma* 39b.

All these events served to warn the priests and the people of the impending holocaust. Josephus observed that "the men of learning" recognized alarm in this situation, and that "these publicly declared, that this signal foreshewed the desolation that was coming upon them." They knew right then, that when the Glory left the Tabernacle, "they must move the camp" while the Lord would go before them, as a Good Shepherd leading them to new ground. (Exodus 40:36 - 37) Just as they had done previously, they took measures to protect all of their sacred articles that happened to be "portable." This included the Red Heifer ashes. (More about this in a later chapter.)

This situation just described is what makes this entire story exciting in this day and age. (Please stay tuned!) But, first we must continue to lay the foundation for the story describing this ceremony, its importance and its messages. Several descriptions of what constitutes being "unclean," etc. are given in Verses 11 through 16.

We pick up our narrative again by starting at Verse 17.

Defining "Living" Water — Verse 17

"And for an unclean person they shall take of the ashes of the burnt heifer of purification for sin, and running water shall be put thereto in a vessel:"

We come now to the actual use of the ashes as a "purification for sin." The ashes; i.e., "blood" of this unblemished and innocent creature, must be mixed with "living" water. That is, "running" water must be moving, flowing, active; in fact, pouring and stirring at the same time for the mixing. *Talmud Sotah* 16b and the *Chumash*[34] at Numbers 19:17 explain that the water must be taken directly from a source of "living (i.e., moving) water" such as a spring or stream. The water then must be stirred as it is poured into a vessel. It must not be poured into another vessel before being mixed with the ashes. Next, a small portion (maybe just a "pinch") of ashes are placed on top of the water and stirred in.

An obscure footnote under *Parah* 5:2 instructs that the ashes of the Heifer must be mixed with running water and that mixture then is used for "washing" those who are ritually "unclean." This includes persons with leprosy, those who have touched or have come near a bone or a dead body and other acts. Similarly, the water used for the ritual bath (*Mikweh*) under the Law must also be "living" water; and as with the Heifer ashes, it must also come from a natural flow of water. – No cisterns or cattle ponds!

It is explained that during the Babylonian exile, no Jewish captives were able to avoid the uncleanness of the dead. Their Babylonian masters probably had little respect or patience for the "fussy" burial practices of their Israelite slaves. Besides, they didn't have the Red Heifer ashes in Babylon. Now, the Rabbis did not take this quest for "cleanness" in any casual context. An extremely complex procedure therefore came into use upon their return to Jerusalem.

Without going into all the details in the *Talmudic* provisions for this procedure, the water must of course be collected by a "clean" person. So, since there were no clean persons after seventy years as captives, they had to literally "grow" clean persons. — Yes, children! —

Why children? — Children could be "grown" clean if they were raised without ever being defiled by handling any of the deceased or even by unknowingly walking over an ancient, unmarked, "uninsulated" grave.

There was an exposed area of bedrock in Jerusalem that had a large vacant chamber of natural rock formation beneath. Therefore, even if there might have been an ancient unknown grave beneath it, the void of air space under "clean" stone then served to "insulate" from uncleanness of a grave, just as provided by the arches of the *Heifer's Gangway Bridge*.

(Now, you're not going to believe this!) – A courtyard and living quarters were constructed on this "clean" bedrock. When a new Red Heifer was to be sacrificed, pregnant women were selected to come to this rock to deliver their babies and to rear them above the rock so the children would be ritually "clean" and could then be qualified to serve in collection of the water for purification from the Pool of *Siloam*. (Far—Out!!)

We may glimpse the serious nature of this endeavor by noting another detail given in *Talmud, Kethuboth* 106a. It is stated that the construction of dwellings, food, provisions and other support for the mothers and the "babes" was provided through a unique but thorough arrangement. The mothers received lodging and "wages" from Temple funds; whereas, the "notable" (i.e., wealthy) women of Jerusalem supplied food, clothing, diapers, utensils, etc. as a charity.

Children selected as candidates for handling the sacred ashes were subject to the utmost strict ritual cleanliness. They were supervised and raised under those restrictions from their pre-natal days until they reached about eight years of age. A footnote indicates that revered and much praised 11th century French Rabbi, Rashi, wrote that the children were maintained in this fashion until they were 12 years old.

A specific child was selected for each Red Heifer "candidate" because the Rabbis had to select the *very* best heifer from all that could be found. There was also the possibility the entire ceremony could be rendered "invalid" through some error and a new Red Heifer then would have to be selected. (See "Eleazar Sprinkeleth" — Verse 4.) The children were then placed on "doors" resting on oxen ("insulated" again!) and carried to the pool. Each child was given a ritually "clean" cup, which he lowered into the pool to draw some of the "living water." Eventually one heifer was selected as "perfect;" and that one child's water was then allocated for the ashes of *that* Red Heifer, having been previously assigned for *that* child. (Whew!!)

The child would take of the ashes of *that* "red cow," which were then mixed with *his* sacred water. According to *Parah* 3:1, the mixture was stirred in a vessel of stone, dried earth (mud), or ordure (animal dung). *Yoma* 2a says the vessel was of cobblestone (or dung). Nevertheless, each of these materials is decreed under the Law to be "insusceptible to uncleanness" – (Well,...uhh,...maybe!) – Extreme, but touching. They were trying so vigorously to please the Lord, but going about it in all the wrong ways — by "works."

Significant also is the origin of the water used with these ashes. The source is the nearest "living" water supply on the Temple Mount, of course. *Parah* 3:2 directs this to be the Pool of *Siloam*, where Jesus healed the blind man. This pond is fed water through an underground aqueduct (Hezekiah's Tunnel) flowing from Spring Gihon just outside the wall of the City.

This ritual we are about to describe may seem even more bizarre than any yet discussed; but remember, *nothing* "unclean" must ever come in contact with these ashes. After all, the ashes are used to make things or people ritually "clean." The "laws" of *Talmud* are much more exacting and stringent than the Law as stated in Bible verses from the book of Numbers. In fact, this part of the statutes is so bizarre and so intricate that we have attempted to condense the procedure in the interest of minimizing *Talmudic* tedium as an act of mercy toward our readers. It is derived from *Sukkah* 21, *Zebahim* 113a and *Parah* 3:2, 3

Briefly then, an adult ties two hyssop branches, one to the tip of each of the horns of a male goat, without touching the tips. The "clean" child then mixes a pinch of ashes with the water in the stone cup. He then holds the cup so as to dip the hyssop tips into the mixture. While seated face-to-face with the goat, the High Priest now taps the goat on the nose as described in *Parah* 3:3. The startled goat then jerks his head downward; thereby causing his horns to "flick" (sprinkle) forward at the High Priest seated in front of him with the purifying mixture of living water and ashes of the Red Heifer. — *Voila!* — The High Priest is now clean! This Priest can now cleanse others and the process continues.

At this juncture it is necessary that we should point out that these purification Laws are not to be applied in everyday life. The purification was required mostly for persons who wished to enter the Sanctuary – the Temple courts. Otherwise, we could have the impression that the Jewish people were completely "hamstrung" by these Laws. Certainly they were very restrictive; although, God did not intend to make their lives miserable through His Law. The Priests and the Rabbis have taken these statutes to the extremes, causing even Jesus to lose patience with their pious attempts at "perfection."

In summary:

The water used for sprinkling must be "living" (flowing) water, not stagnant.

It should be collected from the Pool of Siloam by a person who is "clean".

When it is to be mixed with these Holy Ashes, the water must also be flowing ("living") as the ashes are stirred in.

All this must be accomplished using a vessel that is "insusceptible to uncleanness."

No unclean person must ever touch the ashes or even the vessel containing them, lest the ashes be forever contaminated as unclean.

All through this study, the words of Jesus describing Himself as "the living water" must surely be ringing in our ears...and in our hearts! Here we are reminded that faith, as "living water," if it does no "work" — does not "irrigate" by moving, witnessing, flowing to other "seeds" – it will not bear fruit. Instead, it is stagnant and will become putrid after a time; even if it is occasionally "stirred."

But the more real danger is that such torpid faith may actually stunt or rot and destroy new "seeds." During our Earthly ministry we should strive to see that our faith "flows" and that our "works" will "irrigate" to produce new, good fruit. These kinds of works shall stand uncharred at the Judgment Seat of Christ. All "wood and stubble" will be consumed and the ashes blown away as chaff before the wind.

Purified by Blood and Living Water — Verses 18 and 19

"And a clean person shall take hyssop, and dip it in the water, and sprinkle it upon the tent, and upon all the vessels, and upon the persons that were there, and upon him that touched a bone, or one slain, or one dead, or a grave:

And the clean person shall sprinkle upon the unclean on the third day, and on the seventh day: and on the seventh day he shall purify himself, and wash his clothes, and bathe himself in water, and shall be clean at even."

Our objective is not really aimed at striving after all this *Talmudic* detail. Rather, we are attempting to see Messiah and/or God's Holy Purpose in all this. We wish also to highlight for Christians any spiritual meaning that is unseen by the Jewish people themselves

We have just finished the discussion of procuring the ashes and the water. It was shown earlier that children had to be raised "clean" and then were carried to the Pool of *Siloam* and there collect "living water" and to mix the ashes initially because nobody else was "clean." Now, in these two verses, some adults by this time have been ritually cleansed using the water obtained by the children at *Siloam*. A clean person now takes hyssop and dips it in the water mixed with the ashes. Then comes the sprinkling with the hyssop.

Parah 11:9 specifies that *three* hyssop stalks are used for the sprinkling and each stalk shall contain *three* buds. (And, there will be NO plucking of excess buds!) Again, we see God's number for holiness as *three*. It is certain that the Jewish people practiced these rituals without knowingly dramatizing yet another indication of the Holy Trinity. This indication of the Triune concept appears many times in this most Holy of Jewish rituals. The same indicator appears throughout all Scripture too frequently for coincidence, most would agree. What a pity the Jewish people do not see this.

In Jewish tradition the hyssop is a symbol not so much for humility, as we have observed in regard to Jesus. Rather, hyssop is more a symbol for spiritual purification from sin, as noted under Exodus 12:22. A footnote in the *Pentateuch and HafTorahs*[25] refers to Psalms 51:9, which is Psalms 51:7 in the KJV. This is a less familiar portion of that oft quoted Psalm written by King David, probably at the time when he was confronted by Nathan the prophet concerning David's sin with Bathsheba:

"Purge me with hyssop, and I shall be clean: Wash me, and I shall be whiter than snow."

A description of the hyssop plant[38] specified for this ritual notes that its slender stem has a square cross-section, is free of thorns, has no spreading branches and instead, ends in a cluster of heads at the top. It is reported to have a "highly aromatic odor;" i.e., "fragrant." It is exactly the correct shape and form to be used for sprinkling. This source states that: "No other plant growing in the East is so well fitted for the purpose."

We can see easily through this study how tradition in purification began, especially through the major role played by hyssop in the rites of the Red Heifer. Hyssop is lowly, BUT important. Hyssop was used to smear the Paschal Lamb's blood on the doorposts that night of the Passover in Egypt. (See Exodus 1:22) The Lord evidently regards this lowly little weed and all these teensy-tiny "nit-picky" details with great reverence and would expect us to do likewise.

We should further observe at this point that these same three materials used in the burning of the Red Heifer: cedar, hyssop and "scarlet," also were used in the rite described in Leviticus 14:1 – 32 for cleansing persons who had been healed of leprosy. The pictures and symbolic meanings in the leper cleansing Law are obviously similar to what we have seen for the Red Heifer. However, the leper cleansing details appear to be much more difficult to interpret.

Although some of these "legal" details do not appear in the Mosaic Law as we know it from the *Torah* and from the Old Testament, we are enabled to see some influence of the Holy Spirit in the way the Rabbis implemented the sacrifices. The use of three branches with three buds demonstrates such an example of this positive influence in their worship. Who can say where they received such statutes? Certainly no such details were directed to Moses and Aaron in the Law. We are aware, for example, that Israel and Judah had many prophets who certainly were truthful and righteous men.

Nevertheless, the prophetic exhortations of many of these Saints were never recorded in what we regard as Scripture. We may assume, then, that many of these precepts were handed down through the Lord's prophets, even including some of these "unpublished" prophets who are unknown to us at this time. There are many liturgical details of the Mosaic Law seen here from *Talmud*, but which the *Torah* did not Command. Nevertheless, many would concur that these were precepts ordered from *YHWH* and from no other.

Some historical notes concerning the Red Heifer from the Book of Numbers are of interest at this point. *Midrash Rabbah* Numbers 12:15 states that the Tabernacle was erected three times daily during its "seven days of consecration." Further, it was first erected on *Rosh Hodesh* (New Moon) *Nisan*; i.e., the first day of the first month. The Red Heifer was burned on the second day, and on the third day the water of purification was sprinkled on the Levites (priests) for their cleansing.

Under *Midrash Rabbah* Numbers 13:15 – 16, a discussion of Numbers 7:19 concerning the Hebrew word *hkryb* (pronounced "hikrib" – meaning to offer or to present) asks why the letter *yod* (y) was omitted. This would have resulted as: *hkrb*, consisting of only four characters instead of the conventional five characters for this word. Explanation offers that only four letters are shown in this case to symbolize the four qualifications for the Red Heifer:

- She must be red.
- She must be perfect.

- She must have no blemish.
- She must never have "felt the yoke."

Several qualities that are unique and/or exclusive to the Red Heifer ceremony have been pointed out.

1. The Red Heifer was the only offering that required a specific color for the animal.

2. The Red Heifer was the only offering in which the entire ceremony took place outside of the Temple boundaries; specifically, a Sabbath Limit distant. Just as with the Red Heifer, the entire carcasses of the Sin Offerings and the Atonement Goat were burned atop *Olivet* at the *Miphkad* Altar. However, unlike the Heifer – they were first slain at the Temple.

3. No other sacrifice contaminated the priests who carried out the procedure. The High Priest did not wear his usual Golden Vestments at the burning of the Red Heifer. Instead, he was attired in the identical four-piece, humble, white garments worn by any of the ordinary *kohanim* working in the Temple.

4. The blood applications, sprinklings, etc., of all other procedures were performed either in the Temple or upon the Altar of Sacrifice in front of the *H'ekhal*. Whereas, the Red Heifer's blood was sprinkled by the High Priest as he "gazed" at the curtain ("Veil") covering the Temple doors while he stood looking over the *Miphkad* Altar from the summit of the Mount of Olives. (See Illus. 23: Mt. Olivet viewed from Temple on Crucifixion Day, Page 156, and Illus. 24: Detail of "pit or cavity" in face of Mt. of Olives, Page 157)

5. The ashes of the Red Heifer were of course preserved and used in purification rites. ALL of the ashes and unburned remnants of ALL other animals that were burned either at the Altar of Sacrifice or at the Mount of Olives were "poured out" to cascade down the western slope of *Olivet* (See Illus. 23: Mt. Olivet viewed from Temple on Crucifixion Day, Page 156, and Illus. 24: Detail of "pit or cavity" in face of Mt. of Olives, Page 157)

With attention to the most thorough details, here we must point out that the ancient Hebrew script presented in the *Midrash Rabbah*[37] is not the same as the Hebrew script in the *Masoretic Text* equivalent for Numbers 7:19. For example, the Old Testament word used for "offer" in *Strong's Concordance*[15] is *qarab* (7126) and not *hkryb*; although the same meaning (to offer) is given for *qarab*. This is stated for those readers who might wish to investigate to find the omitted character, *yod*, and would not find it in the word *qarab*. Obviously, the story would not apply unless the word *hkrb* is used.

Details for sprinkling the Heifer ashes and the bathing details for the participants are just too much for us to outline here. Notice again, however, that although this person in Verses 18 and 19 was "clean" before he purified those who were unclean, now he, too, is "unclean," but he shall be clean again "at even." Thus, it is most appropriate that the Old Testament narrative in this portion of our story ends "at even."

Part V – Heifer's Dramas and Types

15

Looking Again at The Gospel

"Living Water" at Bethesda – Bethany, a Leper Colony! – Jesus and "The Ineffable Name" – Jesus <u>Planned</u> His Crucifixion "where ye think not" Prophecies complete at The Cross – Explaining and Locating "Golgotha"

Timing is Everything! – A "Clean Man" & "Clean Place" – Resurrection Proved – What you would have seen at The Cross – Blinded by Tradition

As we mentioned earlier, since we know of the Gospel of Jesus Christ and of His lone sacrifice as one Innocent, we have "20/20 hindsight" in this matter. We now see clearly many pictures of Jesus as our "burnt offering," our Red Heifer. King Solomon and the Jewish sages—Moses, could not have known the Red Heifer was burnt to represent Messiah. You and I can see this now, but there was no way they could have known. — No way. — We can however inform modern Jewish people and Christians about it now, if they are open and led to the Gospel by the Holy Spirit.

But let us apply some of our 20/20 hindsight and our imagination now to examine the Gospel, seeing whether we can bring any new light from our new-found knowledge. If the Red Heifer offering is truly a picture of Messiah, we may see a few new openings that even in small ways relate to Jesus and the Gospel, especially including The Crucifixion.

Remember, Jesus was the most Law abiding of all Jewish people throughout their history. Jesus knew all about the Red Heifer ashes.

Waiting For "*The* Living Water"

Upon examination of new insight from our study of *Talmudic* Law so far, an interesting and beautiful facet is revealed in the Gospel of John and which has some reflection in the Red Heifer ceremony. Without our newly acquired knowledge of *Talmud*, this story and its subtly revealed beauty might never have occurred to many of us.

Another reason for our possibly overlooking an important and touching facet of this story comes from a difference in Biblical translations. Prior to our discussion of this Glorious story from John's Gospel, we need to point out that the verse in John 5:4 is omitted from several "modern" Western Biblical translations. The verse is however included in the King James ("Authorized" Version); having been accepted upon authority of manuscripts from the *Peshitta* or *Syriac*, as in the *Lamsa Bible*. Our discussion will include Verse 4 because it explains more clearly why the disabled people were gathered at this spot. Quoting from the *Lamsa Bible*:

> *"Now there was at Jerusalem a baptismal pool, which is called in Hebrew Bethesda, having five entrances.*
>
> *And at these entrances a great many sick people were lying, the blind, the lame,*
>
> *And the crippled; and they were waiting for the water to be stirred up;*
>
> *For an angel of God went down at a certain time to the baptismal pool and stirred up the water;*
>
> *and whoever went in first after the stirring of the water was healed of any disease he had."*

The Apostle describes the incident in John 5:2 – 9 in which a great crowd of persons who were blind, lame or crippled were hopefully waiting by the pool at *Bethesda*. The very name, *Bethesda*, is the Hebrew expression meaning: "house of mercy." Their hope was to be healed by the waters, which at certain times, would be "troubled" (stirred) by an angel of the Lord. But, alas! – only one of these miserable souls could be healed by this miracle, because only the *first* person who entered the pool after the "troubling" would receive this blessing. Many of these souls could hardly even move unaided, much less "race" to be first in the pool. Here we see a certain futility and yet an inspiring faith in this hope for all who made up that crowd; nevertheless, only one of whom would be blessed by the healing.

Our hearts go out therefore to the man whom Jesus saw lying there, so hopeful in his vigil, yet "hopeless" as well as helpless, in that he had no one to assist him in the "race" to the pool. This invalid had been in that wretched condition for thirty-eight years. Jesus saw him, had loving compassion for the man and healed him immediately — even *before* the waters were stirred — because Jesus is THE Living Water!

So, now we can know a bit more of the significance of this story, and its beauty is even underscored by that understanding. We know, for example, this angelic "troubling" of the apparently otherwise stagnant pool at *Bethesda* was provided to make it qualify as "living water" in the traditional context of Judaic Law. Let us now observe how this fact brings new meaning to the Gospel.

Here they were, then, these lame or halt or blind folks, who had perhaps traveled many miles to try for a chance at this miraculous healing. Many had probably made this futile pilgrimage several times before to no avail. One cannot help but marvel at their faith, but we must also pity their chances – especially the man whom Jesus chose. (Did you catch that?) Jesus *chose* him! – That should give us another "picture."

They were all waiting for the water to become "living;" although, they all knew there would be only one winner in this "lottery." Yet, here was THE Living Water, Jesus —The Lord's Anointed One – Messiah, Son of David — right there in their midst. Instead of having to win that race to the pool on his own (which he certainly could never do!), THE Living Water (Jesus) instead came to the *man*. — *Jesus chose him because he believed!*

Ah! Beloved, how lovely this story is for us who also believe and are healed! In the same way, the healing Grace of our salvation is brought to us by Jesus, THE Living Water. As we lie there with our blindness and our crippled souls, perhaps for even longer than thirty-eight years, some of us still believe we have to win the "race" by some action (works) of our own making. Maybe we think we will be lucky and the Lord will think well of our "good works" and He will then welcome us into "The Good Place." Unfortunately, there are even many professed Christians who also have this same type of futile and flimsy "hope."

Thankfully, there are others of us who, though we lie there in our blind and crippled state, somehow we know that we cannot heal ourselves. Then, along comes Jesus — our Living Water — and if we will just confess our sins; i.e., our "crippled" state, and look up to Him and believe, He heals our withered souls on the spot. We don't have to "do" anything in order to win the "race." Without even our asking, He comes to the door and knocks. And, if we will only ask Him into our hearts, Jesus will extend God's healing Salvation to us on-the-spot. We can then "take up our beds and walk," just as did the man in John's story.

This, I believe, is the message that is intended for us from John's story. But the story is enriched just a bit when we know more about this "Living Water" concept from Jewish tradition and the Law. Jesus had Jewish roots. A profound note in *Sanhedrin* 106b says: "*...The Holy One, Blessed be He, requires the heart, as it is written,...But, the Lord looketh on the heart.*" A footnote refers to I Samuel 16:7.

"You Want to Stay in *Bethany*?!"

Frequently, Jesus is mentioned as having stayed overnight in Bethany, near Mt. *Olivet*, a short distance over the hill from the *Miphkad* Altar. His friend, Lazarus, and his sisters lived in this little hamlet. Jesus is also mentioned as having spent an evening in Bethany at the home of this Simon fellow, a leper. In fact, during the last week of His Earthly ministry, Jesus spent *every* night at Bethany.

That beloved Israeli scholar and archaeologist, Yigael Yadin[6], informs us from the *Midrash* that the Jewish people of the Second Temple period believed that leprosy was transmitted through the air. Since the prevailing winds at Jerusalem were westerly from the Mediterranean, it was considered prudent to require all lepers to reside east of Jerusalem. Yes, east of town! – and downwind!

The Rabbis of the Law (the "lawyers"), as was their usual custom, carried this legalism to extreme. According to *Midrash Rabbah* Leviticus 16:3 – 4, it was unlawful for a person even to walk or stand on the east side of a leper, lest that person should therefore become "unclean." The Rabbis further specify that, if there is no wind, a person must approach no closer than four cubits (about two meters) on the east side of a leper. However, if there is a wind (of *any* intensity), then a person must not approach the downwind side of a leper within one-hundred cubits! — About fifty meters!

This same *Midrashic* text goes on to rule that "he shall dwell by himself," with a footnote explaining that the leper must not mingle even with any *other* unclean persons. We point to these strict Rabbinical ordinances as an example of how far apart were Jesus and the Rabbinical "lawyers," who are so often chastised in the Gospels.

It is certain that we could, given enough time, locate *Talmudic* Law that would define the Scriptural origin of such teaching. Usually this is done by using *a single verse* from the *Torah*, frequently taken out of context with its original and intended meaning, in order to serve as a foundation for some vain, pious, self-righteous, "man-made" doctrine. (This practice should sound familiar to many Christians.)

Jesus, on the other hand — the Author of our Salvation — implored the Rabbis, as if to say, "Please, — just stick to the Law as Moses received it from My Father. There is nothing in His Law saying lepers are to be abused and reviled and condemned in this way." If we examine Chapter 13 of Leviticus for the Law concerning lepers, we will see (as always!) that Jesus is right. But, — the Rabbis did not listen.

So, as you may have guessed, Bethany was located "safely" to the east of Jerusalem, "downwind" on the far side of the Mount of Olives — *and it was the local leper colony!* That verse about Simon, the leper, in Bethany is a Biblical understatement. And, Lazarus — a "Bethanite" — was probably a leper. Lazarus had most likely died of the ravages of that dread disease when Jesus raised him from the tomb after four days. Bad enough a leper! – But in the tomb four days! – (No wonder he "stinketh!") Considering the Jewish concern that the disease was transmitted through the air, can't we just imagine the anxiety of His disciples as Jesus went *each night* to stay with friends in Bethany?...("But, Master! – Must we stay again in Bethany?...er,...uhmm...You know!)

Perhaps we would be slack if we did not point out that, in the Bible, "leprosy" does not necessarily in all cases refer only to the plague that we moderns call leprosy. That chronic bacterial infection actually is more correctly identified as "Hansen's Disease." It is not transmitted through the air and is in fact not highly contagious. Even so, the horrific symptoms of Hansen's Disease are what so often have been so dramatically and tragically portrayed as that dreadful ailment in movies. This is especially the case with Hollywood versions of "leper colonies" during Biblical times, such as *Ben Hur* and others. Rather, if we concentrate on the details in Leviticus 13, for example, we will find there are a variety of "plagues" of the skin that are called "leprosy" in Scripture.

Biblical descriptions of leprosy also include such contamination of garments and buildings, mentioning "green" or "reddish" color in Leviticus 13:47 – 59 and 14:37. These statements suggest a type of mildew or fungus.

A somewhat profound observation is given in The Companion Bible[10] pointing out that use of cedarwood, scarlet and hyssop for purification of the leper (Leviticus 14:4) deals with the tallest tree (cedar), denoting Pride – and the lowliest herb (hyssop), denoting Humility. Since leprosy was believed to be a punishment for sin caused by pride, it was deemed appropriate that humility was necessary to provide the cure. Then, the scarlet or crimson represented blood, which was of course required to overcome sin. The parallels here with the Red Heifer ceremony are obvious and inspiring.

Further evidence concerning leprosy in the life of Lazarus is provided through an interesting statement in *The Encyclopedia Americana*[18]. Under "leprosy" it is stated that as early as C.E. 72, a Christian religious order, *The Order of Lazarus*, was founded to provide compassion and care for persons suffering with that disease. The encyclopedia instructs that the order was named for Lazarus, the beggar, who desired the crumbs from a rich man's table. (Luke 16:20 – 31) The writer assumes that the "sores" on this wretched person were caused from leprosy, although Scripture does not verify that idea. However, the Lamsa Bible[22], translated directly from the original Aramaic language of the *Peshitta*, uses the word "boils" instead of "sores." Chapter 13 of Leviticus mentions "boils" as a symptom of Biblical "leprosy." Although it is a debatable point, this could be leading to a stronger conclusion that this has to do with Lazarus of Bethany because there is no evidence even implied to say the beggar in Luke's Gospel was a leper.

Considering the evidence that has been presented here, therefore, it appears instead more likely that *The Order of Lazarus* was named for Jesus' friend, Lazarus in Bethany, rather than for the beggar in the referenced parable. Moreover, giving that name to this early Christian order seems to reinforce the history, as we have shown, that Bethany was indeed a leper colony and that it is probable that Lazarus was a leper. Thus, it is evident once again that our knowledge of Scripture has been veiled; especially, by our lack of knowledge about Judaic Law and tradition.

To the writers of the New Testament, it was common knowledge that Bethany was a town of lepers. They never bothered to emphasize the fact. – Everybody knew that! Why labor the point? They knew the Law and all the justifications for assigning Bethany as a place for lepers. Those writers must have felt that the situation just needed no discussion.

So, now we learn that Jesus was a type of the Red Heifer and He stayed in Bethany overnight and spent His last night praying at or near the *Miphkad* Altar at the garden called *Gethsemane* on *Olivet*. Some pieces are starting to fit together in what may be another picture.

"Maybe He *IS* Messiah!"

Jesus declared in Luke 6:5 that He was Lord over the Sabbath. He also announced that He was sovereign over the Law and made a point of demonstrating this several times, thus drawing bitter disapproval from the "lawyers" and Pharisees. Now, what if Jesus had not bothered to be "cleansed" after having been among all those lepers? And then He comes into the City...even the Temple! – "Aiii!! — This man has got to go!"

The Gospel does not record all of Jesus' remarks, but just listen to your imagination for a moment. What if He had claimed to others, just as He had said to His Disciples, about the significance of His blood? He had said earlier (John 4:7 – 10) that He was "living water," a well-used expression in the Red Heifer rites. What if Jesus had dropped such "innuendos" as He rode that donkey past the *Miphkad* Altar and across the Heifer's Gangway Bridge into Jerusalem?!

Knowing the Jewish teaching background in this area now, can't you just picture the Rabbinical "lawyers" rushing over to inform the Jewish religious hierarchy about how Jesus was violating the "Law." We can now almost hear them "tattling" and "hissing" about how Jesus even reclined at table with a leper, walked through the whole town of Bethany — while the wind was blowing! – etc., etc., etc. And, yes! – He even had the *chutzpah* to say that He is "The Son of Man" and that He is the "Lord of the Sabbath!"

These kinds of remarks in combination with His other acts indicating He "might" be Messiah would have stirred the ire of the Judaic priesthood as air pumped to a forge! Then, that deal with the moneychangers at the Temple would have been just too much! ("I tell you,...this man has got to go!")

Jesus and "The Ineffable Name"

On a number of occasions in the Gospel, Jesus is quoted as having spoken "The Ineffable Name;" i.e., *YHWH* – "I AM" or *Yahweh*" which is a form leading to *Jehovah* or God. Within Jewish Law (Leviticus 24:16), this was a very serious form of blasphemy for any unauthorized person to speak "The Divine Name" – the *Tetragrammaton*. Uttering "The Divine Name" in a blasphemous manner was punishable by death. The Name of God was so sacred that the Rabbinate ordered that only certain highly honored High Priests were authorized to speak "The Name" during worship. The alternate Name to be used was: *Elohim* or *Adonai*.

Somewhat early during His ministry, Jesus is quoted as having spoken The "I AM" during one of His many confrontations with the Pharisees at the Temple. That occasion for Jesus having committed this alleged act of blasphemy is given in John 8:58.

"*...Before Abraham was, I AM.*"

The rulings of *Yoma* 69b state that uttering the Ineffable Name "outside the limits of the Temple" is punishable by death. However, there seems to be no hard and fast Scripture or *Talmudic* Law prescribing that ruling. If it had actually been a "statute" under His Father's Law, it is *very* unlikely that Jesus would have violated it. Jesus' respect for The Father's authority is therefore a reliable indication that it is, after all, merely a "traditional" ruling. Nevertheless, Jesus skirted even that punishment in a "legal" sense, because He was at the Temple when this occurred. And, – "traditional" or under the Law – even so, the Pharisees were ready to stone Jesus to death right then. He escaped their wrath by hiding Himself until His would-be executioners departed. – It was not yet "His Time."

Another incident in which Jesus again committed this most egregious offense is when Jesus was being questioned by Caiaphas, the High Priest during the morning after His arrest. Jesus remarks are recorded in Mark 14:61 – 63;

"*...Again, the High Priest asked Him, and said unto Him, 'Art thou the Christ, the Son of the Blessed?'*

And, Jesus said,'I AM: and ye shall see the Son of man sitting on the right hand of power and coming on the clouds of Heaven.'

Then the High Priest rent his clothes, and saith, 'What need we any further witnesses?'"

As if that were not enough, Jesus carried His "Offense" even farther just in case Caiaphas "wimped" away from that one. So, in answering "blasphemously" as He did by taking the claim that He was Messiah, Jesus committed a capital offense. *Sanhedrin* 56a requires that a person who pronounces "That" Name in a blasphemous manner (Mark 14:61 – 62) shall be put to death. However, *Mishnah* 7:5 of *Sanhedrin* 55b is emphatic that: "the blasphemer is not guilty until he pronounces The Name."

Witnesses at the trial probably referred to Jesus' earlier remarks in their testimony to the priests, accusing Him of having spoken the "Ineffable Name" concerning Abraham. But then, in what had to have been the ultimate *chutzpah*, Jesus boldly repeated the act before Caiaphas, the High Priest. At the uninformed and casual depth that most of us have in reading our Scriptures, we Christians seem to assume that Caiaphas ripped his garment as a dramatic expression of his wrath at this blaspheming impostor.

Not so. – This is another small example of just how Jesus, with His intimate knowledge of the Law, prearranged His activities in such a way to bring about application of a principle of the Mosaic Law during His Earthly ministry. Jesus therefore pronounced The Ineffable Name after being accused as a blasphemer. Under the statutes of *Sanhedrin* 56a, while standing judgment over an accused blasphemer, the priest was *required* to stand up and rend his garment. Jesus knew this and therefore guided the confrontation with Caiaphas in such a way to produce this exact result as a fulfillment of the Law. (Yes – Every "jot-and-tittle"!)

The Name of God was NEVER to be spoken other than at Holy occasions. Even some Christian groups today consider that it is maybe somewhat slightly less than "blasphemous" to utter or write the name: GOD. Certain conservative Jewish teachers and even some Christian leaders in modern times do not pronounce the Name of God. These groups instead will use *Hashem* or *Adonai* or other names to refer to the Almighty. They carry this act of respect even further when, in their writing, they avoid using all of the letters in His Name. They write the Almighty's name as G_d.

The Scriptures do not of course relate all of such "arranged" fulfillments that Jesus wrought. Nevertheless, here is just one such little drama to tell us that Caiaphas was not just "losing it" when he ripped his robe. Caiaphas was "keeping" the Law. Jesus pressed him to do just that. So, the High Priest had a "capital offense" from Jesus right there in his own residence. (Matthew 26:57 – 66) It is fairly certain that the priest's residence was not within the bounds of the Temple.

This foregoing little Gospel drama is another of countless such applications of the Law in Jesus' Gospel. *Sanhedrin* 56a instructs that, if a "blasphemer" utters the Divine Name, the judges are to *"rend their clothes."* The footnotes attached to this passage actually mention Jesus by name and refer to His "Trial," the judges, etc. Not often does *Talmud* ever mention Jesus by name. Several other expressions are used instead, with most *Talmudic* scholars knowing full well Who is being discussed. We bring this to the readers in order to demonstrate how even the most seemingly trivial and mundane *Talmudic* Laws can be found referenced in the Gospel.

We should pause appropriately at this juncture to ask a fair question: "Why was Jesus so intent upon drawing fulfillment of such seemingly trivial *Talmudic* Laws?"

Speculation is the only approach that I am aware of for an answer to this *very* fair question. It is therefore "speculated" that Jesus exercised such thoroughness in these fulfillments to demonstrate to the Jewish people that He was in fact their long-awaited Messiah; The Anointed One; The Redeemer. It could be expected that His People would have recognized His identity because these events were reflections of ALL of the Laws they had been "keeping" for centuries before Jesus' arrival. It would seem that they should have "made-the-connection." Many Jews at the time did in fact recognize that Jesus IS Messiah. However, we realize that many others of the Jewish people have not recognized their Messiah – not at Jerusalem in C.E. 30 – and not for more than nineteen-hundred years since that time.

Therefore, we can only speculate again that when Jesus comes in Glory and Power to claim His Kingdom, they WILL look upon these events and will see their significance within the Law. They probably will marvel at how they have missed these signs – because, as we

"At Evening, Before the Entire Congregation"

The traditional site for what Christianity has called "The Last Supper" has been at "The Upper Room," a spot quite logically near the Church of the Holy Sepulchre in the Old City of Jerusalem. Consulting all the evidence we have presented, we might be tempted to declare that The Last Supper took place in an "Upper Room" somewhere in or nearby the village of Bethany instead of Jerusalem. This is especially logical considering the Scriptural evidence showing that Jesus and the Disciples spent *every* night during that week of The Passion in Bethany. Nevertheless, Scripture is clear that Jesus directed His followers to go into The City, where a man would show them an "upper room." (Luke 22:12) We therefore must conclude that the room was in fact "somewhere" in Jerusalem.

After that Last Supper, Jesus went to "*Gethsemane*" to pray. Although the present traditional site is not far distant, the C.E. 30 position of this garden may have been very close to the place of the Red Heifer burning, the *Miphkad* Altar. More than enough evidence from Part III and subsequent paragraphs strongly indicate that *Olivet* summit was the site of The Crucifixion. We have also shown the site of the Red Heifer burning was near *Olivet* summit.

That location certainly satisfies the Scriptural descriptions saying that Jesus suffered:

"nigh to the City " (Jerusalem) — from John 19:20, and

"without the gate" – from Hebrews 13:12

It is significant to observe that "*the gate*" is not to be confused with The East Gate of the Temple (Nicanor's Gate), but instead most likely refers to the East Gate to the City, as opposed to just any of the other gates. The East Gate was the main approach to this Holy City, *in that day*, because it led directly to the Holy Temple, the centerpiece of Jerusalem, itself. This prominence in Jerusalem geography and status is also highlighted in that this principal approach to the City was the same road Jesus took on His Triumphal Entry. It was named *The Descent of the Mount of Olives*, and coursed past and very near the *Miphkad* Altar and wound down the western *Olivet* slope to the Heifer's Gangway Bridge, through the East Gate to the City and on to the approaches to the Temple itself. (See Illus. 20: Jerusalem as it Appeared in 70 C.E., Page 153, and Illus. 23: Mt. Olivet viewed from Temple on Crucifixion Day, Page 156)

First century Roman law called for crucifixion to take place at or near the place of arrest or at the site of the crime. Jesus deliberately therefore may have arranged to be arrested at the same locale where His "offense" occurred. For example, we know from Luke 19:38 – 39 that the joyous throng shouted:

"Blessed be the King that cometh in the name of the Lord!"

as Jesus rode from the Mount of Olives into Jerusalem. The Pharisees "rebuked" Jesus because He did not restrain His followers from actually proclaiming Him as a "King."

Thus, did Jesus in effect, accept this lofty Royal Title. By saying nothing about being King, but declining a denial, Jesus was interpreted by the Jewish hierarchy as having made a de facto acknowledgment of the crowd's claim.

This violation of protocol turned out to be a capital crime against Rome, as well as a "blasphemy" in the view of the Jewish clergy. Pilate initially could *"find no fault in Him."* (John 19:4) But, it was treason to claim to be a "King" in the Empire that Caesar alone ruled. The angered and desperate Temple hierarchy reminded Pilate that he should not forget his loyalty to Caesar. This incident was then cited at the "trial," persuading a wavering and hesitant Pilate to condemn Jesus for the crime of sedition and sentenced Him to death on The Cross. (John 19:7 – 16)

During that night of His arrest, Jesus probably arranged to be arrested at the very same spot where the "challenge" to Caesar's sovereignty took place. This presumably would have been in a "garden" at or near the *Miphkad* Altar and along that same roadway Jesus took when He entered so triumphantly into Jerusalem. In this way, Jesus "arranged" to satisfy *both* the Roman legal criteria for the place of His execution; i.e., the place of the "offense" as well as the place of His arrest. In this way, He would have made certain that He would be "offered" at the place of *His* choosing in order that He would have properly and Completely and Perfectly fulfilled the Law.

Jesus knew *exactly* what He was doing. He knew well all the precepts of Roman Law, *Talmudic* Law and Herodian Law. Jesus selected the *Miphkad* Altar proximity as the place for His Crucifixion, by deliberately arranging to be apprehended and arrested at that precise location. This was not just a chance encounter negotiated by Judas with the Temple guards. Jesus was in Complete Control of the situation. He even selected and recruited the traitor who would treacherously live in His midst and who would then ultimately betray Him! – Yes! Jesus CHOSE Judas to betray Himself! (John 6:70 – 71)

After all, Jesus IS God! — Would God just leave it to Pilate or Judas or some centurion to choose where His Supreme Sacrifice would be given?! – (Think about it.)

Just so some of you won't think I have gone "over the edge" in my enthusiasm, we can verify this *Miphkad* Altar/Crucifixion connection by referring to three passages from Scripture:

Ezekiel 8:16

"...with their backs toward the Temple of the Lord, and their faces toward the east;..."

- Therefore, **the Temple (and the veil) faced toward east. — There can be no doubt!**

Mark 13:3

"And as He sat upon the Mount of Olives over against (i.e., facing) the Temple,..."

- Therefore, **Jesus (or anybody else) surely faced the Temple and the veil** and, particularly, the door of the Temple (See note following.) – **"as He sat upon the Mount of Olives." — There can be no doubt!**

Matthew 27:51 – 54

"...the vail of the Temple was rent in twain...the earth did quake...and the rocks rent...and the graves were opened...Now the centurion, and they that were with him, watching Jesus, saw the earthquake, and those things that were done,..."

Note: A translation[22] from 2nd century Aramaic manuscripts says, in all three Gospels relating to this event (Matthew 27:51, Mark 15:38, Luke 23:45):

"...the curtains at the door of the Temple were torn..."

With few exceptions, most Christian commentaries are mistaken in identification of "the veil." Their error is spawned by their unfamiliarity and often downright contempt for Rabbinical writings. Most Christian writers incorrectly describe the veil (or "curtain") as separating the Holy Place (Sanctuary) from the Holy of Holies. Actually, in the Second Temple two "veils" were in place for that function, as verified by the *Mishna* of *Yoma* 51b – also in *Tamid* 29b, Note 5. (See Illus. 21: Detail of the 2nd Temple, Page 154) Whereas, *Yoma* 51a and *Kethuboth* 106a confirm that a huge 60 ft. x 30 ft. "curtain" or "veil" covered the doors of the *H'ekhal*. This curtain is the only "veil" that could have been seen from the Mount of Olives at The Cross or, for that matter, even from outside of the Temple Sanctuary – the *H'ekhal*, itself.

Josephus[4] describes it as the "Babylonian Curtain" [*Wars* 5.5.4 (212)] that covered the doors of the *H'ekhal*. This "veil" is further confirmed in Exodus 36:37, described as "an hanging" of blue and purple and scarlet to cover the door of the Tabernacle.

An additional oversight concerning the Veil exists in that it is consistently omitted from models of the Tabernacle or the Temple. It can be speculated that the Rabbinical authorities have refused access to pictorial details in order to prevent the sacrilege that would result if the Veil were to be copied, either in paintings or by replicas. Nevertheless, contributing to our ignorance concerning the Veil(s) of the temple is the total absence of any pictorial or even verbal description of the design, appearance or detail.

An interesting discussion in the *Gemara* of *Zebahim* 55b, Note 7 explaining that the curtain over the entrance was required because the doors of the *H'ekhal* were open on Feast Days, the first day of the month and on all Sabbaths. The Rabbis justify this measure because: "It is indecorous for the priests to look into the *H'ekhal* while they are engaged with the sacrifice. Hence, it is open, and the sacrifice is valid." This is therefore legal, notwithstanding the fact that the (open) doors are respectfully covered by the Veil (or "curtain" — also Part II, Para. 6).

The earthquake at The Crucifixion (Matthew 27:51) probably caused all *three* of these massive, heavy Veils to tear, thus resulting in a spectacular scene of the brilliant "fire" or Glory of the Lord (*Shekhinah*) to be viewed by the centurion standing at The Cross on the Mount of Olives. It is logical, therefore, that the centurion and his soldiers "feared greatly" at this sight – having confronted Almighty God literally face-to-face! (See Matthew 27:54 and Part III, Para. 9)

Now, let us pause to ask *HOW*(?) they "*saw those things that were done*" — Why, of course: They *saw* the earthquake. They *saw* the opened graves. And yes, they *saw* the Veil (or curtains) rent from top to bottom. — The Word of God says that they "*saw*" all "*those things.*"

> **Therefore, the centurion and the others saw the Veil at the door of the Temple rent-in-twain.** In fact, they saw all of "*those things*" from east of the Temple at the top of the Mount of Olives. That is the *only* place possible from which they could have seen "*those things.*" — **There can be no doubt!**

This fact can be emphasized further as we demonstrate how difficult it was for any persons, other than Jewish men, to see the Veil. *Talmud - Shekalim* 8:5 informs us that twice each year a new Veil was made for the Temple and was displayed atop the roof of the colonnade buildings bordering the Temple courts *in order to permit public viewing from the summit of the Mount of Olives!* This display was provided in order that the public, including even Gentiles, could observe the magnificent beauty and colors of each new Veil. Otherwise, after the Veil was installed before the doors of the Temple, it could be seen only by Jewish men as they brought their sacrifices to be slain at the Court of the Israelites. (See Illus. 21: Detail of the 2nd Temple, Page 154)

Gentiles were forbidden to enter any of the Temple courts. Jewish women, children and Jewish lepers were forbidden to pass beyond the Court of Women. Women and children were forbidden even to ascend the steps leading upward to the East Gate. As they stood below, they could not look over this rise to see the Veil, even if the gate were open. At best, they could only get a peek at the top portion of that 30 ft. by 60 ft. expanse and again, only IF the sun were at its 9 a.m. position to illuminate the Veil without being shaded by the Portico above. (See Illus. 21: Detail of the 2nd Temple, Page 154 and Illus. 17: Detailed Elevation of 2nd Temple, Page 150)

So then, other than that semi-annual viewing atop the colonnade roof, the *only* place where the public could *surely* see the Veil would have been from the place of burning at *Olivet* Summit, the *Miphkad* Altar — known locally as "*Golgotha*" or "place of the skull." If one stood at that very spot at 9 a.m. with the sun at its proper elevation, etc. near the season of either Passover or *Rosh Hashanah* on a Sabbath or Holy Day or on the first day of the month, the East Gate would be open and the Veil could be seen in its full glory of wondrous scarlet and blue and purple. BUT! – Only one or two persons could observe the Veil from *that* spot during a time-span of just a few minutes because, as we have explained, the High Priest had to stand at a precise location – *"directing his gaze carefully"* – since he had such a small field of view. And again, this had to occur at about 9 a.m. – "the third hour of the day" – when the sun would be beaming directly on the Veil. (See Illus. 17: Detailed Elevation of 2nd Temple, Page 150, Illus. 18: Elevation Profile of Temple and Temple Mt., Page 151, and Illus. 19: Elev. Profile: Temple Mt., Kidron VLY., Mt. Olivet, Page 152)

It is likely that "ordinary" citizens – and especially Gentiles – were forbidden to tread that ground where the priests stood. It is obvious then, for a large public attendance, not everyone could stand and be able to sight through the East Gate opening at *that* spot. Further, the public would need to avoid treading past the many graves nearby (awaiting their Messiah!) –

lest they would become "unclean!" Thus, with the Veil arrayed on the rooftops, it was therefore much more convenient and ritually less "profane" for the public to observe and admire the Veil from most any spot on *Olivet* summit north or south of the *Miphkad* Altar.

Another indication that The Crucifixion was at the Mount of Olives is brought forth by the fact that there were graves at the site. Even today that mount is covered with the graves of Jewish dead who are awaiting their Messiah. Yes! – Ever since about 520 B.C.E., with Zechariah's announcement (Zechariah 14:4) that Messiah would stand on the Mount of Olives "on that day," religious Jews and even many secular Jewish persons have chosen that western slope of *Olivet* for their place of burial. There they can rest as they await their Redeemer upon that Holy mountain across the valley from the Temple Mount

The Apostle John provides a subtle but powerful eyewitness testimony concerning the Mount of Olives as The Crucifixion site. Chapter 19 of John's Gospel describes a few of the several Messianic prophecies that were fulfilled at The Crucifixion. Specifically, these are:

- Dividing His clothes and casting lots for His robe – (Psalms 22:18 / John 19:24)
- Gall and vinegar given for His plea of thirst – (Psalms 69:21 / John 19:28)
- None of His bones was broken – (Psalms 34:20 / John 19:36)
- "They shall look upon Me Whom they have pierced." – (Zechariah 12:10 / John 19:37)

This latter statement from the prophet Zechariah has always been of some puzzlement and confusion to the Rabbis because, throughout Chapters 12 and 14, Zechariah repeatedly refers to all those things that the Lord will accomplish "on *that* day." In other words, the Jewish scholars of Jesus' time (and even today!) thought all of Zechariah's latter day prophecies would be fulfilled simultaneously, "on that day." John believed that he actually was witnessing that fulfillment; although, in truth he was witnessing only a part of it. The remainder of the prophecy will be fulfilled gloriously on another and *much* later "day." Please permit me to explain.

Zechariah spoke of "that day" when *all* of Jerusalem will be besieged by *all* the nations (Zechariah 12:3) and when the Lord will destroy all those nations. (Zechariah 12:9) Then, through the prophet, the Lord further describes that as the "day" when "they" (Jewish people) *"...will look upon Me Whom they have pierced, and they shall mourn for Him as one mourneth for his only son."* (Zechariah 12:10)

Later in this narration, in Zechariah 14:4, the Lord is still speaking of "that day" when He will defeat the nations, when He says: *"And His feet shall stand in that day on the Mount of Olives, which is before Jerusalem on the east,..."* — then continuing with the earthquake, etc.

For centuries, Jewish worshipers have believed and still believe that all of Zechariah's prophecies about the arrival of their victorious Messiah will occur on a *single* "day." In fact, they believe this will occur on the Day of their Resurrection. (Daniel 12:1-2) Ever since Zechariah's prophecy (520 B.C.E.) and even continuing today, multitudes of Jewish dead have been buried in the cemetery on the Mount of Olives...so they can be there to greet

Messiah, Son of David, when He arrives! For that same reason, it is most likely that Joseph of Arimathaea purchased his family crypt (or tomb) on the Mount of Olives.

Whereas, Christians know from the Gospel that Jesus will return and indeed His feet will stand on the Mount of Olives "on that day" and the mountain will *"cleave in the midst thereof"* in fulfillment of Zechariah's prophecy. Christians should know also that all Jewish people will *then* mourn when they see Jesus because they did not first recognize that One Whom they (and we!) had pierced.

John was recording several prophecies that he saw fulfilled at The Crucifixion. Although he didn't mention all of Zechariah's prophecy, completely ignoring the earthquake (Matthew 27:51), but he did say they looked "upon Him Who was pierced." We can be certain that indeed there was *"a great mourning in Jerusalem,"* just as the prophet wrote (Zechariah 12:11 – 14), even though John did not mention this and a few other details of that prophecy. The most important point is that John (God's Word) says that portion of Scripture was fulfilled at The Cross; i.e., Zechariah 12 – 14, *"on that day!"*

But, what about the defeat of "the nations?" No nations were defeated. – Certainly not even Rome was defeated on that day when John saw these things fulfilled. So, it may be that "the nations" (i.e., gentiles) were defeated in a figurative way. We must rationalize such a conclusion because this statement is from The Word of God. It cannot be compromised. If it says they were defeated, then they were defeated – if only in a figurative or emblematic sense.

Having written his eyewitness account *after* The Crucifixion, in retrospect John must have thought "the nations" were defeated when Jesus defeated death and sin when He was raised from The Tomb, *which also was on the Mount of Olives!* Evidence of this claim is recorded by the 4th century historian, Eusebius, in Reference 11. True, there was an earthquake at The Cross; although, the mountain did not actually *"cleave in the midst thereof,"* etc. Neither did any *"living waters"* issue forth from beneath the Temple, on the *"right side of the House."* Neither did the "living waters" at that time course their ways to "the nearer sea and the hinder sea," as described by the prophet in Zechariah 14:8.

John and the disciples may well have been confused that day, but God's Word is *never* confused! John said the Scriptures were fulfilled, and he was certainly correct, including the part about Messiah standing on the Mount of Olives. He only omitted the earthquake, the living waters and the defeat of the nations, which therefore may have been considered fulfilled figuratively three days later with the earthquake and Jesus ("living water") on the morning of The Resurrection.

But John thought he had seen "that day" when His Lord was "pierced," and with the "wounds in His hands." (Zechariah 13:6) Yes, John surely believed he also had seen all the rest of those fulfillments, including seeing His Lord "standing" on His Cross on the Mount of Olives. It is almost as if John were saying: "And there we were, up on the Mount of Olives, seeing these things being fulfilled, just as it had been foretold by the prophets."

Regarding the other parts of Zechariah's prophecy, some were fulfilled "that day" in a figurative or symbolic way; although, some surely were fulfilled literally and physically.

After all, Jesus — THE "Living Water"— indeed came forth three days later from a tomb on the Mount of Olives. But the Gospel says they *were* fulfilled. I cannot think of any way that part about Messiah "standing" on the Mount of Olives could have been fulfilled other than as a literal and physical historical event.

Of course, you and I realize now, that Jesus will (again) fulfill *that* part of Zechariah's prophecy literally when He returns on the clouds with Power and Great Glory and stands (again) upon the Mount of Olives, this time literally to defeat the nations of the world at Jerusalem "on that day." But John also viewed The Crucifixion as that fulfillment because he said as much in his Gospel. And, — t*hat certainly had to include Jesus standing on the Mount of Olives.*

Some will say, "But how can you say the Tomb of Jesus was on the Mount of Olives? – Have you never heard of The Church of the Holy Sepulchre? – or The Garden Tomb?"— True, each of those popular sites has been identified traditionally as the Tomb of Jesus for many years not only by the local tourist guides, but also by many famed, knowledgeable and noble scholars. (Sorry, but they are mistaken.) Part of the explanation follows.

In the first place, *both* of these tombs obviously cannot be at the correct location. At least one of these must be incorrect, if it is to be assumed that The Crucifixion took place nearby. In fact, *neither* site can possibly be "correct" because, by the Law (Leviticus 24:14, 23; Numbers 15:35), any execution had to be *"without the camp."* This expression, "without the camp" means the place must be at least "a Sabbath Day's journey" from the Holy of Holies. The Law commands that, during the Sabbath, Jews shall travel no farther than a distance of 2000 cubits or about 1000 yards. Location of the Holy of Holies is known to have been "somewhere" on the Temple Mount. In fact it has recently been identified[7, 47] by Prof. Asher S. Kaufman as the Dome of the Tablets. (Illus. 19: Elev. Profile: Temple Mt., Kidron VLY., Mt. Olivet, Page 152 and Illus. 20: Jerusalem as it Appeared in 70 C.E., Page 153)

We explained earlier that this statute of the Law already had been violated perhaps many times by having executed persons within a Sabbath Limit from the Holy of Holies. Nevertheless, Jesus was fulfilling the Law *Perfectly!* – whereas, those violations of the statute were done by persons who had little or no regard for the Law. They were not doing *anything* Perfectly!

Since Jesus fulfilled all of the Law, this included Numbers 19:9 which required that the ashes (represented by Jesus' corpse) must be *"without the camp in a clean place."* A tomb of hewn stone at *Olivet* summit and which never before had contained a dead body therefore would satisfy the Law of Numbers 19:9 for the Red Heifer. Since both of the present popular and traditional tourist sites are nearer than a Sabbath Day's journey from the Temple Mount and both are west of the Temple Mount, neither qualifies. This single facet is only one of several pieces of evidence that demonstrates to all except the most rigid and "stiff—necked" traditionalists that Jesus was crucified and entombed on *Olivet* summit. However, there is even much more evidence available to show this.

Scriptural evidence proves that The Crucifixion took place on the Mount of Olives. There is also a preponderance of evidence available from historical and archaeological sources[2, 3, 4,]

5, 9, 11 that agrees with the Scriptural conclusion. Those same sources describe another remarkable event, which is the Glorious Withdrawal of The *Shekhinah* Glory from the Temple and Jerusalem, and which is closely relative to this story. However, that data is already presented in Part I. Nevertheless, it should be noted here that not *one* strand of evidence, Scriptural or historical or archaeological, has ever been found which would support *either* of the traditional "tourist" locations for The Crucifixion. I realize 1900 years of traditional teaching is difficult to overcome—but, there it is—for all the world (and "Believers") to see when they search for the Truth.

The foregoing information, especially, sparks interest in all these things of the Gospel that *might* relate to the Red Heifer. Although there is no direct mention of this connection in the New Testament, Jesus' movements and actions in the vicinity of the *Miphkad* Altar would certainly have struck a discordant note with the "lawyers." Then, when we consider His arrest in that same area and factor in the Roman legal procedure mentioned, the possibility of "mere coincidence" must surely fade.

Still skeptical? – Well, there is a very similar Jewish sacrifice that provides another even more dramatic clue. Most Believers agree that the Paschal (Passover) Lamb is another obvious "type" of Jesus. A male lamb "of the first year," unblemished and without spot, slain outside the camp, "...*the whole assembly of the congregation of Israel shall kill it in the evening.*" (From Exodus 12:6) As a direct fulfillment of this, Jesus was killed as "*the whole assembly of the congregation of Israel*" watched. He died at the "ninth hour" or about 3 p.m., considered as "evening" in many cultures even today. This was also precisely the hour for slaying the Passover lambs, in accordance with the Law. (*Aboth* 5:6)

Reference 25, under Exodus 12:6, explains that the literal Scriptural language leading to our English translations as "evening" (or sometimes "dusk") actually means "between two evenings;" although it is better translated as "toward evening." Further, *Talmud* states the "first evening" is the time at which the sun's heat begins to wane, at about 3p.m., and the "second evening" begins at sunset. Josephus recorded that the Paschal Lamb was slain between the ninth and the eleventh hours; i.e., from 3 to 5 p.m.

If you have been to Jerusalem, you are well aware that only one locale is visible to "*the whole assembly of the congregation*" from the Old City...You guessed it! — *Olivet* summit! And it is definitely "outside the camp" — two thousand cubits outside, to be precise!

Moreover, another facet of Roman crucifixion practice was to "stage" the execution where it would be seen by all. It was, in fact, "required viewing" for the citizenry. In this way, Rome dramatized her hardness, power and omnipresence in order to keep vanquished subjects in line. What better place than that Holy mountain, *Olivet*? In the "evening" (at 3 p.m.) *Olivet* summit can be seen from the Old City of Jerusalem in clear detail by everyone, without having to squint into the sun.

One critic has objected to the *Olivet* site on basis that The Crucifixion as well as many other Roman executions was "along a main road into Jerusalem." This is claimed as an indication showing that Gordon's Calvary, The Garden Tomb, etc. is the authentic site since in the present day, the "Road to Damascus" passes closely to the points mentioned. This view is borne of poor scholarship in assuming that the "main roads" entering and departing Jerusalem today are the same as they were during the first century. Scholars who would adhere to that claim are overlooking and/or are ignorant of the fact that the Heifer's Gangway Bridge (Illus. 20: Jerusalem as it Appeared in 70 C.E., Page 153) was the most prominent thoroughfare entering Jerusalem at the time of Jesus. The roadway named *The Descent of the Mount of Olives* (Luke 19:37) wound its course from *Olivet* summit, most likely passing near the *Miphkad Altar* and down the slope to enter the Heifer's Gangway. The importance of the route so described is obvious because that roadway led straight into the East Gate of the City, and in turn, led into the Temple itself.

This fact alone dramatizes that importance as a desirable feature of the Mount of Olives site for the Romans' motives because of its proximity with a major thoroughfare approaching Jerusalem. Traveling The Descent of the Mount of Olives, many travelers nearing the Holy City by arriving from the South or the North, but especially those from the East, would tour down this road, many crossing the Heifer's Gangway Bridge to enter The City. (See Illus. 20: Jerusalem as it Appeared in 70 C.E., Page 153) These travelers would receive a stern reminder of Rome's power as they became exposed to the horrendous spectacle of these Judeans dying on crosses, easily seen from that road.

For centuries there has been a great question among Christians concerning the exact location of "*Golgotha*" or "Calvary," which are the Biblical names for the "Place of the Skull," as derived from Aramaic and Greek, respectively. We have already shown that The Crucifixion most likely took place at or very near the place of burning of the Red Heifer (*Miphkad* Altar) on the Mount of Olives, but why call it "Place of the Skull?"

An argument appears in *Talmud*, *Yoma* 68 and *Zebahim* 105b, concerning the place for the burning of the Atonement goats and the bullocks and goats for the sin offerings. (Exodus 29:14, Leviticus 4:11-12, 16:27) Second century Rabbi Jose claims these burnings took place north of the City. However, two first century Rabbis had stated that those animals were burned east of the Sanctuary at the summit of the Mount of Olives, *at the same place where the Red Heifers were burned!* Not only do the first century Rabbis appear to have the better argument in this debate, but they also have increased credibility through having lived a few decades closer to the time when the sacrifices were still being conducted in the Temple. A note points out that the phrase "poured out" in Leviticus 4:12 literally means: *"it must be a place where the ashes naturally pour down."*

Now, let us consider that ALL of the ash remains of the animals from the burnings of the *daily* sin offerings and the Atonement goats and bullocks were deposited east of the Sanctuary and at the summit of the Mount of Olives. Also remember this was practiced over a period of almost 1000 years accumulated during the period of Solomon's Temple and during the time of the Second Temple. We can see a very clear circumstance that led to the Judeans having called this the "*Place of the Skull.*" Since the skull is about the only recognizable part remaining after an animal is burned on a fire, *that place probably was strewn with literally thousands upon thousands of skulls!*

By describing this locale as a place "where the ashes *naturally* pour down," *Talmud* is referring to such a requirement from the Mosaic Law in Leviticus 4:12: *"...where the ashes are poured out,..."* This of course indicates that the spot had to be located on a somewhat steep incline, such as exists near *Olivet* summit. (You can feel this in your legs on that mountain!)

Some critics question why the Gospel writers did not specifically identify the Mount of Olives as the place of The Crucifixion. We have substantiated that John, in so many words (in John 19:37), alluded to *Olivet* by pointing at The Cross as fulfillment of Zechariah's prophecy: *"They shall look upon Me Whom they have pierced."* (Zechariah 12:10) also: *"And his feet shall stand in that day upon the mount of Olives..."* (Zechariah 14:4) We have proposed that the Aramaic *"Golgotha"* was such a familiar local name for the place with all those skulls, that Judeans would have deemed it superfluous to mention that it was on *Olivet*.

For example, a local writer in New York City, *addressing New Yorkers* about the Statue of Liberty, would sound rather silly if he described it as being on Staten Island...in New York Harbor. — (Can't we just hear them?!)

"Whaddaya mean?! – Everybody in New York knows that! — Gimme a break, already!" Another example: Scripture *never* states that Capernaum is on the shore of the Sea of Galilee. Everybody *knew* that! – By similar reasoning, then it was unnecessary in the minds of Matthew, Mark, Luke and John, to mention that *Golgotha* was on the Mount of Olives western slope. — *Everybody* knew that!

We 20th century Christians must remember that the Gospel writers were *very* familiar with Jerusalem. Even though, except for Luke, they were "country boys" from Galilee, they had visited Jerusalem many times. They could have had NO thought that they were compiling The All-Time Best Seller of All Time for publication "unto the uttermost parts of the World." Neither could they have envisioned that their writings would be printed in several dozen languages and to people who had never even seen nor perhaps ever would see Jerusalem. They wrote in a "local" context, with the Holy Spirit inspiring them to write it just as we see it today. Maybe the Lord wanted to see if you and I would merely follow "tradition," or if we would study Scripture and find the Truth for ourselves.

Even the most deeply entrenched skeptic should decline any accusation of "relying on coincidence," etc. in considering these three facts:

1. Jesus went to pray and was then betrayed and arrested in a *garden* on the Mount of Olives. - Matthew 26:36 – 50, Luke 22:39 and John 18:1 – 3
2. Jesus was crucified in a *garden*. — John 19:41; and,
3. Jesus was entombed in *that same garden*. — John 19:41

Admittedly, we can only presently assume all three events took place in the same "garden," even considering that the last two are confirmed Scripturally. Nevertheless, based upon relative elevations, orientation and distances between the Mount of Olives and the Temple Mount, we will demonstrate how these locales match exactly with literal Scripture and the precise statutes of *Talmudic* Law.

Further intriguing detail dramatizes the importance of this garden. The footnotes of *Hallah* 1:8 set forth a very clever, but legal "loophole" concerning a provision for s–t–r–e–t–

c–h–i–n–g the Sabbath Limit beyond the prescribed two thousand cubits. Called "the *erub* of cooked foods," this measure permits a family or group of persons, *on the day preceding the Sabbath*, to place a cache of prepared food at a distance of one Sabbath Limit (2000 cubits) from their intended destination on the Sabbath itself. Under this clever but devious statute, the party then *may travel any desired distance on the Sabbath Day* in order to reach their cache of food. *Talmud* rules that this "leniency" is justified *because food is considered as one's private domain*, as if it were within a person's house or tent. From that point where the food was stored they may then make their journey of one Sabbath Limit (about 1000 yards), having complete impunity under the Law.

This may at first seem trivial, yet outrageously devious and calculating. However, we must remember that the Law was composed during the time of the Israelites in the wilderness as they lived surrounding the Tabernacle with their camp. The distance ("as-the-crow-flies") from the Tabernacle diagonally to the most remote corner of the camp was about two thousand cubits. Hence, a Sabbath Day journey was all of the distance one needed during those days to travel on the Sabbath; i.e., to the Tabernacle at the center of the camp. There was therefore a legitimate and logical explanation of the distance. The formal statute is found in Numbers 35:5 as a limit of distance beyond their towns that could be traveled on the Sabbath, to be applied of course when they came into The Land.

However, after the Israelites came into the Promised Land, what may seem at first to be a "ruse" leading to the *erub* (pronounced like *Arab*), became necessary for practicality. It is obvious that ALL Jewish worshipers at that time could not have lived within a Sabbath Limit from the Tabernacle and thereby remain in compliance with the Sabbath travel laws. The problem would have been especially acute centuries later during the feast days when Jerusalem was crowded with obedient pilgrims coming to the Temple from throughout Judea. This "accommodation" is therefore instituted even near modern synagogues as a "practical" solution to a "legal" problem. The principles applied here can further augment our identification of The Crucifixion site, in addition to answering a doubt that has been cast regarding the traditional *Olivet* site of The Ascension.

Continuing, *Erubin* 23a rules that the food may be stored at:

- A place that is private, or at least semi–private.
- A garden.
- A courtyard.
- A large court, if it is planted with trees.

This description could fit the locale of a place such as the *Miphkad* Altar, which we propose was at or very near the place of The Crucifixion and *may have been*, at that time, the olive grove and garden called *Gethsemane*. It already has been shown that this place would have been much nearer *Olivet* summit than the present site of that name.

Some scholars and theologians have scoffed at any claim that tradition proposes for authenticity of the Chapel of The Ascension at *Olivet* summit. Their criticism is based on

Luke 24:50, stating that Jesus went out from Bethany (which was about two miles east of Jerusalem and more than a mile east of *Olivet*) and then He departed into Heaven.

Again, as always, the *literal* Word of God is pure — but it must be searched carefully, thoroughly and diligently in order to test the Truth, especially as Truth compared with "tradition."

Acts 1:12 states that immediately following Jesus' Ascension:

"Then returned they unto Jerusalem from the mount called Olivet, which is from Jerusalem a Sabbath day's journey."

So, did Jesus ascend from just some indiscriminate point near Bethany (on the reverse side of the mountain) or did He in fact ascend from the traditional locale at the summit of the Mount of Lives? Further, what was so significant for Luke, the writer of Acts, to state that the point was *"from Jerusalem a Sabbath day's journey?"*

A subtle and very convincing indication of the *Olivet* Ascension is presented in Acts 1:11. Angels declared to the Disciples *"...this same Jesus, which is taken up from you into Heaven, shall so come* **in like manner** *as ye have seen Him go into Heaven."* The phrase, *"in like manner"* indicates that He *"shall so come"* to this very same place! We know, from Zechariah 14:4 of course, that Jesus "shall so come" to the summit of the Mount of Olives:

"And His feet shall stand in that day upon the Mount of Olives."

Please notice here, in the quote from Acts 1:11, His Ascension into Heaven is stated *twice*, actually repeating the phrase "into Heaven" within the same sentence for emphasis. This emphasis is intended to clear our minds to the fact that Jesus will return from Heaven to that very same place from which He had ascended into Heaven *"in like manner"* — from the Mount of Olives.

We must consider now the vital fact that Jesus could fulfill the Law of the Red Heifer, as well as many other facets of the Law, only by being crucified and entombed at *Olivet* summit. Any other place just will not fit. Even the present treasured and revered olive grove, called "The Garden of *Gethsemane*," is much too far down the slope and therefore is too near the Holy of Holies to be qualified under the Law. The place must be "outside the camp;" i.e., beyond one Sabbath Limit from the Holy of Holies. Moreover, one could never be able to see the Veil from that popular Christian pilgrim stop, which lies almost at the very foot of the Mount of Olives, and which is much less than one Sabbath day's journey from the Holy of Holies as recently located by Prof. Asher Kaufman[7, 47]. Much more evidence indicating the *Olivet* Crucifixion will be presented in the remainder of this chapter.

Two thousand years ago then, there was unquestionably a "garden" very near *Olivet* summit, at which all of the Scriptural accounts, the facts and the Law would fit into place. In fact, Eusebius[11], fourth century church historian known as "the father of ecclesiastical history," wrote of "the cave" (presumably Jesus' Tomb) at *Olivet* summit. Eusebius described that point as having been beloved and revered as **the most important place of worship for the earliest Christians at Jerusalem.**

These kinds of Scriptural records, history, archaeology and elementary logic just will not support consideration at either of the two "traditional" Crucifixion sites, namely: the Church of the Holy Sepulchre or near "Skull Hill," Gordon's Calvary, the Garden Tomb, etc. — Sorry, they just don't fit the "picture" or the facts.

Nevertheless, regardless of "the facts," tradition or the Law, it should be extremely difficult for any Believer to agree that God would sacrifice His only Son, our Red Heifer, at just some indiscriminate place out behind the back door of the Temple! They should need to consider the fact also that *all* of the Jewish sacrifices, which certainly do point to Jesus, were conducted in front (east) of the Temple. And, that most important rite of ALL Jewish Temple ordinances was conducted due east of the Temple at a distance of one Sabbath Limit. It would then just seem logical that God would also place that most important Sacrifice of ALL Sacrifices...YES!!...east of the Temple. But, of course, some may need to think about all this for just a bit. After all, it is not easy to persuade against nineteen centuries of traditional belief.

So, there is no "mystery" concerning location of the site of The Crucifixion. We have presented an overwhelming amount of hard evidence to verify that Jesus was in fact crucified near the summit of the Mount of Olives. Moreover, if Prof. Asher Kaufman's location of the Holy of Holies is correctly positioned at the Dome of the Tablets, then The Crucifixion was due east of that humble little structure at a distance of about 2000 cubits and just below *Olivet* summit. (See Illus. 26: Temple Mt., Contoured Mt. of Olives, Page 324.)

More precise location of The Crucifixion site is obtained by applying measurements using Asher Kaufman's[7, 47] Standard (Moses') Cubit. The *Mishnah* of *Kelim* 17:9 teaches that the Sabbath Limit is determined using the Standard (Moses') Cubit = six handbreadths. This length, as substantiated by Kaufman's measurements = 42.8 cm. A "correct" Sabbath Limit then, = 1985 x 42.8/100 = 850 meters.

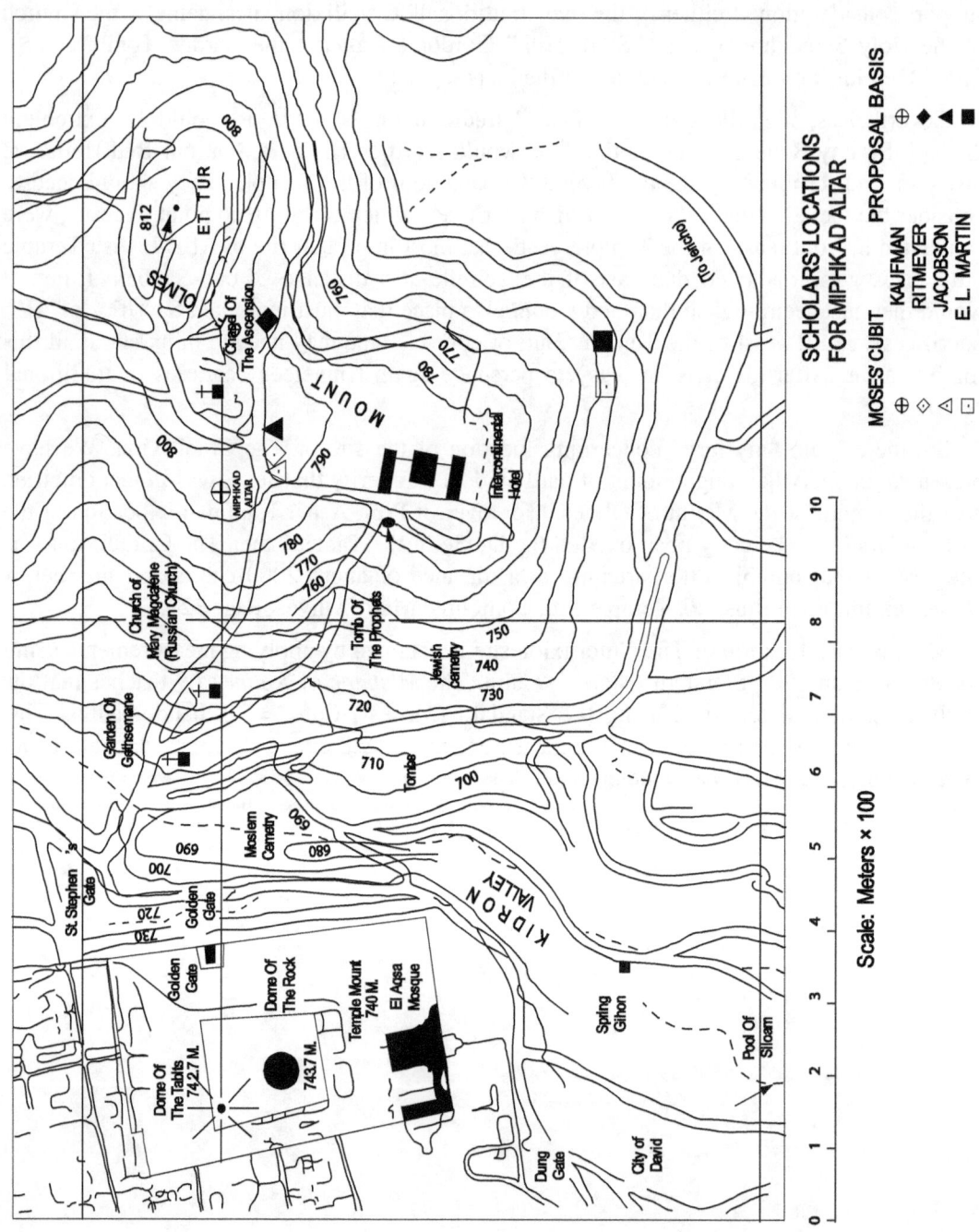

Illus. 26: Temple Mt., Contoured Mt. of Olives

Illus. 26: Temple Mt., Contoured Mt. of Olives, Page 324, is marked by a line extending eastward at a distance of 850 meters from the Dome of the Tablets. The contours then reveal the location of The Cross and the *Miphkad* Altar to be at an elevation of about 795 meters. The summit proper, in the Arab village of *et Tur*, is at 812 meters, far back from where the western slope drops toward the Kidron Valley below.

Closing this discussion, it must be said that proposing that The Crucifixion took place at the summit of the Mount of Olives is an enormously controversial position. The preponderance of traditional teaching has, for centuries, claimed the site at the Church of the Holy Sepulchre, and many Protestant factions during the past 20th century and extending to the present have claimed Gordon's Calvary as that Holy site. The near proximity of the revered Garden Tomb increases their loyalty to that site.

It is disturbing therefore to analyze the opposition of these scholars in the face of irrefutable Scriptural evidence. It is well-known that many of these teachers have been escorting large groups of tourists to these sites during several decades, declaring or at least implying their authenticity. We must observe what is their "practical - business" situation through this controversy. It is obvious that local tourist factions in Jerusalem would be severely upset, were these theologians to suddenly reject the traditionally popular "tourist" sites in favor of the Mount of Olives.

Notwithstanding the "business" objection, it is further apparent that some of these opposing scholars refuse to acknowledge the *Olivet* Crucifixion simply because it causes them to be embarrassed. They are embarrassed because for many years or even decades they have been teaching their "followers" that one or the other of the traditional sites is authentic. Some of these scholars even sponsor guided tours to Israel and then show their followers these proclaimed sites. *Finally, they are embarrassed by the Truth!*

The scholars proposing such teaching have been (and are) highly acclaimed and credentialed. We must respect their credentials and backgrounds; although, we must insist that they have erred in several areas that we have shown. *Both* of those popular sites certainly cannot be correct. We have presented ample evidence showing that, in fact, *neither* of these traditional positions can be correct. Again, there is not one particle of evidence, Scriptural or secular or archaeological, supporting either of the traditional sites. Contrastingly, we have displayed overwhelming evidence for the *Olivet* site, much of which has not previously been presented. Nevertheless, it has become apparent that we cannot convince any persons who, for whatever reason, simply do not *want* to believe the evidence that we have provided supporting the *Olivet* site – no matter the quantity of evidence or how well-founded it is.

These teachers are fearful of reaping the wrath, rejection and ridicule from peers and colleagues as well as damaging their credibility by admitting their ignorance about the Truth. Irony will eventually emerge when they finally will be forced to accept the Truth. The longer they delay acceptance, the more embarrassment and loss of credibility shall they suffer. In sympathy for their predicament, however, we shall point out later in this chapter what *may* be the Lord's Holy Reasoning and Justification for having permitted our prolonged ignorance about the True site of The Crucifixion.

Having discussed my work on these subjects personally with one university professor and Christian TV personality who is well-credentialed in Christian-Judaic theology, he agreed with all of my findings about *Shekhinah* and The Crucifixion. Nevertheless, he declined to "stand-up" with me. There appears to be no other reason for his "dodging" the Truth, other than the "business" motivated position. However, I can understand why he would not wish to jeopardize his career and why he would not wish to confront his fellow "professionals" who oppose the *Olivet* Crucifixion claim.

In the matter of overcoming traditional teaching with Truth, it may be fitting to insert a quote from Israel's most honored sage, the philosopher Maimonides, noted in Rabbi Joseph Telushkin's recent invaluable Jewish text[39]. In the reputedly greatest work of Maimonides, *The Guide to the Perplexed*[40], in Part II, Chapter 25, that Jewish icon stated his goal regarding Truth:

> *"When I have a difficult subject before me...and can see no other way of teaching a well-established truth, except by pleasing one intelligent man and by displeasing ten thousand fools, I prefer to address myself to that one man and to take no notice whatsoever of the condemnation of the multitude."*

"What Time For The Burning?"

Middoth 2:4 instructs that the High Priest must "direct his gaze carefully" in order to see the door at the front of the Temple. Here, we must be mindful that the thick Babylonian curtain — or "Veil" — was hanging in place to cover the door of the Temple. (Exodus 26:36) Two "veils," perhaps much lighter and thinner, separated the Holy Place from the Holy of Holies inside the Temple. (Illus. 23: Mt. Olivet viewed from Temple on Crucifixion Day, Page 156) Let us ask, then: "At what hour would the Red Heifer burning be planned in order that the High Priest could see the Veil as he sprinkled the Red Heifer's blood seven times *directly before the Tabernacle?*"

Most tourists visiting Jerusalem want to get a snapshot (or a video!) of Jerusalem's Old City before their luggage is even up to the room! That scene is, after all, one of the most beautiful and most popular panoramas to be seen on this Planet. However, those who are patient to wait for their tour guide to schedule that marvelous sight will find that he has wisely scheduled it for the next morning —first thing! The reason is, of course, because at that time the Old City, the Dome of the Rock, the East Wall, etc. will be painted in bright golden sunlight just as the sun rises over *Olivet* summit behind their backs.

In fact, the best "photo-opportunity" occurs at about 9 a.m., when the earliest and best light appears after burning off the early morning mountain haze. This also is about the only time when the priest would be able to see the Veil through the open East Gate. *Mishnah* 2:4 of *Middoth* tractate instructs that the High Priest must "direct his gaze *carefully* to see the door of the *H'ekhal* (Temple) at the time of the sprinkling of the blood." This means that, from a distance of almost 1000 meters, he is "sighting" through a rather small opening. The Veil must be completely bathed in sunlight. — No shadows,...not even on the stairs ascending to the *H'ekhal*. The sun must not be too high or the Veil is shaded by the Portico above — or too low and it becomes shaded by the lintel across the top of the East Gate in front. (See Illus. 17: Detailed Elevation of 2nd Temple, Page 150, Illus. 18: Elevation Profile of Temple and Temple Mt., Page 151, and Illus. 19: Elev. Profile: Temple Mt., Kidron VLY., Mt. Olivet, Page 152.)

Continuing, he would need to select a time of year when the sun would be directly behind the priest; i.e., due east. This was necessary in order that he would have the sun's rays passing straight against the Veil, without being shaded by the gate or the Portico. Otherwise, if he chose to conduct this rite in, say December — the sun would be too far to the south; or in June — too far to the north. In either case, the Veil would be partially shaded on the right or left by the column structures at each side of the East Gate. Within *Talmudic* law, it is absolutely "profane" if a shadow should come across the Veil or even the stairs leading up to the *H'ekhal*, during this most Holy ceremony. Then yes, the sun must be *directly* behind the priest, and in *good* weather — no clouds — preferably in Spring rather than Autumn. – Why not Autumn??? – Would the hyssop have buds in Autumn? — No way! — It *was* Spring!

Almost as if by "coincidence," then Jesus went to The Cross, not only during the Spring Season, but at the Passover. At that time the sun would be at or near its Vernal Equinox. It would be then "astronomically" centered" on an east-west line to bring its rays straight and <u>PERFECTLY</u>! through the opened East Gate. In this way, the sun was lined up to illumine the brilliant colors of the blue, purple and scarlet Veil at "the third hour of the day," as Jesus was being "lifted up."

And so, again Jesus had scheduled the precisely correct and marvelous, Holy Timing for His Holy Offering as our Red Heifer. The Red Heifer Ceremony was a picture of Jesus' Most Holy Offering at the summit of the Mount of Olives, at the *Miphkad* Altar, where the ashes were "poured out" – and in the Spring (Passover) Season of the year – when the hyssop was of course in its budding season. – EVERYTHING was scheduled and conducted PERFECTLY ! – What a Savior!!!

"Why Did The Temple Face Toward East?"

Why wasn't the Temple built to face north – or south – or west, or whatever? Why did they not face it toward Mount Horeb or Mount Nebo or some other revered landmark from the Jewish historical/religious tradition? — Why east? The primary and obvious answer to this logical and probing question is of course given in the very first ordinances and specifications for the Tabernacle in Exodus 38:13 - 15 and again in Numbers 3:23 and 3:38. These verses specify that the entrance to the Holy House and the approaching gates are on the east side of the court. The Lord had in fact specified that His Holy House would face eastward.

But, again — even though this was a commandment from the Lord, — WHY did He ordain that the Temple should face east? Our answer is found within the *Talmudic* law for this ceremony.

First, as we have already shown, the Temple had to be oriented such that the Veil would not be shaded, neither by the lintel across the top of Nicanor's Gate nor by the wall at either side. The priest must view the entire Veil, illuminated in sunlight. (No shadows!) Then, the Temple must be faced in such a way that the sun's rays will pass uninterrupted through the open gate and against the Veil, without casting a shadow on the Veil or even on the steps approaching the *H'ekhal*. (Otherwise, "It would be profane.") It was believed that a shadow indicated presence of a demon. (*Yebamoth* 122a) This requirement obviously provides only the choices of facing either west or east, and then only as limited by the equinox seasons previously described.

Another requirement growing from the aforementioned statute is that which dictates that the sun must be elevated at approximately forty-five degrees to avoid shading the Veil with the overhanging portico. This mandates that burning the Heifer must take place at a point east of the Temple at "the third hour" of the day (9 a.m.), because only at that hour will the sun be elevated at forty-five degrees above the horizon in order to avoid "profaning" with shadows and still satisfy all requirements.

Let us consider: If it were not "profane" to have the Veil shaded, why not burn at the ninth hour? The ninth hour is the beginning of "evening" in Judaic tradition as well as in many other societies even today. If the Heifer were to be burned "at even," and if the priests and the other participants must all remain "unclean until even," then a "legal" problem arises. May these "unclean" assistants now return "to the camp" just as if nothing had happened? In order to be consistent with the other "rules" we have seen, it would hardly seem logical that the participants would not face some sort of restriction or penalty for having become "unclean." (We can't just let them go home right away!)

Well, maybe we can make them stay "outside the camp" overnight, and they can return as "clean" the next morning. — *No!* — The Lord says they shall return "at even." — That is *not* morning! — Well, OK. Then, how about the next evening? Can we let them return at that time? — *No!* — The Lord says they will return that *same* evening. (See Numbers 19:10)

OK, then. — That does it. — The burning *must* be conducted in the morning "at the third hour of the day." The only way that can be done in order to accomplish all of the Law of the Red Heifer is by performing the ceremony *east* of the Temple and only if the Temple is facing *east*. Now we know at least one reason explaining why the Lord commanded that His Sanctuary should face east. Examination of the sketches showing the Temple and its topographical orientation will assist the reader in following the intricacies of these details which, although they are complex, do contribute to the Glory of His Plan.

Again, I realize this is all very technical and complicated, but please remain patient, folks; because we have just found another "picture" at The Crucifixion. Jesus was crucified at the "third hour" (Mark 15:25), which was *about 9 a.m.* Also, He was crucified on the eve of *Pesach* (Passover), which arrives with the first full moon of Spring — when the sun and the moon *both* come up over the Mount of Olives *directly east of the Temple*.

It should be obvious at this point that "Someone" sorted through a lot of detail in order to lay out the Temple architecture and its location in such a way that all these angles and heights and directions would provide the required view for the Priest. It did NOT happen by coincidence! We recall that all of these details of cubits, walls, distances, etc. were specified by the prophet Ezekiel Chapters 40-44 about 550 B.C.E. as the dimensions for the Temple that was to be built for arrival of Messiah, Son of David, upon the return of the enslaved Israelites from Babylon to Jerusalem.

The Temple architects implemented these dimensions precisely. They set the lintels over the gateposts, extended the court lengths, stairway, heights, etc. with rigid precision in order that the vitally important Law of the Red Heifer ceremony would be fulfilled without error. It was by no "coincidence" that Ezekiel had lined everything up with the summit of the Mount of Olives and the Temple Mount to precisely coordinate the correct profiles of the terrain, gates, courts, etc. to "fit" the Law of the Red Heifer ceremony.

It was, again ! – certainly not by coincidence that the priest could stand eastward at a Sabbath Limit from the Temple at *Olivet* summit and "*direct his gaze carefully*" to look through the East Gate and see the Veil at the door of the Temple. Neither was it by any coincidence that, when so positioned "carefully" at the third hour of the day he would see the sunlit beautiful, stunning colors of the Veil. – **All** of it had been designed by The Master Architect of The Universe! – (Please study Illus. 15: Plan of Second Temple (by Dr. A.S. Kaufman), Page 148, through Illus. 24: Detail of "pit or cavity" in face of Mt. of Olives, Page 157)

That remarkable design would integrate the Sabbath Journey, the "sight-picture" for observing the Veil illuminated by sunlight, at the "third hour," etc., etc., etc. to fit the Law not only for the Red Heifer, but also for all of the sacrifices and even to the Ultimate Sacrifice of *Y'shua* at The Cross. As we study it now, we can understand and appreciate that all of this was Divinely ordained by the Master Architect of The Universe, centuries, perhaps eons earlier.

Only after studying this as we have done here, can one understand that all of the Temple design and the Law that has been applied here was ultimately intended to become fulfilled in The Crucifixion, The Ascension and the Glorious Return of the Lord to Jerusalem. These thoughts emphatically reveal further the Infinite and Eternal Glory of God in this drama. Only a "Divine Architect" could have designed such an intricate and Magnificent Plan – to be prepared in order to Glorify Himself and His Only Son!

"Let Us Find A 'Clean' Man"

We have identified Christ's Church as the picture of the "man that is clean," as represented in Numbers 19:9 – 10. But, **WHO** portrayed that person at The Crucifixion?

– "The Church" had not even been born! – Why, of course it was Joseph of Arimathaea! – Anybody could guess that! Scripture states repeatedly that this was an honorable and just man. He could then, by most accounts, qualify as "a man that is clean."

We should further note at this point that Joseph's tomb which he had volunteered for Jesus would also qualify as being "clean" because it was hewn in stone, wherein never man before was laid." (Luke 23:53) Earlier we noted the "cleanness" of hewn stone in Judaic Law. Since no other corpse had ever been placed in that tomb, here again is another very important criterion for status as "a clean place."

We also must underline the requirement that the "clean place" must be *"without the camp"* as commanded in Numbers 19:9. The importance of the location of The Tomb regarding this part of the commandment will be shown later.

Nevertheless, some might be moved at first to question whether Joseph's motives were truly pure. Remember? Joseph approached Pilate to request that since Jesus already was dead, that he be permitted to remove Jesus from The Cross for burial. Joseph made this plea because God's Law forbade leaving an executed "blasphemer" to hang overnight "upon a tree," and especially since their Sabbath was fast approaching. (Mark 15:42 – 43; also review Deuteronomy 21:22 – 23 and *Sanhedrin* 47a)

The referenced passage from Deuteronomy is a remarkable example of God's application of His foreknowledge to the Law given to Moses and the Children of Israel. When He issued this statute God knew the Son of Man later would be put to death for "blasphemy" and that He would be hanged from a tree, and that He would be dead before sundown. The Lord knew this righteous man, Joseph, would at that time be prepared to apply and to fulfill that item from the Law. Pilate of course played a part in this, but could have known nothing of what actually was accomplished. In many ways we have shown during this study, that it is obviously apparent that God knew all these things were going to become fitted to the "burnt offering" of His Only Son, Jesus of Nazareth.

Now, Pilate usually strove to promote good will toward the Jewish hierarchy, especially the *Sanhedrin*. So here was Joseph, a member of that esteemed council, requesting Jesus' corpse under a principle of Jewish law. Or maybe he was even asking that he be permitted to bury this man's body as a sort of "convenient accommodation" in order to help the Roman procurator present to the Judeans an image of a "kinder and gentler Rome!" — Pilate could not have resisted such an offer. — He did not like to "make waves." Traumatic incidents in Judea during his "watch" would not bode well on Pilate's Fitness Evaluation at the Home Office! And perhaps Pilate thought this might "square" him with his wife and others who had cautioned against ordering this innocent man to be put to death on a cross. Joseph cut a clever deal, some might suggest. — But, W H Y would Joseph do this???

If these thoughts cause us to suspect Joseph's motives, let us now consider a Jewish tradition of that era which could be even more suspect toward a somewhat bizarre but clever and selfish motive. A story in the Old Testament which continued into the tradition of the Second Temple is discussed in *Talmud Sanhedrin* 47a, stating that it is not good for a wicked man to be buried alongside the bones of a righteous man. The Rabbis explain the justice in this ruling is established from the incident in II Kings 13:21, in which a man being buried in the grave of Elisha was miraculously returned to life when his corpse touched the bones of the prophet. It would be very unjust then, for a wicked man to experience this miracle, should it ever recur. That possibility must therefore be avoided by interring together only those persons of similar righteousness. (Honest! — That is what it says!)

Talmud footnotes further offer that, according to tradition, the man who was raised from Elisha's grave was the old prophet of Beth El in I Kings 13:11 – 31, indicating that this man also was righteous and was therefore deserving of the miracle. *Hullin* 7b provides a spirit-warming note on this same tradition. After seeing Rabbi R. Phineas perform a miracle, another Rabbi remarks that since miracles surely demonstrate the power of the righteous during their lifetimes, *how great must be the power of the righteous after death!* – (Something to think about.)

Joseph knew all these rulings and traditions. So, we may now consider several options in Joseph's "offer" by examining possible motives:

- The people would not be justified in being angry with Joseph for being a traitor or a "lackey" to the Romans for trying to please Pilate; because it was the traditional practice to bury "similarly righteous" persons in a common tomb or grave.

- For the same reason, Pilate would not have been suspicious of Joseph's motives, because Pilate knew something of Jewish tradition and was actually fascinated with Judaism, albeit distantly.

On the other hand, however:

- If Joseph *knew* and *believed* Jesus was Messiah and would actually rise from The Tomb on the first day of the week, then Joseph's nice new family tomb up on the Mount of Olives would be used during only that single Jewish weekend and would not even be soiled by any putrefaction.

  "...neither wilt Thou suffer Thy Holy One to see corruption." (From Psalms 16:10)

- The fact that there was no corruption of Jesus' corpse is evidenced on the Shroud of Turin. And, this is besides the fact that they did not even have time to complete preparations of His body with the anointing, etc. (Mark 16:1)

- Joseph was certainly more aware than most concerning the righteousness of Jesus. Just suppose Joseph therefore made this a really sure-fire "win-win" transaction by speculating that perhaps he and/or even some of his kin might later be raised to life, if "by chance" they should just maybe happen to be laid in The Tomb to touch against the bones of Jesus. This provision might be made as a bit of insurance just in case, even though He was surely righteous, "maybe" Jesus was not actually Messiah after all. This could also provide "insurance" just in case "maybe" Jesus would not really rise from The Tomb after three days, as He had Promised.

- Joseph was known to be an honorable man and, notably as a member of the *Sanhedrin*, was most likely of *anyone* who could be trusted to refuse permission to those Jewish zealots who might try to steal away the body of Jesus, and then later to claim, "He IS risen!" It was well known among the people that Jesus had foretold of His Resurrection. Oh, yes! Then Joseph, with the help of the assigned

- guards at the sepulchre, could be trusted to make sure no Galilean "monkey—business" took place at his family tomb.
- Maybe Joseph wanted "to cover all bets," as we say. Maybe Joseph had closed an unmatchable "can't—lose" bargain. After all, how could he lose?! — And, how could Pilate lose?!...**DEAL!!!**
- However, the Word of God says we need not have any sarcastic, skeptical or suspicious negative speculations about Joseph's motives, because Scripture (Luke 23:50 – 51) says Joseph was in fact "good" and "just." Moreover, Joseph had the very best and the most "righteous" justification toward asking for the body of Jesus under the most sacred Law of the *Torah* in Deuteronomy 21:22 – 23. The Lord commands:

"And if a man have committed a sin worthy of death, and he be put to death, and thou hang him on a tree, His body shall not remain all night upon the tree, but thou shalt in any wise bury him that day; (For he that is hanged is accursed of God;) That thy land be not defiled, which the Lord thy God giveth thee for an inheritance."

We can now of course understand the Lord's Purpose in issuing this commandment to the Children of Israel. The Lord, in His foreknowledge, knew it would be necessary to have this Law in place in order that the death and burial of Jesus would be followed by His Resurrection on the third day after His death. This was a vital requirement, which had to be in concert with several others of the Lord's Promises and which could not be rescinded for any reason. Jesus *had* to be taken down from The Cross and be placed in The Tomb *before sundown that day* in order that the Law would be completed Perfectly. In this way, Friday would be counted as a *full* day, under the Law of *Megillah* 20a, and as the *first* day of His *three days* in The Tomb!

It is an established fact that crucifixion victims often struggled against that slow strangulation for several days before death finally brought mercy. They were then left on the cross for days afterward in a rotting display to terrorize the subdued citizenry of nations that the Romans had overcome. Had this "incident" occurred in any other Roman province, say Egypt or Gaul or Britain, those three corpses might have been left for several days as a "display" and a feeding for carrion.

The Romans however, including Pilate, had some amount of admiration and respect for the religious "laws" of the Judeans and therefore consented to their wishes on this festival of Passover. This Law applied to the two thieves as well, the Roman soldiers having hastened their strangulation by breaking their legs. The Law has further validity in this case because each of these *three* were hanged "on a tree;" i.e., a wooden cross. Some scholars[9] even conclude that all three men in fact were hanging on the same tree. This Law was maintained and completed then as both thieves (or "malefactors") soon expired and were taken down for burial before the Sabbath began as that Jewish day ended at sunset.

Thus, God had all of this planned down to the finest detail since "before He laid the foundations of the Earth." When the Lord issued this statute to Moses and the Children of

Israel in the *Sinai* (1500 B.C.E.), He had this elaborate Plan in mind — which was to reach fulfillment 1500 years later. This was certainly not by "coincidence" and was not a "fanatical accident." The Lord planned all this and He knew exactly how, when and where it would be completed. The Lord also arranged that this "good" and "just" man, Joseph of Arimathaea, would appear in this minor but important role in the drama as "a man who is clean."

One question so far unanswered is: WHY?? was THIS Joseph assigned to this role? Were there no other men of Jerusalem or Bethlehem or *Emmaus* or other nearby villages who also were "clean" ?

Of course there were other men, equally righteous and (as we have shown) maybe even more righteous than this Joseph. BUT — God chose THIS "Joseph" because he just "happened" to have:

- A hewn stone tomb; i.e. — "a clean place,"
- that no corpse had ever defiled, (again~ "a clean place.")
- near the summit of the Mount of Olives,
- which was just slightly more than a Sabbath Day's journey from the Holy of Holies, (i.e., "without the camp")
- and yet, it also was nearby the place of The Crucifixion in order to permit this obedient Jew to travel from *Olivet* summit over to Pilate's residence, to return to lay Jesus to His rest in The Tomb. Then, there would still be sufficient time remaining for Joseph to travel to some nearby place before the Sabbath began, and then to eat the Passover. Without tarrying along the way, he was able to accomplish all this in the space of maybe three hours; from about 3 p.m. until 6 p.m.; i.e., from the ninth hour until the twelfth hour. Jesus died at 3 p.m. The Sabbath began at 6 p.m.

Joseph had what it takes! — The right stuff! We must now understand that the Lord was *very* selective to have prepared – before the beginning of Time! – such a man as *this* Joseph. The Lord had all of this planned just as He said, — right down to the last "jot and tittle." We certainly may not! criticize His selection of The Cast!

We have shown agreement, therefore from Scripture, which confirms that Joseph was "good" and "just." And even IF all of Joseph's motives had not been noble, God cast him as the "clean" man in this drama, who was to "lay up" the ashes (Jesus) *"without the camp in a clean place."* He was obedient to the Lord and, by all accounts, obeyed all of these Laws. He had already been offered and accepted a "win-win" covenant from the Lord Jesus – *because Joseph believed!*

Jesus offers you and me that same "win-win" contract. — **IF YOU BELIEVE**, please sign here.

X_____ — YOU CAN'T LOSE! —

The "Casting" Director

Perceivably and logically, many Christians initially will wince at even the thought of casting the centurion in the role of Almighty God, or even as the High Priest. One of their first counter-strokes will be to quote some of the many references in Acts and Hebrews that refer to Jesus Christ as "our High Priest." For example, from Hebrews 6:20, "...*even Jesus, made an High Priest for ever after the order of Melchizedec.*"

Nevertheless, I propose that God appointed the centurion to that role – even though he was a Gentile – because he was to be the official of the highest rank in attendance at the occasion. This superiority of rank is a type of the High Priest at the burning of the Red Heifer; and, ultimately, it also is a type mirroring the Supreme Authority of Almighty God, Master of the Universe. And, as we reported earlier in Chapter 2, the High Priest (as God, The Father) officiated as the ranking member at the offering of the Heifer.

Yes, as a Roman officer, the centurion outranked everyone else in attendance at The Crucifixion. Pilate was absent, King Herod was absent and Caiaphas (the High Priest) was absent. All of them shunned public exposure at implementation of their shameful works against this gentle Rabbi from Nazareth in Galilee. They were rightfully fearful of the public wrath; for each of them knew Him to be innocent.

Within constraints of the most candid reasoning, Jesus could not simultaneously take the role of both the Heifer and the High Priest. Besides, in the eyes of the Father, Jesus truly "out—ranked" ALL present. To the world, nevertheless, He became the lowest ranking person at the scene. In His agony and jeered by the crowd, they even cursed and spat upon Him; although, they could not have known **WHO??** Jesus was, even as He forgave them. Punished as a "blasphemer," under the Law of *Sanhedrin* 42a, Jesus was executed publicly in the nude as a further humiliation. Even the other two victims, the thieves, ridiculed Jesus as they all three struggled, gasping for every breath in their torturous resistance against death. — How much lower could anybody's humiliation descend?

Just imagine for a moment and picture the intense emotional stress Jesus must have felt as He knew in advance that ALL of the Temple sacrifices represented the Ultimate Sacrifice that was His destiny. It is nearly impossible for us to contemplate His degree of humility, most especially as He realized that His own death on The Cross was to supply a Sacrifice to replace and supersede ALL other sacrifices. Knowing these things, and still Jesus never boasted about the meaning of these things. – That kind of Humility could only be acquired and retained by God!

In these comparisons, once again we see the veritable Infinity of our Savior's humility as He laid down His life for our sins. He did this in spite of the fact that He was completely without sin. Still, each of us is totally guilty (in the eyes of a Perfect God) for being guilty of even one sin. He did this also in spite of the fact that He is Master of the Universe and we are nothing, barely ranking above ants or even amoeba.

Humility in these proportions is simply incomprehensible to man. However, the Lord Himself did cast, write, produce, direct and even took a starring role in this drama. We cannot argue with God about why He chose that centurion to play His character; nor can we question why God chose to "star" in the humble role of a "victim."

Some Questions Concerning "A Clean Place"

A few discerning skeptics and critics have thoughtfully questioned why the Jews would have permitted The Crucifixion to be conducted at the *Miphkad* Altar. – Would not that sacred shrine be considered "a clean place?" However, we recall that the priest who slays the Red Heifer is "unclean" because he has touched something that represents sin. Remember? He is "unclean until evening." Someone else asks, "If anything representing sin is 'unclean,' are not the Red Heifer's ashes then 'unclean' as well?"

Risking gross understatement, we must recognize here that the Law is *very* complex in this situation. A fair explanation appears in *Yoma* 68b, stating that the ashes are clean even though the priest surely is defiled by a representation of sin. *Talmud* explains that, although the ashes may even contain lumps of charred (unconsumed) flesh, it is no longer an animal (bullock, heifer, goat, etc.) *after it is burned*. The ashes (including other residue) therefore are holy (i.e., "clean") because they have been sanctified by having resulted from a burnt offering. Nevertheless, the priest is not sanctified and therefore is "unclean."

Those ashes are sanctified as holy by The Holy One, blessed be He, just as Jesus became "unclean" by taking on all of our sins, even though He is holy. This is, again, that gorgeous picture in which one pure, innocent and unblemished life is given into "uncleanness" (i.e., death) in order that its holy remains can be used to wash away all "uncleanness" from all others, each of whom is totally "blemished" and "unclean." The ashes of an unblemished but dead ("unclean") Red Heifer therefore are used to purify the "unclean," just as a Perfect Jesus met death and became "unclean" when He took on our sins in order that He could purify us.

Nevertheless, the ashes of the Red Heifer had to remain "clean." This was accomplished simply by burning any new Red Heifer on the *Miphkad* Altar, along with the existing ashes, in a hewn stone vessel having a void of air space beneath. Then, "a clean man" took the ashes to "a clean place," etc. (More on this later.) The ashes of the Red Heifer were therefore "clean."

Now, here is where the Law gets really "tricky." The slope immediately in front of the priest where the Heifer and the sin offerings were burned was called the place "where the ashes are poured out," and it was "a clean place" and which was "without the camp." (Leviticus 4:12) It was also called the *Miphkad* Altar; albeit, only when the Red Heifer was burned at that spot. *Talmud* is clear (*Yoma* 68b and *Zebahim* 106a) that *all* of the ashes from *all* of the Temple sacrifices were also "poured out" at that point. (See Illus. 23: Mt. Olivet viewed from Temple on Crucifixion Day, Page ,156 and Illus. 24: Detail of "pit or cavity" in face of Mt. of Olives, Page 157)

The Red Heifer was not technically a "sacrifice," and of course its ashes were not "poured out." Moreover, it is important to note that only the *Miphkad* Altar and the ground where the ashes were poured was "clean." *Talmud* rules in this manner because only the "dead" animal material at that point was clearly "sanctified" because it had been consumed by fire and therefore would no longer "defile." Nevertheless, the priest who burned the offerings at that spot was rendered unclean because he and his garments were exposed to the carcass *before* the burning.

Yoma 68b emphatically describes that position as a steep slope, where the ashes, skulls, bone fragments, etc., as they were "poured out," would cascade down the western face of *Olivet*, facing the Temple. In fact, this debris was not comprised solely of the ash remains from the burnings at *Olivet* summit. By far, the greater proportion of this pile was contributed from the ashes and remains from the Altar of Sacrifice at the front of the Temple. The ashes from that Altar were carried *daily* and poured out at this same place, which was "without the camp" and was the place *"where the ashes are poured out."* (Leviticus 6:10 – 11)

The skulls of many animals would not have been completely consumed by the fire, simply because of the significantly greater mass of the skull. Therefore, surviving bone fragments and the skull of the Heifer were pulverized using stone hammers, then sifted through stone sieves. Here we recall that stone that has not been cut with iron tools is "clean." The pulverized remains were then divided into three parts: one portion to the priests, one part deposited on the Temple walls and the third scattered on the Mount of Olives. (Parah 3:11)

However, the skulls, remnants, chunks, etc. from the Altar ashes of the Temple sacrifices were left included with the total ash content and were not processed in any way. These everyday burnings then would have left the skulls virtually intact. The ash residue pouring down that slope, was accumulated from *all* of the burnt offerings during one thousand years of Temple sacrifices. As we remarked earlier, there would have been *thousands* upon *thousands* of *skulls*! – clearly indicating why this spot could have been called *"Place of the Skull"* — i.e., *Golgotha* or *Calvary*. (See Illus. 23: Mt. Olivet viewed from Temple on Crucifixion Day, Page 156, and Illus. 24: Detail of "pit or cavity" in face of Mt. of Olives, Page 157)

Certain critics of this work have countered any claim that Jewish Law would have tolerated Jesus and the thieves having been put to death at the *Miphkad* Altar because it was a "clean place." And, they are surely correct in that judgment. However, the place where the High Priest (or the centurion) stood was back several meters from the *Miphkad* Altar and the slope and was not "a clean place" because this is where the Priest stood to kill the heifer and to sprinkle the Red Heifer's blood. Under the Law, the Heifer was still intact at this point and had not yet been consumed as a "burnt offering" – even though it certainly was dead.

It is certain, however, that the centurion and The Cross would have stood at the same spot location where the priest stood as he sprinkled the blood toward the Temple. We have shown, in Illus. 24: Detail of "pit or cavity" in face of Mt. of Olives, Page 157, that it was a few meters back from the slope "drop-off," which plunges downward and westward toward the Temple. We have shown earlier that this was, in fact, the *only* location from which the centurion could have seen the Veil, just as the Priest must "direct his gaze carefully" in order to see it.

Concluding then, the *Miphkad* Altar certainly was a "clean place," because it was the spot where the sanctified ashes were "poured out" according to Leviticus 4:12. However, the blood spattered ground behind that point; i.e., where the High Priest "sprinkled," had to have been the spot where The Cross stood. That was not "a clean place" and therefore could have been a place for Roman execution as well as being acceptable to the Law.

Merely having been carved out of stone and having held no previous corpse did not, in and of itself, qualify The Tomb of Joseph of Arimathaea as "a clean place." However, as we have proposed, since Jesus' body (as the ashes) was laid in a clean place as fulfillment of Scripture (Numbers 19:9), then His Tomb most certainly had to have been "a clean place" as well.

So, now we must further determine how that Tomb could have qualified under the Law. As we noted earlier, the Rabbis ruled that as long as a dead air space existed between a person and the soil beneath, that person was "insulated" against touching any grave (even an unbeknownst prehistoric grave) that might exist under his path. (*Parah* 3:2 and 3:6) Further, we cited the Israelites who returned "unclean" from Babylon and even had to raise "clean babes" by creating on—site prenatal care, delivery facilities, a nursery, living quarters and a day-school atop a stone chamber.

Talmudic Law is thorough on this point by actually specifying the exact minimum air space required in order to provide this insulation from uncleanness. *Sukkah* 21a instructs that the air space above that which is unclean must be a minimum of one handbreadth, which is one sixth of a cubit, about 4 inches or 10 centimeters. It is appropriate that we should point out that the Garden Tomb would not qualify as "a clean place." Since it contains only a single space for a corpse, located at the floor of the tomb; hence, it has no "insulating" air space beneath. It therefore would not qualify under the Law.

We see that a hewn stone chamber therefore must also have a void of air space beneath in order to "insulate" from any grave that might be in the soil below the rock. Scholars[13, 14, 23] describe the Jewish practice of carving multiple "niches" or "benches" or "berths" in the limestone walls of the sepulchre, thereby providing space for several burial niches in a single tomb. These same references point out that "The Tomb of the Prophets" and other nearby tombs from the Second Temple era located atop *Olivet* had been constructed in this manner.

It is noted that such tombs were very much preferred by families of means, especially during the Second Temple period, so that even in death, all the family could be together to await Messiah and The Resurrection of the dead! And, as we have said, the most popular spot for this vigil by faithful Jewish families was (and still is!!!) on the Mount of Olives, and preferably near the summit! It surely follows that the tomb reserved for a family of the Temple aristocracy, such as Joseph of Arimathaea, would have been just such a tomb.

Now, we can see that since the body of Jesus was the first to have lain in His Tomb, and if He were placed upon one of the upper "berths" (or niches), there indeed would have been a void of air space beneath Him as provided by the empty berth below! – Hence, it was a "clean place" in every respect within the Law.

Some will ask, "Well, why would Joseph even care whether Jesus were laid in a 'clean place?' Would Joseph go to the trouble to put Jesus in an 'upper berth,' as you say, just so Joseph's tomb would qualify in providing Jesus with a 'clean place' – just so He could fulfill this Law?" — I am confident that Joseph never had such a thought. He just took Jesus to The Tomb and placed His Body on one of the niches *at a convenient height*, where preparation of His Body could be completed after the Sabbath.

Just as I do myself, those who suffer chronic lower back pain will know the most comfortable and convenient height would be at about waist level above the floor of the crypt. According to archaeological evidences[13,14,23], there would most likely have been at least one niche and maybe even two niches below waist level. This would have provided ample dead air space beneath Jesus' corpse in order to have achieved compliance within the Law concerning a "clean place."

It is probable that Jesus' interment in Joseph's tomb was intended to be only temporary, and a generous act of compassion as the Sabbath approached. Later, Jesus' family would have had the body properly prepared and buried at their own choosing. Joseph just took Jesus to The Tomb and placed Him on one of the niches where they could conveniently finish preparation of His body after the Sabbath. — God was in control. Joseph was surely obedient to God's Will and Purpose; although, he probably did these things unawares.

We certainly cannot prove that Jesus rested in a tomb having such berths or that His was one of the "upper berths." Up to this point in our discussion, we have made a convincing case claiming that Jesus fulfilled the Law very thoroughly in this rite. We can therefore claim without hesitation that, if Jesus was fulfilling the Law of the Red Heifer, He would most certainly have been placed in that hewn stone chamber so as to have a void of air space underneath. This is not Gospel, but it is the Law! Joseph did not plan it that way. — God planned it.

All this Jewish preoccupation with "cleanness" brings us to the first of two very important reasons for considering against "Gordon's Calvary," located nearby the Garden Tomb, as the place of The Crucifixion and Jesus' burial. (See Illus. 26: Temple Mt., Contoured Mt. of Olives, Page 324) This first consideration is pointed out by that beloved Israeli scholar, the late Yigael Yadin. In his studies of the Second Temple period, Prof. Yadin[6] noted that the latrines for the local Essenes were located northwest and just outside the City Wall at the time of Jesus. That means that Gordon's calvary and the garden Tomb are in that vicinity! – With this fact we can note that serious, observant Jews would have *never!* buried their loved ones adjacent to the latrines. This would especially be true for a wealthy and religious man such as Joseph of Arimathaea, who was also a member of the *Sanhedrin*.

Secondly, responsible, knowledgeable and respected archaeologists have determined that tombs in the vicinity of the Garden Tomb (and including the Garden Tomb) date from the eighth century B.C.E. That period would have been during the time that "Jerusalem" was actually the City of David, and which was located southeast and outside the walls of Jerusalem as they stood during the time of Jesus. We must also observe that the eighth century B.C.E. was about two-hundred years before Zechariah gave his prophecy that Messiah would arrive at *Olivet* summit. After Zechariah revealed this, and even continuing today, worshipful Jews as well as many so-called "traditional" Jews have longed to be laid to their rest in that ground to await their Redeemer. As we have said, it is most likely that Joseph of Arimathaea would have followed that same tradition.

Nevertheless, some would argue to counter this claim by referring to recent recovery of the bones of Caiaphas[21], the High Priest. The grave of Caiaphas was found southeast of Jerusalem and not on the Mount of Olives. This "untraditional" burial of Caiaphas may be explained by the likelihood that Caiaphas, just as were most of the High Priests of that period, was of the *Sadducean* sect. It is well known that *Sadducees* did not believe in the Resurrection and Caiaphas therefore would *not* have looked forward to that Blessed Jewish Hope! It is perhaps noteworthy to observe that Judaism even today is split on the "question" of a life after death. If one reads the Word of God from the prophet (Daniel 12:2), it is difficult to see why any could doubt there is life after death.

While we are on this subject of The Tomb and The Resurrection, we present some thoughts for skeptics to ponder. We can demonstrate, through the most elementary logic, that the fact of Jesus' Resurrection actually is documented by what the Bible and historians do **NOT** say. Please just consider for a moment some situations surrounding the fact that Jesus' Body had "disappeared" from The Tomb.

- The Temple priests bribed the Roman guards at The Tomb, paying them to say that His body had been stolen away by Jesus' followers. (Matthew 28:12 – 15)

- Routinely, the Jewish religious hierarchy vigorously dispatched zealots all over Judea and even into Syria to seek out and punish Jewish people who had become Christians or joined any other rebellious Jewish sect. Before his conversion, the Apostle Paul is known to have been one of these "bounty hunters." (Acts 8:1 – 3 and 9:1 – 2) Israel has always maintained a marvelous intelligence network; and this is Biblically confirmed as one of the chief reasons why Israel often is able to overcome enemies who vastly outnumber her armies. Certainly this hallmark prevails equally today as well.

- Uncharacteristically then, in the face of such determination to discredit a "false" Messiah, and who appeared to threaten the very existence of Judaism, Jewish authorities strangely did **NOT** organize any exhaustive search for Jesus' corpse. They could have tortured the Disciples in order to locate His corpse and thereby eradicate all claims of this group. They could have skinned them alive. They could have stoned them or burned them. But,...**NO!** ...They did not!

- So, **WHY??** then, did the priests **NOT** undertake a search for Jesus' body???! – **WHY??** did they **NOT** torture the Disciples and other followers to reveal His concealed corpse???...**WHY??**

- The answer is so simple and so obvious and so powerful, that actually it *proves* unquestionably the FACT of The Resurrection by means of the most ordinary logic.

- The Temple priests did not order a search for Jesus' body simply because they and everyone else in Judea already knew that He had appeared to hundreds of persons in His Risen Body! (Luke 24:31 – 48 and I Corinthians 15:4 – 8)
- There was then no need to search for the corpse of a living, walking, talking PERSON, whom literally hundreds of people already had seen out of The Tomb and at many places throughout Judea and even Galilee!
- When we stop to think about this, the searchers really would have appeared quite ridiculous if they had scoured every village and the countryside to search for the corpse of a person who was at that same time being seen by hundreds of people all around Jerusalem and even in Galilee!
- Then, of course, He ascended into Heaven after forty days. So there really wasn't much point in searching after that time either!

Were You There?

In order to feel some of the drama and pathos of that Glorious hour, picture now if you will, the scene that a Judean would behold upon facing eastward from the Temple at the "ninth hour of the day" – 3 P.M. at *Olivet* summit. You can see three crosses erected by the Romans for crucifying a "blasphemer" and two thieves near the same point where the ashes of the burnt offerings are poured out. Plunging downward and outward on *Olivet*'s western slope, like unto a tower of tears, one can see a lengthy trail of ashes, bones and skulls having been accumulated from all the burnt offerings during one thousand years of Judaism's Temple worship and Altar sacrifices. (See Illus. 23: Mt. Olivet viewed from Temple on Crucifixion Day, Page 156, and Illus. 24: Detail of "pit or cavity" in face of Mt. of Olives, Page 157.)

It was as if the Lord were actually punctuating all of Judaism's sacrificial worship by presenting a finale pointing to the ultimate meaning of all of those offerings. However, for reasons known only to God, Jewish people appear actually to have been blinded from seeing that which now should be so clear to us.

Reflecting on all the other "pictures" and "Law," we have seen in this most Holy ritual, does anybody still doubt that Jesus was fulfilling the Red Heifer ceremony *"as a purification for sin?"* Just a little imagination could tell us some more things which may have happened and which would reflect an even more detailed fulfillment of the Law — every "jot and tittle." Please consider these now.

In order to ease driving the ¼ inch spikes and to avoid splitting the wood, holes likely were pre-drilled into the timber of The Cross. Then, perhaps the spikes were driven with two strokes of the mallet for each hand and with three strokes to a single spike through both feet. *That is a total of seven times.* Swinging a mallet or hammer requires hand/wrist action very similar to movement of the priest as he "sprinkles" the Red Heifer's blood with his finger seven times.

Precise description of this hand/wrist motion is detailed for sprinkling, again *seven times*, the blood of the he-goat or the bullock at the daily sin offering in *Yoma* 15a. In fact, the gesture specified for these sprinklings is to be *ke-mazlif*, "like the swinging of a whip"; i.e., "a lasher." This dramatic detail from *Talmudic* Law also may be a reflection of the vicious scourging which Jesus suffered from the whip-like *flagellum* in the hands of a "lasher" before He went to The Cross. However, at that occasion there were many times more than seven lashings. Further, we may see another reflection of the Law in the hyssop reed that was used to give Jesus the "spunge." (John 19:29) And, as we have said, He probably was nailed to a *cedar* Cross.

The soldier, then, probably swung the mallet "seven times" as the blood was being spattered *"directly toward the Tabernacle."* All this *may* have taken place then, in accordance with the ordinances of *Talmudic* Law and *exactly* as Zechariah had foretold: *At the summit of the Mount of Olives* — while the spikes were driven — as He lay bound with "meqeg *rope of bast"*— on the ground among the *hyssop* weeds — nailed to a *cedar* Cross — *with His head to the south* – and as He turned *His face toward the Holy of Holies* — just before The Cross was *"lifted up"* at the *"third hour"* and His *crimson* blood was *"poured out"* upon the ground flowing down *"where the ashes are poured out"* – *"as a purification for ALL sin!"*...AMEN!!!

We have indicated all of these features throughout our discussion of the Red Heifer ceremony. Even though at this time we must rely on mere speculation as to details of what occurred at The Cross, it is of course obvious that all of these details relating to The Crucifixion are reflections of the Red Heifer ceremony.

So, now we know why Jesus was crucified at the third hour. It certainly was not just because that may have been a convenient time for the Roman garrison detail and it was not just at some indiscriminate location *behind* the Temple! The Crucifixion was planned *at that time* and *at that place*, as arranged by Jesus in order that He could accomplish His mission to completely and Perfectly fulfill the Law pertaining to the Red Heifer as well as the Passover Lamb, the Atonement Goat, the Sin Offerings and ALL of the Altar offerings. — We can say with confidence: *"It was no accident!"*

We have shown further that it was "no accident" when God selected Joseph of Arimathaea in this drama as a man who was "clean." We also have observed how thoroughly the Law of the Red Heifer was fulfilled, right down to the gathering and storing of the "ashes" (Jesus) in this heretofore unnoticed drama. Critical accusations such as "mere coincidence" or "tabloid garbage" or "Christian nonsense," etc. must surely suffer a quick and final demise after we regard all of these fulfilling events and circumstances that we have presented.

At this point we should recognize and discuss the traditional claim of many respected scholars who believe that the Dome of the Rock is the site of the Jewish Temple. This has been a popular belief for centuries and continues for many even today. However, through the Law of the Red Heifer and by examining the *Zion* and *Olivet* topography, it can be proved once-and-for-all that the Temple could *never* have stood at that site. The key to this solution exists in the line-of-sight extending from east to west relative to the terrain contours between the Mount of Olives and the Temple Mount

Some critics will immediately and desperately jump to a speculation that the contours of the Kidron Valley/*Olivet*, etc. may have changed over the span of nineteen centuries. Geological evidence[24], however, suggests that even after many earthquakes, only very slight change in topography and contours has taken place over this time.

The most convincing reason for eliminating the Dome of the Rock exists in the fact that the High Priest would not be able to see the Veil as he sprinkled the Heifer's blood toward the Temple. This is because, standing at a distance of two thousand cubits "outside-the-camp," the Priest would be standing too far eastward and over the brow of the hill, so-to-speak, actually *behind* the Mount of Olives. There are several more reasons applying to this same truth, involving recent archaeological discoveries, location of the Jewish Cemetery, Zechariah's prophecy and other factors. Nevertheless, these are too detailed for discussion here. However, we should note that the correct length of the cubit measurement is extremely critical to any research of this problem.

Continuing, we have seen Jesus (as the ashes) laid in a "clean place," which was a tomb of "hewn stone," and which had never before contained a corpse. If it had been used previously, this of course would have rendered The Tomb unfit because it would have been "unclean" under the Law. According to reliable ancient historians[11] as well as modern Church historians[9], location of The Tomb agrees with that confirmed by our evidence and by Scriptural evidence and indeed would have been "without the camp." We have shown logical and reasonable likelihood that Jesus' burial tomb was also near *Olivet* summit, about a Sabbath Day's journey from the Temple – and was again, "outside-the-camp."

Reference sources[13,14,23] also agree that Palestinian tombs of the first century often were hewn from limestone, with multiple niches or "berths" carved into the walls. This feature is included in The Tomb of the Prophets and other tombs that can be visited today and are located at the summit of the Mount of Olives. (Illus. 20: Jerusalem as it Appeared in 70 C.E., Page 153)

Another indirect verification toward locating *"the place where the ashes are poured out"* is seen in the current and obvious proliferation of dense vegetation extending down *Olivet*'s western slope (See Illus. 3: Old City of Jerusalem and Mt. of Olives, Page 19 and Illus. 10: Church of Mary Magdalene (Russian Church), Page 59). The large volume of ashes and remains from many centuries of sacrifices would have contributed a rich nutrient content to that soil. Aerial photos reveal a well-defined strip of trees, brush, etc. extending downward from the Church of The Ascension, straight across to the Temple Mount, and centered toward the Dome of the Tablets. The remainder of *Olivet* is comparatively void of vegetation. It is further significant to note that this strip of vegetation does not extend toward the Dome of the Rock. Instead, it is about 100 meters north of that axis. – Yes, toward the Dome of the Tablets.

Some geologists[24] propose that this growth pattern is stimulated by centuries of earthquakes and landslides along that seismic fault which extends through where *Olivet* "*shall cleave in the midst thereof.*" (Zechariah 14:4) They go on to say that all this seismic activity has loosened the soil and strata sufficiently to encourage excellent moisture content even in Jerusalem's rather arid climate. This condition then promotes growth and may be at least partly responsible for the increased vegetation[32].

Nevertheless, we must not overlook the effects of pouring ash remains, charred flesh remains, etc. down that hill over a period of more than a thousand years (950 B.C.E. — C.E. 70). First, there was sparse growth while ashes were dumped daily over that slope. Presently however, that particular strip of vegetation extending down the western slope of *Olivet* effectively has multiple layers of fertilizing nutrients from ash remains having been applied during a millennium!...Think about it!"

We could never have seen this beautiful drama and these fulfillments of the Law without comparing the Law of the *Talmud* with the Gospel of Jesus Christ. It is no wonder that "super-intellectual" King Solomon could not explain the Red Heifer blood, ashes and cleansing. How could he?! — Solomon knew every tiny scrap of the Law, but Solomon did not see Jesus fulfill the Law as we are privileged to see at this time. The beauty of this ancient and forgotten ritual that has been concealed for all these centuries perhaps has been reserved and preserved for us as a sort of love letter from the Lord Jesus. It may be that He is revealing this to us at this time because of the nearness of His Coming.

These comparisons of Law and Gospel could not have been mere coincidence. The Lord went to a lot of effort to plan, design, organize, provide and execute this drama *just for us!* – *Believers!* – This is notwithstanding the fact that, while He was doing all this, Jesus also suffered horrible humiliation, pain and death as punishment for **OUR** crimes. – Crimes that He did not commit. We must be certain therefore that we ignore this Holy ceremony no longer.

The Lord mandated Jesus to pay for the sins of man by fulfilling (or "completing") all of the Law. Premium among Jewish Temple worship were the *most* Holy sacrifices: the Sin Offerings, the Atonement Goats, the Passover Lambs and, chiefly, the Red Heifers. In order to Completely and Perfectly fulfill the Law, the Passover Lamb is required to be selected as an unblemished yearling male from the flock *on a specific calendar day of a specific calendar month;* i.e., the 10th day of the first Jewish month, *Nisan*. Furthermore, he is to be slain *on a specific day* and at *a specific time of the day;* i.e., the 14th day of *Nisan* between the sixth and the ninth hour of the day. All of the remaining most Holy sacrifices require that the entire carcasses of these animals shall be burned to ashes *at a specific location* relative to the Temple; i.e., *"where the ashes are poured out"* at *Olivet* summit.

So, now do you see?! — Jesus paid for our sins so that we can appear sinless and therefore "clean" before the Father. God prescribed the Law in order that, regardless of their sins, men could become Holy by obeying His Law, but only by repenting and offering sacrifices when they fell short. And yet, no man could be completely obedient to keep the Law and thereby "earn" Salvation via his own works. God therefore answered this dilemma exactly as He had Promised to Abraham in Genesis 22:8. God provided Himself — the Lamb for the Sacrifice — in the form of His only Son. Jesus fulfilled the Law for us as **THE** Ultimate Gift from Himself as well as from The Father.

We have just seen that He did not limit the Gift by providing Himself merely for a single Jewish sacrifice. At The Cross, Jesus played out His role as the sacrifice for completing and superseding ALL of the sacrifices prescribed in the Law. ALL of the lambs, goats, heifers, bullocks, rams, doves—and yes, even the grain offerings, the First Fruits. And, don't forget the broken second *matzah* wafer, the *Afikoman*. — Everything! in the Law points to Jesus.

However, since The Crucifixion, no man needs to "do" anything anymore in order to be acceptable to God. Actually, men could never have accomplished this via their own "works," because men are not even *nearly* Perfect – and everything that is acceptable to God *must* be Perfect.

Forty years after The Crucifixion the Temple was destroyed. It was then no longer possible for the Jewish people to have continued their sacrifices at that time; although, we do realize that Judaism will in the Last Days resume the sacrifices during The Tribulation. (Daniel 9:27) — It was as if God had said to the Jewish people and to the World at that time:

> *"You no longer need the sacrifices. They didn't cleanse you anyway.*
>
> *They were only substitute offerings that pointed to The Lamb. He has made all the sacrifices that any of you will ever need."*

- Nobody needs to kill the Passover Lamb any more. – Messiah died in his place.
- Nobody needs to offer the Sin Bullock. – Messiah paid for the sins of ALL of us.
- Nobody needs to kill the Atonement Goat. – Messiah atoned for ALL of our sins.
- Nobody needs to offer any of the lambs, goats, bullocks, rams, doves or anything else. – Messiah was offered instead. – He died in *your* place. – He has paid it ALL.
- Nobody needs to burn a Red Heifer again. – Messiah was "burned" to make ALL of you as clean in My sight — For ever."

Therefore, for almost two thousand years, it has not been necessary to continue the sacrifices. Seven years before Messiah arrives, the sacrifices will be resumed as God tests the Jewish people during the Tribulation. However until that Day, the sacrifices are just not required. — Jesus of Nazareth paid and completed ALL of the sacrifices and the Temple Law — Completely and Perfectly.

We have shown, therefore, that Jesus did fulfill all of those sacrifices as Messiah, Son of David – Completely and Perfectly by being slain at the ninth hour on the 14th day of *Nisan* and as specified at the summit of the Mount of Olives. This was done in obedience and dedication to an ordered, detailed, complex Plan commanded by His Father. There was no other choice. There was no other time and no other place and no other way at which He could satisfy ALL of these Laws as commanded by His Father.

What a Savior!!! — Isn't God Great?!! — General Douglas MacArthur — even C. B. De Mille — Steven Spielberg — nobody! – could ever have written and staged a drama to equal this. And we have been missing it for 1900 years! Lazily and complacently, we have been following tradition instead of searching and "testing" the TRUTH.

From Whence Cometh These Errors?

Curiosity should cause us to ask WHY?, during all these centuries, we Christians have been so far off-the-mark in our location of the place of The Crucifixion. From what we have seen, the evidence points unflinchingly to *Olivet* summit for that most Holy scene.

History tells us that the traditional locale at the Church of the Holy Sepulchre was first identified to Helena, mother of Emperor Constantine. Local Jewish "tourist guides" escorted her to visit that site during her first pilgrimage to the Holy Land. Later, the story goes, Constantine claimed to have had visions which "authenticated" that spot as well as several other locations as Christian "Holy Places." (See *Secrets of Golgotha*[9] – Ernest L. Martin, pgs. 126-127)

For whatever reasons, Christian theologians and archaeologists at that time overlooked Chapter 27 of Matthew or they could never have been so thoroughly hoodwinked. And besides, who was going to argue with Emperor Constantine?! – Or his mother?! – Even the stalwart Bishop Eusebius was eventually forced to knuckle under to this concept from his Emperor's "Divine Revelation." And so, the die was cast and set. For all these centuries, we have been following this phony tradition.

It is with bitter irony that we Christians must confront the tragic barbarism and slaughter of Jews, Muslims and Christians extending from the early 11th century until almost the 14th century during the Crusades[50]. Destruction of the Church of the Holy Sepulchre at the dawn of the 11th century ignited Christian wrath and began a series of futile and desperate expeditions to recover Jerusalem and what we now realize was a falsely proclaimed "Holy Place."

Many centuries afterward, of course the Church of the Holy Sepulchre eventually was recovered and restored as a treasured Roman Catholic Holy site. Following the Balfour Declaration (November, 1917), Jews, Muslims and Christians have dwelt in Jerusalem in relative harmony. There have been a few eruptions of religious fervor to produce threats and even occasional violence. Even the 1967 Six Day War relinquished continued Islamic autonomy on the Jerusalem Temple Mount by the ruling *Waqf* authorities.

Mistaken identity of the place of The Crucifixion persists, nevertheless. More recently, during the 19th century, a purportedly more "modern" and more "accurate" location, competing with Catholicism's more traditional and more popular site, was proclaimed by Britain's hero of Khartoum, General Charles Gordon. This locale serves as more of a Protestant sanctioned site; since Catholicism, then as now, has dominated and claimed the Church of the Holy Sepulchre as the "official" location of Calvary (or *Golgotha*) as well as the place of Christ's Tomb.

This distinguished military leader, General Gordon, viewed an outcropping northwest of the Old City and saw pockets and depressions in the soft limestone face of the cliff strangely shaped to the appearance of a "skull." Gordon enthusiastically and "blindly" concluded: "This must be the place!" – Now, Gen. Gordon was not an archaeologist, nor did he profess having such knowledge. But, he was a national heroic figure — and, then as now, it was considered in very "poor taste" (as well as very bad for one's "health") to contradict war heroes (especially generals or emperors!) about religion or warfare or anything else!

It is not at all likely that Gen. Gordon was aware that the area he had chosen was in proximity with the site of the Essene's latrines during the first century! Sadly also, the general was not familiar with the centurion's line-of-sight to The Veil, as related by Matthew. There is no record that would indicate that Gordon had been misled by any knavish "tourist guides." He apparently misled himself by looking so eagerly for what he *wanted* to see, rather than looking for the Truth.

A few decades later and perhaps inspired by similar romantic but blind enthusiasm, some Christians found an empty tomb nearby "Gordon's Calvary," which today is popularly and reverently referred to by many eager and enthusiastic Christian pilgrims as "The Garden Tomb." Romantic tourist enthusiasm toward this site sadly has been promoted and stimulated by Christian clergy who escort Holy Land group tours. Thus, "starry eyed" Christians have been misled about the authenticity of these places, but have held on to these traditional locales with a romantic fervor that will surely not bend easily to the Truth. Tradition is powerfully addictive. Nevertheless, we still need to determine WHY the Jewish survivors at Jerusalem would have sought deliberately to deceive Christian pilgrims, especially the mighty Roman Emperor Constantine! — That required great *chutzpah*!

When we remember that the Jewish people of the third and fourth centuries were eagerly and faithfully waiting for their Temple to be restored, the rationale for their boldness becomes obvious. When and if the Temple were restored and the burnt offerings, Red Heifer burnings, etc. were resumed, *the Jewish authorities would not have wanted Christians or anyone else up there erecting shrines, conducting tours, selling T-shirts!, gawking around, tramping over graves in the vicinity of their Miphkad Altar at Olivet summit.* – So, local Jewish "tourist guides" took these naive, wide-eyed Christians by-the-nose and led them in exactly the *opposite* direction from the True position — to the west side of The City, instead of eastward to *Olivet*.

It well may be that all this is the reason for the Lord having permitted delay in publication of this book for several years. If Christians suddenly awaken to the fact that The Cross was at *Olivet*, and if a restored Temple worship were to resume the burnt offerings at *Olivet*, just imagine what might be the reaction within Judaism and Islam. To say the least, this would be an "explosive" situation!

This discussion should in part explain why we, and our scholars, have been so inaccurate for so long a time concerning the place of The Crucifixion. After all, the Lord has "permitted" our ignorance to prevail in order to accomplish His Holy Purpose. Nevertheless, from what we have presented, the evidence is overwhelming to indicate *Olivet* summit as The Crucifixion site. We mortals need not squirm and be fearful of releasing the Truth in this matter. The Lord's Will shall advance this predicament to whatever destiny suits His Purpose.

An equally thrilling and equally dramatic story in Chapter 9, reveals precisely why Jesus died "*at the ninth hour*" and just how the centurion was able to see the Veil at that hour. We can tell you that story also was no accident.

Despite all the details, "pictures," man-made "laws," speculation, whatever, both the Old Testament and the New Testament present us the same "bottom-line:" We can cleanse others with the blood and living water of our burnt offering, Jesus Christ. But, we must also repent and believe and accept our own "washing." Although we most surely do have our Salvation through His Grace, we still are living in a sinful world and are not ourselves without sin at this time. So then, we still are "unclean until even" – the same as the "man who was clean" and who gathered the ashes. Then, in the "evening" of the age, when the Lord Jesus comes to claim His Kingdom, as we accompany Him with our newly glorified, resurrected and purified bodies, we shall all be without sin and, yes —"clean." Then, at "evening," (the evening of the Age) we will all be permitted to "return to the Camp" — Heaven, that is!

Hallelujah!!!

16

Ashes? Who Needs Them?

Altar Incense & Anointing Oil Found –Jewish & Christian Indifference – Heifer in Jewish Worship – Compare Old vs. New Testament – Why Jewish Graves on Mt. of Olives? – Jewish Abortion Ruling – Surprising Jewish Eschatology – Biblical "Types" of Jesus – Need MANY Ashes!

As **you might** expect, after their prolonged exile and a nearly two thousand year void in their Temple worship, many Jewish teachers have "fallen away" from any notion of importance toward the ashes of the Red Heifer. Some sympathy for Jewish lack of understanding of this importance can be extended, because earlier we noted that even the wisdom of King Solomon could not decipher this riddle.

Nevertheless, we have presented convincing evidence showing why Christians should recognize that importance. A few news releases in recent years tend to demonstrate Orthodox Jewry's renewed interest in the Red Heifer, especially since a cask of the Priests' anointing oil (*Shemen Afarshimon*) was discovered in 1988 and a 600 kilogram (1323 lbs.) cache of genuine Altar Incense (*Qetoret*) was unearthed in 1994 by archaeologist/minister, Rev. Vendyl Jones at The Cave of the Column in *Qumran* during his quest for the Heifer ashes.

Rev. Jones has pointed out that the date of discovery for each of these articles, in addition to his finding the ancient ruins of *Gilgal*, have all three occurred on the 10th day of the first month, *Nisan*. In the Law (Exodus 12:3 - 8), that was the day for selecting an unblemished male of the first year *"from the flock"* – later to be slain and prepared for the Passover Feast. The 10th of *Nisan* was also the day of Israelites' entry into the Promised Land (Joshua 4:19) and for Jesus' Triumphal Entry into Jerusalem. (See Chapter 20 – Really *"3 Days and 3 Nights?"*)

The dates for these discoveries are much more than just coincidental. We have shown that the 10th of *Nisan* is very significant in the Passover and of course in The Crucifixion as well. An Israeli Rabbi, Menachem Burstin[33], has observed: "It is certainly significant that the very first items found (by Rev. Jones) were the Holy Anointing Oil and the Altar Incense. This is consequently important because in the *Torah* those items were the very first things that *HaShem* commanded Moses to make."

The more typical and traditional view within Judaism, however, has been more inclined just to ignore the entire matter. Sadly, this is true about the majority of Christianity as well. Two popular Jewish encyclopedias[8, 48] present the popular, traditional view of the Rabbis, saying that no plausible reason can be found for conducting the Red Heifer Ceremony in modern times. It is as if they say, "Well, you know – that was OK for Moses and the People in the *Sinai*, but now..."

Some go on to say that all discussion of the Red Heifer should be abandoned. We have even heard one knowledgeable, beloved and well-known Hebrew Christian televangelist register contemptuous remarks toward any who would profess interest in the Red Heifer. We must pray for his awakening. He just doesn't know any better.

Midrash Rabbah Numbers 19:5 adds that Satan has accused the Jewish people by asking questions about the Red Heifer and other Commandments on the Law. The discussion in *Midrash Yelamrnedenu-Hukkath*[7] closes by declaring that meanings of those commandments will be learned only in the next world. We hope here to have shown that we need not wait that long, IF we will only compare the Gospel of Jesus Christ with the Law.

Lest we begin condemnation against all Rabbis, for a tragic lack of spirituality in those few, we must note that some do take a more reverent position. These believe that the Law pertaining to the Red Heifer is to be regarded as a *chukkah* (pronounced: khuk` ah). Where a *chukkah* is defined in *Talmud* as a classic example of a commandment that has no rational explanation for its existence; and yet, it *must* be obeyed because it is a Divine Statute, as we have pointed out. These observant Rabbis instruct that this Law is one of those that Satan and Gentiles will use in order to ridicule the Jewish people, accusing them of hypocrisy and thereby demonstrating dilution of their religious loyalty.

Another indication that observant Jews do not deserve harsh criticism on this subject is derived from the study of their scheduled Sabbath readings from the *Torah*. Every year, on the Sabbath following the feast of *Purim*, *Megillah* 29b-30a explains that the Red Heifer portion shall be read from Numbers 19. The Rabbis have rationalized this as necessary in order to direct attention of the people to the need for "ritual cleanness" in preparation toward offering the Paschal Lamb. We see from these thoughts that responsible, worshipful Jewish people certainly have not ignored the Red Heifer.

Jewish awareness of the pictures of Jesus Christ in this Holy ritual is observed in more than a few Jewish commentaries. Christians will observe with genuine surprise that at least one Jewish source[26] notes that Christians consider that the blood of Jesus can be compared to the blood of the Red Cow because it removes "spiritual defilement;" i.e., "dead works."

With contrasting irony, at least one conservative Evangelical commentary states that the Red Heifer has no bearing toward the Sacrifice of Jesus Christ. The ceremony is described as "just an obsolete Jewish ritual." A typical demonstration of this kind of "blindness" is shown in Christian commentaries concerning what some Western Biblical translations have called "the water of separation." (Ref. Numbers 19:9, 13, 20, 21; 31:23) Some have rendered this as "water of impurity" or "water of uncleanness," as if to say it is something repugnant. Some commentaries then carry this "separation" in a negative sense as indicative of the Jewish people's separation from God. Other negative interpretations concerning Judaism have been drawn as well. Intentional or not, this brand of seemingly Christian judgmental intolerance has fueled and promoted anti-Semitism within the Church.

Actually, *"the water of separation"* is a rather crude, and therefore inappropriate translation. This fact is evidenced when we examine these same verses in English translations from the Hebrew *Torah* and in the Aramaic (or *Syriac*) *Peshitta*[22]. Here, we find that *"the water of sprinkling"* or *"water for purification"* stands as more accurate translation. We can only now speculate as to how this error was formed when we consider vocabulary limitations in languages such as ancient Biblical Hebrew and Aramaic.

Conservative commentaries, then, have seized upon this "separation" as something abhorrent and rejecting. They direct this as a sort of "Divine chastisement" against Judaism and the Jewish people, manifested as a "separation" from God.

We continue our study by comparing some of the other more familiar Jewish sacrifices and personal "types" with the pictures portrayed in the Red Heifer ceremony. Using that Biblical foundation then, we hope to demonstrate why the Red Heifer ashes count so vitally in prophecies relating to the Last Days.

Certain scholars have pronounced the following comparison of the two major components of our Holy Bible:

- Old Testament: World Corruptible
- New Testament: World Incorruptible

And, some Christian teaching continues this concept by pointing out that the Old Testament "died" at The Cross and, as would follow, the New Testament was "born" at The Cross. This concept reflects again a picture of Jesus Christ as we have often shown in the Law and in the Temple sacrifices.

The Old Testament (Jewish *Tanakh*) gave men a very regimented plan for living a Godly life. This plan was to be delivered to all men through the Jewish people, and which they have accomplished within the limits of their frail human capabilities. Much of the laws and values preserved in our modern societies worldwide have their origin from the Law as given to Moses. Given, that the laws and democratic forms of government came to our Judaic–

Christian societies from the Greeks and Romans. Nevertheless, Greece and Rome adopted many of these values as they "conquered" the Jews. As we would say: The Law of Moses "rubbed-off" on them!

But men, including the Jewish people, would not (and actually could not) follow that Law via their own human works, because the works of men are unclean, even under the most noble intentions, ever since that original sin of Adam. In order that God could save men from death brought about by their "uncleanness," our Lord Jesus Christ presented His own life at The Cross as the final payment under the Law to cleanse men of their uncleanness.

Some might then ask: "God must have known that men could not keep His Law. So then, WHY did God even give Moses and The People the Law?" — God could not accept sinful men unless they would repent and be redeemed of their sins. So, God gave the Law in order to lead men to repentance and atonement for their sins, IF they keep the Law. – Well – **NOT EXACTLY!** – We know of course that men *cannot* keep the Law. But God *can* keep it because He IS Perfection. He kept it as The Son, in the Person of Jesus of Nazareth, by mirroring ALL of the sacrifices under the Law with His death on The Cross.

At The Cross then, it might be said that, figuratively, the Old Testament (Judaism) "died" and has been in a "Hellish" condition throughout the scattering of the Jewish people to the nations during these past two "days" (of two thousand years). Again, the Jewish people actually have been *sacrificed* as God's offering (as a type of Jesus) to cleanse the Gentiles through their suffering ("smiting" or "bruising") during these past two "days." This was a fulfillment of the prophecy from Hosea 5:15 – 6:2. The Lord had said that He was "going back to His place" and that the Jewish people would be "smitten" or "bruised" or "torn" or "wounded" or "stricken" for "two days," but that in the third day He would "raise them up and they would be in His sight."

Another parallel of types is seen in that a fully Righteous and Innocent Jesus was "offered" to the World by His Father and was obedient in going to The Cross and His sacrificial death at the hands of the World. (Matthew 26:39) Similarly, even observant and sincerely worshipful (righteous) Jewish people have been "lifted up" by God to be "crucified" as a "type" of both Jesus and the Red Heifer and as an example lesson to the Gentiles (the World) who have conducted the sacrifice (burning) by literally creating a sort of "Hell on Earth" for the Jewish people during the past two "days" of one thousand years each. In obedience to the Lord their God, these faithful Jewish people have remained steadfast in their worship of a loving Father, despite all their suffering through these centuries. Clearly in this drama, faithful Jewish people are cast as a "type" of the Innocent Lamb of God.

In a preceding chapter we discussed tradition concerning Jewish hopefulness in looking forward to burial at the Mount of Olives Cemetery in order to be present to greet Messiah at His arrival (Return!). That tradition, discussed in *Kethuboth* IIIa, has another facet revealed in the belief that no Jewish dead who are interred "outside The Land" (*Eretz Israel*) will be resurrected. Then, the *Gemara* of *Kethuboth* IIIb continues discussion on this ruling by stating that in fulfillment of Daniel 12:1-2, "the just will break through the soil and rise!"

"And many of them that sleep in the dust of the earth shall awake, some to everlasting life, and some to shame and everlasting contempt."

Here we can understand that *"the just"* are those righteous Jewish people of the "Elect" who faithfully have been honoring God and have genuinely repented and have longed for their sins to be Redeemed by Messiah. These are the Jews who will be raised *"to everlasting life."*

Jewish people who live in distant lands and who also have means to deal with the expense, can arrange to have their remains sent to Israel and prepared for burial at the Mount of Olives. In this way then, when Messiah comes, they can just "break through" that *Olivet* soil and meet Him. Otherwise, they reason, if a person's grave is in, say New Zealand or southern Argentina, they would have to "burrow" through the entire diameter of the Earth! in order to "break through the soil" and greet Messiah at Jerusalem!!!

For this reason then, an even more bizarre tradition has been implemented in order to accommodate those of the Jewish faithful who cannot afford the expense required to have their remains sent from *"the far corners of the Earth whereto I have scattered thee."* Many of these instead will have a small vial of soil from Israel or even from the Mount of Olives placed in their caskets. Certain Jewish sources[20, 42] and especially the *Shulcan Aruch*[43] even provide detailed instructions for sprinkling the precious soil beneath, around and on top of the corpse. Then, "legally", they are "technically" in The Land and on the Mount of Olives as well! – And obviously, they will need only to "break through" a tiny amount of soil! – (This procedure may be quaintly amusing to Gentiles; although, it is touching in its sincerity and faith.)

This teaching is even more specific regarding who is qualified to "rise" by declaring that the ruling even includes miscarriages! In case you have wondered – as I had wondered: "What is the Jewish position on the matter of abortion?" Then, we need wonder no longer. As demonstrated by this feature of *Talmudic* Law, Judaism long ago had considered the human embryo to be a living person, even while still in the mother's womb. And, since miscarriage of a fetus can occur at any time during the term of pregnancy, this means that life exists for that "human" from the very moment of conception! – (We certainly need not wonder "WHO" ever gave them that idea?!)

The picture portrays a type of The Resurrection of Jesus in that Judaism and the Old Testament finally are returned to life when Messiah, Son of David, arrives to begin what Judaism calls "The Messianic Age," and what Believers call "The Kingdom Age." The Old Testament then is "resurrected" as a newly glorified and incorruptible body (a "new" creature again) after two days (i.e., two thousand years) when Christ Jesus returns in Glory, and descending to the Mount of Olives as Messiah, Son of David. Their Old Testament Scripture, the *Tanakh*, will at that time reveal to them its True meaning – that which they had initially misunderstood and therefore had tragically rejected. Also "in that Day," the Jews will begin their New Covenant when they are reunited at last, incorruptible with Christ's Church after those same two "days."

Other Pictures And Types

One must stand back to contemplate and marvel here at the Lord's unmatchable art and feelings as a poet and dramatist. Who but the Lord could ever have composed such a drama? This drama actually develops as a beautifully complex and intricate matrix, with a composite overlay consisting of the stories of: Creation, Joseph, Jonah, Isaac, the Atonement goats, the Red Heifer, the Passover Lamb and perhaps a few others. These Biblical entities will now be presented as "types" to portray the story of Messiah, The Desire of All Nations, The Lord's Anointed One, Jesus Christ.

The Creation

The "lights of Heaven" were created on the fourth day of Creation~ (Genesis 1:14 – 19) and man was created on the sixth day (Genesis 1:24) After the sixth day; i.e., man's "day," the seventh day began as a day of rest — the Lord' s Day. Christ Jesus, "the Light of the world," as a reflection of the "lights of Heaven," arrived on Earth symbolically during the fourth "day;" i.e., four thousand years after Adam. Messiah's arrival, then, occurred four "days" after Adam and two "days" before the ending of The Days of Man; i.e., the six thousand years of man's dominion on Earth – the sixth "day." Jesus shall return to rule His Kingdom at the end of the sixth day and beginning the seventh day — the Lord's Day! – (See Illus. 6: Chronology of Principal Events in This Work, Page 33)

At this point we desire to point out some significant teaching from Jewish tradition, as recorded in *Talmud* and dated even from before Jesus Christ. These teachings come as no surprise to Christians, but it is somewhat surprising to see these coming from even the most ancient Jewish sources. Indeed, many of the teachings of Jesus are of *Talmudic* origin. After all, Jesus came to fulfill the Law — which is mostly what *Talmud* is about.

First, in tractate *Pesahim* 54a, it is announced that seven things were created (or designed) before God created the world. Specifically, these seven items are: The *Torah*, Repentance, the Garden of Eden, *Gehenna* (Hell), the Throne of Glory, the Temple and *The Name of the Messiah!*

Christians would of course point out that Messiah — Jesus — the second One of The Trinity, actually existed even before anything was created. (John 1:1 – 3) Believers would further note that *"Heaven and Earth shall pass away,"* but the Words of Jesus will never pass away! (Matthew 13:31) Nevertheless, maybe one of the several names of Jesus (one of which is even yet unknown to us! – Revelation 19:12) was not assigned until the Sixth Day — perhaps His name *Y'shua* (or Jesus). This timing at the Sixth Day of The Creation would certainly be appropriate since God created man on that day and *Y'shua* is God's name as a "Man." The Rabbis point out that the name of Messiah, the King's Son (Psalms 72:1) *"shall endure for ever, and has existed before the sun!"* – (Psalms 72:17) So, it can be reasoned that Jewish and Christian teaching are not so far apart on this point.

Tractate *Pesahim* 54a footnotes[2] go on to say that these seven things comprise prerequisites for the ordained purpose and progress of mankind in this world. The *Torah*, as the Supreme source for man's learning, presents the concept of repentance ("to err is human") and when men fail, they have "a second chance" and may "rise again!" The Garden of Eden represents reward and of course *Gehenna* (Hell) is the symbol of shame and punishment. *Talmud* continues, saying that the Throne of Glory indicates God's goal of The Creation in which the Kingdom of God (symbolized by The Temple) shall be established "on Earth as it is in Heaven." Then, at the End of Days, *Talmud* declares that the Name of the Messiah represents: *The certainty that God's Purpose ultimately will be achieved.* — AND, EVERYBODY SAID, "AMEN!"

One could say, from all this again, that Jewish theology and Christian theology are actually not so very far apart. Now, it just occurred to me, that perhaps we have just seen a clue as to that "secret" Name of the King of Kings that Revelation 19:12 says "...*and He had a name written, that no man knew...*" – Maybe that name is just what the Rabbis said; i.e., *"The Certainty That God's Purpose Ultimately Will Be Achieved."*

Christians will again be surprised to learn even more facts about Messiah which Jewish people have believed and studied for thousands of years! – and which Christians also know about Messiah — Jesus. Tractate *Kethuboth* 111a says the Jewish Messianic Era will commence with the return of the Jewish people from exile to The Land (*Eretz Israel*). Continuing in *Kethuboth* 112b, *Talmud* says: "all the wild trees of The Land will bear fruit."

Sanhedrin 98a presents a footnote that quotes the beloved Jewish teacher, Rashi from the 11th century, who said to "watch for the time when Palestine becomes very fertile." He then says this means that the arrival of Messiah will be very near at that time. — And, he adds:

"There can be no clearer sign than this!"

During your next visit to Israel, listen and examine carefully as your Israeli guide describes how Israel's crops have flourished. Please observe, also, how Israeli farmers have prospered and how the land has "prospered" agriculturally since their return in 1948 to this desert land, which the previous tenants had for so long abused and neglected. – Israel IS now green!

But, there is even more! Tractate *Kethuboth* 112b also states that Messiah will arrive after a time of troubles and disasters that will occur in rapid succession! In at least a dozen places in *Talmud* it is stated emphatically that arrival of Messiah will be preceded by the Battle of *Gog* and *Magog* (End-Time invasion of Israel – Ezekiel Chapters 38 and 39) and *will be the very worst period ever for the Israelites to pass through.!*

Now, please don't go away just yet, folks! – because the best is yet to come! The story we are about to reveal may be the most heartbreaking and yet the most heart — "leaping!" story we shall ever see in Jewish tradition. Jewish teaching says there are *two* Messiahs. From *Sukkah* 52 we learn that one of these is Messiah, Son of "Joseph," and the other is Messiah, Son of David, who is The Redeemer.

Apparently, *Talmudic* scholars received this from some "unpublished" and therefore presently unknown Prophets, and they have assumed this refers to a person having been born of the tribe of Joseph. (After all, how could the Messiah be born just as the son of a mere carpenter with the name "Joseph"?! – Makes no sense!) The Rabbis lament that Messiah, Son of "Joseph," was to have been the "precursor" (predecessor) of Messiah, Son of David. But, then they sadly relate that the Messiah, Son of "Joseph," was slain! Jewish teaching from *Sukkah* 52a further declares that *both* of these Messiahs are — guess what?!...

CARPENTERS!!!

Christians would agree that yes, Jesus also was a carpenter as an apprentice as well as being the "Son of Joseph," a "carpenter" of Nazareth. And yes, Jesus was born of a virgin mother (Isaiah 7:14) and to parental lineage that also makes Him a "Son of David." And yes, Jesus was slain — "pierced" — for *all* of the transgressions of *all* people. Jesus was actually the "precursor" of Himself, as He will someday soon arrive at the Mount of Olives to redeem Israel and to be seen as "The One Who was pierced for our transgressions." And yes, at that moment Jesus will claim His Kingdom as Messiah, Son of David!

In the teachings of *Sanhedrin* 97a, the Rabbis further lament that Messiah, Son of David, was expected to have delivered the Jewish people from their oppressors 4000 years after Adam or 2000 years after Abraham. In other words, Jewish teaching says that Messiah "should have come" about 2000 years ago, or at about the time that you and I would call "the time of Jesus!" Disappointed and with some regretful sense of guilt, — the Rabbis say — *"Alas, He has delayed because of our many sins!"*

At one point a Rabbi announces: *"All the predestined dates for Messiah (or Redemption) have passed, and the matter now depends only on repentance and good deeds."* (From *Sanhedrin* 97b) Believers would agree with all except that part about "good deeds." Moreover, Believers would point out that God is not a liar. It is obvious, therefore, if "All the predestined dates for Messiah have passed;" *then, Messiah must already have arrived sometime in the past!*

If God said Messiah would be here at that time, then He **WAS** here! – You can Believe it! Earlier we showed how Daniel's prophecy of "the seventy weeks" (Daniel 9:24-27) had predicted the exact day of Messiah's arrival. Jesus rode into Jerusalem on that exact day! At the end of this discourse, *Sanhedrin* tractate quotes: *"Happy are all they that wait for Him!"* (From Isaiah 30:18) Sadly, and without even their knowing it, sincere and worshipful Jewish people then wait hopefully for that *same* "One" Whom we Believers await!

Through our tears of mixed joy and compassion for these blinded Jewish worshipers, we now continue our study of other pictures and types of Jesus, first by referring to the story of Joseph, son of Jacob.

Joseph

Vivid parallels with the life, suffering and resurrection of Jesus can be seen in Joseph's betrayal (for a few pieces of silver!) into slavery by his own brothers; his exile into Egypt; his tempting by Potiphar's wanton wife; his innocent suffering; his escape from "death;" then his final vindication, victory and kingdom with reunion and mercy for his brothers, even after their slowness in recognizing him. Joseph rescued both of his families (Israel and Egypt) from worldly famine and death. All of these events parallel the life of Jesus. Jesus delivers both Israel and Gentiles (the World) from spiritual famine and eternal death.

Jonah

The ordeal of three days and three nights in the belly of the fish is often termed as a picture of Christ's time in The Tomb.

Isaac

Although offered by his father, Isaac was supplanted by the ram in the thicket until "*God will provide Himself, a Lamb for the burnt offering.*" (From Genesis 22:8)

Please observe a subtlety in this Scripture that we have marked with a suggested punctuation of Abraham's remark. The King James translation says, *"...God will provide Himself a lamb for a burnt offering:..."* — i.e., implying that God would provide a lamb for *Himself* or by *Himself*. Whereas, we have indicated a more specific interpretation of this phrase by placing a comma after "Himself." With the comma placing the phrase following in apposition, the meaning of the sentence then indicates that God will "*provide Himself*" as the Lamb.

The foregoing interpretation has credence in that it makes more sense because God at that time actually provided a *ram* for the burnt offering instead of a *lamb* (and instead of Isaac!) We also must realize there actually was no punctuation in the earliest Scriptural writings as originally transcribed, whether in Hebrew, Aramaic or Greek. Not until the ninth century, in fact, was *any* punctuation developed, even for the earliest Greek texts. (See App. 173 in Reference 10) Many Bible verses therefore must be evaluated carefully concerning the proper and most logical interpretation under applications of modern punctuation. In just this single example, we have demonstrated that meaning of a sentence can be profoundly altered by only a mere comma.

Since Abraham "*saw the place afar off*" (Genesis 22:4), it had to have been at *Olivet* summit, rather than the traditional place at the Temple Mount, often termed "Mount *Moriah*." This is because only *Olivet* is visible from "afar off" – even from as far as *Masada*! (About 53 km. or 33 mi.). Abraham was approaching "the land of *Moriah*" (the present vicinity of Jerusalem) from Beersheba, far to the south. Viewing panoramic photographs or even a cursory examination of relief maps, contours, elevations, etc. reveals that the Temple Mount (Mt. *Zion*) lies in the lowest portion of the terrain, as viewed from that southern approach *or from any other approach direction.*

The Temple Mount sits almost as if it were at the bottom of a "bowl" relative to the other peaks surrounding it. Whereas, the Mount of Olives towers far above *all* nearby peaks and terrain. Our conclusion is that Isaac was "offered" atop *Olivet*, but the ram was sacrificed at what we know as the Temple Mount. Our interpretation is that God "provided Himself" as the Lamb on Passover, about 30 C.E. *at that very same spot* where Isaac was offered on the summit of the Mount of Olives!

The Two He-Goats

The goat to be sacrificed on the Day of Atonement (*Yom Kippur*) was chosen from either of two he-goats by the High Priest's drawing of two lot pieces from an urn (*kalpei*). One goat stood in front of the Priest on his right and the other goat stood to his left. One lot piece was labeled "For the Lord," and the other was labeled "For *Azazel*;" i.e., "scapegoat." After the urn was shaken to separate the lot pieces, the priest, while blindfolded, reached into the urn and drew out one lot piece in each hand.

If the lot labeled "For the Lord" came up in the Priest's right hand, this was considered a "happy omen." (*Yoma* 4:1) In that case, the goat on his right would be slain as the goat "For the Lord" to atone for Israel's sins. Its entire carcass: flesh, hide, horns, dung and hooves were then burned atop the Mount of Olives at the place *"where the ashes are poured out"* — at the same place where the Red Heifers were burned. It is significant to note from *Yoma* 35b that the Atonement Goat was slain by the Altar as it lay with its head to the south and with its head turned to face westward; i.e., toward the Temple – reflecting the same positioning as specified for the slaying of the Red Heifer. (See *Parah* 3:9)

The other goat, the "scapegoat," was led from the Temple by a priest, carrying Israel's sins away from Jerusalem and was then released to freedom in the wilderness. Although our culture considers a "scapegoat" as one who, albeit virtually without any fault in a matter, has been sacrificially punished for the misdeeds of others, we can easily see that quite the opposite is the case for the Biblical scapegoat. *Azazel* (pronounced: Az-ah-zale`) is the Hebrew word meaning: goat of departure. He is actually the he-goat that is released – through no merit of his own. A specific route was assigned for this departure, beginning by crossing the "*Azazel* Bridge" and continuing on a road leading southeastward away from The City. (See Illus. 20: Jerusalem as it Appeared in 70 C.E., Page 153)

The *Mishnah* of *Yoma* 6:1 instructs that the two he-goats are required to be alike in appearance. This goes on further to say that they must even be of the same coloring, the same size, weight, etc. — unless one goat was purchased one day after the other. It is clear, however, from Rodkinson's edition[16] of *Talmud* that "*it is a merit*" if both goats are purchased on the same day. The remainder of this *Mishnah* and the *Gemara* following present a lengthy and tedious discussion of various procedures to be followed in the event that one goat dies before the ritual, etc., etc., etc. Nevertheless, in its "purest" form, this statute requires that the two Atonement he-goats definitely shall be of like appearance.

However, in our story this image is carried even further, as documented by footnotes of *The Companion Bible*[10] at Luke 23:18. This source reveals that the early Alexandrian theologian and martyr, Origen (186-253 C.E.), translated the name "Barabbas" in Matthew 27:17 as *Jesus bar Abbas*. Origen documented that both young men (Jesus and Barabbas) had the same given name: *Yeshu* (in Aramaic) or *Y'shua* (in Hebrew). The name has since become "Grecian-ized" and later "Angli-cized" to become Jesus.

It is noteworthy that the literal Aramaic meaning of *bar Abbas* means "son of a distinguished father," or more literally, a "high" father. It may then be speculated that Barabbas as a surname was passed on to us by early translators in order to spare us from confusion with the other Jesus, the TRUE Son of **THE** Most "Distinguished" Father! –

THE Most High Father!

More detailing of Barabbas as the type of the Scapegoat (or *Azazel*) is revealed when we consider what must have happened to Barabbas immediately after his release. It is most likely that this man, having been convicted as a rebel and a murderer in violation of Roman law (Mark 15:7); although freed, would have been escorted swiftly across the *Azazel* Bridge and out of the country, maybe even out of Rome's jurisdiction. Moreover, an undesirable and apparent incorrigible such as this person surely would have been forbidden ever to return to Judea, under penalty of death.

Now, when we examine closely the Scriptures detailing the Law for the Day of Atonement in Leviticus 16:21 – 22, this picture of Barabbas as the *Azazel* develops even further. The Scapegoat was to be sent away "by a fit man into the wilderness." Some remains of the *Azazel* Bridge were reported to have been unearthed a few years ago. The Temple priests complied with this directive by assigning one priest to lead the goat by way of the specified route, crossing the *Azazel* Bridge and continuing southward to the fields and rocks and hills near Bethlehem, which was at that time a "wilderness."

A respected Jewish source[25] notes that the most appropriate translation of the word *Azazel* would have the meaning "dismissal" or "entire removal." The word is described as having been the ancient technical term that referred to the entire removal of sin and guilt from the community. The reference further explains, from the *Torah* in the *Masoretic Text*, in which Verse 22 says the goat shall bear "*all their iniquities unto a land which is cut off;*" i.e., cut off from Israel, so that the animal could not wander back "to the camp." Thus, the live goat, representing Israel's sin and guilt, was being sent away never to return; i.e., "entire removal."

Then, complying with these statutes, the *Azazel* was led far into the wilderness, where he would be permitted just to run wild, eventually perhaps to join up with a herd of other wild goats. His escort, the priest, was charged to see that the animal reached freedom far from Jerusalem, that no harm would befall him *en route*, that no little shepherd boys would "adopt" him into some local herd, and generally to insure that the goat would not return to Jerusalem.

After the countryside (wilderness) around Jerusalem had become very populous during the later period of the Second Temple, this part of the ritual became difficult to uphold unless the goat was taken a much greater distance from the City for release. This procedure therefore became corrupted; wherein the goat was taken to a high cliff and was cruelly slain by hurling it to its death. This was their way at that time of insuring that the goat did not return.

Nevertheless, we know Barabbas was given the same type of exiled freedom as was specified by the Law for *Azazel*. Very likely, Barabbas was escorted out of the country, perhaps beginning his journey southward to Egypt, traveling across the *Azazel* Bridge toward Bethlehem. It is significant to remember here that the Temple priests and the Jewish people on that fateful day almost 2000 years ago were completely unaware that these Laws of the Day of Atonement were being fulfilled before their very eyes as The Precious Lamb of God was being slain "For The Lord" and for us! on The Cross. Neither the Priests nor the Jewish people could have known that all these circumstances we have noted were aimed toward Barabbas filling the type of the Scapegoat. It is certain as well that they were also unaware that Jesus was fulfilling the type of the He-goat that was slain "For The Lord" on their most sacred Autumn feast, *Yom Kippur*. It all happened almost as if it were "by accident." However, you and I know that it was NO accident!

Yom Kippur is then a picture of the "trial" of Jesus before Pilate. The Roman Procurator, albeit unwittingly, acted out the role of the High Priest as he "drew the lots" by asking the crowd to select from two young men, both having the Aramaic name "*Yeshu*," as to which *Yeshu* would be crucified and which *Yeshu* would be given his freedom. The crowd also unwittingly acted out the role of the two lot pieces as they divided into two distinct groups, depending upon which young man either group proposed for release by Pilate. As a result of a preponderance of vocal encouragement from one side of the crowd, Pilate then "turned-up-the-lot" by assigning *Yeshu bar Yusef* of Nazareth to be the burnt offering "For the Lord." Pilate then released *Yeshu bar Abbas* as the "Scapegoat" (*Azazel*) – hence, as "the goat of departure."

Noting the detail by which Jesus fulfilled the Law in other portions of this study, one could further and confidently speculate that:

- *Yeshu bar Abbas* and *Yeshu bar Yusef* of Nazareth probably had the same hair color, at the same length and style, same eye color, same complexion tone and color, same sandal size.
- They probably were of the same age, height, weight and build; i. e., Barabbas was Jesus' double!
- Probably they even wore robes of the same color, texture and cut.
- Jesus probably was standing at Pilate's right hand; and Barabbas probably was standing to Pilate's left.
- And yes, one could wager with confidence that they were "purchased" on the same day. Barabbas probably was arrested on the same day Jesus was arrested.
- God just does things that way.

The Passover Lamb

At that first Passover, the "firstborn" of the Children of Israel were kept from the Angel of Death sent by God's "Firstborn." They were protected by having sprinkled the Paschal Lamb's blood (with a hyssop branch) on the doorposts of their dwellings. (Exodus 12:22) This is an obvious picture of Christ reflected as: *"Your lamb shall be without blemish, a male of the first year..."* (From Exodus 12:5) Again, *"...and the whole assembly of the congregation shall kill it in the evening."* (From Exodus 12:6) We have shown fulfillment of both of these verses The Crucifixion of Jesus, the Holy Lamb of God. (See Hebrews 11:28)

Born In A Manger

It is appropriate at this point to observe another subtle but powerful reminder of the constant and consistent humility of Jesus as indicated in the Temple sacrifices. Almost all of the animal sacrifices, with the exception of the doves, were what we would term "barnyard animals" or "farm animals." All of the sheep, goats, rams, bullocks and heifers were birthed in very humble circumstances as compared with human births. At the very minimum within Western cultures, most of us were born at least in a bed in a house. With few bizarre exceptions, such as autos, taxis, elevators, etc., we should agree that most moderns from our Western societies are born in the Delivery Room of a hospital, with all the "high-tech" trimmings, trained personnel and state-of-the-art equipment.

But, none of this was for Jesus, The Precious Lamb of God. — No — Instead, He was born on a bed of straw on the floor of a stall for horses or cattle or goats, etc. And, instead of a "Delivery Room," Jesus was gently placed in a manger for feeding beasts. He had no crib with sterilized sheets, stainless steel frame. No high-tech monitoring equipment with colored computer screens. No nurses scurrying in spotless uniforms and cushion soled shoes.

Jesus chose to be delivered in the most humble surroundings — exactly as were the animals offered as the sacrifices that represented Himself. How many of us could even have thought to have been so humble?! – Especially, if we had created The Universe!!!

Three Crosses at Calvary

We must not overlook the picture that is manifested by the presence of the three persons who were lifted up to be crucified at Golgotha on that tragic but Glorious Passover, C.E. 30.

As a review of Luke 23:33 – 43, the first thief vents hostility as he chides Jesus, saying: (From Luke 23:39)

"If thou be the Christ, save thyself and us."

This thief (or "malefactor") represents "the world" as he rejects any idea that Jesus is dying for his sins, despite the fact that Jesus was innocent and without sin. The first thief was looking only for what Jesus could do for him right now! – in a worldly context.

The other thief, who had actually joined earlier in this worldly "railing" against Jesus (Matthew 27:44), evidently had come to realize afterward that Jesus really was "Somebody Special." The second thief then admonishes his henchman: (From Luke 23:40 – 41)

> *"Dost not thou fear God, seeing thou art in the same condemnation? And we indeed justly; for we receive the due reward of our deeds; but this man hath done nothing amiss."*

Then acknowledging, accepting and appreciating the Eternal Promise of Jesus, the second thief delivered the "bottom-line" for all of us, saying from Luke 23:42:

> *"...Lord, remember me when Thou comest into Thy Kingdom."*

Exhibiting with this statement, a simple, childlike faith that Jesus was his Redeemer, the second thief witnessed his belief and acceptance of Jesus. Jesus thereupon accepted this clear affirmation and comforted the man with His Words of Promise: (From Luke 23:43)

> *"...Verily I say unto thee, today shalt thou be with me in paradise."*

- Jesus, of course, is our picture of His Gospel and the Red Heifer (represented as the ashes) in that He died as a Perfect Innocent in order that all of us (*none* of whom is innocent) can be cleansed of our guilt before God.

- In the first thief we see a picture of the priest who slays the Red Heifer, representing the World to which God offered Him, but which "received Him not." A great irony exists in that Jesus is actually dying because of the sins of this man (and for all of our sins as well). Sadly, however, the man is indifferent to His sacrifice.

- The second thief then, is a picture of *"a man that is clean,"* in that he now accepts the Gospel (ashes) of Jesus; i.e., *"lays them up in a clean place."* Since he has the Gospel of Christ in his heart, his heart is now "a clean place." He then offers its message to his companion.

We should take note of the fact that at least one respected source[10] presents a conclusion that five – not three – persons were crucified. This notion seems outrageous. Nevertheless, the objective in this teaching appears to have been generated by a desire to remove or discredit an alleged Biblical "discrepancy" which could seemingly arise in that two "thieves" are mentioned in Matthew 27 and Mark 15; although, two "malefactors" are described in Luke 23. However, it seems to me that John 19:18 made it clear enough by stating,

> *"...and two other with Him, on either side one, and Jesus in the midst."*

And after all, John is the only one of the Twelve who is known to have been at The Cross. It is my own opinion that this empty argument in Appendix 164 of Reference 10 could actually create more doubt by striving to prove against what appears to be obvious: i.e., only two other persons were crucified with Jesus: two "thieves" – OR – two "malefactors"...whatever. – *"On either side one, and Jesus in the midst."*

If unbelievers choose to count that as a Bible "discrepancy," there is nothing in the Scriptures or that you or I can tell them that would alter their choice. Nevertheless, let us not in desperation ...s - t - r - e - t - c - h... Scripture just in order to make a point or to try to "fit" Scripture to satisfy doubters. As we have just witnessed, The Word of God is well capable of defending Itself on His Own Words!

With the believing thief as "the man who is clean," we have seen yet another picture at The Cross, which would be unseen without the comparison with the Law of the Red Heifer. This is, of course, only one man's view of this interpretation. Others may observe a different picture; although, we offer this for your consideration.

The Red Heifer

We have shown this burnt offering to be probably the most important, the most profound and the most beautiful of all these pictures of Jesus as Messiah. Many unbelievers and skeptics would label these numbers and pictures as mere coincidence and ignorance in superstitious religious fanaticism. We reserve the right to disagree.

But, Why Do We Need Those Ashes Now?

Without stating a reason, at the beginning of this discussion it was said that imminent recovery of the Ashes of the Red Heifer is important to both Jews and Christians. Why are those ashes so important that we need them NOW? – after nineteen centuries?

An indirect reason for this is because God never breaks a Promise. He *never* forgets anything He has Promised, yet He *always* forgives us when we *frequently(!)* forget our promises to God. Although we can *never* match any of God's qualities, we Glorify God whenever we even try to be just a little bit like Him in our small Worldly ways. We must remember that He told Moses that *those* ashes from that very *first* Red Heifer were for a statute *forever*, a *perpetual* statute. God's use of those words means that, in His eyes, *those* ashes will *always* be Holy. – "But why do we need them NOW? – Can't the Jews just burn a new Red Heifer?"

Answering the first question first: In Daniel 9:27 we are told that near the "end of days," three and one half years after he is revealed, Antichrist will cause the sacrifices and offerings ("oblations") to cease. Antichrist is not revealed yet, but he cannot stop those sacrifices unless first they are started again. Even with the questions raised earlier regarding location of a Temple or a Tabernacle; i.e. the "Sanctuary," we know the sacrifices *will* be resumed at that time. Further, and most important, regardless of where the Sanctuary will be located, the priests and the Temple must be sanctified and purified by *those* ashes. Moreover, there can be neither Priests nor Temple unless they are purified by *those* ashes.

The second question can be answered by recalling that Moses was instructed that some of those ashes of that very first Red Heifer, burnt about 1500 B.C.E., are to be held in perpetuity...forever! So, the Jewish people of today must find the urn (*Kalal*) containing the ashes of all Red Heifers ever burned. Otherwise – No ashes! – No Sanctuary! – No sacrifices!

A less obvious reason for urgency toward finding the Red Heifer ashes is because as the imminent Return of Jesus Christ draws nearer, there will be an eventual resumption of Temple worship. This will create a huge demand for purifications with the ashes of the Red Heifer because everyone and everything is presently "unclean." The return of Jewish Temple worship, sacrifices, etc. is therefore certain to deplete their supply of ashes unless they burn several Red Heifers early during the first three-and-one-half years of The Tribulation. (Daniel 9: 27) Many prophecy scholars teach that the battle of *Gog* and *Magog* (Ezekiel, Chapters 38 and 39) will occur early during The Tribulation and perhaps soon after Antichrist is revealed. (This is *not* the battle of Armageddon.)

The key to this subtlety concerning an early need for more ashes is given by the prophet Ezekiel. Briefly, the armies of *Gog* will be so severely mauled during their defeat "*upon the mountains of Israel*" that only one sixth of their number will survive. (Ezekiel 39:2). Then comes the cause for nearing depletion of the ashes, from Ezekiel 39:13:

> "*Yea, all the people of the Land (Israel) shall bury them;...*"

Yes! There will be so many dead soldiers from *Gog*, *Magog*, *Gomer*, etc. that seven months will be required for the Israelis to bury all of them in order "*that they may cleanse the Land.*" (Ezekiel 39:12) We may be certain that at this time the Jewish people in Israel will have returned to worship under the Mosaic Law. This fact is evidenced in that they will have resumed the sacrificial offerings at this time. We know from Daniel 9:27 that the sacrifices will be resumed, because after 3½ years into the Tribulation:

> "*...in the midst of the week he (Antichrist) shall cause the sacrifice and the oblation to cease.*"

Therefore, under the Law, all those Jewish persons who bury the dead must be purified afterwards by the Red Heifer's ashes, if they are to return to "cleanness" under the Law. We have earlier noted that only a minute quantity of ashes is mixed with the "Water of Sprinkling." Nevertheless, over one million Israelis burying probably hundreds of thousands of dead enemy soldiers is going to require an awesome quantity of ashes. Recent political "ebb and flow" in Israel has indicated a present and strengthening inclination toward Jewish orthodoxy and a national return to observing the Mosaic Law. For example, have you noticed that there are no longer any "girlie" pictures on the advertisement posters, etc. at Jerusalem bus stops? And, *El Al* Airline flights no longer depart on the Sabbath or on the eve of the Sabbath. – Better get ready! – Amen!

The recent collapse of the Soviet Union understandably has caused some students of eschatology (i.e., theology of "The Last Days") to question whether "*Gog* and *Magog*" really are from Russia. Jewish teaching from *Talmud* makes no specific identification of these people in terms of modern ethnicity. However, *Yoma* 9b does identify "*Gomer*" (Ezekiel 38:6) as people who eventually became what we know as Germany.

Talmud identifies *Gog* as representative of the vast group of "heathen" nations that will come against Israel in the Last Days just before the arrival of Messiah, Son of David. (See *Pesahim* 118a and/or *Sanhedrin* 94a) Ezekiel 38:15 makes it clear that this force is coming from lands to the north of Israel. Here we discourage against the popular tempting notion derived by some eschatology scholars who use Biblical names such as: *Rosh* (Russia), *Meshech* (Moscow) and *Tubal* (Tobolsk). Referring to historical peoples and lands in this way, suggests a connection with modern identities of nations and/or cities having names that are phonetically similar.

Using more scholarly principles, we could select a number of nations to the north of Israel as candidates to represent *Gog* and *Magog* with other nations of this evil force. The first might be the mountainous region of the Caucasus, which was the original habitat in ancient times for the greatly feared "Scythians." This people is described by historians as being a most horrible, loathsome horde of evil barbarians. At this time those people could best be counted as from regions of what is now Southern Russia and some of her former satellite nations of the Soviet Union. Several familiar names emerge for this region from today's troubled headlines. Within only a short distance (500 miles) from the center of the region are: Armenia, Azerbaijan, Chechnya, Dagestan, Georgia and Iran. Also nearby are: Turkey, Iraq, Iran, Kazakhstan, Syria, Turkmenistan, and Uzbekistan.

Seemingly endless warring between ethnic and religious factions in that area has confounded civilization for centuries. During modern times the region has been especially "explosive" for Russia because of the strategically vital access that Russia *must* retain through seaports on the Black Sea. It does not require a great amount of imagination to understand how this will be possible, especially considering events of today, including the recent conflicts in Afghanistan, Pakistan, Kashmir, Iraq and "who-knows-where-next"?! History in that troubled area is moving at a rapid and threatening pace. There could very soon be a huge force coming against Israel from that distressed and unstable zone.

However, this northeast direction also could be extended to indicate China as the leader nation of this group. The Lamsa Bible[22] does in fact identify "*Gog*" as China. We are of course aware that China *presently* has a huge army of 200 million men and that a future military force of *exactly* that number is identified in Revelation 9:13 – 16, that will approach from the east; i.e., from "*the great river Euphrates.*"

Some difficulty arises with the Chinese conclusion, however, because the Chinese and other Oriental peoples are descended from the same branch of Noah's family as are of course the Jewish people and many other people of the Middle East. The Chinese also are then descended from Noah's eldest son, Shem. Whereas, *Meshech*, *Tubal*, *Gomer*, etc., identified in Ezekiel's prophecy, are names of grandsons of Japheth. *Talmud* in fact emphasizes that these are Japheth's descendants. Japheth was of course the youngest of Noah's three sons and is identified as the ancestor of the so-called European ethnic groups. Nevertheless and despite China's Semitic roots, that nation has now and will continue to demand more and more oil and other strategic materials as China emerges awesomely as a huge military/industrial/political World power during the next few decades.

Convincing evidence for identifying Russia as *Gog* appears in Jewish history presented in the writings of Josephus[4] *Antiquities* 1.6.1 (123). That respected 1st century historian identifies "*Magog*" as the Scythians and "*Gomer*" as "*Gall*" which comprises present regions including parts of France, western Germany, Netherlands, Belgium, Switzerland and Northern Italy. "*Meshech*" is labeled as "*Mosoch*" and is described as "Cappadocia" (Acts

2:9 and I Peter 1:1), which was in the eastern regions of Asia Minor. "*Tubal*" is identified by Josephus as "Thobal" and as "the Iberes" which is the region of (formerly Soviet) Georgia, with its capital, Tbilisi. This example would appear to support at least some of the theory using phonetic similarities of names; although, perhaps merely through coincidence.

Concluding, the implication is then slanted more toward "*Gog and Magog*" as a European group, coming from "somewhere" to the north of Jerusalem. We have intended to show here that one should use caution instead of making a firm identification of this evil horde. If nothing else, this should be a lesson to teach us not to be overly confident concerning our abilities to interpret prophecies of the End-Times with "pin-point" accuracy – (because we may receive a surprise occasionally when we are way off-target).

Nevertheless, the real reason for Christians to have interest and excitement over all this is because we are now so near God's fulfillment of events leading up to the Return of Jesus as King of Kings and Lord of Lords. All these things *must* happen and *will* happen before His Glorious Return at the time His Kingdom will be established. — So, we know we are getting close!

> *Orthodox Jewish worshipers, too, should be excited because, after nineteen centuries, they are so near to having Temple worship again. The time of the Gentiles will be complete! More than one Yeshiva school in Jerusalem presently is training young men of Levite birthline in the intricacies of the Temple sacrifices. Also, it is not just a rumor when it is said that the Israelis have been preparing articles for the Temple and the sacrifices. An organization known as The Temple Institute is principally involved in this activity. Recent reports have even described public displays of some of these furnishings. They aren't kidding! They are getting ready! We cheer them on! Yet, we grieve and agonize over those who are yet unsaved.*

17

Who is "Indiana Jones?"

*Red Heifer Ashes **WILL** be Found! – Searcher Inspired Movie Character*

"Signs" Warned Priests to Hide Precious Temple Articles – Challenging, Frustrating, Fascinating Search – Breeding "Red Cows" in Israel

Recovery of the Red Heifer ashes is believed to be imminent, thanks to obedient and faithful efforts by a team of Israeli and American Biblical archaeologists. The chief organizer and leader of this effort is Rev. Vendyl M. Jones, minister/archaeologist from Arlington, Texas. Sharing that leadership initially, was the late Shlomo Goren, distinguished former Chief Rabbi of Israel. It is possible that other search teams are working as well. Rev. Jones states[33] that his first ambition at the age of nine years was to find the Ark of The Covenant and Israel's Holy Tabernacle that was kept with the Ark.

Although controversy surrounds the claim that Rev. Jones' exploits inspired producer George Lucas and director Steven Spielberg to create the well-known motion picture character, *"Indiana Jones."* Rev. Jones' ambition later was transferred toward finding the Ashes of the Red Heifer. Nevertheless, Vendyl Jones' real life search for the Ashes of the Heifer is arguably more exciting than any movie "fairy-tale" about the Holy Ark.

The first excavation began in 1967, after becoming aware of an engraved copper scroll discovered in Jordan in 1952. The scroll consists of three thin copper sheets, nearly eight feet in length and embossed in ancient Hebrew, describing the location of the urn (the *Kalal*), which contains the sacred ashes. Although the scroll is kept in a museum in Jordan; scholars, including Vendyl Jones, have been permitted to read and decipher the directions for finding this hidden treasure – much like a "treasure hunt."

Almost as exciting as the prospect of recovering the ashes is another secret that the Copper Scroll describes as hidden with those ashes. During the final forty years leading up to the Judean rebellion, just before the Romans began the siege of Jerusalem, several incidents ("signs") occurred concerning the Temple. These events brought Heaven-sent warnings to serious and watchful Jews that a disaster was looming. (See Part II, Para. 7) Apparently the Jews' foreboding prompted them to remove the most precious and sacred items from the Temple, including the Red Heifer ashes.

An implied message on the Copper Scroll indicates the Judeans apparently moved many items, such as the *Menorah* (candlestick), Altar of Incense and other items out of Jerusalem and cached them in caves near the Dead Sea. Replicas of the Temple furnishings probably were placed in the Temple in order to delude the Roman conquerors. Alluding to this possibility is a statement on the Jordanian scroll of copper saying that hidden with the *Kalal* is another scroll that gives *"the measurements to all things hidden."* Such a maneuver is not at all surprising, considering the priests' previous experience when King Nebuchadnezzar looted all of the Temple articles and displayed them as victory trophies in Babylon. (Jeremiah 52:12 – 23; Daniel 5:1 – 2)

This is taken then as an indication that instructions for locating those other precious relics are hidden with the ashes. (What a joke on the Romans, if they had paraded so triumphantly into Rome with all those Judean "treasures" which actually were phony gold-plated replicas!)

Recent reports[49] have surfaced Israeli suspicions that some or all of the Second Temple articles of worship are hidden in caves beneath the Vatican in Rome. After all, Titus and his Grand Theft of such items has been memorialized for centuries since 70 C.E. in sculpture on the Triumphal Arch of Titus on Rome's *Via Sacra*. Fascinating eye-witness accounts are quoted from persons claiming actually to have seen items such as the *Menorah* and even a blood-spattered Veil in those catacombs of Rome. Needless to say, tensions are increasing between Jewish and Roman Catholic authorities concerning negotiated retrieval of these precious and Holy articles. However, it remains to be seen whether any of those articles are authentic or, as we have speculated, they are merely phony replicas. The Temple authorities had plenty of warnings toward impending doom for the Temple. The Rebellion began in 66 C.E. and grew steadily more violent and threatening concerning Rome's shortening patience with this Jewish challenge to the Empire's sovereignty in Judea. As they saw Roman patience decline, the priests would have known to replace the precious with counterfeit.

An encouraging and sensible statement about recovery of the Temple items is given in that same report[49]. The author quotes an e-mail response from the *Israeli Ministry of Foreign Affairs* to a query regarding the rumored Vatican cache. The Ministry, in effect, concludes that of course Israel looks forward to recovering those Temple treasures. However, they do not anticipate that such will take place *"before the Coming of Messiah."*

We shall limit the story of the search because that adventure is equally as complex as the story of the ashes and would certainly furnish enough material for a fair sized book by itself. Briefly then, the place of search is a mountain bordering *Wadi HaKippa,* a dry river-bed at a short distance west of the northern end of the Dead Sea. This location is just slightly north of the *Qumran* cave where the Dead Sea Scrolls were found. Perhaps you have seen recent newspaper and magazine articles reporting on Jones' discovery of an urn that contains a fluid that Jewish authorities have verified to be the precious perfumed oil that was used for anointing the Temple priests.

The Copper Scroll identifies the hiding place as a cave with a chalk floor, a double entry and facing eastward. After searching several months, Jones located just such a cave, "The Cave of the Column," on *Wadi HaKippa.* Excavation of the cave was initiated in 1981 and continues to this date. Progress has been limited at almost "glacial" speed as judged by the time standards of men. God, however, has the project proceeding right-on-schedule — at His Eternal Speed.

Desert climate at the Dead Sea is of course an impeding factor because the blistering heat of the region limits "dig" operations to the months of November through March. Numerous equipment failures, Israeli/Palestinian political turmoil, bureaucracy "hassles," shortages of funds, cave-ins and other human frailties also have contributed to remaining "on-schedule." They also have conducted this venture with "blood, sweat and tears"— literally.

The Copper Scroll and other sources identify the *Kalal* as an urn of copper and brass. This is probably only a decorative chalice and a more durable support for the somewhat fragile container of the ashes, which we know is made of dried-out mud, dung or stone. At one relatively recent point in their exploration, the team enjoyed a high note of encouragement when a borrowed NASA "hi—tech" metal detector identified a concentration of brass and copper directly ahead of their excavation progress at a distance of only a few meters!

Earlier we noted that secular news media has shared in the excitement of a few of Jones' discoveries at the *Cave of the Column.* Israeli Rabbinical authorities have confirmed that Jones on 1 April 1988 recovered a cask that contains the perfumed anointing oil, *Shefar Afarshimon.* The oil is still in perfect condition, even after having been hidden away during nineteen-hundred years in the Dead Sea region. The formula for making this preparation was closely guarded in Temple times and was used for anointing the High Priests and the kings of Judah. (Kings of the rebellious nation, Israel, were not anointed.)

We also described the Altar Incense, *Qetoret*, the "red stuff" that was reported by secular sources as well. A large cache of this precious substance was found on 1 April 1992 near the entrance to this cave that Jones and his crew have been working during already the past few decades. Recovery of this substance is equally as important as is that of the oil toward the prophesied and imminent resumption of Temple worship by the miraculously restored nation of Israel during that seven years ("week") of Tribulation. (Daniel 9:27) It is vital to restored worship with the commanded Temple rites, at the start of that Tribulation "week," that both of these materials are recovered in their original form and purity. Apparently, that goal has been achieved through this discovery by Vendyl Jones. In the chapter following, we shall explain why restoration of the Temple itself is not actually a requirement for resuming the sacrifices, etc. The same or similar procedures will be used as were followed on both previous occasions when the children of Israel returned to The Land, *Eretz Israel*.

In later portions of this book we have presented much more detail concerning the oil and the incense. Some previously unreported or obscurely reported miracles associated with these materials are also described.

Many scholars will accuse against Vendyl Jones that he is a "loose cannon" or a "renegade" or other negative statements. Some such comments came even from other ministers who claim to be his friend. I can say only that Rev. Jones has been most truthful and responsive to our requests and inquiries. Admittedly, I do not agree with some of his theological views – nor would he necessarily agree with all of mine!

Nevertheless, I am convinced that God has surely anointed this man to complete His Purpose for Israel and the World concerning the ashes of the Red Heifer. Regardless of any human faults, Jones' discovery of the Altar Incense and the Holy Anointing Oil are sufficient to convince me of his genuine acceptance by the Lord for this task. He deserves our respect for his dedication to that task and for what he already has discovered. God does not always "anoint" those whom men might have chosen to implement His Purpose.

A much more detailed and comprehensive history of Vendyl Jones' saga is available from Karen Boren's book[41] *Messiah of the Winepress – Christ and the Red Heifer*. She has presented a much more detailed coverage of much of the background activities associated with providing Israel with a strain of Red Heifers. This includes a few American cattle ranchers who are devoted to that task.

Mentioned earlier, the Red Heifer's ashes already may have been recovered or surely will be very nearly recovered by the time you read this. But there is more to come. We need to examine how we may expect this recovery to impact Israel, Judaism, Islam, Believers and "the World."

18

What Happens After the Ashes are Recovered?

Secular Media Notice – Islam on Temple Mount – Scholars Must Defy Tradition – Heifer Ceremony Defines Temple Site – Olivet Contour Lines Confirm Temple Site – Fleming's "Lower Gate" – Ashes Are "Poured Out" – Where is "the Holy Place"? – Third Temple to be built "speedily" – NO Ark! – Awaiting Messiah and the Third Temple – The "Watergate" Story – Errant Shepherds misled Israel – 3rd Day and 7th Day meanings

In previous chapters we have shown why the ashes *must* be found and we have established that they *will* be found because all prophecy *will be fulfilled* and these ashes are required for that fulfillment. – So, it's simple! — *They will be found!*

Certain Orthodox Rabbis are understandably looking forward to that recovery with great eagerness. For example, they actually have organized a procession to celebrate by carrying the sacred *Kalal* around The Wall of The Old City when the ashes are brought into Jerusalem. At last report these marchers were planning to sing certain of the Psalms during the planned celebration.

Occasionally, articles about Israel's search for "red cows" have appeared in secular media: *Time, New Yorker*[29] and various local newspapers. A group of farmers in the mid-western U.S. are reported to be raising herds of cattle with nearly pure red coats to ship to Israel. Israeli farmers plan then to breed those cattle to eventually produce a PURE Red Heifer. At last report, the one Red Heifer "candidate" that authorities had evaluated as "pure" later showed to have grown a few white hairs on her coat. – Alas! Too bad! – Back to the breeding corral.

But what happens next is anybody's guess. Although the ashes have been hidden for these many hundreds of years, and it is *guaranteed(!)* they will be found, but the Temple cannot be rebuilt before "the" time. It is well known that the third most holy shrine of Islam, the Dome of the Rock, rests only one hundred meters from where the Holy of Holies would be at the Dome of the Tablets. Orthodox Judaism would consider it a perversion to erect the Temple or even the Tabernacle within view of a Muslim shrine or any monument or building glorifying any religion other than Judaism. Moreover, any move to conduct any Jewish worship next to a shrine of Islam would be taken as an act of **WAR!** ... *Jihad!* ... Holy War!

Throughout this discussion we have highlighted the fact that the Red Heifer burning is the single most important Jewish ritual. It should be noted that Islam also points to the importance of the "Red Cow" in very dramatic ways. This is first indicated by the fact that the first *surat* (chapter) and the very oldest chapter of the *Quran* (or Koran[19]), the Holy Book of Islam, is *Surat al-Baqarah* — "The Cow." This was the very *first* work written by their prophet, Mohammed, as he promoted this new faith among the Arab peoples.

Although it is plain to see that he is referring to what Scripture calls the Red Heifer, Mohammed refers to the animal as "fawn-colored" rather than red. (Another translation says it is yellow.) Mohammed wrote: "... *her color is very bright ... She is a cow neither old nor young ... She rejoiceth the beholders ... She is a cow not worn by plowing the earth or watering the field; sound, no blemish in her."* (*Koran*; Surat 2:69)

It has been said that Islamic tradition underlines this importance of the Red Cow by stating that whoever finds and holds the ashes of the Cow, burned by Moses and Eleazar, will rule the world! This chapter title then is not mere coincidence, in that the conflict between Israel and the Islamic nations may therefore be even more profound than the obvious disputes concerning existence of Israel as a nation, Arab lands, the Temple Mount, Dome of the Rock, etc.

Currently, a great contention exists among archaeologists and historians concerning the True position of the Jewish Temple site. During the past several centuries at least, the most traditionally accepted locale has been the Islamic shrine known as the Dome of the Rock. This shrine, in fact, is proclaimed as the third most holy site in Islam, being worshiped as the place from which Muslim tradition claims that Mohammed, accompanied by the angel Gabriel, ascended into Heaven on a winged horse.

This seems strange, in that Mohammed's tomb is at the second most sacred Islamic holy site, located at Medina[8] in Saudi Arabia. Further doubt comes from the majority of historians who note that the prophet was never known to have been even within hundreds of miles from

Jerusalem. The City of Jerusalem is never mentioned by any recognizable name in the Muslim's Holy Book, The *Quran*. Some Islamic interpretations of verses from *Surat* 17, referring to the "distant mosque" (or temple), are claimed as references to the former location of the Jewish Temple at *"Urusalim."* Muslims of course claim this was at the present location of the mosque at the Dome of the Rock. We shall report that even a few errant non-Muslim scholars have agreed with the Muslim claim.

The Dome of the Rock is typical of many Islamic holy sites, in that it rests over a reputed holy site that is also revered by a "rival" religion. Another prime example of this "dog-in-the-manger" policy is the Chapel of The Ascension on the summit of the Mount of Olives. When 12th century Arab leader Saladin, and later, Turkish Sultan Suleiman I – the Magnificent conquered Jerusalem, Muslims initiated vigorous campaigns to "colonize" many Jewish and Christian holy sites as Muslim holy places. Best known of these is of course the Dome of the Rock.

In 1982 Prof. Asher Kaufman produced very convincing evidence[7, 47] that the Jewish Temple site is not beneath the Dome of the Rock, but is instead about 100 meters northwest of that point, humbly and serenely "waiting" beneath an unimposing little cupola called "The Dome of the Tablets." More recently, in 1992 and again in 1996, Dr. Leen Ritmeyer[27, 28] has proposed that the Dome of the Rock is in fact the site of the Temple and is in direct conflict with Prof. Kaufman's conclusion; although, it is most certainly in line with tradition.

We should note here that most geologists agree there has been only slight alteration of the Temple Mount/Kidron Valley/Mount of Olives topography over the past several centuries. This becomes very important during any study concerning the Law for the Red Heifer, as we already have demonstrated. It is significant therefore to observe that Prof. Kaufman did laboriously consider the Red Heifer Law and its inherent topographical criteria from the very beginning when he did his analysis. Conversely, Dr. Ritmeyer and other scholars apparently either ignored or were unaware of any import regarding that ancient rite being connected with the Temple location.

At present, one cannot absolutely *prove* that Prof. Kaufman's location is correct. Nevertheless, close examination of evidence from all such proposals reveals a preponderance of credibility for Prof. Kaufman's claim, as opposed to finding almost no credibility for other proposals. Principal among the factors indicating this conclusion are the requirements stipulated in the Law for the Red Heifer ceremony. **Conformance with the Law of the Red Heifer cannot be over emphasized in any search for the location of the Temple.**

IF we knew positively the exact location of the *Miphkad* Altar, for example, it would necessitate only a simple surveying operation to determine the precise location of the Temple site. Thus, location of the Temple can be verified (or refuted) by analyzing carefully all details of the Law for the Red Heifer. Similarly, IF we could prove that Prof. Kaufman's location of the Temple site is accurate as proposed at the Dome of the Tablets, it would also be relatively simple to survey the location of the *Miphkad* Altar. It could be surveyed to a distance of a Sabbath Limit; i.e., about two thousand cubits due-east of the Holy of Holies.

By elementary surveying technique, I located myself at or very near what I believe may have been the *Miphkad* Altar site. *Parah* 4:2 describes the place as a "pit" or cavity in which the "red cows" were burnt on the Mount of Olives. The location surveyed is at the correct elevation and distance (1000 yards) on a due easterly alignment from the Dome of the Tablets. This area is level and somewhat of a clearing in the midst of thick underbrush (hyssop, too!) and remote from any buildings. A relatively level area appears as if it had been "scooped" out of the hillside at a point where the slope is very steep. It looks as if it "could" be the spot. (See Illus. 26: Temple Mt., Contoured Mt. of Olives, Page 324)

The Temple entrance, according to the cubit size, dimensions and location as presented by Dr. Ritmeyer, could never be seen from the *Miphkad* Altar if it were at 2000 cubits distance eastward from the Dome of the Rock. Using Ritmeyer's cubit dimension, a point located 2000 cubits eastward would fall beyond (actually "behind") *Olivet* summit. There are several additional details from Dr. Ritmeyer's thesis that cannot be supported by the Law or by archaeological data at that region. Another important objection is seen in that neither Ritmeyer's analysis nor a more recent work by Dr. David Jacobson[30, 31] provides a Temple location that is compatible with location of the *Miphkad* Altar at a place of burning "where the ashes naturally pour down." (See Leviticus 4:12 and *Yoma* 68b)

The proposals of both of those scholars yield sites for the *Miphkad* Altar that are on essentially level ground on top of or even behind the Mount of Olives. It would be physically impossible for the High Priest to be able to see the Veil of the Temple from such locations, considering that his field-of-view would be from behind or *through* the intervening mountain profile. (See Illus. 19: Elev. Profile: Temple Mt., Kidron VLY., Mt. Olivet, Page 152)

None of the Temple sites proposed by scholars other than Asher Kaufman fit the specifications under the Law as it fits the contour lines of the Mount of Olives. (See Illus. 26: Temple Mt., Contoured Mt. of Olives, Page 324) The position of the *cohain* (the priest) must be at the correct distance, location and elevation in order to satisfy all of the criteria given in The Law. All of the other proposing scholars have ignored the Law of the Red Heifer, which is so undeniably vital to verifying the site.

Dramatically, the contours from Survey of Israel define the slope where the ashes would "naturally pour down" and would flow directly and appropriately *toward* the Temple. In contrast however, if the Temple were located at the Dome of the Rock as tradition has claimed over many centuries and even as some recognized scholars have agreed, an entirely different result is rendered. If the *Miphkad* Altar were located on *Olivet* directly eastward from the Dome of the Rock, and if the larger cubits of those scholars claiming the Dome of the Rock as the site were applied, a fundamental obstacle to their theory arises. The priest would be unable to "direct his gaze carefully" to view the door of the *H'ekhal* as he sprinkled the blood.

This fact alone is enough to disqualify The Dome of the Rock as the Temple site. However, there are several other reasons that disqualify *es-Sakhra* as the site. Several of the reasons are summarized in Appendix G – "Temple Site". Dr. Ritmeyer's proposal for *es-Sakhra* is severely impacted by the exceptionally long "Royal" cubit he employs, more than seven "handbreadths." He is "locked in" with the Royal cubit = 52.5 cm. because his entire thesis is based upon that cubit dimension by the way he has justified it from certain of the dimensions of the Temple Mount Platform.

Applying Ritmeyer's Royal cubit at a distance of 1985 cubits (1042 m.) from the rectangular depression indicated on *es-Sakhra*, (Dome of the Rock), the priest would be unable to see the door of the *H'ekhal*. The contours on Illus. 26: Temple Mt., Contoured Mt. of Olives, Page 324, clearly demonstrate that at such distances the priest would be far back on the "flat" at the summit or possibly even on the reverse (!) slope of the mountain. The black diamond symbol below the word: "Ascension" on the Illus. 26: Temple Mt., Contoured Mt. of Olives, Page 324, shows the resulting position for Dr. Ritmeyer's proposal with the Dome of the Rock as the Temple site and using the much larger Royal cubit. The view of the priest westward and *downward* to the Temple Mount would be blocked by the intervening earth as he attempted to "gaze" toward the door. From that point, the contour lines indicate that the ashes – ignominiously, aimlessly and without pattern – would "pour down" to the southeast and down the *back* (eastern) slope of the mountain – actually *away* from the Temple!

Such a configuration in itself hardly seems in line with a theme that displays an obvious commonality in *all* of the Temple sacrifices. That is, a consistent theme is evident in that with *all* of the offerings at the Mount of Olives, the ashes and characteristics of those rituals are pointed *directly at the Temple* – not in some unseemly, almost random and purposeless direction – and, especially, not *away* from the Temple!

Applying the Standard "Moses' cubit" for the Sabbath Limit distance in Ritmeyer's analysis would certainly improve the priest's view somewhat and affords interesting comparison with Asher Kaufman's analysis. Ritmeyer's position for the *Miphkad* Altar is marked by a clear diamond symbol on Illus. 26: Temple Mt., Contoured Mt. of Olives, Page 324. Nevertheless, from examination of the contours at the south end of *Olivet*, it still appears that the priest would be too far back on the "flat" to permit clear line-of-sight to the front of the *H'ekhal*. Moreover, the ashes poured out from that location would tumble down the slope in a southwesterly flow, instead of directly toward the Temple.

David Jacobson's proposal[30, 31] also maintains the location of the Holy of Holies within the bounds of The Dome of the Rock. However, Jacobson's location is centered somewhat to the rear (west) of *es-Sakhra* itself. Multiple objections similar to those for the Ritmeyer proposal emerge for that of Dr. Jacobson; although Jacobson applies a cubit of more realistic length = 18 in. (46.5 cm.). At 1985 cubits, this places the *Miphkad* Altar somewhat nearer the *Olivet* slope, shown on Illus. 26: Temple Mt., Contoured Mt. of Olives, Page 324 by a black triangle symbol. Nevertheless, it remains doubtful that the *kohain* (priest) would be able to sight the curtain at the door of the Temple, which is uncompromisingly required for the ceremony of the Red Heifer. The ashes poured from that point; although they would flow to the southeast in this case, they would, again, course down the slope in a random and meaningless direction and not directly toward the Temple.

The Temple site as proposed by the late Ernest L. Martin[46] is deserving of mention at this point. Prof. Martin located the Temple near Gihon Spring, about 300 meters south of the Temple Mount. Martin has claimed that, during the 1st century, high ground had been built up in the area presently known as the City of David. He proposed that the Temple of Herod was atop that high ground and somewhat northwest, but nearly directly above Gihon. Martin based this claim on some credible historical accounts, some Scriptural references and a few assumptions. He maintained that the built-up area supporting the Temple was leveled when the Temple was destroyed.

A counter argument is given by the fact that no remains of such a huge build-up has ever been found. Additional argument is drawn from the testimony of the *Siloam* Tower, the ruins of which remains today nearby the Pool of *Siloam*. That feature is at an elevation similar to the Pool of *Siloam* (650 m.), all of which is at approximately the same elevation as that of Gihon Spring (680 m.). The tower testifies to the effect that the present topography of that portion of the Kidron basin is relatively unchanged from what it was in the first century. Several geologists have offered that same conclusion.

Martin employed a cubit = 18 in. = 45.72 cm. It can be seen from Illus. 26: Temple Mt., Contoured Mt. of Olives, Page 324, that the terrain directly east of Gihon Spring, at what would have been the *Miphkad* Altar and marked by a black square, is on almost level ground and at elevation of about 730 meters. This is again based on a Sabbath Limit of 1985 cubits from the Temple. If the Temple were, as represented in Martin's sketches, atop that formerly built-up ground at an elevation similar to that of the Temple Mount; i.e., approx. 700 meters, the *cohain* would be standing at almost the same level as the Temple. And, since the *Miphkad* Altar would have been on what amounts to level ground, there would have been no slope for the ashes to "naturally pour down." The ashes therefore would not have "naturally poured down" toward the Temple nor indeed, would they have poured in *any* direction whatsoever.

The white square symbol and white triangle mark the position for the *Miphkad* Altar if Moses' cubit were applied for the Sabbath Limit from Martin's and Jacobson's proposed Temple sites respectively. No improvement in the situation is gained from such a change for either proposal.

On Illus. 26: Temple Mt., Contoured Mt. of Olives, Page 324, we have marked locations of what would be the position of the *Miphkad* Altar, at one Sabbath Limit distance from the Holy of Holies for each of the proposed Temple locations by: Jacobson, Kaufman, Martin and Ritmeyer. We should point out that none of the other three scholars opposing Kaufman has made any consideration of the requirement for the *kohain* to see the curtain at the door of the *H'ekhal*. Moreover, only Kaufman's Temple location is "punctuated" by the presence of Fleming's "Lower Gate" pointing *very* convincingly toward the Dome of the Tablets. Neither did any of the other three even mention Dr. James Fleming's remarkable discovery nor its importance in the quest for locating the Temple site. – There have been proposals on the subject from other scholars for which time and space will not permit discussion here.

Let us consider now the Divine Pattern commanded for the most Holy of the Temple sacrifices; i.e., those whose remains are burned at the *Miphkad* Altar near the summit of the Mount of Olives. –

- The sprinkling of the Heifer's blood is directly *toward the Temple*.

- The priest, as he sprinkles, "directs his gaze carefully" *toward the Temple.*
- The ashes from the Atonement Goat and the daily Sin Bullock are "poured out" and "naturally pour down" *toward the Temple.*

Then, with such an obvious and powerful theme as that shown for the most Holy sacrifices, it just seems fitting that the ashes from the Altar of Sacrifice that are poured out at the *Miphkad* Altar atop *Olivet* also should "naturally pour down" – YES ! – *toward the Temple!*

The contour lines indicate that a sort of "finger" extends from Professor Kaufman's proposed site of the *Miphkad* Altar westward and *directly* toward the Dome of the Tablets. The "poured out" ashes would then "naturally" cascade down that finger as "a Tower of Tears" toward the Lord's Holy Temple. We have shown convincing evidence that the Blood of Jesus also was "poured out" and to then "naturally pour down" that *same* slope from that *same* point. – What could be more fitting? – What could be more Glorifying of His receiving the sacrifices of His People and Glorifying of His ULTIMATE Sacrifice at that *same* place on that Holy Mountain?!

The opposing scholars also appear to have been rather cavalier in their selection of the length for the Standard cubit as whatever seemed to be "convenient" for their analysis. Kaufman's cubit is in agreement with the Biblical dimension from more precise translation of Ezekiel 40:5 in the *Peshitta* (See Lamsa Bible[22]) and with the cubit size given in *Kelim* 17:9. More importantly, however, is the fact that Kaufman's cubit is even confirmed by measurements of numbers of ashlars still visible on the Temple Mount.

A significant and recent archaeological discovery that should be highlighted in this argument has also been ignored or overlooked. Just a few years before Prof. Kaufman began his search for the Temple (1969), a remarkably "fortunate" accident befell a young graduate archaeology student in Jerusalem. As he was setting up his camera tripod, preparing to photograph the Mount of Olives, the rain-soaked earth gave way beneath his feet. James Fleming plunged downward several feet, falling into a Muslim gravesite in front of Suleiman's ("Golden") Gate in the East Wall. The sight that greeted him below the ground revealed arch stones of a much earlier gate that is directly beneath Suleiman's Gate. All of the other proposals also have ignored Dr. James Fleming's "Lower Gate" discovery, which points to the Dome of the Tablets *like an obedient and faithful bird dog!*

In conclusion, there appears to be much more reason to believe the true Temple site is at the Dome of the Tablets rather than at the more "popular" location, the Dome of the Rock. That conclusion is derived based not only upon an overwhelming preponderance of evidence in favor of Prof. Asher Kaufman's site at the Dome of the Tablets, but also because of many errors and omissions in the proposed alternate locations.

In recent years there have been all sorts of unconfirmed "Gee-Whiz" rumors and "undercurrents" claiming that the Israelis already have Temple stones cut, etc., etc. And, as mentioned previously, they actually have proudly displayed several recently produced Temple articles. (No rumor!)

So, will all of Jewry defy all of Islam and the Mosaic Law by building the Temple under their present topographical/political/religious, etc, situation? Or, as former Israeli Prime Minister Menachem Begin replied when asked about this dilemma, he shrugged and suggested, "Maybe there will be an earthquake!" As a matter of fact, recent reports[45] from Jerusalem describe warnings from local authorities, such as "danger of major collapse" at the Temple Mount. One notably visible defect is a "bulge" and large cracks observed in the southern wall and the eastern wall also shows damage.

Charges fly back and forth between Rabbinical authorities and the Muslim *Waqf* (Temple Mount Authorities). Israeli reports accuse the *Waqf* of carting off and dumping debris from unauthorized excavations of sensitive archaeological sites. Muslims, in turn charge Jewish archaeologists and engineers of "undermining" the Temple Mount, so sacred to both faiths.

Meanwhile, Jordanian groups attempt to mediate and balance this delicate confrontation to keep the peace. Studies by Jordanian, Israeli and Egyptian engineers, architects and geologists are under way, however, Israeli engineers blame much of the damage and threat upon natural flow of rainwater through the centuries and, especially, the recent (27 Feb 2004) earthquakes and "heavy snowfalls" during recent Winters.

So, maybe there will be an "earthquake" to settle the Temple Mount dilemma much sooner than we think. Moreover, damage from "heavy snowfalls" turns our attention to the prophecy about Messiah's Return in Lamsa's Bible[22] for the phrase that strangely was omitted from our Western Bibles in Luke 21:11, which says "... *and the winters will be severe.*"

We just don't know how that Glorious Scenario at His Coming is going to play out. But somehow the sacrifices *will* be resumed, perhaps in a Tabernacle or in a rebuilt Temple. — Guaranteed!

Where Is The "Holy Place"?

This present Jewish vs. Islamic confrontation regarding the Temple Mount has been a great puzzlement to Biblical prophecy scholars for centuries. However, there may be an answer to this quandary provided in that revered and invaluable study source from a century ago, *The Companion Bible*[10].

Much of the puzzle stems from a single verse spoken by Jesus in the Gospel of Matthew 24:15 – 22, warning the Jewish people to escape for their lives by referring to the coming "*abomination of desolation*" when a Messianic impostor (Antichrist) will stand in "the holy place." This of course refers to Daniel's prophecies in Daniel 9:27, 11:31 and 12:11. Quoting Matthew 24:15,

> "*When ye therefore shall see the abomination of desolation, spoken of by Daniel the prophet, stand in the holy place, (whoso readeth, let him understand:)*"

Translation of Matthew 24:15 comes from *hagios topos* as the Greek equivalent for "holy place." All other translations in the New Testament from *hagios topos* are definitely referring to *the Temple area*, as opposed to the Holy Place within the *H'ekhal*; i.e., the "sanctuary." (See Acts 6:13 and 21:28) When referring to the Holy Place and the Holy of Holies in the Temple sanctuary (Illus. 15: Plan of Second Temple (by Dr. A.S. Kaufman), Page 148), the Greek plural noun equivalent of *hagia* (the holies) is used instead of an adjective and appears without the equivalent plural noun *topon* (places). (Hebrews 9:12 and 25)

The confusion for those of us who are limited to only the English language arises from the fact that each of these two Greek usages is translated simply as "holy place" in all of the New Testament references listed. Therefore, elementary logic combined with common-sense and consistency, seems to indicate that where our Bible says, *"in the holy place"* (from *hagios topos*), Matthew 24:15 is in fact referring to *the Temple area*, instead of the Holy Place within the *H'ekhal*.

The footnotes for Matthew 24:15 in Reference 10 refer to footnotes under Matthew 4:5 where explanation is given for rendering of the Greek word for "temple." The equivalent phonetic English pronunciation: *hieron*, for the Greek (ιερον) is used for "temple" in Matthew 4:5. Such Greek usage, which also can mean: *holy place*, therefore implies that this location is maybe somewhere in the vicinity of the Temple Mount or possibly even in the Holy City, Jerusalem, nearby. The notes further state that Arabs even today sometimes refer to the City of Jerusalem as *el Kuds* (Arabic: the Holy Place) because the Jewish Temple (Sanctuary) twice was located there and because Islam's sacred Dome of the Rock is presently nearby. (Illus. 20: Jerusalem as it Appeared in 70 C.E., Page 153) Yes, – (and this should not be surprising to us!) — Muslims as well as Jews and Christians regard the entire Jerusalem area as "a Holy Place."

According to tradition, the "pinnacle" mentioned in Matthew 4:5 is actually referring to the southeast corner of the City Wall. This is the place where Satan carried Jesus and challenged Jesus to demonstrate His Deification by leaping off the wall, apparently to His death, but then to be rescued from the fall by legions of angels. (Matthew 4:5 – 7) This is also the same place from which James (brother of Jesus) was martyred when he was thrown to his death in a plunge of about 250 feet to the floor of the Kidron Valley below. The tomb of James is nearby and just below *"The Pinnacle of the Temple."* (See Illus. 20: Jerusalem as it Appeared in 70 C.E., Page 153.)

Theodotion, a scholar of the second century who was involved in the fourth revision of The *Septuagint*, wrote that this "pinnacle" is the place where Antichrist will stand to bring "the desolation." (Matthew 24:15) As we have shown, the pinnacle is within the bounds of the environs of Jerusalem and does therefore easily qualify to be called "a holy place" within a local traditional context. Intending no disrespect for Theodotion, nevertheless, the lesson here could be for us in these latter days to not insist upon any definite pin-pointing of where that infamous usurper will stand *on that day*.

Who Needs An Earthquake?!

This debate continues by centering on the *two* Greek words used for "temple" in Scriptural writings of the New Testament. The phonetic English equivalent *naos* is used for the Greek (ναό ς) when referring to the Holy House, the *H'ekhal*; i.e., the Sanctuary that is comprised of both "The Holy Place" and "The Holy Of Holies." (See Illus. 15: Plan of Second Temple (by Dr. A.S. Kaufman), Page 148) However, when Scripture refers to the Temple grounds, buildings and the vicinity at large (including "the pinnacle"), the Greek, *hieron*, is used. Matthew 4:5 says: "*... and setteth Him on a pinnacle of the (hieron) Temple;*" which clearly therefore does not refer to **THE** Holy Place which is in The Holy House, The Temple Sanctuary, The *H'ekhal*, etc. Rather, the Greek *hieron* instead refers to the general vicinity, which *can* and *may* refer to The Pinnacle Of The Temple as the place where Antichrist will stand *on that day*.

Paul's use of the word *naos*, however, prompts us to pause to examine II Thessalonians 2:4, "*... so that he as God sitteth in the Temple (naos) showing himself that he is God.*"

Paul is speaking of Antichrist sitting in the Temple (*naos*) proclaiming himself as God. We *could* gain the impression here that Antichrist will actually sit in the *H'ekhal*. However, the Greek rendition shows multiple use of the preposition "as", which could be interpreted as: 'sitting *as if* he were God, seated in the Temple of God.' Paul's less than formal writing style frequently uses *naos* as a figure of speech; such as comparing our bodies as being a Temple (*naos*) of God. Nevertheless, Paul sometimes employs *hieron* for the same type of metaphor.

For example, I Corinthians 3:17 is translated as: "*... which temple (hieron) ye are.*"

Whereas, I Corinthians 6:19 says: "*... know ye not that your body is the temple? (naos) ...*"

Some will say, "Well, it's all Greek to me!" Nevertheless, we must remember that God's word is TRUE and without confusion. Maybe He does not presently wish us to know all of His Plans in this picture. We must be cautious to avoid being so dogmatic that we insist on certain limits, processes, details, etc. concerning exactly how HIS PLAN will reach fulfillment.

Especially regarding this latter reason, therefore, we should not worry ourselves about the Dome of the Rock, earthquakes, Islamic confrontation, etc. Then, to go along with that concept and based upon the Master's own words in Matthew 24:15, from the Greek *hagios topos*, one logical conclusion emerges. It appears that Jesus was speaking of the Temple vicinity and not the Holy House itself or the Gospel would have said as much, using either *hagia* as "Holies" or *naos* as "Temple."

The foregoing discussion is presented in order to demonstrate that the term: "holy place" is not necessarily referring to that portion of the Holy House itself – the Temple – the *H'ekhal*. The resumption of Jewish Temple worship most certainly will resume sometime after Antichrist is revealed and before Jesus returns. Nevertheless, as we have said, the Israelis *may not* need to rebuild the Temple atop the Temple Mount, as of old. Such a move would of course inflame the Moslem world. Instead, they *may* elect to begin the sacrifices, etc. at a reconstructed Tabernacle. Add to this possibility the Jewish restriction against building the Temple next to a "heathen" shrine on the present configuration of the Temple Mount, and the "Tabernacle solution" appears even more likely and less threatening politically and militarily.

Before we depart from this subject, it should be reported that the original (Aramaic) Scriptures, as translated by George Lamsa[22], state Matthew 24:15 as follows:

"When you see the sign of uncleanness and desolation, as spoken by the prophet Daniel, accumulating in the holy place (whoever reads will understand);"

This translation, rendered from the oldest and therefore the most authoritative Biblical manuscript source – the *Peshitta* – reads slightly different than the King James (so-called "Authorized") version, by saying "accumulating" instead of "stand." This could be so interpreted and would seem to fit more appropriately with the "holy place" being a region or an area rather than a particular "spot" in the Holy Temple.

Apparently, therefore, the man of sin will commit the abomination perhaps at some point on the Temple Mount, but maybe not in the Temple, itself. This means that Judaism may not *necessarily* even need to erect a Temple or even a Tabernacle on the Temple Mount at that time in order that Scripture will be fulfilled. Nevertheless, they *must* still resume the sacrifices before Daniel 9:27 can be fulfilled. – But how can they do that without a Temple? – What about the Law? ... **HOW???**

A logical suggestion answering "HOW?" is maybe the Israelis return to "Temple" worship by first using a Tabernacle. An obvious rationale for this choice comes from Revelation 6:14, 16:18 – 20. These verses describe the "Great Earthquake" that will be *"...such as was not since men were upon the Earth,... and every island fled away, and the mountains were not found."* In short, just prior to Jesus' Glorious return, Earth will be leveled. – Not a wall will be left standing *anywhere* on Earth! There will no longer be any problem with mosques on the Temple Mount. (See Is. 24:20; Ezek. 38.18)

Jewish teachers believe that the Temple described in Ezekiel 47:1 is the Temple that Messiah will build "speedily" when He comes. (*Rosh Hashanah* 31a) Jewish liturgies include prayers at every weekly *Shabbath* service and at Passover, petitioning that the Temple *and* Messiah "will come *speedily* in our day." In fact, Orthodox Jews pray *daily* for the Temple to be restored. Christians of course would agree that, in Jeremiah 3:17, the Lord is most certainly speaking of what they call "The Kingdom Age;" i.e., after Jesus returns, because He says that *all* nations shall be gathered unto Jerusalem at that time. So, it follows that maybe Jesus *will* build the Temple *"speedily"* when He comes! According to this logic, former Prime Minister Begin was correct when he remarked, "Maybe there will be an earthquake!" – However, from Revelation 16:18 – 20, we know it is not a *"maybe"*!

Some scholars point out that the Rabbis already have even the Temple stones prepared – ready to rebuild a Third Temple. It is proposed and / or rumored that the stones are prefabricated, identified and marked, much the same as would be for a set of *Lego* construction toys. This thought is intriguing if for no other reason that a well-concealed mystery surrounds the process used for cutting the stones. This is especially challenging since whatever process is employed must accomplish the task with strict precision – and – **it must be done without use of *any* implements, tools or materials containing iron!**

Notwithstanding that restriction, however, let us just consider for a moment what happens if that Biblically prophesied earthquake of the Last Days or even Menachem Begin's earthquake "option" levels the Temple Mount, the mosques – **everything**! A very "practical" problem arises because reconstruction crews will **not** be able just to go up there and scrape off the debris and rubble with bulldozers, backhoes and earth movers.

Remember? – Iron implements must **never** even so much as *touch* a stone of the Temple, lest it be "disqualified." A depth of rubble and debris would stand at about at least 7.50 meters or about 24.50 feet. This is because the floor of the *Azarah* (Court of Women) is that depth lower than the *Shethiyah* – which is at the level of the entire *H'ekhal* floor.

A painstaking and time-consuming and extremely cautious task would be required for removal of that much earthquake debris in order even to begin construction. The "painstaking" process necessarily must be done, *literally*, "spoonful-by-spoonful" in order to recover – *undamaged and untouched by any iron tools!* – any Temple articles, artifacts, etc. that might be buried in the construction site. Again, this must also be done while not defiling any buried Temple stones with iron tools. Needless to say – assigned archaeologists must perform this "dig" with brass or plastic or wooden "spoonfuls!"

Moreover, it is likely that any and all workmen involved in reconstruction of the Holy House must *also* be ritually "clean" themselves as well! We must concede, however, that a specific *Talmudic* ruling for such a requirement so far has not been sifted from the Law during our research. Nevertheless, from the precision, Holiness and rigidity in the Law in the areas we *have* encountered in this study, it would appear *very* likely that such a restriction would be in force. The Judaic requirements for "purity" in *any* regard to the Holy Temple certainly may not be minimized or overlooked.

For these stated reasons and very "practical" considerations then, the so-called "supernatural" rebuilding "speedily" by Messiah begins to make a lot more sense than any "hasty" or "impure" effort by Jewish zealots – no matter how sincere and worshipful their motivation. Besides, rebuilding of Israel's Holy Temple by man's puny and awkward means would require *years* to complete!

It is important that we should pause to correct a mistaken impression that most Gentiles have, especially we Christian Gentiles, concerning the Temple at Jerusalem; i.e.,

THE Temple as mentioned in Scripture in Jewish worship. The Temple (or The Tabernacle, earlier in the *Sinai*) was the Earthly Residence of Almighty God – not just a synagogue or in any way similar to a "church" building, as so many seem to believe.

We probably derived this impression in part by having heard our Jewish friends talk about "going-to-temple" in much the same way as we Christians speak of "going-to-church." Another way this impression is distorted for Christians is by the names that some Jewish congregations have given to their synagogues, such as "Temple so-and-so." We will hear a Jewish person casually mention "going to Temple" or we read notices about services at "Temple _ _ _ _ _." We therefore quite naturally think of this in our own Christian frame of mind, such as "going-to-church." (And, you may be surprised to learn that many Jewish congregations even have what they call "Sunday School.")

Serious Christians, who are rightfully and vitally concerned and interested in Jewish worship, should be informed and aware of the unique and Holy stature of "THE" Temple in Jerusalem. It was *not* a synagogue. It was not anything approaching a "church" building (or even a revival tent! Only the priests could enter the Sanctuary and only the High Priest could enter God's Private Chamber — the Holy of Holies – only once each year on the Day of Atonement, *Yom Kippur*. Only Jewish men were permitted even in "the front yard" (Court of the Israelites) where the animals were slain before being offered upon the Altar of Sacrifice. Of course, Jewish women, the children and all Jewish lepers could pass no farther than the Court of Women, as bounded by the immense Eastern Gate ("Nicanor's Gate"). Women and children were prohibited even to ascend the semi-circular stairway approaching the Eastern Gate. (See Illus. 16: Isometric View of 2nd Temple, Page 149, and Illus. 21: Detail of the 2nd Temple, Page 154)

Jewish congregations, dating from 1500 B.C.E. until the first century, worshiped at the Tabernacle or **THE** Temple. There they did not just sit in little rows of pews and listen to sermons from their Rabbi — as in a synagogue. Still, when they did attend their synagogues, – Yes – they worshiped in a fashion somewhat similar to that of our church services. Please remember then, THE Temple of the Jews at Jerusalem was *not* just a building at which the congregation gathered for worship. It was God's Holy House, which was built according to His specifications and for His Holy Residence alone. He "lived" there. NOBODY else lived therein. The Temple is a Holy Chamber and it is The Only One. — There is no other.

Let us recall that the Israelites worshiped at the Tabernacle (tent) of Moses during their forty year journey to the Promised Land. Since they are even now returning to *some* requirements of the Law, it is fitting at this time that Israel would again *first* worship at a Tabernacle. As soon as they are able to resume observing the *full* ordinances of the Law, as they did previously after returning to The Land, they worshiped in the Tabernacle during the Exodus and in The Promised Land until the Temple could be rebuilt. And, as we have shown previously, the Tabernacle or The Temple, the priests, and the utensils must first be purified by the ashes of the Red Heifer mixed with Living Water of Purification. Some Jewish teachers today faithfully and eagerly observe that they will not need to rebuild the Temple, because, they believe, the Lord their God will build it! (More about this later.)

Scripture presents at least one clue that the resumption of the sacrificial offerings will take place in a Tabernacle. Referring to Amos 9:11 – 15,

"In that day I will raise up the Tabernacle of David that is fallen, ..."

Some modern scholars of prophecy have heralded Verse 13, in which the Lord proclaims:

"... the plowman shall overtake the reaper ..."

Agricultural "miracles" have been occurring throughout the reborn land of Israel over the past few decades, including this rapid growth cycle that was forecast in the writings of the prophet, Amos. Israeli farmers sometimes have as many as three or four harvests in one year!

Not all of these crop successes can be attributed to the Israelis' advanced irrigation technology, the resourceful *kibbutzim* workers and their brilliant prowess in agriculture. (Somehow, they are receiving Help!)

Lest critics oppose these claims of fulfillment on the basis of their being "out-of-context," please examine Verse 15. The Lord says that this "Day" and all this agricultural "bloom" will appear in Israel at a time, which He says:

> *"And I will plant them upon their land, and they shall no more be pulled up out of their land which I have given them, saith the Lord thy God."*

Yes, the Lord their God "planted" them upon their land in 1948. Further, Ezekiel 37:25 sounds an echo of this same permanence of Israel, speaking of that final rebirth of the nation, *"they shall dwell therein for ever."* We have witnessed the return of the scattered Jewish people to their land, along with the prospering of that land. The prophecy from Amos says, literally, they shall return "in that Day" to worship at a Tabernacle. Moreover, they know also that it will truly be "the Tabernacle of David" because — remember what their Rabbis taught (from *Sanhedrin* 98a) about signs for coming of Messiah? — "Watch for the time when Palestine becomes very fertile, there can be no clearer sign than this!" *that Messiah, Son of David is near!!!*

The sacrifices can be resumed by locating and erecting a Tabernacle, in accordance with the Law from Exodus, at a suitable location somewhere in Israel. Just as before. – Maybe even at Shiloh! This would mean, however, the Tabernacle still must be purified by the ashes of the Red Heifer. Otherwise it is just another tent! And, if any more Red Heifers must be burned, the Israelis will still have to follow all of the Law we have outlined from *Parah* tractate of *Talmud*. The tent must face eastward, the burning must be at a point 2000 cubits distant (east) from The Holy Of Holies, with a view to the un-obscured and un-shaded curtain, etc., etc.,

Now, some will ask, "But, even if they find the Heifer Ashes, how can the Jews resume Temple worship? — Won't they first have to find the Ark of the Covenant?" There has been much speculation and discussion concerning the Ark, and many people understandably are excited. Their excitement is whetted every time they read or hear a rumor from some source that says the Ark has been located here or there, or The Ark is hidden away in this place or that, etc.

In recent decades, a certain amount of speculation, approaching so—called "tabloid" sensationalism, has suggested that the Ark is under the Temple Mount or in Ethiopia or Iraq –- or one of the most recent of these reports says the Israelis already have the Ark and are hiding it somewhere until "The Time!" On this thought we should consider the logic involved in such a proposal. It seems strange indeed that the Israelis would have the Ark now (or even know its whereabouts); whereas, they did certainly not have access to the Ark when they had the Second Temple. If they knew its location then, why did they not recover it for the Second Temple? – That idea just does not make sense.

Based upon a single passage of Scripture, we may be confident that there will be *no* Ark in the next Temple (or Tabernacle) just as there was no Ark (nor even a replica) in the

Second Temple. Hear now what is said about disposition of The Ark during "the Day of the Lord" in Jeremiah 3:16 – 17:

"And it shall come to pass, when ye be multiplied and increased in the land, in those days, saith the Lord, they shall say no more, 'The Ark of The Covenant of the Lord;' neither shall it come to mind: neither shall they remember it; neither shall they visit it; neither shall that be done any more."

At that time they shall call Jerusalem the throne of the Lord; and all the nations shall be gathered unto it, to the name of the Lord, to Jerusalem; neither shall they walk any more after the imagination of their evil heart."

In addition to the Scriptural evidence concerning the absence of the Ark, at least two historian sources also record that the Holy of Holies was void of the Ark. Josephus *Wars* 5.5.5 (219) says of the Holy of Holies: "In this there was nothing at all." This fact is echoed in *Yoma* 5:4, 53b. – Nothing was in the Holy of Holies ... *Nothing! Middoth* 1:1 agrees that although the term "Mercy Seat" was retained pertaining to the Temple rites, the High Priest sprinkled the blood of the Atonement Goat on the Foundation Stone (*Shethiyah*). Since that is where the Ark formerly had rested, the *Shethiyah* was the only appropriate place to sprinkle the blood, because there was no Mercy Seat because there was no Ark.

As a side note, *Talmud* Rabbis (*Yoma* 5:4 and 54b) declare: "the world was founded at this spot." They refer to several Scriptural verses as basis for this claim. Noting this from Job 38:6 –

"Whereupon are the foundations thereof fastened? or who laid the corner stone thereof;"

The *Gemara* goes on to say that the world was created with *Zion* as the starting spot. Here they refer to Psalms 50:1-2 –

"A Psalm of Asaph. The mighty God, even the LORD, hath spoken, and **called the earth from the rising of the sun unto the going down thereof. Out of *Zion*,** the perfection of beauty, God hath shined."

There is even a Judaic theme on the subject of The Creation, saying in a footnote, that *Zion* was Created first from "the centre," and around it the other soil, stones, continents were built until the Earth's formation was complete. Here, the reference is to Job 38:37-38 –

"Who can number the clouds in wisdom? or who can stay the bottles of heaven, When the dust groweth into hardness, and the clods cleave fast together?"

One comment, attributed to the noted scholar, Rashi, suggests that there was first a framework and which became filled and solidified from all sides toward the "centre." The footnotes continue, adding that this is an amazing agreement with "modern theory" saying the Earth was created by *"solidification of vapours"* and thereby showing that this *Talmudic* narration testifies this *"gradual creation"* to God's Will.

Ezekiel Chapters 41 – 47 describe the Temple that was to be built to await Messiah. Upon returning to The Land after their captivity in Babylon, Zerubbabel built the Second Temple exactly in accordance with the measurements and specifications given through Ezekiel. They followed Ezekiel's directive from the Lord right down to every cubit and wall and gate. They even made the folding doors at the entrance, hinged exactly as instructed in Ezekiel 41:23 – 24. (See *Middoth* 4:1.)

This point is illustrated further in that the Temple architects also named a gate at the southeast corner of the *H'ekhal* based upon the prophecy of Ezekiel 47:1-2. It was called the WATERGATE! – *Shekalim* 6:3 inquires: "... and the water gate. Wherefore was its name?"A Rabbi replies: "... because through it the waters trickled forth and in the hereafter they will issue out from under the threshold of the House ..." – referring to the prophecy from Ezekiel 47:1 – 2.

Yes! – The Jews of the Second Temple were expecting Messiah to arrive when the "living waters" would issue "... *out from under the right side of the House* " (See Illus. 21: Detail of the 2nd Temple, Page 154) Ezekiel made this prophecy while the Jewish people were captives in Babylon. They were praying to be released and that they would then return to a "renewed" Israel. They derived this interpretation from the words of Ezekiel 3:16, saying: *"... when ye be multiplied and increased in the land, ..."*

We must indicate the significance of their adhering to the specifications from Ezekiel. The Jewish leaders of that time, then, built a Temple that will be very much like the Third Temple. We know that Messiah will actually occupy His Temple that will be just as Ezekiel had described ! The Temple Plan shown in Prof. Asher Kaufman's detailed layout in Illus. 15: Plan of Second Temple (by Dr. A.S. Kaufman), Page 148, IS the plan of the Third Temple as well as what has been shown for the Second Temple.

The Jews of the Second Temple period, however, fervently prayed and believed that Messiah, Son of David, was going to come to that Temple which King Zerubbabel had built precisely as Ezekiel had specified. Nevertheless, Ezekiel did not call for an Ark to be installed in the Holy of Holies because Ezekiel and the Jews who built the Second Temple were obedient to the Lord's Commandment from Jeremiah 3:16, saying: "*... neither shall that be done any more."*

Further circumstantial evidence on withholding the Ark is presented by what Scripture does not say. For example, *none* of the Old Testament prophets succeeding Jeremiah ever mentioned the Ark. Jeremiah said: "... *neither shall it come to mind* ..." After Jeremiah, the Ark is never again mentioned by any of the later prophets of the Old Testament. It is mentioned only twice in the New Testament:

- Hebrews 9:4 describes Moses' Tabernacle, of course being an historical description from the Old Testament (*Torah*).
- Revelation 11:19, describing disposition of the Ark in Heaven:

    "*And the Temple of God was opened in Heaven, and there was seen in His Temple the Ark of His Testament;*"

Some conservative Christian theologians have used this absence of the Holy Ark to claim as proof that God did not reside in the Second Temple as His Divine Presence (*Shekhinah*).

This claim is easily refuted, however, by Scripture from both Old and New Testaments, as follows:

- Haggai 1:8 and 2:7 quote the Lord's encouragement to King Zerubbabel:

"... build the House and I will take pleasure in it and be glorified, saith the Lord."

"... and I will fill this House with Glory, saith the Lord of hosts."

- Zechariah 1:16 quotes the Lord's Promise to Jerusalem upon their return:

"... I am returned to Jerusalem with mercies:

My House shall be built in it, saith the Lord of hosts, ..."

- Matthew 23:21 quotes Jesus speaking concerning the Temple:

"And whoso shall swear by the Temple, sweareth by it and by Him that dwelleth therein."

- John 2:16 quotes Jesus referring to where His Father "dwelleth:"

"... make not My Father's House an house of merchandise."

- In Luke 24:53, after The Crucifixion, the Disciples worship at the Temple:

"... were continually in the Temple, praising and blessing God ..."

Many places in the book of Acts the Disciples are described as worshiping at the Temple. Then, please ask yourself: "Would Jesus' Disciples have worshiped at the Temple if they had known that God, the Father, were not there?" That would have been a vain and pointless sacrilege! These references show that the Holy One in fact did still sanctify His Holy House, even after The Crucifixion, ... but yes,... without the Ark.

The argument that *Shekhinah*, the Glory of the Lord, did not reside in the Second Temple is refuted by means of referring to the Greek of Matthew 23:21. The Greek word naos, earlier described, is used here and is known to represent the Holy House – the *H'ekhal* – the Holy Temple – the Sanctuary. Jesus referred to *"Him that dwelleth therein"* THAT House. It is *certain* that NOBODY other than Almighty God dwelled in His Holy House.

Although the Glory of the Lord did still reside, He did not manifest His Divine Presence as greatly and as wonderfully as He had done in Solomon's Temple. Many of the previous miracles of Solomon's Temple did not repeat in the Second Temple; although, some others did reappear and remained until The Crucifixion. Then sadly, as the Rabbis of *Talmud* and *Midrash* lament, *all* miracles were taken away "forty years before the Temple was destroyed" in C.E. 70. (See *Yoma* 51 and Chapter 7)

So, why didn't they at least place a suitable replica in the Holy Chamber? The answer is, again, — because the Lord had commanded them: "Neither shall *that* be done any more!" And, nothing has altered that Commandment since that time, nor will it be altered now or in the future. And, if they conducted sacrifices, etc. without The Ark during the time of the

Second Temple, then why would they need it now? Besides, the Lord had said there would be no Ark after Jerusalem and the Temple would be destroyed by King Nebuchadnezzar.

It appears that the Lord made it plain enough that, "in that day", there will be NO Ark. They won't mention it — They won't even *remember* it! – It just won't be there. — Instead, "saith the Lord", they shall call Jerusalem *"The Throne of the Lord!"* Besides, does anybody *really* believe that, while Jesus is reigning as King of Kings and Lord of Lords at Jerusalem, He is going to live in a golden box?! – When He returns *"in like manner,"* He is not going to be seen as a "fire" or a "cloud" this time. He is going to be seen with His same Glorified Body – the same as when He appeared to His followers after The Resurrection and when He ascended into Heaven.

It is reasonable to inquire: "Why would the Lord *not* want His Holy Ark to be in the Second Temple?" – We propose that the answer to that inquiry is obtained through thoughtful consideration of:

- Ezekiel's vision detailing specifications of the rebuilt Temple. (Ezekiel 40-46)
- Chronological order and timing of Temple prophecies and history.
- Comparisons of Ezekiel's descriptions with Josephus' and *Talmud* descriptions of the Second Temple.

As we discussed earlier, the returning Jewish exiles from Babylon believed – fervently! – that they were rebuilding that Temple at which Messiah, Son of David, would arrive to conquer their perpetual foes and to redeem their Salvation from sin. The Lord had told them in Daniel's prophecy (Daniel 9:24-27) that The Redeemer would arrive 483 years (69 "weeks" of years) after the proclamation to rebuild The City, and which eventually was granted by Artaxerxes I about 450 B.C.E.

So, there they were back in *Eretz Israel* ready to rebuild. There was no need for Messiah, Son of David, to live in that "golden box"! It is significant, also, to observe that the Lord's Godhead is more Glorious in Messiah – Jesus – than in *Shekhinah* who resided with the Ark. The Rabbis assumed, rightly, that they were building the Temple in compliance with the Lord's specifications as received from Ezekiel. No Ark is mentioned in Ezekiel's vision. God knew they would need NO Ark – EVER ! – But, there is still more to this argument.

Some will argue that Scripture is referring only to the Kingdom Age (after Christ's return) concerning absence of the Ark, *"... when ye be multiplied and increased in the Land, ..."* etc., etc. This argument then would claim that since Israel has not yet been "increased," they could surely have the Ark when Israel resumes the sacrifices during The Tribulation just preceding His return.

That argument can easily be countered by noting that the primary reason for there having been no Ark in the Second Temple was because Israel had broken The Covenant, which of course the Holy Ark represented. Their chastisement for this failure was the withholding of the Ark from their midst. Israel was being obedient to the Lord's Commandment from Jeremiah 3:16. Yes! — *Obedient!* – Many Christians seem often to forget that the Jews of the Second Temple truly believed their Messiah was coming to *that* Temple. They enthusiastically believed that Temple was built for the arrival of Messiah, Son of David.

They followed the detailed instructions from Ezekiel Chapters 40 – 47 right down to each and every cubit and wall and gate. (Sadly, we know that their Messiah, Jesus, indeed *was* there – *"but they knew Him not."*)

At this present date, however, serious Jewish worshipers are even more hopeful for Messiah's Coming and for their Promised "increase." They have no reason to place an Ark in this new Temple (or Tabernacle) any more than the Jews of the Second Temple had for the Ark in 500 B.C.E. They have no more reason now than the Second Temple Jews had for disobeying after the Lord told them: "*... neither shall that be done any more."* Israel was then obedient at least to that Commandment and she will be again.

A cautioning note from the *Talmud* Rabbis on interpretation of Scripture is given in *Menahoth* 27a. Here it is stated that when the Lord uses the words *"statute"* or *"shall be,"* this indicates "absolute indispensability of the rites connected therewith." In other words, God insists that *"it shall be!"* or in this case, *"shall not!"* Please go back now, and count how many times the Lord says *"shall not"* with reference to the Holy Ark. We know that when the Lord repeats a directive, it is for emphasis! – He Always says what He means, and He Always means what He says...Always!

Let us therefore avoid directing our well-intentioned hope and excitement and zeal toward recovery of this Holy, but "extinct" artifact. Rather, we should be searching and finding those truths that are important to His Coming — those things which He says *"shall be."* I do not wish to bring contention or confrontation with any of my Brothers whose intentions are certainly pure, although apparently mistaken. It is evident that Scripture already has "literally" eliminated this entire argument

At least we can be certain that Orthodox Jewry in Israel is very serious about resuming the Temple sacrifices. There has been an increasing frequency of reports in top-line news magazines and newspapers, especially a report[29] about the Israelis researching cattle embryos, herd surveys, etc. in the United States, Europe, South America, South Africa and other locales. Essentially, these report only that Israelis are *"seeking to breed heifers with red coats."*

Not surprisingly, few of these reports contribute much on the significance of these "cows" such as we have uncovered in this study. Neither do they explain the fact that the Israelis still must first have the ashes of that very first Red Heifer that was burned by Eleazar, 1500 B.C.E. Nevertheless, their Rabbis are well aware of this, because "*... **it shall be** unto the children of Israel, and to the stranger that sojourneth among them, **for a statute for ever.**"* (From Numbers 19:10)

So, only the Rapture of the Church, recovery of those precious ashes and the emergence of Antichrist remain to occur before completion of The Plan for arrival of His Kingdom. — *The Israelis don't need any earthquake or a war to overcome the problem of the Temple Mount!* – No Problem!

To summarize, then:

- A Tabernacle can be erected, but need not be on the Temple Mount, where it would presently conflict with the nearby Islamic shrines.

- The animal sacrifices and the oblations can be resumed in a Tabernacle that will have been purified by the ashes of the Red Heifer.
- Temple worship can be conducted, just as it was in the Second Temple, with the absence of the Ark Of The Covenant.
- The "*abomination of desolation*" can still take place as Jesus indicated, perhaps at "The Pinnacle of The Temple," or at some "holy place" on the Temple Mount or possibly even in The Old City of Jerusalem, (but not necessarily in a rebuilt Temple or even in a Tabernacle).

Praying for the Third Temple

Most Gentiles are unaware of the Jewish fervor and faith with which modern Jewish Faithful pray and await rebuilding of their Temple – what they call the "*Third Temple*." One of the more visible and effective organizations promoting such activity is *The Temple Institute*, headquartered of course in the Jewish Quarter of The Old City of Jerusalem.

On their website at – www.temple.org.il – a recent update (19 Sept 2005), authored by Rabbi Chaim Richman[51], explained that a part of Temple worship includes sounding a silver plated *shofar* on days of fasting and to call upon God's help in times of trouble, war, strife, etc. The update goes on to report that this silver plated *shofar* symbolizes the past year (2005), where Israel has had numerous occasions to warrant that call. Many prayers have been offered at the Western Wall, the *Kotel Hamaravi*. We shall paraphrase his text, for the most part, rather than making a direct quote.

Since the Israelis have had several deadly attacks in the past few years, it is stated that "we are all yearning to hear the message of 'good tidings' that is brought by the *shofar* that is plated with gold." This golden *shofar* brings the herald-blast for Redemption. The Rabbis then urge the plea:

> "*Sound the great shofar for our redemption. Bring us to Zion Your City with song, and to Jerusalem, Your Holy Temple, with everlasting joy!*"

The narrative continues with comment that two fervent prayers arrive with this blast:

First –

> *May we merit True freedom! – To be a free people in our own Land. May this truly become the state of the Jewish People, who dwell in security in every corner of their own Land, with pride of nationhood, subservient to no one.*

Second –

> **May we also merit construction of the Third Holy Temple**, *to be built by all of us. We shall be united as one man, go to the quarries and bring huge stones to raise the walls of the Temple that have now lain so desolate for thousands of years. We shall go up to Lebanon, and bring cedars, to rebuild the Temple at Jerusalem.*

The Rabbis further encourage that they believe *"no prayer goes unanswered."* They trust that *every* prayer finds its place *"on high,"* and there it *will* be accomplished – but, perhaps seeming that it is unanswered. – Nevertheless, it *will* be completed in the future.

Before we leave this question of the rebuilt Temple or a Tabernacle, we should at least be curious to ask, "What does Jewish teaching say about the rebuilding of their Temple?" Although it seems strange indeed, *Talmud* refers only to some problems that will arise when the Temple is rebuilt. The problems result because of some rather obscure and seemingly "trivial" statutes within *Talmudic* Law. Nevertheless, we must again caution ourselves against launching scorn, ridicule or judgment of any kind toward Jewish people in their implementation of the Law, which after all, was given to them by *YHWH*.

The problems of most concern appear from the possibility that God may answer one of Judaism's most fervent and persistent prayers. During all these years the Jewish people have prayed about their Temple, asking: *"May it be rebuilt speedily in our days."* This phrase prayerfully accompanies frequent entries in *Talmud* concerning the Temple. (See *Ta'anith* 26b) Here we also should mention that another frequent and fervent entry seen in *Talmud* is a similar phrase requesting a "speedy" arrival of Messiah!: "May He arrive *speedily* in our days!" This phrase is sometimes a part of the liturgical procedure (*Haggadah*) at the annual Passover supper, the *Seder* and in parts of the Sabbath morning liturgy in the synagogues *every week*.

Applying semantics, the Rabbis reason: "Since The Holy One, blessed be He, has so far not answered our persistent and faithful prayer that He rebuild the Temple 'speedily,' (i.e., soon) after its destruction, surely therefore whenever He does finally answer our prayers — as He surely will — He will then build it 'speedily,' (i.e., in a very short time)." Some Rabbis teach that the rebuilt Temple will be "wrought by the Hands of Heaven" — supernaturally. (See *Rosh Hashanah* 30a) It follows then, the Rabbis surmise, that the Temple for Messiah might be built so "speedily" as even *"in the twinkling of an eye!"*

This "speedy" reconstruction brings on some "problems" in keeping the Law, especially for the Temple priests. For example, *Ta'anith* 17 points out that the Temple might be rebuilt suddenly at a time when the priests' hair is too long. This unkempt condition would then render them unfit to take part in even the dedication, which they would also desire to be accomplished "speedily." Then comes the obvious question, followed by typically tedious *Talmudic* trepidation concerning just when, where, how, by whom, etc., etc. can their trailing tresses be trimmed? Finally, one Rabbi wisely suggests that they just settle the whole matter by keeping their locks at the proper length *at all times!* – (You know, — just in case!)

A few other "sticky" problems emerge regarding "the eating of the new corn" (*Sukkah* 41a) and an absolutely "mind — boggling" statute concerning the eating of eggs! (*Bezah* 5b) Jesus, it seems, had far more patience with those "lawyers" than any of us could ever be gracious enough to offer.

We must observe here that modern Judaism is not unanimous at this time in expecting to rebuild their Temple or Tabernacle or resuming the animal sacrifices, etc. The four principal denominations within Judaism: Orthodox, Conservative, Reformed and Reconstructionist –

have diverse doctrines regarding this matter of animal sacrifice and resumption of Temple worship. Nevertheless, we know that one "Day" they will indeed be "unanimous" on these questions when Messiah occupies His Temple!

Many Jewish teachers still believe that the Temple will be rebuilt by Messiah, as "wrought by the Hands of Heaven." Many Christians would support that view, in that the so — called Millennial Temple will be built upon the return (Arrival!) of Messiah. This is the Temple that was described by the prophet Ezekiel (Ezekiel 47:1) and which will have "*living waters*" issuing from under the threshold on the right side of the House. A few years ago, there were reports of a tremendous and mysterious underground water source under the Temple Mount in Jerusalem—near and beneath the future site of "the right side of the House!" — Hallelujah!

One of the primary reasons for NOT referring to "the Third Temple" regarding the "NEXT" Temple or Tabernacle or whatever place of worship where the "*oblations and sacrifices*" will resume is that Temple or Jewish place of worship – *whatever it is* – will *not* be fully consecrated to the Lord. – There are a few extremely vital reasons for this lack:

- *Shekhinah* will not have occupied it, because *Shekhinah* will only arrive when Messiah Jesus arrives to claim His Kingdom – three and one half years later, to be precise.

- This "Temple" – even if it is to be an actual Temple – will be desecrated at "*the abomination of desolation*" by Antichrist.

You may observe in Illus. 21: Detail of the 2nd Temple, Page 154, that the Second Temple also had a gate called the "WATER GATE" on the "right side of the House." This is just one of many features indicating that the Jews who built the Second Temple (later remodeled by Herod) actually believed that they were building that Temple for Messiah. More evidence of that belief is seen when we closely examine dimensions and other features of the Second Temple, as described in Scripture as well as by Josephus, in *Talmud* and other Jewish historical sources.

We demonstrated earlier that the Jewish people in the first century were *expecting* Messiah to arrive, at *Olivet* summit, about two—thousand years ago. And, it is well that the Rabbis *should have been expecting Messiah*, because five centuries earlier the prophet Daniel had told them the exact time of His arrival!

Daniel's famous prophecy of "the seventy weeks" (Daniel 9:24 – 27) in Verse 26 reveals the exact total "weeks" of years, counting from "*the commandment to restore and to build Jerusalem unto Messiah*" – until, it says, "*shall Messiah be cut off.*" The total number of "weeks" (each of seven years) is sixty-nine – or 483 years. Then, Messiah should have been "*cut off*" 483 years after the Persian King, Artaxerxes, issued "the commandment" during the Jewish month of *Nisan* in 453 B.C.E. (Nehemiah 2:1 – 10)

Applying corrections to all of the calendars for the intervening centuries, the 483 years were accomplished as the Jewish people reached the fateful year of C.E. 30. Jesus of Nazareth was "cut off" (crucified) on the 14th day of the Jewish month *Nisan* — *exactly* 483 years after King Artaxerxes had issued his decree during the twentieth year of his reign. (See App. 91 of Reference 10) These matters are not what some would call "fanatical coincidence." The dates of these events are a matter of historical record. Holy Scripture and documented history declare that Messiah arrived at *Olivet* summit *"right on time!"*

Some will ask: "Well, how do we know for certain that the Jewish people of the first century were expecting Messiah and that they knew that was the day?" During the first century B.C.E. – the time of Herod the Great – there was a prominent Judaic teacher named Hillel the Elder. Hillel's most prestigious disciple was Rabbi Jonathan ben Uzziel, who is described in *Megillah* 3a as having composed the *Targum* (paraphrasing interpretation) of the Prophets. A footnote adds that this Rabbi used paraphrasing to its greatest advantage in making clear interpretations of these prophecies to his readers. In the *Talmudic* discussion it is said that a voice "went forth" from the Lord, chastising ben Uzziel for having revealed "My Secrets to mankind." More specifically, it is explained that the criticism was leveled because ben Uzziel had explained Daniel's prophecy of the Seventy Weeks (Daniel 9:24 – 27) in which *"the date of the Messiah is foretold"*!

Therefore we know that, in response to what they had learned from earlier teachers of Messianic prophecy, the Jewish people were waiting for Messiah because they knew of this prophecy and others that told them to *expect* Him *at that time*. Sadly however, many of them did not recognize Him at that time. And, sadly again, it was because they were "blinded" by tradition, which had crept into their teaching and into their minds and hearts. They were lazily receiving only what their Rabbis (and *their* Rabbis, etc.) had taught from "tradition," instead of reading and studying God's Word to find the Truth for themselves. Christians, too, must be wary of complacency and of being deceived by tradition from "errant shepherds."

We must point out at this time that modern Jewish teaching admonishes any who would attempt to analyze the prophecies relating to the coming of Messiah. *Sanhedrin* 97b scolds: *"Blasted be the bones of those who calculate the end."* A footnote confirms that the reference is to predicting the time of the Messiah.

Joyfully!, however, many faithful and worshipful Jewish people still are waiting for Messiah. Although Jewish pride would surely drive them to deny it, worshipful Jewish people await the same One we Christians await. These we must encourage, in order that this time they will not only "wait" and "expect" Messiah, – but *this* time they will also **WATCH!!!**

A "Clean" Building

If the modern Israelites indeed are on the verge of recovering the ashes of the Red Heifer after nineteen centuries, they are faced with that same problem that existed upon their return from Babylon after perhaps only about fifty years. – The problem: After 1900 years of the People having been "scattered" throughout the nations and with the absence of any purification rites, NOBODY is "clean" now! — Remember? — If *any* person who *ever* walked across a grave, whether a known gravesite or perhaps one from thousands of years ago in prehistoric ages, that person is "unclean" under the Law of Numbers 19:16. This would mean that almost nobody on Earth is "clean" because almost everyone on the planet "could have" walked across such a grave, whether intentionally or not. So, *nobody* is "clean" under the Law. Nevertheless, whoever handles or touches those sacred ashes *must* be clean.

Within the Law then, this means the Jewish people have a really "sticky" problem – a problem that affects *all* of those with Vendyl Jones' archaeological team who are engaged in recovering the ashes. As we pointed out earlier, no unclean person must *ever* come in contact with the ashes. Several in Jones' party are Gentiles – and *that* is a problem. Gentiles are, by definition, unclean! – *No Gentile must ever touch those ashes or even the urn containing the ashes!* Neither Jones nor any of his Gentile workers nor any other Gentile can be permitted to lift that precious cache from its hiding place. But, neither can any Jewish person – man, woman or child – of today's world be permitted to touch even the urn, the *Kalal* – because *nobody* is presently clean under the Law!

Readers probably will think my imagination is "working overtime," but maybe Jewish people need to be bringing up some children over "the place of the stone" right now, as we speak. That was the place we described earlier where "clean" babes were raised for overcoming this same problem upon the return from the Captivity in Babylon. But, where is that place? Israeli archaeologists should be searching the Old City right now to locate that vital site. Who knows? – They may already have located it and in fact they already may have the "clean" babes, the oxen and the "doors" all ready and waiting for Vendyl and his workers to find the ashes. Or, Yes! – It is even possible that the team already has located the ashes, BUT ! – Remember – NOBODY is presently "clean."

Karen Boren[41] points out that the Israelis already have a plan for avoiding any defilement while moving the ashes. The plan is to have young Jewish lads pass braided hyssop strands through the eyelets of the *kalal*. The *kalal* would then be carried on poles to a place where they can be protected after discovery and removal from their hidden cache. This carrying procedure is limited as appropriate *only* for transport of the ashes. Whereas, NOBODY who is "unclean" may be permitted to touch the ashes or even the actual "clean" bowl containing the actual ashes. Therefore it is emphatic that "clean" babes must be available to remove the precious ashes and to place a "pinch" of ashes into a "clean" bowl of pure, living water. This procedure would then be the start of a process to purify priests or others, in order to begin the purification of *all* of Israel. – In the discussion to follow, we shall describe that intricate process.

Maybe the stone chamber no longer exists, or at any rate, what if they can't find it? Or, what if the chamber lies in a section of the Old City that is forbidden or at least is inappropriate for such Jewish activity. Examples of where such restrictions exist are the Muslim Quarter, the Christian Quarter and the Armenian Quarter? What will they do? – What *can* be done? – How can they find someone who is clean?

Now you are really going to think I have gone "off-the-deep-end!" One modern "practical" solution to this perplexing problem is to have certain Jewish mothers bear and rear their children in a specially-constructed building, preferably in the strict Orthodox *Me'a Shearim* region of Jerusalem. The foundation could be constructed so that an air space would always "insulate" a person from the ground beneath. Again, as on the Heifer's Gangway

Bridge, the foundation would be constructed in such a way so as to provide two levels of alternate air spaces (of at least one "handbreadth" each) to "legally" isolate occupants of that building from any unknown grave that might lie beneath the foundation. (And, who knows where there might be a former grave in Jerusalem after 1900 years and dozens of conquerings?)

Illus. 27: Clean Babes, Foundation, House, Page 406 depicts one foundation arrangement that could result. It is apparent that the alternating beams would lead to a somewhat complex structure, meaning also that it would be costly to construct – especially using only "clean" materials! Nevertheless, we can be sure that these disadvantages will not deter serious, worshipful Jewish people from keeping the Law.

The children born and reared in this building cannot be permitted to just venture outside the building and into the yard or the streets. They must of course always be carried out of the building in order that their feet must never touch the ground, lest they become defiled by any unknown grave. This rather awkward and intricate, but "legally" vital arrangement then, after a few years, would provide young children who could qualify as "clean" persons. These could then become candidates to be that first person who will lift the precious *Kalal* from its niche whenever it is found. According to Reference 29, there may be an activity presently under way in Jerusalem to provide "clean" children as we have described.

As before, when the Israelites returned from Babylon, they devised a very elaborate procedure for reinstituting this purification rite. At that time, as well as the present, NOBODY was clean. The "clean" children were carried on doors on the backs of oxen to draw "living water" from the Pool of *Siloam*. The procedure from that point on and leading up to "cleansing" of that first adult was described earlier as pecking the goat on the nose, etc.

There may be now a temptation for some to scoff or ridicule these Jewish interpretations of the Law as just so much "nit-picking." We must learn not to fall into that temptation. We must not view all this as silly or unnecessary. It is very important to Jewish people because the Lord gave them the Law. — They didn't just invent this requirement to satisfy their own vanity or piety. Serious Believers who love the Jewish people and who also love and understand the important place the Jewish people hold in these last days should be curious to learn how the Israelis will accomplish these things. We know they already are making preparations. All this is very intriguing and "mind-tickling," but we have no way of knowing all of the details in these mysteries because they are secrets between the Lord and His Chosen, whom He has "elected" to be present at His coming. Those shall be there to *"look upon Me Whom they have pierced."*

Mishnah 8:5 of *Shekalim* tractate records that the Veil was braided of seventy-four cords of twenty-two threads each, resulting in a beautiful curtain over three inches thick and sixty feet long by thirty feet wide. This considerable task was performed by "eighty-two young damsels." – *Shekalim* 8:4 teaches that when the Veil was new and before hanging, or if it became defiled by some unclean substance, the Veil (or "curtain") was immersed in one of several cisterns beneath the Temple courts for cleansing. Because of its great weight and size, three hundred priests were gathered to immerse it

Now, we can believe they already may have eighty-two "young damsels" braiding the Veil, right now! At any rate, they had best get started soon! But, perhaps the Temple will not be built *"until the time of the Gentiles be fulfilled."* This has not yet been fulfilled because the (Gentile) Supreme Muslim Council (*Al Waqf*) does, after all, still hold official jurisdiction of the Temple Mount. This, despite the fact the Israelis have regained control of Jerusalem and The Old City. Nevertheless, as we suggested earlier, maybe a Tabernacle will be erected and which also would require all those same Temple furnishings, utensils, etc. – We shall see.

Washed And Purified — At Evening

We have shown in many ways how the Red Heifer is a "type" of Jesus: pure, innocent and untainted by "the World." This type symbolism continues in this ancient and Holy drama by washing away sins ("uncleanness") via "blood and living water." In fact, as our "Red Heifer," Jesus Christ is the centerpiece of this story, which involves three characters before the burning and three characters afterward.

Earlier we identified three characters during the burning as representing:

- God – the High Priest
- The World – the priest who slays and burns the "Gift" from God.
- Jesus – The Gift; i.e., the Red Heifer.

We "pictured" the burning as The Resurrection — with nothing but ashes (the Gospel) remaining in the Empty Tomb (as a "clean place").

After The Resurrection (burning), there are again three characters to behold:

- He that watcheth — God, watching the World "consume" His Gift.
- He that burneth — The ungrateful World, which "knew Him not."
- He that gathereth — The Church, that now harvests the "ashes."

Hey! That's Us!

More of this picture can be seen in Numbers 19:9 where "he that gathereth" is a man who is ritually "clean." Nevertheless, despite his having been "clean" *before* he collected the ashes, this man now is not clean enough to enter the camp and mingle with "the congregation" after he has participated in this Holy ceremony. (Verse 10) No, he must now wash his clothes and *"be unclean until the even,"* just as will all the other participants we have discussed in this Holy rite.

Then, at evening he may return to the camp as a "clean" member of the congregation. Apparently, "the man who was clean" became "unclean" as a result of having handled the ashes of the dead Heifer. This is both disturbing and puzzling, because we have seen this man as a "type" of the Church, comprised of the faithful saints of Jesus Christ. Maybe the message here is that ALL Believers, no matter how righteous or "clean" we appear, are after all still unclean with sin even as we "harvest" in His Holy Name and for His Purpose.

It would follow that we would then become "clean" at "The Evening of the Age" – i.e., at Christ's Coming. This is reasoned on basis that at that time we will have our new, Glorified, Pure, "Clean" bodies. But again, as with King Solomon, we must concede that we cannot be absolutely certain that we have a complete understanding of this picture of types. The Lord has retained some of His Mystery in this drama that will be revealed to us later.

Now, I know some of those of "the Church" are going to be really taken aback by any suggestion that they are not really "clean" right now! After all, they have been washed in the blood of Jesus. —But, please stay with me.

Yes, this man is a type of the Church; however, this concept which considers Believers as sinful; i.e., "unclean," will disturb folks who believe they have no sin now since they were washed with the blood of Jesus. But we are at present only ritually clean as a result of having accepted His righteousness and having been washed (baptized) in His Holy Name, only *ritually* clean. Of course, we *will* be washed clean ("without spot") when we meet His Father — in the "Evening" of this Age! – So, until then — while we are yet in this sinful world, we Christians also are tainted by sin. The Apostle John said it best in I John 1:8,

"If we say that we have no sin, we deceive ourselves, and the truth is not in us."

Also, many unbelievers are mistaken in the belief that Christians profess "purity;" and then they use our faults to condemn us and our faith. I admire that bumper sticker that reads:

Christians are not Perfect – just Forgiven!

Yes, if we repent of our sins, Jesus will wash all of us clean, "without spot" — at evening. However, in the meantime we must continue to "gather the ashes" and remain "outside the camp" and we are actually "unclean" until the "evening." We of the Church are now ritually clean, but we won't be totally clean "until even," when we throw off this corruptible carcass and exchange it for that which is incorruptible. And all "in the twinkling of an eye!" (From I Corinthians 15:51 – 54)

Further description of the Church is implied in that this man who is clean shall lay up the ashes *"without the camp in clean place."* This may refer to the Church as it takes its stand in a position of righteousness (a "clean place") before the World ("without the camp") while upholding and delivering the Gospel (ashes) of Jesus Christ.

Returning to Verse 9: *"... it is a purification for sin."* The Church leads the World to the Gospel that they may have "a purification for sin." Yes! We gather the "ashes" (Gospel) of Jesus and "sprinkle" (witness) with "living water" (our faith and our "walk") to demonstrate and Glorify His purifying, saving, Grace-donated sacrifice that paid for ALL sin for ALL men for ALL Time. So, we must now continue to "sprinkle" His "ashes" mixed with "living water" faith (keep it flowing!) to help others to become clean at **EVENING!** – When He comes!

At the same time we must remember that even we who "sprinkle," are "unclean until even." (Numbers 19:21) Therefore, we are not ourselves yet really "squeaky clean;" and we must remember also to do our "sprinkling," not as a haughty cedar, but as a lowly but Holy three-branched, triple-budded, common, ordinary, humble, no-name hyssop weed. (This, beloved, is the toughest part!)

Earlier, in our second chapter, we explained several "pictures" of the Gospel as portrayed in the ceremony of the Red Heifer in Numbers 19. However, we stopped after the cleansing and the return to the camp at evening, by "the man who gathered the ashes." (Numbers 19:10). Moreover, we identified Joseph of Arimathaea and "the church" as types representing this "clean" man.

At this point we must examine the picture that symbolizes those who perform the purification rite by sprinkling "living water" with the ashes and hyssop. (Numbers 19:11 – 19) A subtle and beautiful picture is revealed in these verses; however, it is rather complex. We shall therefore simplify briefly here for consideration and thought, beginning with Verse 11 –

"He that toucheth the dead body of any man shall be unclean seven days.

This may depict the fact that man is in a sinful world, represented as death. Man will be in that World and exposed to its sinful dominion for seven thousand years – seven "days."

Continuing, we come to Verses 18-19 –

"And a clean person shall take hyssop, and dip it in the water, and sprinkle it upon the tent, and upon all the vessels, and upon the persons that were there, and upon him that toucheth a bone, or one slain, or one dead, or a grave:

And the clean person shall sprinkle upon the unclean on the third day and on the seventh day: And on the seventh day he shall purify himself, and wash his clothes, and bathe himself in water, and shall be clean at even."

This picture presents a formula of sorts that deals with *"three days"* and with *"seven days."* These periods suggest a link with the prophetic scenario that was presented in Chapter 6. Here, you can almost guess what is coming. The third day could refer to the time of Messiah's appearance, which at about 4000 years after Adam, was at the end of the *third* "day" (after Adam) and the start of the *fourth* "day." Further, Jesus was raised from the Tomb on the third day; and upon this the entire Gospel rests. Then, as we noted earlier, the seventh day signified the Kingdom Age (or Millennium) when Jesus will rule the Earth for 1000 years; i.e., The Lord's Day.

Verse 11 states that any person who touches a dead body *"shall be unclean seven days."* This may be a picture of man's fall into sin through Adam and the 6000 years (six "days") in which man shall live with sin (shall be "unclean"). Then, in the beginning of the seventh day (the Kingdom Age, man shall be without sin; i.e., "clean"

We must point out a Jewish custom here that is well known to scholars of prophecy. The Jewish Law counts any *part* of a day as an *entire day*. This custom is illustrated in detail by an example from *Talmud — Megillah* 20a. (Now, you know where they got the expression:

"*the whole Megillah!*") Here it is explained, from a commentary by the noted Jewish scholar, Maimonides, that daylight begins (in Mosaic Law) 1 1/5 hours before sunrise, as the first streaks of light appear on the eastern horizon.

This same measure is stated in Pesahim 4a, which declares: "...is observed for one day only; *and part of the day is as the whole of it.*" These passages then state that when something must be accomplished on a given day, if it is done after daylight "it counts as done"; i.e., it is considered as having been accomplished *during the complete day that is dawning.* This principle becomes critically important as we continue.

Verse 12 emphasizes that the "unclean" person must purify himself (i.e., have himself sprinkled with the ashes) on the *third* day and on the *seventh* day after contact with any remains of the dead. The remaining details are presented in Verses 16 through 22. Rightly, Verse 18 instructs that the sprinkling must be done by "a clean person."

The picture of purification ("sprinkling") on the third day would of course reflect from the "washing" of all Believers through their faith, won as a result of the Resurrection of Jesus at dawn on "the third day." (Mark 16:9) The further sprinkling on the seventh "day" may refer to our final purification, which occurs at the "dawn" of the seventh day, the Kingdom Age or what Judaism refers to as the Messianic Age. At that time and on the occasion of the Rapture of the Church, we will receive our "purified" bodies—"*we shall be like Him.*" (From I John 3:2)

The emphasis noted in Verse 12 was the key "day", which was the *third* day. Even if he is "sprinkled" on the seventh day, nobody will be rendered "clean," unless he also was "sprinkled" previously on the third day. This Law therefore is reflected in a somewhat complex "picture" by the fact that Jesus overcame sin ("sprinkled" us) for our Purification; at the end of the third "day" after Adams death. Here a "day" is 1000 years. Adam died after having lived almost 1000 years. (Genesis 5:5) Jesus died and was Resurrected about 2000 years (two "days") later.

The sequence of requiring this sprinkling *before* the seventh day testifies that without Purification accomplished on that "third day" through Messiah (Christ Jesus), one cannot become "clean" before The Father. This means that one must repent of his sins and must believe in and longingly, eagerly(!) wait for Messiah. Just as important, they also must love Him, must obey Him, must be "sprinkled" by His "ashes" – which were "raised up" on the third day in order that each of us may become a purified, new person at His Second Coming — at the dawn of the seventh day (6000 years) after Adam. – The Kingdom Age. This will be the "evening" of man's dominion on Earth – when all is at Peace – "*at even.*"

Continuing in Verse 19, the "clean person who "sprinkles" the unclean must: "*wash his clothes, bathe himself in water, and he shall be clean at even.*" Now, he has just sprinkled "the unclean" during the *seventh* day. He therefore must purify himself by bathing, etc. in order to become clean "at even" of the seventh day; whereas, those whom he sprinkled could have been purified as early as dawn that *same* day.

Throughout the discussion, we have identified the "clean man" as Christ's Church, and surely Christ dwells within those who truly comprise "the Church." This therefore could be the picture of the Lord Jesus and His Church at the end of the Kingdom Age ("evening"), on the seventh day after Adam, when "the unclean" and all *"death and hell were cast into the lake of fire."* (Revelation 20:13 – 15) Jesus then "washes" Himself and the Church by ridding ALL of His Creation from ALL sin. Now then, *everybody* is "clean."— Pure, forever! – HALLELUJAH !!!

Notice the beautiful symmetry we have reached at this point. At the beginning of this drama, even though He was Himself "unclean," the High Priest (God) was the *only* One who was permitted to return to the camp (Heaven) after the burning of the Red Heifer (Jesus). This is a reflection of the fact that God returned to Heaven after the sacrifice of the Son, Jesus. Now, after all is complete at the close of the drama, the One who served as our Red Heifer is also our High Priest (Jesus) and He is the *only* One who remains to be purified. In other words, Jesus will not feel "clean" until the last sin has been cast into Hell. Jesus will wait until every soul has chosen either to be washed by His blood in order to be accepted as "clean" or to not accept His washing and instead to be "cast into the lake of fire" – to be burned as leaven.

There is another symmetry reflected at the beginning of the drama in the fact that Jesus, as our Red Heifer, took on our sin and was cast into the "fire" as He was borne on The Cross at the summit of the Mount of Olives. This is again a reflection of the burning of the Red Heifers and the Sin Offerings, etc. on the *Miphkad* Altar at *Olivet* Summit. Then, at evening of the seventh "day," The Heifer (Jesus) now throws sin into the fire. — A fire that will never be put out. — IT IS FINISHED!!

If we now assume that the Red Heifers and the Sin Offerings represent sin and consider that Jesus took on our sin when He was thrown into the "fire," watch what happens. Jesus, at "evening" of the seventh day, takes the role of:

- *The High Priest* — as He brings an unblemished, Perfect sacrifice (the Heifer) to be destroyed by fire as He "throws" His own Power (cedarwood) and Humility (hyssop) and Blood (crimson wool) into the fire to be consumed with His own Pure body bearing our sins. Symbolically, as He is nailed to The Cross, He "sprinkles" His own Holy Blood seven times toward the Veil before His Father's House as the spikes pierce His flesh.

- *The Other Priest* — as He offers ("slays") Himself by intentionally incurring the self-righteous wrath of the unbelieving Priesthood as He treads across "palm branches" to "kindle" their zeal to have Him put to death. He presents Himself, Innocent, to be slain by the World.

- *The "Clean Man"* — as He "gathers" His Victory over sin proclaimed in The Gospel (the ashes of the consumed Heifer) and places it in His Church ("a clean place") from where He then "sprinkles" (preaches), using His Humility (hyssop) and His Faith ("Living Water") through His Church to the World in order that they may have "a purification for sin."

Then, His Victory is complete. And yet, His Humility also is complete. Jesus has played ALL of the roles in this drama, including the very lowliest role, as the Red Heifer. He waits now until all of His little ones are "clean" before He (The Victor, Himself!) becomes "clean." This has to be what could be called "Super Humility!" His Humility is Constant and Infinite. His Completeness is Constant and Infinite. His Mercy is Constant and Infinite. Jesus IS Infinity! — God IS Infinity! – Infinity IS God! — Jesus IS God! – There IS no other!

Standing-tall, but Bowing-low

There is a sermon of sorts in the symbolism of the Red Heifer ceremony that we wish to share with you. Since that rite and the *Miphkad Altar* figure so prominently in the *Shekhinah* story, it seems fitting that we should present it here.

We are drawn in this theme to the cedar tree and the hyssop plant, used in the ceremony for the burning. In Jewish tradition, the cedar of Lebanon, stately and tall, is often a symbol of haughtiness, while the hyssop, in contrast, is a symbol of humility. (See Reference 16.) These two opposite "pictures" provide a message.

When men or nations begin regarding their own "stature" and "tallness," God usually causes them to be "brought low" in order that they may again become more like the hyssop — lowly, plain, lacking "color" and inconspicuous. "Tallness" and "stature" are especially regarded as "wicked" in God's eyes when we attribute our "comeliness" and our "sheen" and "image" to our own creation rather than by His Grace and to His Purpose.

When we begin "preening" (individually or as nations) before our peers and then solicit and/or savor men's lauding of our *own* "magnificence," we surely are provoking the Lord to chasten us and to bring us back down to earth.

We must then be reminded that we are ALL a part of His Creation. ALL are created for His Purpose — and "increased" only through His Hand — certainly not by our *own* puny and ill-guided efforts. When we begin to say, "I AM what I AM because of what I AM!," we are "tempting" God to diminish the increase that He alone has given us.

In the past few decades, as well as throughout the Bible and all of history, there are many examples of "kings" and nations who have been "brought low" as the hyssop. We need not mention names. I am sure you can think of some (nations and "kings") who have been in the headlines as recently as yesterday.

We also must notice that some of these same "kings" and nations have been "brought back" from their lowly estate as the hyssop, to rise again to become "tall and stately" once more. And then, if they do not become too haughty and begin "preening" again, the Lord may permit them to remain "tall," *if* they also regard and obey Him.

God presents some learning examples for us through His messenger, Zephaniah 3 (NASB):

His warnings:

(Verses 1 & 2) Woe to her who is rebellious and defiled, The tyrannical city! She heeded no voice; She accepted no instruction. She did not trust in the Lord; She did not draw near to her God.

His "Rod":

(Verse 6) I have cut off nations; Their corner towers are in ruins I have made their streets desolate, With no one passing by; Their cities are laid waste, Without a man, without an inhabitant.

His Healing:

(Verses 11–13) ...and you will never again be haughty;

On My holy mountain.

But I will leave among you

A humble and lowly people,

And they will take refuge

In the name of the Lord.

...For they shall feed and lie down

With no one to make them tremble.

Jesus also gave us a similar but brief instruction on this theme:

"For everyone who exalts himself will be humbled, and he who humbles himself will be exalted." Luke 14:11 (NASB)

Can we possibly comprehend or appreciate the humility of Jesus, who IS God, as He approached the Temple where His Divine Presence also dwelt? Here He stood in debate with the doubting Pharisees, who were unaware they were actually scheming to trap the Great "I AM" concerning the Law that *He* had written! No *ordinary* man could have resisted the urge to quip, "Shall I ask My Father to come out and convince you?"

Learning from these examples, we should pray that He would give us strength to "stand tall" like the mighty cedar — resisting the worldly "winds" of temptation, "modern change," conformity, and "lusts." We should "stand tall" in our faith against these worldly rages in order that we demonstrate (witness) our strength in our Lord before "the world."

Further, we should pray that He would show us how to remain humble as the lowly hyssop concerning our "increase" brought about by His Heavenly "winds" of Wisdom, Grace, and Strength. Pray also that we would not become a "haughty" cedar, showing pride before the eyes of men. Pray we remember that before God we are merely hyssops. HE is the Cedar.

Our best example is the Lord Jesus. He is our tall and stately Cedar, although His stance is as the hyssop. Only Jesus is worthy to stand tall. He is justified to haughtiness, but He is not.

* * * Jesus bows at our feet that we may worship Him. * * *

"Worthy is The Heifer!"

We have drawn much from Jewish tradition in this study. I was particularly moved upon first learning of the Jewish belief in the power of blood to overcome death. Although he conceded that even his wisdom could not decipher the meaning of the Red Heifer ceremony, I certainly am not even in the same league as *Shlomo ben David* (King Solomon). Nevertheless, I believe there are at least a few facets of the Red Heifer burning that are understandable to a mere man when we consider that burning as a "picture" representing the Gospel of the Lord Jesus Christ. It is my prayer that readers will also share this understanding and will agree with at least a few of these "pictures."

Appendix E presents some detailed interpretations of these pictures that are too intricate and too complex to be included with the main story. Earlier we stated that some Evangelical Christian authorities decline to agree that the Red Heifer ceremony is a "picture" of Jesus Christ as Messiah or even that it has anything in connection with Jesus. Having seen the various features of the Law for the Red Heifer, readers can now observe for themselves whether those critics have a convincing argument. We propose a New Testament verse, which with very brief examination, testifies that the Red Heifer is a legitimate type of Christ. Hear now what is said in II Corinthians 5:21 –

> *"He made Him who knew no sin to be sin on our behalf, that we might become the righteousness of God in Him."*

Like the pure and unblemished Red Heifer, Jesus actually became our sin, notwithstanding the fact that He was certainly pure and without sin. Again, like the Blood of Jesus purifies us – even sinful as we are – the Heifer's blood (ashes) purifies those who are "unclean." What should be obvious to all is nevertheless hidden from those who are blind.

Nowhere is Jesus' Blood Redemption compared more profoundly with that of the Red Heifer than in Hebrews 9:12 – 15 –

> *"Neither by the blood of goats and calves, but by his own blood he entered in once into the holy place, having obtained eternal redemption for us.*
>
> *For if the blood of bulls and of goats, and the ashes of an heifer sprinkling the unclean, sanctifieth to the purifying of the flesh:*
>
> *How much more shall the blood of Christ, who through the eternal Spirit offered himself without spot to God, purge your conscience from dead works to serve the living God?*
>
> *And for this cause he is the mediator of the new testament, that by means of death, for the redemption of the transgressions that were under the first testament, they which are called might receive the promise of eternal inheritance."*

Another example is presented in the commentary in *Midrash Rabbah* Exodus 17:2 where King Solomon is quoted in a profound observation that is pertinent to our subject. Solomon says the regal cedar tree and the lowly hyssop plant are equal in the sight of God. This most learned man and noted regent of Israel observed that the hyssop was used in many of Israel's most holy rites. In the Red Heifer offering, the stately and powerful cedar and the meek and lowly, homely hyssop are of equal importance.

King Solomon remarked that the humble hyssop was used to smear the lambs' blood on the doorposts during that first Passover night when God redeemed Israel. Citing that event, the noble monarch proclaimed: "He performeth miracles with the smallest things, and through the hyssop which is the smallest of trees, did He redeem Israel." Solomon therefore observed that each plant was of equal importance to God. On basis of these thoughts Solomon declared that these two plants of totally opposite "status" are used "to teach you that the small and the great are equal in the sight of God."

King Solomon implies that it is precisely because of its lowly status that the Lord chose to instruct His People to use this humble weed in several of His more important rituals. Specifically, these are: smearing of the Paschal Lamb's blood on the doorposts to preserve from death Israel's firstborn; the Red Heifer ceremony; the cleansing of lepers.

Of course we realize that all this "*Talmudic* trivia" and "Law" is very rigid and complex. However, this Law was contracted between Israel and Almighty God; and when we strike a bargain with Him, *it is forever!* – No turning back, and no refunds!

He has offered all of us the best bargain anyone will ever see! — EVER!!! Jesus is that "Bargain." He is yours just for the asking, if only you will believe that He **IS** Messiah. No "hassle" over price! (It's already been paid!) – No "deposit." – No "return." – You get to keep everything He has ever given you ... forever! – No "payments." – Absolutely "nothing to buy." – No "credit references." – FREE "Deliverance," too! – And this is not one of those "limited offers," folks. – Everyone is invited! Your only obligations are to Love Him and to live for His Purpose and to accept His Love. – And, besides all this, His Father still backs it with a "Written Warranty" stating that His entire contract with you is "Guaranteed" – Yes! – **F0REVER!!!** ... Such a Deal! ... What a Salesman! – HOW could you resist?! ...You have only to believe and invite Him into your life ... But you do have to believe and invite Him. – And, listen ... He will continue to make this offer to any and ALL Faithful "customers" until "Closing Time!" – And you needn't be concerned about the familiar clause: "Only while the supply lasts." — This supply will last ... You guessed it! — **FOR EVER!!!** – And folks, don't forget — a special Bonus Gift is awaiting all of you who act **RIGHT NOW** to accept His Generous Offer. (See II Timothy 4:8)

Well, OK — there is just one "catch." – Just as we sing in that well-known hymn, "I Surrender All" – You must surrender *everything you want* in this World, so you can let Jesus give you *everything you need* in this World. Then, at "Evening," He will give you *everything He has* in the World to come — riches beyond your wildest dreams! And, your odds for becoming an Eternal Winner in this Divine Sweepstakes are ONE to one, between Jesus and you. You just have to LET Him make you a Winner. Now, the choice is up to you. (And again, NO PURCHASE IS NECESSARY!) You don't have to DO anything but believe and invite Him.— BUT, if you persist with your hesitance, doubt and "sales resistance;" if you just won't accept His offer of His Eternal and Infinite Love for you, then He will also reject you on that "Final Day of the Sale" (Closing Time). He has Promised His "Steady Customers" an even Better(!) Deal at His New Store in The Very Best Part of Town. If you continue to delay and then later try to call Him after Closing Time, you will just hear a recorded message:

"Sorry, that number has been disconnected."...

You will then be – as He says in Exodus 14:13 – *"No more forever!"*

This is why you must learn to love the Lord (and your Neighbor!) right now. You must learn to accept and adore His Son's sacrifice. Jesus Christ is your "Red Heifer." Only through His death, Resurrection and Grace can you have "a purification for (your) sin." Jesus already loves you! He even died for you! So, P L E A S E ! Love Him N O W, before it is too late. (It's already much later than you think!)

We have referenced much from the Judaic work, the *Babylonian Talmud*, in our discussion of Jesus and the Law. A comforting note for "new" Believers is presented in *Berakoth* 34b, quoting from Isaiah 57:19, *"...Peace, peace to him that was far and to him that is near ..."* The Rabbis hold "him that *was* far (from the Lord, that is)" in highest esteem because of their interpretation of this Scripture. The person who has returned to a life of penitence after having been a "backslider" is known as a *ba'alei tshuvah*. It is said that a wholly righteous person "cannot stand" in a place where a penitent Jew, a *ba'alei tshuvah* stands. *Talmud* points out that, since "him that was far" is mentioned first, the Lord has an increased Joy toward that person who at first was "far" from penitence; i.e., who had been non-religious and has later in life come close to The Creator. The person who has always been "near" has had less to overcome, since he has been penitent and observant all his life.

Rabbi Joseph Telushkin[39] presents an example in which many a *ba'alei tshuvah* has confided to him that he truly suffers the loss of savoring lobster and shrimp. On the other hand, however, persons who were "near" have been brought up in strictly observant *kosher* homes and therefore never experience any sense of deprivation. They are never tempted; whereas, those who formerly had been "far" must now overcome the temptations again to be "far."

This story should once again remind us that our Lord, same as the Red Heifer, was valued at a very high price. His sacrifice, "burning" and "ashes" are not to be ignored. The ashes of the Red Heifer are not to be ignored either; because of their symbolism mirroring the Lord Jesus and because of their importance concerning His Coming Again. When we see Him, we will say: "Worthy is The Lamb!" – I wonder if we may also say: *"Worthy is The Heifer!"*

Meanwhile as we wait, Believers must be watchful, eager, prayerful, excited, but obedient! We should be waiting as a bride waits – with her "lamp trimmed." We should be submissive as a bride and humble as a hyssop.

"Even so, come Lord Jesus."

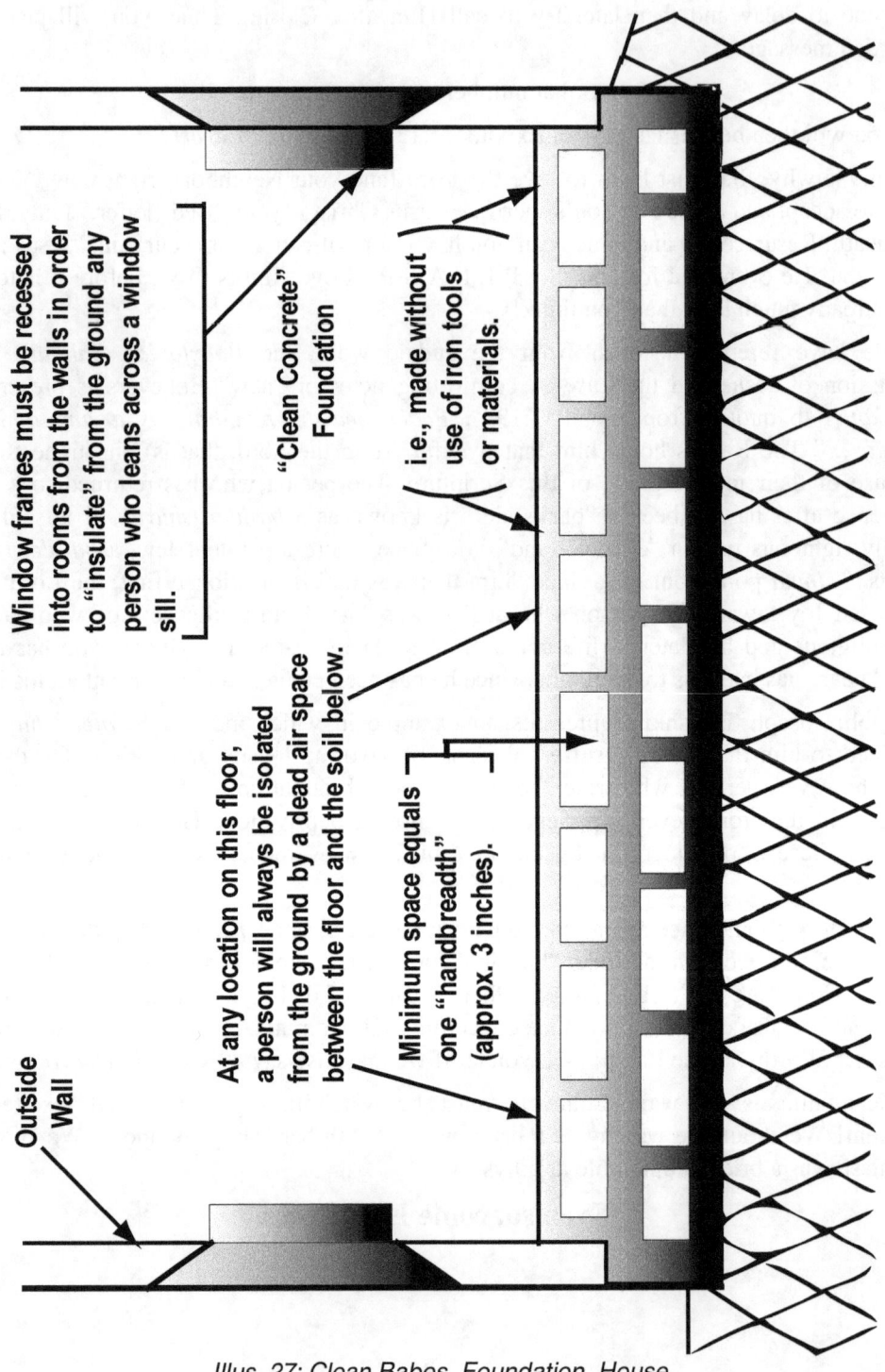

Illus. 27: Clean Babes, Foundation, House

References and Bibliography for: The Red Heifer

(References are noted as superscripts in the text)

1. *Halley's Bible Handbook** – Twenty Fourth Edition, pg. 532 — Zondervan Publishing House, Grand Rapids MI 49506 – May 1976

2. *The Babylonian Talmud** – Quincentenary Edition, The Soncino Press, Limited, 123 Ditmas Ave., Brooklyn NY 11218 — 1978

3. *Midrash* Rabbah*, The Soncino Press, Lt'd., 123 Ditmas Ave., Brooklyn NY 11218 —1978

4. *The Works of Josephus** – New Updated Edition, (Translated by William Whiston, A.M.), Hendrickson Publishers, Peabody MA 01961 — 1987

5. *The Fire And The Cloud* – Revised and Updated Edition, Robert F. Reiland, Xlibris Corp., Philadelphia PA – 2003

6. *The Temple Scroll** – Yadin, Yigael, Biblical Archaeology Review, Biblical Archaeology Society, 4710 – 41st Street NW, Washington DC 20016 — Sep/Oct 1984

7. "Where the Ancient Temple of Jerusalem Stood"*– Kaufman, Asher S., Biblical Archaeology Review, Biblical Archaeology Society, 4710 – 41st Street NW, Washington DC 20016— Mar/Apr 1983

8. *Encyclopedia Judaica** – Keter, Inc., 4400 Park Avenue South, New York NY 10016 — 1972

9. *Secrets of Golgotha* – Martin, Ernest L., Academy For Scriptural Knowledge, P.O. Box 25000, Portland OR 97225 — 1988

10. *The Companion Bible** – Kregel Publications, Division of Kregel, Inc. P.O. Box 2607, Grand Rapids MI 49501 — 1990

11. *The Proof of the Gospel* – Eusebius, (Ed. and translated by W. J. Ferrar), Book VI, Chapter 18 —— Baker Book House, Grand Rapids, MI 49506 — 1981

12. *The Interlinear Greek—English New Testament* – Berry, George R., Zondervan Publishing House, Grand Rapids, MI 49506 — 1976

13. *Manners And Customs Of The Bible* – Freeman, Rev. James M. – Logos International, Plainfield, NJ — 1972

14. *Harper's Bible Dictionary* – Achtemeier, Paul J. (Editor), Harper & Row, Publishers, San Francisco CA — 1985

15. *The New Strong's Exhaustive Concordance Of The Bible** – Strong, James, Thomas Nelson Publishers, Nashville TN — 1990

16. *New Edition of the Babylonian Talmud** – Michael L. Rodkinson (Editor), The *Talmud* Society, Boston MA — 1918

17. "The Garden Tomb – Was Jesus Buried There?" – Barkay, Gabriel, , Biblical Archaeology Review, Biblical Archaeology Society, 4710 – 41st Street NW, Washington DC 20016 — Mar/Apr 1986

18. *The Encyclopedia Americana* – Americana Corporation, New York NY – 1955

19. *The Koran** — (Translation by J. M. Rodwell — Published by: Everyman's Library, Distributed by: Dutton, New York NY — 1978

20. *Laws and Customs of Israel* – Published by: Shapiro, Valentine and Co., 81 Wentworth Street, London, England — 1949

21. *Burial Cave of the Caiaphas Family** – Greenhut, Zvi, – Biblical Archaeology Review, Biblical Archaeology Society, 4710 – 41st Street NW, Washington DC 20016— Sep/Oct 1992

22. *Holy Bible — From the Ancient Eastern Text** – Translated from the Aramaic of the *Peshitta* – George M., Lamsa, – Harper & Row, Publishers, San Francisco CA — 1984

23. "The Tombs of Silwan" – Shanks, Hershel – Biblical Archaeology Review, Biblical Archaeology Society, 4710 – 41st Street NW, Washington DC 20016 — May/Jun 1994

24. "Earthquakes in Jerusalem and the Mount of Olives Landslide" P. 119 – Levitte, D. & Wachs, D., – Israel — Land and Nature, Vol. 9, No. 3 — Spring 1984

25. *The Pentateuch and HafTorahs* – Hertz, Dr. J. H. (Compiling Editor) – 2nd Edition – Soncino Press, London — 1965

26. *The Torah — A Modern Commentary* —The Union of American Hebrew Congregations — New York NY — 1981

27. "Locating the Original Temple Mount"*– Ritmeyer, Dr. Leen, Biblical Archaeology Review, Biblical Archaeology Society, 4710 – 41st Street NW, Washington DC 20016 – March/April 1992

28. "The Ark of the Covenant: Where It Stood in Solomon's Temple"* – Ritmeyer, Dr. Leen, – Biblical Archaeology Review, Biblical Archaeology Society, 4710 – 41st Street NW, Washington DC 20016 – March/April

29. *The New Yorker* – Wright, Lawrence — pp. 42—53 – July 20 1998

30. "Sacred Geometry — Part 1" – Jacobson, Dr. David, – Biblical Archaeology Review, Biblical Archaeology Society, 4710 – 41st Street NW, Washington DC 20016— July/August 1999

31. "Sacred Geometry — Part 2" – Jacobson, Dr. David, – Biblical Archaeology Review, Biblical Archaeology Society, 4710 – 41st Street NW, Washington DC 20016– Sept/Oct 1999

32. "Earthquakes in Jerusalem and the Mount of Olives Landslide" P. 120 – Levitte, Dov and Wachs, Daniel – Israel Land and Nature, Vol. 9 No. 3 – Spring 1984

33. Researcher – Vendyl Jones Research Institutes – P.O. Box 120366 – Arlington TX 76012-0366 – September 2002

34. *The Chumash – The Stone Edition* – Sixth Edition – Compiling Ed. Rabbi Nosson Scherman – Mesorah Publications, Lt'd. – Brooklyn NY – 1996

35. *The Online Bible CD-ROM** – Cross Country Software – Niagara Falls NY – 2003

36. *The Soncino Talmud CD-ROM** – *Davka* Corporation – Chicago IL – 2002

37. *The Soncino Midrash CD-ROM** – *Davka* Corporation – Chicago IL – 2002

38. *1999 Smith's Revised Bible Dictionary* – on The Online Bible CD-ROM[35]

39. *Jewish Literacy* – Rabbi Joseph Telushkin – Wm. Morrow & Co., Inc. – New York NY – 1991

40. *The Guide to the Perplexed – Moses Maimonides*, translated by Shlomo Pines – University of Chicago Press – Chicago IL – 1963

41. *Messiah of the Winepress* – Christ and the Red Heifer – Karen Boren – Beit *Parah* Publishing – Provo UT 84603-0676 – 2002

42. *The Jewish Book of Why*, Vol. I, pp. 55 – Alfred J. *Kolatch* – Johnathan David Publishers, Inc. – Middle Village, NY – 1997

43. *Code of Jewish Law* – (Kitzur Schulchan Aruch) – A Compilation of Jewish Laws and Customs – Chap. CXCIX:2 – R. Solomon Ganzfried – Translated by H. E. Goldin – Hebrew Publishing Company – New York NY – 1927

44. *The Holy Scriptures* – The Jewish Publication Society of America – New York NY –1916

45. "How Solid is the Temple Mount?" – Michael Shurkin – Biblical Archaeology Review, Biblical Archaeology Society, 4710 – 41st Street NW, Wash. DC 20016 — Jul/Aug 2004

46. *The Temple that Jerusalem Forgot* – Ernest L. Martin – Academy for Scriptural Knowledge Publications – 2000

47. *The Temple Mount – Where Is The Holy of Holies?* – Kaufman, Asher S. – Har Ye'ra'eh Press – Jerusalem – 2004 – Distributed by: RUBIN MASS, Ltd – P.O. Box 91009 – Jerusalem 91009 Israel

48. *The Jewish Encyclopedia* – Isadore Singer, Ph. D., Managing Editor – Funk and Wagnalls Company – New York and London – 1910

49. *The Temple Menorah – Where is it?* – Steven Fine – Biblical Archaeology Review, Biblical Archaeology Society, 4710 – 41st Street NW, Wash. DC 20016 — Jul/Aug 2004

50. *The Rugged Beauty of Crusader Castles* – Adrian Boas – Biblical Archaeology Review, Biblical Archaeology Society, 4710 – 41st Street NW, Wash. DC 20016 — Jan/Feb 2006

51. Newsletter from The Temple Institute – Rabbi Chaim Richman – 24 Misgav Ladach St. – Jewish Quarter 97500, Jerusalem, Israel – temple@temple.org.il – www.temple.org.il – 19 September 2005

* – CD-ROM's with various translations of the Bible, *Talmud*, *Midrash* and other Judaica as well as the *Quran* and many other articles are available from various software firms and on the Internet.

Part VI – Hidden Gospel Mysteries

19

Secrets Hidden in The Passover

Seder symbolism explained – Matzahs shape clues – Star of David "invented" – Messiah "hidden" in Seder – The place settings – Afikoman a "picture" of Messiah

Several secrets have been hidden from the Jewish people during the past several centuries; actually, since the Middle Ages. In this part of the book, we shall uncover these secrets principally by means of this author having "de-coded" an ancient *Haggadah* (Passover instruction handbook) discovered by a beloved Rabbi several years ago in Europe.

More secrets are revealed through the author's research of literally dozens of *Haggadoth* from Judaica libraries. It should come as no surprise that several more secrets are revealed through careful study of Scripture, both from the Old Testament as well as the New Testament.

It is hoped that many new ideas will be inspired both for Christians and for Jewish people concerning the Passover *Seder* and how it should be viewed by both Faiths, having this new knowledge. Since it is a fairly complicated story, several sketches are provided to illustrate details and to assist in following the narrative.

Introduction

We are going to study the Jewish Passover, with primary emphasis on the details of the Passover evening meal, the *Seder*, about which most Christians are sadly uninformed. The sadness is brought about by the fact that we have missed much of the Glory of God's beautiful plan of Salvation because we have not seen the drama of this spectacular "picture" of Christ. In most recent years, more and more Christians, however, have been participating in Christian sponsored Passover ceremonies, *Seders*, and have been gaining greatly increased knowledge of the Passover compared with awareness of previous generations of Christians for this Jewish Holy day.

However, we can have even more appreciation for this Holy rite if we study the Law in order to reveal signs in this holiday that point directly to Jesus as Messiah, but which tragically have been hidden from the Jewish people. Sad to say, most Christians are also unaware of these things simply because they are not familiar with Judaism and the Jewish Law that Jesus "Lived."

Most Jewish people who observe Passover and *Yom Kippur* (Day of Atonement) do so with even more fervor than most Christians exhibit at Christmas and Easter. Jewish families have an even older tradition than Christians can claim. (3500 years vs. 1900 years) Still, Jewish Passover celebrants have maintained and preserved *almost all* of the statutes and rituals of that feast throughout all of those 3500 years.

We encountered, however, at least one statute that has been omitted since cessation of Temple worship. Earlier, in Chapter 13, we learned that the Red Heifer Ceremony is detailed in *Midrash Rabbah* Exodus 19:2, where it was stated:

> "...those who would eat the Passover must be purified by the ashes of the Red Heifer;"

But, in order to practice the purifications with the ashes of the Red Heifer, Temple worship rites must be resumed. Therefore, since the Jewish people no longer can conduct worship at their Temple, they must be pardoned for not observing this practice at their Passover celebrations.

Regardless of this omission from the "pure" Law, the Jewish Passover meal or *Seder* (Hebrew: order) appears to outsiders as being much more dramatic and "religious" than, say, any Easter Sunday dinner or even the Holy Communion, Lord's Supper or Eucharist, which surely are inspired by that Last Passover "Supper" with Jesus and His Disciples. Christians have no celebration even minimally comparable with the Jewish *Seder*.

Moreover, each of the several Jewish denominations and nearly all members of nearly all Jewish families *worldwide(!)* observe this holiday in unison and *uniformly*, with few minor differences. Indeed, the foregoing sentence is NO exaggeration. Recent demographic surveys have discovered obscure Jewish remnants in almost every nation and continent. Jewish people have been found even in some of the principally Buddhist or Muslim countries of Asia. The Jewish remnant from Ethiopia is a well-known story. These isolated Jewish families are found to be still observing most of their Feasts and traditional holidays.

Even if they observe no other Jewish holidays, most do observe the Passover. For example, a 1996 survey[44] among Chicago area Jewish families reported that 93 percent of those surveyed observe Passover; although, only 43 percent had joined a synagogue congregation. An estimate for Israeli observance[42] states that 99 percent of the Jewish people in Israel celebrate "some kind of *Seder*." It is further remarked that 82 percent do not eat prohibited foods during that Holiday. The apparent emphasis at Passover is especially dramatized by the fact that only 79 percent of Israeli Jews "keep *kosher*" and only 44 percent fully observe *kashrut*; i.e., taking only "clean" foods.

The principal reason for Jewish uniformity in this observance is the preservation of the Hebrew *Haggadah*. (Hebrew: narration) The *Haggadah* is a booklet detailing instructions for the *Seder* and which retains most of the original stringent detail given to Moses and the People at that very first Passover in Egypt.

Importance and prestige of the *Haggadah* is established in that it has been published in the most versions, editions and printings of any book in all of Jewish history. To illustrate, consider that the research for this Part of this book, alone, was conducted through more than one-hundred English translated *Haggadoth* (plural) volumes, located in just *one* Judaica library[48] at a state university nearby. It is overwhelming to our imagination to consider just how many *Haggadoth* may exist worldwide in scores of languages.

The fact that today these *Haggadoth* are virtually unadulterated as compared to much earlier versions is especially remarkable after all those centuries of persecution, flight, scattering, torture and abuse from Gentile nations all over the Earth.

The *Haggadah* is, of course, the Jewish "instruction handbook" or "script" for conducting the Passover *Seder* meal. It directs who does what, who says or sings what, when they say it or sing it, when they eat this or that, when they do this or that, etc. To most Christians and even many Jewish people, the bigger question is **WHY?** do they do these things? Certainly, the *Haggadah* dutifully informs Jewish participants as to **WHY?** all this for some of this rite. However, many Jewish folks still do not really understand or accept any of the multiplicity of answers given by Rabbinical authorities in the myriad of *Haggadoth*. Many do not even care as to **WHY?** – They *are* Jewish! – So, they proudly and loyally declare:

"It's **TRADITION** – That's all that matters!"

At this juncture it is interesting to note the derivation of the word: "*Haggadah*." It is said[45] to be drawn from Exodus 13:8, begins: "*Ve-haggadta le-vinkha...*"

"And thou shalt tell thy son in that day, saying: 'It is because of that which the Lord did for me when I came forth out of Egypt.'"

Nevertheless, we wish to point out some very important details that may have been in the original (Exodus) *Seder* and which later must have been dropped from all known *Haggadoth* presently available. After all, *the* oldest known *Haggadah*[21] dates back only to the 14th century – a comparatively "recent" date relative to 3500 years of Judaic history. However, the "clue" that inspired this entire section came from an observation on another ancient *Haggadah* that was seen by the late Rabbi Max Stauber, who told evangelist/ archaeologist

Rev. Vendyl M. Jones[22] of what he had seen in the ancient *Haggadah*. Rev. Jones wrote of Rabbi Stauber's description, noting that the three *matzah* wafers were placed at the father's or leader's place setting in an intriguing and specific order of positioning that does not show in modern *Haggadoth* and Jewish *Seder* practice.

Unfortunately, Rev. Jones was unable to "document" his find as to the identity of R. Stauber's source or museum (or ???), an approximate printing date, etc. Please understand, therefore, this work is based on that thin reference from Rev. Jones and upon further speculation on my part as to a meaning for such *Seder* procedures. Nevertheless, we submit that there are a few more "clues" to verify this now "hidden" procedure. Further, we offer our readers the choice to decide whether our interpretation "*could* have been" as Moses originally observed the Passover or whether all this is just coincidence and/or contrived through somebody's overactive imagination. We believe that after readers review the evidence, they will reject any likelihood of mere "coincidence."

Geometric Clues

Vendyl Jones' observations from Rabbi Stauber's notes, were as follows:

- The father's place setting has the 1st (lowest) *matzah* pointing away from the father,
- The 2nd (middle) *matzah* points toward the father.
- The 3rd (upper) *matzah* points, again, away from the father.
- Jones goes on to say that initially the *matzah* wafers were triangular. Evidence of that fact shows in Jewish encyclopedias. Then, so the story goes, during the Middle Ages, Christians began telling Jewish people that the three *matzah* wafers, each having *three* points and *three* equal sides was "obviously" indicating The Holy Trinity, The Triune God – The Father, The Son (Jesus) and The Holy Spirit. This observation is based on a principle of Scriptural numerology in which "*three*" is the Divine Number, symbolic of Holiness.
- That was "Enough, already!" for the Rabbis. The Jewish Rabbinate rejects the idea of a Divine Messiah or a "Trinity" on the basis from Deuteronomy 6:4 – "...The Lord our God is *one* Lord." It therefore is not difficult to understand why they defended against this Christian Evangelizing "onslaught" by immediately and thereafter proclaiming that *any* other shape *except* triangular would be used. We see, for the last several hundred years, then, – only round or square or maybe even hexagonal *matzah*, but NO triangles! (The Rabbis declare: "We will hear no more about that "Trinity!")

Now, for the clues revealed through the logic concerning just HOW a *matzah* wafer could "point" toward any particular direction or object. Let us first consider the instruction that each wafer is to "point" in a specific direction at the *Seder* Table. Then, we should ask, "How can a round *matzah* point anywhere?!" By the way, in Judaic symbols or emblems, the circular shape is symbolic of the world.

Next we should ask, "In which direction does a square *matzah* point?" Even if a square is oriented with its sides at the diagonal, as with a diamond shape, it will "point" both toward and away from the Father.

Round or Square Pointing Which Way? <u>Triangle?</u> Yes!

On the other hand; – YES! – A triangle can be oriented such that one of the points would be "pointing" in a specific direction from the father's place at the table.

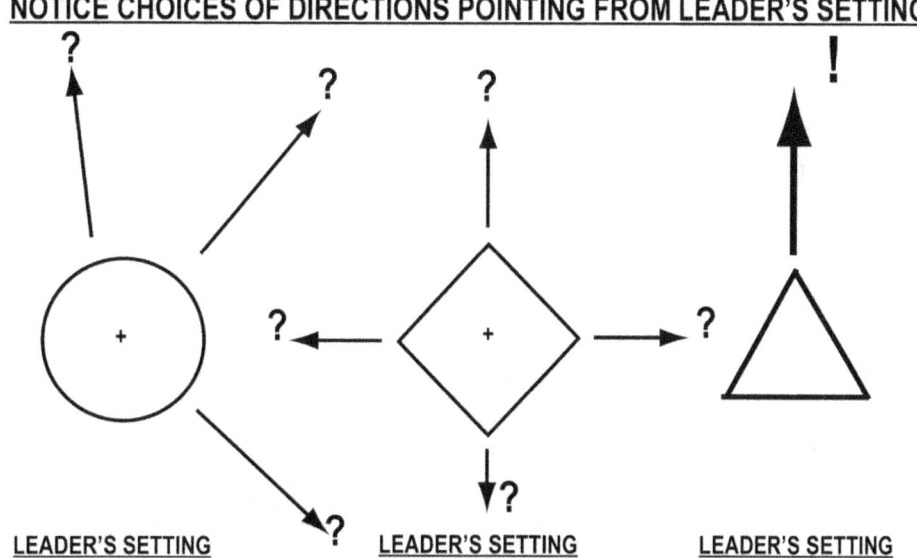

Illus. 28: Round or Square Pointing Which Way?

This is true even in the case of the "equilateral" triangle, in which all three sides are of equal length and all three "points" are enclosed by equal angles, each of 60 degrees. (See Illus. 28: Round or Square Pointing Which Way?, Page 417 above) One source[29] mentions that sketches in some *Haggadah* manuscripts from Medieval times show the *matzah* as triangular as well as in other forms.

God (perhaps scratching images in the sand or even engraved upon a stone!) must have actually shown Moses how they were to make the unleavened bread for that first Passover; although, no details are presented in the *Torah* Scripture, God must have directed Moses to make triangles with equal sides. And, God must have said something like:

"Make the cakes like this, with three equal sides. Punch little holes in the dough, like this and bake them on a grate.

And, I want each house to bake three matzah cakes of that sort; and the leader of their supper shall stack the cakes at his place at the table, like this, etc., etc."

Somebody, presumably God, must have given Moses these detailed instructions that the Jewish people have followed very closely for literally a few thousands of years. It is doubtful that they would have been so faithful and diligent in keeping the Passover traditions if some patriarch (even Moses) had merely "invented" these details.

Illus. 29: Corruption of Seder Matzah Symbolism, Page 444, shows the change of traditional *matzah* shapes over the centuries, finally reaching the square *matzah* we buy today from supermarket shelves. It is easily understood how square sheets would be more efficient than triangular dough sheets in modern bakery machinery, shipping logistics, etc.. Nevertheless, it is sad to consider the loss of the beautiful symbolism we later shall see provided by the triangular *matzah*. Moreover, the sadness is magnified when we realize how much Jewish people miss by not being able (or "willing") to see the pictures that Christians are enabled to see in this.

Still, let us inquire: "What specific clue might lead us to believe the *matzah* was originally triangular?" A clue of subtle reference is recorded in well-known Jewish encyclopedias, referring to the ancient customs of the *Seder*. They casually mention only that in Europe during the Middle Ages, "various" *matzah* shapes were used, *including triangular!* We offer, therefore, that the triangular *matzah* was in fact used during the Middle Ages when Christianity (and "the Church") began to grow strong in Europe. Christians saw immediately (and excitedly!) that they could point out something "obvious" of which Jewish people were not aware. So then, some Rabbis urgently put out the word to "avoid that Trinity stuff" by revising their *matzah* shape.

It is significant to note that the "banishment" of the triangular *matzoth* from the *Seder* and Jewish adoption of the Star of David as the official emblem[39] of Judaism both happened during the Middle Ages, perhaps within a few years of each other. It may be speculated that adoption of the *Magen David* as Judaism's emblem most likely occurred before the triangular shape for the *matzoth* was replaced by round or square shapes. Jewish people have no clear notion today as to the source of the design known as the Star of David. *The Jewish Book of Why*[42] presents a brief history of the shape, dating back to Roman times, but states that the origin of their emblem is "cloudy."

It would have taken a while, perhaps even several decades during the Middle Ages, to incorporate such a radical change to a different *matzah* shape throughout all of Judaic Europe. At that period, 1000-1500 C.E., it would have been especially difficult to accomplish this in a timely fashion, considering the limited communications of that time. Besides, traditional religious liturgy, doctrine, etc, is extremely resistant to *any* change. (Just try it sometime! – For example, as when changing to a "new" hymnal for a long established congregation, or worse! – for *all* churches in your denomination!)

However, the Rabbis neglected to conceal what is perhaps the strongest and yet the subtlest clue, comprising the most convincing evidence for triangular *matzah*. It can therefore be named an *"indelible clue"* simply because Jewish authorities could not go out and retrieve and revise all *Haggadoth* "overnight" to conform to this newly required "avoidance." This powerful, yet subtle clue is still evident today in nearly all of the *Haggadoth* in our Judaica libraries. – They have not been successful in "rubbing-it-out"!

At this point it is appropriate to point out that in addition to signifying Holiness, the number "three" – as well as the triangular shape – is the most fundamental number in the laws of Creation as well. For example, three is the ideal number of supports for any object – such as the three-legged milking stool – which is stable even on the rough ground in a barn yard. Two supports are definitely unstable without an additional brace or tie. And, if you have ever sat at a "wobbly" four-legged table, you understand that four supports are unstable unless the surface is PERFECTLY flat or, even if it is flat, all four legs must be EXACTLY the same length. Three is therefore the PERFECT number of supports.

The three basic "forces" encountered in The Creation consist of:

Tension

        i.e., "pulling" something apart – such as a breaking a rubber band.

Compression

        i.e., "pushing" something together – such as mashing putty.

Shear

        i.e., "slicing" apart – such as when we "cut" a deck of cards.

Another principle supported by the number three is found in the techniques of composition encountered and applied throughout the field of art. A dominant triangular pattern in an art form is considered to provide one of the more interesting composition choices. Artists and photographers alike therefore often strive and/or design to produce arrangements of figures, objects, colors, etc. in triangular patterns. And, yes – there are *three* primary colors – red, yellow and blue. Indeed, this list can and does go on and on!

But, now – GET THIS ! – In all art forms, the triangle is used to indicate power and authority to the object(s) in the pattern! Throughout all parts of this book we see more and more evidence of God's Power and Authority represented through this number "three." – YES ! – It comes as no surprise that since God is The Master Artist of His Universe! – He uses His Number Three to signify His Power and Authority to His People Israel in the *Seder*.

During our research for this work, we examined over one hundred *Haggadoth*, dating from the 18th century and up until the present time. Now for the clue! – Nearly all of these – particularly the older ones! – specify that the second *matzah* is simply to be broken and "the *larger* piece" (or some say "the larger half") becomes what is known as the *Afikoman*. This is stated, just as a matter-of-fact, as if it were *obvious* that one piece would *always* be larger. It is likely that phrase has been handed down through all *Haggadoth* through the centuries.

For example, the procedure following is from one recently published *Haggadah*, dated 1988, stating: *"It is the larger part of the middle matzah that is concealed."* Others just direct the *matzah* to be broken in "half;" and "the larger half" is to be wrapped in the napkin and hidden as the *Afikoman*. (Get that? – The larger *half*!) A person should pause here to ask HOW ??? can there be a "larger" half of *anything*!

If it is intended to break some object into "halves," the natural inclination is to break the object at the middle. Referring to Illus. 29: Corruption of Seder Matzah Symbolism, Page 444, we see this sort of "natural inclination" resulting with an *obviously* "larger" piece when a triangular *matzah* is broken casually at its "middle."

On the other hand, it can be seen in that same Illus. 29: Corruption of Seder Matzah Symbolism, Page 444, that one must *intentionally* "manipulate" in order to break off a larger piece from a circular or square *matzah* or any other symmetrical shape. Thus, for those shapes, it is likely that unequal "halves" will result ONLY if there is actually a *contrived* effort to produce a "larger half" instead of breaking it at the "middle" and leaving it to chance. In many cases, one might need actually to examine the pieces very closely to discern which is the larger piece from two pieces broken from a circular or square *matzah*.

This "larger half" phrase then is the "indelible" clue that yields subtle indication that the *matzah* was at one time in its history broken across the middle and that it was most likely an equilateral triangular shape. This procedure of course would have been perfectly natural in producing a larger piece on one side of the break at the middle seam of a triangular wafer as we have shown rather dramatically in Illus. 29: Corruption of Seder Matzah Symbolism, Page 444. We have emphasized the subtle yet vital import of this larger piece. Still, this is no proof; although, it is powerful circumstantial evidence pointing to a triangular "verdict."

Nevertheless, some very modern *Haggadoth* have corrupted this importance in the *Seder*. Some specify breaking into unequal "halves" or some even state, in a somewhat Cavalier fashion, *"Just break off a piece and wrap it."* – or – *"Break the matzah and wrap one of the pieces."* – having no mention of a larger or smaller piece. Here we have seen just a brief time bracket showing how the *Seder* has been corrupted over the centuries. However, lest we be accused of harshness or ridicule against Jewish tradition, please remember and note that despite corruption of these minor details, the "Big Picture" of the *Seder* is in fact still relatively close to the original when we consider there has been 3500 years of opportunity for decline in the *Seder* tradition.

Another historical source[20] presents an example of triangular shapes in Jewish baking as the *Hamantaschen* cakes made for the *Purim* holiday. The symbolic Jewish food for *Purim*, and still in use today, is this three-cornered pastry filled with poppy seeds, prunes, apricots or other fruits.

Triangular-shaped dumplings (*kreplach*) are served during the *Shavuot* holiday as well as during *Purim* and *Hoshana Rabba*. It is also served as a pre-fasting dish prior to *Yom Kippur*. One Jewish source[42] acknowledges that "three" is a "prominent number in Jewish tradition." It is pointed out, for example, there were *three* patriarchs: Abraham, Isaac and Jacob and that this is the reason for the three corners in the *kreplach*. The Jewish Scripture (*Tenakh*) has *three* sections: *Torah*, Prophets and Holy Writings. There are *three* family divisions of the Jewish people: *Kohanim*, Levites and *Y'israel*.

There appears, therefore, to be no traceable reason for the triangular shape of these pastries, other than perhaps, again, the Biblical numerology connection mentioned with the number, three. We do know that these shapes date back to having been established by Jewish people in Europe, probably during the Middle Ages. The name, *Hamantaschen*, ("Haman's pockets") is a German (or *Yiddish*) form referring to Haman, the arch-villain in the story of Esther, who lined his pockets with wealth stolen from the Jews in Persia. (Esther 3) Hence, the name, "Haman's Pockets." This further verifies that Jewish use of triangular pastry shapes extends far back into Jewish history.

Further influence toward triangular shapes appears in several *Haggadoth*[1, 12, 40] with arrangement of articles on the *Seder* plates. (See Illus. 42: Seder Plate Arrangements: Various Haggadoth, Page 457) Listed with each arrangement are the symbolic meanings for each of the articles. A broad variation of interpretation is seen through the traditions and teachings from each of these authors. These are but a few of the many arrangements seen in researching for these *Seder* items; nevertheless, most do include some sort of triangular and/or six-pointed pattern. It is interesting to note that microscopic studies[46] of snowflakes reveal this same feature involving six-pointed or six-sided shapes. (Actually, this should come as No Surprise, considering Who designs them!)

Concluding from the facts presented, we believe it is fair to state that "some evidence" exists for the triangular *matzah*; although, it constitutes no actual "proof." After we present the remainder of the "possible" meanings for triangular *matzah*, we hope readers will join with us in our excitement about what is revealed through this evidence.

The *Seder* Table

Considering Rabbi Max Stauber's observation on the "pointing" of the *matzah* wafers from the father's place at the head of the table, we refer now to Illus. 30: Position: 1st (Lower) Matzah at Seder Table, Page 445. Several symbolic meanings can be derived from the information noted this far and which, we believe, are much too representative and important to be categorized as "coincidence."

First, since the father is seated at the head of the table, he is symbolic of God, The Father, and His Place represents Heaven. The places of others at the table then represent "the World," since they are His subjects. God, The Father, is "speaking" to the World as He leads the *Seder*, especially in the manner that He demonstrates His Story using the *matzah* at His Place, as we shall describe in detail following.

The *Matzah*

Of course, the *matzah* is "unleavened" bread, containing no yeast or fermentation. Many observant Jewish people believe that unleavened bread, often called "the bread of affliction," was specified only "*because they were in a hurry!*" when the Jews departed Egypt to escape Pharaoh's tyranny. Their assumption would appear at first to be well-founded because, in fact, a statement to that effect is found in the *Haggadah*. However, this would be a shallow rationale; because *Talmud* Rabbis (*Rosh Hashanah* 3b or Reference 2) make it emphatically clear that the leaven (*hametz*) is symbolic of sin and/or "haughtiness" and it therefore must be purged from all Jewish households before the Passover. Reference 45 notes that certain Rabbis have observed that leavened bread in fact has a "puffiness" that is representative of "haughtiness."

Significantly, Jewish men, whom God assigned to proclaim the Law (Exodus 13:9), are responsible for the baking of the *matzah*, at least by supervising the process. Under the strictest directives, it must be baked in a darkened room, during a period of less than eighteen minutes, extending from the kneading until removal from the oven. This is specified in order to retard fermentation of the dough. It is evident from all these rigid requirements and because the entire procedure must be completed in eighteen minutes, that baking of the *matzah* could be a stressful operation. Moreover, if there are any mistakes, the entire procedure must be restarted from the beginning. – It must be accomplished *perfectly!*

Preferably, the water is to be drawn cool from a well at twilight and left to stand overnight. The water must not be used before daybreak; although, the sun's rays must never fall on it. Even in modern times an exultant procession winds through the Old City of Jerusalem to the Pool of *Siloam* to draw water on the evening before Passover. No salt may be added to the dough. The baking fire is kindled using willow branches saved from the *Sukkoth* (Feast of Tabernacles) from the previous Autumn.

It is said[4] the cool, stilled water retards fermentation, but further introduces the ideas of death and consequent distance from God. These, in turn, are balanced by the fire's warmth and the eighteen minutes. Sabbath candles are lighted eighteen minutes before sunset. Furthermore, it is stated that, unlike wine, which is wet, colorful, tasty, "tangy," fluid and unstable; unleavened bread is: dry, colorless, bland, flat, brittle and unchanging.

The author's (Ruth Freedman) contrasts in[4] are further illustrated (very controversially!), as she says men prepare "unchanging" *matzah*; although, women are responsible for "changeable" leavened bread. As with women, "the fruit of the vine," and leavened bread become "culture" through words and events; although they cannot reach a permanent status because they are unstable. Although, meat, men and *matzah* reach a stable state via The Great Transformer, as He creates the materials and then forms the completed stable result. (It is probably very fortunate that a man did not originate such remarks about women!)

Looking back upon all these baking instructions, it is evident that God had no intentions that the *matzah* should ever be produced in factories with machines. He wanted all Jewish fathers to prepare their Feast bread in their own homes. Judging from all we are seeing and are about to see, it appears that God wanted Israel *always* to bake this bread in each Jewish home, just as they did for that first Passover.

Making the wafers in the homes and by manual means into triangular shapes in earlier times would not have drawn any thought toward "industrial efficiency." The fact that *matzah* is now machine-made and square, instead of homemade and triangular, is done in order to avoid the obvious "suggestion" of The Trinity in addition to being more convenient and easier to manufacture. This situation of course follows the pattern of nearly all religions, in that we have opted for "convenience" rather than for God's Intent and Purpose.

Jewish tradition teaches that the perforations, made with a spiked wheel called a *reidel* (Illus. 35: Equal Perforation Spacing = Triangular Pieces, Page 450), are placed to enhance aeration of the dough to prevent rising, to keep it flat and thin and to further retard fermentation[11]. However, most Christians would note that the *matzah* is "pierced" and "striped," suggesting the obvious Messianic references to the flagellation, beating, spikes and spear in The Crucifixion of *Y'shua* of Nazareth, as prophesied through the Prophets Zechariah and Isaiah –

"They shall look upon Me, Whom they have pierced" – From Zechariah 12:10

"With His stripes we are healed." – From Isaiah 53:5

Equal sides and equal angles forming the points of an equilateral triangle; definitely bring the suggestion of The Holy Trinity. The shape tells Christians that God is manifested as One God in Three Persons, all of whom are equally ranked; although, The Father is *always* first.

Most Jewish people and even many Christians have difficulty understanding (and accepting) the concept of the Triune God; i.e., what we Christians call the Holy Trinity: God, The Father – God, The Son – and God, The Holy Spirit. Jewish teaching of course has always opposed this teaching and has emphasized, from Deuteronomy 6:4 –

"...the Lord is our God, the Lord is One."

One of the most effective explanations of the Trinity may be offered applying water as a demonstrating analogy. Water is actually the chemical compound: H_2O – and can also be identified as "dihydrogen oxide" – although, scientific "purists" might insist that it is just plain "hydrogen oxide." But, that argument aside – YES ! – It is a chemical compound consisting of two parts hydrogen and one part oxygen (Notice – a total of "3" parts).

This material appears in three forms: as a liquid, as a solid or as a vapor.

- The liquid, we call *"water,"* or *"rain,"* or *"mist."*
- The solid, we call *"ice,"* or *"snow,"* or *"sleet."*
- The vapor, we call *"steam,"* or *"fog,"* or *"clouds."*

Each of these forms is actually made up of what we call "water," and yet, each form is seen differently from the other two and is NOT seen as "water." The chemical make-up for each material is *still* H_2O, and yet, we almost always think of H_2O *first* as "water" – a liquid. Notice also, each of the *three* forms appears in *three* more forms within its own category; e.g., the liquid form is seen as water, rain (droplets) or mist, but they are **ALWAYS** water, and **ALWAYS** H_2O. If God could create His "water" material to be a "trinity," but consisting of only ONE compound, He surely could take this concept for His Own Holy Forms to be three different persons who are in fact the same ONE Person. – Something to think about.

Jewish *Haggadah* discussions offer a broad variety of reasons and meanings for three *matzah* wafers. For example, the most popular explanation is that they represent "Kohen" (upper *matzah*), "Levi" (middle) and "*Y'israel*" (lowest); representing the three sections of the House of Israel. In this same order, representatives for each of those sections even today are called up to receive the *Torah* at *Shabbath* services in synagogues[3]. During the Middle Ages, *matzah* was about one fingerbreadth in thickness[5]. In Jewish traditional practice, the wafers are to be no thicker than "one fingerbreadth" and are of course much thinner in the case of modern commercially baked *matzah*.

An interesting opinion on the derivation for three *matzahs* is found in *Talmud – Pesahim* 116a. The Rabbis teach that the blessing for the unleavened bread must be said over just a piece of the *matzah* only, not over a whole one. This is to be a symbol to emphasize Israel's poverty in Egypt. Hence three pieces of *matzoth* are required: two because every festival and the Sabbath require two loaves, and a third which is broken, so that the blessing may be recited over *that* piece. We will demonstrate that a much more beautiful and meaningful symbolism exists for these *matzoth* and which will be far more Glorifying of God than is this traditional view.

One Judaica source[1] states that some traditional Jewish congregations, in order to better appreciate the *matzah* taste, abstain from eating any *matzah* during the entire month preceding Passover, starting after *Purim*. The Rabbis require abstaining from *matzah* at least for the day preceding the *Seder*, saying: "Whoever eats *matzah* on the day before Passover is to be compared to a man who makes love to his fiancée in his father-in-law's house." Another Judaica source[6] observes that wine is used as a symbol of sanctification; although, it truly suggests the possibility of intoxication and debauchery. She asks how wine can symbolize liberty when so many are enslaved by alcohol. Answering her own question, the author states that no object or substance is intrinsically good or bad. Its quality or character is determined by how well it is used – or how it is misused.

Some Haggadic Themes

In order to enter our discussion in the best attitudes for our minds and hearts, it is agreeable first to listen to some general comments on the rite of the *Seder* from Jewish sources.

The Passover *Seder* is to be joyous occasion. However, it is noted in Reference 7 that all are to participate with dignity. The *Seder* is not to be a noisy, boisterous or even gleeful celebration. Unlike *Purim*, for example, it is to be more of a symposium: with reading of the Exodus story, the questions, the answers. Secreting away the *Afikoman* and the subsequent search is as close to "fun" as one should reach.

Jewish sages forthrightly affirm the *Haggadah* as having a Messianic message and hope, although many Christians would agree that Jewish people neither see nor understand the message. The present and continuing Jewish Hope for the Coming of their *Meshiach* (Hebrew: Anointed; English: Messiah) is abundantly clear, as we shall see later in the *Seder* liturgy. Nevertheless, it goes without saying that *Seder* participants have absolutely NO understanding of the Gospel portrayal that is so prominent throughout this feast. Our purpose is to explain and demonstrate that portrayal for what may be the first time. The Passover *Seder* is the story of Jesus Christ, extending from before the beginning of Time until the Life in the World to come.

One source[8] states that mentioning the Exodus actually brings the coming of *Meshiach*! – AMEN! – Further, it is declared that while the redemption from Egypt is forever remembered in the *Seder*, that event will be forever eclipsed by the redemption that *Meshiach* brings to His People! – and again, AMEN!

Although "three" is certainly God's Number of Holiness, the number "four" is prominent throughout the *Seder*: four cups of wine, four sons, four questions. Four is the number of "the World" in Biblical numerology. (Four seasons, four compass directions, etc.) It is not certain that any "worldly" significance is connected with that number concerning the four sons or the four questions. Nevertheless, it is certain there is a "connection" regarding the four cups of wine. In part, Jewish sages have referred to four sentences giving promises to Israel in Exodus 6:6 - 7, announcing each of the cups. Additionally, we have introduced a symbolic "punctuation" by the four cups, marking three 1000 year "days" in the chronology of Messianic Promise, as noted in Illus. 37: Seder – 1st Day in Messianic Period in Israel, Page 452, and Illus. 38: Seder – 2nd Day in Messianic Period in Israel, Page 453.

In modern Jewish tradition, a "fifth cup" (preferably a large goblet of wine) is placed in the center of the table. This is the "cup of Elijah, the prophet," whom all Israel eagerly and prayerfully awaits, looking forward to his announcing the Coming of Messiah. Although there is certainly a Scriptural reference to Elijah as a precursor to Messiah (Malachi 4:5); Jewish tradition[42] has overlooked that assurance by reasoning that since Elijah did not "die" a physical death, he will come to herald arrival of Messiah.

Christian interpretation has been of course that Malachi 4:5 was fulfilled by John the Baptist who was a "type" of Elijah in the way he lived in the wilderness, eating "locusts and wild honey" and ministered and was followed as a righteous messenger for God. And, of course he did announce the Coming of Messiah before he baptized *Y'shua* at the Jordan. (Matthew 3:1 – 17)

Elijah's cup is not included in all *Haggadoth*. Centuries ago there was a Rabbinical dispute over whether there should be four cups or five cups. No agreement could be reached and therefore, as a compromise with the minority, the fifth cup was added; although it is filled but not drunk. Because of the belief that Elijah will herald the coming of Messiah, the fifth cup came to be known as the Cup of Elijah. Ancient Jewish legend[9, 41] tells that Elijah will resolve all doubts and disputes about this as well as other questions regarding the *Seder*.

It comes as no surprise that some conservative Christian "tea-totallers" prefer to believe that the Passover wine – *"fruit of the vine"* – used by Jesus and His Disciples was actually just non-alcoholic "grape juice." Certain Evangelical Christian teachers, quoting Greek vocabulary and other scholarly sources, have gone out of their ways, in attempts at s-t-r-e-t-ch-i-n-g Scripture to find corroborating support for claiming that "Jesus would NEVER take strong drink!"

Our research of this question shows that such, however, is not the case. A respected and thorough Jewish source[43] explains that although fermented "fruit of the vine" (wine) is "*kosher*" for Passover; other alcoholic beverages such as beer, scotch whiskey, rye, etc. are not acceptable because they are made from grain and not from grapes ("*fruit of the vine*") The discussion adds that other ingredients, such as potato or fruits may be used for the Passover beverage in accordance with the Law.

Jewish teaching further reasons to presume that such ingredients qualify because they are "fruit of the ground" or "fruit of the tree" and are therefore of like stature as "the fruit of the vine." This exercise in Jewish legal wrangling leaves us to wonder why grapes, potatoes or apricots are acceptable, but barley or hops are forbidden. ALL are "fruit-of-the-ground." The foregoing is typical as an example of Rabbinical/*Talmudic* devious and calculating thought process that is often applied in order to "stretch" for a practical or more "convenient" alternative.

Torah makes very clear which persons are *not* to be seated. Exodus 12:43 states:

> "And the Lord said unto Moses and Aaron: 'This is the ordinance of the Passover; there shall no alien eat thereof.' "

Rabbi J.H. Hertz[47] teaches that the "alien" refers not only to those who have not entered the covenant of Abraham, but also is directed at any Israelite "whose deeds have alienated him from his Father in Heaven." The interpretation has added prestige in having been forwarded from the 11th century scholar, Rashi. Hertz declares that the occasion is: "to be a distinct *Israelitish* observance."

Christian worshipers receive a similar admonishment concerning their participation at the Lord's Supper. No person is to come to the table of Holy Communion or Eucharist unless that person is "*right with the Lord*." The observance is Holy and must not be reduced to status of a "ritual." It is not to be entered just because it is offered and everybody is going up there to take the crackers and the wine. – Or, because "It won't look right if I don't go," etc., etc.

Paul issues such a warning in I Corinthians 11:20 – 29. It is likely that Paul's training as a Jew influenced his specific cautioning in verses 27 – 29 –

> "Wherefore whosoever shall eat this bread, and drink this cup of the Lord, unworthily, shall be guilty of the body and blood of the Lord.
>
> But let a man examine himself, and so let him eat of that bread, and drink of that cup.
>
> For he that eateth and drinketh unworthily, eateth and drinketh damnation to himself, not discerning the Lord's body."

The word "unworthily" means that a person must not partake, for example:

- If it is done during or in the presence of gluttony and/or drunkenness.

- If there is no observance of The Crucifixion and Resurrection of Jesus Christ – especially if there is no belief in those redeeming acts of our Savior.
- If it is done in mockery.
- If it is done in a careless, wicked or irreverent manner.
- If it is done in order to promote a "religious" image for the participant(s).
- If it is done in order to accommodate the wishes of a spouse, friend or other.
- If it is done under guilt or un-repented sin.

And, just as in the admonishment from the Rabbis at the *Seder*, the occasion should not end abruptly with a call such as: *"On with the entertainment!"* – It is to be a solemn and Holy occasion. If any participants do "sup" unworthily, they crucify Christ again, and they are therefore guilty of His blood, instead of being cleansed by it.

We should be aware that, despite modern "permissiveness" and Jewish/Christian alliances – "political correctness," etc. – even for promotion of "good-will," etc. – the Law emphasizes by means of repetition that inclusion of any "alien" or "uncircumcised" (i.e., non-Jewish person) is forbidden at the Passover meal. (Exodus 12:43, 48) The qualifications from *Torah* for limiting participants at the *Seder* are specific. – As if Exodus 12:43 had veiled its true intent, Verse 48 repeats the message for emphasis, making the Lord's statute undeniably clear, saying: *"...but no uncircumcised person shall eat thereof."*

These statutes may put Gentile Christians in an embarrassing position if they should receive an invitation to attend a *Seder*, even under the most gracious intentions from a Jewish host. It is difficult to recommend a proper, tactful, "gentle" response to this invitation, which most Gentile Christians – especially – would certainly consider a high honor. It is probable that Jewish observance of this statute would occur only among Orthodox Jewry, and not so likely with Reformed or even Conservative congregants.

Perhaps, with supplanting of the Law by the New Testament, Gentiles are surely "circumcised" in God's view. However, it is not clear whether Jewish hosts are "legally" free to include Gentiles unless they also agree that Christian Gentiles indeed are "circumcised" via their New Testament faith! – A difficult position for which we can offer no easy solution.

Some final thoughts are offered on the reverent attitude to be present at the *Seder*, as attested by comments in various *Haggadoth*.

- The *Seder* offers a rich opportunity for study of the *Torah*. The sages[10] tell us: "Three who have eaten together at a table and have not discussed the *Torah* are as though they had eaten of the sacrifices to the dead. But three who have eaten together at a table and have spoken words of the *Torah* are as though they had eaten from God's own table."
- The doctrine that the Children of Israel are the Chosen People is not true merely because it is an article of faith. Rather, it is an article of faith because that doctrine is true. The logical consequence of thirty-five hundred years of a unique and

fascinating history for the Children of Israel is mirrored in an experience unparalleled in any other society[11].

- An earthly employer requires his workers to serve him. Whereas, the Master of The Universe appointed us His servitors, then He tends us, tenderly, taking care of all our needs[11].

The Father's Place Setting

We shall discuss each of the three *matzah* wafers, its position and its "hidden" meanings. Principally, the three wafers in this discussion portray the actions of Messiah as He obediently carries out The "Threefold" Plan of His Father. Later we shall discuss other pictures seen in the *Seder* array of *matzah* wafers (or plural, *matzoth*). We should point out that the "pictures" described are interpreted from impressions seen by this author and may or may not be supported by other sources.

- **1ˢᵗ (lowest) *matzah***

   The "first" *matzah* is the "lowest" because it is first to be laid on the plate of the father or the *Seder* leader. Referring to Illus. 30: Position: 1st (Lower) Matzah at Seder Table, Page 445, we note that the triangular wafer points away from the Father. Although the 1ˢᵗ *matzah* represents God, The Father (because He is "first"), He "points" as if He were "commanding" the action of The Son, Messiah, descending into the World to save mankind from their manifold sins. Earlier, we mentioned that, in Jewish symbolism, the circular shape denotes The World. This message is carried forth by the plates at the *Seder* table, as shown in Illus. 30: Position: 1st (Lower) Matzah at Seder Table, Page 445, Illus. 31: Position: 2nd (Middle) Matzah at Seder Table, Page 446, and Illus. 32: Position: 3rd (Upper) Matzah at Seder Table, Page 447. Messiah is therefore shown departing from Heaven into "the World," as *Y'shua ben Yusef* of Nazareth. Doing this, He fulfilled many Scriptures, only a few of which are:

   - Being born of a virgin (Isaiah 7:14 and Matthew 1:18 – 22)
   - As the Son of God (Psalms 2:7 and John 3:16 – 17)
   - Descended from the House of David (II Samuel 7:12, 13, 16 and Matthew 1:6 – 16)
   - Birthed in Bethlehem Ephrathah (Micah 5:2 and Matthew 2:15)

- **2ⁿᵈ (middle) *Matzah***

   The 2ⁿᵈ wafer (Illus. 31: Position: 2nd (Middle) Matzah at Seder Table, Page 446) represents The Son of God in The Trinity, and now points toward Heaven. This action depicts The Son, Messiah, returning to His Father's Place (Heaven) after having been in The World to make payment for the sins of men. He accomplished this by Perfectly completing His Father's Law, which men could not keep. It is well to note also that the middle wafer is centered between the other two, just as

Messiah is the "central" figure in all of Scripture. Nothing in Scripture could hold or make sense without the Salvation brought by Messiah to sinful mankind. It is fitting to observe here that the 2nd *matzah* is broken before any *matzah* is eaten and enjoyed during the meal. This is a reflection of the fact that Believers could not "enjoy" Salvation until after *Y'shua*'s Body was "broken" for us. (See Illus. 38: Seder – 2nd Day in Messianic Period in Israel, Page453)

- **3rd (upper)** *Matzah*

    Illus. 32: Position: 3rd (Upper) Matzah at Seder Table, Page 447, presents the 3rd wafer, now pointing again away from The Father in Heaven. And, as before, even though the 3rd *matzah* is symbolic of God's Holy Spirit, He is "pointing" the movement of Messiah's return to the World, claiming His Eternal Kingdom in Victory over sin.

The *Magen David*

No historian to date has been able to trace the origin of the Star of David, (Hebrew: *Mogen David* or *Magen David*) that best-known emblem of the Jewish people and the Nation of Israel. By placing the triangular *matzoth* as directed in the ancient *Haggadah*, that six-pointed star practically "leaps" to our recognition in Illus. 33: Final Arrangement of Matzoth at Seder Start, Page 448. We can, however, only speculate that is how the star got its name. Perhaps more rightly, it should have been named "Star of Moses," since Moses may actually have been the first to see it when God gave Moses that very first *Haggadah* on the eve of that very first Passover.

Nevertheless, we see here in Illus. 33: Final Arrangement of Matzoth at Seder Start, Page 448, not only a possible source of that revered emblem, but also a dramatic portrayal of The Holy Trinity. Each of three wafers is symbolic of One member of The Trinity, and yet, each wafer itself is emblematic of all three *Equal* members of The Trinity, depicted by three *equal* sides and three *equal* angles. All this, the One Triune God presents to man as One star with man's number (six) for its points in order that man can "see" God! Many should agree that this is too much for coincidence. Who but God could ever have thought of such a device?!

The *Afikoman*

As stated earlier, the 2nd *matzah* is "central" to God's story of dealing with sinful mankind through Messiah. We see this "centering" most emphatically in the *Seder* portrayal through the 2nd (middle) *matzah*, because much more is happening and much more is to be said about the 2nd *matzah* than about either of the other two wafers in this drama,

We must point out that several Jewish prophets had foretold that Messiah would be "broken" or "cut off. In fact one of those prophets, Daniel 9:24 – 27, told the Jewish people the exact date when "The Anointed" (Hebrew: Meschiach; English: Messiah) would be "cut off." Our depiction of the 2nd *matzah* as Messiah to be "broken" is therefore not a frivolous choice.

Illus. 34: Breaking Afikoman from 2nd Wafer, Page 449, shows the 2nd *matzah* broken in two pieces. The piece that receives the most attention is of course the larger piece, the *Afikoman*. However, let us first examine the smaller piece, especially since now it can be seen in a new light, because it, too, is triangular – Holy.

The smaller piece, in the Jewish tradition, is called the "bread of affliction" or "poor man's bread" This provides an obvious reference to the Israelite's miserable plight in Egypt leading up to the night of the "Passover" by the Angel of Death. Nevertheless, in our search for more spiritual meanings in the *Seder*, let us consider what the smaller piece might represent.

Instead of being just a piece of *matzah* broken off, it is now smaller but truly, again, an equilateral triangle. In watching for symbolism in the *Seder*, we see something not present when other *matzah* shapes are used. The smaller piece, because it is an equilateral triangle, now continues to represent The Triune God. This is remarkable since the "point" was broken off from the 2nd wafer, which represents Messiah, The Son, as One of The Trinity. (Are your brain cells getting just a bit tired?!) – Please "hang-in-there." – God never said He did anything in a simple fashion.

Continuing, the smaller piece is portraying The Son as Messiah in a now Glorified Body, returning ("pointing') to Heaven, back at the Place of His Father. This happened after He was "broken" and left His mortal body in The Tomb for three days. This is truly a picture of *Y'shua* as we know Him from the Gospel in the New Testament. Jewish people probably were doing this since their first *Seder* in Egypt. But how could they have known what it meant? In fact, how can they know even now, unless they "know" Messiah?

At this point we must point out a symbolic "gesture" described in the Gospel and which points again to Jesus' death as dramatized in the Passover. Immediately before the second *matzah* is "broken," the person conducting the *Seder* is instructed to *"wash his hands without pronouncing the benediction,...."* Here we are reminded of Pontius Pilate's "gesture" of washing his hands to absolve himself of complicity and any responsibility in sentencing Jesus to be put to death – in fact, "broken." (Matthew 27:24) This picture from the Jewish Law appears to match the Gospel in that Pilate also pronounced no "benediction" as he sentenced Jesus to The Cross. It is interesting, however, to observe that in all subsequent stations through the *Seder*, the leader is to wash his hands and pronounce the benediction:

> "Blessed art Thou, O Eternal, our God, King of the Universe, Who bringest forth bread from the Earth."

There is a "traditional" story that says Pilate was recalled to Rome shortly after The Crucifixion, and that until his death by suicide, he suffered severe depression and was continually washing his hands!

It is somewhat surprising that at least one Jewish source[13], however, recognizes that early Christians understood, *after* The Crucifixion, the most obvious of the symbolism we have described. It is explained in these same terms that those Christians knew the 2nd wafer represented the broken Body of their Lord, just as He had declared before He died. Again – It is most surprising to see this observation being acknowledged by a Jewish source.

It is further noted that Rabbi Gamaliel, leading Jewish teacher at that time as well as mentor to Saul of Tarsus, was undoubtedly aware of this new meaning applied to the Passover symbols by *Y'shua's* followers. Legislating strong resistance to such thought, Gamaliel therefore ordained that Jewish people *everywhere* were to be reminded regarding what *he* (Gamaliel) had ordained as the *original* symbolism of these items at each *Seder*. This was done lest anyone might become confused or forget! Those original symbols were the *Kohen*, *Levi* and *Y'israel* parts that we discussed earlier. This also may have led to transferring the supper until after the explanations of the *matzah*. Under Gamaliel's revised *Haggadah* then, nobody would eat this ritually important supper without first affirming the "proper" and authorized meanings for the symbols. – (According to Gamaliel, that is!).

The next station in the Passover drama is the wrapping of the "larger" piece, which is called the *Afikoman*, derived from the Greek "*epikomion*," described[12] as meaning a "festive procession." Judaic tradition offers several theories explaining the origin, purpose and meaning for the *Afikoman*. Reference to a "festive" occasion probably arose during the time when Greece controlled Palestine. By that time the Children of Israel had long forgotten why(?) they called it *Afikoman*. Even today Jewish celebrants can only speculate about why(?) they break it, wrap it and hide it away, etc.

One interesting theory offered by many *Haggadoth* claims the wafer is broken to signify the Israelites' skimpy rations during slavery and during their forty years through the *Sinai*. Further, they indicate that "breaking bread" also indicates hospitality, "inviting the needy to share and eat with us." It has been suggested[14] that the *Afikoman* is wrapped in a napkin to symbolize the Israelites carrying their personal belongings, wrapped in garments and toted over their shoulders while exiting Egypt. This thought is referenced to Exodus 12:34.

Jewish folks have several interesting theories for why the 2nd *matzah* is broken. Reference[1] writes that the 2nd *matzah* is "the bread of poverty." It is broken in two because poor people are accustomed to breaking their bread into pieces in order to share it. A somewhat less romantic version reasons that the poor usually break off a piece of their bread and put away the other piece for the next meal. We would hope that our stated reasons for the "breaking" will reflect a much deeper meaning.

Jewish tradition via another source[42] has trivialized the symbolism of the *Afikoman*, saying the ritual dates back only 700 years and was instituted as a sort of entertainment for the children at the *Seder* "to make it more exciting." Even if that stated origin is fact, it remains that a vivid "picture" of Jesus Christ is painted: showing He was "broken" – He was "hidden away" – and later He will be "found" and "enjoyed" by all righteous persons at His Resurrection.

In our more spiritual outlook, we see a vivid and emotional picture of the Death, Burial and Resurrection of *Y'shua* of Nazareth. That impression is powerfully suggested even by the very manner in which the *Afikoman* is wrapped in the napkin, then hidden away "in a place not known," and to be found and enjoyed as dessert at the end of the meal.

First, the "broken" (crucified) body of the man who was literally "photographed" on the *Shroud of Turin* is believed by many to be a genuine photograph of *Y'shua ben Yusef* of Nazareth, whom we call Jesus Christ. That homespun linen cloth was wrapped over the body of that man in *exactly* the same manner as the *Afikoman* is wrapped; i.e., folded in the middle over itself, rather than at right angles to that direction. (See Illus. 37: Seder – 1st Day in Messianic Period in Israel, Page 452) – Dare we suppose that is coincidence?!

Some critics will charge that the Shroud of Turin cannot qualify for such a comparison because, they say, Jesus' body would have been "wrapped" in strips of cloth. Some would claim that such a burial preparation is implied in the story of Lazarus (John 11:44). This charge can be refuted by the fact that Joseph had insufficient time for the "traditional" wrappings because he was in a rush to return home before the Sabbath arrived. Because of the approaching Sabbath at sundown, Jesus was laid to rest in haste. The claim of "strips" is also refuted by quotes from Jewish Law listed earlier in Chapter 12. Gospel quotes from: Matthew 27:59, Mark 15:46 and Luke 23:53 – all state that Jesus was *"wrapped in a linen cloth."*

This was to be, after all, a "temporary" entombment in Joseph's family crypt. When the women returned on the next morning, they had planned to prepare His body properly and had perhaps made arrangement for a permanent place of interment. They therefore laid His body on this piece of homespun linen and draped it over His full-length supine corpse as a measure of haste. Without their being aware of it, Jewish *Seder* celebrants repeat that same handling of the napkin for the *Afikoman* – representing the "broken" Body of Messiah.

Detailing the roles of the *Seder* participants in this drama, the father is to hide the *Afikoman* "in a place not known" while one of the children or a guest is sent out of the room. God, The Father, has indeed hidden *Y'shua's* mortal body "in a place not known." – It has never been found – nor will it *ever* be found.

The child or guest, who must later find the *Afikoman*, would seem to be a picture of Israel who will, at the end of days, "find" Messiah, who at that time will have arrived in His Glorified Body at the Mount of Olives. (Zechariah 14:4) Meanwhile, the other *Seder* celebrants represent "the World" that continues to watch as Israel searches passionately to find their Messiah. Finally, when Israel does find Messiah, all the World and Israel will rejoice and be blessed by His Kingdom. That happy occasion is then dramatized by the assembled participants, eating the *Afikoman* as a "dessert" for a blessing to all present at conclusion of the meal.

Closer examination reveals additional symbolic meaning for the *Afikoman*. We demonstrated earlier, in Illus. 34: Breaking Afikoman from 2nd Wafer, Page 449, that the *Afikoman* can be broken into three equilateral ("Holy") triangular shapes. Each of the triangles contributes to repeating the message presented by the manner of placing the *matzahs* at the father's place setting. That is, each of the triangles at the ends of the *Afikoman* points from what would be the "base" – the longer edge – of the wafer. The triangles at each end point "downward" from the base as if to portray Messiah coming to the World to fellowship with man. And, surely He will have done this on two occasions when Jesus Completes His Mission to man on Earth at His Second Coming.

The middle (or "Second") triangle similarly portrays Messiah's departure (Ascension) from the World as it points upward from the base of the broken *matzah*. Indeed, there appear to be almost limitless possibilities of "typology" or "pictures" that are revealed in this Holy and enduring Jewish festival.

Continuing our study in typology of this drama, Illus. 34: Breaking Afikoman from 2nd Wafer, Page 449, reveals additional symbolic meaning for the *Afikoman*. The point representing the "Son" was broken off and returned to the Father's Place as Messiah's Glorified Body. But the remaining piece, the *Afikoman*, still has two "points." The point at the father's right hand symbolizes God The Father as manifested by His *Shekhinah* (Divine Presence) who resided visibly in the Holy of Holies behind the Veil in Israel's Temple. *Shekhinah* remained in the World, then, with the Jewish people until forty years after The Crucifixion, finally ascending into Heaven just before the Temple was destroyed.

The Holy Spirit, the other "point" on the *Afikoman*, also remained in the World, dwelling in the souls of the Apostles, the Disciples and with all Believers, and even continuing today. Although, since the *Afikoman* has only two points, it is therefore not "Holy" and cannot enter Heaven. It is instead "hidden" in the World, rather than going to the Father's Place. However, the smaller piece, representing *Y'shua's* risen, Glorified Body, is triangular and therefore "Holy" and is returned to the Father's Place until a later time.

We do pray our readers' brain cells are not fatigued by this deep, complex symbolism, but there is much more to derive and examine. God, the Sovereign of All Mathematics, designed His Trinity so that it could never be completely broken; i.e., it would always remain a Trinity and Holy, no matter how it is broken. Satan, much less of a mathematician, although nevertheless persistent, continues in attempts to break The Trinity because it is Holy (triangular). Satan persistently and consistently fails at this because he evidently does not understand a most simple geometrical corollary.

When *any* triangle is broken, at least *one* triangle remains. (See Illus. 34: Breaking Afikoman from 2nd Wafer, Page 449) In fact, when an equilateral triangle is broken symmetrically in the manner shown in the illustration, one piece *always* remains as a smaller equilateral triangle, as demonstrated with our 2nd *matzah*. Even more Glorious, however, even the other piece – the isosceles trapezoid or truncated equilateral triangle – can still be broken into *three* equilateral triangles! This can be seen as formed by the double-dashed lines through the *Afikoman*. This means the *Afikoman* can still remain "Holy," even when its parts are broken as shown, just as *Shekhinah* and the Holy Spirit remain Holy, regardless that Satan may "break" them.

At this point one must stand back in awe and just humbly admire our God who devises such marvelous "coincidence" for us to behold in these images. God is not a magician, but rather we should see Him as THE Supreme Scientist and Supreme Mathematician. – He has just proved it!... Again!

In modern times, the hiding and finding of the *Afikoman* has taken rather a light spirit or an air of levity that is actually inappropriate for the *Seder*. Considering, however, the Jewish lack of pure understanding of this rite, we can empathize with any apparent lack of reverence.

Typical of the loss of meaning is registered in several *Haggadoth*[16] explaining the playful manner of the children in this act. It is said that the custom of encouraging the children to "steal" the *Afikoman* and hide it is based on misinterpretation of the *Talmudic* instruction: "the *matzah* are eaten hastily so that the children should not fall asleep." (From *Pesahim* 109a)

Another playful participation is described in which the children are permitted to assist in baking the *matzah* by letting them operate the *reidel* to puncture the dough, as discussed previously. This task would be more interesting and more fun (challenging) if lines of perforation were made parallel to each of the three sides of a triangular *matzah* as we have shown in Illus. 35: Equal Perforation Spacing = Triangular Pieces, Page 450. This feature would of course also facilitate breaking off additional triangular pieces. We have done so for sake of simplicity in most of our illustrations, instead of spacing the perforations parallel to only one side.

More serious, and more reverent comments from several *Haggadoth* are listed following:

- "It is to be a silent, reflective act."
- "During the *Yahatz* (breaking, etc.), no word is spoken, no benediction is uttered before it is broken."
- "The larger piece is hidden, for more is hidden than is revealed."
- "We are, as with the broken *matzah*, incomplete. Our children in their searching, are extensions of our own searching to become complete.' "The *Afikoman* represents the Paschal Lamb, eaten in the time of the Temple. It was the last course of the meal, that its flavor might linger in the mouth." (See Reference 17)

It would seem that this last statement reflects very closely toward the picture we have interpreted in this study. Indeed, the *Afikoman* is (or was) thought of as a "type" of the Paschal Lamb, whom we Believers think of as a type of *Y'shua*, our Messiah. Already, we have shown many symbolic parallels indicating *Y'shua* as The Lamb and the *Afikoman*. Some scholars would point out that the *Afikoman* also can portray a "type" of Israel in the *Seder* drama. Many would agree that too many comparisons appear here for this to be considered as mere coincidence or "statistical random selection."

After Breaking the Middle *Matzah*

The picture in Illus. 36: Arrangement: Matzoth After Afikoman is Broken, Page 451, has generated a very subtle but important change by pointing the wafers just opposite of their orientation *before Yahatz* – breaking the *Afikoman*. This demonstrates that, *after* The Crucifixion (i.e., the "breaking") of Messiah, the two remaining whole wafers are presently "pointing" the actions of God, The Father and God, The Holy Spirit. Whereas, just the actions of Messiah were portrayed by all three wafers *before Yahatz*. Also, the "broken" Son's Glorified Body (the smaller piece) is now pointing back to Heaven, as He returns to His Father. Each wafer therefore is indicating the action of One member of The Holy Trinity after the "breaking" of The Son, Messiah. The 1st (lowest) wafer shows God, The Father, returning to His Place (Hosea 5:15) as the Divine Presence, *Shekhinah,* when He withdrew from the Temple, C.E. 70. The Holy Spirit is portrayed by the 3rd wafer now pointing back to the World as He ministers to mankind through the Church after The Son went back to His Father's Place.

In this sequence are shown some subtle traits of The Triune God that we have not yet addressed. Notice that the 1st *matzah*, depicting God, The Father, is "lowest" (beneath) the other wafers, but He IS First! – Observe also that:

- The Father's wafer is placed first on the plate.
- The Father "supports" the other Two of The Trinity.
- The Holy Spirit "covers" the other Two of The Trinity.
- The Son "completes" the other Two of The Trinity as He is "centered between them: in Heaven, in The Word, and in The World.

It must be observed that during any "works" of God, when One of His Trinity is absent from the other Two, His full Presence still remains in effect. God is omnipresent. This is seen in Illus. 36: Arrangement: Matzoth After Afikoman is Broken, Page 451, where we see that even after breaking the 2nd wafer, the full star shows even when only the 1st and 3rd *matzah* wafers are present in unbroken form. (The Supreme Mathematician!,...Again!)

For example, when His Son was "in the world," The Father and His Holy Spirit were still in Heaven, in full Glory, Presence and Power. Similarly, when His Son returned to Heaven, His Holy Spirit was dispatched, during what we call "The Church Age," to work with righteous men "in the world." The Father and His Son remain in Heaven in His full Presence, Glory and Power.

A Glorious summary of The Crucifixion, Resurrection and Ascension of *Y'shua* of Nazareth, as well as pictures of both the Church Age and the Kingdom Age, is portrayed by the *Seder* and presented in Illus. 37: Seder – 1st Day in Messianic Period in Israel, Illus. 38: Seder – 2nd Day in Messianic Period in Israel and Illus. 39: Seder – 3rd Day in Messianic Period in Israel, Pages 452, 453 and 454. A third drama is presented in Illus. 40: Seder Matzoth Show God, Holy Spirit, World, Page 455, summarizing the actions of God, the Father and God, the Holy Spirit in the World during this present "Church Age."

A fourth story is related concerning the role of God's People, Israel, through the ages, portrayed in Illus. 41: Seder Matzoth Show God Leading Israel, Page 456. The foundational clue to deciphering this overall meaning of the *Seder* is found in the Four Cups. Each cup marks the end of one "Day" and the beginning of the next "Day" in each of *three* "Days" with *three* individual and distinct stories seen in the *Seder* drama,

The 1st "Day" of these three dramas is presented in Illus. 37: Seder – 1st Day in Messianic Period in Israel, Page 452. Principally, we have shown the story of The Crucifixion and burial in The Tomb, all taking place before sundown on 14 *Nisan*, the Day of Preparation. Upon this day the Paschal Lamb, a male of the first year and without blemish, is to be slain before the entire congregation "at evening" – i.e., "the ninth hour" or about 3 p.m. – the exact hour of *Y'shua's* death upon The Cross. (Matthew 27:46 – 50)

Further, it would hardly seem to be coincidental that we also see the first "day" or period of Israel's "smiting," which started when they began their disobedience by not observing the Sabbatical Law. The Israelites ceased to "*rest the land*" as they had been Commanded to do (Leviticus 25:2-5) for one year of each seven year period. Soon afterward Israel was "broken" into two nations, as Israel and Judah, carried into captivity and eventually "scattered" (buried) among the nations. (See Illus. 41: Seder Matzoth Show God Leading Israel, Page 456) Judah, the smaller piece, was God's Holy remnant – symbolized by the triangle.

From Hosea's prophecy (Hosea 6:1-2),

"Come and let us return unto the Lord: for He hath torn , and He will heal us; He hath smitten, and He will bind us up. After two days will He revive us: in the third day He will raise us up, and we shall live in His sight."

So, it should be no surprise that observant, studious Jewish people, after the "two days" are now anxiously expecting Messiah, Son of David, to bring soon their Redemption and the end of their "smiting." We know that Israel is to be "smitten" for two Days, in which each "day" consists of one thousand years. In parallel to Hosea's forecast, this 1st Day also depicts the 1st "day", of 1000 years, of what Believers have called the Church Age. During this period the early Church was persecuted and scattered to begin its Holy Work in the World.

Gentile Christians seem often to forget or ignore the fact that Jewish men and women actually started what we call "the Church." They were viciously persecuted and scattered at the time. The smaller triangular piece may represent those Christians who were given to become the martyrs of that "day." They were righteous and holy, thus represented by a triangle in this picture.

A tragic recollection tugs at our heartstrings and pinches our tear ducts as we now drink that 1st Cup, the "Cup of Sanctification." It is now evident *Y'shua* alluded to the meaning of this cup when He prayed at *Gethsemane*, shortly before He was arrested, saying in Matthew 26:39 –

"Father, if it be possible, let this cup pass from Me."

The 2nd Day is outlined as the *Seder* continues in Illus. 38: Seder – 2nd Day in Messianic Period in Israel, Page 453. As we have said, this depicts both *Y'shua's* 2nd day in The Tomb and the 2nd day of The Passover (which is the 1st Day of Unleavened Bread, 15 *Nisan*) as well as Israel's 2nd "day" of smiting, since God went "back to His Place." (Hosea 5:15) That period, of course, has consisted of the past 1000 years of the Church Age.

Rabbi Max Stauber, whom we recognized earlier as having discovered profound information about the Passover *Seder* in an ancient *Haggadah*, had this to say about the significance of the *Afikoman*. R. Stauber observed that Israel was "broken" when the Temple was destroyed and The People were "scattered." Then, Israel was "hidden away" for "two days" (two thousand years) by being "smitten" and removed from the world scene as a nation. In 1948 The People returned to The Land, *eretz Israel*, and the nation of Israel was miraculously restored to its sovereignty. And so Israel, symbolically as the *Afikoman*, was "found" again and has been "enjoyed" by The People as every Jewish person worldwide takes justifiable pride in the fact that they once more have their Beloved Homeland which God had Promised to them.

A rather touching observation from one *Haggadah*[18] says drops of wine are dropped from the 2nd Cup for each of the ten plagues of Egypt as they are counted during the *DAYENU*, Illus. 38: Seder – 2nd Day in Messianic Period in Israel, Page 453. A finger is dipped into the wine and then drops are placed in a saucer; suggesting the "Finger of God" which wrought the plagues on Egypt. Many Christians would argue that God does not bring evil events against men. Egypt therefore, through her sins against the children of Israel, actually empowered Satan to deliver the plagues on herself.

Some believe that it was during the *Maror* portion of the *Seder*, which we call *The Last Supper*, that Jesus dipped the *matzah* (some translations say "*morsel*") into the *maror* and/or *charoset*. (See Illus. 42: Seder Plate Arrangements: Various Haggadoth, Page 457) At this point, *all* participants dip a "morsel" of *matzah* into the *charoset* and *maror* (bitter herbs). Alfred Edersheim[49] and David Stern[50] both express that opinion concerning which portion in the ceremony this incident occurred. – John 13:26 states:

"Jesus answered, 'He it is, to whom I shall give a sop, when I have dipped it.' And when he had dipped the sop, he gave it to Judas Iscariot, the son of Simon."

Edersheim points out that *all* persons at the table would have had the "*morsel*" or "*sop*" – thus leaving it questioned about whether Judas actually was obviously indicated as the betrayer at that time. Jesus then gave the morsel to Judas, thereby revealing (perhaps only as "20/20 hindsight") that Judas was the one who would betray Jesus.

Significance of this move is seen from the *Haggadah* in that the *Dayenu* is intended to bring remembrance of the deliverance of the Israelites from their bondage in Egypt. This is compared then as a picture of Christ delivering men from the "bondage" to Satan that their sins would surely bring. Christ had to suffer for our sins in order to deliver us from the bondage of sin. Judas was of course His instrument for causing Him to suffer what was, after all, our punishment. The "picture" then continues as Judas' actual eating the *matzah* represents his "eating" the Paschal Lamb. We recall here that the *matzah* represents the Paschal Lamb and Jesus represents the Paschal Lamb of God. – (We hope all this didn't make you dizzy!)

Another source offers that decreasing the level of wine points to the diminishing strength of the Egyptians during the plagues. However, *Midrash Rabbah – Eichah, Lamentations, Part 24 (Prologue)* and *Sanhedrin* 39b say on the day the Egyptians drowned, angels were forbidden to sing praises. This would be as if God had said, "My creatures are drowning in the sea, and you want to sing praises?!" *Haggadah* reminds us here that even in the midst of jubilance over our victories, some pleasure must be sacrificed in memory of our fallen enemies *who also are God's creatures!* – God is heartbroken when any of Humankind are suffering or dying. We could wish that we and our allies might have had this sort of counseling at the close of our many wars.

The 3rd Cup in Illus. 39: Seder – 3rd Day in Messianic Period in Israel, Page 454, is the "Cup of Redemption," that heralds the ending of the 2nd Day as well as the beginning of the 3rd Day, at sundown on 16 *Nisan*. "*On the morrow after the Sabbath;*" i.e., sunrise the next morning, the priest waves a sheaf of grain gathered from the first Spring harvest (usually barley) for the Feast of First Fruits. It was on that morning that *Y'shua* arose from The Tomb as The First Fruits of The Resurrection. When He accomplished that, our Redemption was completed. *Y'shua* overcame the Death which awaits all of our souls, if we die without accepting His Payment for Redemption of our sins. "*The soul that sinneth, it shall die.*" (Ezekiel 18:20) Thus, *Y'shua* will put to death that Ultimate Lie authored by Satan: "*...You shall not surely die.*" (From Genesis 3:4)

The 3rd "Day" is further dramatized for the nation of Israel. After their two "days" (two thousand years) of smiting, Israel is Promised to be "raised up." (Hosea 6:2) In that "Day," *Y'shua* shall govern the World from Jerusalem, where He will dwell with His People. And Oh!, how the *Haggadah* adoringly and eagerly awaits Messiah, Son of David – their Redeemer. From the *Haggadah* liturgy, we have excerpted in Illus. 39: Seder – 3rd Day in Messianic Period in Israel, Page 454, several familiar Messianic phrases of Hope from Holy Scripture, which Jewish worshipers call the *Tanakh*; i.e., Gentiles' "Old Testament."

We had discussed earlier that the Jewish *Talmud* and *Midrash* many times declare: "our Rabbis teach" that Judaism has been faithful to pray for Him to arrive "speedily" (soon) to build His Temple. All during now these many centuries, it is obvious their prayers have been heard by The Almighty. They reason therefore that their prayers will be answered not by His "speedy" (soon) arrival, but instead that Messiah, Son of David will actually build the Temple "speedily" (i.e., quickly) – as in the twinkling-of-an-eye, when He does arrive. In this way, Jewish people are confident the Lord will answer their prayer – *one way or the other!*

As we advance through this study of the *Haggadah*, we encounter several Biblical quotes that are very familiar to Christians. It is interesting to discuss the Jewish origin of these phrases and statements. Near the conclusion of the meal, the leader gives thanks by saying:

"*Blessed art Thou, O Eternal, our God, our King of The Universe, Who bringest forth bread from the Earth.*"

Followed by:

"*Blessed art Thou, O Eternal, our God, King of The Universe, Who sanctified us with Thy Commandments, and Commanded us to eat unleavened bread.*"

These blessings are said over all of the remaining *matzah* wafers.

Later, as a sort of "dessert" after the meal, the leader takes the larger piece of the second (middle) *matzah* (i.e., the *Afikoman*) and breaks it. He then distributes pieces to the participants. No food is eaten after this. This station in the order is the *Tzafon*, and is most likely the point at which I Corinthians 11:24 describes Jesus saying:

"*And when He had given thanks, He brake it and said, 'Take, eat: This is My Body, which is broken for you...'* "

And, as emphasized throughout, all participants then close the meal, as instructed, with the Blessed taste of the *matzah* in their mouths.

Next, before the pouring of the third cup of wine, the leader pronounces a wine blessing, with:

"Blessed art Thou, O Lord, our God, Who createst the fruit of the vine."

After the blessing, the *Cup of Redemption* is filled with wine.

After a final Blessing of wine, the Fourth cup – the Cup of Hope – is poured. The cup is drained. The celebration is then closed by all participants proclaiming, in unison – Joyfully! –

"NEXT YEAR IN JERUSALEM!"

Before departing, several most plaintive pleas for their Messiah are given, such as:

"May The Holy One send us the Messiah speedily."

"May He Who is most merciful make us worthy to attain the days of Messiah, and eternal life in the World to come."

No less than twelve times in some narrations, the participants urge The Holy One:

"...soon rebuild His House speedily, speedily, soon, in our days."

Also appearing throughout this closing portion of the *Seder* are several Biblical phrases familiar to Christians, and which sincerely reflect the Messianic Hope of the Jewish people:

"The stone which the builders rejected, hath become the chief cornerstone."

"This is the day The Eternal hath made. Rejoice and be glad in it."

"Blessed be He Who cometh in the Name of The Eternal."

"He causeth the dumb to speak; He looseth those that are bound; He supporteth the fallen; He raiseth up those who are fallen down."

"Every mouth shall adore Thee; And every tongue shall swear unto Thee; Every knee shall bend unto Thee; Every being shall bow down before Thee; And every heart shall revere Thee; And all inward parts and reins shall sing psalmodies to Thy Name."

"Who is like unto Thee?"

Revised liturgy is specified in certain portions of the narration for *Seder* nights that happen to occur on Friday night, on Saturday night or on a weekday night. Many *Haggadoth* comment lengthily on this portion of the *Seder* concerning Messiah.

Many of the prayers at the *Seder* include words pleading to The Holy One, asking: *"that Messiah will come speedily in our day."* It is clear that many Jewish people have waited lovingly and longingly for Him for many centuries, just as Believers await eagerly the same

One. Jewish worshipers say[19] they wonder how long will He tarry? Still, for millennia, they have expected Him momentarily. – (Does this sound familiar?)

They agree that His Coming has got to be the best kept secret of all time! – Messiah, Himself, said, "*Only The Father knoweth*" (From Matthew 24:36). Jewish sages agree that when He comes, there will be no hunger, no wars, no strife, no jealousy, universal prosperity, blessings in abundance. And, note this: The world will be *totally* occupied in acquiring knowledge about *God*.

The narration continues in the reflection that their Messianic hope has continued to beacon through the gloom of their exile. It is said that everyone, by his actions, is intimately involved either in hurrying or in delaying the arrival of Messiah. Each one of us counts in this. Together we can help restore "cosmic harmony" and aid in bringing the beginning of the End of Days.

Surely, the hearts of all Believers must be warmed in the knowledge that Jewish brethren share these same thoughts in welcoming Messiah, Son of David. And, remember – Jewish people are doing this "welcoming" of Messiah at each Passover – *every* year. That same hope is further echoed by placing of a cup for the prophet Elijah at the table. This is done of course, because Elijah is to herald the arrival of Messiah!

We Christians also are *supposed* to be continually and eagerly awaiting His Coming again as we give *Y'shua* His Remembrance at every Lord's Supper, Holy Communion, etc. The Apostle Paul reminds and admonishes us –

"For as often as ye eat this bread, and drink this cup, **ye do shew the Lord's death, till He come.***" (I Corinthians 11:26)*

Still, how many Christians do we know who are indifferent or even are horrified at any mention of the End of Days?

We again remind ourselves that the *Haggadoth*, and many *Talmud* statements (*Pesahim* 19), seriously emphasize that *"We must finish the meal with the taste of the Paschal Lamb in our mouths and nobody shall say, 'On with the entertainment!' – It is a solemn occasion."* That is, the *Afikoman* is eaten lastly, to be savored by all participants as a sort of dessert; although, *matzah* certainly is not very tasty or sweet. Although mentioned previously, we should recall at this point that the *Afikoman* actually represents the Paschal Lamb. Unleavened bread of the *Afikoman* at the end of this sacred rite signals the humility and love of God which He wishes to leave with men as a final thought at His Supper.

As we examine closely the narration of the Last Supper (*Seder*), beginning at I Corinthians 11:23, Paul makes it very clear that he is speaking of that last night:

"*...the same night in which He was betrayed...*

...After Jesus broke the bread and had given thanks, He said,...take, eat: this is My Body, which is broken for you: this do in remembrance of Me.

After the same manner also He took the cup, when He had supped, saying, 'This cup is the new testament in My blood: This do ye, as oft as ye drink it, in remembrance of Me.'"

Paul continues in Verse 26:

"For as often as ye eat this bread, and drink this cup, ye do shew (proclaim) the Lord's death until He come."

During that last *Seder*, Y'shua instructed His followers: *"As oft as ye drink this (or eat this), do in remembrance of Me."* (from I Corinthians 11:24 – 25) Yes, He was saying that once each year at their Passover *Seder*, when they snap the *matzah* in two pieces and eat their *matzah* and drink their wine, they are urged to "remember" *exactly* what all that means. However, we can be fairly confident that upon that tragic and dramatic night of their last *Seder* with The Master, the Disciples "had no clue" about what all that REALLY meant. They had been taught since childhood that the *Seder* was "for a remembrance" of their flight from slavery in Egypt to their freedom in the Promised Land.

We can just imagine the wonderment the Twelve must have felt that night when *Y'shua* took bread and broke it, saying, *"This is My Body, which is given for you."* When *Y'shua* snapped that middle *matzah* with a loud c-r-r-a-C-K!!!, their startled, dumbfounded expressions must have been as if to say, "Master, do You mean after all these centuries, when we break the 2nd *matzah*, that *matzah* is symbolizing you, Lord?! – How can this be?!" – (Or, maybe at the time they thought *Y'shua* was just "talking.") We know, of course, the Disciples at the time did not really understand or believe *Y'shua* was *really* going to be crucified and was *really* going to rise from the Tomb on the third day.

After *Y'shua* had risen – Yes! – then they finally began to know what it all meant. Later, as interpreted by some Christians in Acts 20:7, the early Church repeated at least part of the ceremony on the first day of each week (Sunday). This has come to be known as "The Lord's Supper." Many Christian denominations serve "Communion" or "The Eucharist" or "The Lord's Supper" frequently during each year, and some observe actually *every* Sunday.

A Christian (Gentile) misunderstanding has surfaced during our examining of that last *Seder* with His Disciples. *Y'shua* said, "...*this do ye*, **as oft as ye drink it**, *in remembrance of Me.*" Then, "*as oft*" means: When you do *this* on each Passover. *Y'shua* did not "command" the Disciples to practice that ritual *every* Sunday, as some Christian doctrines have interpreted. That practice was adopted later by the first century Church. The practice is certainly intended to honor Messiah and it is undeniably a noble practice, but He did *not* "command" *Christian Gentiles* that it be done every Sunday or at *any* time.

If *Y'shua* "commanded" anybody to do this, He commanded all Jewish *Seder* celebrants to remember it was He whom they were symbolizing each Passover "*as oft as **you** break this matzah, drink this wine, etc.*" In fact, everything *Y'shua* ever remarked in the Gospel was addressed directly to *Jews* – *always* in a Jewish context and *always* on Jewish occasions. Sadly, there has been and continues to be much strife, judging and accusation from Christians in doctrinal disputes because of this simple and unfortunate Gentile application and misunderstanding of a *very* Jewish rite.

Again, there is surely nothing inappropriate or unworthy about observing that Remembrance more than once each year at any occasion. Nevertheless, Jesus certainly never "commanded" that it be done other than by Jewish worshipers at their Passover *Seder*. Christians would do well to "remember" each time just what He was talking about and exactly what all of it *really* means. This work is intended to bring to Christians that kind of awareness about the "pictures" of *Y'shua* in the Jewish feast days.

If we pause to contemplate all the spirituality and sincere reverence demonstrated here for the Lord on this day, we should be able to understand why the 15th of *Nisan* is a "special" Sabbath. Christians should especially have empathy toward worshipful Jewish people in their loving and hopeful vigil for Messiah, Son of David. Their devotion and zeal for Messiah is almost worthy of envy. If only they could know right now WHO actually He is!! – They will, however, surely know Him when He arrives. – *Returns !:*

> "*...and they shall look upon Me Whom they have pierced, and they shall mourn for Him, as one mourneth for his only son,...*"

Zechariah 12:10

> "*And one shall say unto Him, 'What are these wounds in thine hands?' Then He shall answer, 'Those with which I was wounded in the house of My friends.'*"

Zechariah 13:6

The *Seder* is completed at drinking the 4th Cup and the reading of the *NIRTZAH*. Finally, all the celebrants join in accepting God's Mercy and in giving thanks and blessing Him for all things for all time. A final burst of Jewish joy and hope and thanks is given as all declare in unison their desire that their next *Seder* will be ...

"NEXT YEAR IN JERUSALEM !"

Believers could add that we will say this at the end of the 3rd "Day" when we drink that 4th Cup and *everyone* – Jews and Christians – will shout:

"NEXT YEAR IN THE NEW JERUSALEM!"

Closing Remarks

Two of the remaining illustrations, Illus. 40: Seder Matzoth Show God, Holy Spirit, World, Page 455, and Illus. 41: Seder Matzoth Show God Leading Israel, Page 456, are mostly self-explanatory. These are included because they demonstrate just how far-reaching and how thoroughly God had planned the Passover Supper to teach men about Himself.

If you wish to try the triangular *matzah* shape for yourself, it can be cut to that shape from ordinary commercial square *matzah* with relative ease. After marking the cutting lines at the proper angles, use a hacksaw on a cutting board, carefully and very gently cutting the brittle wafer to an equilateral triangular shape. Using three *matzah* wafers, you can then demonstrate to yourself and to others how this story unfolds in such a beautiful manner to Glorify God and *Y'shua*.

As I look at this work, I am certain that the intricacy, symmetry, geometric Perfection, Drama, Passion and Order of this story is not a work that can be attributed to a mere human. Surely, anything this Glorious had to be wrought from a Divine Mind, Heart and Hand. To accuse this design of being coincidence or imagination is outright ludicrous. It would seem that if the Children of Israel did not originally conduct the *Seder* in this fashion, they certainly *should* have done it this way! Moreover, the *Seder* should surely be conducted in this manner after Messiah does arrive. Maybe this could help Jewish people (and other folks) have a better understanding of The Trinity.

We have made some apology for the complexity shown. However, God makes no apologies. Nothing God has ever done for His Chosen People could be classified as simple. He probably figures: "They are an intelligent and resourceful People. – It's not to worry! – They can handle it!"

It is our hope that after Jewish persons read this, they will know just how Holy the Passover *Seder* truly is. We further hope that Christians will, after reading this, have a better understanding of the Jewish Passover and *Seder*, and most importantly, what it all means! The next time they are given those tasteless, papery Communion wafers, or soda crackers or even soggy store-bought bread at The Lord's Supper, Holy Communion or Eucharist or Blessed Sacrament, etc., we hope they will at least reflect on how the *matzah* should **CRR-RACK**! – We hope both faiths will remember and savor the true meanings of this sacred supper and will love the stories it represents.

We are certainly aware that some will not agree with our interpretations of the pictures presented here. Some may even be offended. We offer that which we have received. We acknowledged at the beginning that we have only thin evidence to support the foundational story of the Father's Place Setting. Nevertheless, it can be said without apology, that even if the *Seder* was *not* originally conducted in this manner – **IT SHOULD HAVE BEEN!**

There may be even more pictures or different interpretations than what we have presented. We welcome, therefore, any criticism or correction that will make this story even more Holy and more Glorifying of The Author – The Great "I AM."

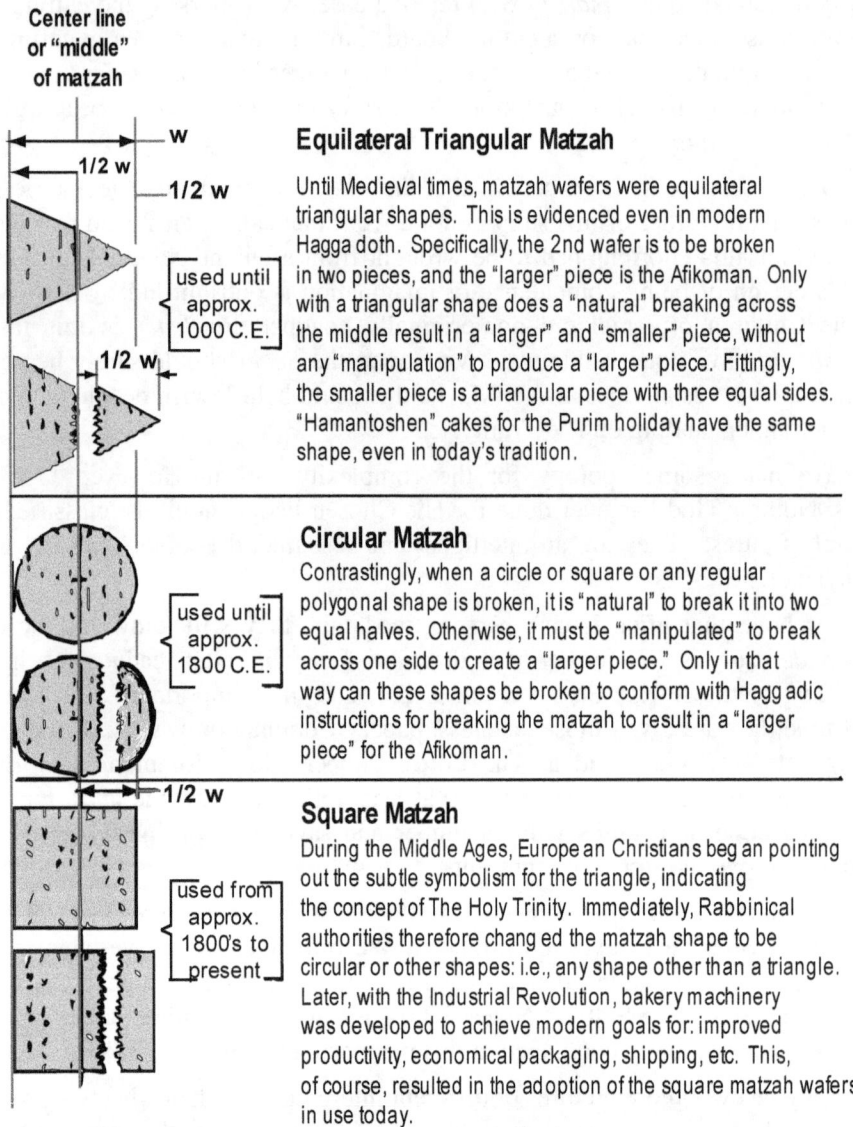

Equilateral Triangular Matzah

Until Medieval times, matzah wafers were equilateral triangular shapes. This is evidenced even in modern Haggadoth. Specifically, the 2nd wafer is to be broken in two pieces, and the "larger" piece is the Afikoman. Only with a triangular shape does a "natural" breaking across the middle result in a "larger" and "smaller" piece, without any "manipulation" to produce a "larger" piece. Fittingly, the smaller piece is a triangular piece with three equal sides. "Hamantoshen" cakes for the Purim holiday have the same shape, even in today's tradition.

Circular Matzah

Contrastingly, when a circle or square or any regular polygonal shape is broken, it is "natural" to break it into two equal halves. Otherwise, it must be "manipulated" to break across one side to create a "larger piece." Only in that way can these shapes be broken to conform with Haggadic instructions for breaking the matzah to result in a "larger piece" for the Afikoman.

Square Matzah

During the Middle Ages, European Christians began pointing out the subtle symbolism for the triangle, indicating the concept of The Holy Trinity. Immediately, Rabbinical authorities therefore changed the matzah shape to be circular or other shapes: i.e., any shape other than a triangle. Later, with the Industrial Revolution, bakery machinery was developed to achieve modern goals for: improved productivity, economical packaging, shipping, etc. This, of course, resulted in the adoption of the square matzah wafers in use today.

Illus. 29: Corruption of Seder Matzah Symbolism

Secrets Hidden in The Passover 445

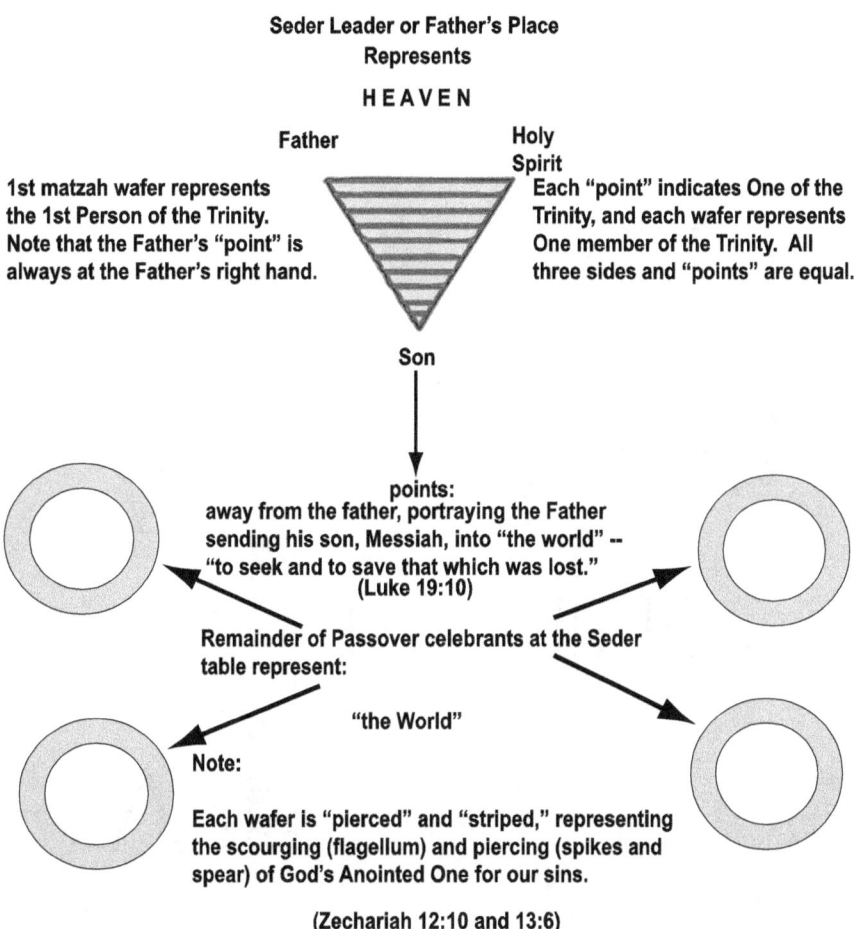

Illus. 30: Position: 1st (Lower) Matzah at Seder Table

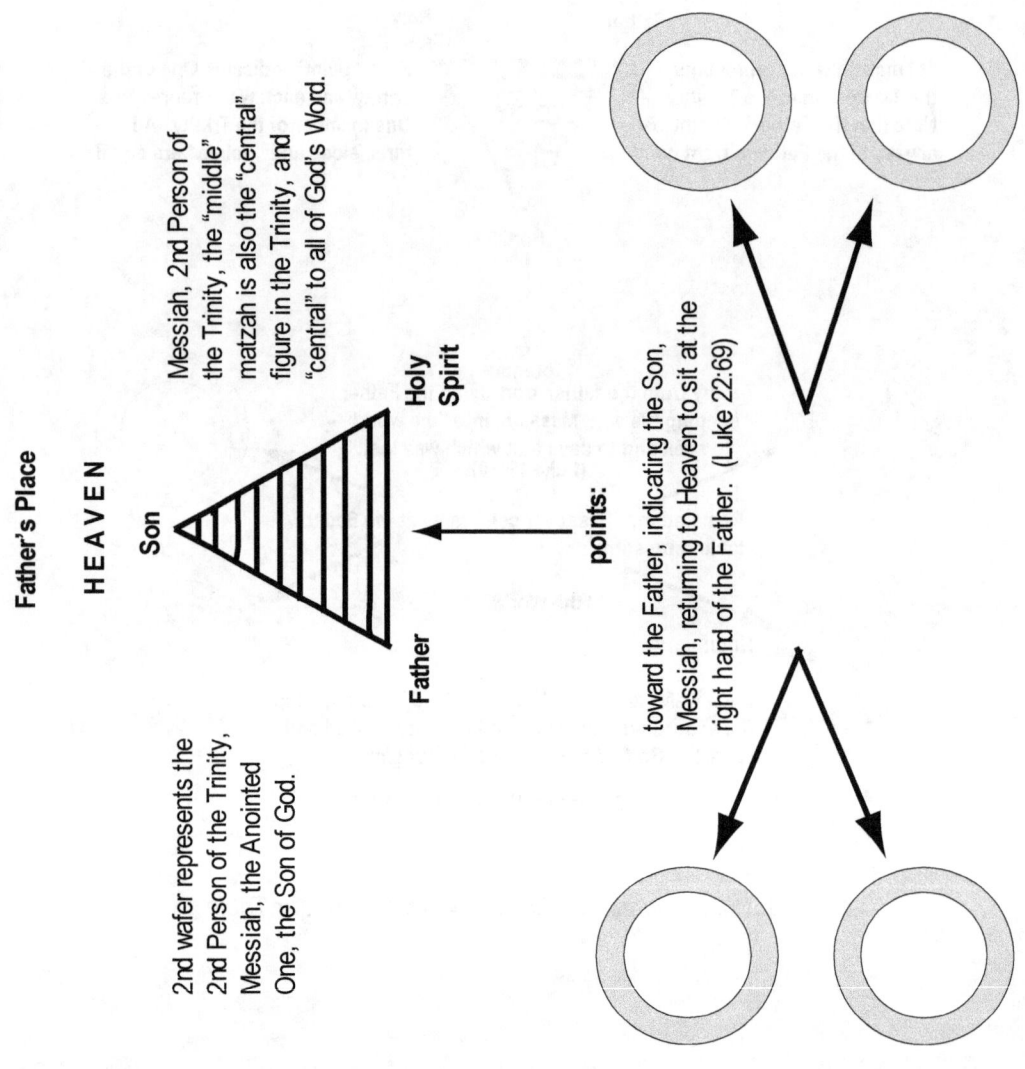

Illus. 31: Position: 2nd (Middle) Matzah at Seder Table

Secrets Hidden in The Passover **447**

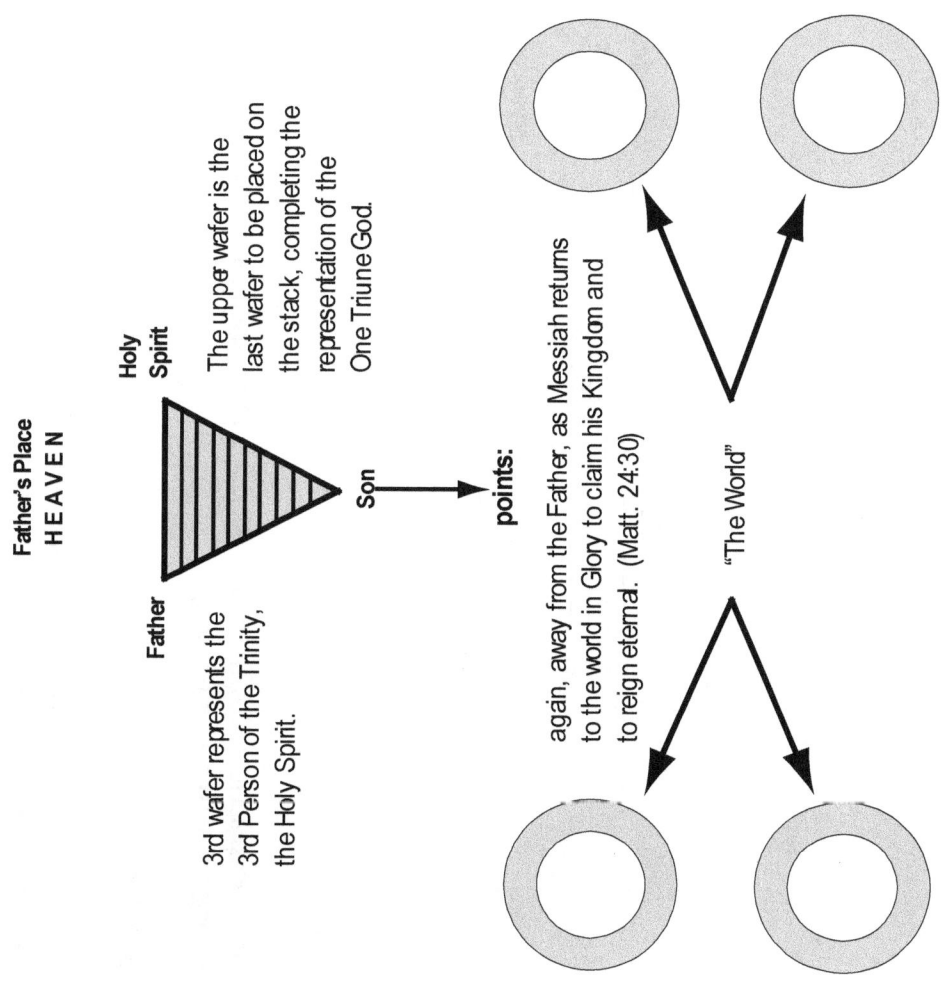

Illus. 32: Position: 3rd (Upper) Matzah at Seder Table

448 Jesus and the Third Temple

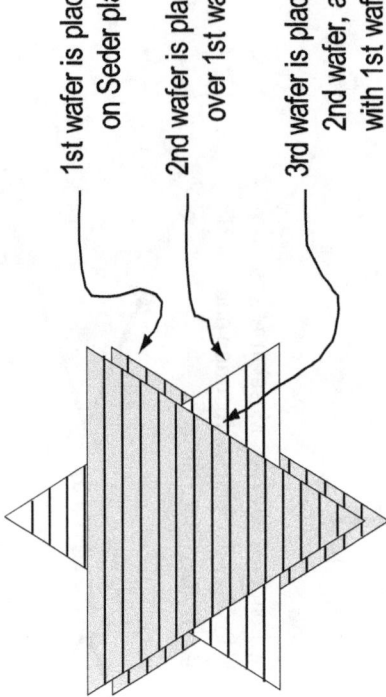

HEAVEN
(Father's Place)

1st wafer is placed on Seder plate.

2nd wafer is placed over 1st wafer.

3rd wafer is placed over 2nd wafer, aligned with 1st wafer.

Note:

The resulting figure, called The Star of David (Hebrew: Magen David), may actually have been originated at Moses' First Passover.

Summary:

Three triangular, equilateral matzah wafers at the Seder Table portray three major Scriptural Events manifested through the Central Person of The Trinity; i.e., Messiah, God's Anointed One. The wafers further manifest all three Divine Personages of The One Triune God.

Illus. 33: Final Arrangement of Matzoth at Seder Start

Secrets Hidden in The Passover   **449**

HEAVEN
Son
(body)

Messiah's Glorified Body is risen from The Tomb and ascends into Heaven.

Smaller piece also represents The One God in three Persons, via three points and three equal sides.

Father Holy Spirit
(soul)   (spirit)

Messiah's Earthly Body, hidden away in The Tomb, folded within a napkin of fine linen. (Luke 23:5)

(Afikoman)

Larger piece is folded in a napkin, hidden away and later eaten.

(soul)   (spirit)
Father   Holy Spirit
(Shekhinah)

Notes:

-- The three points of the wafers indicate the Soul, Body and Spirit represented by the members of The Trinity as: Father, Son and Holy Spirit.

-- The Son's Earthly (mortal) Body, the Afikoman or larger piece, then represents only The Father and The Holy Spirit, since both still remained in the world after Y'shua's Resurrection. The Father dwelled 40 more years in the Temple as Shekhinah (Divine Presence). The Holy Spirit dwelled in Apostles and the Disciples and continues to occupy today in <u>all</u> Believers.

-- Afikoman also depicts the death, burial and resurrection of Messiah. Since the Afikoman no longer was triangular, because The Son was broken away, it no longer was complete and could not therefore enter into Heaven. Whereas the smaller piece IS triangular and complete and IS in Heaven. Satan, thus by breaking Messiah's Body, was unable to destroy His completeness (Holiness), because when any triangle is broken in two, one triangle <u>always</u> remains.

-- Breaking the Afikoman from the 2nd wafer portrays "breaking" the body of "The Anointed" (Messiah), who was "cut off" (Daniel 9:26).

Illus. 34: Breaking Afikoman from 2nd Wafer

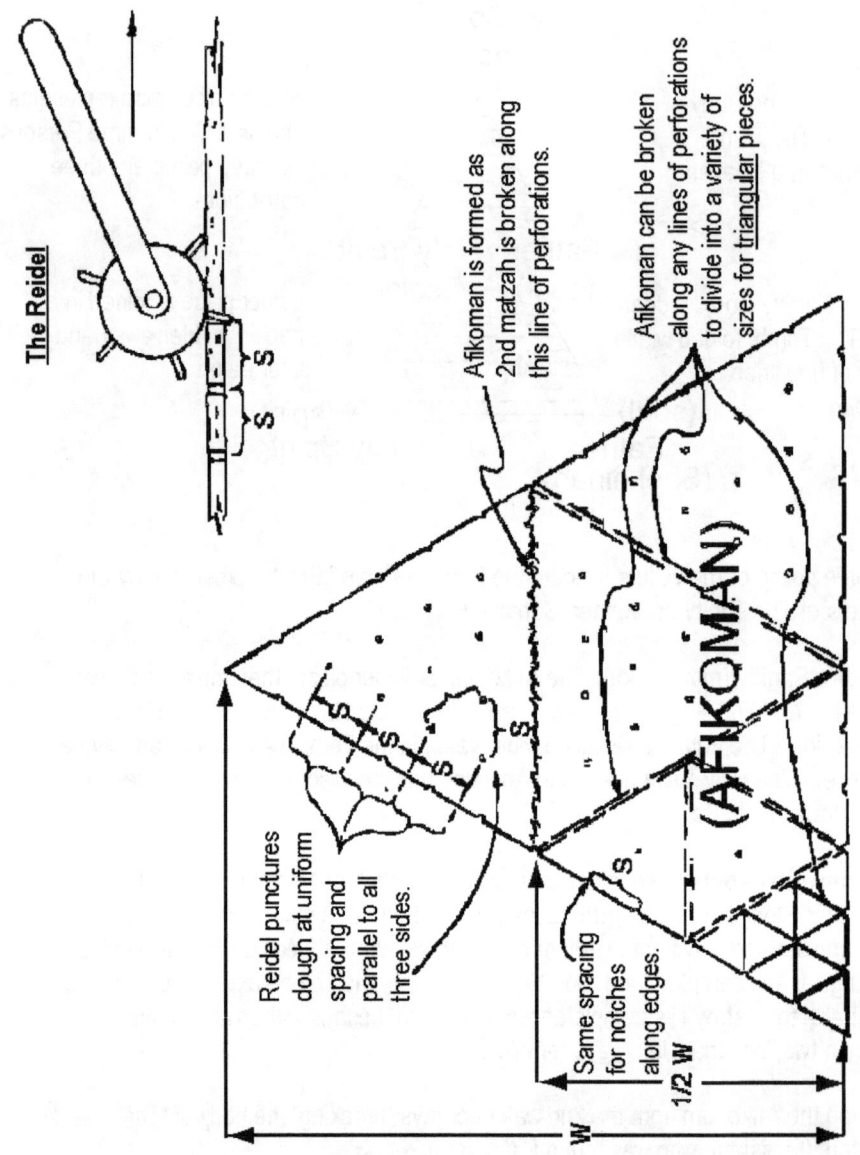

Illus. 35: Equal Perforation Spacing = Triangular Pieces

Secrets Hidden in The Passover   451

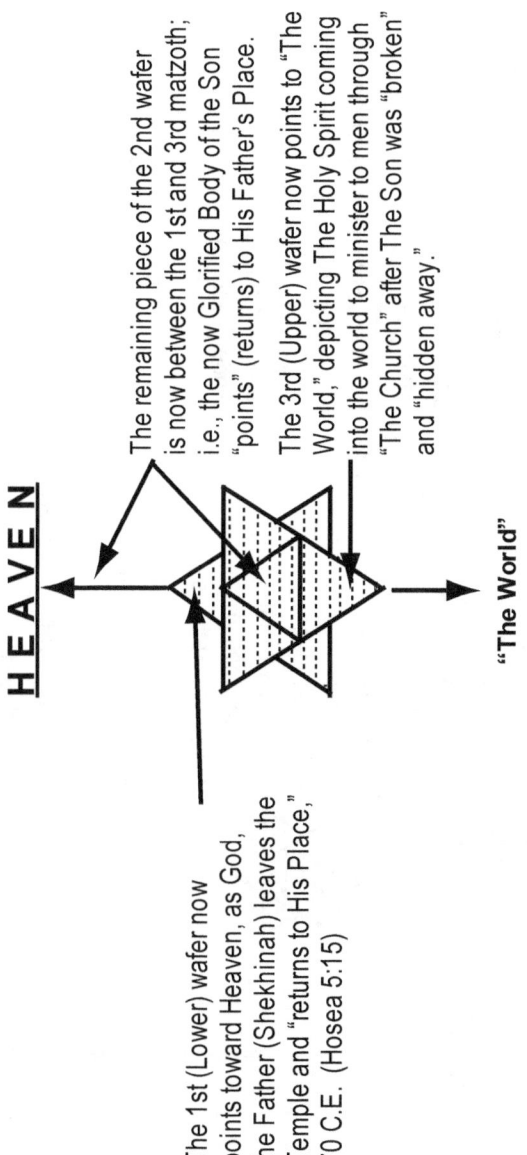

Illus. 36: Arrangement: Matzoth After Afikoman is Broken

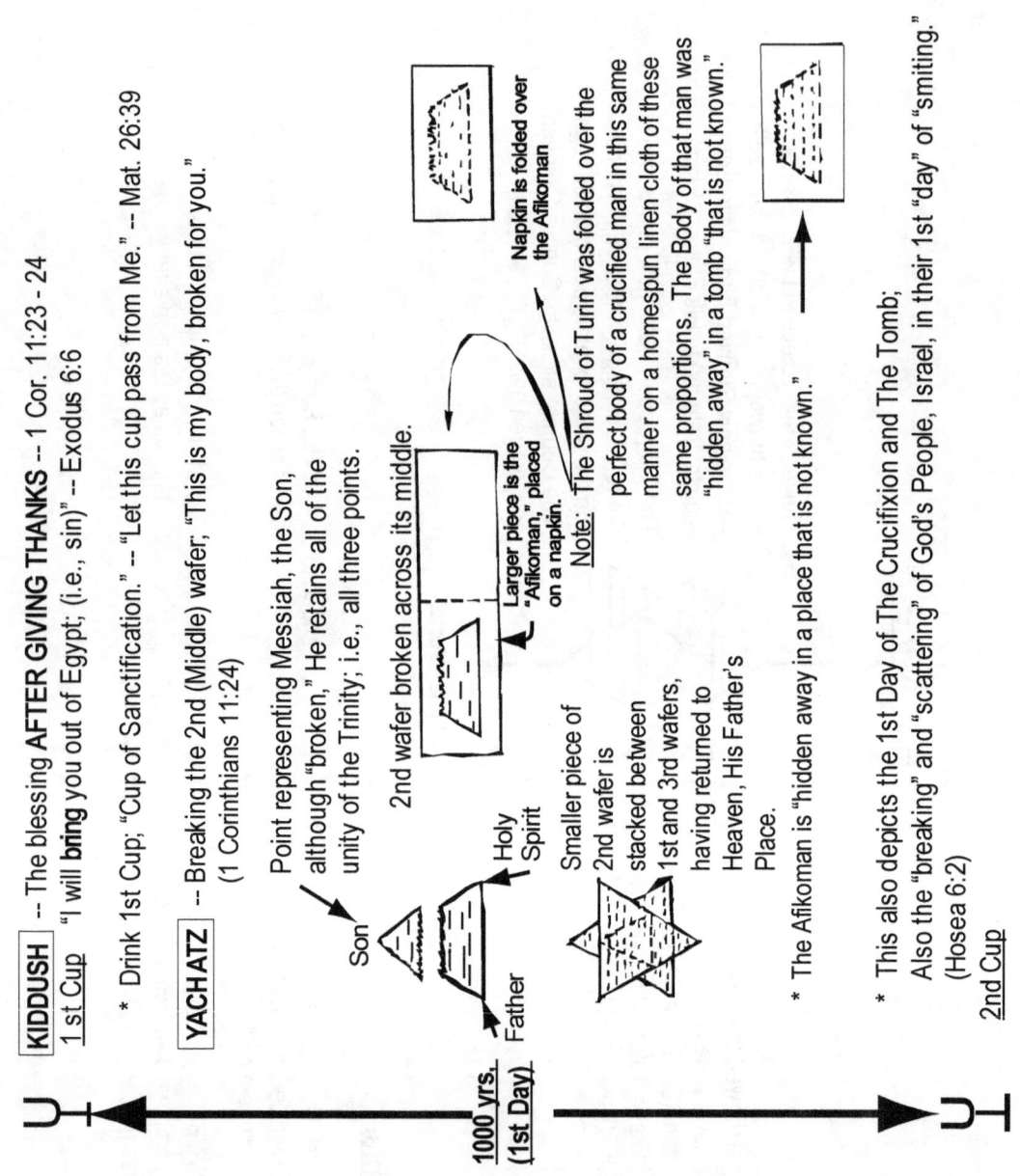

Illus. 37: Seder – 1st Day in Messianic Period in Israel

Secrets Hidden in The Passover 453

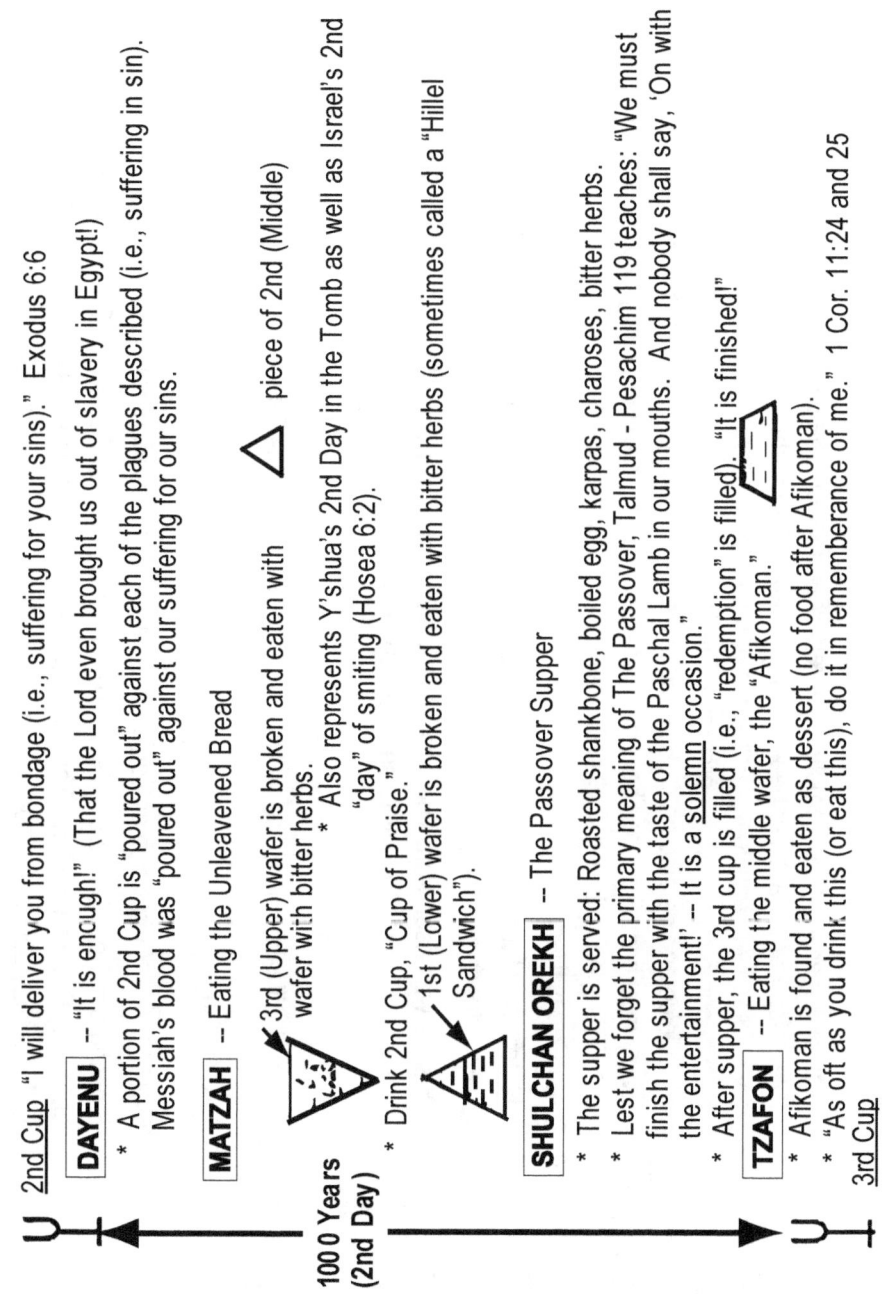

Illus. 38: Seder – 2nd Day in Messianic Period in Israel

3rd Cup "I will redeem (i.e., rescue, save) you. -- Exodus 6:6

* Drink 3rd Cup, "Cup of Redemption."

* A plea is made for the Temple to be rebuilt and for Messiah to arrive "speedily." (Many familiar phrases appear as this is read to the celebrants.) "...He is thy help and thy shield...I will walk in the Presence of the Lord...the stone which the builders rejected hath become the chief cornerstone. This is the day which the Lord hath appointed; we will rejoice and be glad on it...Blessed is He who cometh in the Name of the Lord.... Every mouth shall adore Thee; every tongue swear unto Thee; every knee shall bend unto Thee; every being shall bow down...who is like unto Thee?"
* 4th Cup is filled.

1000 Years (3rd Day)

Note: Israel will be "redeemed" two "days" after Messiah's body was "broken." Messiah's kingdom, through Israel, will reign for one "day" afterward.

* Y'shua was risen from The Tomb "on the third day." -- Luke 24:46
In the 3rd "day," God will raise Israel up. Hosea 6:2

4th Cup "I will take you to Me as My own People." -- Exodus 6:17

* Drink 4th Cup

NIRTZAH -- "Affirmation of God's Acceptance" (Abbreviated from Haggadoth)
Blessed are thou, O lord our God, ruler of the world. ...have mercy, O Lord our God, upon Thy People Israel, on Thy holy city, Jerusalem, on Zion, Abode of Thy Glory... Rebuild Holy Jerusalem speedily in our time...for Thou art the Good Lord, Who does good to all, and we thank Thee...Blessed art Thou, O Lord...
* <u>NEXT YEAR IN YERUSHALAYIM!</u>

Illus. 39: Seder – 3rd Day in Messianic Period in Israel

Secrets Hidden in The Passover **455**

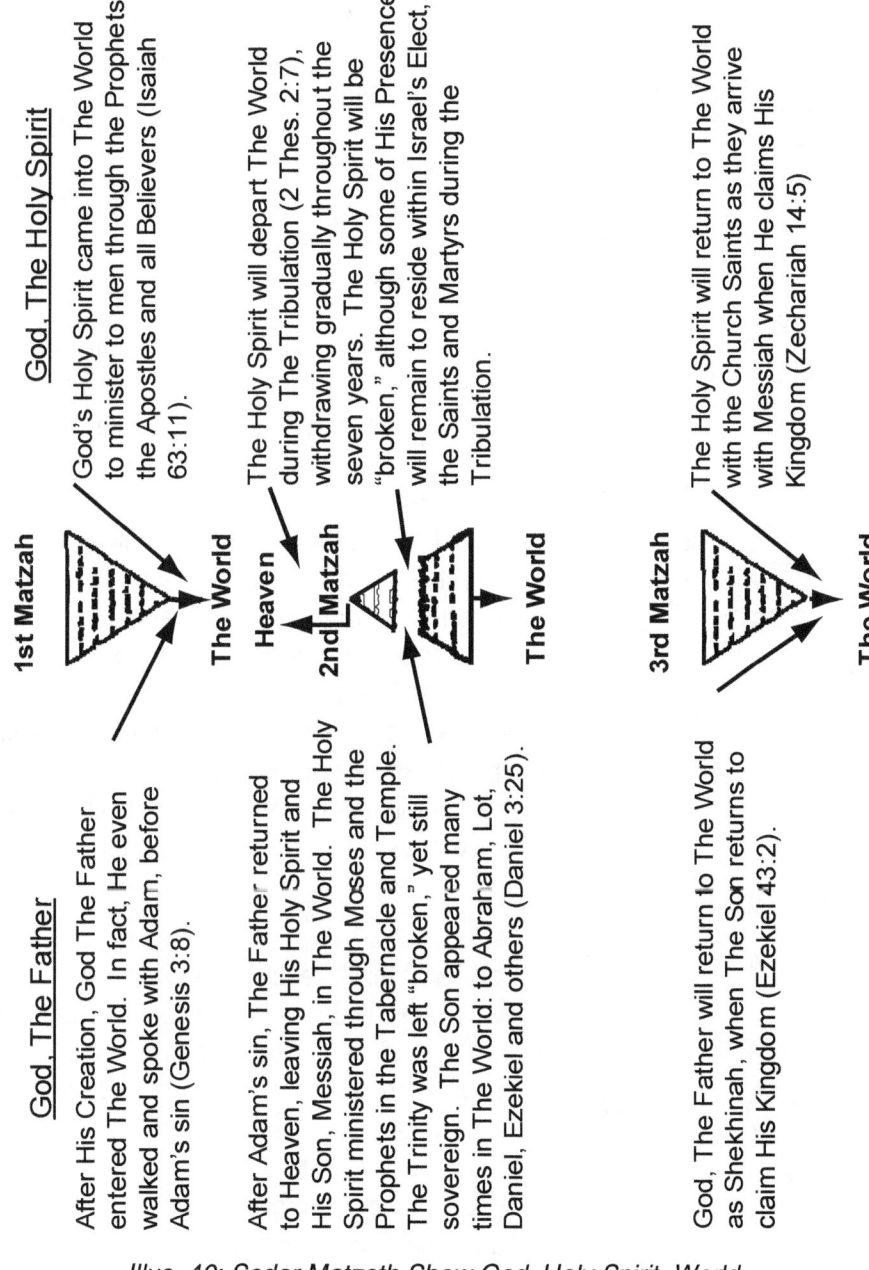

Illus. 40: Seder Matzoth Show God, Holy Spirit, World

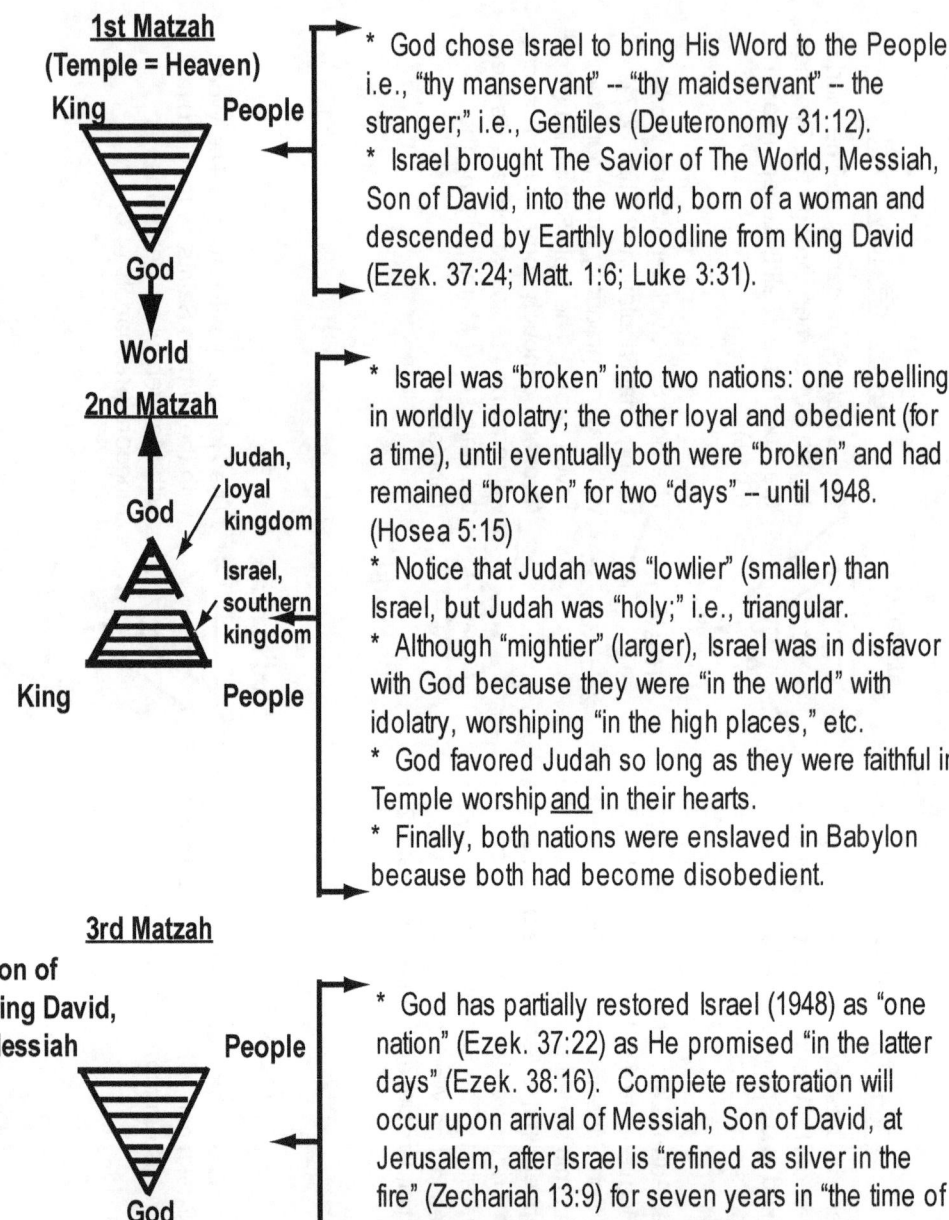

Illus. 41: Seder Matzoth Show God Leading Israel

Secrets Hidden in The Passover   457

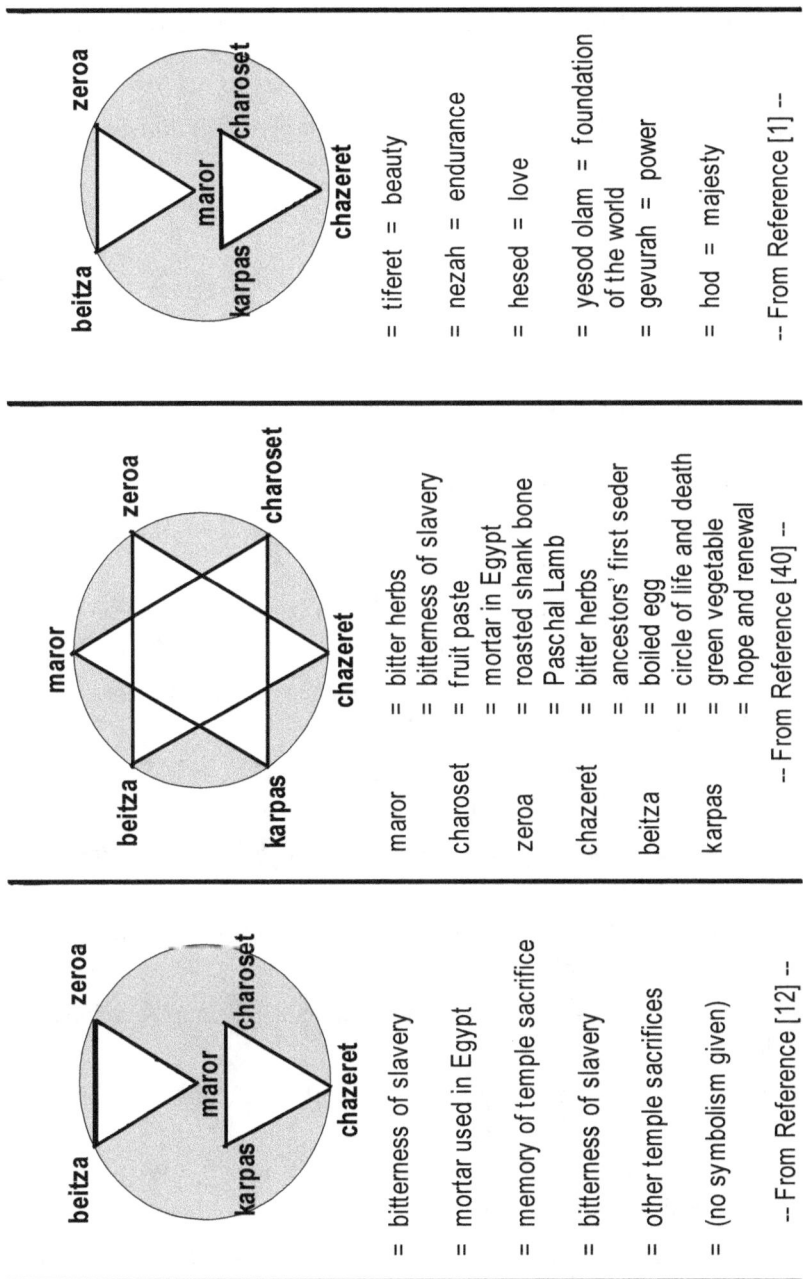

Illus. 42: Seder Plate Arrangements: Various Haggadoth

References and Bibliography for: Secrets Hidden in the Passover

(References are noted as superscripts in the text)

1. *Passover* – pp. 43-54 – Mordell Klein – Leon Amiel, Publisher –New York NY – 1973

2. *Babylonian Talmud*, Quincentenary Edition – The Soncino Press London, England – 1978

3. *Passover Haggadah* – pp. 6 – Rabbi Morris Silverman – Prayer Book Press Hartford CT – 1959

4. *The Passover Seder* – pp. 86 – Ruth Gordon Freedman – University of Pennsylvania Press – Philadelphia Pa – 1981

5. *The Passover Anthology* – pp. 88 – Phillip Goodman – The Jewish Publication Society of America – Philadelphia PA – 1961

6. *Passover Haggadah – The Feast of Freedom* – pp. 24 – Rachael Ann Rabinowicz – The Rabbinical Assembly – 1982

7. *Polychrome Historical Haggadah for Passover* – pp. xv – Jacob Freedman, D.D. – Jacob Freedman Liturgy Research Foundation – Springfield MA – 1974

8. *The Sinai Haggadah* – pp. 11 – J.H. Sinason – G.J. George & Co., Lt'd,. – 47 Milmark Park, London, England – 1978

9. *The Passover Haggadah* – pp. 11 – Nahum N. Glatzer – Schocken Books, Inc. – 342 Madison Ave., New York NY – 1973

10. *Passover Haggadah* – pp. viii – Rabbi Morris Silverman – Prayer Book Press – Hartford CT – 1959

11. *Passover Haggadah* – The Feast of Freedom – pp. 25 – Rachael Ann Rabinowicz – The Rabbinical Assembly – 1982

12. *A Feast of History* – pp. 253 – Chaim Raphael – Simon & Schuster – New York NY – 1972

13. *A Passover Haggadah* – pp. 10 – Herbert Bronstein – Central Conference of American Rabbis – New York NY – 1975

14. *Passover Haggadah – The Feast of Freedom* – pp. 27 – Rachael Ann Rabinowicz – The Rabbinical Assembly – 1982

15. *The Fire And The Cloud* – Revised Edition – pp. 42-43 – Robert F. Reiland – Xlibris Corp. – Philadelphia PA – 2003

16. *The Passover Haggadah* – pp. 17 – Phillip Birnbaum – Hebrew Publishing Co. – New York NY -

17. *Hagada* – pp. 5 – J.D. Eisenstein – Hebrew Publishing Co. – 1933

18. *A Guide to Passover* – pp. 54 – Isaac Levy – Jewish Chronicle Publications – London, England – 1958

19. *Passover Haggadah* – The Feast of Freedom – pp. 92 – Rachael Ann Rabinowicz – The Rabbinical Assembly – 1982

20. *The Joys of Yiddish* – pp. 299-300 – Leo Rostein – Washington Square Press – 1970

21. *A Lesson of Survival in Sarajevo* – Edward Serotta – Los Angeles Times (as reported in The Palm Beach Post) – 3 April 1996

22. *Will The Real Jesus Please Stand?* – pp. 2-24, 2-25 – Rev. Vendyl M. Jones Institute of Judaic-Christian Research – Arlington TX – 1983

23. *Passover Haggadah – Deluxe Edition* – Maxwell House of Kraft General Foods, Inc. – 1995

24. *A Passover Haggadah For Christians* – Ed. Bruce J. Lieske – The Lutheran Church Missouri Synod – St. Louis MO – 1973

25. *A Sephardic Passover Haggadah* – Rabbi Marc D. Angel – KTAV Publishing House, Inc. – Hoboken NJ – 1988

26. *On Wings Of Freedom* – Rabbi Richard N. Levy – KTAV Publishing House, Inc. – Hoboken NJ – 1989

27. *A Passover Haggadah* – Michael Strassfeld – The Rabbinical Assembly – Conservative Judaism, Vol. XXXII, No. 3 – New York NY – Spring 1979

28. *Jewish Encyclopedia* – Funk & Wagnalls Co. – New York NY – 1904

29. *Universal Jewish Encyclopedia* – published by: Universal Jewish Encyclopedia – New York NY – 1939

30. *Passover Haggadah* – Rabbi Hirsh Myski – Gross Bros. Printing Co., Inc. – Brooklyn NY – 1976

31. *The Haggadah* – Arthur Szyk – Massadah and Alumoth – Jerusalem and Tel Aviv, Israel – 1960

32. *San Diego Woman's Haggadah* – Women's Institute For Continuing Jewish Education – San Diego CA – 1980

33. *The Rylands Haggadah* – John Rylands – Harry N. Abrams, Inc. – New York NY 1988

34. *Israel Passover Seder* – Rabbi Menachem M. Kasher – American Biblical Encyclopedia Society – New York NY – 1950

35. *The Passover Haggadah* – Rabbi Adin Steinsaltz – Carta Publishing – Jerusalem, Israel – 1983

36. *The Shalom Seders* – compiled: The New Jewish Agenda –Adama Books – New York NY – 1984

37. *The Exodus Haggadah* – Rabbi David A. Wortman – United Jewish Appeal Rabbinic Cabinet

38. *The Union Haggadah* – Central Conference of American Rabbis – 1923

39. *The Encyclopedia of Jewish Symbols* – Ellen Frankel and Betsy Franklin Teutsch – Jason Aaronson, Inc. – Northvale NJ – 1992

40. *A Passover Haggadah As Commented By Elie Wiesel* – pp. 10 – Simon & Schuster – New York NY – 1993

41. *Jewish Literacy* – pp. 586 – Rabbi Joseph Telushkin – William Morrow & Co., Inc. – New York NY – 1991

42. *The Jewish Book of Why* – Alfred J. *Kolatch* – Johnathan David Publishers, Inc. – Middle Village NY – 1981

43. *The Second Jewish Book of Why* – Alfred J. *Kolatch* – Johnathan David Publishers, Inc. -Middle Village NY – 1985

44. *Chicago Tribune* – Part 2, Page 8 – "Lessons of the Past, Hope for the Future" – Maria T. Galo – 21 June 1996

45. *The Interactive Haggadah* CD-ROM – Jerusalem Multimedia Productions, Lt'd. – Jerusalem, Israel – 2003

46. *www.SnowCrystals.com* – Website all about snow crystals and snow flakes.

47. *The Pentateuch and HafTorahs* – Hertz, Dr. J. H. (Compiling Editor) – 2nd Edition – Soncino Press, London — 1965

48. *Price Library of Judaica* – George A. Smathers Libraries – University of Florida Gainesville, Florida

49. *The Life and Times of Jesus the Messiah* – pp. 824 – Alfred Edersheim – Hendrickson Publishers, Inc., Peabody, MA – 1994

50. Jewish New Testament Commentary – David Stern – Jewish New Testament Publications, Inc., – P.O. Box 615 – Clarksville, MD – 21029

20

Really "3 Days and 3 Nights?"

A complex controversy is easily settled by the Truth of what Scripture says and from The Law – Christians argue about a Jewish occasion without knowing the Jewish "rules" that apply – More thorough understanding of The Crucifixion is gained by observing the Jewish principles involved — Jesus fulfilled The Law on The Cross

Christians have debated for centuries about how Jesus completed three days and three nights in The Tomb. The question arises in the traditional *and* in the Biblical scenario, where Jesus was placed for burial on Friday just before sundown, then He arose early Sunday morning. That is a period of only about thirty-six hours. – This is far less than seventy-two hours that would be required to span three days and three nights. Many Christian teachers have struggled and striven with Scripture and with logic to explain that Jesus' body was placed in the grave Wednesday evening. Others "calculate" that it must have been on Thursday evening. These well-intentioned scholars are of course trying to make the scenario come to "three days and three nights;" although they attempt this within the culture of Western concepts of time.

Their chief motivation seems to be a desire to refute potential claims of critics who might say Jesus was in The Tomb perhaps only a bit less than 36 hours with the Friday-to-Sunday scenario. Another motivation is their intent to "prove" that God's Word is to be taken "literally." With their Western "bent" on timing of days and nights, they cannot accept that a Friday burial actually will be in compliance with "literal" Scripture in stating that Jesus was raised "on the first day of the week." – Sunday. Actually, neither the "Wednesday" nor the "Thursday" version agrees with "literal" Scripture in the Gospel scenario of those days and nights. Literal Scripture is clear that Jesus was in The Tomb before sundown on the day of His Crucifixion. (Luke 23:50 – 56) Scripture is also clear that Jesus was raised *"early the first day of the week"*; i.e., Sunday. (Mark 16:9)

The chief failure of these scholars is in fact caused by their using our Western concepts of days and nights in their "calculations." They are so desperate to prove their own personal version as the only valid solution that they commit grave errors and do not even achieve what they intend to show. For example, if Jesus were entombed on a Wednesday just before sundown, and then raised at dawn on a Sunday, He would have accrued a total of 4 nights and 3 days in the grave within a Western time tradition. Or, if he were placed in The Tomb on a Thursday just before sundown, and raised on the following Sunday at dawn, He would have been in the grave 3 nights and 2 days in Western tradition. So, what ever happened to the *"three days and three nights"*?

We shall investigate this problem, uncovering their folly and demonstrating how Scripture is "literally" accurate when we remember the writers were Jewish! – And, they used ONLY Jewish applications of the Law in determining "days" and "nights."

Then, of course some will say this argument is of no importance. – "It doesn't affect our Salvation, etc., etc." – We of course agree that this contention has no import concerning Salvation; although, it is important that we derive the Truth in all Biblical matters to whatever extent is attainable. There are many facets of this analysis that are Glorifying to God and to Jesus Christ. Such matters are therefore not to be ignored and cast aside with indifference.

It's "Only" A Question of "Time"

"Was it Really Three Days and Three Nights?" – If a person believes the Gospel in Matthew 12:40 is truly the Word of God, there can be only an enthusiastic and affirmative answer to this question. Nevertheless, Christians continue in strife over this challenge, each side defending its position as based on "The Word of God." And, since all of their debates are in fact based upon God's Word, none of these righteous folks are questioning that Jesus was in The Tomb "three days and three nights." Rather, they struggle with each other concerning **HOW** did He do it?!

The contention generating this strife of course begins with the traditional story that Jesus was in The Tomb "Friday" at sundown and that He arose "Sunday" morning; and thereby comprising a period of only about thirty-six hours. Whereas, in Matthew 12:40, if Jesus lay in The Tomb conforming to our Western concept of "three days and three nights," this would have spanned three complete 24 hr. periods or seventy-two hours. Of course, unbelievers and skeptics use such apparent "Biblical discrepancies" to accuse against our witness for The

Gospel. Even without that obvious battle, Believers need to be armed with the Truth of The Gospel and must not be confused nor hesitant to defend it. This cannot always be accomplished if Believers hold always to "Tradition" — i.e., what has always been taught. We will attempt to determine and explain what is "tradition" and what is "truth" in this matter.

First, the apparent reason for the argument is founded on the vast void existing in many Christian's minds (and hearts) concerning knowledge of the Mosaic Laws of Judaism. Christians tend to forget that our Holy Bible is, after all, a VERY Jewish book! Along with that same failing, Christians seem to forget also that Jesus and the Disciples were Jewish! The thoughts, philosophy and customs of the Bible must therefore be viewed in a Jewish sense rather than in our Western Gentile context. Another abundant fuel to this argument is our undeniably human trait that leads us either to repose comfortably in traditionalism *or* to be skeptical about things that do not follow the way we have been taught. – Aha! – Traditionalism, again!

All of us tend to rely on what we have been taught by our mentors and peers, rather than "digging" to find the facts and to reason toward finding the Truth on our own. The "digging" requires lots of work and patience and time. Then sadly, our "human" peers and mentors will reject us, no matter how "brilliant" is our analysis, if we express beliefs that do not agree with their beliefs that of course were founded in turn on traditional teaching from *their* mentors and peers.

So, at considerable risk of rejection from our peers, but "hungering" for Truth, we are going to do some "digging" to answer our theme question. We invite you to join our search for The Truth.

When Did Jesus Arise?

At this point we need to take aid from the accompanying charts to diagram the Jewish calendar and the precise timing of the events involved. Illus. 43: Chronology of Passion Week, Page 503, Illus. 44: Days, Events for Feast of Unleavened Bread, Page 504, Illus. 45: Western & Jewish: 3 Days, 3 Nights in Tomb, Page 505, and Illus. 46: Western & Jewish: 3 Days, 3 Nights, Page 506, are provided as an aid to our readers, listing chronologically the significant events of that final week, enabling us to identify and track through each day leading to The Resurrection.

- Illus. 43: Chronology of Passion Week, Page ,503 presents a chronological tabulation of the events of that week along with the referenced Gospel verses establishing the events.

- Illus. 44: Days, Events for Feast of Unleavened Bread, Page 504, lists events and references for the Feast of Unleavened Bread, so fundamental to the fulfillments shown by Jesus' Final Week and therefore vital to this investigation of that week.

- Illus. 45: Western & Jewish: 3 Days, 3 Nights in Tomb, Page 505, lists chronologically in the right-hand column the sequence of these events as they must be in order to fulfill the Law as well as avoiding any contradiction between Scriptures and in conformance with the Law and simple logic. The Left-hand column displays the scenario as proposed by a highly respected Biblical commentary source, which is nevertheless shown to be in error in several instances.

- Illus. 46: Western & Jewish: 3 Days, 3 Nights, Page 506, repeats the same order of events as required to be in conformance Biblically and with logic as presented in the right column of Illus. 45: Western & Jewish: 3 Days, 3 Nights in Tomb, Page 505. The left-hand column of Illus. 46: Western & Jewish: 3 Days, 3 Nights, Page 506, describes a scenario that has become popular among many Bible scholars who, through various motives, desire to demonstrate that Jesus was in The Tomb a complete *"three days and three nights"* as would be counted in our modern Western Gentile culture.

Readers are urged to closely examine and study these charts as the text is read. This should not be done with haste. The analysis is very complex and many faceted. Our Lord went to a great deal of effort to arrange and sequence all these events and dates to produce His Perfect and Complete Fulfillment of the Law. We mortals cannot hope to decipher His Work by expending minimal or casual effort.

Scripture is abundantly clear concerning certain elements of the timing regarding two of the events we shall investigate. That is,

　　a. Jesus was entombed sometime just before sundown on the evening of *"the day of preparation"* which is 14 *Nisan* on the Jewish calendar (Matthew 27:59 – 62)

　　b. Jesus arose from The Tomb sometime around dawn on *"the first day of the week"* – which we call Sunday. (Mark 16:9)

If we were able to derive from the Gospel the day and the hour or even the approximate hour of Jesus' entombment and the hour of His Resurrection as well, we could possibly end this study after a very brief discussion. Possibility of this early solution to the argument in this study exists in that *only* by either of two ways could Jesus have been three *complete* "Western" days and nights (i.e., 72 hours) in The Tomb.

　　1. If He had been laid in The Tomb on Thursday morning and had risen at the same hour Sunday morning – ("the first day of the week") or,

　　2. If He had been laid in The Tomb on Wednesday just before sundown and had risen Saturday evening just before sundown.

There can be no argument that if there were any deviation from either of the aforementioned sequences, the result would not have completed "three days and three nights" in The Tomb in Western tradition. There can be no consideration that it was "about" (approximately) three days, or approximately three nights. The Law of the *Torah* is not subject to "approximations." And *Torah* is, after all, what Jesus fulfilled, going to a lot of effort to do so, – *"every jot and tittle."*

The Gospels all agree that Jesus was placed in The Tomb just before sundown. The Gospel further confirms that He was laid there on 14 *Nisan*, "the Day of the Preparation" for the Passover. (Exodus 12:6; Luke 23:54 – 56, John 19:14, 19:31, 19:42) Therefore, option (1) or any other morning burial option is eliminated without any argument. We must then search for evidence stating or deriving the time of His Resurrection. All four Gospels agree that Jesus was raised "the first day of the week." All say Mary Magdalene "came unto the sepulchre" at sunrise; although John 20:1 says: "*...cometh Mary Magdalene early, when it was yet dark,...*" Mark 16:9 confirms this with: "*...Jesus was risen early the first day of the week,...*" Then it was very early "Sunday" morning. Later we shall see the importance of John's description.

There is agreement that Mary arrived at The Tomb early around sunrise on the first day of the week. Matthew 28:1 – 7 gives the most detailed account, saying that Mary saw the earthquake, the stone rolled away and the Angel who directed her to "*go quickly, and tell His disciples that He is risen from the dead.*" However, this alone does not say Jesus *arose* at dawn. It is implied by all four Gospels, as well as being supported by traditional interpretation, that Jesus arose some time *just before Mary arrived at The Tomb.*

Otherwise, if Jesus had arisen the previous evening ("Saturday") just before sundown, as with option (2), this could seem to conform with the exacting seventy-two hour entombment proposed. We must inquire then: **WHY** would Jesus arise at dusk and then sit up all night to wait until next morning, appearing to His followers twelve hours later? – Remember? The Angel said "*go quickly and tell His disciples.*"

A second and very powerful implication that Jesus arose at dawn is given in the continuing detail of Matthew's narration in Chapter 28. Verse 11 tells of the guards going into Jerusalem *that morning* to inform the Chief Priests of "*all the things that were done.*" At this point we must acknowledge that Jesus did not need to have the stone rolled away in order to exit The Tomb. He could easily just glide through the walls with His new and Glorified Body, as He frequently demonstrated on later occasions

Regardless of whether Jesus came out of The Tomb or even had been "stolen away" during the night, we must ask also: If "*all those things that were done*" occurred at dusk, then **WHY** would the guards wait until dawn to report this? (Maybe they were afraid of the dark?!) Common sense tells us that as soon as "those things were done," they would have *immediately* raced into the city with the news – as they in fact did that morning — *immediately* after the women departed to inform Jesus' Disciples. The "watch" went into the City to tell the chief priests "all the things that were done." (from Matthew 28:11)

Then, in Verses 12-15 we find that the priests bribed the soldiers to lie, saying His disciples "*came by night, and stole Him away while we slept.*" Their untruthful answer saying it happened "at night while we slept," means it is obvious that they really did not know until morning that The Tomb had been opened. In Truth, The Tomb actually was not opened until dawn when they saw the stone being rolled away, the earthquake, the angel and "those things that happened." (Matthew 28:1 – 2) This description along with exercise of simple logic easily voids any claim that Jesus arose at sundown Saturday evening. Therefore it had to have happened at dawn on the first day of the week, *just as the Scriptures say!*

Option (2) then, is given its final demise because "before sundown" the previous evening (Saturday) would not have been, in the Judaic Law, "the first day of the week." This would be in opposition to Scripture from Mark 16:9, saying: "*Jesus was risen early the first day of the week.*" If Jesus had risen *after* sundown on Saturday (counting that time as "early the first day," etc.), counting back 72 hours would bring us to a Wednesday burial just *after* sundown. Luke 23:54 affirms that a Sabbath was approaching as Joseph of Arimathea was placing Jesus in The Tomb. Then, if Joseph had done this after sundown, he would have been in violation of the Sabbath by having placed Jesus in the Tomb (i.e., "working") after the Sabbath had begun.

Reference 1 and some other sources have said "early on the first day of the week" means just after sundown as the new (Jewish calendar) day began. That would be a "Saturday" night. By adopting this interpretation that Jesus was raised "Saturday" night, these scholars are of course attempting to show "three days and three nights" in their Western tradition by timing His rising to be of that exact duration following a "Wednesday" Crucifixion.

They of course have fallen into the very awkward error of having timed *more* than the three days/three nights interval sought. We all KNOW, from John 19:42, that Jesus was placed in The Tomb *before* sundown "Wednesday" if they choose that day in order to "fit" their interpretation. Therefore He would need to arise *before* sundown Saturday (not after) in order to set the exact time as they intend – as well as being in keeping with the "daylight" requirement to be emphasized throughout this subject. And, one thing we have observed in Jewish thought is that very little tolerance is allowed for the "inexact." Again, Scripture is firm that Jesus "was risen early the first *day* of the week."

As we shall demonstrate, Rabbinical thought deems the word "day" to mean *during daylight* – not after sundown, as the timing of these scholars would require. Earlier we showed that Maimonides had even declared that "daylight" was "official" at 1 1/5 hours *before* sunrise. Surely, these scholars are "struggling" to make Jewish thought fit Western Gentile Christian thought. Such a goal is not attainable without studying diligently and thoroughly to define *Jewish* thought in these matters.

And, we realize that some will say, "Well, do we really care about all this Jewish Law and Rabbinical 'thought'? – Why should all this detail concern Christian Gentiles as long as we believe in the Resurrection?" – It matters because Jesus IS Jewish. We are missing much of the Glory of His fulfillment of "His" Law unless we learn HOW the Law was fulfilled. These things are somewhat concealed within the Scriptures and in ancient Jewish writings that we have studied in this work. The work is certainly tedious and challenging, but satisfying in its completion. Hopefully nevertheless, the work is Glorifying of God, centered upon Jesus Christ and edifying to the Church.

Jesus "gave up the ghost" at the ninth hour of the "day" – or in Western tradition, what we would call 3 p.m. The traditional Jewish way of counting hours of the "day" – i.e., daylight hours – was to begin with the first hour of the day at what we would call 6 a.m. or 0600 hours. Then, *early the first day of the week* would have been *early* in the morning (i.e., "the morrow") shortly after sunrise.

How do we know "the morrow" denotes an early hour? – This is a well-known term for such timing noted in Rabbinical writings, such as *Talmud* and *Midrash*. It's origin apparently is drawn from Scripture at Leviticus 23:15 – 16 as follows:

*"And ye shall count unto you from **the morrow after the sabbath**, from the day that ye brought the sheaf for the wave offering, seven sabbaths shall be complete;"*

In this verse *"the morrow"* would perhaps seem to refer to an undetermined daytime period on the day following the Sabbath day. It can be seen, however, that *"the morrow"* refers to the early morning through close examination of Verse 16 –

*"Even unto **the morrow after the seventh sabbath** shall ye number fifty days; and ye shall offer a new meat offering unto the Lord."*

This is because, in comparing these two verses it is shown that the "counting" begins at the start of the day (*the morrow*; i.e., when "*tomorrow*" begins) rather than just on the "day" after the Sabbath.

At this point we see what perhaps is the origin of Westerners' confusion about Jewish "*dates*" and Jewish "*days.*" The Jews spoke of a "date" (such as 14 *Nisan*) as "the fourteenth day of the month." Nevertheless, that "date" began at evening at what they refer to as "*the first hour of the night*" and went on to completion of that "date" on the next day at the end of "*the twelfth hour of the day*" following. The "day" is of course referring to the daylight hours. In order to overcome this confusion, then, in our study of this Gospel narration we must always distinguish carefully between "date" and "day."

It may be helpful to readers who are unfamiliar with Jewish Biblical time concepts to provide an explanation at this juncture of our work. In fact, it is helpful to keep these Jewish time "rules" in mind as we read at any point in Scripture.

- On any given "date" – such as, for example, the 12th "day" of the Jewish month, *Nisan* – the "hours of the night" would come first. This is because the 12th of *Nisan* begins at sundown; i.e., about 6 p.m. – (as the 11th of the month is coming to an end).
- The "1st hour of the night" would be from what Westerners call 6 p.m. until 7 p.m.
- The " 12th hour of the night" would be from what our Western clocks would register as 5 a.m. until 6 a.m.; i.e., at about the time of sunrise.
- The "1st hour of the day" would then be from what we call 6 a.m. until 7 a.m.
- And finally, the 12th hour of the day" (of the 12th of *Nisan*) would extend from 5 p.m. until 6 p.m. – that is, about the time of sundown, where the next day – the 13thof *Nisan* – would begin.
- As an example from the Gospel, "the third hour of the day" – when Jesus was lifted up on The Cross – was at what we call 9 a.m. And, "the ninth hour of the day" – when Jesus "gave up the ghost" – was at what we call 3 p.m. – all on the 14th of *Nisan*. Then, as Joseph of Arimathea was hurrying to prepare Jesus for

burial, the Sabbath was approaching and would begin at 6 p.m. that evening as the 15th of *Nisan* was about to begin.

- Readers are reminded that the Law counts anything done during the daylight hours is to be counted as if it had been done during an entire 24 hour day and a night. (Ref. *Pesahim* 4a and *Megillah* 20a)
- In Jewish reckoning, then "three days and three nights" *could* be counted for an event, even though it actually had taken place during only slightly longer than 36 hours!

We sincerely hope that this time summary will be helpful as we proceed through the remainder of this work, where there will be multiple examples such as these.

Yoma 82a presents a note explaining Jewish criteria for stating the "hours of the day." Every day, summer and winter, was divided into twelve hours; and likewise, every night also was divided into twelve hours. When using the sundial, the hours of daylight, however, vary in duration dependent upon the time of year. In December an hour may consist of forty minutes, in June maybe ninety minutes. It must be remembered and considered that during the Winter months there is less daylight in any 24 hour period; and in Summer there is more daylight. These phenomena of course would greatly influence the performance of sundials.

In the Jewish months, *Nisan* and *Tishri*, (usually around April and September, respectively) an hour would have about sixty minutes. The first hour of the "day" would be from six a.m. to seven a.m., the second hour from seven a.m. to eight a.m. "At the second hour of the day" would thus correspond to about eight o'clock in the morning. Similarly, the first hour of the night is from six p.m. to seven p.m., etc. Applying this stated criteria, therefore as derived from *Talmud*, we confirm that "early the first day of the week" clearly means early morning and not "early" as the calendar "day" began; i.e., "evening." – (Gentiles who would hope to decipher Jewish *Talmudic* concepts must learn to *think* Jewish!)

It is doubtful that any of the Gospel writers would have neglected to announce it, had Jesus arisen just after sundown on a Saturday as the calendar DATE of "the first day of the week" (Sunday) began. Since we know He was placed in The Tomb just prior to sundown, this would have exceeded 72 hours; i.e., three days and three nights. – Nobody saw Him until early morning. – Nobody – All eyewitnesses confirmed Mark's statement that "early" meant in the early morning hours – not early in the evening hours. It is therefore apparent that Jesus had risen about the time when Mary reached The Tomb at sunrise, but "*while it was yet dark.*"

And again, **WHY** would Jesus sit up all night to just wait around The Tomb for twelve hours? Nevertheless, the best reason for rejection of any "after sundown" proposal is that by Sabbatical Law Joseph of Arimathaea was "driven" to have Jesus' Body placed at rest in The Tomb before sundown, when the Sabbath would begin. (Luke 23:50 – 56). Very simply, the seventy-two hour criteria accordingly would not hold with such timing.

We have proved, therefore, that Jesus was not in The Tomb seventy-two hours. Consequently, some would say Scripture is in error! – But that is not possible! Scripture never said Jesus was in The Tomb seventy-two hours. Western Christian Gentiles have reasoned that idea from their own cultural method of dating and viewing "days" and "nights." Scripture says He was in The Tomb "three days and three nights." Many learned and respected (Western) theologians have taught that when Scripture says "three days and three nights," it means that literally. They claim it comprises three complete 24 hour days and nights, totaling seventy—two hours. We have just introduced irrefutable proof that, in the case of Matthew 12:40, that statement certainly is not accurate.

The challenge to Western timing becomes even more obvious when we consider that Scripture also says that Jesus would be raised ON or DURING the third day. Very simply, it is impossible to do anything for three complete days and three complete nights AND to then terminate that activity DURING the third day. We shall discuss this problem in greater detail later.

Another example of how Gentiles can easily become confused by Jewish thinking appears in the Law for the Feast of Unleavened Bread, shown in Illus. 44: Days, Events for Feast of Unleavened Bread, Page 504. If the First Day of Unleavened Bread were really on the 14th of *Nisan*, there would be a total of eight days instead of seven; because Scripture says clearly, the last and seventh day is "the twenty—first at even." (Exodus 12:18)

Ironically, modern Judaism has added to our confusion in this feast by the fact that many Jewish congregations do in fact observe the feast for eight days instead of the Biblically specified seven days. We shall explain this modern twist later in this text. (Refer to: How could the "Last Supper" have been a "*Seder*"?)

Referring to Illus. 44: Days, Events for Feast of Unleavened Bread, Page 504, we observe that last "evening" meal is after sundown of 20 *Nisan* and is therefore actually on the 21st. Then, counting back seven nights, the first partaking of unleavened bread is at night on 15 *Nisan*; i.e., just after sundown of 14 *Nisan*.

The question is finally cleared-up **for the Biblical version** of the feast when we realize that the lamb for the Passover meal, the *Seder*, is killed on the 14th "at even." This pure, unblemished, yearling male of the flock is called "the Paschal Lamb." The meal obviously cannot be after sundown as the 14th begins; i.e., before the lamb is even slain. Instead, the meal is served after sundown as the 15th of *Nisan* begins.

Exodus 12:8 truly solves the problem, saying "*they shall eat the flesh in that night*" that is, after sundown of the 14th, which then becomes the 15th. Sundown is at "the twelfth hour of the day" or about 6 p.m. in our Western tradition. The "first hour of the night" is then about one hour after sundown or about 7 p.m. The 15th of *Nisan* is more correctly the "First Day of Unleavened Bread" because that is the first day on which the Passover *matzah* is eaten. Leviticus 23:5 – 6 also verify that the lamb is killed on the fourteenth and the unleavened bread is eaten on the 15th.

Gentiles must use the most deliberate caution therefore when interpreting Scripture that has been written by men who kept time much differently than we moderns and who used only sundials and hourglasses instead of our modern mechanical/electrical timepieces and our modern calendars. They had entirely different perspectives on viewing time as compared with our modern "Space Age" Western Gentile view. Indeed, we shall experience many more of these same types of Jewish "timekeeping" in this discussion.

The Schedule of Events

From the Scriptural references in the accompanying charts (Illus. 43: Chronology of Passion Week, Illus. 44: Days, Events for Feast of Unleavened Bread, Illus. 45: Western & Jewish: 3 Days, 3 Nights in Tomb and Illus. 46: Western & Jewish: 3 Days, 3 Nights, Pages 503, 504, 505 and 506) we can see great agreement on timing of nearly all events. An apparent exception is found in the case of Jesus' "cleansing" of the Temple, driving out the moneychangers, etc. Specifically, if we assume Mark's narrative (Mark 11:9 – 15) is chronological, it reads as if Jesus cleansed the Temple on the day following His Triumphal Entry. Furthermore, Mark 11:11 seems to indicate that, on His first day in the Temple, Jesus just sort of "looked around." Hence, it is evident that Mark's description is not necessarily chronological; otherwise, it would be considered in conflict with the other two Gospels on this event. Please study Illus. 43: Chronology of Passion Week, Page 503, carefully on these points.

Only the most finite and careful scrutiny of the Gospels will reveal the Truth in these matters. Matthew 21:12, Mark 11:15 and Luke 19:45 all agree on the event of the moneychangers, except that casual notice of Mark's narrative would seem to indicate that event (Mark 11:15) occurred on the day following the Triumphal Entry. This implication emerges because that verse follows Verse 12, telling of their night in Bethany and of Jesus being hungry the next morning. Matthew 21:18 tells of Jesus' hunger; although, it is clear this is not on the morning of the Triumphal Entry. Rather, it is the following morning, 11 *Nisan*, which began with the withering of the fig tree: Matthew 21:19, Mark 11:20.

Further evidence that the hunger was expressed on 11 *Nisan* is noted in that Matthew, Mark and Luke all concur that was the same day of:

- The Pharisees asking of Jesus "authority."
- Jesus answering their query regarding Caesar's coin.
- The earthquakes, wars, famines at His Coming.

Lastly, what should be the most convincing evidence stems from the fact that all three Gospels close the narration for that day, saying: "*after two days is the Passover.*" This statement seems to have been made at the close of the "day" of 11 *Nisan*, or possibly even after sundown, which would have been 12 *Nisan*. In either case, all three Gospel writers leave the impression that this was taking place *after* the "day's" activities on 11 *Nisan* – Jesus' second day in Jerusalem The mutual agreement of chronology on all these other events would seem to indicate that only Mark's description of the "riot" of the moneychangers is out of sequence.

Luke also deviates from chronological sequence, as more of a "biographer;" whereas, Matthew seems to have kept the most accurate "log" of events, times, etc. An example is seen in Luke 13:34 where Jesus wept for Jerusalem; although, Luke tells of this while relating the activities of the group when they were not even yet arrived *"nigh to Jerusalem."* (Luke 19:11) Matthew describes that same occasion as having occurred after they had arrived, during Jesus' second day, 11 *Nisan*. (Matthew 23:37)

We should note here some of the personal background of these Gospel writers. These things are important to Believers as well as to critics and doubters or to any who would pursue study similar to ours. Matthew was the only one among these three being discussed who was actually one of The Twelve who accompanied Jesus through all this time. Notice that, although John surely was one of The Twelve, John did not write of the details we are evaluating at this point. (Please see Scriptural references in Illus. 43: Chronology of Passion Week., Page 503)

Many of the more authoritative New Testament commentaries agree that the moneychanger incident described in John 2:15 obviously occurred at the beginning of Jesus' ministry; i.e., much earlier than that event described in the Synoptic Gospels. Matthew, however, was indeed on hand with The Master while all this transpired. Matthew took great care to note as a daily log all these details that are now so important to this study.

Mark was possibly present with Jesus during part of this time; although, he was very young at the time and really was not a part of the core of this group. Many scholars conclude that Mark had heard these stories from Peter and the others when he was a young lad. Everything Mark recorded is the Truth and really happened, but apparently it did not happen necessarily in the order that he told of these events in the Gospel.

Similarly, Luke was a skillful writer, but he as well was an outsider during this week we scour so carefully. Luke was a friend brought into Discipleship by Paul at a considerable time after The Crucifixion. At the time of The Crucifixion Paul was not a follower of Jesus. As we are aware, Paul was actually a zealous and enthusiastic persecutor of the earliest Christians. Luke came along later after Paul's conversion. Again, we must emphasize that the absence of Mark and Luke from that "inner circle" of The Twelve in no way detracts from their reliability toward having recording in Truth "what" happened, but no doubt Matthew had a far better opportunity for knowing "when" and in what order these things had happened.

We must logically conclude therefore that Mark just "got-ahead-of-his-story;" i.e., before the riot instead of on the following day, as related both by Matthew and by Luke. This tenuous deviation from our Western custom of writing chronological narratives leads some scholars to add an extra day in the sequence, thereby resulting in erroneous interpretation.

Some scholars and sources[1] have claimed there were two cleansings on those two consecutive days, on the basis of Mark's narrative. They have even taken the desperate track of claiming two processions or "entries" into Jerusalem on the basis of Matthew 21:1 – 9, "implying" that He entered from Bethpage on the 9th of *Nisan* and later on 11 *Nisan* from Bethany. (John 12:1) Some readers may recall that this same brand of "desperation thinking" was described earlier for the ludicrous declaration that five crosses were raised at *Golgotha* in order to "defend" Scripture having said there were two "thieves" and there were two "malefactors."

Those who are familiar with the geography of the Mount of Olives should agree it is obvious that Bethpage and Bethany were very closely neighboring villages. Although the precise location of Bethpage on the Mount of Olives is not known, most scholars believe Bethpage was somewhat nearer Jerusalem than was Bethany. In fact, Mark 11:1 says it best: *"And when they came nigh unto Jerusalem unto Bethpage and Bethany at the Mount of Olives..."* Since he mentions Bethpage first, Mark, in so doing, then implies that they arrived in Bethpage *first* as they approached from Jericho.

The fact that Matthew mentions only Bethpage and John mentions only Bethany certainly does not mean there were two separate events, given the close proximity of these two hamlets. Upon reading all four Gospels in parallel, it is evident that the ass was obtained upon their arrival at Bethpage from Jericho (Mark 10:46 – 11:1) and they spent that same night (Sunday, 9 *Nisan*), before the Triumphal Entry, at the home of Lazarus in nearby Bethany. (John 12:1 – 12)

The single occurrence of each event is further evidenced as we inspect Illus. 43: Chronology of Passion Week, Page 503, considering that some of these events were so dramatic, that if they had occurred twice, there would surely have been mention of that excitement and its significance by at least one Gospel writer.

One example is the overturning of the moneychangers' tables. That was a virtual "riot!" – exciting! Another example is of course the Triumphal Entry. Had there been two days on which He roused the townsfolk to throw down their garments, cut down branches and shout "Hosannas," we could reasonably expect at least one writer to have noted significance of such a repetition. We therefore consider each of these events occurring chronologically as a single event. Whereas Matthew and Mark seem to account for activities of each day, Luke and John do not. For example, Luke 19:47 says, *"...and He (Jesus) taught daily in the Temple,"* without detailing what he taught each day."

In order to survey these events truthfully, it is apparent that some traditional concepts of this Final Week will be cast out. Early in the sequence it is shown in Illus. 43: Chronology of Passion Week, Page 503, that the Triumphal Entry occurred on the second day of the week, Monday. The tradition of "Palm Sunday" is in error because the party had to arrive at Bethany on 9 *Nisan* at evening in order to have been at Bethany "six days before Passover." (John 12:1) Here the "Passover" refers to the Passover meal (*Seder*) which occurs after sundown and which is actually 15 *Nisan*. Counting back six days *before* Passover then becomes 9 *Nisan*. Therefore they would have traveled to Bethany from Jericho (approximately 13 miles) on that 9 *Nisan* "Sunday;" if only because they could not have made a journey of that distance on the Sabbath. In the Law, a "Sabbath day's journey" is about 2000 cubits, or just a trifle more than half a mile. Jewish persons are not permitted to travel farther than a Sabbath day's journey during the Sabbath.

John 12:1 states that the group, *en route* to "go up to Jerusalem," arrived at Bethany "six days before the Passover." A walking journey of about 13 miles from Jericho to Bethany would have taken somewhat longer than four hours at a "normal" pace of 3 miles per hour and without stopping to rest tired, sandaled feet. Thus, the journey to Bethany would have consumed the greater part of their day, likely six to eight hours, allowing for breaks and lunch. Then, since the approaching Passover was to be on a Saturday, we can count back six days to determine that they departed Jericho on a Sunday and arrived at Bethany that same evening. We could estimate that they began their trek about 8 a.m. and perhaps arrived at Bethpage/Bethany about 3 or 4 p.m., just in time for supper at the home of Lazarus. (John 12:1 – 2)

Although the Gospels of Matthew, Mark and Luke are consistent in saying that Jesus procured the donkey upon their arrival at Bethpage, John 12:12 – 15 makes it clear that Jesus rode into the Holy City *the next day*, which would have been Monday and *not* Sunday.

> "**On the next day** *much people that were come to the feast, when they heard that Jesus was coming to Jerusalem,*
>
> *Took branches of palm trees, and went forth to meet Him, and cried, 'Hosanna: Blessed is the King of Israel that cometh in the name of the Lord.'*
>
> *And Jesus, when He had found a young ass, sat thereon; as it is written, 'Fear not, daughter of Zion: behold thy King cometh, sitting on an ass's colt.' "*

Moreover, it is significant that none of the Gospels states that the Triumphal Entry was on "the first day of the week." On the basis of Jewish Sabbath laws pertaining to travel, we have been able to show that the Triumphal Entry actually had to have taken place on a "Palm Monday." The "Palm Sunday" tradition apparently was started in connection with the same proposal discussed in Illus. 45: Western & Jewish: 3 Days, 3 Nights in Tomb, Page 505, or other theories attempting to justify "three days and three nights" in a Western context of time. In fact, one fairly detailed analysis[1] of that Tragic Week attempts to make the case that Jesus was entombed three days and three nights, totaling 72 hours in traditional Western time. That highly respected source therefore has concluded that the party traveled from Jericho to Bethany on a Saturday; i.e., the Sabbath. We have just shown that traveling that distance on a Sabbath is prohibited under the Law. – And, Jesus was NOT in the practice of violating ANY of His Father's Laws! We can be confident therefore that they traveled to Bethany on the 9th of *Nisan*, which was a Sunday – and, "*six days before the Passover.*"

Some might thoughtfully inquire: "What principle mandated Scripture to specify that Jesus would be in The Tomb *three* days? – Why wasn't it four days? – Or, two days?" Although there may be no connection for this question, there is a Jewish traditional superstition relating to a corpse three days after death. *Midrash Rabbah* Genesis 100:7, *Midrash Rabbah* Leviticus 18:1 and *Midrash Rabbah* Ecclesiastes 12:6 – 7 discuss the ancient Jewish belief that the soul of a corpse does not depart and/or frequently returns to the body ("hovers") for three days after death.

Edersheim[21] explains that much of this Jewish concern with the significance of three days is derived from Scripture. An example cited is from Genesis 22:4, in which Abraham on the third day of his journey to the land of *Moriah* "*saw the place afar off*" where he was directed to offer his son, Isaac. Edersheim points out that the Rabbis interpret this importance from several Biblical events associated with Israel – and, especially regarding resurrection of the dead. Hosea 6:2 is such a reference. Another is taken from Genesis 42:17, in which Joseph held his brothers in prison three days to convince Egyptian officials that they were not spies.

Midrash Rabbah is referenced because it says: *"...The Holy One, blessed be He, never leaves the righteous in distress more than three days."*

Another example indicates from *Midrash Rabbah* Leviticus 18:1 – *"For three days [after death] the soul hovers over the body, intending to re-enter it, but as soon as it sees its appearance change, it departs, as it is written, When his flesh that is on him is distorted his soul will mourn over him."*— (Referring to Job 14:22).

It was reasoned therefore that the person was not *completely* dead and therefore not legally dead until the soul had departed after three days. The ravages of *rigor mortis* and putrefaction were thought not to have been extreme until that interval had been passed. Then, the soul was believed to depart before the body became extremely disfigured. It has been rationalized that perhaps Jesus wished to demonstrate that both He and Lazarus were in fact "completely and legally" dead – thereby echoing Jewish tradition – by being interred three days, or in the case of Lazarus: *four* days! – Whhewwy!

It was also important to His Mission that Jesus scheduled His final seven days such that they would not be interrupted by a weekly Sabbath. He arrived at Bethany on the day following the Sabbath in order to allow Himself five *complete* days in Jerusalem before His death. He entered the City precisely on the 10th day of *Nisan* in order that, by the Law given in Exodus 12:3 - 6 and *Pesahim* 96a, the priesthood would "select" Him on *that* day to be slain as a type of the Paschal Lamb of God. The Priests then applied these Laws as they tested ("watched") Jesus during those four days, just as they also were required to "watch" the Passover Lamb. During that time the Priests learned of course that Jesus was Pure before He was slain *"before the congregation in the evening of the fourteenth day."* This sequence requiring selection of the Lamb on the 10th day of *Nisan*, to be slain on the 14th day is further described in *The Jewish Book of Why*.

Otherwise, His movements for at least one day would have been somewhat restricted by the rigid Sabbatical Laws. Jesus had many things to accomplish during that last week. He could not afford to lose time or momentum. Furthermore, His Father did not want His Son's Most Holy of Holy Days – The Crucifixion —- diluted or distracted or obscured in any way by another "Holy Day" leading up to that MOST Holy Day. We shall explain later why *this* Sabbath was what Jewish tradition identifies as a "High Sabbath." Indeed, that first night and day of Rest in The Tomb was to be the Highest Sabbath of All "High" Sabbaths!!

Could the "Last Supper" have been a "*Seder*"?

It is important to take note of some terms, which if we misunderstand them, may cause confusion in the Gospel narratives on this last week. Specifically, the phrases: "day of preparation," "Passover" and "first day of unleavened bread" should be addressed. One reason for possibility of confusion is seen in the fact that Jesus and The Twelve did not have their Passover *Seder* ("Last Supper") at the same time as residents of Jerusalem observed the Passover.

Scholars have pondered for centuries over this seemingly inconsistent observance of perhaps the second most sacred Jewish holiday, *Yom Kippur* being the most sacred. Jewish historians[2, 3] explain that, upon the return from Babylon, outlying regions of Israel, such as Galilee, were located remote and distant from Jerusalem and the Temple. Jewish folks in such regions therefore were allowed *two* days for observance of Passover, instead of just one day. This was permitted because the Jews had to count the days of their months beginning with the first day at each new moon. The Israelites made attempts to relay official notice of the New Moon by using signal fires atop hills and peaks, smoke signals, etc. from the worship center at Jerusalem; although, not always with success. Because of inclement weather, smoke, etc., it was not always possible to determine reliably the day of the New Moon; i.e., the first day of the month.

The Rabbis therefore ruled that those faraway places, such as Galilee, would celebrate Passover season for eight days instead of the Biblical *"seven days of unleavened bread."* (Exodus 12:15) In this way they could be confident they had not *missed* the proper day. (See Illus. 44: Days, Events for Feast of Unleavened Bread, Page 504) This same latitude of using two days is practiced by some Jewish groups even today for Passover as well as for *Rosh Hashanah*, which falls on the first day of the month, *Tishri*. The extra day is also added for the holiday of *Shavuot*, and for the same reason, being *the possibility of uncertainty in outlying communities for determining the first day of the month*. A detailed discussion of these matters is presented in the Introduction of *The Jewish Book of Why*. Jewish Rabbinical thought on this matter seems to be: *"Better too early than too late!"* Or, equally conservative: *"Better too many days than not enough!"*

For example, most Orthodox and Conservative congregations have observed the two days of Passover, especially since the *Diaspora* (scattering to "the nations"). Many Reformed congregations observe the second day as a "Community *Seder*," where a large gathering is assembled for a large number of *Seder* participants, inviting virtually any who wish to attend. We mentioned earlier that inviting any "uncircumcised" participant at the *Seder* is in violation of the Law specified in Exodus 12:48.

There even may be some obscure statute in *Talmudic* Law that permits "outlanders" this latitude of eight days even when they are in Jerusalem. It is obvious that Jesus and His Disciples applied some such ruling, because they surely did celebrate that Holy Feast as the 14th of *Nisan* began. Jerusalem "regulars" had their Passover meal as 15 *Nisan* began, just after **THE** Holy Paschal Lamb of God had been placed in The Tomb. Moreover, the difference between the two Passover dates is implied in John 2:13 and 11:55, where it is said: *"the Jews' Passover was nigh at hand."* This is a subtle implication that the *"Jews' Passover"* would be that date when the feast was celebrated in Jerusalem, and not to include the earlier date for observance by groups away from Jerusalem.

Moreover, we know that Jesus was "Lord of the Sabbath" (Luke 6:5) as well as Sovereign over all the rest of the Law. Jesus therefore had authority to rule His own Passover date in favor of the "practical" consideration that He was going to be unable to observe the next evening because of His impending death as the Paschal Lamb on Jerusalem's "Day of Preparation." On the morning of that day of 14 *Nisan* the Rabbis of Jerusalem were burning all the leaven that had been searched out of all the homes during the night before, as Jesus was on "trial." The leaven, in fact representing sin, passion and corruption, was burned at "the third hour" that morning as Jesus was being "lifted up." (See Reference 4, pg. 256)

This practice was conducted in compliance with Exodus 12:15, saying, in part:

"...the first day ye shall put away leaven out of your house;..."

Emphasis is to be placed on the word "day." The Rabbis interpret that "day" means the leaven must be destroyed (burned) during the daytime. A practical procedure results therefore that the houses are searched for leaven during the night previous. It has been ruled by the same logic that the leaven must be placed upon a fire at the third hour of the day in order that it will have the best opportunity to burn completely by the end of the daylight hours.

A "parallel" with Jesus' "trial" and The Crucifixion appears in this Jewish practice of removing and destroying all leaven on the Day of Preparation, 14 *Nisan*. During the night before, all of Israel was searching and collecting the leaven found in their households. Meanwhile, during that same night, the Jewish hierarchy "searched" to find Jesus and examined Him during the trial to determine if He was possessed of any "leaven" (sin.) Of course, Jesus was devoid of ANY sin; nevertheless, He was unjustly convicted of sin and was "collected" by Caiaphas, the *Sanhedrin* and Pilate to be "burned" (put to death, destroyed) as "leaven" to represent our "corruption, passion and sins."

Earlier we highlighted the fact that Jesus "gave up the Ghost" just as the Paschal Lambs were being slain in the Temple at this same hour in compliance with Exodus 12:6 and as detailed by the Law in *Aboth* 5:6. Both of these Passover rites – burning the leaven and slaying the Paschal Lambs – were being performed while Jesus was on The Cross to fulfill those items of the Law. After all, Jesus had to fulfill ALL of the Law, including the Passover. He was actually substituted as the "leaven" to be burned at the third hour and as the Paschal Lamb, to be slain on 14 *Nisan* at the ninth hour, "at evening, before the entire congregation." (Also see Reference 4, pg. 254)

Jesus then could have said: "Yes, I know that all of Jerusalem will eat the Passover *Seder* tomorrow night. (15 *Nisan*). However, we must celebrate on the night that begins 14 *Nisan* because I cannot fulfill it at the same time I eat it. I am entitled to first celebrate the Passover with My Disciples so that I can demonstrate to them what it is I am going to fulfill. I am Sovereign over the Law." Either of these principles could be applied to explain how Jesus, being Sovereign over the Law, and with The Twelve being from Galilee, justified celebrating Passover a day earlier than was observed at Jerusalem on the night of His death. We can see that this "two-day Passover" tradition was pre-ordained probably a few hundred years before Jesus was born. The Lord had Glorious Foreknowledge of the Events that were ordered to take place in Jerusalem "on that day," knowing Jesus and The Twelve would need an extra day for *their* Passover and its Most Holy *Seder*.

It does appear that this group was discerning these different dates, because "six days before Passover" in John 12:1 is certainly referring to the Jerusalem Passover. If John had been referring to the night of the Last Supper (i.e., *their* Passover), he should have said, "six days *until* Passover." – not "before Passover." We confirm this by counting back the days, noting from Scripture the activities taking place each day. (See Illus. 43: Chronology of Passion Week, Page 503) The "six days before" statement referenced could not have been on 8 *Nisan* because the Sabbath travel Laws would have prohibited travel from Jericho to Bethany (or Bethpage) on that date, which was a weekly Sabbath day. In this way we can confidently establish the days of the week with the *Nisan* calendar days, counting from that Sabbath night in Jericho.

Which "Law"?

When the Disciples asked Jesus where they should "prepare the Passover" (Matthew 26:17) this was said to have been "the first day of unleavened bread." This is repeated in Mark 14:12 and Luke 22:7 – 8, where they add that this was the day for killing the Paschal Lamb. There is apparently a "loosening" of terms here. The Paschal Lamb is to be killed on the "Day of Preparation" – which for these Galileans was to be 13 *Nisan*, before sundown, about 3 p.m. How do we know this was the 13th of *Nisan*? – We remember that these Galileans had an extra day for this feast and they were to commence one day early – in order not to be too late!

That night, *after* sundown, 14 *Nisan* arrived and was the time of *their* "High Feast," *their Seder* — *their* ("Galilean") Passover meal (the "Last Supper"). And at *this* time *their* first partaking of unleavened bread occurred. This was "technically" then, 14 *Nisan*, at night, just *after* 13 *Nisan* had ceased. For these Galileans then, 14 *Nisan* was again "technically" *their* "first day of unleavened bread."

Although the principle is not discussed in the Gospel, an interesting feature of the Law would have been "kept" by Jesus on the day preceding His *Seder* (14 *Nisan*) because of His status as a "firstborn." Both *The Jewish Book of Why*[20] and the *Shulcan Aruch*, Chap. CXIII:6 direct that any firstborn person must fast during the day preceding the Passover. Reference 20 states that the firstborn must fast in memory of the "firstborn" that were spared by the Angel of the Lord as he slew all of the firstborn of Egypt at the first Passover.

Since their "Galilean" *Seder* (The Last Supper) would have been Thursday night, Jesus therefore would have been fasting and devoid of *any* food during what we would call "Wednesday" night until "Thursday" night, as listed on the right-hand sides of our charts, Illus. 44: Days, Events for Feast of Unleavened Bread, Page 504, and Illus. 45: Western & Jewish: 3 Days, 3 Nights in Tomb, Page 505. This was the day during which, while they were at Bethany, the Disciples asked Jesus: *"Where wilt thou that we prepare for thee to eat the Passover?"* (Mat. 26:17) Jesus then ended His fasting and ate the Passover with the Twelve at their "Galilean" *Seder* Thursday night, as 14 *Nisan* began after sundown. In these modern times, this practice of fasting by the firstborn is called *Siyum* or *Siyum Massechta*.

In fact, *all* Jewish persons are forbidden to eat *matzah* (unleavened bread) during the entire day preceding the *Seder*. Rabbinical disdain for ignoring this taboo is voiced in Reference 3, where it is said: *"A man who eats matzah on the day before Passover shall be like a man who makes love to his fiancée in her father's house."* Some Jewish groups even today abstain from *matzah* during the entire month prior to Passover; i .e., from *Purim* until Passover.

All this "legalism" concerning partaking of the *matzah* is generated because the *matzah* represents the Paschal Lamb at the end of the meal. At that time the last piece of *matzah*, called the *Afikoman*, is eaten as a sort of dessert. It is to be savored and enjoyed by all the celebrants as the final, most Glorious part of the meal. Jewish teaching insists the taste of the *matzah* is more enjoyable as well as more spiritually rewarding if each person has not tasted *matzah* for at least one day prior. Here we need to once again repeat the admonition from *Pesahim* 19 instructing that each person at the *Seder* must: *"finish with the taste of the Paschal Lamb (i.e., the Afikoman) in his mouth. And nobody shall say, 'On with the entertainment!'"* The Passover *Seder* is a most highly Blessed and Solemn occasion for all Jewish People. (It is *not* an occasion for revelry.)

Of course, many Christians are aware that the *Afikoman*, the broken middle piece of *matzah*, represents the "broken" Body of Jesus as The Paschal Lamb of God – for Israel and for all the rest of us! — Yes, this part of the meal is a Most Blessed and Solemn Occasion.

As we explained, the "proper" or "Jerusalem" dates for the Day of Preparation and the Passover "Feast Day" (Sabbath) were more Biblically observed on 14 and 15 *Nisan*, respectively, as shown in Illus. 44: Days, Events for Feast of Unleavened Bread, Page 504. Our charts have used the Jerusalem dates because these are the dates Jesus fulfilled as The Paschal Lamb and they are therefore more important and governing in this study. This is only one very "simple" example testifying to the often overwhelming complexity of Mosaic and *Talmudic* Law. Oftentimes for Christians, there is a temptation to ignore or even ridicule all such devious and tedious *Talmudic* technicalities. Nevertheless, we must not be deterred in our search for the Glory of God's Plan, which is so cleverly "hidden" in the legal Judaic labyrinths throughout all this complexity.

Fulfilling The Law

Why should we Christians struggle to solve this puzzle? – Because we should be motivated to learn HOW Jesus fulfilled the Law. – *That's why!* – Too often neglected in studies of The Crucifixion is examination of the Ultimate and Final Purpose for the sacrifice of Messiah on The Cross. There is no mystery as to that Purpose. Jesus fulfilled ALL of the Law in order to pay for ALL sins of ALL people. Upon His death, it was no longer required that man should atone for his sins through shedding the blood of goats, bulls, etc. in the Temple. "Jesus Paid It ALL!" Jesus in fact declared this concept in John 14:6, saying:

"Jesus saith unto him, I am the way, the truth, and the life: no man cometh unto the Father, but by me."

By this, Jesus said He had done ALL that was to be done with bulls and goats, etc. and that through His Completion of these Laws, men could now "cometh to the Father" if they accepted His Completion. His Crucifixion at *Golgotha* represented each of the Jewish sacrifices, down to the finest detail — to the last "jot and tittle."

The mystery is seen in HOW Jesus fulfilled those Laws. Jesus died as a Complete and Perfect replacement for all the bulls, goats, rams, doves, etc. that were slain in ANY and ALL of the Jewish sacrifices. The Law is very specific concerning the time, method and purpose for slaying each of those animals. These specifications extend to meticulously detailing even the motion of the priest's hand as he sprinkles the blood on the Altar. It is to be done in the manner as one swinging a whip or a lash, as at a scourging of a crucifixion victim with a *flagellum*, for example. (*Yoma* 53b) *Talmud*, in fact, states the words: *"by imitating the movements of a lasher."* (*Yoma* 15a)

If we really believe that Jesus died for our sins, then we should be eager to learn these marvelous and revealing details concerning how He fulfilled the Law and why He had to die for us in order to accomplish that. No man is worthy on his own merits to come before God, because all men are sinful and God is without sin. God therefore gave the Jewish people the Law in order that they could see the result of their sins and repent. Men cannot "keep" the Law because men are impure. Only God is Pure. A tainted man cannot "pay" our Pure God for his own sins because the payment would be tainted as well. A Perfect God could never accept a tainted and therefore imperfect payment. Pure and "without spot," therefore, God Himself came to pay for *all* of the sins of *all* men through *His* "keeping" of His own Law.

Each time Satan accuses against one of us, God can now point to this Pure and PERFECT Completion of His Law. The required payment against ALL of our sins has been paid in FULL and Satan therefore can no longer accuse in such instance. – Our Just and Merciful God **ALWAYS** wins in these continual "jousts" with Satan!

Jesus said (Matthew 5:17) "...*I am not come to destroy (the Law), but to fulfill."* And, that is exactly what He did every day of His life. Nowhere is His Perfect and Complete fulfillment of the Law witnessed more than in the seven days extending from the Triumphal Entry to The Resurrection. By the way, the number "seven" in Biblical Numerology[1, 10] is the number of Perfection or Dispensational Fullness. Jesus completed ALL of the Law by being the right Person to do the Right Thing at the Right Place at the Right Time. And, Jesus, who IS God and who IS Pure, is the ONLY Person who has the Authority and the Capability to Complete His Own Law and thereby make PURE, FULL and PERFECT Payment for the sins of men. This feat *had* to be consummated Perfectly. Otherwise, God could make NO claim against Satan that ALL sin had been washed Clean and Pure. Yes, Jesus fulfilled the Law Perfectly and Completely. And, again – we MUST hunger to know how He accomplished that.

Jesus gave us a picture of this as He insisted that the Disciples "let" Him wash their feet. (John 13:5) Think about all the Earthly pleasures Jesus could have enjoyed if He had bent to the temptation to use His Power. He could have had what the World would call "everything!" The most humble act a man can perform is to exchange his own life for the lives of others. That is the ULTIMATE act of...Yes, God kneels in humility at *our* feet as He washes *our* sins and gives *us* His Complete Rest.

Satan can claim only those men who then do not accept God's washing of their sins. Unless we study His Law, we cannot know or understand how the Lord accomplished this. It would seem that we should at least be curious, if not admiring.

All of His fulfillments are of vital importance to study of The Gospel. However, there are so many of these that we must limit this discussion to those seen in Scripture for the seven Days of Unleavened Bread. As we shall later demonstrate, these dates are key to any study regarding the number of days and nights in The Tomb as well as the days leading up to that time. Illus. 44: Days, Events for Feast of Unleavened Bread, Page 504, is presented to assist in our understanding of these dates.

Continuing now in Illus. 44: Days, Events for Feast of Unleavened Bread, Page 504, the Law of the Passover begins on the 10th day of the first Jewish month, *Nisan*. Exodus 12:1 – 5 commands that each Jewish home will select a yearling, an unblemished male lamb or goat on the 10th of *Nisan*. Jesus fulfilled that portion of the Law as an unblemished male, having just reached the Jewish age of maturity at about thirty years of age.

Jesus was "selected" for His Sacrifice on the 10th day of *Nisan* when the priests decided that He must die after having accepted the crowd's proclamation as Messiah (Matthew 21:9) and then having driven the moneychangers from the Temple. (Matthew 21:12) The priests were furious because this "pretender" had disrupted their subsidy that had become a Temple "business." All of the circumstances and timing of the events leading up to this period worked together for His "selection" to occur on 10 *Nisan*. No other day would He have permitted *Y'shua's* fulfillment of Exodus 12:3, which specifies that day for selection of the Paschal Lamb.

On the 10th day of *Nisan, Y'shua* entered Jerusalem, was proclaimed as Messiah by the people and disrupted the foul practices of the High Priests and scribes in His Father's House. Therefore, on that date the authorities then decided Jesus must be killed, despite the fact they *knew* Jesus was "unblemished." (Mark 11:18) – Yes, Jesus was our Paschal Lamb.

Next, Exodus 12:6 orders that *"ye shall keep it* (the lamb) *until the fourteenth day of the same month."* This four day period is set aside for observation of the animal to make certain he does not have some as yet unseen symptoms of an illness, lameness or other defect, which would surely disqualify him as "blemished." And so, during that four day period, we see Jesus going into the Temple each day, teaching, being closely examined and tested and questioned and scrutinized by the Scribes, Priests, *Sadducees*, etc.

These "legalizers" continually tried to trap Him. They tried to stump Him. They tried to show inconsistency in His teaching. They tried to expose Him as a blasphemer and a Messianic impostor. They absolutely could not accomplish *any* of those goals. They could find no fault or "blemish" in Him. They even bribed false witnesses against Jesus. (Matthew 26:59) Nevertheless, they finally had to just give up even trying to find a fault in Him. (Matthew 22:46) – Jesus had proved, then that He was "acceptable" as the Lamb.

Then, on 14 *Nisan* — "the day of preparation" for the Passover, the Paschal Lamb was to be slain. Exodus 12:6 directs: *"...the whole assembly of the congregation of Israel shall kill it in the evening."* In many cultures even today, "evening" begins about 3 p.m. in the afternoon, or what the ancients called "the ninth hour of the day." Jesus then completed this part of the Law, having been crucified in view of *"the whole assembly of the congregation"* and having died at the ninth hour on 14 *Nisan*. (Matthew 27:46)

Jesus fulfilled even much more of the Law than we could ever describe in just a few pages or even in a complete book. The Law of the Red Heifer (Numbers 19) and the Atonement Goat (Leviticus 16) are but a few of other statutes of the Law that were completed on that day. We should recall here that God, the Father, ordained in His foreknowledge all this detail of Law as a "picture" of the Prime Sacrifice the Son of Man would ultimately fulfill as He *"provided Himself as the Lamb for a burnt offering."* (Genesis 22:8)

Briefly then, the next day as 15 *Nisan* began at sundown, the Passover meal (*Seder*) began just after sundown. Thus, the 15th of *Nisan* is "the first day of unleavened bread."

Jesus became the Paschal Lamb and was buried just before sundown while the unleavened bread (*matzah*) was being prepared. By the Law, the *matzah* must be prepared in less than eighteen minutes after all the ingredients are assembled, because that is the time at which fermentation begins. Jesus probably was laid in The Tomb eighteen minutes before Sunset. This would have been just about enough time for Joseph of Arimathaea to walk perhaps a little less than a mile to his home in Jerusalem before the Sabbath began. (Luke 23:51 – 56)

The Body of Jesus, pure and without sin, but "broken," lay in The Tomb as our unleavened *Afikoman* until He was raised on the third day. We know from the Shroud of Turin[11] that His Body suffered no putrefaction, as prophesied in Psalms 16:10. Of course, the theme question we are addressing concerns just *when* that third day occurred. One of the keys to answering that question is contained in the Law of the Passover; although, it seems that even some Jews as well as a few Christians have disagreement on this part of the Law.

The point in debate here concerns the "Sabbath" of Leviticus 23:11. The instructions of Leviticus 23:5 – 11 call for *"an holy convocation"* on the 15th of *Nisan*, the day of the *Seder*. On that day *"ye shall do no servile work therein"* – thereby making that day a "Sabbath." It may be helpful here to explain that, although the weekly Sabbath is always on a Saturday; this "Passover" Sabbath could fall on any "day" of the week, but it was always on the 15th of *Nisan*.

The Feast of First Fruits is described in Verse 11 as being *"on the morrow after the sabbath."* Then the 16th of *Nisan* is the day of the Feast of First Fruits of Verse 10 because it is the "morrow" that follows the "Sabbath" of the 15th. In the same way, then, the Feast of First Fruits also can fall on *any* day of the week.

However, some still argue that First Fruits is to be "the first day of the week" following the Passover; i. e., the first Sunday after Passover. Here the reasoning is that the first day of the week is *"the morrow after the sabbath"* because it follows the *weekly* Sabbath Day (Saturday) and is judged therefore to be the correct day for the Feast of First Fruits.

Jewish sources[4] inform us that the *Sadducean* sect insisted on this latter option and the Pharisees upheld the former interpretation. Many Christians today are divided along the same lines on this question as well.

It is interesting to note that a number of Jewish translations of *Torah*, especially among the earlier versions, render Leviticus 23:15 as follows:

*"And ye shall count unto you from **the morrow after the day of rest**, from the day that ye brought the sheaf for the waving;..."*

Most of these same versions, however, have translated Verse 11 with the familiar *"...morrow after the Sabbath."* Hertz[4] observes that "the day of rest" is a "better" translation from the Hebrew text. No explanation is offered as to why "Sabbath" is used in Verse 11, but "day of rest" is used in verse 15.

Nevertheless, it would seem that the wordage referring to *"an holy convocation,"* and especially, *"no servile work"* commanded on 15 *Nisan*, indicates this surely is an *extraordinary!* Sabbath. Moreover, Exodus 12:14 proclaims the 15th of *Nisan* as a *"feast by an ordinance for ever."* The Rabbis refer to it as the "Feast Day" because it is most certainly a Holy day. This is dramatized further during the Priests' decision in "selecting" Jesus for death, when in considering that His execution might stir the people unfavorably, they cautioned that it be *"not on the Feast Day!"* (Matthew 26:5)

It should come as no surprise after all, that a strong implication toward solution of this entire argument is provided in the Gospel of Jesus Christ, from Mark 15:42 –

*"And now when the even was come, because it was the preparation, that is, **the day before the Sabbath**,"*

The way the language of this verse is constructed and with the usage presented, it is stated as if to confirm that, yes, the preparation was *always* the day before the Sabbath – with "the Sabbath" of course being the day of the *Seder, the First Day of Unleavened Bread,* etc. Since it is clear that the 14th of *Nisan* – *"the preparation"* – could fall on any day of the week, this is stated as if to say "the Sabbath" mentioned here is *not* the weekly Sabbath; i.e., Saturday.

It appears that Jesus chose to avoid this debate altogether, by arranging for *that* Sabbath to satisfy both the Pharisaic position and the *Sadducean* position. Through means of modern technology we are able to trace the days of His "week" to determine that the 15th of *Nisan* that year was a Feast "Sabbath" that occurred on the weekly Sabbath day. In this way, neither side could complain about which day was the Sabbath!

In Jewish tradition, when the Sabbath of the 15th of *Nisan* falls on the regular weekly Sabbath (Saturday), it is indeed a *High Sabbath.* (See John 19:31) The Passover *Haggadah* (instruction) has some exclusive words that are spoken in the liturgy when these Sabbaths coincide. On such occasions, it is *"a more Holy feast."* We could agree it was most appropriate that this feast was indeed a "High" Sabbath and was truly "a more Holy Feast" when it was completed by our Lord Jesus. As stated earlier, this was the Highest of "High" Sabbaths...EVER!

It is indeed regrettable that Christians have such contention and strife over such matters as we have discussed. Many would say that all these things are not important anyway. And, we would assuredly have to agree that such arguments certainly are not important to our Salvation through Jesus Christ. Nevertheless, it is important to awareness of Believers that Jesus fulfilled ALL of the Law so completely and precisely. If we therefore wish to acquire that awareness, then we must address ALL of the details and Marvelous Precision that our Lord implemented in these fulfillments. Ignoring these details and shoving them aside as just so much *impedimenta* is diminishing of His Glory and Majesty and is certainly unbecoming to Christian scholarship.

Continuing on these fulfillments, Jesus fulfilled First Fruits by being raised as the First Fruits of The Resurrection. Jesus was the first "man" to be resurrected in a new Glorified Body in defeat of Death. He accomplished this on the 16th of *Nisan* which was "*the morrow after the Sabbath,*" in accordance with the Law of Leviticus 23:11.

In Jewish tradition, the "morrow" meant after daylight; i.e., as the "day" began, as distinguished from the sunset at evening previous when the *calendar* "day" began. It was necessary that the "morrow" began at an hour such that sufficient time would be available to harvest the grain and return from the field, delivering it to the priest at the Temple (Deuteronomy 26:2). Moreover, the grain sheaf would need to be brought promptly in order that the stalks and leaves would not wilt and become limber. It was to honor the Lord and to be crisp and *fresh* from the harvest in His Presence.

Here we can picture Jesus on the day of His Glorious Resurrection. Jesus was raised and "waved" before the Lord in His Glorified Body. He was not even to be touched by Mary at The Tomb. His Body was the First Fruit of The Resurrection. Jesus fulfilled the Feast of First Fruits by being the first "man" to be resurrected in an Eternal and Glorified body, just as you and I will be raised on that Glorious Day!

Although the "legal" pathway is obscure at this time, Jesus also must have fulfilled the "seven days of unleavened bread" in some way. (Illus. 44: Days, Events for Feast of Unleavened Bread, Page 504) Exactly forty-nine days later, Jesus fulfilled the Feast of Pentecost (*Shavuot* or "Weeks") when He sent the Holy Spirit to "anoint" the Disciples with tongues of flame, commissioning them to begin their ministries. Jesus has yet a few more of the Seven Feasts of Jehovah to fulfill when He comes in Glory to receive His Kingdom. These are: Feast of Trumpets (*Rosh Hashanah*), Day of Atonement (*Yom Kippur*) and Feast of Tabernacles (*Succoth*). He will fulfill ALL of those remaining Feasts with exactly the same criteria and with the same precision and Glory as He has previously fulfilled these first four Feasts we have traced.

As a review, the seven Feasts of Jehovah are listed in order as they occur during each year on the Jewish "Religious" calendar, with the Hebrew name followed by the "popular" English name and the date of celebration. –

- *Pesach* – Passover – 14-21 *Nisan*, except 15-21 *Nisan* at Jerusalem – March/April
- *Hag Hamatzah* – Unleavened Bread – (Included as part of Pesach/Passover)
- *Yom Habikkurim* (Also: *Lag B'Omer, Terumoth, Hallah*) First Fruits – 16 *Nisan*
- *Shavuot* – Weeks or Pentecost – Seven weeks after 16 *Nisan*
- Rosh Hashanah – New Year or Feast of Trumpets – 1 Tishri – Sept/Oct
- Yom Kippur – Day of Atonement – 10 Tishri
- Succoth – Booths or Tabernacles – 15 Tishri

- Already fulfilled by *Y'Shua ben Yusef* – Jesus of Nazareth – 30 C.E. – At Jerusalem

Before we discuss the remaining Feasts it is vitally important that we take notice of the criteria that was set as precedent for those first four Feasts. First, consider the fact that ALL of these first four Feasts were fulfilled in Jerusalem. ALL were fulfilled ONLY to Jewish people and ALL were fulfilled on the exact date and in the same order as they appear on the Jewish religious calendar. Remember, ALL of those first Christians were Jews. No Gentiles were involved in any of these fulfillments. Any Gentiles that may have been present – even the Roman soldiers at The Cross — were merely "bystanders." ALL three of those remaining Feasts will be fulfilled *in Jerusalem*. ALL will be fulfilled ONLY to the Jewish People. ALL will be completed exactly on the proper day and ALL will continue to be fulfilled in exactly the same order as they occur on the Jewish religious calendar.

We must pause at this point to explain, however, that present day Judaism does not hold to these same Jewish calendar dates for some of these feast days. For example, *Yom Habikkurim, Terumoth or Hallah* (First Fruits) is not observed by some groups. Instead, many Jewish people today observe *Lag B'Omer* on the 33rd day after the second day of Passover. This is a sort of memorial for a plague that occurred, striking down many thousands of students of the Rabbinical sage, Akiba. It is sometimes called *Scholars' Day*. There is no Biblical justification for such an observance.

Along this same vein of thought, instead of observing 16 *Nisan* as the Feast of First Fruits, modern Judaism observes *Shavuot* (Weeks or Pentecost) as the Feast of First Fruits. A Jewish person who has studied *Torah* and the Law would of course be familiar with all of the dates and celebrations we have put forward. However, if you were to discuss these fulfillments with a so-called "traditional" Jewish person with only casual knowledge of Scripture, it would quickly be pointed out to you that your understanding of the Jewish calendar and Feasts is severely in error! It is vitally important to this subject, then, to keep in mind the fact that our discussion is based *strictly* upon the Biblically stated assignments of these days from *Torah*. Although traditional Judaism has made some changes, it is hardly reasonable to believe that God has changed His Calendar! – Gentiles can become really perplexed by all these sorts of things!

Here we remind ourselves that God told the Children of Israel that *Nisan* is "*the first month.*" (Exodus 12:2 and Esther 3:7) *Rosh Hashanah*, the Jewish New Year, occurs on 1 *Tishri*, which is the first month of the Jewish "secular" calendar. However, *Tishri* is the seventh month of the Jewish "religious" calendar. It is interesting to note that the final *three* Feasts of Jehovah occur, and therefore will be fulfilled, during that seventh "religious" month, *Tishri*. We must observe here God's Placement of His Holy Number – *three* – approaching completion of fulfilling His Feasts. His final *three* Feasts are: *Rosh Hashanah, Yom Kippur* and *Sukkoth* (Tabernacles or "Booths.")This He also does by reaching His Number of *seven* for His Holy Perfection at the Final Completion of His Feasts! – Again! – God just does things that Way!

Contrary to the well-intentioned teaching of some of our most respected and learned Christian teachers of Bible prophecy, the "Rapture" or "taking away" of The Church (I

Thessalonians. 4:16) will not occur to fulfill *Rosh Hashanah* or Feast of Trumpets. Remember? – Jesus said: *"...for the Son of man cometh at an hour when ye think not."* (Luke 12:40) We are not therefore to be expecting His Coming on any specific date. Believers are instructed by this to be ready at ANY time!

Instead, by again reviewing the "precedent" in the criteria for fulfilling the Seven Feasts of Jehovah, the remaining feasts must be fulfilled as follows:

- in Jerusalem – (Not in the U.S.A., Canada, Europe, South America, etc.)
- only to Jewish people — (Not to Christian Gentiles)
- on the exact date required in the Law for that Feast on the Jewish calendar.
- in the exact order specified in the Law on the Jewish religious calendar.

Thus, we have seen the first two key elements of the fulfillment criteria are not satisfied using a theory teaching that the Rapture of the Church will manifest fulfillment of the Feast of Trumpets (*Rosh Hashanah*). However, there are some Old Testament prophecies, as yet unfulfilled, that will fit *all* of the categories. One of these foretells the *"gathering up"* of the Jewish people when *"the great trumpet"* sounds its call.

The "Jewish Rapture"

On that day *"the great trumpet"* will sound, and *"those scattered"* (ALL Jewish People, living and dead) shall then be *"gathered up one by one"* from *"the four corners of the Earth."* (See Isaiah 27:12 – 13, Zechariah 9:14 – 17, Mark 13:24 – 27) Therefore, the Feast of Trumpets *will* be completed when ALL Jewish survivors of the Great Tribulation (His "elect") will be translated bodily; "raptured" – if you will, to Jerusalem to greet Messiah, Son of David (Jesus) when He arrives (Returns!) to claim His Kingdom.

Now you are asking, "But, you said the living and the dead." We must recall here that when these prophecies were spoken it was assumed that ALL or nearly all Jewish dead would be buried at the Mount of Olives. There they would lie at rest "in the Earth" to await Messiah in response to the prophecy of Zechariah 14:4 and would not need therefore to be "translated" to Jerusalem. These prophecies were given before the "scattering" through the *Diaspora* and into the past 1900 years, during which many Jewish dead had not been able to arrange for interment at the *Olivet* Cemetery. Millions of Jewish dead are "scattered" throughout the nations. It would seem that the Lord mercifully withheld many of the depressing details in this prophecy from His Chosen.

The two remaining Feasts after Trumpets, Day of Atonement and Feast of Tabernacles, will be fulfilled ten and fifteen days later, respectively. Again, these also will be fulfilled not only to the Jewish remnant that will survive the Tribulation; but also to ALL other righteous Jews – both living and dead. This is the Day of The Resurrection, which Jewish worshipers prayerfully anticipate on each *Yom Kippur*. On this Day, their most sacred Holy Day of the year, the prayer of each Jewish person is that his or her name shall be: *"sealed in the Book of Life for ever."*

The solemnity and Holiness of this Feast is dramatically emphasized by Hertz[4] by means of two entries under Leviticus 23:16 – 32. One comment states that confession of sin is the most essential and characteristic element in the services during *Yom Kippur*. Another comment suggests rich Blessings for Israel from this most sacred Holiday. It is claimed that no other nation – ancient or modern – has any ritual or ceremony even approaching *Yom Kippur* as regarding "religious depth." It is described as a day for purification and turning from sin. Forgiveness is granted then, through Grace from a Merciful God, who holds penitence in esteem as high as that of guiltlessness itself. The latter comment is attributed with credit to the prestigious 1st century Jewish philosopher, Philo of Alexandria.

On the Day of Atonement (10 *Tishri*) Zechariah's prophecy will be fulfilled when: "...*they shall look upon Me Whom they have pierced*..." (Zechariah 12:10) as Messiah arrives at the summit of the Mount of Olives. (Zechariah 14:4) Multitudes of Jewish dead in the Mount of Olives Cemetery have been eagerly and prayerfully waiting to greet the arrival of Messiah ever since Zechariah had delivered his prophecy, 520 B.C.E.. At present, those burial plots are in such high demand and in such short supply that wealthy Jewish people pay $50,000 for one plot. To me, this fact alone indicates that Jewish worshipers are serious(!) about wanting to be there to greet Messiah when He arrives at the summit of the Mount of Olives "*on that day!*" — Yes, Jewish Believers await the same ONE we Christian Believers await. They just do not realize that ONE is Jesus of Nazareth and that He is the ONE God whom they love and worship as we do.

It is significant to note in Judaism that *Sukkoth* or Tabernacles is also sometimes called *Chag Haasif*, meaning: "Festival of Gathering" – "As when you gather in the yield of your field." It is truly Glorious and remarkable to observe here that at that time Jesus will "gather" all the "yield" of His "Harvest" of Believers – both Jewish and Gentile!

On 15 *Tishri*, the Feast of Tabernacles, ALL nations will be "gathered" to rejoice in Jerusalem with the Jewish people at the Kingdom of their Messiah, who will then rule the Earth in Perfection and Glory for one thousand years. ALL seven of the Feasts of Jehovah will have been fulfilled to the Jewish people, and fulfilled in Jerusalem and exactly on the right dates, with each in its proper order and exactly on Schedule!

Traditional "Days" and "Nights"

In attempts to rationalize the Biblical timing of The Crucifixion, Christian Gentiles have proposed varying proposals to explain how *Y'shua* spent "*three days and three nights*" in The Tomb. In their ignorance of Judaic Law and tradition, scholars have instead applied Western, Japhetic Christian timing of these days and nights. We shall present two such "scenario" proposals that purport to explain the timing; although, each uses different criteria and results in a different answer.

"It must have been on a Wednesday!"

We have chosen to demonstrate what is wrong about the traditional "Western" three days and three nights in the scenario for The Passion Week before we discuss the correct, "Jewish" scenario. Illus. 45: Western & Jewish: 3 Days, 3 Nights in Tomb, Page 505, depicts the Jewish calendar dates alongside our Western days of the week proposing a Wednesday Crucifixion in the left-hand column. The scenario described here is from an established and respected source[1] which would at first appear to present an excellent argument, until one examines the details closely. The correct scenario that emerges from literal reading of Scripture and from the Judaic Law given to Moses is presented in the right-hand column of Illus. 45: Western & Jewish: 3 Days, 3 Nights in Tomb, Page 505.

Nearly all Bible translation versions agree, on basis of John 19:31, Jesus died on 14 *Nisan* "*the day of the preparation.*" (Exodus 12:6) Counting back to "*six days before the Passover*" (John 12:1 – 2), on 9 *Nisan*, Jesus and the Twelve would have traveled from Jericho to Bethany on a Friday, arriving at the home of Lazarus just as the weekly Sabbath began at sundown. After sundown, on the Sabbath starting 10 *Nisan*, Mary would have violated the Sabbath by "working" as she anointed Jesus with oil and wiped His feet[6] with her hair. (John 12:1 – 2) This day could not be, therefore, 9 *Nisan* or six days before the Passover because counting back from The Crucifixion, 10 *Nisan* would have been a Sabbath night if 14 *Nisan* had occurred on Wednesday as taught by Reference 1.

Observing Illus. 45: Western & Jewish: 3 Days, 3 Nights in Tomb, Page 505, we see that the days of the week are established by counting back "three days and three nights" (in a Western context) from The Resurrection on Sunday – "the first day of the week." (John 20:1) This feature is the basis for this proposal, founded upon a desire to make Scripture fit and "make sense" (i.e., "prove" it really was three days and three nights), but within our Western concept of days and nights. In order to do this, proponents must force violation of the Law and/or force Scripture into self-contradiction. These Christians try, albeit with righteous intentions, to defend Scripture against critics who, as with themselves, neither understand nor appreciate the Judaic Law given to the Jews by *YHWH*. Ironically, this position leads to a well known "trap" used by these same critics, in that they are constant in their enthusiasm, watching and waiting for other Christians to present Biblical interpretations that result in self — contradiction within Scripture.

One such futile "making-it-fit" example is found in a so-called Biblical "inconsistency" between the two "thieves" of Matthew 27:38 and Mark 15:27 versus the two "malefactors" of Luke 23:39 – 43. This one scholar therefore proposes there were FIVE crosses at *Golgotha* instead of only three, claiming there were Jesus, two thieves and two malefactors. Such careless scholarship, in striving to "prove" Scripture's unerring consistency, instead exposes a scholar's ignorance by completely ignoring John 19:18 –

"*Where they crucified Him, and two other with Him, on either side one, and Jesus in the midst.*"

What could be more clear?! – There were *three* crosses. – Next, we might expect somebody will propose there were even *two* Crucifixions, as based upon Matthew, Mark and

John saying the place was called "*Golgotha*;" whereas, Luke said it was "*Calvary*." We illustrate these ridiculous approaches in order to introduce the type of "thinking" that has generated these theories leading to claiming The Crucifixion occurred on a Wednesday or a Thursday. As we will demonstrate, such struggling to make Scripture "fit" our Western traditional concepts of time, location, manners, customs, lifestyles, etc. usually lead to ridiculous Biblical teaching that invites well-justified criticism from doubters and unbelievers. – Serious Bible scholars *must* learn to *think* Jewish! – Moreover, they must learn to THINK! – period! – instead of just blindly accepting all of the traditional Bible teaching concepts they have been taught previously.

In order to attempt "fitting" this scenario with the Gospel, some devious and therefore doubtful interpretations are made, which in turn then fuel the doubts and criticisms of unbelievers and skeptics. For this study we have listed:

1. A claim that two entry processions were made into Jerusalem: One from Bethpage on Friday, 9 *Nisan* (Matthew 21:1 – 2) and finally the Triumphal Entry from Bethany on "Palm Sunday," 11 *Nisan* (Luke 19:29 – 38). As already explained, Bethpage and Bethany were "twin-cities." This is certainly thin evidence toward claiming there were therefore "twin" entries into Jerusalem. Jesus and His group traveled from Jericho, arriving and passing through Bethpage. They continued on to Bethany nearby and spent the night. The Triumphal Entry occurred next day.

2. Along with (1), it is taught that Jesus cleansed the Temple by routing the moneychangers on *both* of those "Triumphal Entry" days as well. The second riotous event in the Temple is claimed on basis of Mark 11:15, which must certainly be out of chronological sequence. Otherwise somebody surely would have recorded that Jesus committed that act on two occasions during that week.

3. This sequence finally must reason that Jesus was raised just before sundown on 17 *Nisan* (Saturday) in order to log exactly three days and three nights in The Tomb – exactly seventy-two hours. Already we have shown that the Gospel accounts, coupled with simple logic, reveal that He was raised in the "wee hours" just before dawn "on the first day of the week" (Sunday). However, this theory could never stand with that Truth because that would add another twelve hours – another "night" making His entombment a total of three days and *four* nights.

In this scenario, Jesus would have had an uncommonly "busy" day on the 9th of *Nisan*. Here we are asked to believe that *in just one day*:

- Jesus and The Twelve walk from Jericho, or a place nearby, to Bethpage/Bethany, a walk of about 13 – 15 miles.
- Jesus directs His men to negotiate for loan of a donkey;
- Jesus makes an initial (but not "Triumphal") entry into Jerusalem;
- Jesus marches into the Temple and ejects the moneychangers;
- Jesus heals the blind and the lame at the Temple.

- Jesus returns to spend the Sabbath night at Bethany.

Many would agree that would have made rather a "full" day. And remember, Jesus was not the type to rush through a place, "flitting" from one person to another, "glad-handing," giving out "small talk" – such as so many modern "party animals." He would have to stop and teach and talk and heal and comfort all those He saw along the route. Jesus did not "flit." This much activity would have been a bit much for just one day – and even more a challenge when we consider that He had to hike at least two miles from Jerusalem back to Bethany before the Sabbath began at sundown that Friday evening. We also must allow for at least a few hours of that day if the group had walked even half of the thirteen-mile jaunt from Jericho.

Next, we are asked to consider the unlikely sequence in which, on one day (9 *Nisan*), Jesus enters Jerusalem with shouts of "Hosannas;" and ejects the moneychangers. He spends the next day, the Sabbath, at Bethany. Then a day later (11 *Nisan*) He makes a second and even more Glorious and "Triumphal" entry into the City and gets on the moneychangers *a second time!* All this is twisted and concocted in order to justify an additional day and is mostly based on Matthew's mentioning of both Bethpage and Bethany; along with Mark's somewhat disjointed and non-chronological narrative.

By adding the extra day, this theory disrupts the timing revealed in a very important verse: *"After two days was the Feast of the Passover, and of unleavened bread."* (Mark 14:1) This carries a somewhat colloquial Jewish reference to the beginning of the Passover Holiday as *"the First Day of Unleavened Bread."* This was actually *"the Day of Preparation"* for the Jewish Passover – 14 *Nisan*. According to the scenario in Reference 1 and as shown in Illus. 45: Western & Jewish: 3 Days, 3 Nights in Tomb, Page 505, that sentence was spoken on 13 *Nisan* during the Tuesday evening at the home of Simon, the leper.

We can be certain also that the reference was to the Jerusalem Passover, because in the next verses of both Matthew and Mark the Priests are cautioning that Jesus must be killed *"not on the Feast day"* – for the Passover in Jerusalem – which would have been 15 *Nisan*. We recall from Leviticus 23:7 that the 15th is a day of *"holy convocation"* and on that Feast day *"ye shall do no servile work"* Since the Passover Feast was the 15th, then if this had been spoken on the 13th, Passover would not have been *after* two "Western" days, but actually would have been *after* only one day. The key word here is *"after."* Timing in this scenario is too "crowded" therefore to be in agreement with Scripture.

We should pause here to observe the Priests' reasoning toward urgency and haste on the night of the "trial" – 14 *Nisan*. The priesthood hierarchy did not want this unpleasant episode, with high possibilities of riots erupting, to mar in any way the approaching seven day Holy Season. They had to get this troublesome Galilean arrested, tried, sentenced, executed and buried *before* "the Feast Day" – 15 *Nisan* – which began at sundown Friday evening of the 14th. After all, that evening as 15 *Nisan* began, all of Jerusalem – including King Herod, High Priest Caiaphas and all the priests, were to sit at table to celebrate and enjoy their *Seder*.

They barely had time to bring about all these events by staging the entire scenario on 14 *Nisan*. It began as Jesus was arrested on the night as 14 *Nisan* began and ended with His burial in The Tomb just before sundown as 14 *Nisan* closed. Truly, it had to be finished before "the Feast Day." This was truly "lynch—mob justice," forged out of Jewish desperation to preserve a religious Holiday that God had devised to Honor and Glorify the One being punished in this ordeal. Here we must weep with God as we contemplate this Infinite irony.

Well-deserved sympathy can be granted to any scholar who painstakingly would attempt to dissect and decipher this last and Most Holy Week. Principal among factors contributing to the frustration in this task is some ambiguity brought through Gentiles' ignorance and Jewish "flexibility" concerning the terms: "Feast of the Passover" and "First Day of the Feast of Unleavened Bread." (Matthew 26:2 and 17; Mark 14:1 and 12) The explanation is very complex and will require your utmost patience.

In a colloquial fashion, Jewish people often traditionally refer to the "Day of Preparation" (14 *Nisan*) as the "First Day of Unleavened Bread" or as "Feast of the Passover." They do this despite the fact that *technically* those events occur *after* sundown, *after* the 14th day closes and becomes 15 *Nisan*. This technicality is supported in Leviticus 23:5 – 6, where it is said that the 14th of the month is "*the Lord's Passover and the 15th is the first day of "the feast of unleavened bread*." A more "technically correct" description would be that the 14th is the Preparation for the Lord's Passover. His Angel of Death did not actually "pass over" Israel's first-born until that night – after sundown – then, technically the 15th of *Nisan*. Illus. 43: Chronology of Passion Week, Page 503, and Illus. 44: Days, Events for Feast of Unleavened Bread, Page 504, show this situation in graphical form.

One modern translation[12] of the Jewish Scriptures (*Torah*) from the Masoretic text renders Leviticus 23:5 – 6 as follows:

*"In the first month, on the fourteenth day of the month, at twilight, there shall be a **passover offering** to the Lord, and on the fifteenth day of that month the Lord's **Feast of Unleavened Bread**. You shall eat unleavened bread for seven days."*

The expression, "passover offering" is a more accurate term describing the fact that killing of the lamb is on 14 *Nisan*; and is logically followed by "the Lord's Feast of Unleavened Bread" on 15 *Nisan*. That "Feast" is of course the *Seder* meal.

Further substantiation comes from Exodus 12:6 – 8,

"And ye shall keep it until the fourteenth day of the same month; and the whole assembly of the congregation of Israel shall kill it at dusk.

And they shall take of the blood, and put it on the two side-posts and on the lintel, upon the houses wherein they shall eat it.

And they shall eat the flesh in that night, roast with fire, and unleavened bread; with bitter herbs shall they eat it."

Each Jewish family is directed to kill the Paschal Lamb "at dusk" or "even" or "twilight" (the Law says this is between 3 p.m. and 6 p.m.) on 14 *Nisan* and then to eat its flesh and the unleavened bread *that night*, which of course is 15 *Nisan*, because *"that night"* is *after* sundown when the 14th ends and the 15th begins.

The ancients were not as precise as we moderns regarding day, evening, night, etc. They were nevertheless very observant regarding the ending of the day at sundown. Referring again to Illus. 44: Days, Events for Feast of Unleavened Bread, Page 504, we can see that the seven days of unleavened bread ordered in Exodus 12:18 *must* begin actually the night of 15 *Nisan* (which is called the 14th "at even"). Otherwise, if the first meal of unleavened bread were on the 14th, ending on the 21st with the seventh and final meal would comprise *eight* meals and eight days instead of seven, as directed in Scripture. However, eight days of unleavened bread are permissible, but *only* for Jewish persons who are in distant regions, such as Galilee (in order that they should not miss the proper day).

Nevertheless, further difficulty in deciphering the calendar sequence of that Most Holy Week is brought with the extra day for Passover for those outlying territories such as Galilee. This measure has existed within Jewish tradition[13, 14] since the return from Babylon, approx. 520 B.C.E. For example, Mark 14:1 says: *"after two days is the Feast of Passover and Unleavened Bread."* This text is actually referring to the "Jerusalem" Passover "Day of Preparation" in the traditional and "colloquial" manner earlier described, as opposed to the "technical" manner for identifying that day.

Later, in Mark 14:12 the Disciples ask The Master, *"Where shall we prepare the Passover?"* They ask this question on the day that Scripture earlier identifies as "the first day of unleavened bread." Clearly, they ask this in the "traditional" fashion, because it is obvious this is *technically* their "Galilean" Day of Preparation. Since that had to be the day before *their* Passover *Seder*, which was "The Last Supper," it had to have been 13 *Nisan* because their *Seder* was that same night after sundown and "technically" then 14 *Nisan*. This complexity is further entangled by the fact that here, just eleven verses later, the text now refers to *their* Galilean Passover as permitted in their Jewish tradition — 13 *Nisan* — instead of the Jerusalem Passover.

Another aberration of timing in the Western scenario as proposed in the left-hand column of Illus. 45: Western & Jewish: 3 Days, 3 Nights in Tomb, Page 505, concerns the Disciples' preparation for their (Galilean) Passover. Matthew's narrative clearly establishes that this was done the next day following the night at Simon's home. That would have been, according to the scenario as proposed in Illus. 45: Western & Jewish: 3 Days, 3 Nights in Tomb, Page 505, on 14 *Nisan* — too late for *their* (Galilean) *Seder*; i.e., "The Last Supper," which occurred most certainly shortly *after* sundown, as 14 *Nisan* was beginning. Their lamb had to have been killed at 3 p.m. 13 *Nisan*, just *before* sundown. These sorts of errors in this proposal render it unsupportive of Scripture and/or the Law and must therefore be discredited.

However, as we have shown, the entire plan for achieving a 72 hour interval is discredited by claiming Jesus was raised before sundown on Saturday. Scripture could not be more clear in stating this is incorrect, by saying in Mark 16:9:

"Now when Jesus was risen early the first day of the week..."

One remaining objection to the theory under discussion is a blatant disregard for fulfillment of the Law through the Feasts of Jehovah. The two entries into the City and two "cleansings" of the Temple completely ignore any requirement that Jesus be chosen as The Type for the Paschal Lamb on 10 *Nisan*. This routine has Jesus resting in Bethany with 10 *Nisan* as the Sabbath. At the same time, as discussed, it would portray Lazarus' sister, Mary, as having violated the Sabbath[6], "working" as she wiped anointing oil from Jesus with her hair. Somebody would have surely criticized Mary and Jesus likely would have defended her for that. He did defend her seeming extravagance (John 12:3), but not her "work." Jesus did not need to defend her "work" because Mary was *not* anointing Him on the Sabbath.

If anyone is tempted to correct the 10 *Nisan* fulfillment by arranging to put 9 *Nisan* on a Saturday, that theory will encounter more Sabbath violations. The citizenry would not have been free to "cut down branches" to place in Jesus' path as He entered the Holy City. (Matthew 21:8, Mark 11:8) Neither would *"those that bought and sold"* (moneychangers, etc.) have been able to perform their "work" on the Sabbath. And finally, The Pharisees would surely have had plenty to squawk about, had Jesus taken the affront to heal the blind and the lame in the Temple(!), if that day had been a Sabbath. (Matthew 21:14) To their credit, the originators of the theory presented were evidently aware of avoiding these Sabbath violations in Jerusalem and the Temple on 10 *Nisan*. For that reason, they had Jesus spending the Sabbath at the Home of Lazarus in Bethany. They nevertheless did forget that anointing Jesus and wiping Him dry would also constitute a violation. (We should all be elated that we are not under the Law!)

In their "zeal" to establish three Western days and nights, this plan completely overlooks the fulfillment of First Fruits on 16 *Nisan*. Ignoring the Law of the Feast of First Fruits is seen in teaching that Jesus arose on 17 *Nisan* as that weekly Sabbath had ceased. Indeed, He did need to rise and to be seen *"on the morrow after the Sabbath"* in order to be "waved" as the sheaf in completion of Leviticus 23:11. Nonetheless, that delay of twelve hours would upset the requirement for three nights by instead spanning *four* nights. Jesus was raised *"early on the first day of the week"* (Sunday) – not at the 12th hour of the seventh day, as this theory would have to prescribe in order to conform to a precise 72 hour interval in The Tomb.

Again, **WHY** would Jesus just sit there for twelve hours(!) in the Jerusalem Cemetery from sundown until daybreak?...and **WHY** would the guards wait 12 hours to report the stone being rolled away? – It just does not make sense. – Several other doubts for this proposal are noted in Illus. 45: Western & Jewish: 3 Days, 3 Nights in Tomb, Page 505, as well. A major defect of this scenario is that it results in having Jesus in the grave FOUR nights and THREE days! – Please note also that this plan has Jesus resurrected on (i.e., during) the *fourth* day instead of on the *third* day, as He had prophesied. (Matthew 16:21) We shall later discuss this error in detail.

"Or, maybe it was a Thursday!"

Another "Western" concept for achieving three days and three nights is presented in Illus. 46: Western & Jewish: 3 Days, 3 Nights, Page 506. This theory also is frequently proposed by well-intentioned and sincere Believers as they attempt to convince critics and doubters that there is no contradiction within Scripture, whenever that failing is alleged concerning the "three days and three nights." They implement this merely by adding one more day into the scenario. In this way, the three days and three nights are "almost" salvaged by appointing Thursday as 14 *Nisan* for The Crucifixion instead of the traditional Friday. Nevertheless, this solution retains at least some veracity by calling for The Resurrection to have occurred on "the first day of the week."

Without close examination, this proposal might at first appear to offer a credible explanation of how three days and three nights were accrued. This story comes very close to fulfilling the Law on the proper days; although, it makes no effort to explain the timing detail for the days and events preceding The Crucifixion. For example, "six days before Passover" could not have been the time for travel to Bethany/Bethpage because it would be too far distant from Jericho for journey on a Sabbath[7], thus conflicting with Scripture, which affirms that they did travel on that day.

Although Jesus is "Lord of the Sabbath" (Luke 6:5) and certainly He *could have* traveled on that day with impunity, He did not violate Sabbatical Law. Neither would Jesus have caused even His Disciples to corrupt the Law of His Father. He was falsely or ignorantly accused of such, but always won His debates with "the lawyers." John 12:1 – 13 clearly states that Jesus traveled to Bethany, arriving the day *before* His Triumphal Entry. Again, *none* of the Gospels describes the Triumphal Entry as having occurred on "the first day of the week" – Sunday. It is reasonable to expect at least one of them would have indicated this if, in fact, that had been the case.

Next, a Thursday Crucifixion followed by the Sunday morning Resurrection does result in three nights; although, with only slightly more than two days in The Tomb. This proposal follows the *Saducean* rendition of First Fruits (if they even considered that) by placing that fulfillment "on the morrow after the (weekly) Sabbath" (17 *Nisan*) instead of, properly, after the "day of a holy convocation" at 16 *Nisan*. This proposal also has the questionable timing of The Resurrection on the fourth day instead of on the third day. (Matthew 16:21) Later we shall demonstrate that "questionable" is a word that is too charitable in this case.

Three Jewish Days and Three Jewish Nights In The Tomb

OKAY – So, how *do* we get three days and three nights? We know the Bible is infallible as the Word of God; and yet, there is this question that can spawn doubts and/or contention about this inconsistency within our Western way of dealing with days and nights. In the scenario described following, we will demonstrate how "working within the Law" helps our understanding of Scripture as well as understanding the Hebrews who wrote it *reflecting their own culture and traditions.* The right—hand portions of Illus. 45: Western & Jewish: 3

Days, 3 Nights in Tomb, Page 505, and Illus. 46: Western & Jewish: 3 Days, 3 Nights, Page 506, portray the sequence of events in a perspective derived from literal Scripture as well as being aligned with Jewish *Talmudic* Law. (You know, – the "lawyers.") This sequence is presented to provide illustration of those principles and statutes required for fulfilling the Law as well as providing a comparison reference vs. the Western teaching we are criticizing.

We now must show just *how* Scripture can stand unquestioned on the claim of Jesus having been in The Tomb three days and three nights. Jesus said He had come to fulfill the Law. (Matthew 5:17) Everything He did therefore came under the Law that was given to Moses; the calendar, the Sabbath Laws, the dietary laws – *everything*. Jesus was never talking about days, nights, etc. in the way we Western Gentiles think of these matters. As we will note, the Law had some very strange ("weird") concepts, which Jesus nevertheless upheld and used constantly, because Jesus IS a Jew!

An example illustrating this variance of Jewish thought concerning "day" and "night" is described by Alfred Kolatch[22] with reference to birthdays and dates of death for Jewish people. If a person is born on a "Thursday" night; i.e., just before midnight – say on July 26th – his birthday actually will be registered in Jewish annals as "Friday," July 27th. His "Jewish Birthday" then is July 27th. Similarly, if a Jewish person dies at 9:15 p.m. on a Thursday night, July 26th, the date registered on his "Jewish" death record is July 27th. The explanation for this seemingly puzzling procedure is simple when we recall that Jewish dates begin at sundown – not at midnight.

Illus. 45: Western & Jewish: 3 Days, 3 Nights in Tomb, Page 505, and Illus. 46: Western & Jewish: 3 Days, 3 Nights, Page 506, diagram the timing and events for accomplishing "three days and three nights" comparing two "Western" concepts vs. the Jewish method. We already have shown why the Western views are invalid. We present these comparisons to equip readers with a graphic evaluation for reaching a positive conclusion on this question. The Western concept in Illus. 45: Western & Jewish: 3 Days, 3 Nights in Tomb, Page 505, is taken from a respected, venerated, beloved reference[1], albeit presenting an erroneous teaching regarding these events.

The concept detailed in Illus. 46: Western & Jewish: 3 Days, 3 Nights, Page 506, is usually proposed by righteously intentioned Christians who have some knowledge of Scripture, but who attempt to "squeeze" Scripture into agreeing with their own preconceived notions and/or traditional "Western" thought. Through this study, we would pray to encourage these sincere Christians to enrich and expand their Scriptural awareness and reinforce their witnessing by studying Biblical history, customs, Judaic tradition and, especially, the linkage connecting the Old Testament and the New Testament. There is also found among some dedicated Christians a bent toward defense of what they believe to be unwarranted accusations of "Biblical discrepancies." These so-called "discrepancies" are actually nothing of the kind, but instead, are actually incorrect interpretation of Scripture, frequently brought about by our western misunderstanding and/or ignorance of Jewish thought and tradition.

The argument just described persists among Christians despite the fact that there is a wealth of documentation showing that eastern civilizations do not count "days" in the same fashion as that of our western cultural practices. John W. Haley's priceless work, *Alleged Discrepancies of the Bible*, points out that *"Orientals" count any part of a day as a full twenty-four hour day*. This of course typifies that condition just described. Many Scripturally aware and well-intentioned, although uninformed Christians have adopted this erroneous interpretation of what constitutes a "day" or especially a day of the month in the *Jewish* inspired Gospel of Jesus Christ – Who is, after all, a Jew.

Megillah 20a teaches that anything *"after dawn counts as done"* in a full 24 hour "day." That is to say, if anything is done after dawn and during the daylight hours, it counts as if it had been done during that *complete* 24 hour period; i.e., *"a day and a night."* We should recall here that a Jewish "date" begins at sundown and closes at sundown twenty-four hours later. But, we must observe that a Jewish "date" such as the 10th "day" of *Nisan*, is not equated with a *"day"* beginning just after midnight, as in our modern English language. When Judaism speaks of "day," it is referring to "day time" – not a "date" on the calendar. Likewise, when Judaism refers to "night," it means after sundown – "night time." Earlier, we saw application of this ruling from Exodus 6:8. The lamb is killed "in the evening" – i.e., between 3 p.m. and 5 p.m. of the 14th of *Nisan*. Then, it was said: "And they shall eat the flesh in *that night*,..." which was of course, on the next "date" – the 15th "day" of *Nisan*, which begins after sundown – after dark – at *night*.

The Rabbis apparently rationalize this measure on basis from several Laws, including a principle (*Megillah* 20b) applied in "reaping the *omer*" of grain for the Priest's wave of the First Fruits. (Leviticus 23:10) The Priest is required to wave a sheaf of grain from an "*omer*" (about one tenth of a bushel) from the first grain harvest of Spring. This he must do "*on the morrow after the Sabbath*." (Leviticus 23:11) Here, the Sabbath is the "*day of an holy convocation*," 15 *Nisan*, which is the Passover "Feast Day." The "morrow" after the Sabbath is then the next morning after the Sabbath has ceased and is actually at 6 a.m., the first hour of the "day" – the 16th of *Nisan*.

A practical consideration in the timing of this procedure concerns the distance that the sheaf may need to be transported. The sheaf must sometimes be carried over a significant distance after harvesting. Nevertheless, the sheaf *must* be delivered to the Temple at Jerusalem before daybreak on 16 *Nisan*. This is brought about by the very logical possibility that the crops at or near Jerusalem will not yet be ripe for the harvest. That possibility is increased by the cooler climate at Jerusalem's mountain locale. Indeed, "going up to Jerusalem" is a literal fact – not just a figure of speech.

The *Gemara* and footnotes of *Menahoth* 64a detail that on occasion the sheaf had to be brought from either Lyyda (now Lod) – about 30 miles west of Jerusalem – or from Assaker (now Nablus) – about 30 miles north of Jerusalem. It is explained that from such a distance it is preferable to bring corn as the *omer*, because barley "would lose its freshness" after such a journey.

These considerations very likely prompted the Pharisaic Rabbis to reach the logic for harvesting the *omer* immediately as the Passover Sabbath of 15 *Nisan* began. Only a few of the Judeans owned chariots or even horses. Therefore, in order to transport the *omer* about 30 miles during darkness, presumably on foot, the trip would require about 12 hours. Departing with the harvested *omer* at about 6 p.m. and walking 30 miles at about 2 ½ m.p.h., arrival would be about 12 hours later at about 6 a.m. – Then, at or just before dawn, the *omer* would have arrived at Jerusalem barely in time for the priest to "wave" it "on the morrow after the Sabbath" – on 16 *Nisan*, as Commanded.

Talmud teaches that the Rabbis have "relaxed the Law" under many circumstances, but especially for *this* Sabbath. One such law that was relaxed by a Rabbi Simeon ben Nanus is mentioned in *Erubin* 105a. Simeon emphasized his authority for judgment in such matters, saying that although he had once relaxed the Sabbath Limit, he would not permit "tying a knot in a broken harp string" during any Sabbath.

Earlier we had mentioned the controversy in which the *Sadducees* opposed the waving of the *omer* on the 16th of *Nisan*. The Pharisees countered by pouring derision upon the *Sadducees* because of their errant position. We see evidence of this in the scenario that takes place during harvesting of the *omer*, as described in *Menahoth* 65a.

At dusk on the evening of 14 *Nisan*, a crowd was assembled to witness the ritual and to take issue against the *Sadducean* view. As the sun lowered and the Passover Sabbath (15 *Nisan*) and darkness began, the reaper called out: "Has the sun set?" – The crowd replies: "Yes!" – He repeats each question twice, and each time the crowd answers: "Yes!" – "With this sickle?" – "Yes!" – Into this basket?" – "Yes!" – "On the Sabbath?! – "Yes!" – "On THIS Sabbath?" – "YES !" – "Shall I reap? – "Reap!" – Again, the reaper asks: "Shall I reap?" – The crowd assures him again: "Reap!" – And, a third time he asks: "Shall I reap?" – The crowd assures him again: "Reap!" – And, a third time he asks: "Shall I reap?"

"Yes! – Yes! – Yes!"

This little drama delivers a sarcastic response to the opposition sect. Further, this dialogue is somewhat similar to that exchange spoken between the priest and the assembled crowd at the burning of the Red Heifer. – "Is this cedarwood?", etc., etc.

The *omer* therefore is gathered as 15 *Nisan* begins immediately after sundown, to permit night transport into the "wee" hours of morning – perhaps as far as thirty miles. This timing reduces the possibility that the leaves and stalks might wilt. It would be profane to wave a sheaf of wilted grain for this thankful gesture to the Lord. Through this principle then, "somehow" the Rabbis have reasoned that whatever is done after daybreak counts as having been done during all of that 24 hour day. We might say here that Jesus "beat the lawyers at their own game!" by remaining in The Tomb three Jewish days and three Jewish nights as permitted under the *Megillah* 20 statutes.

For many people, all this may seem to be just so much "hair-splitting" or "nit-picking" or "gnat-straining." Although these things are difficult for us Gentiles to fathom, it is nevertheless a part of the Law that Jesus completed. Jesus is Glorified more by every "jot-OR-tittle" of the Law in which we can show how He has completed it.

Continuing, once again we must observe that in the left-hand column of Illus. 46: Western & Jewish: 3 Days, 3 Nights, Page 506, if Jesus had been placed in The Tomb Thursday evening just before sundown as 14 *Nisan* was closing, then He would need to have risen from The Tomb just before sundown (Sunday evening) as 17 *Nisan* was closing in order to have completed three "Western" days and nights or seventy-two hours in The Tomb.

We are familiar with the fact that the Jewish calendar begins each "date" at sundown because God ordained: "*...the evening and the morning were the first day*" — from Genesis 1:5. Earlier, *Megillah* 20a says "our Rabbis teach" that dawn begins 1 and 1/5 hours (or 1 hr. 12 min.) *before* sunrise, "*as the first streaks of light are seen.*" This would be at the time when the very first "hint" of daylight or the first streaks of gray light are seen on the eastern horizon – when the first "glimmer" of dawn appears.

Now, *this next is of utmost importance.* — This means that Jesus, having risen maybe less than an hour before sunrise ("*when it was yet dark*" — John 20:1), still would have "qualified" under the Law as having been in The Tomb for the *complete* "Jewish" day and night on that first day of the week, as specified in *Megillah* 20a. Again, this is because "dawn" was ruled under this statute from *Megillah* 20a as arriving 1 hour and 12 minutes *before* sunrise. Jesus arose legally therefore "after dawn" and still met the Law even though "it was yet dark."

Taking this further, to the day of The Crucifixion; since He was laid in The Tomb *before* sundown (which is *after* dawn), *Megillah* 20a says Jesus was right then "legally" in The Tomb for one complete Jewish night and day on 14 *Nisan*. It was "counted as done" even though He had only just died and was actually in The Tomb perhaps not even an hour (maybe only eighteen minutes!) before sundown at the very close of that Jewish day.

Earlier we remarked on the importance of John 20:1 saying: "*when it was yet dark.*" We have verification here that Jesus then arose with "credit" for a full day and night. Despite His rising "when it was yet dark," as the first gray streaks of dawn began to appear, Jesus "legally" arose after the "official" dawning of daylight. Shown in Illus. 46: Western & Jewish: 3 Days, 3 Nights, Page 506, and Illus. 14: Scenario of the End of Days, Page 119, and in spite of His having been in The Tomb only about thirty-six hours, when all of the "Jewish" days and nights are accounted, **Jesus was in The Tomb for a total of three days and three nights, thereby fulfilling Matthew 12:40.**

And, remember also that **Jesus was raised from the grave ON the third day,** and thus fulfilled many verses of Scripture that had prophesied this detail of The Resurrection. Later we shall explain that being in the grave three days and three nights AND being raised from the grave ON (during) the third day is mathematically impossible. Nevertheless, we have shown that through the maze of Rabbinical *Talmudic* maneuvering, it IS possible – even though it is in fact mathematically impossible!

In our summary we shall explain why it was significant that the scenario we have demonstrated under Jewish Law is the only plan in which Jesus also fulfilled His own prophecy by being resurrected "*on* (during) *the third day.*" (See Matthew 16:21 and others)

Some will accuse persons attempting analysis in the depth we have pursued as "unimportant Jewish trivia" or "straining-at-the-gnat" (Matthew 23:24) or "contentious nit—picking." However, God does not always make things "simple" for man. He gave man a brain partly for purpose that man should think! These details are important, if for no other reason, than to demonstrate how precisely Jesus indeed fulfilled the Law of His Father. Imperfect men certainly could never meet the requirements of God's Perfect Law. Jesus therefore "met" the Law for us. Should we not then wish to see how He did it? –Should we not marvel at how He did it? – Heaven forbid that we would just ignore these things or shrug them off as "obsolete Jewish religious rituals!" We must strive and clamor and "dig" to see these things. How else are we to see FULL Truth of the Gospel? – NONE of us could be saved from God's Eternal and Infinite Judgment without Jesus having completed the Law, which certainly we could NOT complete.

Jesus (God) did not Plan all these things just by letting events, days, hours fall wherever they might alight on His Calendar. Neither did God nor The Son of Man leave it to the Chief Priest or Pilate or a Roman centurion to decide when, how and where and in what manner these things would happen. They were decreed an "eternity" before these dates by The Great "I AM" in consultation and consensus with His Son, Jesus, and the Holy Spirit. We may tempt His ire and judgment if we choose to ignore His Plan or if we lack sufficient ambition to study it.

These two examples show how some scholars try to bend and twist Scripture to conform with our traditional modern Western Gentile concepts of everyday human life. By this "squirming" and "wriggling" and "squeezing" and "cramming," they are trying to "force" agreement with Scripture. One of the first rules any competent mechanic learns is: "Don't force the parts!" — If the parts do not fit, it is usually because they are the wrong parts, or the right parts in the wrong place, or parts installed in an incorrect position, or installed in the wrong order, or parts that have been fabricated incorrectly or parts that have been damaged. Very rarely is it ever necessary for a "successful" mechanic to "saw" or "file" or "grind" or "twist" or "bend" a legitimate part in order to make it fit. Here we have seen examples of each of these errors.

Following are five Scriptural passages from the Gospel that we must examine thoroughly:

- **Matthew 12:40** – *"For as Jonah was three days and three nights in the whale's belly; so shall the Son of man be three days and three nights in the heart of the earth."*

- **Matthew 20:19** – *"And shall deliver Him to the Gentiles to mock, and to scourge, and to crucify Him; and the third day He shall rise again."*

- **Mark 8:31** – *"And He began to teach them, that the Son of man must suffer many things, and be rejected of the elders, and of the chief priests, and scribes, and be killed, and after three days rise again."*

- **Luke 23:53 – 54 (excerpted)** – *"And he took it (Jesus' Body), and wrapped it in linen, and laid it in a sepulchre, And that day was the preparation, and the Sabbath drew on."*

- **Mark 16:9** – *"Now when Jesus was risen early the first day of the week, He appeared first to Mary Magdalene, out of whom He had cast seven devils."*

We began our discussion by pointing out that this argument is kindled by the words: *"three days and three nights in the heart of the earth"* from Matthew 12:40. Seemingly, a Biblical conflict or so-called "discrepancy" emerges because there are no less than ten verses in the King James Version telling of Jesus being raised "the third day" or "ON" the third day. These verses are: Matthew 16:21, 17:23, 20:19 – Mark 9:31 and 10:34 – Luke 9:22, 18:33, 24:7, 24:46 and I Corinthians 15:4.

Hardly any reasonable person would dispute that "raised the third day" or "raised on the third day" means simply and clearly that He was raised "during" the third day. We must also take notice here that Mark 8:31 in the King James Version quoted here, says Jesus shall rise again "*after*" three days." The Lamsa translation from the *Syriac* or *Peshitta* Scriptures is taken from much older manuscripts than those used for the KJV and is considered by many scholars[1] to be the most authoritative Scripture available. Lamsa shows ALL of these verses saying Jesus arose "ON" the third day. So, we have what would at first appear to be a Biblical "inconsistency" caused by a semantic nuance overlooked by the KJV translators.

Highly regarded Hebrew Christian scholar, Alfred Edersheim[21], clarifies the interpretation of "the third day" to eliminate the "inconsistency." Edersheim explains that, in the Jewish manner of reckoning, this language means: *on the third day after His death* – as Friday, Saturday, Sunday. Again, "ON" – "DURING" – not "AFTER" the third day.

BUT – in ALL of the twelve translations consulted – Matthew 12:40 says Jesus was in The Tomb "*three* days and three nights." – Whereas, He could not have been in The Tomb three complete days and nights (72 hours) if He departed The Tomb during the third day. – How can this be?! – As the saying goes:

"You can't have it both ways!"

Very simply, there can be no interval of "three days and three nights;" (i.e., 72 hours in the western context) if the interval ends DURING the third day. *That is mathematically impossible!*, because this means the interval ends during the third day. — For example, since Mark 16:9 affirms Jesus "*was risen early the first day of the week*" (Sunday morning), He would then need to have been placed in The Tomb *early Thursday morning* in order to have achieved fully three days and three nights. (See Illus. 46: Western & Jewish: 3 Days, 3 Nights, Page 506) Counting then from Thursday until Sunday would have made Sunday the *fourth* day. – Jesus did NOT rise "ON" the fourth day! – He arose "ON" the third day!

One other obvious choice is to count from the time Jesus was placed in The Tomb. If He were placed in The Tomb during Thursday at dusk, then He would have to be raised Sunday evening at dusk in order to accrue three full days and nights. Again, that would say He was raised ON the fourth day instead of the third — and, Jesus was raised early the morning of the first day of the week (Sunday) – *not at dusk!*

It is important to take notice of the fact that Jesus fulfilled this entire "three days and three nights" by accumulating the *absolute minimum* amount of time required to accomplish that interval under the Law. It is almost as if He were "rubbing-it-in" for the *Talmudic* "lawyers"! – (Who says God doesn't have a sense of humor?!)

He was placed in The Tomb just a short time before the end of "official" daylight (approx. 6 p.m.), thereby receiving "credit" for one entire "day and night" of 14 *Nisan*. Similarly, Jesus was risen from The Tomb perhaps only minutes after the "official" daylight (approx. 6 a.m.) for the First Day of the Week, 16 *Nisan*. In that way, in accordance with *Megillah* 20a, He received credit, again, for that entire "day and night" – 16 *Nisan*.

All of His actual hours in The Tomb for 14 *Nisan* and 16 *Nisan* added to a complete 24 hour day and night (Saturday) on 15 *Nisan* comprised a total of only about 36 hours, and yet – as we have shown under the Law – this amounted to three *complete* "days and nights"! He could not have achieved three days and three nights by having spent any less time in The Tomb. And yet, He accomplished three complete Jewish days and three complete Jewish nights by applying the Rabbinical Law **PERFECTLY** in this matter – in the minimum amount of time. – That feat, in itself, is certainly Glorifying of God in a way we have never seen before!

Some other defenders of the "Western" scenarios then fall into a very similar trap, as they come in with slightly different timing, offering: "Well then, Jesus probably was buried just after sundown and then was raised after sundown three days later; i.e., "*early the first day of the week.*" We know this futile move will not complete their puzzle because Scripture is clear that Jesus was laid in The Tomb *just before sundown*, as the day was ending. The Gospel of Luke is very thorough in reporting that Jesus was laid in The Tomb *before* the women "rested the Sabbath day." (Luke 23:56) Then under this scenario, in order to accrue a complete (72 hr.) three days and three nights, Jesus would have been raised just before sundown Monday evening instead of "early the first day of the week." Thus, a concept using Western days and nights in this story simply will not stand with the Truth of Scripture.

Summary & Conclusions

So, if we believe God's Word is True, we must accept that Jesus was in The Tomb "*three days and three nights*" (Matthew 12:40), and that Jesus was raised (during) "*the third day*" (Matthew 20:19), and He was risen exactly as it had been prophesied that Jesus "*after three days shall rise again*" (Mark 8:31), and that Jesus "*was risen early the first day of the week.*" (Mark 16:9) We have demonstrated that the *only* way Scripture cannot be seen to conflict over these four statements is by applying the Law to this timing instead of trying to "fit" Scripture to our modern Western Gentile cultural concepts.

An important and profound comment is found from Reference 19 in the commentaries for Matthew 12:40. The commentary from Barnes' New Testament Notes is especially significant in the arguments we have explored. Barnes explains that Jesus was in the grave actually during two nights (Friday and Saturday) and during a part of three days (Friday, Saturday and Sunday). It is observed that the computation is strictly in accordance with the Jewish mode of counting "three days and three nights."

And, THE FOLLOWING IS MOST IMPORTANT:

Barnes continues that:

If the "three days and three nights" had not been counted properly, the Jewish scribes surely would have caught such an obvious fault, and these critics "rightly" therefore could have accused the Savior as being a false prophet. This because it was well known to them that Jesus had spoken this prophecy. (Matthew 27:63) Such accusation, however, never was made. It is plain, therefore, that what was meant by Jesus' prophecy was in fact accomplished. In computing time, it was a well-known maxim among the Jewish people (from Megillah 20a), that ANY part of a day was to be counted as a complete 24 hour day.

Some may accuse us of quibbling or "nit-picking" or "gnat-straining" as we insist the words "ON the third day" mean that day was not yet completed when Jesus was raised. Nevertheless, we have shown that ALL of the literal Word in Scripture can and does have full agreement that Jesus was in The Tomb three days and three nights. We have shown also that it is Glorifying of God, not just that He accomplished this; but in HOW it was done through His PERFECT compliance with His Law. As I have said: *"He beat the Rabbis at their own game!"*

It is important for Believers to resolve this conflict, if for no other reason than to be in a position to counter the claim of a "Biblical discrepancy" from critics. It is of further importance, as we declared early in this work, because Believers need to understand HOW Jesus fulfilled the Law – not just being content in the knowledge that He did it. Further significance is seen in this detail in that it is edifying to Jewish people who have been "blinded" from seeing their Redeemer during all these many centuries. Sadly, the Jewish people – no matter how sincere they may be in loving God and in observing Judaism's Feasts, the Law, etc. – have NO inkling as to what the Law represents. Equally sad, the same can be said of most Christians as well.

The Law Represents Jesus as Messiah in Every Way!

What better motivation could Believers have for learning about the Law?! – Believers therefore are urgently instructed in Romans 1:16 to exercise a priority on "edifying" Jewish people about the Gospel –

"For I am not ashamed of the Gospel of Christ: for it is the Power of God unto Salvation to every one that believeth; **to the Jew first,** *and also to the Greek."*

And, let us remember, there was a host of critics in Judea trying desperately to "catch" Jesus in misinterpreting or distorting the Law. And, these critics were the scribes and the Pharisees who were very knowledgeable concerning Jewish computation of "days and nights." It was well known to Jesus' critics that He had said (Matthew 27:63) that He would arise from the grave "after three days." If His timing had not matched the Jewish computation mode, Jesus thereupon would have been identified as a false prophet. That charge was never made because those "critics" were fully aware that any part of a day was to be counted as a whole day.

We are charged to take notice of the fact that Jesus completed application of this Law by having spent only the exact amount of time necessary for fulfillment. He was not in that Tomb one minute longer than what was required to accomplish *"three days and three nights"*

– finally being raised *"on the third day."* Jesus was meticulous and overwhelmingly thorough in fulfilling this part of the Law.

This argument finally can be put to rest, as always, by Scripture. That Scripture is from Mark 16:9, which says, Jesus was risen *"early the first day of the week."* That is not just before sundown, which would have been mandatory if the interval were measured *exactly* three days after Jesus was laid in The Tomb. It is my opinion that most, if not all, persons who would insist on the "72 hour entombment" are unaware of this verse, because Jesus obviously was placed in The Tomb late in the day – not early!

A well-known and proven adage says that if Scripture seems to contradict itself, it can only be because men are misinterpreting one or both of the verses that are alleged to be in conflict. The most effective solution therefore is to let Scripture interpret Scripture. We know from Scripture, Jesus was laid in The Tomb just before sundown (not morning) and He *was* raised DURING *"the third day."* (Matthew 20:19) And, in compliance with the Law of *Megillah* 20a, this had to be after He had accrued *"three days and three nights"* in The Tomb. (Matthew 12:40. When we understand the Law in this matter, there simply is no conflict within Scripture.

So, the *only* way this conflict can be resolved is by coming to realize these are not Western days. – They are, instead, "Jewish" days – the kind of days that are counted in *Megillah* 20a. Everything fits Perfectly and, *most importantly*, there is no conflict within Scripture when we use these Jewish "days." All of the dates are consistent, all of the Feasts are fulfilled on the proper dates and there are no violations of Sabbatical Law, etc. (It is neither proper nor necessary that we should need to "saw" or "grind" or "twist" or "bend" to make everything fit!)

The right side portions of Illus. 45: Western & Jewish: 3 Days, 3 Nights in Tomb, Page 505, and Illus. 46: Western & Jewish: 3 Days, 3 Nights, Page 506, demonstrate that Jesus was in The Tomb three "Jewish" days and three "Jewish" nights and was raised ON the third day. Once again Scripture has demonstrated that Scripture is Perfectly capable of interpreting Scripture. It means what it says and it says what it means.

So, nobody needs to show that Jesus was in The Tomb "three days and three nights" by showing Him crucified – "maybe" on Wednesday – or, "maybe" Thursday. We have shown, in fact, that *neither* of these two ideas even result in "three days and three nights" in the grave! Nobody should be trying to make Scripture "fit" our Western Gentile cultural concepts and philosophies. – Remember??? – Jesus IS Jewish!

We have shown that Western concepts of "days" and "nights" fit neither the Law nor the Gospel Scripture; whereas, the Jewish concept fits Perfectly. Jesus IS Jewish. Jesus lived Perfectly through a completely Jewish life, a Jewish death and a Jewish burial. We must accept this and study His life from its Jewish perspective whenever we study the Gospel and the Old Testament. Otherwise, we will encounter confusion and doubt – which are not a part of God's Word.

Really "3 Days and 3 Nights?" **503**

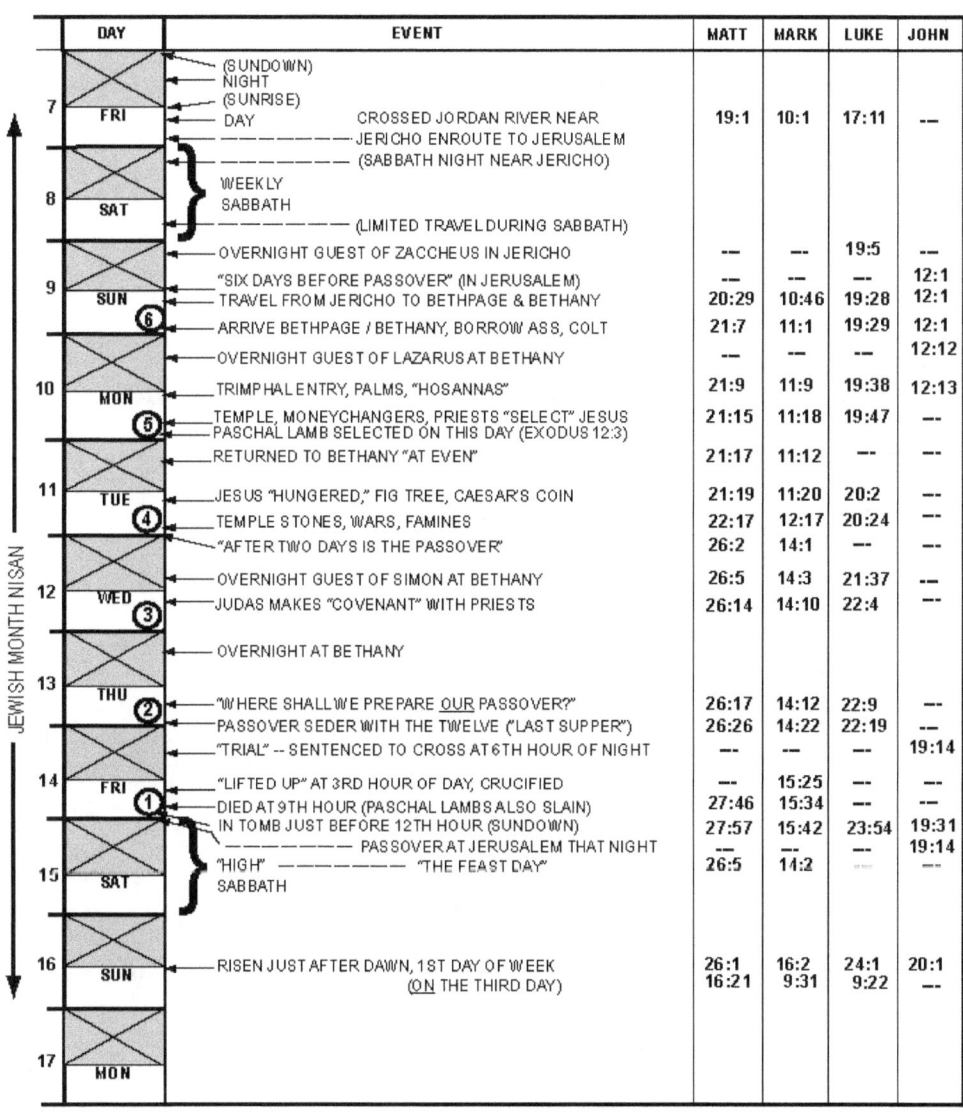

Illus. 43: Chronology of Passion Week

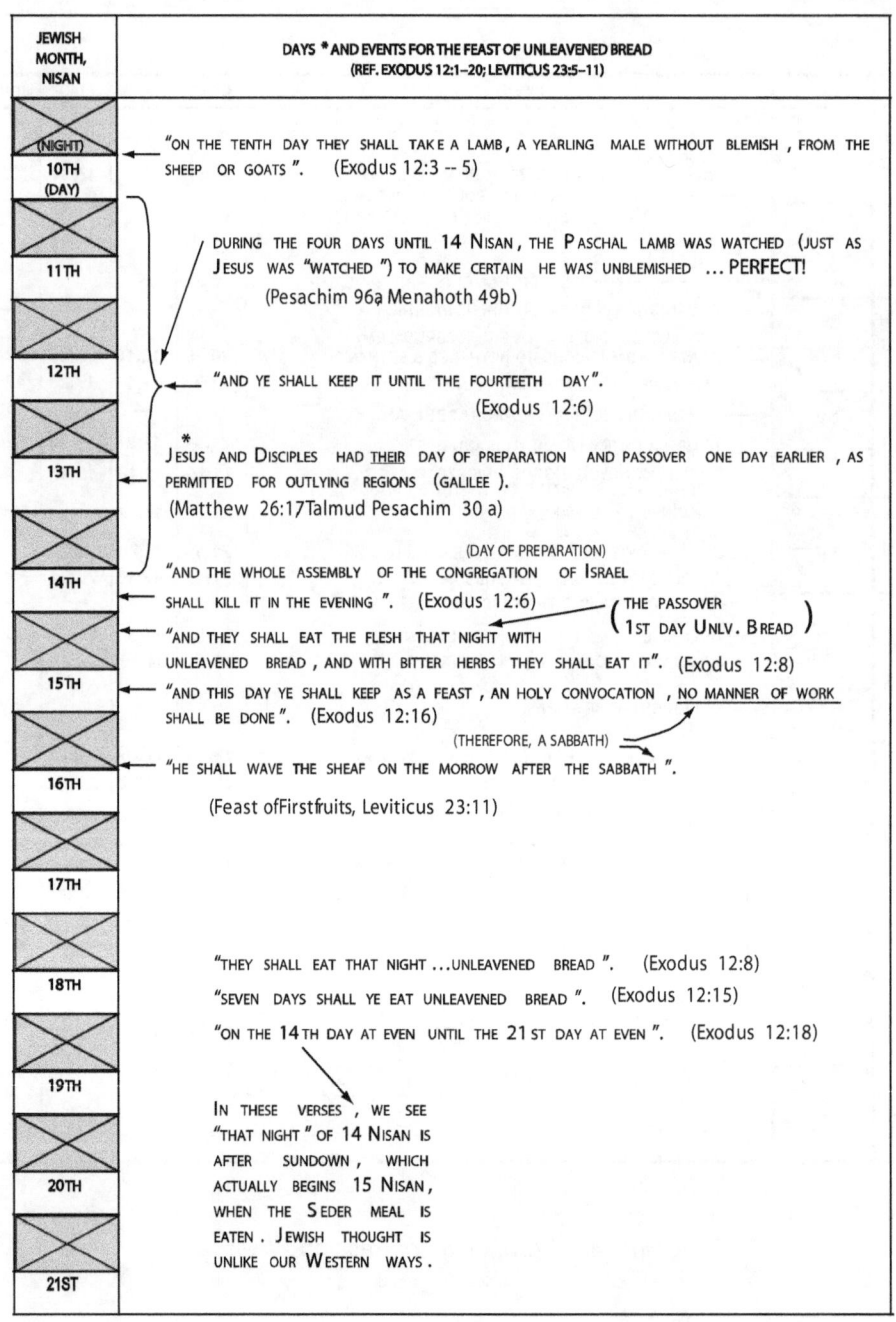

Illus. 44: Days, Events for Feast of Unleavened Bread

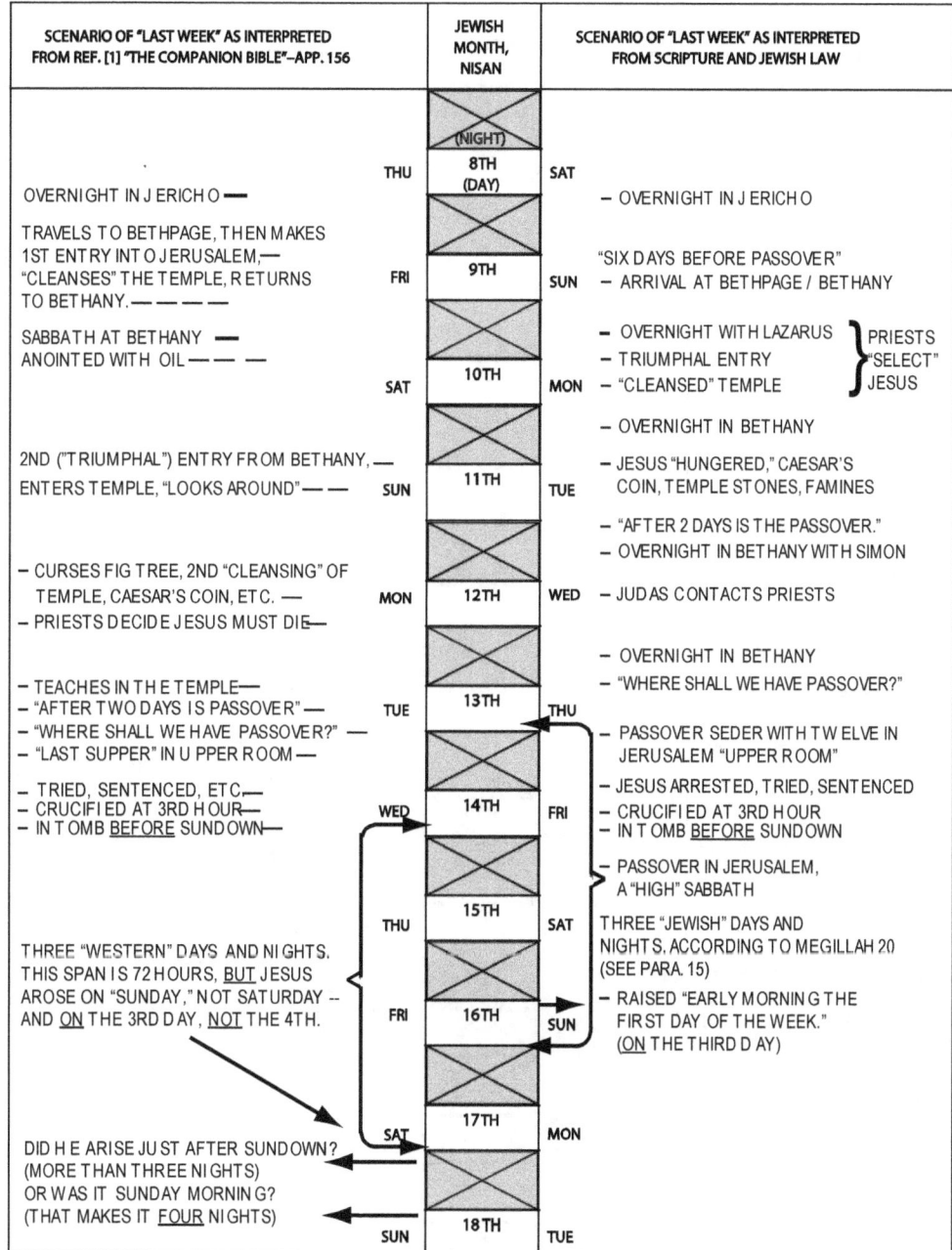

Illus. 45: Western & Jewish: 3 Days, 3 Nights in Tomb

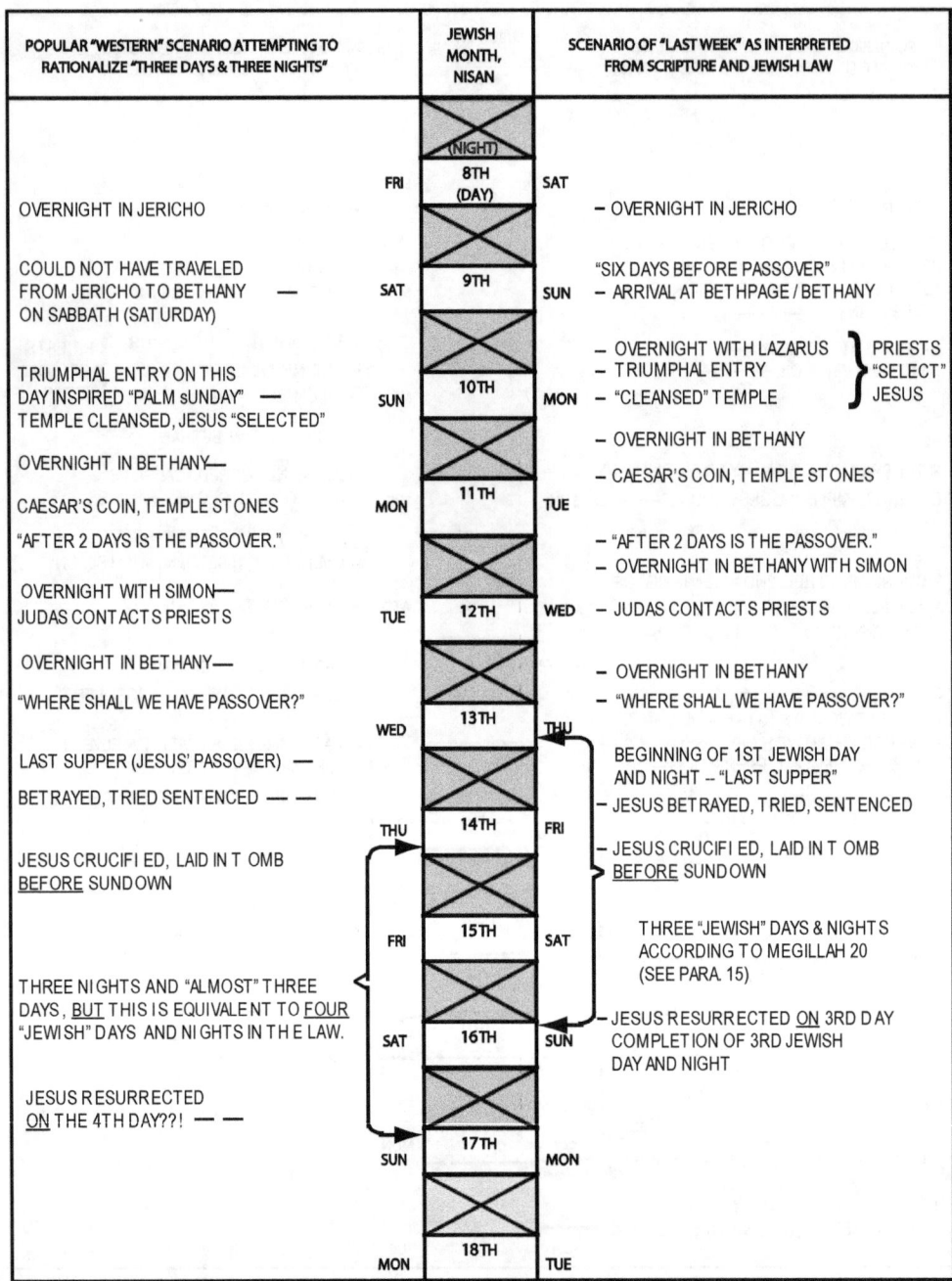

Illus. 46: Western & Jewish: 3 Days, 3 Nights

References and Bibliography for: Really "3 days and 3 nights?"

(References are noted as superscripts in the text)

1. The Companion Bible – Kregel Publications — Grand Rapids MI — 1990

2. A Feast of History – Chaim Raphael – Simon & Schuster – New York NY – 1972

3. Passover, pp. 46 – Mordell Klein – Leon Amiel, Publisher – New York NY – 1973

4. The Pentateuch and *HafTorah*s, Second Edition Ed. J.H. Hertz The Soncino Press — London —- 1965

5. The Babylonian Talmud, Quincentenary Edition — The Soncino Press London – 1978

6. Code of Jewish Law – (Kitzur Schulchan Aruch) — "A Compilation of Jewish Laws and Customs" – Vol. II, Chap. LXXX, Item 58, pp. 98 – R. Solomon Ganzfried – Hebrew Publishing Company – New York NY – 1927

7. Code of Jewish Law – (Kitzur Schulchan Aruch) – A Compilation of Jewish Laws and Customs" – Vol. II, Chap. XCV, Item 1, pp. 141 – R. Solomon Ganzfried – Hebrew Publishing Company – New York NY – 1927

8. Code of Jewish Law -— (Kitzur Schulchan Aruch) – A Compilation of Jewish Laws and Customs" -— Vol. III, Chap. CXIII, Item 5, pp. 33 – R. Solomon Ganzfried – Hebrew Publishing Company – New York NY – 1927

9. The Fire and The Cloud, Updated & Revised Edition — Robert F. Reiland – Xlibris Corporation – Philadelphia PA –2001

10. Dispensational Truth — Clarence Larkin – Rev. Clarence Larkin Estate – Glenside PA — 1918

11. Verdict On The Shroud — Kenneth E. Stevenson and Gary R. Habermas – Servant Books – Ann Arbor MI – 1981

12. *Torah* (New Jewish Version) Revised Printing – Jewish Publication Society – New York NY – 1967

13. The Jewish Book Of Why, pp. 185 – Alfred E. *Kolatch* – Jonathan David Publishers, Inc. Middle Village NY -— 1981

14. The Jewish Book Of Why, pp. 248 – Alfred E. *Kolatch* – Jonathan David Publishers, Inc. Middle Village NY -— 1981

15. Jewish Literacy, pp. 582 — R. Joseph Telushkin – William Morrow and Company, Inc. New York NY – 1991

16. Kitzur Schulchan Aruch, Vol. III, Ch. CXIII, Items 6, 7, pp. 33 – R. Solomon Ganzfried, Translated: H. M. Goldin – Hebrew Pub. Co. – New York –1927

17. The Interactive *Haggadah* CD-ROM – Jerusalem Multimedia Productions, Lt'd. – Jerusalem, Israel – 2003

18. Alleged Discrepancies of the Bible; pp. 413 – John W. Haley – Whitaker House – Springdale PA – 1980

19. On-Line Bible – www.onlinebible.net – 2003

20. The Jewish Book Of Why, pp. 186 – Alfred E. *Kolatch* – Jonathan David Publishers, Inc. Middle Village NY –— 1981

21. The Life and Times of Jesus the Messiah, pp. 907 – Alfred Edersheim – Hendrickson Publishers, Inc., Peabody MA – 1994

22. The Jewish Book Of Why, pp. 10– Alfred E. *Kolatch* – Jonathan David Publishers, Inc. Middle Village NY –— 1981

21

God's Favorite Aroma

Remarkable discovery of the Holy incense that was burned on the Altar of Incense in the Temple – Relatively unknown to the general public – Christian indifference noted – A serendipitous find associated with searching for the Red Heifer ashes.

Jewish Rabbinical authorities in Israel have affirmed that some material recovered by a Dead Sea archaeological team is incense of the kind that was used in the Altar of Incense in the Second Temple. By means of chemical analysis, all ingredients of this "red stuff" have been identified at this writing. The excavation has been proceeding for several years at a spot called "*The Cave of the Column,*" where this team has been searching for the Ashes of the Red Heifer. The locale is nearby the cave where the famous Isaiah Scroll was discovered in 1947.

Talmud - Kerithoth 6a and Encyclopedia Judaica list fifteen substances comprising the incense for the Altar that stood in the western end of the Holy Place in front of the Veil. (See Illus. 22: The Sanctuary of the 2nd Temple, Page 155) The reddish brown, powdery substance is made from all of the proper constituents, as confirmed by scientists at *Bar Ilan University* in Israel by means of the chemical analysis mentioned. Among those ingredients are several aromatic perfume resins as well as at least three different varieties of cinnamon. Some of these same perfumes were also used to make the Holy Anointing Oil that was used for anointing High Priests and Kings. The prominence of cinnamon in this mixture accounts for the reddish brown coloration mentioned.

Exodus 30:34 lists only four specific ingredients for the incense; although, twice repeating "sweet spices." *Talmud* says the incense must be made with *"things whose smoke arises and fragrance spreads."* It also contains *Ma' Aleh' Ashan*, meaning: *"That which makes the smoke ascend."* This material contains *kippat ha-yarden*, which is believed to be from the Cyclamen bulb plant. But! – the most *exciting*(!) ingredient yet described is from the plant, *Leptadenia pyrotechnica*, which contains among its several constituents, nitric acid.

Nitric acid is used in some liquid rocket propellants as an oxidizer. Burning then releases nitrogen oxides, which produce red smoke! This then was added to the incense in order to cause it to emit red smoke as it burned. *Encyclopedia Judaica* tells us that the red smoke alluded to the power of blood to overcome death.

We must take note that cinnamon would cause a pleasant aroma to arise from the blaze. The Rabbis in *Talmud - Yoma* 19b tell a glorious story that illustrates just how robust and appealing must have been the aroma from burning of the incense at the Temple. They write that the goats in Jericho, 13 miles to the east of Jerusalem, would sneeze at the odor of the incense. Its smoke was carried eastward from Jerusalem by the prevailing westerly breezes rolling off the Mediterranean Sea. The women of Jericho did not have to use perfume because they were clothed in this sweet fragrance of cinnamon and frankincense sweeping into their city from the Temple, miles away in Jerusalem. The brides in Jerusalem in those days of course had no need for the usual perfumes, etc. to prepare themselves for their husbands. Just imagine, if you enjoy the sweet savor of freshly baked cinnamon rolls or raisin bread, cinnamon toast, etc., how delicious this mixture of cinnamon, perfume and spices must have smelled. (The Lord surely must love cinnamon as much as we do!)

Part VII – Miracles, "Acts" and "The End"

22

A Miracle Overlooked

Vendyl Jones unearths a cask of Holy Anointing Oil –Another discovery made during the quest for the Red Heifer ashes — The miracle associated with this oil is virtually unreported in Jewish or Christian scholarship – A clue that the priests foretold doom.

The secular news media has shared in the excitement of a few recent discoveries near the Dead Sea. Israeli Rabbinical authorities have confirmed that a joint American/Israeli archaeological team has recovered a cask that contains perfumed anointing oil, the *Shemen Afarshimon*. The discovery was reported a few years ago in at least one major U.S. news magazine. The oil is still in perfect condition, even after having been hidden away in the climate extremes of the Dead Sea region for nineteen centuries. This preparation was closely guarded in Temple times and was used for anointing the High Priests and the kings of Judah. (Kings of the northern rebellious nation, Israel, were not qualified for anointing with this oil.)

We wish to share with our readers the story of a Divine miracle that was associated with the Holy Anointing Oil. The Rabbis describe this marvelous event in *Talmud - Kerithoth* 5b and *Horayoth* 11b. We must point out that this miracle occurred *only* with the anointing oil that was prepared by Moses during the 40 years trek through the *Sinai* wilderness. That cask of oil was placed in the Ark of the Covenant when it was hidden away just before Solomon's Temple was destroyed in 586 B.C.E.

Modern scholars have determined that the Temple priests wisely anticipated that disaster was approaching before Titus actually launched his siege in 70 C.E. Most or nearly all of the important Temple articles therefore were hidden away in caves in the *Qumran* area. Hopefully they would be recovered when Messiah arrived to rebuild the Temple. (It is likely that Titus' Legions "captured" only replicas of the true and precious articles of the Holy Temple before it was destroyed.) It is certain that we cannot *prove* that the cask recently discovered actually contains that oil which was used in the Second Temple. Even so, qualified scientists have verified that the oil in the vessel now discovered certainly was made from the same Biblically specified ingredients for the *Shemen Afarshimon*.

Originally, Moses prepared a volume of oil equal to twelve *logs*; wherein a "log" is a liquid volume equal to 549 cubic centimeters or "about the space of six eggs." Then, the total volume of oil made by Moses in the wilderness was 12 x .549 = 6.588 liters or about 1.75 gallons. The Rabbis ask us now to consider how much oil the pot would have absorbed, and how much the roots of the several spices would have absorbed, and how much oil would have been burned in the fire during the boiling of the roots.

Keeping these factors in mind, now here is the miracle. Despite all the conditions listed above, that same volume of 12 "logs" of oil sufficed for anointing *all* of the Tabernacle components (priests, curtains, altars, veils, etc.) as well as *all* of the other furnishings and accessories. Even so, the level of oil remained at 12 logs even after the anointing of Aaron and all of his sons throughout the seven days of their consecration as priests. *Incredibly, the level of oil was not reduced even after almost 1000 years of anointing High Priests and kings.* (1500 B.C.E. to 586 B.C.E.) *Talmud* reports that "Our Rabbis" said: *"This oil remains for the time to come."* – In other words, it was to last forever!

They refer here to Exodus 30:31 –

"This shall be a holy anointing oil unto Me throughout your generations."

There appears to be a very subtly implied message in this line of Scripture, as stated in the Hebrew script for the word "*This.*" Since, in the Hebrew language, numerical values are assigned to each of the letters of the alphabet, we can decipher the full meaning that the Lord had written in this verse. The Hebrew word for "This" in the Scripture quoted above, is *ZeH* and is formed by the Hebrew alphabet letters *zayin* (for Z) and *he* (for H), joined by the "e" vowel and pronounced as in "eight." Now, adding the seven (for *zayin*) plus a five (for *he*) gives the word a numerical value of twelve. *Talmud* explains that the value of "twelve" beginning this sentence in the Holy Scriptures is not mere coincidence. Rather, it means "this quantity was preserved;" i.e., the twelve "logs" of oil were preserved.

Talmud has revealed herein a miracle that, to many, would seem to surpass the Miracle of the Lights, which is celebrated by the Jewish people as *Chanukah* (or *Hanukkah*). The oil for the Lampstand at *Chanukah* lasted for nine days; whereas, Moses' Anointing Oil lasted for about one thousand years! Why have we never heard of this?! – Simply because mostly only a very few Jewish Orthodox scholars study in *Talmud*. Moreover, almost NO Christian scholars study *Talmudic* writings, much less do even those engage in *Talmudic* thought! –

Because of these voids in our scholarship, there are plenty more as yet unreported "gems" where this came from!

23

"The Acts" of The Apostles

First Christians were Jews! – Temple not like synagogue or church – Temple customs – Temple miracles – Israel's Righteous Priest – Messiah, WHEN ?! – Forty years of woes follow The Crucifixion – Shekhinah Departs – Promised Disaster arrives

The Acts of the Apostles describes the earliest days of the Church of Jesus Christ, beginning at The Ascension of Jesus and ending with banishment of Paul to Rome. Believers can have a better understanding and appreciation for study of the Book of *"The Acts of the Apostles"* if we consider some of the events involved with the Jewish Temple worship during the first century C.E. After all, the *first* Christians were Jews! – The term: "Christians" had not yet even been invented. During these days God spoke to His People Israel through these events in the Temple and actually spoke to them, literally, just as He had spoken to them during the forty years of the Exodus from Egypt through the *Sinai*. (Deuteronomy 4:33) The speeches to the Jewish hierarchy by Peter and by Stephen (Acts 2:14 – 41, 7) amplified what God was telling His People about their Messiah in much more subtle ways.

We will review the history, function and practices at the Temple and discuss certain "signs" which God gave to the Jewish people at this time, immediately following The Crucifixion. We shall demonstrate contrast between the reigning High Priests of Jesus' time compared with some earlier and very righteous High Priests. Further, we shall discuss perhaps for the first time for many of you, the final climactic Event that set the stage for the coming Church Age.

The Temple

Gentile Christians sometimes think of the Temple as a type of synagogue, where worshipers would sit in pews, almost as in a church. This belief is doubtlessly fostered by present day names for synagogues, such as: *Temple Israel, Temple Sinai, Temple Beth Shalom*, etc. and by hearing our Jewish friends and congregants stating, "I went to Temple Saturday."

The Temple was the Earthly dwelling place of Almighty God, the Father.

It was – shall we say – His own little Earthly condominium, built by the Jews at Jerusalem to His Own Specifications. (Haggai 1:8 and 2:7) The dimensions of the main building or the *H'ekhal* (Sanctuary) were only 30 ft. wide by 90 ft. long, with God's actual dwelling chamber – the Holy of Holies (*Kodesh ha-Kodashim*)– only 30 ft. square. God's Divine Presence, whom the Jews call *Shekhinah or Shechinah*, dwelled as a pillar of cloud by day and as a pillar of fire by night, just as first described in Exodus. (Exodus 13:21) – And, we must address something that disturbs many Gentiles. – *Shekhinah* appeared **ONLY** to Israel. (And *still* they "wavered!")

The two courts of the Temple were much larger in area. The Women's *Azarah* (Court) had a usable walking area of about 1600 sq. meters, compared with only about 300 sq. meters of floor space in the *H'ekhal*. The approaches to the Temple were of even greater expanse, the largest being from the south and being used by the largest proportion of worshipers.

It is interesting to note (from *Middoth* 2:2) that *all* who entered the Temple courts must turn to their right upon stepping through the entry gate. After entering, they were required also to *always* make right turns (*clockwise*) – *no matter in which direction they wished to travel!* This was done as they circuited the courts and as they eventually exited at a gate that was to be to the right of the gate at which they had entered. This meant that if a course to the left was "mandatory" for any reason, it also was mandatory that the person must rotate to his right in order to reach the point at which the journey could be resumed.

Let us consider in Illus. 21: Detail of the 2nd Temple, Page 154. A line drawn on , for example, a person who wished to proceed from the Chamber of Oils to the Chamber of Wood. And, let us say the center of the Women's *Azarah* was severely crowded so as to prohibit walking north past the stairway or diagonally across the Court. In such a situation, he would need to walk eastward to the Chamber of Nazirites, and from that point travel north to his destination at the Chamber of Wood. -- HOWEVER ! – He must *not* make a left turn at the Chamber of the Nazirites. At that point of his journey he must make a "3/4" turn to his right – 270 degrees, clockwise – then continue northward to his intended destination.

As is typical of *Talmudic* Law, nevertheless, an exception was made for persons to whom "something untoward had happened." In this way, if a person saw an acquaintance turn to the left, he should inquire of his friend: "Why do you go around to the left?" The other would reply, for example, that he mourned the death of a loved one, or his property had been stolen, he had suffered a business setback, etc.

A more "practical" reason for the right turn policy, however, was brought about because of dense crowding in the courts, especially on feast days, etc. "One-Way-Traffic" was of course far more efficient. The one-way traffic/right turn concept was of equal or even greater advantage for the priests as they performed their ministrations and duties: within the *H'ekhal*, in the process of taking sacrifices from the slaughterhouse to the Altar, etc. Their travel, for example, in ascending and descending the Altar ramp was a potential cause for a traffic problem. These statutes are presented in "painful" detail in *Yoma* 15b, 52b and *Sukkah* 48b. Especially intricate are the moves and steps required for the High Priest as he enters the *H'ekhal* and proceeds to approach and pass between the two Veils as he enters the Holy of Holies to make atonement before the Lord.

In the Tabernacle and with Solomon's Temple, God actually lighted the fire for the Altar of Sacrifice, just as He had done for Elijah atop Mt. Carmel. (I Kings 18:23 – 38) Also, we recall how the Lord had shown His pleasure and approval as the "cloud" filled the House when Solomon's Temple was dedicated. (II Chronicles 5:13)

Josephus *(Antiq. 15.11.7 (425)* relates a story about miraculous event during the rebuilding (or "remodeling") of the Temple by King Herod –

"It is also reported, that during the time that the temple was building, it did not rain in the daytime, but that the showers fell in the nights, so that the work was not hindered. And this our fathers have delivered to us; nor is it incredible, if any one have regard to the manifestations of God. And thus was performed the work of the rebuilding of the temple."

There were many other miracles associated with the Temple and which are described in ancient Jewish writings. For example, *Yoma* 21a reports ten miracles that existed in the Temple.

- There was never even one fly in the slaughterhouse area during their sacrifices.
- The column of smoke from the Altar ascended vertically, despite the fact there might have been a forty-knot gale through the valley.
- No rain ever quenched the fire upon the Altar.
- But, perhaps the most spectacular miracle was the way there was always room for all worshipers to lay prostrate on the ground in the Temple court during certain prayers on the Day of Atonement, *Yom Kippur*. **This occurred despite the fact that the court was filled to standing room only!**

Earlier in the book, a report of the miraculous "silent" opening of the East Gate (Nicanor's Gate) was presented. An additional miracle associated with Nicanor's Gate is described in *Yoma* 38a. Nicanor, a wealthy benefactor supporting restoration for the Second Temple, contracted a firm in Alexandria to build the gigantic 60 ft. x 30 ft. doors of wood and brilliant Corinthian bronze. Upon the return voyage to Israel, the ship encountered violent and threatening seas. Intending to provide improved stability (lower center-of-gravity) for their vessel, they cast one of the doors overboard into the sea. But, no relief was gained.

As the crew prepared to slide the remaining door across the gunwale and overboard, Nicanor, clinging to the door, protested: "Cast me in with it!" – The crew complied with his wish without hesitation. As he was lashed to the door, the gale ceased immediately. Nevertheless, Nicanor was profoundly grieved at having lost the first door. However, as the ship approached the dock at the harbor of Acco at the northern coast of Israel, that *first* door popped out from beneath the hull and was thus miraculously retrieved.

When the Second Temple was later "remodeled" by Herod, all gates except that East Gate were covered with gold leaf. Nicanor's (East) Gate was retained with its original brilliantly golden hued Corinthian bronze – mostly because of this miracle.

Priests and "Signs"

During the fourth century B.C.E., the time of Alexander the Great, Israel had two of the most righteous High Priests ever to hold that revered office. The first was Simeon ben Onias I, more popularly known as Simeon the Righteous or Simon the Just, whose tenure lasted forty years and who was so respected that even the Greek conqueror, Alexander the Great, honored him.(*Yoma* 69a) and came to worship and to praise Israel's God. (Josephus 11.8.5 [336])

This priest is said to have been one of the last survivors of "Jerusalem's Great Assembly." This Rabbinical body of leading scholars led Israel's rededication to *Torah* during the 6th to the 3rd centuries B.C.E. Their leadership brought the Jewish people back from their lengthy absence from Temple worship during their captivity in Babylon. Scripture indirectly refers to that period in Nehemiah 8 – 10.

An amount of conflicting references among historians surrounds the name of this man. There is no known specific reference to this man by *this* name in Scripture. Some historians refer to a man who many believe is this "Simeon;" although, he is said to be Jadduah or Jaddus. In fact, "Jadduah" (or Jehoiadah) is one of those men (Nehemiah 10:21) who was active in forming the Great Assembly and in formulating their "covenant." (Nehemiah 9:38)

The conflict of names could possibly be a result of Greek infusion into Jewish culture during the period. It is indeed unfortunate that more of the qualities and merits of this "Simeon" are beyond our reach at this time. He was evidently a very righteous and worshipful priest, well-deserving of the titles: Simeon, the Righteous or Simeon, the Just. It would be a safe "bet" that Simeon was one of those "saints" who were raised up from their graves when "the rocks were rent," etc. at The Cross. (Mathew 27:51-54)

Following Simeon was Yohanan Hyrcanus with the unmatched tenure of eighty years. These two stalwarts were the last High Priests to have been ordained by God Himself. After this time, the office became so corrupted that eventually, by the time of Jesus, High Priests such as Caiaphas and his father-in-law, Annas, actually purchased the position from Roman officials.

Simeon was evidently highly regarded by the Lord as well as by the public, including even mighty figures such as Alexander. During the tenure of Simeon, God demonstrated His approval of Simeon *and* Israel in the way He provided miraculous "signs" in Temple worship. (God knew His People always looked for "signs!") *Talmud* records (*Yoma* 39a) "Our Rabbis taught" that, during Simeon's reign, the following signs were present:

- The lot piece for the Atonement Goat "for the Lord" always came up in the Priest's right hand.
- The Westernmost Candle of the *Menorah* was the candle closest to the Lord's Divine Presence, *Shekhinah*, in the Holy of Holies. That candle always was burning after all other six candles had burned out, even though it was always lighted before the others.
- The "Crimson Strap" from the Scapegoat (*Azazel*) always turned white as snow after the goat reached the wilderness, carrying the sins of Israel. This was a sign indicating that Israel's sins had been forgiven. *Talmud* Rabbis point out from Isaiah 1:18 as to why this miracle was manifest – *"...though your sins be as scarlet, they shall be as white as snow;..."*
- The two logs for the Altar *always* continued to burn for a full day of offerings. The Law (*Yoma* 26b) permitted that *only* two logs could be added to the fire each evening.
- The "breads" from the shewbread, at the size of an olive, *always* were enough to...satisfy the priests' hunger for a full day.

During the years after Simeon and extending until the time of Jesus, these signs would "sometimes" appear, and sometimes not, but when they did appear, this was taken as a "good omen." Nevertheless, the Rabbis are unified in their grief, emphasizing the fact that "*during the forty years before the Temple was destroyed,*" NONE of these encouraging signs EVER appeared again! Strangely, the Rabbis never mention that climactic Event in C.E. 30 that occurred in Jerusalem "*forty years before the Temple was destroyed!*"

The Time(s) of Messiah(s)

We know from Daniel 9:24 – 27 that Messiah was to appear 483 years (seventy "sevens" of years) after Nehemiah received the commandment to return to Jerusalem and rebuild the City. Of course the Jewish people knew: *This was the time!* – Moreover, an earlier (although "un-published") prophet had revealed that Messiah would arrive two "days" (2000 years) after Abraham. The Jews then knew "again" that was surely the time for Messiah – i.e., during what we now call the first century.—Yes! They were marking off the days on their calendars!

But the Jewish scholars were confused in a lot of ways. First, they expected Messiah to arrive as a great conqueror who would liberate them from their oppressors. (Certainly not a lowly Galilean carpenter's apprentice!) *Talmud Sukkah* 52a and *Sanhedrin* 97 demonstrate that further confusion came from that prophet's declaration that there would be two Messiahs – first, a "precursor" Messiah, son of Joseph and then Messiah, son of David – who would actually be the One who would redeem them. They believed the first Messiah was to be a "son of Joseph" as from the tribe of Joseph. It certainly never occurred to anyone that He would descend from a "son of David" (Matthew 1:20) who would be a carpenter named Joseph! – And, from the hamlet, Nazareth – of all places! – (Confusing??!!) – But, isn't *this* neat?! – The prophet said that both Messiahs would be...Guess What?!...***carpenters***!

On this subject, *Talmud* goes on to say that Messiah, son of Joseph was "killed." (The Rabbis never say anything about the personal identity of the One who was "killed'") Then it says: *"Because of our sins, Messiah, son of David will delay for two more 'days.'"* They rationalize this of course from Hosea 5:15 – 6:3. – The Rabbis then lament that all the dates for Messiah have passed and that "*we can now only be redeemed by our repentance and by our good deeds.*" (See *Sanhedrin* 97b) From all these things, it would seem that God has deliberately blinded the Jewish people – even those who truly love Him – for His own unfathomable reasons. – We cannot judge the Jews.

"Forty Years Before The Temple Was Destroyed"

Applying appropriate corrections to the Gregorian calendar, the Crucifixion occurred about C.E. 30. The Temple was destroyed in C.E. 70. The Rabbis of the *Talmud* have much to say about this period, which began a worldwide assault against Judaism and began the "scattering" (the *diaspora*) of the Jewish people among all the nations of the Earth. Nevertheless, they *never* refer to the date of The Crucifixion. Instead, with lamenting, they passionately refer to this period as "forty years before the Temple was destroyed." – Now, it doesn't take a "rocket scientist" to figure out what grievous and traumatic event happened in C.E. 30 to begin this terrible period and ending with Titus' siege of Jerusalem in C.E. 70.

During those forty years, *Talmud* Rabbis grievingly affirm that the "signs" they had seen earlier; i.e., during the tenure of Simeon the Righteous, NEVER appeared.

- The *lot piece* for the he-goat "for the Lord" NEVER came up in the right hand.
- The *Westernmost Candle* NEVER outlasted the other candles.
- The *Crimson Strap* on the Scapegoat's throat NEVER turned white.
- The *two logs* for the Altar NEVER burned for a full day of sacrifices.
- A morsel of *shewbread* NEVER was enough to satisfy the priests.

The very absence of these "signs" had to have been a "sign" in and of itself. More specifically, in *Shabbat* 22b it is stated, the Rabbis had reasoned during the centuries before that the miracle concerning the Westernmost Candle indicated that *Shekhinah* "rested over Israel." Consequently, they observed that when the Westernmost Candle no longer outlasted all the other candles, this was a certain indication that Israel's Beloved *Shekhinah* was preparing to depart the Temple! Apparently they had recognized the warning associated with absence of this sign previously, as in leading up to the occasion of when Solomon's Temple was destroyed in 586 B.C.E.

Of great importance to our study in the Book of Acts is a statement in Acts 6:7, saying, *"...a great company of the priests were obedient to the faith."* And why would the priests not be impressed?! – They were present in the Temple as these things were happening and they were in the best position therefore to witness the total and complete "removal" of these signs, which were looked upon to bring good omens to Israel. Many of them *had* to have understood that these things happened just after that Galilean "impostor," *Y'shua* of Nazareth, had been put to death and after His followers had claimed that He was risen from death.

That great Rabbinical sage, Gamaliel I, said it very well in Acts 5:38 – 39, where he cautioned the Jewish authorities that all this may have been from God and they had best not be too aggressive in persecuting Jesus' Disciples.

"And now I say unto you, Refrain from these men, and let them alone: for if this counsel or this work be of men, it will come to nought:

But if it be of God, ye cannot overthrow it; lest haply ye be found even to fight against God."

Gamaliel, we should note, was the teacher and mentor of Saul of Tarsus, who later ignored his teacher's admonishment, aggressively having persecuted Jews who had strayed to Christianity. (Acts 8:1 – 3 and 9:1 – 2) Nevertheless, Gamaliel's student became a newly converted Apostle in this new Faith, known to us as Paul. Paul of course "haply" learned *not* to "fight against God"! We can only wish that Gamaliel had lived to see his pupil, Paul, making sure this new movement did NOT "come to naught."

The Ascension

The "traditional" site of Jesus' Ascension is at the summit of the Mount of Olives. Some Biblical commentators scoff at recognizing this site on basis of Luke 24:50 having said Jesus led them as far as Bethany, which is believed to have been about one mile to the southeast beyond *Olivet* summit. Nevertheless, in Chapter 4, we explained how the *"erub of cooked foods"* from *Hallah* 1:8 probably was applied in order for the party of Jesus and His Disciples to have traveled "legally" on the Sabbath to *Olivet* summit from Bethany.

Acts 1:9 – 12 also implies strongly that Jesus ascended from *Olivet* summit at a point about 2/3 of a mile (i.e., "a Sabbath Day's journey") from Jerusalem.

"Which also said, Ye men of Galilee, why stand ye gazing up into heaven? This same Jesus, which is taken up from you into heaven, shall so come in like manner as ye have seen him go into heaven."

The words *"shall so come in like manner"* would indicate the spot at *Olivet* summit, because we *know* from Zechariah 14:4 that *"His feet shall stand in that day upon the Mount of Olives."* From these verses then, we can deduce that Jesus is going to *"so come"* to the Mount of Olives, as He returns *"in like manner"* as when He ascended. In the discussion to follow we shall encounter even more substantiation that the "traditional" Ascension site is in fact the True location.

Shekhinah Withdrawal and Ascension into Heaven

At this point we should note a few historical dates and events following The Crucifixion that led up to this most spectacular and significant and Holy Event and which has been so long ignored by both Jewish and Christian scholars.

- James, the (half-) brother of Jesus, was the designated leader of Christians as Bishop of the Church at Jerusalem. James was martyred by the Jewish hierarchy in C.E. 62. He was thrown from the *"Pinnacle of the Temple"* to be dashed upon the rocks in the Kidron Valley 250 ft. below. Still alive, he then was stoned by the mob and finally and mercifully clubbed to death with "a fuller's beam," borrowed for the occasion. James was noted to have been one of the most righteous of "ordinary" men. Many historians have referred to him as James the Just. He was known as "the man with camel's knees." That name was assigned to James because his knees were so callused (as are the knees of a camel) from continually praying on his knees before the Lord.

- Christians began mass exit of Roman Judea upon the death of James. After all, they concluded, if Jewish zealots murdered James the Just, what could be the chances for others who were less-righteous?!

- The Jewish Rebellion that eventually led to bringing Titus' Great Siege, began C.E. 66. At 3 a.m. on the morning of 8 *Nisan*, just a few days before Passover of that year, Israel's *Shekhinah*, the Divine Presence, withdrew from the Temple on a Glorious, although very "public" occasion. That Holy and Spectacular Event is described by the Rabbis (*Midrash Rabbah Eichah* 25 – Proems and *Talmud – Rosh Hashanah* 31a) and by Flavius Josephus. His movements were *exactly* as had been foretold by the prophet's visions, as described in Ezekiel Chapters 10 and 11. However, there were some Glorious details that were reported by the renowned first century historian, Josephus; although, apparently were not revealed to Ezekiel. The beginning of that Holy and Glorious Event was witnessed by a large party of Temple priests on the 8th of *Nisan*, as they were preparing the Holy House for the Passover that was to be celebrated six days later. Flavius Josephus (Wars, 6.5.3/ 288-300) reports: *"So these publicly declared, that this signal foreshewed the desolation that was coming upon them."*

- The Rabbis report that later, on the Day of Pentecost following, *Shekhinah* returned into the Temple for just one last look and then departed **due eastward** to the summit of the Mount of Olives. A line drawn on Illus. 26: Temple Mt., Contoured Mt. of Olives, Page 324, **due eastward** from Prof. Asher Kaufman's recently discovered Temple site, at the *Dome of the Tablets*, passes directly through the "traditional" site of Jesus' Ascension, the *Chapel Of The Ascension*.

- The Rabbis woefully and tragically record that *Shekhinah* "sat" at *Olivet* summit for three and one-half years, pleading with Israel to: "*Return unto Me and I will return unto you.*" (Malachi 3:7)

- After the three and one-half years, around the time of *Hanukkah* C.E. 69, *Shekhinah* ascended into Heaven from *Olivet* summit, saying: "*I will go back to My Place.*" (Hosea 5:15) God did thereby Glorify Jesus and His Resurrection and even "punctuated" the fact that Jesus IS Messiah by having ascended into Heaven from the very same spot where forty years earlier Jesus had ascended from *Olivet* summit. (See Illus. 3: Old City of Jerusalem and Mt. of Olives, Page 19)

- Just a few months later, in the Spring of C.E. 70, Titus and his Roman legions began the horrible siege of Jerusalem, eventually bringing destruction of The City and the Holy Temple.

If it had not been clear to the Jewish people during the preceding forty years that a grave error had been committed with putting to death that gentle Galilean Rabbi, it should have been *abundantly* clear after these Events.

Josephus notes that the spiritually "stupid" looked upon this Event as a good "sign." Since the Lord had even left the Temple Gate open, these ignorant wretches believed He was "*opening them the gate of happiness.*" But those who were spiritually awake understood this was showing the Temple was no more God's Holy Residence and their security in His Presence was also departed. Moreover, they knew that when the "*cloud*" or the "*fire*" moved away, it was time to "*move the camp.*" (Exodus 14:19)

Just a few months later, Titus brought his legions to the outer limits of the Holy City and began the siege that would scatter Israel "to the nations" (Deuteronomy 4:23 – 27) for 2000 years. (Hosea 6:1) Although long ignored, this Event in fact had been recorded almost two thousand years ago by the Rabbis of *Talmud* and *Midrash*, and by esteemed historians Josephus and Eusebius.

Some Conclusions

- During those 40 years, God "tested" the Jewish people who had actually "experienced" their Messiah. Many found their Messiah at that time; although, the Jewish people who have followed them would wait until a much later time to find Him – when He stands upon the Mount of Olives "in that day." (Zechariah 14:4)

- God nurtured the Church through these Events, warning them to "leave the camp." – "Forty years before the Temple was destroyed," God showed ALL of the Jewish people at Jerusalem that they had made a terrible mistake – in C.E. 30.

- But, God showed the World that He forgave the Jews their mistake as He remained in the Temple forty years after the mistake.

- God forgave repentant Jews, "for they knew not what they did," (Luke 23:24) and has preserved their culture and religion through 2000 years of bitter persecution and has resurrected their nation Israel, in preparation for arrival of their long awaited Redeemer – Messiah, Son of David.

We should note that neither the *Shekhinah* Event nor the destruction of Jerusalem and the Temple is reported in the New Testament. Jesus had prophesied that both Jerusalem and the Temple would be destroyed with "...*not one stone upon another.*" (From Luke 19:42 – 44 and 21:6) The Glorious occasion of the *Shekhinah* withdrawal was *forecast* through Ezekiel's "*visions of God.*" (Ezekiel 10 and 11)

Although many respected scholars have argued bitterly over this point, we may conclude from the most simple logic that *all* of the New Testament books, except Revelation, therefore were written *before* these two cataclysmic and traumatic Events occurred. The logic is derived from the fact that it is a *very* safe bet that the New Testament writers certainly would not have hesitated to have "rubbed-it-in" on unbelieving Jews at the time, if they had seen this prophesied destruction. They would not have missed such an opportunity to point out that, Indeed! – their Master had forecast that destruction. Neither would they have shirked from telling the World **WHY!!** *Shekhinah* had selected *that* spot for His Ascension. But most importantly and obviously, Christians at Jerusalem at that time would not have hesitated to point out that these Events were manifesting a Divine Judgmental Punishment against an unbelieving Israel after having rejected their Messiah.

References for Part Seven: See References and Bibliography for Departure of Shekhinah.

24

Jewish Concept of the World to Come

Time for the "Third Temple"—Rabbis inconsistent on "Messianic Age" – Christian Eschatology Connections – Explaining "types" of Persons & Events – Mt. of Olives and the "Jewish Rapture" – Rabbis KNOW what terrors are coming! – Profound questions for Rabbis – Last Days Scenario – <u>THINKING</u> about "Paschal's Wager"

We recognize that significant differences exist between Jewish people and Christians concerning *"The World to Come"* or *"The Last Days"* or *"The Time of the End"* – or what Christian theologians refer to as "eschatology." That period in future history also has come to be known as *"The Day of the Lord."* Nevertheless, it is considered important that we address the Jewish concept(s) because Jewish anticipation of the arrival of Messiah has been prominent throughout most of our study in this book.

Even during the time of Jesus, there were at least two factions within Judaism regarding the subject that *Talmud* usually calls: *"The World to Come."* We understand, for example, from the New Testament that the *Saducean* sect had serious differences with the Pharisees on this subject. The Pharisees seem to have believed in a life after death; although not actually the same as our Christian concept of That Blessed Hope. The Pharisees actually held to a quite "literal" acceptance of the Holy Scriptures. They believed in a "latter day" resurrection in accordance with Daniel which would bring all *righteous* Jewish people to everlasting life if their names were *"inscribed in The Book of Life."*

Controversy within Christian eschatology is centered upon the question concerning the timing of Jesus' Return; i.e., relative to the seven years of The Tribulation that will immediately precede Jesus' arrival, especially. Some who argue against a "Rapture" of Believers point to the words of Revelation 1:7 –

"...every eye shall see Him,..."

They argue that Believers will be on Earth to see the event described in Mark 13:26:

"...they shall see the Son of man coming in the clouds with great power and glory."

These folks are in denial of those calamitous events that will occur during The Tribulation and, especially, the wholesale martyring of Christians by Antichrist. Moreover, these do not understand that "they" in that verse are those persons on Earth who have survived the horrendous years of The Tribulation. It is likely that only a "handful" of Christians (if any) will survive to see His Coming. However, those who do survive The Tribulation will see His arrival, just as Scripture has described.

The "anti-Rapture" argument brings an accusation that the "Rapture Faction" would claim that Jesus is coming twice! – The Truth is, however, that we (Believers) are actually "going up" to meet Jesus when we are caught up *"to meet Him in the air"* before The Tribulation begins. (I Thessalonians. 4:16 – 17) –

"For the Lord himself shall descend from heaven with a shout, with the voice of the archangel, and with the trump of God: and the dead in Christ shall rise first:

Then we which are alive and remain shall be caught up together with them in the clouds, to meet the Lord in the air: and so shall we ever be with the Lord."

Later, at the end of the seven years of Tribulation, we will return to Earth as His saints, to arrive with Jesus (I Thessalonians 3:13; Jude 1:14) in Victory as He claims His Kingdom.

"To the end he may stablish your hearts unblameable in holiness before God, even our Father, at the coming of our Lord Jesus Christ with all his saints."

It is important to note that the Rapture of "the Church" is NOT Christ's Second coming! – Again, – at that time Believers will be GOING "upward" to meet Jesus. NOBODY on Earth will see Him at that time. This is the time at which He will come *"as a thief in the night."* (I Thessalonians 4:15) Although, seven years later, His actual "Second Coming" will consist of Jesus Coming to Jerusalem, a Second time to His People – the Jewish People! And, referring to all who have survived The Tribulation and are on Earth at THAT time – YES! – "every eye shall see Him" as He comes " with great power and glory." – It is vital to the study of eschatology to keep these facts in mind.

Throughout this book, we have frequently referred to "types." One of the best examples of such is the story of Joseph sold into slavery in Egypt as a "type" of Jesus – as well as many other types we have introduced. In Biblical scholarly pursuits this approach has been labeled as "typology." Although some scholars and even laypersons look upon typology with scorn and / or mild contempt, it must be remembered that these "types" were ordained by God – and, not by man's clever imagination. There are plentiful and important lessons in Biblical scholarship to be derived from typology, especially for any who would study eschatology.

The Great Flood of Genesis, in Chapters 6 through 8, is certainly easily recognized as a "type" of The Tribulation that is to come before Christ returns. God judged the Earth with the Flood; just as He will again judge the Earth with the punishments of The Tribulation. At this point in our discussion, we wish to present several "types" of events from The Great Flood and other Biblical historical events with "types" that were repeated later or will be seen during The Tribulation. It will be shown that God is a Great supporter of "precedent," as are lawyers and judges in our secular world.

PRECEDENT EVENT	REPETITIVE EVENT
First Temple destroyed on 9th day of Av.	Second Temple destroyed on 9th day of Av.
Enoch (a Gentile), who "walked with God" was "not found" (taken up).	"Type" of (Righteous) Christians, who will be "not found" (taken up) at the Rapture.
(Righteous) Methuselah died before The Flood.	Righteous who die before The Tribulation.
Noah's family, preserved through The Flood, were a type of the Jewish People.	Remnant of the Jewish People to be preserved through The Tribulation to greet Messiah at Jerusalem.
Righteous Noah and his family repopulated Earth after destruction by The Flood.	Righteous Remnant of Tribulation survivors will repopulate a "scorched" Earth.
Jesus Ascended into Heaven from *Olivet*.	*Shekhinah* ascended to Heaven from *Olivet*.
Jesus AND *Shekhinah* will RETURN together to Jerusalem at *Olivet* Summit.	
Graves were opened, Saints arose at The Cross at the earthquake.	Righteous Jewish dead will be "gathered up" from their graves.
Phillip, a Righteous Jew, was "translated" from Gaza to Azotus.	Righteous Jewish survivors of The Tribulation will be "translated" to Jerusalem from the four corners of Earth. ("Jewish Rapture").
Temple was rebuilt BOTH times after its having been destroyed.	Temple will be rebuilt again for Messiah, Son of David, who will rule the World from Jerusalem for 1000 years.

As we discuss this "Jewish Resurrection," we should address the statement from Romans 11:26 – *"And so all Israel shall be saved:..."* If this meant that each individual Jewish person would be saved, it would indeed be in conflict with other Scripture, such as Daniel 12:2, saying:

"And many of them that sleep in the dust of the earth shall awake, some to everlasting life, and some to shame and everlasting contempt."

This Scripture then leads us to the following Promise announced through the prophet in Ezekiel 20:38 –

"And I will purge out from among you the rebels, and them that transgress against me: I will bring them forth out of the country where they sojourn, and they shall not enter into the land of Israel: and ye shall know that I am the LORD."

It can be seen from these verses that "All" Israel includes only those whose names are written in The Book of Life. There is no conflict within Scripture, therefore, because by this time the Lord already will have judged Israel to determine which of the children are His. Many Jewish people will be saved for His Glorious Kingdom at this juncture. However, many others will be cast out because they had no desire to have their names written in the Book. They have only cold hearts against God. Again – that was their choice. – This is no different than it is in the case of Christians. – We have chosen to be with God. We love Him because He first loved us. – God does not reject those who do not Love Him. – They reject themselves!

And so, instead, all this means God will remove Godlessness and sin from Israel as He establishes His New Covenant with His People. This will occur when Messiah, Son of David, arrives to setup His Earthly Kingdom, to rule the Earth from Jerusalem for one thousand years. This will be His Sabbatical "Day" of Peace and Rest as the seventh to follow man's six "days" of Earthly dominion – encompassing a host of evil and suffering.

The *Sadducees*, unfortunately, comprised much of the Jewish priesthood and the wealthier and therefore most influential families of the day. Scholars and historians, as well as Matthew 22:23 and Mark 12:18, have informed us that the *Sadducean* sect did not believe in a resurrection of the dead. This would at least in part offer explanation as to the location of the burial ossuary containing the remains of that most infamous High Priest, Caiaphas, discovered in 1990. His burial was not in the traditional Jewish Cemetery atop the Mount of Olives, but was instead at a seemingly random location in a valley south of the Temple Mount. (Ref. Biblical Archaeology Review – Zvi Greenhut – Sept./Oct. 1992)

By contrast, in this study, we have repeatedly referred to the fact that "observant" Jewish people during Biblical times were most likely Pharisees, such as Joseph of Arimathea and Nicodemus. They were interred so as to be eagerly awaiting Messiah's arrival at the Mount of Olives *"on that day."* For that reason, ever since Zechariah's prophecy (Zechariah 14:4) about 500 B.C.E. and even continuing today, there has been a reverent desire among modern "observant" Jewish people to be buried at that Jewish Cemetery to await their Redeemer.

However, within present Jewish teaching and even in *Talmudic* discussions, there is no clear definition of any Jewish position on the subject of "the next life." The Rabbis seem to prefer not to discuss any eventuality for the future. However, during *Tshuvah* season, many Jewish people greet each other with the Blessing: *La shana tova tikatevu*, meaning: *"May you be inscribed (in the Book of Life) for a good year."* Nevertheless, we have uncovered a few revealing passages from various Judaica that might offer some understanding of Jewish anticipation of "The World to Come."

It appears that a preponderance of Jewish teaching looks to a later life during The Messianic Age, which Christians know as The Millennial Kingdom Age; i.e., Christ's 1000 year reign on Earth. Jewish teaching observes that it is only this later life that has been revealed by the prophets. (They don't have John's Revelation!) They don't really have much to say about "What comes after Messiah?" Jewish teaching does not emphasize nor even give much discussion to words such as: "Eternity" or "Everlasting," etc.

However, *Berakoth* 17a gives a rather vivid description of "The Future World" that is "not like this world," for it will be a life where there will be:

> *"...no eating nor drinking nor propagation nor business nor jealousy nor hatred nor competition, but the righteous sit with their crowns on their heads feasting on the brightness of the Divine Presence, as it says, And they beheld God, and did eat and drink."*

The Rabbis of course are not unified within these Jewish eschatological positions, to any greater extent than Christian theologians agree in eschatology. The Rabbis do seem, however, to appreciate the anticipation of a life in "the World to come," and which they believe will follow what they term as the Messianic Age. For that later period they say (from *Shabbath* 63a): *"but as for the world to come, the eye hath not seen, O Lord, beside thee what He hath prepared for him that waiteth for Him."*

A footnote at this passage refers to Isaiah 64:3, in which it accurately states that conditions of the future world are described somewhat vaguely in *Talmud*. In general, it states the future world is the opposite of this world. In *Berakoth* I:5, "this world" is opposite in comparison with the days of Messiah.

The *Mishnah* I:5 is found in *Berakoth* 12b and presents a thoughtful discussion involving subtle use of words in such *Talmudic* themes concerning the "future world."

> *"For it says: That thou mayest remember the day when thou camest forth out of the land of Egypt all the days of thy life." [Had the text said,] 'the days of thy life' it would have meant [only] the days; but 'all the days of thy life' includes the nights as well. The sages, however, say: "The days of thy life refers to this world;* **'all the days of thy life' is to add to the days of the Messiah."**

A further quote is offered from a scholar, G. Moore, in one of his works stating that in Judaism, any attempt to coordinate Jewish notions of the hereafter "imposes upon them an order and consistency which does not exist in them."

In this same passage from the earlier referenced *Shabbath* tractate, an interesting phrase appears that does have a "connection" with John's Revelation, saying: *"Because it is written, Gird thy sword upon thy thigh, O mighty one, Thy glory and thy majesty."* This is of course reminiscent of Revelation 19:16 –

> *"And He hath on His vesture and <u>on His thigh</u> a name written, KING OF KINGS, AND LORD OF LORDS."*

Much of the Jewish involvement in the Last Days already has been discussed in this work. We have shown how *Talmudic* teaching divides the "six days" of man's Earthly dominion. This is followed by their recognition that Messiah (the "Anointed" one) would arrive "two days" after Abraham's time. That date was to have been what we call the First Century – Yes! – *The Time of Jesus!* We pointed out that His arrival was prophesied even more precisely by Daniel 9:26 – *even to the exact day!* We discussed the Jewish confusion and doubt concerning Messiah, son of Joseph, "who was slain." The Rabbis never identify that One Who was slain. But then, the Rabbis sadly acknowledge: *"Because of our sins, Messiah, Son of David, has delayed two more days."*

That date, extending "two days" forward from the 1st century, of course brings us to the present time, the 21st century, for anticipation of Messiah's arrival. Rabbis agree that Jewish people should now be watching for their Messiah. Nevertheless, *Talmudic* discussion led to a statement by other Rabbis saying: *"All the predestined dates for Messiah have passed."* These thoughts, although conflicting, draw a conclusion that a person, knowing these things, must ask whether they believe that God has lied or whether Messiah has already come and was "overlooked"?!

Jewish knowledge of the Last Days seems to come to a halt at this point, but their Hope is strong! – They are presently STILL faithfully awaiting Messiah, as evidenced in their worship that we have quoted; and, especially as the Jewish dead rest in their faithful vigil at the Mount of Olives cemetery! Frequently in the Gospels, Jesus addresses the "lawyers" and admonishes them for their often pious, hypocritical interpretations and applications of the Law. It is intended in this book to demonstrate here that Jesus applied the most detailed and precise adherence to obedience of those statutes in His completion of the Law. The most broad and yet the most rigid of these statutes appear as demonstrations showing Jesus' fulfillment of the Law as it applies in the Red Heifer ceremony.

Much of what the Rabbis say about the Coming of Messiah, Son of David will indeed sound very familiar to anyone who has studied eschatology. Moreover, our readers will easily recognize many of the conditions described by these anxiously and eagerly expectant Rabbis as existing in our modern World today.

Hear now some of what the Rabbis of *Talmud* have to say about the times leading up to the coming of Messiah, from *Sanhedrin* 97a –

- Thus hath R. Johanan said: in the generation when the son of David [i.e., Messiah] will come, scholars will be few in number, and as for the rest, their eyes will fail through sorrow and grief. Multitudes of trouble and evil decrees will be promulgated anew, each new evil coming with haste before the other has ended.

- Our Rabbis taught: in the seven year cycle at the end of which the son of David will come-in the first year, this verse (*Amos 4:7*) will be fulfilled: And I will cause it to rain upon one city and cause it not to rain upon another city; in the second, the arrows of hunger will be sent forth; in the third, a great famine, in the course of which men, women, and children, pious men and saints will die, and the *Torah* will be forgotten by its students; in the fourth, partial plenty; in the fifth, great plenty, when men will eat, drink and rejoice, and the *Torah* will return to its disciples; in the sixth, [Heavenly] sounds; in the seventh, wars; and at the conclusion of the *septennate* the son of David will come.

- R. Joseph demurred: But so many *septennates* have passed, yet has he not come! — Abaye retorted: Were there then [Heavenly] sounds in the sixth and wars in the seventh! Moreover, have they [the troubles] been in this order?! (*Footnote –*

Either Heavenly voices announcing the advent of Messiah, or the blasts of the great Shofar; from Isaiah 27:13). Earlier we interpreted that these verses from Isaiah, among others, *"when the Great Trumpet (Shofar) shall sound"* refer to the next fulfillment of a Jewish feast, namely: Feast of Trumpets.

- *[Wherewith thine enemies have reproached, O Lord, wherewith they have reproached the footsteps of thine anointed.] (From Psalms 89:52)* it has been taught, R. Judah said: in the generation when the son of David comes, the house of assembly will be for harlots, Galilee in ruins, Gablan lie desolate, the border inhabitants wander about from city to city, receiving no hospitality, the wisdom of scribes in disfavour, God-fearing men despised, people be dog-faced (*Footnote: without shame*), and truth entirely lacking, as it is written, Yea, truth faileth, and he that departeth from evil maketh himself a prey. (*From Isaiah 59:15*) What is meant by 'yea, truth faileth'? — The Scholars of the School of Rab said: This teaches that it will split up into separate groups and depart. (*Footnote: Probably meaning that there will be so many conflicting opinions as to what is the truth as to render it, for all practical purposes, inaccessible.*) What is the meaning of 'and he that departeth from evil maketh himself a prey? — The School of R. Shila said: He who departs from evil will be dubbed a fool by his fellow-men.

- It has been taught: R. Nehorai said: in the generation when Messiah comes, young men will insult the old, and old men will stand before the young [to give them honour]; daughters will rise up against their mothers, and daughters-in-law against their mothers-in-law. The people shall be dog-faced (*without shame*), and a son will not be abashed in his father's presence.

- It has been taught, R. Nehemiah said: in the generation of Messiah's coming impudence will increase, esteem be perverted, (*Footnote: I.e., none shall esteem another. Another opinion: even the most esteemed shall be perverted and deceitful.*) the vine yield its fruit, yet shall wine be dear, (*Footnote: Everyone will be drunk, so that in spite of the abundant yield, there will be a scarcity.*) and the Kingdom will be converted to heresy (Footnote says: Converted to *Christianity*) with none to rebuke them. This supports R. Isaac, who said: The son of David will not come until the whole world is converted to the belief of the heretics. (Christians) Raba said: What verse [proves this]? it is all turned white: he is clean. (*Footnote: Leviticus 13:13.– This refers to leprosy: a white swelling is a symptom of uncleanness; nevertheless, if the whole skin is so affected, it is declared clean. So here too; when all are heretics (Christians), it is a sign that the world is about to be purified by the advent of Messiah.*)

NOTE: *The conversion to Christianity is a reflection from a famous verse in the Gospel from Matthew 24:14 –*

> *"And this gospel of the kingdom shall be preached <u>in all the world</u> for a witness unto <u>all nations</u>; and then shall the end come."*

It would appear here that Jesus was teaching right out of *Talmud!*

Jewish Concept of the World to Come 535

- Our Rabbis taught: For the Lord shall judge his people, and repent himself of his servants, when He seeth that their power is gone, and there is none shut up, or left: (Deuteronomy 32:30) the son of David will not come until denunciators are in abundance. (*Footnote: 'When He seeth that their power is gone' is interpreted as meaning that they will be at the mercy of informers; then God will judge his people — redeem them through the Messiah.*) Another interpretation [of their power is gone]: until scholars are few. Another interpretation: until the [last] *perutah* (smallest Roman coin) has gone from the purse. Yet another interpretation: until the redemption is despaired of, for it is written, there is none shut up or left, as — were it possible [to say so] — Israel had neither Supporter nor Helper. Even as R. Zera, who, whenever he chanced upon scholars engaged thereon [I.e., in calculating the time of the Messiah's coming], would say to them: I beg of you, do not postpone it, for it has been taught: Three come unawares: (*Footnote: Lit., 'when the mind is diverted.' Messiah, a found article and a scorpion. – Hence by thinking of him they were postponing his coming.*)

- R. Kattina said: Six thousand years shall the world exist, and one [thousand, the seventh], it shall be desolate, as it is written, And the Lord alone shall be exalted in that day. (*From Isaiah 2:11*) Abaye said: it will be desolate two [thousand], as it is said, After two days will He revive us: in the third day, He will raise us up, and we shall live in His sight. (*Footnote: From Hosea 6:2 – the 'two days' meaning two thousand years. Ref. Psalms 90:4. and quoted below.*)

- It has been taught in accordance with R. Kattina: Just as the seventh year is one year of release in seven, so is the world: one thousand years out of seven shall be fallow, as it is written, And the Lord alone shall be exalted in that day,' and it is further said, A Psalm and song for the Sabbath day, (*Ref. Psalms 92:1*) meaning the day that is altogether Sabbath — (*Footnote: I.e., the period of complete desolation.*) and it is also said, For a thousand years in thy sight are but as yesterday when it is past. (*Footnote: Psalms 90:4; thus 'day' in the preceding verses means a thousand years.*)"

- The *Tanna debe Eliyyahu* teaches: The world is to exist six thousand years. In the first two thousand there was desolation; (*Footnote: I.e., no Torah. It is a tradition that Abraham was fifty-two years old when he began to convert men to the worship of the true God; from Adam until then, two thousand years elapsed.*) two thousand years the *Torah* flourished; (*Footnote: I.e., from Abraham's fifty-second year until one hundred and seventy-two years after the destruction of the second Temple. This does not mean that the Torah should cease thereafter, but is mentioned merely to distinguish it from the next era.*) and the next two thousand years is the Messianic era, (*Footnote: I.e., Messiah will come within that period.*), but through our many iniquities all these years have been lost. (*Footnote: **He should have come at the beginning of the last two thousand years; the delay is due to our sins.***)

> Elijah said to Rab Judah, the brother of R. Salia the pious: 'The world shall exist not less than eighty-five jubilees, (*Footnote: Of fifty years.*) and in the last jubilee the Son of David will come.' (*Footnote: [Messiah. The belief in his Davidic descent is already mentioned in the Song of Solomon 17:21.]*) He asked him, 'At the beginning or at the end?' (*Footnote: Of the last fifty years*) — He replied, 'I do not know.' 'Shall [this period] be completed or not?' (*Footnote: I.e., if at the end of the jubilee, shall it be at the beginning of the fiftieth year or at the end thereof?*) - 'I do not know,' he answered. R. Ashi said: He spoke thus to him, 'Before that, do not expect Him; afterwards thou mayest await him.' (*Footnote: He will certainly not come before then, but may delay a long time afterwards.*)

It is easy for any Christian who has studied eschatology to observe that several features of The Tribulation period have been described here in *Talmud* in very profound and insightful detail. Typical of such writings are found in *Pesachim* 118a, where we read such expressions as: "the pangs of Messiah" and "the suffering which must precede His Coming." The Rabbis dutifully describe conditions that will exist when "the Son of David comes." They relate how "Our Rabbis taught that in the seven year cycle before the Son of David will appear, etc." This dialogue is heart-breaking for Christians to encounter as we see how God has concealed Messiah from our Jewish brethren.

From this it can be concluded that Jesus, in describing these times and conditions, certainly had brought forth these things from Jewish teaching. His hearers would definitely have recognized it as such. This demonstrates just how long a time the Jewish teachings on this subject have been in place. This is surely NOT new!

Of course, the most exciting statement here for Christians, we have placed in bold type, saying Messiah, Son of David: **should have come at the beginning of the last two thousand years; the delay is due to our sins.** This shocking acknowledgment is not just a random sentence in *Talmudic* writings. This same reference to when He "should have appeared" is occasioned at about three different tractates in *Talmud*.

One is pressed to wonder if this teaching is still recognized by the Rabbis and/or how they explain it to their people. Because, Yes! – This says Messiah "*should have come*" two thousand years ago! – And, Yes! – Jesus of Nazareth WAS here at that time and Jesus fits ALL of the Messianic prophecies that He chose to fulfill at THAT time. However, the Jewish teachers were confused and perhaps even a bit "stiff-necked" to have insisted that He should fulfill ALL of the prophecies at that time – especially to include throwing off their bondage and ejecting the oppressive Romans from *Eretz Israel*.

Earlier, in Chapter 18, we discussed the 1st century scholar, Jonathan ben Uzziel, who was severely chastised by the Rabbinate for having "spilled the beans" – so to speak – by having explained in clear terms the timing in the prophesy of Messiah's Advent as revealed in Daniel 9:24 – 27. As a result, existing today are *Targumim* for ALL of the canonical Scriptural books, EXCEPT that Daniel, Ezra and Nehemiah have been "omitted." Earlier in this book we have demonstrated the importance of these books in Messianic prophecy. This is especially the case with Nehemiah and Daniel in "timing" of the seventy "weeks." Also, we pointed out that the Rabbinical Authority had declared a curse upon anyone who would dare attempt to "calculate" the time of Messiah's appearing.

After hearing of the aforementioned Rabbinical teachings on their Messianic expectancy, we are moved then to present several facts to the Jewish people, as follows:

- Scripture and history clearly confirm that Jesus of Nazareth WAS at Jerusalem on the exact date that had been prophesied for Messiah ("The Anointed") to arrive.
- Jesus of Nazareth accomplished ALL of the tasks that had been predicted for Him, except for that of defeating the nations that will surround Israel during the Last Days with the intent of destroying her. Jesus healed the sick, made the blind to see, taught in parables – everything! – except that the time for Messiah's annihilation of Israel's enemies lay far in the future. – That is, until now!
- Immediately after Jesus was crucified, during the 1st century, the Rabbinical authorities forbade scholars to "calculate" when Messiah was to arrive.
- This indicates that the Jewish authorities knew that Messiah already had been there – and right on time!
- This means further that the Rabbis do not want their people to know that Messiah had in fact arrived; although, He was killed. Therefore, some of their scholars have reasoned that Messiah has "delayed" His Appearance until "two more days" (two thousand years) after the 1st century.
- The Rabbis have acknowledged that "all the predestined dates" for the coming of Messiah have already passed.
- It is therefore evident that, either today's Rabbis are too confused and blinded to understand and comprehend all these facts, or they have hatched a "cover-up" – because...
- ***They do not want their people to know that Messiah has already been here!***

I sincerely hope and pray that the action (and/or "inaction") of the Rabbis has not been a deliberate cover-up.

We already have accounted for the omission of Daniel's prophecies from the *Targumim*. Additional testimony of sorts under the same Rabbinical motivation is derived from *Talmud*, the *Mishnahs* and *Midrash Rabbah*, revealing what appears to be a deliberate Rabbinical "omission" of Messianic reference in those Judaica sources.

Daniel's prophecy of "the seventy weeks" is without dispute the most remarkable prophecy in Scripture. As we have shown, Daniel 9:24 – 27 proclaimed the day of arrival of "The Anointed" – Messiah – at Jerusalem. That fact should qualify that passage for several mentions as reference in these sources.

There are sixty-five tractates comprising as many as seventeen volumes in the *Babylonian Talmud*, and yet only ONE reference to Daniel 9:21 – 27 is listed. That entry is in *Shabbat* 55a and concerns only the messenger role of the angel, Gabriel. – NOTHING about the

Advent of Messiah! There are ten sections distributed through ten volumes in *Midrash Rabbah* and not even *one* reference to this marvelous prophecy is included!

This obvious omission of such a vital Scripture from Jewish theology seems to indicate that this void was *not* accidental! Jonathan ben Uzziel compiled his *Targum* of the prophets during the 1st century. Regrettably, it does appear that the Rabbis have withheld reference to that Scripture because they did not want to face admission of the tragic mistake that was wrought at Jerusalem on the Passover in the year 30 C.E. They apparently devised the "curse" and avoidance of study of the subject in order to serve as an alibi for having hidden the "mistake." They are saying: *"Oh, we can't talk about that. – It is forbidden!"* – (We wonder: "Just Whom do they think they are foolin'?")

So, again – the Rabbis must confront these profound questions:

- Was or was not Messiah here at that time when God had said He would come?
- If we say Messiah did not come at that time, aren't we saying that God lied ?!
- But, if "Someone" came who met "almost" all of the Scriptural prophesies about Messiah, maybe we should at least have given Him "benefit of doubt."
- Maybe we just didn't understand or were too bound with tradition to "see" Messiah.
- Still, if Messiah DID come, then certainly the Lord our God surely did NOT lie!
- So, then – If Messiah did come to us, then why are we still waiting for Messiah, Son of David?"

This Jewish misunderstanding and blindness is perhaps the Greatest Tragedy of all mankind, through all the Ages.

Even so, we are moved once again to declare *emphatically!* – Judaism and Christianity are the ONLY faiths whose God has Substantiated – Verified – Guaranteed! The Truth of His Word by instituting prophetic forecasts of Events that have and WILL in the future come to pass. – NO other religion, cult, or "faith" can show evidence to make and support such a claim. Why should anyone doubt that God will continue to bring about these events that have not yet occurred?

One of Daniel's most profound prophecies has often been misunderstood, especially by some overly enthusiastic Evangelical prophecy teachers. The Scripture concerned is Daniel 12:4 –

"But thou, O Daniel, shut up the words, and seal the book, even to the time of the end: many shall run to and fro, and knowledge shall be increased."

These well-intentioned, but misinformed teachers, have allowed that *"many shall run to and fro"* refers to the great advances in transportation that exist in our day. We travel "to and fro" in fast automobiles, ships, jet aircraft – rockets, even! And, then these teachers point to the phrase: *"knowledge shall be increased"* as an obvious End-Times reference to the remarkable technology progress we have achieved in all fields: medicine, engineering, construction, communications, astronomy, space exploration – *all* of science, in fact.

Nevertheless, many scholars point out that a "more scholarly" and consequently more accurate rendering of Daniel 12:4 means that during those times approaching "the Day of The Lord" –

- Rabbis will be going "to and fro" through the Scriptures, comparing events with prophecies, tying Scriptural events to the predicted conclusions, etc.
- Those studies of Scriptural prophecies will then have the result that "knowledge shall be increased" concerning arrival of Messiah, the Day of The Lord and the World to come.

This "more scholarly" approach is especially noteworthy as we contemplate what will take place among those Jewish teachers who will be "gathered up" on that Day when "The Great Trumpet shall sound." As they are gathered-up to Jerusalem on 1 *Tishri*, they will have ten days together in which to discuss (and debate!) as they go "to and fro" through the Scriptures that predict these events. Surely, their "knowledge shall be increased" such that they will know their Messiah when He alights on the summit of the Mount of Olives to claim His Kingdom.

Jewish teachers are of course presently NOT scouring through the New Testament, nor even in their *Tanakh* for eschatological input. *Talmud* teachings in fact state (*Shabbath* 138b) that Daniel is saying that they shall search "to and fro," but will not find "The Word of the Lord." They base this conclusion on Amos 8:11, which declares in part that there shall be a famine in The Land –

> *"Behold, the days come, says the Lord God, when I will send a famine in the land, not a famine of bread, nor a thirst for water, but of hearing the words of the Lord;"*

We have evidenced previously, however, that that the Rabbis knew of many of these prophecies even before the time of Jesus. – The exact date of His Arrival, for example! The events still to be fulfilled await us and their timing is revealed through diligent study of BOTH the "Old" (Hebrew: *Tenakh*) and the New Testament. A summary identifying all of those Events and their sequence should be of help to our readers. Following is a listing of those Events that will describe participation and/or relationship with the Jewish people in those times.

- The next Event to take place in the "End Times Scenario" is the "catching away" or "Rapture" of Believers to be with the Lord. There is no timed sequence or date associated with this departure of Christians from Earth. Suddenly, without warning, mysteriously, thousands upon thousands of Christians from all walks-of-life, all ages, all nations, all over the Earth will supernaturally disappear, as if into thin air. Clothing will be left at each person's last position on Earth. Stockings will be in their shoes, shoelaces will still be tied, snaps, Velcro or other devices still fastened in place. Underclothing will be inside of shirts, blouses, trousers, skirts. Buttons and zippers and belts will still be fastened. Even watchbands, bracelets, neckties, scarves and necklaces will still be fastened. Eyeglasses, wallets, jewelry, contact lenses, implants of all types, dentures, tooth fillings and anything we were not born with will be left behind – lying right where the person had been standing, sitting or lying. This will be the same type of startling evidence that was seen by Peter and John; i.e., the "grave-cloths" in The Tomb! Because of this last reason, alone – the "left-behind" evidence. – it will be EXTREMELY difficult for ANYONE to dispute to witnesses of these Events. The witnesses will insist that, just as had been long prophesied, these people were taken away by the Lord to be with Himself!

- The Western nations – in particular the United States – will be thrown into chaos, since many of their officials in high positions in government and the military were Christians and will have disappeared at this time. The United States will be at least temporarily "out-of-action." As a result, without its customary protective shield from the United States, a vulnerable Israel will then become especially "nervous" and Muslim forces will see an opportunity to eliminate the nation of Israel once and for all.

- At some time afterward, maybe seconds – maybe even a few years – The World will be on the brink of global conflagration as inflamed by continued and ever increasing violence between Israel and the Islamic nations and peoples. Suddenly, a charismatic, but little-known world leader will arise from a relatively small nation of minimal influence and shall forge a seven-year treaty purported to protect Israel from her hostile neighbors. This measure will delude most people into believing that Peace at last has been achieved in the troubled Mid-East. Israel will trust that security for her borders is guaranteed by the treaty provisions to be enforced by the newly arisen World leader. In the New Testament he is identified as: "Antichrist" or "666." This treaty will most likely be formally recognized on the date of *Yom Kippur* – The Day of Atonement – 10 *Tishri* on the Jewish calendar. This single Event signals the start of a period that *Talmud* Rabbis have recognized for centuries as the worst period that Israel ever has or ever will endure. The period of the last seven years (The Tribulation) just before arrival (Return!) of Messiah, Son of David is well known by scholars to be of terrible portent for Jewish people living at that time.

- MOST IMPORTANT ! – At this same time, the treaty will authorize Israel to resume Temple worship, with resumption of the animal sacrifices, all of the Feasts of Jehovah, etc. As a result of their acquiring this new-found security and acceptance, Israel will probably not even take notice of the sinister implications that apply to this "Mr. Wonderful." The Temple rites may be conducted in a restored Tabernacle, rather than actually in a rebuilt Temple on the Temple Mount. The priests will need to purify themselves as well as all of these Temple worship articles by sprinkling "living water" mixed with the ashes of the Red Heifer.

- Israel will, for a time, consider herself confident about her security under this treaty. Ezekiel describes Israel's security complacency at this time, saying they are a nation of "un-walled villages." In other words, Israel will believe she has, at last, nothing to worry about from her neighboring Islamic nations. Israel's "guard" will be down.

- Soon afterward, a "consortium" of nations will scoff at the treaty provisions imposed by this new World leader and will hold his authority in contempt. They will plan an invasion of Israel from the north. Specifically, the consortium, Biblically identified as *Gog* and *Magog*, will consist of: Russia, many of the Eastern European nations, along with Libya, Iran, Syria and others. Their aim will be to capture the "Land Bridge" that Israel occupies connecting Africa to Asia; thereby obtaining control of the world's oil supply as well as the strategic value of the Suez Canal. But, more importantly to the Islamic nations: Their goal will be to annihilate the Jewish people; or at least to terminate Israel's status as a nation and to drive the Jewish people from what the Arab and Palestinian people consider to be "the Arab Lands"!

- These invading hordes will be smashed as they reach "the mountains of Israel" (Lebanon). In fact, 5/6 of their forces will be annihilated either by a nuclear strike from Israel's neutron bomb or by a natural disaster – most likely the latter. Very likely, however, there will be a nuclear exchange between the ocean-bounded Western nations (i.e., "*them that dwell carelessly in the isles*") and the mostly "land-locked" invaders' consortium, led by *Gog* and *Magog*. God's Word from Ezekiel 39:6 says:

"And I will send a fire on Magog, and among them that dwell carelessly in the isles; and they shall know that I am the Lord."

- Nevertheless, this new World leader will emerge unscathed through this slaughter and most people will marvel at his charisma, power and magic, which he has credited to himself as a result of his remarkable success and survivability. – In order to delude The World, God is going to make Antichrist "look good"!

- A huge "power vacuum" will exist since the United States, Great Britain, Germany, France and other prominent nations (dwelling carelessly in the isles) will have been devastated to greatly reduced military, economic and political strength as a result of the nuclear war – World War III – i.e., *Gog* and *Magog*. The new leader, Antichrist, "666" – will fill the power vacuum and gain control over virtually the entire globe.

- The Earth shortly will become a "living Hell" with ever increasing earthquakes, floods, storms, diseases, famines, wars and rebellions, lawlessness, oppression under this "666" regime. Jesus described the times we currently experience (2000-2005) as "the beginnings of sorrows." At present we can see the "beginnings" of what will be much worse as time goes forward. The entire seven-year Tribulation period is also known as "The Time of Jacob's Trouble." In Jewish theology it is well known that a terrible time for the Jewish people will precede the Coming of Messiah, Son of David.

- Three and one half years after the seven-year pact, "666," will "speak against the Most High." He will perform some defiling act in the Jewish place of worship and will proclaim himself as God. The Jewish people will of course recognize at once that he is a fraud and actually *"the abomination that maketh desolate."* In response, he will stop Israel from their conduct of Temple worship. He then will turn upon the Jewish people and will begin hunting them down for extinction worldwide, just as during WW II in Europe. Jewish people will have to hide wherever they are able in order to escape death. This onslaught most likely will begin on the date of the Passover, 15 *Nisan*, which will then be three and one half years after the seven-year "covenant" with Antichrist began. That is, it will be in "the middle of the week" (of seven years) as stated in Daniel 9:27

- A large contingent of Jewish refugees will flee to what is currently known as the ancient city of Petra, a city of 65 sq. miles area, literally carved out of stone cliffs and located just across the Israel border in Southern Jordan. As a result of circumstances presently not understood, somehow Jordan (i.e., *"Edom, Moab and Ammon") shall escape out of his* (Antichrist's) *hand."* (Daniel 11:41) This remnant of Jewish people therefore will be preserved at Petra during the remaining three and one half years (1260 days, forty-two months, "time and times and half a time," etc.) – The time of "Jacob's Trouble." Very likely, they once again will be fed with that Heavenly bread which they called: manna; and they perhaps will obtain water from a nearby artesian well. The well is "traditionally" claimed to be where Moses *"struck the rock."* An aqueduct, extending from the well into Petra, exists there even today.

- At this same time, Antichrist will require every person worldwide to have an identifying "mark" placed either in the right hand or in the skin of the forehead. Nobody will be able to buy or sell anything unless he has the required "mark." Many persons will at first herald this mark as a boon toward improved law enforcement, albeit at some sacrifice of civil liberties. For example, persons will be required to log on a computer with that mark. This will be a deterrent to many "hackers." Further, would-be terrorists will be identified by the mark if they should attempt to board any aircraft or ship, etc. – A very negative thought accompanies this seemingly "beneficial" edict in that ANY persons who refuse the mark will be beheaded. Moreover, ANY persons who accept the mark will be forever doomed from ever receiving Salvation from God.

- During this next three and one half years there will be 12,000 Jewish men from each of the twelve tribes who will have received the Holy Spirit and who will travel worldwide, ministering the message of Salvation through Jesus Christ, Israel's Messiah and Savior of all men. Many people will be saved through the faithful works of these Jewish evangelists! — Sadly, however, most of these brave souls will be martyred rather than accepting the "mark" of Antichrist.

- This period also will bring horrible events on this Earth, such as have never before existed, nor will ever again. The sun will be blotted out for a time, but it also will be seven times brighter for a time. The moon will shine as the sun! As we have stated, it will be possible to get a "moonburn!" Earthquakes, wars, disasters, famine, disease will reach such proportions that we cannot comprehend, much less describe! Jewish people will still be hunted down by Antichrist.

- The Earth will have suffered to such an extent by this time that almost no survivors will exist. Nevertheless, a "remnant" will be preserved. On the date of *Rosh Hashanah* – The first day of the seventh month, *Tishri* – Feast of Trumpets. About three and one half years after the sacrifices were abolished, "The Great Trumpet will sound" and Jewish people, living and dead, will be "gathered up" and "whisked" supernaturally to Jerusalem from wherever they happen to be all over the Earth! – Yes! – This will include even the Jewish dead being "gathered up" from their graves! There, during the next ten days, they will rejoice that God has preserved them and they will share at learning the Scriptural passages detailing the arrival of Messiah to rescue and to Redeem them from their sins.

- Meanwhile, a huge army marshaled from virtually all of the nations of the Earth will assemble on the plain of *Megiddo* north of Jerusalem. They will gather to organize and implement an attack against the Jewish people, all of whom will be at that time in Jerusalem. On the 10th day of *Tishri*, Day of Atonement – *Yom Kippur* – these armies will advance to surround and trap all of the surviving Jewish people in Jerusalem.

- On this same day, ALL peoples of the Earth will observe a brilliant and Majestic Light approaching from the east. Actually, ALL of the peoples of the Earth for several days have been fearfully watching this spectacle approaching Earth. As it nears, men will become increasingly awe-struck because NOBODY ever before had ever seen ANYTHING such as this! At last they will recognize that the figure illuminating the eastern horizon is Jesus, returning upon the clouds and in Great Glory, clothed in white and with feet of brass. He will be accompanied by the Divine Presence of God – *Shekhinah* – and by a multitude of "lesser" lights – His Saints – comprising ALL of His Believers from throughout the Church Age. These will appear in their new and Perfect resurrected Glorified bodies. "They will be like Him !"

- All the Earth's peoples will see Him and they will know that He is The King of Kings and Lord of Lords! – They will be greatly awed by the sight of Him coming in such never-before-seen Beauty – Glory – Power – Magnificence...Indescribable! – Every knee shall bow, every tongue confess – that Jesus Christ is Lord!

- He will alight on the summit of the Mount of Olives and the mountain will divide at the center. In a flash ! – He will annihilate Israel's enemies that surround The City. A huge river of "Living Water" will emanate from the Temple Mount and flood the entire region from the Mediterranean Sea to the Dead Sea. In fact, the tiny Dead Sea hamlet, *En Gedi*, will later become a prosperous fishing village!

- The Jewish people who had been transported and gathered at Jerusalem will at that time see their Messiah. They will recognize that He WAS that One who had been nailed to a Cross and had been "thrust through" with a spear when He was with them much earlier. For this reason they will mourn as never before because they will then realize it was He whom they had rejected when He was with them in the first century – C.E. 30.

- Five days later, 15 *Tishri* on Feast of Tabernacles – *Sukkoth* – Messiah will establish His Messianic Kingdom on Earth for one thousand years. He will thrust "The Evil Inclination" – Satan – bound in chains into a "pit" – "for a little season."

- His Saints will assist during His Millennial rule. Jerusalem will be the World Capital. There will be total Peace on Earth –No disease – No war – No disasters – No famine – No crime – No lawyers! – No politicians! – NO PROBLEMS ! – With the absence of evil, disease, wars, famine, etc., people will live to an age of about 1000 years – just as did the Patriarchs (Methuselah, etc.) before The Great Flood.

- However, at the end of the "little season," Satan will be released from the pit to roam the Earth again, "*seeking whom he may devour.*" – from I Peter 4:8. This will be to test those whom have lived only in Christ's Perfect World, without temptations toward The Evil Inclination." In this way, all men who have ever lived, at some time will have been exposed to the menace of Satan's wiles and will have been "tested" – i.e., confront the choice to accept God or Satan.

- At The Great White Throne God will judge men "*according to their works.*" Those whose names are not written in The Book of Life will be cast, along with Satan and his demons, to suffer eternally in The Lake of Fire.

- The names of all His Saints will be written in The Book of Life and they will ascend with Him to The New Heaven and The New Earth to The New Jerusalem to be with the Lord for Eternity.

- A Chart showing this scenario, with Scriptural references is included to follow.

Jewish Concept of the World to Come

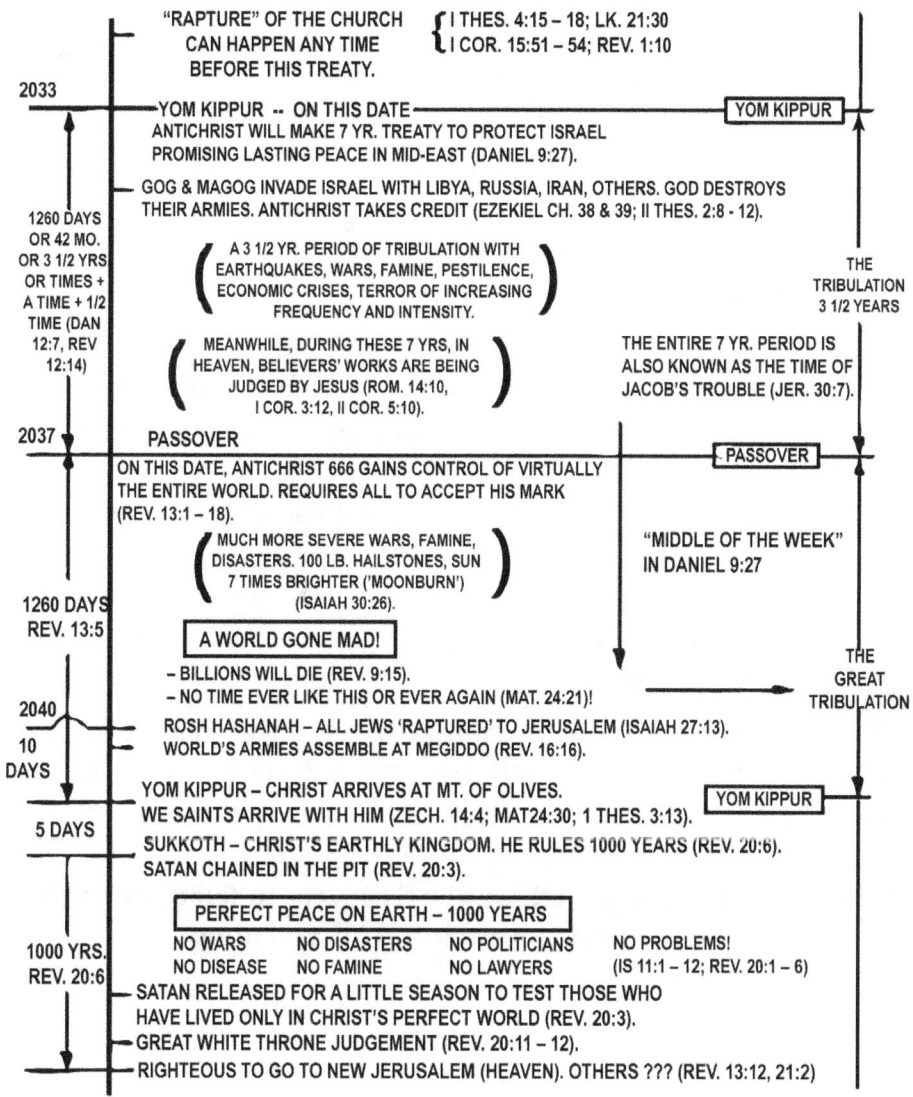

Illus. 47: Scenario of Messiah's Arrival and Kingdom

Something to Think About

We have presented a wealth of evidence showing that Jesus of Nazareth is Messiah. Any persons who still are reluctant or skeptical about believing and trusting Jesus, here are some thoughts that those persons MUST consider. –

Blaise Paschal was a French scientist and mathematician of the Middle Ages. He developed most of the hydraulics laws that we use today. Each time we open a faucet or pour a beverage or flush a toilet or step on a brake pedal, we are employing some of Paschal's laws of physics. He is thought by many scholars to have possessed the most brilliant mind of all the men who ever lived. Blaise Paschal proposed a wager to "test" the truth of God & Christianity. It is called: Paschal's Wager:

- Either Christianity is true or it's false.
- If you bet that it's true, it follows that you believe in God and submit to Him.
- Then if it IS true, you've gained God, heaven, and everything else.
- If it's false, you've lost nothing, but you've had a good life marked by peace and the illusion that ultimately, everything makes sense.
- If you bet that Christianity is not true, and that's correct, again – you've lost nothing.
- But if you bet that Christianity is false – but, it turns out to be true
- then, you've lost everything and you will spend eternity in hell!

The essence of "Paschal's Wager" is:

"I would rather live my life trusting God, and die to find out there is no God, than to live my life insisting there is no God, and die to find out there is!"

Paschal's Wager is something for Believers to tell unbelievers, and for unbelievers to – THINK! about!

25

Go Tell It To the World

Summarizes facts and logic reported – Questions for doubters and skeptics – Hopes for bringing Jewish and Christian people together in understanding – Jesus Christ IS Jewish! — Jesus lived AND died The Law!

Assuming you have read all of the preceding chapters and have received a few new blessings, I wish now to leave you with some thoughts that have occurred as a result of facts brought out by these stories.

A Messenger's Plea

The Departure Event of the *Shekhinah* is the foundation for all other stories of this book. Please do not ignore this Event. Ignoring it would hardly seem likely if you have read through this far. But, please tell others about this beautiful story, even if they won't read it. Stimulate their curiosity. Any Christian or Jew should at least be curious about this story. The sting of rejection and retort is soon forgotten, but the ache of the ignored messenger lingers and remains.

We have pointed out that the *Shekhinah* Event actually played a very important part in God's plan for rescue and preservation of the Jewish and Christian stalwarts who became the remnants to initiate the Church Age. It is indeed ironic that modern "conservatives" of both faiths are embarrassed, thrown off-balance, etc., by this beautiful story — a story that points to why and how their "fore-saints" were alerted to "get out of the camp" before death and destruction inundated Jerusalem and all of Judea.

The more we learn of the Old Testament, Judaic history, customs, the "Law," the more we see of Messiah (hidden) in Jewish culture and religion. That fact should have been quickly recognized as we studied the remaining articles and stories in this book. Christians, so informed, are then more surely equipped for witnessing the Gospel of Messiah to Jewish people. Knowledge and appreciation of Judaism should also promote better understanding between these two closely linked faiths that are also "closely opposite."

By not emphasizing (even avoiding) the Messianic "pictures" and "types" in the Old Testament, we have cloistered Christianity from the Jews. (And not without considerable help from the Jews themselves, occasionally.) Even more tragically, this "cloistering" of our own Messianic view has further blinded the Jewish people from Messiah, because of something most Christians do not notice. Our Jewish friends are watching us and listening to us, especially if our "walk" demonstrates that we "see" something within Judaism that they do not see. (They are naturally curious.)

We should each be curious. Indeed, my own curiosity about the *Shekhinah* Departure Event has led me to manifold blessings about the Lord Jesus in my searches through the Bible and all types of Judaica. My hope would be to find a Jewish student who has a similar curiosity about my Faith and about this Event as well as the other subjects in the book.

It is my hope that, if nothing else, this book will have stirred an interest in the Bible. This work has been, after all, a rigorous and vigorous Bible study. Many Christians and Jews encounter only a handful of familiar verses and Bible stories in their Scriptural education from Sunday School and from the pulpit. Great enjoyment and closeness to the Lord can be achieved by disciplining oneself to read the Bible through — yes, cover to cover. Only in that way can you see His story unfold, showing the plight of the Jews, God's forgiveness of "naughty" Israel, subtle appearances of Messiah, and best of all! — God's Infinite and Eternal Love for Israel and for all the rest of mankind.

After studying the history, spiritual "pictures," archaeology, Judaism, Laws, prophecies, and other facets, such as those we have addressed, the Bible reader is better equipped for "enjoying" the Bible. The reason for this is simply because the reader then "knows what to look for." Otherwise, for example, if he is not familiar with the prophecies, etc., he could read right through Ezekiel, Daniel or other prophets, without ever knowing what it is all about.

The Lord wants to speak with you "one on one" through His Word. He doesn't want you to hear Him only through your "Rabbi." "Rabbis" after all, are only human. God wants to talk with you. The Bible is God talking to you! How many Sunday School teachers or preachers or other "Rabbis" ever told you about the "Dry Bones" prophecy? How many times have you heard that old Negro spiritual rendition? — "*Toe-bone connecta to de foot-bone — Foot-bone connecta to de leg-bone — Leg-bone connecta to de knee-bone, etc., etc.*" Did you know that is about the rebirth of Israel as a nation? (See Ezekiel 37)

On "Palm Sundays," have you ever heard any preacher explain that it was REALLY on a Monday? Or has one ever explained WHY? – on THAT day – all those folks were throwing down their cloaks and palm fronds along the path of that gentle, humble Galilean "carpenter"? (See Daniel 9:24-26) — See what I mean?

However, the reader must believe the Bible is God's Word. If you believe, the Lord has Promised many times that He will help you to understand. (See Proverbs 1:7 and 2:1 – 6) But, in order to read all through the Bible in one year, you must discipline yourself to read about three or four pages every day. Now, that takes about fifteen or twenty minutes. Do you think you could spare fifteen minutes each day for your Creator and your Redeemer? Think about it.

But...How Can We Be Sure?

Though some will misunderstand my motives, I say with all humility: The *Shekhinah* Withdrawal could be the most important Biblical event since the Pentecost. I am not the one to make the final conclusion on this possibility, but it does certainly have important bearing on both faiths, on prophecy, and on our outlook and "watching" in these Latter Days.

We have attempted to answer all of the criticism so far received in written and verbal comment from some very highly qualified Christian teachers. At this writing, although Prof. Asher Kaufman has commented and occasionally corrected my work on archaeological and historical points, I have not yet received any scholarly critique from Jewish theological interests. There can be no doubt that this story is true, both through Scriptural verification and ancient historical records.

- It was prophesied to happen (sometime).
- It DID happen – in 66 C.E.
- The Event alarmed the Temple officials to the extent that it was announced publicly.
- It was documented by several historians who were concerned with Jewish antiquity.

We have also attempted to display truth through the most elementary logic. Again, it is ironic that some of the most "enthusiastic" doubters are Jewish—yet, the secular (and Biblical!) sources are all Jewish.

My favorite answer to stubborn "resistance" to this story, in the face of what I believe to be very hard evidence, goes like this:

- "Well, why are you so sure the Chicago Bears won Super Bowl XX?"
- "Are you kidding? Everybody knows they won!"
- "Well, were you at the game?"
- "No."

- "Well, do you know someone who was at the game?"
- "No, but I saw it on TV and I read the sports page. So did you."
- "Well, maybe the TV was 'faked.' And sports writers get things mixed-up all the time."
- "OK. But I haven't seen or heard anyone who claims to have been at that game saying the Patriots won. Therefore, I think it's fair to 'assume' that yes, the Bears won!"
- "BUT...GEE!' I thought (hoped) maybe the Patriots won."
- "Nope...the Bears!"

That great scholar, Sir Robert Anderson (in *The Coming Prince*, PP. 129) said it very well:

"There is a point beyond which unbelief is impossible, and the mind in refusing truth must needs take refuge in a misbelief which is sheer credulity."

Questions For The Skeptics

It is natural that anyone would be skeptical upon first hearing this story. After all, it is not every day that some unknown engineer steps out to challenge the thoroughness and perception of twenty centuries of scholars and learned theologians.

However, as outlined earlier, documented evidence for this event is much stronger than evidence for many other events of antiquity, including some Biblical accounts. Two sources, who were otherwise fervently dedicated to bitter antagonism, recorded this event in corroborative detail. (This is perhaps the only subject upon which Josephus and the Rabbis of the Second Temple *ever* agreed!)

Following are some questions offered to assist "skeptics" in their search for TRUTH and to serve as a summary of this glorious event:

- Ask those who insist that only Ezekiel "saw" the Glory withdraw to explain WHY?? Ezekiel stated three times that he saw this event as a vision. As the prophet begins this narrative in Chapter 8, he describes it as having been given "in the visions of God," while he was actually in Babylon seated before some of the elders of Judah.
- Ask them also to explain when Ezekiel's prophecy of the Glory's Withdrawal was fulfilled. The accounts described by Josephus and the Rabbis of the *Talmud* and the *Midrash* are the only corroborative documentations we have of such an event. One so-called traditional version would have us believe that only Ezekiel saw that glorious "fire" or "cloud" when He removed from the Temple and went across the Kidron Valley to "the mountain which is on the east side of the City." (Does anybody believe Almighty God would just "sneak" away?!)
- Ask the indifferent skeptic who dismisses or belittles this Holy Event, or who thinks it is contentious and trivial, to explain why the Lord went to all this bother

to appear and to speak and to plead in person with His Chosen after virtually 1,500 years of cloistering Himself from all but the High Priest.

- Ask those who believe God no longer loves the Jewish people, to explain why He has preserved them as a people and has resurrected them as a nation, just as He had Promised He would do after their scattering. (See Ezekiel 37:21 – 22)

- Ask those who doubt because Scripture does not record this Event, to explain WHY?? they believe the Temple was destroyed. That event was recorded only by the same historians who witnessed and recorded the *Shekhinah* Withdrawal. It is not reported as fulfillment in Scripture.

- Ask those who don't accept the credibility of *Talmud* and *Midrash* Rabbis in this matter, to explain why the first-century Hebrew scribes would ever have "invented" this story by recording, documenting, an event that actually punctuates, underscores, "spotlights" and glorifies The Crucifixion, The Resurrection and The Ascension of Jesus and that, by the Jews' own admission, clearly indicates this was a stinging rebuke from the Lord "because they would not."

- Ask those who don't accept credibility of Josephus, who was corroborated by his enemies in this matter, why they believe anything else he has written. Flavius Josephus has been proved, archaeologically and/or historically, to be correct most of the time. (This time, too!)

- Ask those who insist that Ezekiel "saw" *Shekhinah* depart (Ezekiel 8:3) and that He never returned, to explain how Ezekiel was able to "see" *Shekhinah* return to the Temple! (Ezekiel 43:2) especially considering the fact that he was still in Babylon and the Temple had certainly not been rebuilt when that vision was given "*in the fourteenth year after that the city (Jerusalem) was smitten.*" (Ezekiel 40:1)

- Ask those who have difficulty believing the Divine Presence was in the Second Temple, to explain what the Lord had intended when He told Haggai to exhort Zerubbabel to "*...build the House; and I will take pleasure in it, and I will be glorified...Yet now be strong...for I am with you...and I will fill this House with Glory...*" (From Haggai 1:8, 2:4, 7)

- If these insist that Jesus, "*The Desire Of All Nations*," filled the House with His Glory, ask them to explain how Jesus, as a peasant born of the house of David and not a Levite priest, would ever have been permitted to enter the *H'ekhal*, especially the Holy of Holies or even the Holy Place? – Or even the Court of the Priests?

- Ask them to explain who did fill that House with His Glory. (It could only have been the One whom Jesus and Paul said "dwells within.")

- If they "squirm" from this, ask them to explain who was dwelling in the Temple when Jesus said: "*...Him that dwelleth therein...*" (From Matthew 23:21)

- Also have them explain who "pertaineth" to (belongs to) the Israelites, where Paul said: *"...my kinsmen...who are Israelites; to whom pertaineth the Glory..."* Not "formerly pertaineth," but now — circa 57 C.E., the time of Paul's letter to the Romans. (From Romans 9:4)

- Try to keep a straight face as you ask the skeptic to explain why God the Father would sacrifice His Son behind the Temple? (west) when all of the other sacrifices were given (east) in front of the Temple?

- If they still "squirm" at this, ask them to explain how the centurion was able to see that *"the veil was rent in twain,"* especially if he were west of the Temple in the vicinity of the Church of the Holy Sepulchre or the Garden Tomb, etc.

- Or, even if he agrees with the *Olivet* Crucifixion, but still does not believe *Shekhinah* was in the Second Temple, ask him to explain how the centurion could have seen that the Veil was torn, while squinting into the 3 P.M. Sun – and with the Veil having been in the "ninth-hour" shade, 40 ft. back under the 150 ft. high portico. (See Illus. 16: Isometric View of 2nd Temple, Page 149, Illus. 17: Detailed Elevation of 2nd Temple, Page 150, Illus. 18: Elevation Profile of Temple and Temple Mt., Page 151, and Illus. 19: Elev. Profile: Temple Mt., Kidron VLY., Mt. Olivet, Page 152)

- Ask the skeptic to offer some rationale to explain why three of the four Gospel writers reported that the centurion had seen the Veil torn. Why was that Veil so important to their report?

- And now, perhaps the most Glorious of all, ask the skeptic to explain why that centurion and his men were "terrified" and were moved to exclaim:

"Truly this man was the Son of God."

Having formerly served as a soldier in combat myself, I had often pondered why seeing *"those things that were done"* — an earthquake, the opened graves, a torn curtain — would "terrify" and move violent, "macho" Roman foot soldiers to suddenly recognize the Divinity of their execution victim. Of course, we now understand how the centurion saw that the Veil was "rent," as that brilliant "fire" of the Lord's *Shekhinah* burst through the parted veils. It is incredulous that, even after six hours on that Cross, the victim's second unexplainably vigorous shout, would be likely to inspire them to sudden "conversion." But, after their face-to-face confrontation with Almighty God (*Shekhinah*), they were terrified! And they believed!

So far, nobody has provided any plausible counter-explanations for these questions. Neither do the Scriptures explain all of this; although, the historical accounts presented here certainly are supported by those details and circumstances that are presented in Scripture. Can it be there is only one explanation?

We have proposed sensible answers to these questions, which I, too, had to ask myself. The traditional stories hold no truth, but spawn doubt and skepticism while they are based only on assumptions leading to opinion. It is understood that certain perils exist for any who would buck the tide of traditional opinion. Nevertheless, I submit that we have proved this "entrenched" opinion cannot stand in the light of literal Scripture, recorded history, and simple logic.

I have been critical of both Christian and Jewish conservative "traditionalists." I hope not to convey harshness toward critics, and I invite opponents of the validity of the *Shekhinah* story to investigate Scripture and the factual evidence for themselves. Meanwhile, we must pray that God will soon "remove-the-scales-from-the-eyes" of the Traditionalists. We would also ask that He would extend His Healing Mercy concerning the damage that Traditionalism teaching has wreaked through the World with these un-Truths.

The *Shekhinah* story tells Jewish people: "Yes, Jesus of Nazareth is Messiah!" It also tells Christians: "But I forgave them at the Cross, remember?" And the Law was not taken away just then; i.e., the sacrifices and the *Shekhinah* were removed only after the passing of a full generation of forty years. It is as if God had tested that generation who declined "*the time of their visitation*" and then He shut down their Temple. Yes — Forty is God's number for testing.

It is my hope that this book will cause people to think! In that way, all persons will more surely reach the truth.

This story of the *Shekhinah* Event rests on *three* literal Scriptural verses from *three* different writers with recorded works from *three* contemporary, indigenous historical sources. I am open to any who will show me any mistakes in these facts or analyses. "Best-selling writer" Job said:

> *"Teach me, and I will be silent:*
> *And show me how I have erred.*
> *Honest words are not painful,*
> *But what does your argument prove?"*

Job 6:24, 25 (NASB)

So, That's What "They" Want!

Let us take ourselves back in time to Jerusalem in 66–69 C.E. Can you just imagine that scene? Yes, imagine seeing the Lord Himself, the "fire" and the "cloud" — The "I AM" — up on that mountain top speaking to you. Imagine what you would have felt, had you been there to see Him and to hear Him pleading, through a feminine voice, day and night for three and a half years, pleading to His "naughty children" to repent and return to Him.

This was a startling supernatural event. Why have we never heard of this? Today the bookshelves and racks are top-heavy and overflowing with all the "junk-novels" and paperbacks and all categories of "best-sellers." The secular entertainment industry and journalists are inundating us and choking the TV channels and clogging the aisles of our supermarkets and now, even "cyberspace," with stories of the "super-natural," extraterrestrial beings, reincarnation, mysticism, terror, science-fiction, celebrity autobiographies, documented "eye-witness" accounts of "Big Foot," "the Abominable Snow-Man," flying saucers, "aliens," etc., etc.

Women, in the U.S.A. especially, are demonstrating their hunger for "love" by their enthusiastic response to the glut of "junk-novels" and "soap-operas." ("Real-Men" don't watch those, do they?!) Women have been persuaded that their void of what they think is "love" will be filled by this "junk," which is actually a sensual stimulant of sorts. They read about what they think they need — "Love."

Men, we are certainly not much different. Our "macho" search for an elusive "love" is being stimulated (but not satisfied) by the "girlie" magazines, "porno" merchants, etc., especially on the Internet, in a somewhat less wholesome fashion than that of our distaff side. So everybody, it seems, is looking for love...but in all the wrong places.

Our Latter Day culture is literally starving for some kind of assurance, some kind of "link" with the Almighty. (Whoever He is!) They want and need His love, His protection from whatever our "shaky" future holds in store for us. They want to share His knowledge (Whoever He is!) of the future. But, man's nature has not changed much in the past few millennia — because man still wants all of this in a worldly covenant. Man wants it now, but without any commitment from himself to "God." (Whoever He is!)

Man still doesn't realize that the only God who exists has already provided all of these things man needs and is seeking. God has even shared His knowledge of the future with those of us who read and study His prophecies and believe and obey His Word. It's called the Holy Bible. (I often like to refer to it as "The Owner's Manual.")

So, the entertainment industry and the secular journalists have observed and nurtured this "need" in man's hunger for a "God" of some sort; and they are making lots of money filling that need. Then, to satisfy the need, the only commitment required from man is his purse.

Well — so that's what they want! We should give the entertainment/journalism industry a challenge. Let them tell "man" the *Shekhinah* story if he wants adventure, war, mystery, supernatural phenomena, excitement. They could give them an historical drama "mini-series" that would make "*Masada*," "*Roots*," "*Shogun*," and some of the other "block-busters" seem like day school nap-time stories by comparison. Especially if they showed the violence and carnage at the siege of Jerusalem!

The conspicuous difference that contrasts this story with much of modern popular literature, however, is the fact that this story is true. This really happened — 1,900 years ago in Jerusalem — The City of God.

This is a biographical sketch about the most "charismatic," the most all-powerful, the most beautiful, THE most "everything" celebrity of ALL time — Almighty God, Himself! ("Best-Seller" celebrities will now please leave the stage!)

So, is that what they want? Well, here it is — another of many true life episodes in the greatest LOVE story ever told. I sincerely pray that men will be privileged to hear this real-life "happening" about Almighty God before He turns the final pages of "His" Story.

What Should We Do to Tell this Story?

There is great temptation now to go out and start witnessing, through this story, to our Jewish friends about how Judaism and Christianity in 30 C.E. and in 69 C.E. "converged at a point" on the Mount of Olives. But don't forget what was noted in the opening chapter of this work — about trying to be a "bridge." (Don't be surprised if you must endure some stress when you are "run-over" and "walked-on" by some.)

Indeed, God does want this story to be told to Jews and Christians. However, we (Christians) must be very gentle and very patient and very careful about how we present this bittersweet story to Jewish people. Don't rush at them, insisting that they "find" their Messiah through this story. God has surely used the Jewish people as an example lesson to us Gentiles. He has used His Chosen People to teach us, but God did not have them do the teaching. He teaches us through their example. We (Gentiles) should, therefore, do likewise by standing back a little so we let this story be, truly, a lesson-from-God, and avoid making it sound like a lesson from a Christian Gentile.

Drawing Jews and Christians Closer Together"

But why did God wait for so long after Jesus was "offered" until He removed His Divine Presence from the People?

Perhaps God wished to show Israel that He truly did "forgive them for they knew not what they did." (From Luke 23:34) And perhaps God wished also to show us Gentiles that He forgave the Jewish people — just as the first Gentiles were first beginning to accept Jesus as their "sin offering" at about that time.

It appears that the Lord tested that last generation forty years before He scattered them among the nations, to give individual Jews at that tragic period one final opportunity to decide whether Jesus was their own "burnt offering." Many did come to realize Jesus was The Anointed as they observed those Temple signs and were finally warned to "scatter" when *Shekhinah* withdrew from the Holy House. These Jews were kept from the Roman slaughter, then to become a believing remnant who went on to build "The Church" started by Paul and the other Apostles.

Nevertheless, He also preserved a Jewish remnant from the coming generation of those who were still too blind to recognize their Deliverer. This Merciful and Loving Father then laid a "smiting" upon them as He had Promised (Hosea 6:1). Because of their disobedience, He scattered them as a persecuted minority "among the heathen" (Deuteronomy 4:27) as a part of that smiting. But He gave this Promise of His mercy upon individual Jews of future generations in Deuteronomy 4:29 – 31:

> *"But if from thence thou shalt seek the Lord thy God, thou shalt find Him, if thou seek Him with all thy heart and with all thy soul.*
>
> *When thou art in tribulation, and all these things are come upon thee, even in the latter days, if thou turn to the Lord thy God, and shall be obedient to His voice;*

(For the Lord thy God is a merciful God), He will not forsake thee, neither destroy thee, nor forget the covenant of thy fathers which He sware unto them."

Many Jewish people have sought the Lord "with all their hearts," but only God can judge this and only that Jewish individual and the Lord can know if he found God. Christians must stop insisting that Jewish people stop being "Jews" if they genuinely want to find their Lord. Many Jewish people in these "latter days" are finding Messiah Jesus as Lord, but they are finding Him while they remain "Jewish." These are sometimes known as "Messianic" Jews or "fulfilled" or "completed" Jews.

Some others, who have not yet found Messiah, may have been earnestly seeking the Lord, but are still too "Jewish" to see Jesus. Ironically, this may occur partly because we have been too "Christian" in our evangelizing the Jews. They have been watching us. They still haven't forgotten our evangelical approach during the Crusades and the Spanish Inquisition. Neither have they forgotten our "smiting" of their people during the Holocaust.

If you were a Jew, would you seek the Lord your God by becoming a "Christian?" Or would you be proud of your "Jewishness" and your covenantal heritage as a Jew? Some Jewish people may have found "the Lord their God" as Jews (Plan "A"). Many Jewish people have become "Christianized" and have found the Lord. They therefore do have that "Blessed Assurance" (Plan "B"). Those Jews who recently have found the Lord and Messiah as One (Still Plan "B") have also that same "Blessed Assurance" and more — because they are still Jews! These are of course released from the Law and the sacrifices, but they are *still* God's Chosen People...Yes, Jews. Again, if you were Jewish, how would you seek the Lord your God?

Leave the judging of these things to the Lord. Pray that He will teach us how to help Jews find Him. He may "judge" us Christians because we have not really loved the Jewish people by accepting them and even encouraging them to be "Jewish."

Rev. Vendyl Jones offers an explanation on why we Gentiles should be less judgmental toward Jewish people and how we can improve our understanding of their unique covenantal relationship with God. (Quoting from Reference 4, pg. 7 – 60, ref. Acts 5:33 – 40):

Rabbi Gamaliel's words concerning the message of Jesus were: "...*if this counsel or this work be of men, it will come to naught, but if it be of G-d, ye cannot overthrow it, lest haply ye be found even to fight against G-d. And to him (the Sanhedrin) agreed...*" What Gamaliel said of the message of Jesus and Christianity can also be said of the Jew and Judaism. If it were of man, or if Christianity had replaced Judaism, it would have long ago come to naught. The very survival of the Jew, Judaism and Israel is the verification of G-d's perseverance of the people of His earthly economy. All the efforts by Christianity to thwart Judaism and the Jewishness of Jesus have been, by the same formula of Gamaliel, "*to fight against G-d.*" (*Touché* Vendyl!)

One would ordinarily expect modern repentant Jewish people to welcome this *Shekhinah* Event. But, as I have explained, this story seems to cause embarrassment for Jews because it confronts them with the fact that their *Shekhinah* ascended to Heaven from the same place as the Gentile Christians' Jesus had ascended forty years earlier.

Then, ironically and paradoxically, even some conservative / fundamental / evangelical Christians are also embarrassed because this story tells a different version of the *Shekhinah* Withdrawal than they quite innocently have been "assuming" and teaching for all these centuries. (The fact that this story is documented only by Jewish sources doesn't add to their enthusiasm, either!) Actually, we just didn't have all of the available information, simply because this report has apparently been somewhat suppressed, although I don't really know why or by whom. (But we certainly know it was for God's Purpose that it should not be told, at least until now. Maybe others have tried it before.)

We should point out that at least one early Christian historian reported the truth concerning the Withdrawal of *Shekhinah*. Eusebius, a native-born Palestinian Christian of the fourth century and a contemporary of Emperor Constantine I, documented and observed the importance of this event* and left his works for scholars of the ages to follow. He was Bishop of Caesarea in the early Church. His work has had scant notice outside of the most unbiased scholarly interests, primarily because the Church "establishment" has not wanted to hear this. (It's too "Jewish"!) * "The Proof of the Gospel" – Book VI – Chapter 18.

Although Eusebius had accurately described the withdrawal of *Shekhinah* from the Temple and had noted that The Crucifixion took place on *Olivet*, these items from his work have been kept from us by our teachers. This, in spite of the fact that Eusebius is revered by the scholars as "the father of ecclesiastical history!" It seems he was over-ruled by Constantine on these matters after Constantine had employed divination to discover in his "visions" the popularized holy sites we traditionally revere. The "Church" of course went with Constantine and his mother, Helena. These two early Gentile Holy Land pilgrims "discovered" some of our most popular sites, including "Calvary" and "His Tomb," which are due west of the Temple site at the Church of the Holy Sepulchre. Eusebius, too, has been obscured by the powers of "tradition." After all, how was Eusebius going to oppose the emperor of Rome?!

Although this event has been hidden(?), misunderstood(?), or maybe ignored(?) for all these centuries, from God's Word we know also that He does reveal some mysteries to us according to His Purpose:

"He reveals mysteries from the darkness, And brings the deep darkness into light." Job 12:22 (NASB)

Part of those mysteries we had earlier observed as "human" qualities, especially His emotions. We sincerely hope our readers have in fact seen with this story a more approachable and loving Father than they might otherwise have envisioned without having experienced God's Event with Him as it actually happened.

Perhaps now is the time for the mystery of His withdrawal from the Temple to be revealed as an expression of His Eternal Love and His Blessing upon His Church and upon the Believing Remnant of His Chosen. We shall glorify the Lord more by seeking and revealing the truth than by preserving and persisting in error and confusion, "wriggling" and "squirming" to evade or ignore Scripture, fact, and even simple logic.

This book has centered around a discussion wherein we explored the most important Jewish rite of Temple worship – The Red Heifer Ceremony. Its impact of significance to the emergence and Glorification of the Third Temple is underlined. In addition, the importance of how Jesus fulfilled The Law during His Earthly ministry is detailed in ways that, to our knowledge, have never been previously revealed. A dramatic description of the "typology" and "picture" showing the Gospel of Jesus in the Passover *Seder* provides many surprises for almost all readers.

As we close, it is fitting that we recall from John's Gospel a verse summarizing the central message that I believe the Lord had intended to convey to the world through this Holy Event.

> *"For God so loved the world, that He gave His only begotten Son, that whosoever believeth in Him should not perish, but have everlasting life."*
>
> *John 3:16*

The Lord has demonstrated through this Event, after having given His only begotten Son, that he did forgive us and that Jesus is in fact His Son. We who profess to be His own, especially, must become aware of this Event, its importance, and its Glory. We can no longer continue to evade or ignore one of His greatest gestures showing his Infinite, Eternal, Unequaled, Perfect and Perpetual Love for man.

So, now we must swallow our "embarrassment" and "gird up our loins" and get on with it. It is my sincere hope and fervent prayer that the Lord will permit His Glory to be seen, through this event, by "awakened" Jews, Christians, Muslims, and indeed all mankind before His return.

The Glory of God can be seen everywhere, by those who would look for Him in all things.

Appendices and Glossary

Appendix A – Josephus Excerpt

Josephus (Wars) Excerpt Concerning Departure of the Divine Presence from the Second Temple (66 C.E.)

FROM: *The Works of Josephus*
Translated by William Whiston, A.M.
Hendrickson Publishers – Peabody, MA
(From: "The Wars of the Jews," 6.5.3/288 – 300)

The following excerpt from Josephus is only that portion which describes the departure of the Glory of the Lord from the Temple, including some other mysterious events that occurred simultaneously with that event.

"Thus, also, before the Jews' rebellion, and before those commotions which preceded the war, when the people were come in great crowds to the Feast of Unleavened Bread, on the eighth day of (*Nisan*), and at the ninth hour of the night (approx. 3 A.M.) so great a light shone around the altar and the Holy House, that it appeared to be bright daytime; which light lasted for half an hour. This light seemed to be a good sign to the unskillful, but was so interpreted by the sacred scribes as to portend those events that followed immediately upon it. At the same festival also, a heifer, as she was led by the high priest to be sacrificed, brought forth a lamb in the midst of the Temple. Moreover, the Eastern Gate of the inner (court of the) Temple which was of brass, and vastly heavy, and had been with difficulty shut by twenty men, and rested upon a basis armed with iron, and had bolts fastened very deep into the firm floor, which was there made of one entire stone, was seen to be opened of its own accord about the sixth hour of night. Now, those that kept watch in the Temple came thereupon running to the captain of the Temple, and told him of it; who then came up thither and not without great difficulty was able to shut the gate again. This also appeared to the vulgar to be a very happy prodigy, as if God did thereby open them the gate of happiness. But the men of learning understood it, that the security of their Holy House was dissolved of its own accord, and that the gate was opened for the advantage of their enemies. So these publicly declared, that this signal foreshewed the desolation that was coming upon them. Besides these, a few days after that feast, on the one-and-twentieth day of the month (*Iyar*) a certain prodigious and incredible phenomenon appeared; I suppose the account of it would seem to be a fable, were it not related by those that saw it, and were not the events that followed it of so considerable a nature as to deserve such signals; for, before sun-setting, chariots and troops of soldiers in their armor were seen running about among the clouds, and surrounding of cities. Moreover, at that feast, which we call Pentecost, as the priests were going by night into the inner (court of the) Temple, as their custom was, to perform their sacred ministrations, they said that, in the first place, they felt a quaking, and heard a great noise, and after that they heard a sound as of a great multitude, saying, "Let us remove hence..."

Appendix B — *Midrash* Excerpt

Midrash Excerpt Describing the Departure of the Divine Presence from the Second Temple and Jerusalem-66 – 69 C.E.

FROM:

MIDRASH RABBAH

Midrash Eichah Rabbati Petikhta d'Eichah Rabbati (25)

*Introduction to the Midrash of Lamentations (Eichah) Middle Portion of Section **(25)** Proems*

*(Large **BOLD** numbers in the text refer to this author's commentary notes following the end of the Midrash narrative.)*

The Divine Presence moved ten times: From cherub to cherub, from cherub to the threshold of the Temple, from the threshold of the Temple to the cherubim, from the cherubim **4** to the east gate, and from the courtyard to the roof, from the roof to the altar, from the altar to the wall, from the wall **5** to the city, from the city to the Mount of Olives.

- From cherub to cherub, as it is written: (Ezekiel 10:4) *'The Glory of the Lord was raised above the cherub.'*

- From the cherub to the threshold of the Temple, as it is written: (Ezekiel 10:4) *'The Glory of the Lord was raised above the cherub where it was, to the threshold of the Temple.'*

- From the threshold of the Temple to the cherubim, as it is written: (Ezekiel 10:18) *'And the Glory of the Lord left from above the threshold of the Temple and stood over the cherubim.'*

- The phrase 'left from' was not appropriate for this sentence: rather, 'came to' was appropriate. Nevertheless, 'left from' was used, instead. Why 'left from?'

- Quoting Rabbi Akha: 'Like a king who reluctantly **6** must leave his palace, who would leave and come back to caress and kiss the walls of the palace and the pillars of the palace, weeping and saying, "Goodbye, my house – my palace – goodbye, my own precious vessel – goodbye!" In the same way, when the Divine

Presence left the Temple, He returned to caress and kiss the walls of the Temple, the pillars of the Temple, weeping and saying, "Goodbye, my Temple – goodbye, house of my kingship. Goodbye, my precious home – goodbye, my precious vessel – goodbye!"

- From the cherubim to the east gate, as it is written: (Ezekiel 10:19) *'And the cherubim took their wings and...stood at the door of the east gate of the Lord's house; and the Glory of the God of Israel was over them above.'*
- From the east gate to the courtyard, as it is written: (Ezekiel 10:4) *'and the 7 courtyard was filled with the radiant glory of the Lord.'*
- From the courtyard to the roof, as it is written: (Proverbs 25:24)
- *'It is better to live in a corner of the roof than in a large house with a quarrelsome wife.'* 8
- From the roof to the altar, as it is written: (Amos 9:1) *'I saw the Lord standing on the altar.'*
- From the altar to the wall, as it is written (Amos 7:7) *'And it came to pass that the Lord stood by a vertical wall.'* What is meant by "vertical?" Numerically, "vertical" (in Hebrew) is equivalent to the number "71," which is the *Sanhedrin* of 71 members 9 and this is what "vertical" means. *"And the Lord said I am appointing 71."* (Amos 7:8)
- From the wall of the city. Quoting Rabbi Judah, son of Simon:
- As it is written: (Micah 6:9) *'The voice of the Lord calls upon the city.'*
- From the city to the Mount of Olives. As it is written: (Ezekiel 11:23) *'The Glory of the Lord went up from the midst of the city 10 and stood on the mountain which is east of the city.'*

Quoting Rabbi Jonathan: 'Three and one half years the Divine Presence sat **11** on the Mount of Olives, expecting that perhaps Israel would repent, but they did not. And the Divine Presence would speak forth with a *Bath Kol*, saying: (From Jeremiah 3:14, 22) *'Return, naughty children;* and (Malachi 3:7) *'Return to me and I shall return to you'* and, since they did not repent, said (Hosea 5:15) *'I will go back to my place.'*

Of that hour it is said: (Jeremiah 13:16) *'Give praise to the Lord before darkness descends. 12 Before darkness descends on the religious judgment. Before darkness descends on prophecy. Before your feet stumble on the mountains of night. And (before) your search for the light in Babylon. And (before) the devastation into deep darkness in Midian. And (before) the obscurely foggy discourses of Greece...'*

(Here ends the excerpted *Midrash* narrative.)

Following are Author's Commentary Notes on *Midrash Eichah* Narrative.

1. The narrative was translated from the Hebrew, having no generic punctuation code; therefore, brackets, punctuation, quotation marks, etc., have been inserted to improve clarity, flow, and organization of the *Midrash* material.

2. English translations from several versions of the Bible as well as some Judaic works have been used as references throughout this work. However, out of respect for the Scriptural quotes in the *Midrash* as printed and, hopefully, to convey the Rabbi's intended meaning, the *Midrash* wording is used as closely as possible. For example, in Jeremiah 3:14, 22, "*naughty*" children is used, as translated from the *Midrash*, instead of "*back-sliding*" children or other translations appearing in some modern Bible versions.

3. This translation presents the exegesis from this portion of the *Midrash* as completely and as accurately and conscientiously as was humanly possible for the Hebrew translator who assisted in this work. No additions or comments from the translator or this writer are inserted anywhere within this *Midrash* narrative, although quoted verses from Scripture have been inserted as a convenience to the reader.

4. It should be understood that this does not refer to the present Golden Gate in the City Wall, but refers instead to the East Gate of the Temple; i.e., Nicanor's Gate. This same narration in *Talmud Rosh Hashanah* 31a is credited to a Rabbi Judah ben Idi, who declares it in the name of Rabbi Johanan ben Zakkai, beloved sage of Tiberias by the Sea of Galilee during the first century.

At first, one might interpret that Ezekiel is describing the Glory as hovering "*above the cherubim*" that were over the Ark of the Covenant, or perhaps those cherubim that were carved into the cedar panels of the walls in the First Temple (II Chron. 3:7). This conclusion is incorrect, however, because the prophet makes it very clear in Ezekiel 10:15, 20 and 22 that these are "*the same living creatures*" he had seen "*by the river Chebar.*" (Ezekiel 1:1, 3 and 3:15)

Additionally, we know from Jeremiah 3:16 and from Josephus (Wars, 5.5.5/219) that there was no Ark of the Covenant, no acacia wood cherubim over the Mercy Seat, not even a replica, in the Holy of Holies of the Second Temple. Therefore – no wooden cherubim. These were real cherubim, attending the Lord at His withdrawal from the Temple. Regardless of whether the Rabbis (priests) saw the cherubim or not, they were describing the movements of the *Shekhinah* and need not have actually seen any Angelic beings in order to have described this event as fulfillment of Ezekiel's prophecy.

5. It has been assumed that *Shekhinah* passed through the open East Gate as He moved "from the Altar to the wall" on the Feast of Pentecost, 66 C.E. The gate, according to *Talmud, Sukkah* 53b, would have been open since this was a Feast Day. This passing through then, may be interpreted as a fulfillment of Ezekiel 44:3 in which "*...He shall go out by the way of the same.*" (See Chapters 5 and 6.)

It is believed that this refers to the "wall" of the Temple courtyard, rather than the "wall" around the city of Jerusalem. However, it is not clear concerning what is considered as the "city." It may be speculated that there were some dwellings along the route described, on the western slope of the Mount of Olives, in the vicinity of the present sites of the Russian Church of Mary Magdalene and the Church of All Nations, and then on toward the summit.

This speculation is somewhat reinforced by a note concerning the word: "city" in Cruden's Concordance as follows:

In Hebrew usage, a collection of permanent human habitations, whether many or few, especially if surrounded by a wall. The word was also used, as now, metaphorically for the people of a city.

Perhaps the most logical explanation is offered by Professor Martin in that Jerusalem's city limits were extended to a "Sabbath day's journey" (Acts 1:12) from the Holy of Holies. Such a distance, 2,000 cubits by Judaic Law, was about half or two thirds of a mile, depending upon the cubit size. This was established, of course, in deference to the crowds of worshipers who could not all live within the city walls, especially during the feast seasons.

6. In this *Midrash* commentary note, the Rabbi is apparently referring to the subtlety of a nuance in the Hebrew Scripture, which indicates that one is departing of necessity or because of circumstances rather than by choice. (For example: to get out of the way.) The *Midrash* Hebrew literally says: "Like a king forced to leave his palace... ." However, it is neither appropriate nor Scriptural to agree that the Lord could be "forced" to do anything. The *Midrash* text was therefore modified to read "reluctantly must leave" instead of "forced to leave."

7. It appears that the movements and/or "stops" described in Ezekiel 10: 4 may not be in chronological order, whereas the *Midrash* locations are implied to be listed chronologically. It is probably not important as to just "when" the Glory filled the courtyard, whether in Ezekiel 10: 4 or later after Ezekiel 10: 19, because from our Biblical knowledge of the *Shekhinah* Glory in the Tabernacle and from description provided by Josephus we know the brilliance was so intense as to fill the entire Temple and appeared to be "bright daytime." (See Appendix A.)

8. This reference to the "roof " by using Proverbs 25:24 may at first impress one that the Rabbi was stretching things just a bit in order to connect this roof position of the Glory with the Holy Scripture, no matter how remote that connection might be. However, I suppose one could compare Israel, during the Second Temple era, with a "quarrelsome wife," including being confined with her, even in a large house. A footnote in *Rosh Hashana* 31a observes that the "quarrelsome wife" refers to an idol that had been placed in the Temple. Considering these possibilities, then, the verse is not at all far-fetched; in fact, it is surely appropriate.

Other not-so-far-fetched verses are Amos 7:7 and 9:1. Initially, each of these verses, in the opening phrases, appears to be "striving" for the connection. However, as one continues through the rest of the verse or perhaps even the next few subsequent verses, there appear "signals" to connect the location of the Divine Presence during the departure with a Scriptural message of judgment on a disobedient and unrepentant Israel. Once again:

"So shall My word be which goes forth from My mouth; it shall not return to Me empty, without accomplishing what I desire, and without succeeding in the matter for which I sent it." Isaiah 55:11 (NASB)

9. The Midrash text explains that *"anak,"* which is the Hebrew word for "vertical" or "plumb-line," is comprised of the same letters of the Hebrew alphabet that also denote the number of seventy-one (71): *"aleph"*=1; *"nouhn"*=50; *"kahf"*=20; or *"anak"* meaning "vertical." It is then taken by the Rabbi's comment that the passage refers to a *"Sanhedrin,"* because that body was made up of seventy-one Jewish men of high standing and reputation.

As discussed in note **8**, one must consider all of Amos 7:8 and 9 in order to follow this comment:

From verse 8: *"...Behold I am about to put a plumb line*

- ⌐ (a "71")
- ⌐ (a *"Sanhedrin"*)

"...in the midst of My people Israel. I will spare them no longer."

And verse 9: *"The high places of Isaac will be desolated and the sanctuaries of Israel laid waste. Then shall I rise up against the house of Jeroboam with sword."*

The implication could be that the Lord, in His displeasure with the *Sanhedrin* for their poor "shepherding" of His people, will replace them with a new *"Sanhedrin"* or "71." Also, it carries an additional implication that, just as Hosea had warned Jeroboam and Israel of impending doom almost eight hundred years earlier, Israel would again suffer humiliating desolation at the hands of a pagan conqueror.

A speculation for the "71," or new *Sanhedrin*, might be "71" survivors of the coming slaughter and the scattering that was to follow the destruction of Jerusalem in 70 C.E. It may be that the Lord selected 71 "roots," unheralded and known only to the Lord. These would begin a long line of new leaders to "shepherd" and "survive" Judaism through the next 2,000 years of scattering, oppression, struggle, and fugitive-like existence. But this is only speculation. Perhaps some scholar can provide a less speculative interpretation of this statement.

A parallel exists in the New Testament in Luke 10:1 when Jesus appoints seventy disciples to spread the Good News. A *"Sanhedrin"* of sorts was then comprised of seventy plus The One. There was apparently a strong Jewish traditional concept in creating a body of seventy-one men to accomplish the Lord's message to His People. Here again we see Him create a "new *Sanhedrin*" when His Purpose is not being served by the Temple "establishment."

10. Since the "city limits" of Jerusalem had been extended one Sabbath Limit, or about two thirds of a mile eastward, then the Temple was to be considered as it states: in *"the midst of the city."*

11. My Hebrew translator informs me that the word used here for "sit" means literally "to-sit-in-mourning" (as for the death of a loved one), not just to be seated casually. Jewish people refer to this period of mourning as "sitting shiva." Knowing such a detail adds to the drama and pathos of the occasion.

Immediately following where the Lord states: *"I will go back to My place,"* a very exciting prophecy is given in Chapter 6 of Hosea. That continuing portion of the prophecy deals with the timing of Israel's "two days" of suffering after He goes back to His Place. (See "When Did those Two Days' Start," Chapter 6.) Noted earlier, God spoke to Israel on this occasion as a *Bath Kol*; i.e., a feminine voice. (See Glossary and Soncino Midrash – Lamentations XXV, pp. 51)

> 12. There is no documented date of the Rabbinical commentaries in the *Midrash*; however, permit me to speculate as to the time period and what thoughts might be interpreted from the Rabbi's epilogue.

It seems likely that this lament was written soon after the "scattering" had taken place, rather than say, several centuries later. This seems evident because the writer admonishes the people to, "Give praise to the Lord before darkness descends." They certainly knew, after the destruction of Jerusalem and the Temple, that even more "darkness" was coming. My view is, therefore, that this might have been written during the first or second century. This view is further reinforced by a statement from The Encyclopedia Americana (under *Midrash*) which suggests: "When such writings first arose is not known, but the most flourishing period of *Midrashic* exegesis was from about 100 B.C.E. to 200 C.E."

In the commentary following the direct comments on Jeremiah's Scriptural statement, the Rabbi makes some remarks which may be a reflection of his own impression of Israel's future plight based on conditions, political and religious, at that time.

First, *"your search for the 'light' in Babylon"* may refer to some distant hope and yearning for retrieval of the Ark of the Covenant (presumed to be in Babylon, perhaps) in the hope that possession of that precious article might restore Israel and encourage a return of the *Shekhinah* to dwell again with Israel.

Second, *"devastation into deep darkness in Midian"* may refer to the Rabbi's fear that Judaism would be lost for many Jews who escaped to *Midian* (Arabia), because they would be under pressures of heathen pagan religions in a land of unfriendly people. (Yes, even 400 – 500 years before the religion of Islam was born.)

Lastly, *"the obscurely foggy discourses of Greece"* may have been an apprehensive reference concerning the writings and preachments from those strange but devoted followers of that even more strange Rabbi from Nazareth who, years earlier, was executed for blasphemy. Indeed, these discourses were "obscure" and "foggy" to most of the Jews and, indeed, they were given boldly and vigorously (even to Gentiles) in the Greek language, *"even in Jerusalem and in all Judea, and in Samaria, and unto the uttermost part of the earth."* (Acts 1: 8)

NOTE: It is of interest that the Hebrew translator of this *Midrash* text was in no way prejudiced regarding this story. Just like most people, he had never heard of the *Shekhinah* Event nor had he ever read from any other portion of the *Midrash*. At that time, neither of us was aware of existence of, nor did we have available, the Soncino translation in English. Upon reading this story as he translated, however, my Jewish friend confided that he had been "deeply moved" by its tone and by what it says. (Both of us had tears of mixed joy and sadness.)

As we have indicated, this translation has certain variations from the Soncino translation, although, the main theme and essential details remain unchanged. It is our opinion that the translation offered here reflects more of the compassion relative to the tragedy and pathos that was felt by the Rabbis who recorded this event and the emotion and agony experienced by the Lord our God.

Appendix C – Integrity of Josephus

Josephus, "Lover of Truth"
Testimony of the Sages
Regarding Integrity of Josephus

Some critics and skeptics have doubts concerning the integrity of Josephus as an historian. Since his works are a direct source for this story, we should examine what the sages of historical record have to say about this man. It is my intent that by showing some of what is written concerning his credentials from perhaps the most learned of his critics, we can highlight credibility for Josephus' account of the *Shekhinah* event.

Further testimony as to the integrity of Josephus as an historian is continually being revealed by modern archaeological discoveries. Descriptions of ancient Jerusalem, Caesarea, and especially Herod's fortress at *Masada* as rendered by Josephus have been shown to be almost faultless. Recent excavations at *Masada* by Professor Yadin and others have uncovered Herodian works, Roman works and, dramatically, even some artifacts from the zealots who defended so heroically against Roman procurator Silva in 72 C.E.

Direct testimony concerning Josephus' sincerity, his love for the truth, and his love for the Lord is given from his own written statements about God. A fitting summary of his thoughts is derived by scanning the index of Mr. Whiston's work under the word "God."

Here is some of what Josephus has to say about God.

> *God (the true God), His Presence in the Tabernacle...His wisdom, and that He cannot be bribed...His mercy obtained only by religion...His foreknowledge, and that His decrees cannot be avoided...His will is irresistible...without His will nothing can happen...that nothing is concealed from Him...it is dangerous to disobey Him...whether it is easier to serve God or man...He uses beasts to punish the wicked...is not to be imposed on by the wicked...delights not in sacrifices, but in good men...is called on in time of danger, by even bad men...foretells futurities, that men may provide against them...affords assistance only when the case is desperate...delights in those that promote His worship...is by nature merciful to the poor...is omnipresent...His bounty the cause of all men's happiness.*

Surely, most would agree that Josephus knew God.

Finally, let us briefly review the credentials of his best-qualified critic, Joseph Justus Scaliger (1540 – 1609). This sixteenth century French scholar is, by reputation, perhaps one of the most brilliant men who ever lived. In the introduction to Appendix Dissertation 1 of The Works of Josephus, Mr. William Whiston (translator of Josephus' works) says of Joseph Scaliger. "...perhaps the most learned person, and the most competent judge that ever was, as to the authority of Josephus..."

Joseph Scaliger, according to Encyclopedia Americana (1955 ed.), deserves to be called "the father of the science of chronology." It is recorded that Scaliger locked himself in a room and committed to memory the complete works of Homer in twenty one days. He continued by memorizing the rest of the Greek poets in three months and all of published Greek literature in two years. In addition, he possessed equal skill in twelve other languages.

Although brilliant, Scaliger was evidently somewhat arrogant toward his peers and was persecuted throughout his career, especially after having converted to Protestantism at age twenty-two. The quotation to follow is excerpted from Whiston in the Introduction to Appendix Dissertation 1. Hear an appraisal of Flavius Josephus rendered by this outstanding scholar in the *Prolegomena* to his book, *De Emendatione Temporum*, p. 17:

"Josephus is the most diligent and the greatest lover of truth of all writers; nor are we afraid to affirm of him, that it is more safe to believe him, not only as to the affairs of the Jews, but also as to those that are foreign to them, than all the Greek and Latin writers; and this, because his fidelity and his compass of learning are everywhere conspicuous."

Most anyone would be satisfied with a testimonial of such tone.

Both Jews and Christians owe deep respect and gratitude to Flavius Josephus for having given us such a worthy record of Judaic history, customs, tradition, and religion.

Appendix D – Ark of The Covenant

Excerpt From II Maccabees regarding the Ark of The Covenant

As a convenience to our readers, we have excerpted the following uncanonized referenced verses from the so-called Apochryphal Book, II Maccabees 2:4 – 8, from The New English Bible.

"Further, this document records that, prompted by a divine message, the prophet (Jeremiah) gave orders that the Tent of Meeting and the ark should go with him. Then he went away to the mountain from the top of which Moses saw God's promised land. When he reached the mountain, Jeremiah found a cave-dwelling; he carried the tent, the ark, and the incense-altar into it, then blocked-up the entrance. Some of his companions came to mark out the way, but were unable to find it. When Jeremiah learnt of this he reprimanded them. 'The place shall remain unknown,' he said, 'until God finally gathers His people together and shows mercy to them. Then the Lord will bring these things to light again, and the Glory of the Lord will appear with the cloud, as it was seen both in the time of Moses and when Solomon prayed that the shrine might be worthily consecrated.' "

The final authority is of course God's Holy Word, in which He declares His final disposition of the Holy Ark. Please read what Holy Scripture says in Jeremiah 3:16 – 17. We believe the Scriptural disposition provides the only correct conclusion in this matter.

Appendix E — A Trilogy at the Mount of Olives

Red Heifer Ceremony has three "submerged" dramas concealed within, comprising a "trilogy." Each Drama centered about each of the three characters from the central drama – The Red Heifer Ceremony, itself.

Presents more detailed "typology" of characters and events than in Parts IV and V.

Describes intricate relationships between each of three dramas portrayed.

A trilogy, consisting of three individual but closely related plays, can be recognized as these dramas from the Red Heifer ceremony unfold. These three dramas emerge with the "Cast" and "Plots" as follows:

ACT I – <u>The Burning of the Heifer</u> – In the *Sinai*, at morning, the third hour of the day, on the eve of the Passover, about 1500 B.C.E., the time of the burning of the first Red Heifer.

TYPE FROM THE LAW	PORTRAYING
The High Priest	God, the Father, who gave His only Son, Jesus, to the World as a burnt offering for the sins of the World
The Red Heifer	Messiah, the Son – Jesus of Nazareth, the unblemished Lamb of God
A priest who slays the Heifer	The World that slew Jesus, but "received Him not"

ACT II – After the Burning of the Heifer – That same evening, at the ninth hour of the same day – Passover eve, 1500 B.C.E.

TYPE FROM THE LAW	PORTRAYING
The High Priest	God, the Father, grieving at the loss of His Son as our Burnt Offering, returns to the Camp (Heaven)
The Ashes of the Red Heifer	The Gospel of Jesus Christ, which remains now as the sole witness after His "burning" and Resurrection for purification of our sins
The "clean" man, who gathers the ashes and "lays them up" in a "clean" place	Christ's Church learns ("gathers") and spreads ("lays up") and preaches ("sprinkles") the Gospel ("ashes") of Jesus Christ mixed with Faith ("Living Water") for a purification of sins for the World

These are the highlights of meanings that can be seen in this ceremony from what is presented in Scripture along with other reflections from *Talmud* and *Midrash*. King Solomon could not decipher this puzzle simply because he had seen only the first two acts of this drama, just described. Solomon was further hindered in that he did not have the second portion of the "program" (the New Testament) which identified the "players" as we have summarized here. Solomon left the "theater" when he was "called home," during Act II, but the "program" for Part II unfortunately was not available to the "audience" until the close of Act II. It was not his fault, but – (You can't tell the "players" without a "program", folks!) –

The Great Producer kept this program key from His Chosen People for reasons of His Purpose which we cannot understand at this time. – Maybe someday, but not yet.

Most Christians are familiar with The Crucifixion, but they typically have no awareness of the concealed symbolism presented in this three-act drama of the Red Heifer burning. Hopefully, Christians, seeing these first two acts perhaps for the first time, now can look back with their knowledge of the Gospel, to assemble the Glorious third and final act to present the powerful and beautiful messages of The Crucifixion and The Resurrection.

Interestingly, Act III symbolically reflects both Act I and Act II. Similarly, each of Acts I and II reflects and points toward completion and fulfillment in Act III. Note also, each Act and each Scene throughout this trilogy has *three* characters or *three* players. Thus, by means of Biblical numerology, we have a picture of the Holy Trinity. And, just as within the Trinity: One in the trilogy is always first, yet all are equal, but each is required for completion.

Watch here as we summarize the "types" from the Law, the characters, "The Cast" and the scenes for:

ACT III – The Crucifixion, The Entombment and The Resurrection

Scene One: The Crucifixion – The "Heifer" is slain.

Olivet Summit, the third hour of the day (9 a.m.), the eve of Passover, C.E. 30, as Roman soldiers prepare to crucify Jesus along with the two thieves (or "malefactors").

PLAYER	CHARACTER	TYPE FROM THE LAW
The Centurion	As God, the Father, who brings His Son, as the Heifer, to be slain	High Priest, as God
The Crowd	As The World (Jews and Gentiles) *"which knew Him not"*	Priest who slays the Red Heifer
Jesus of Nazareth is lashed to His Cross with *"megeg rope of bast"* as the spikes are driven through His hands and feet	As Messiah (Innocent)	The Heifer, perfect and unblemished, never with a yoke, slain to accomplish our purification for sin

Scene Two: The Entombment – The "Heifer" is burned.

- *Olivet* summit, that same evening, at the ninth hour (3 p.m.) as His lifeless form is taken down from The Cross and laid in The Tomb.

PLAYER	CHARACTER	TYPE FROM THE LAW
The Centurion expresses some regret for his act, saying, *"Truly, this man was the Son of God!"*	As God, the Father, feeling "unclean" in His grief, returns to "camp"	High Priest, as God, returns to "the camp," is "unclean until even."
The Crowd	As The World (Jews and Gentiles) *"which knew Him not,"* crucified Him	Priest who slew the Heifer and burned her in a stone bowl to collect the ashes
Joseph of Arimathaea	As The Church, who *"lays up the ashes* (Gospel) *in a clean place"* to be mixed with Living Water (Faith) to give purification for all "uncleanness"	The "man who is clean" carries the body of Jesus (the ashes) to a tomb *"hewn of stone"* and where no corpse ever had lain; i.e., a "clean place"

Scene Three: <u>The **Ashes** are **Gathered** and **Sprinkled** to **Wash** the **Unclean**</u>.

Translation: (The **Gospel**) is (**Learned**) and (**Preached**) to (**Save**) (**Sinners**).

- *Olivet* summit, at dawn in the morning of the first day of the next week *"on the morrow after the Sabbath,"* as Jesus' Disciples and the women approach The Tomb to prepare His body for the grave, **BUT – THE TOMB IS EMPTY !**

- However!

    God's Holy Spirit IS "clean;"

    dwells IN those who "saw and believed" (The Church);

    they are "clean" through His indwelling

    and may then "sprinkle" (preach)

    with "Living Water" (Faith) and

    "hyssop" (humility) to "purify"

    (save) the "unclean" (sinners)

PLAYER	CHARACTER	TYPE FROM THE LAW
God, the Father returned to His Place (Heaven, i.e., "the camp") after The Crucifixion. He still grieves (feels "unclean") over the loss of His Son and for those who remain unclean (in sin). However, He will be greatly joyous ("clean") later, "at evening," when all of His Blessed are washed "clean"	(As Himself)	The High Priest returns to the "camp" (Temple) after the burning, but is unclean until evening"
The Crowd returned to their homes to enjoy the Passover in the irony of having slain the Precious Lamb of God, who is also the Red Heifer. They continue their worldly pursuits until they are to be judged as "clean" or as "unclean" at evening; i.e., end of the Kingdom	The World	The Priest who slew and burned the Heifer – is now "unclean" and must remain *"without the camp"* (Temple) until evening
The Women at The Tomb, Followed soon afterwards by John and Peter, who were the first Persons to learn ("gather") and preach ("sprinkle") the fact of The Resurrection (ashes/Gospel) because they saw and they believed. – Birth of the Church	The Church	The Man who was "clean" gathers the ashes but is now himself "unclean" and cannot enter "the camp" (Temple) until evening

NOTE 1:

Present, although unseen, throughout this entire drama is the third One of the Holy Trinity, the Holy Spirit. The Holy Spirit is the *only* One of the Trinity who is at all abstract; i.e., at times He has no physical appearance; although, He has appeared to the Children of Israel as a "cloud" and as a "fire" – including as "tongues of flame" at The Pentecost. Nevertheless, even though unseen, He dwells in each of the other Two of the Trinity as well as in each of those who believe. – That's us!

God's Grace and our Faith is delivered to us by the Holy Spirit when we receive the Lord Jesus into our hearts. From that time hence, the Holy Spirit dwells in us. Again, He is still unseen by men who, even if they also believe, cannot discern Him even in our good works. They may think they see Him, but they cannot be sure. This is because, if He truly dwells in us, He dwells in our hearts and cannot be seen by mere mortals. Thus, the Holy Spirit remains invisible to men; although, He is most certainly present just as He is also present in this drama.

NOTE 2:

The women at The Tomb, as well as Peter and John, believed because of what they did *not* see; although, Scripture says, *"they saw and they believed."* (From John 20:8) They "saw" that Jesus was *not* in The Tomb. They knew, therefore, that Jesus had risen, because The Tomb indeed had been sealed shut and was guarded by soldiers. They "*saw*" because of what they did *not* "see"! – And they believed!

NOTE 3:

The High Priest as God, the Supreme One of the Trinity, is the *only* One of the *three* "Players" who appears in all *three* Parts and in all *three* Scenes of the trilogy that we have presented. He is first and He is last and He is always and Forever!

NOTE 4:

Although Scripture does not directly state this, it could be speculated that the Centurion did appear to feel some regret (i.e., represented as "uncleanness") as revealed by his remark at The Cross: *"Truly, this man was the Son of God!"* – He and his men had just put to death a man whom they knew had committed no actual crime. They had seen him thrashed to a pulp by the lash when He had only words of forgiveness for His tormentors. When they drove the ¼ inch diameter spikes through His hands and feet, this man didn't even let out a whimper. Then they saw Him seem to will His own death, as if He were in control – actually giving out a loud shout after hanging on that Cross for six hours. Most men, especially even those stronger and larger than He, would surely have been struggling, writhing in agony, gasping for breath, too weak even to whisper – much less, to give forth with a loud call! – *TETELESTAI!!* – They also were impressed by the other events, including the rending of The Veil at the door of the Temple. All these things may have indicated to the centurion that he had just contributed to the final act of a great tragedy.

WHAT DOES ALL THIS MEAN?

- The Curtain descends at the close of Scene Three (the end of the Church Age).
- At that time, the Cast (those who have been "sprinkled") will be "Called Out" from "backstage" to meet with <u>The Star of the Show</u> at:
- <u>THE GRAND "CURTAIN CALL"</u> that is scheduled for the entire "Cast" to return "at evening" to the "Stage" at *Olivet* Summit where:
- <u>JESUS</u>, the <u>STAR OF THE SHOW</u> ! as <u>THE RED HEIFER</u>, will accept kudos and applause as He takes His place at CENTER STAGE at the summit of the <u>MOUNT OF OLIVES</u> to take His bows, as:

"...they shall see the Son of man coming in the clouds of heaven with power and great glory."

"On that day His feet shall stand on the Mount of Olives..."

"they shall look upon Me Whom they have pierced, and they shall mourn for Him, as one mourneth for his only son,..." ...and

"Every knee shall bow,...every tongue shall confess,..."

YES !...JESUS CHRIST IS LORD!!!

And don't forget! The entire Cast will assemble that Evening for a really great theater party that will blast! for 1000 years! – WOW !!! – Don't miss it! – But, you must be "clean" that "evening."

I know that I shall not have the last word concerning these interpretations that I have offered for this Holy ritual. I do most sincerely invite and urge other Believers to decipher and interpret these verses, as they may receive insight from the Holy Spirit. There may be some additional beauty and meaning that this author has not seen, but which is important to all who believe.

The Red Heifer ceremony *must* have some important meaning for the Jewish people and for the Church. Otherwise, the ritual itself would not have been so vital in Jewish Temple worship and in the Law. Please pray and study to find even more and even deeper meanings for all of us.

Appendix F — Translations from Greek and Aramaic

Compares and explains origin, differences, and authority of Lamsa Aramaic (Peshitta or Syriac) vs. King James Version and so-called "Western Bibles."

Describes history of tragic separation of Church of the East from the West – How it happened? – what were the results?

Explains position of Aramaic as the "language of the people" in Jesus' time.

Numerous times in this work we have referred to the *Lamsa Bible*. (See Reference 8 at close of Chapter 11) Dr. George Mamisjisho Lamsa (1892-1975) was ethnically an Assyrian, and lived in Palestine until World War I. Brought up in the Christian culture in the Church of the East, he became fluent both in speech and in letters with the Aramaic (or *Syriac*) language. Dr. Lamsa devoted the major portion of his life to translation of his native Aramaic into the valued English translation of *The Holy Bible from the Ancient Eastern Text*, also known as the *Lamsa Bible*.

Complaints similar to those leveled by many Christian scholars against *Talmud*, *Midrash* and other Judaica will also be directed against our frequent reference to the *Lamsa Bible* translation. We are well aware that some conservative scholars have strong objection to these sources. Since George M. Lamsa was only a man and, just like the other *men* who have produced Biblical translations of our Scriptures, it is possible that he made some errors. Nevertheless, it is our hope and prayer that critics will refrain from rejecting through prejudice that which can be shown as Truth from Lamsa, *Talmud*, *Midrash*, etc. That is, we hope our critics will observe that well-known caution: *"Please do not throw out the baby with the bath-water!"*

One of the greatest tragedies in the history of Christianity is the division and ignorance that has existed between the Church of the East and that of Western Christianity. Sadly, that division and ignorance continues even today.

There appears to be no single clear event or situation that caused the separation and eventual estrangement between the Church of the East and Western Christianity. Nevertheless, a most significant break occurred around 225 C.E. At that time, some Persian rulers feared that Roman Emperor Constantine's edict of universal Christianity for all his territory constituted a threat to Persian culture and sovereignty. The ensuing merciless Persian persecution of Christians seems to have broken the West away from the East at that time. In addition, there were deep theological rifts contributing to the split, and at a time centuries in advance of Islamic conquest of the region.

Survival of this Aramaic Christian culture has endured, principally because of this isolation, buoyed by their tenacity and fierce, warlike character. Under the circumstances, the survival of that culture might be termed somewhat miraculous. They have survived through rise and fall of several empires through the region, having almost no contact or support from Christians in the West. This isolation is illustrated by the fact that only one bishop and one deacon represented the Church of the East at the Nicene Council, 352 C.E.

After Emperor Constantine I converted to Christianity in 318 C.E., Christians in the Persian Empire were then considered as friends of Emperor Constantine, and therefore as enemies of Persia. Persecution of those Christians began during the 4th century and continued until the arrival of Islam with the Arab invasion of Persia in 632 C.E. <u>*Because of that situation, especially, the Church of the East was prevented from communication and association with Western Christianity.*</u>

It has to be surprising, especially considering the situation in that region at the present time, for Western Christians to learn that the Church of the East today is comprised of Christians in countries such as: Iraq, Syria, Turkey, Pakistan, India, etc., etc. Among the Iraqi Kurds, for example, a significant population of Christians are represented in that society. Obviously, these people undergo heavy persecution as they try to worship and live and work in these predominantly Muslim nations.

Perhaps as an indirect result of those several centuries of separation, our Western theologians have taught traditionally that the New Testament Scriptures were originally transcribed in the Greek language. There seems to be no simple explanation for their motivation toward that belief, other than the idea having been imprinted over all these centuries of TRADITION.

That teaching, however, is not supported by historians of the first few centuries after Christ. Josephus (Antiq. 20.11.2 (263-264), referring to the Greek language, announces: "...for our nation (the Jewish people) does not encourage those that learn the language of many nations,..." Josephus goes on to admit that he experienced great difficulty in speaking Greek because of his native Aramaic accent.

Further disdain for the Greek culture is expressed by the Rabbis in *Talmud – Baba Kama* 82b as they compare learning Greek with breeding swine! – *"Cursed be the man who would breed swine and cursed be the man who would teach his son Grecian wisdom."*

Another rather "spirited" discussion in *Talmud* details the why's and wherefores in uses of languages in Jewish religious writings. The discussion from *Talmud-Megillah* 9a is paraphrased following:

From *Megillah* 9a:

> *Following the view of R. Judah*, it has been taught that: tefillin and mezuzahs are to be written only in Assyrian, but our Rabbis allowed them to be written in Greek, also. I must say therefore, 'Scrolls of the Scripture may be written in any language, and our Rabbis permitted them to be written in Greek.' But, R. Judah said: 'When our teachers permitted Greek, they permitted it **only** for a scroll of the Torah.'* **Thus R. Judah forbade other books of the Scripture to be written, save in the original language.**

*Rabbi Judah ben Ala'i was of the 2nd century, during what is known as the Tannaic period and during which time much of the *Mishnaic Talmud* writings were produced. It seems to be an historical fact that a Greek translation of the Pentateuch (i.e., the aforementioned *Torah* scroll) was made in the time of King Ptolemy Philadelphus of Egypt (285-247 B.C.E.).

A rather convincing statement appears as a footnote in Menahoth 64b, as a part of a discussion about a man who was learned in "Greek wisdom," as follows:

> *"An old man there, who was learned in Greek wisdom, spoke with them in Greek wisdom,..."*

The footnote adds:

> *" 'Greek wisdom', according to Rashi means 'gestures and signs', but most probably it means the Greek language, which was not understood by the people in the city."* (i.e., Jerusalem)

Nevertheless, there is no absolute conclusion in *Talmud* as to whether even *Torah* was written *only* in Aramaic originally. As we study carefully a discussion in *Megillah* 3a, there is some belief among Jewish scholars that there may indeed have been "originals" transcribing both in Aramaic and in Greek at about the same time; although, many historians agree that the *Septuagint* was the first written Scripture and it was completed about the middle of the 3rd century B.C.E. However, it is noteworthy that most scholars are in agreement that the Jewish Scriptures were first only spoken – because at that time it was considered a major sacrilege to transcribe the Word of God.

Reference is made to the 1st century C.E. when a Greek proselyte, Aquilas, made a Greek manuscript (*Targum*) of the Pentateuch under the guidance of Rabbis Eleazar and Joshuah. The narrative further notes that an Aramaic *Targum* of the Prophets' portion of the Holy Scriptures was composed by Jonathan ben Uzziel. Ben Uzziel was a disciple of noted 1st century Rabbinical leader Hillel, who had worked under careful study of works of the prophets: Haggai, Zechariah and Malachi.

Returning from their servitude in Babylon in 520 B.C.E., the Jewish people retained use of the Aramaic (Chaldean) tongue of their masters. It became the language of the people – the "vernacular" for daily life and even in their worship. It is still used by some Jewish scholars today. Both versions of *Talmud* (Babylonian and Jerusalem) as well as the works of Flavius Josephus, were written in Aramaic. A commentary on the book attributed to the prophet Habbakuk, found in a Dead Sea region cave, offers convincing evidence that use of Aramaic in such works has existed at least from the 1st century until the present.

Some respected and impressively credentialed Christian theologians have concluded that the Gospels and the Epistles of the New Testament were written two or three centuries after the time of Christ. That group includes even some who would be considered as adherents to conservative branches of theology. Common sense, however, indicates that those works were completed "on-the-spot" as the events occurred. As discussed in Chapter 23, this fact is evidenced by absence of any mention concerning *three* climactic, historic events of the first century:

- Departure of the Glory of the Lord (Divine Presence; *Shekhinah*) from the Temple in 66 C.E.
- Ascension of *Shekhinah* from the summit of the Mount of Olives, 70 C.E.
- Destruction of the Temple and Jerusalem in 70 C.E.

The writers of the New Testament would not have hesitated to report these *three* events that testified to constitute Divine Judgment against an unbelieving, disobedient and unrepentant Israel. By their very absence from the New Testament, it should be considered obvious that those *three* events occurred *after* the last books of the New Testament were written, with the exception of John's Revelation about 96 C.E.

Lamsa (Harper's) and *The Companion Bible*, compiled by several scholars at the close of the 19th century, both state that the oldest and therefore the most authoritative manuscript of the New Testament is in the Aramaic (or *Syriac*) and is called the *Peshitta*; meaning straight, simple, sincere and true; i.e., "original." Portions of that manuscript, maintained by the Church of the East, are dated as early as 170 C.E. (This is not to be confused with the Eastern Orthodox Church.)

It is truly gratifying and certainly a credit to the dedication of these Believers that they have retained their Scripture version with no alteration or addition through all these centuries until the present day. The preserved integrity of the *Peshitta* is even more impressive considering that the Church of the East consists of about five arguing rival factions. That fact may be viewed in contrast with scores of versions *in many different languages* that have been translated from Greek and Latin. Those texts were made for our Western churches and have undergone constant revisions throughout history and continuing even today. For example, just in the English language during the 20th century there were literally dozens of Biblical translations compiled.

Although some Jewish citizens (possibly even Jesus) spoke some Greek, it was not the "street" language of the day, and certainly it was not the religious language of Palestine. The Israelites wrote their Scriptures only in Hebrew and Aramaic. The *Septuagint* was prepared in the 3rd century B.C.E., but only for the Jewish people in Alexandria, Egypt. The Jews of Palestine didn't read it, principally because most of that population could not read Greek and it was not the "everyday" language of the so-called "working class." Jewish authorities actually condemned the *Septuagint* and even declared a period of mourning against the errors in that text.

Scriptural testimony to Jewish authorities in favor of the *Peshitta* is found in Old Testament quotations from Jesus that match exactly with the same verses in the *Peshitta*; although they do not match the *Septuagint*. An example is a quotation in John 12:40 from

Jesus regarding Isaiah 6:9-10. Compare now the translation from Greek in Verse 10 to be followed by the same verse translated from the Aramaic of the *Peshitta*.

From Greek:

> *"Make the heart of this people fat,*
>
> *And make their ears heavy,*
>
> *And shut their eyes;*
>
> *Lest they, seeing with their eyes,*
>
> *And hearing with their ears,*
>
> *And understanding with their heart,*
>
> *Return and be healed."*

From Aramaic:

> *"For the heart of this people is darkened,*
>
> *And their ears are heavy,*
>
> *And their eyes are closed,*
>
> *So that they may not see with their eyes,*
>
> *And hear with their ears,*
>
> *And understand with their heart,*
>
> *And be converted and forgiven."*

Differences are seen in words, tense and grammar. However, the most significant and vitally important difference exists in the very theme, meaning and emotion intended in this delivery from the prophet. God speaks an entirely different declaration in the Aramaic (original) text.

Jesus and the Disciples perhaps were able to speak the Greek language, but it is unlikely that Jesus taught His Twelve or "the multitudes" in the Greek tongue. The Greek translators and later "modernists" just were not aware of the myriad of subtle nuances in the Aramaic language. Jesus surely was familiar with such speech details and used them constantly. Perhaps of equal importance, the Greek translators were unfamiliar with the several dialects within the Aramaic language. This controversial issue regarding the Aramaic Scriptures may soon be impacted by the recent discovery of the very controversial so-called "James' Ossuary." The ossuary, a stone "box," is engraved with 1st century Aramaic script, stating that it contains the remains of: "James, the son of Joseph and brother of Jesus."

Eminent and distinguished publisher of Biblical Archaeology Review (Pg. 59 – Nov/Dec 2004), Dr. Herschel Shanks, stated that IF the ossuary is found to be authentic, it will demonstrate that as late as the 60's C.E., Christians in Jerusalem continued to adhere to Jewish burial practice. Further, Shanks observes that the Aramaic inscription will show also that Christians were speaking and using the Aramaic language. Dr. Shanks emphasizes that such a validation "is no small matter."

We owe our eternal gratitude and admiration to those scholars who compiled the King James Version. That work has been our "Rock" for Scriptural reference during many centuries and has served as God would order it. Nevertheless, it appears that we have missed some things by our tragic isolation (and even enmity) from our Christian brothers in the Church of the East. Critics have complained about some portions of Lamsa's text. This is to be expected after centuries of traditional "adherence" to the King James Version as the "Authorized" Version.

Although George Lamsa was not Perfect as a man, he has performed a useful and worthy product for our edification in Scripture. Lamsa has pointed to some areas of our traditional text that should be examined. We do not examine the texts to "test" Scripture. Nevertheless, we need to "test" the Truth because both the East and the West have certain theological/doctrinal "interpretations" that influence their texts. Lamsa has provided a way for us of the West to examine what might be termed a "cultural gap" between these two major Christian entities in order to "test" the Truth.

A dramatic example of this cultural gap is seen in the *Peshitta* version of John 3:1-4, in which Nicodemus is puzzled about the expression: *"born again."* In a footnote, Lamsa explains that Nicodemus was a Judean from the local environs of Jerusalem; whereas, Jesus used an idiomatic expression traditionally spoken in His home territory of Galilee. Nicodemus, being from Judah, did not understand that "born again" was an expression that was not to be taken as a literal statement. Lamsa's footnote explains that the meaning of the phrase refers to a change in a person's way of thinking – attitude – lifestyle – i.e., to reform.

Following are a few interesting comparisons between the two references:

<u>Genesis 37:3</u> – Western Bibles tell of Joseph's "coat of many colors." Lamsa's translation reads: "rich robe with long sleeves." The latter would seem a more likely provocation of jealousy and to have been coveted by Joseph's brethren for its practical value on cold nights as they were shepherding their flocks.

<u>Matthew 19:24</u> – Western Gospels quote Jesus saying: "It is easier for a camel to go through the eye of a needle, than for a rich man to enter into the Kingdom of God." Lamsa's Gospel reads: "It is easier for a rope to go through the eye of a needle, . . ." A footnote explains that the Aramaic word (gamla) means "camel," or it also means: "rope." This duplicate meaning probably occurred because, during Biblical times, the hair of camels' tails was used for braiding rope before strands of hemp were used.

It is both amusing and disturbing to note that this flawed "camel parable" has been unknowingly, but innocently promoted by some Bible teachers as a "fable." The story goes that the verse refers to a gate in the wall of The Holy City that was so low that camels would need to "bow" in order to pass through. Then, the message was interpreted to be that a "rich man" must humble himself ("bow") in order to enter The Kingdom. It follows that the traditional message is worthy and by all means acceptable. (And, certainly not restricted to "rich men"!) The irony is that it has been derived through an inaccurate translation of Scripture!

Another Scriptural difference is encountered in the Gospel of Luke 21:11, in which Jesus described the signs of His Return in reply to the query of His followers. The Western texts describe: *"wars and rumors of wars, kingdom against kingdom, earthquakes in diverse places, famines, pestilences, alarming sights, great signs in the heavens."* BUT, then Lamsa's text adds: *"...and the winters will be severe."* – And, we know for certain that Jesus was talking about the winters in Palestine – NOT in Siberia or in Spitzbergen or Minneapolis! In Chapter Six we have presented material regarding importance of this phrase in terms of present day events in Israel.

Nevertheless, Blessed are the scholars who translated our King James Version! They applied their best effort in translating into English from perhaps several cycles of translations from Hebrew, Aramaic, Latin and Greek. Indeed, tracing the origins of these scripts has been and still remains a task that is apparently beyond human attainment. Beloved as the King James ("Authorized") Version has been for centuries to the Christian world of the West, it does hold some apparent translation errors shown by comparison with the *Peshitta*. Some of these errors have precipitated bitter controversy among Christian theologians. The fact that the superior authority of *Peshitta* has not been accepted universally or even by a significant percentage of Christians makes resolution of such controversies tenuous at best.

One outstanding example of such contentious strife is evidenced in comparing *Peshitta* with the Authorized Version in Psalms 22:1, Matthew 27:46 and Mark 15:34. Western Bibles render Psalms 22:1 in the first sentence as:

"My God, My God, why hast thou forsaken Me?..."

Lamsa translates as:

"My God, My God, why hast thou let Me to live?..."

The corresponding verses in Western texts of the Gospels of Matthew and Mark of course repeat verbatim the words from Psalms 22:1. However, the Lamsa translations of Matthew 27:46 and Mark 15:34 actually show Jesus as having been provided with the answer to the troubled question of Psalms 22:1 –

"My God, My God, for this I was spared!"

(i.e., "This was My destiny!")

Our Western translation is from the Greek translation of the original Aramaic text; whereas, Lamsa has translated directly from the Aramaic. Somehow the non-Aramaic translators made a few errors. The authority of the *Peshitta* can be verified in that there can be no contradiction in Scripture. Jesus could not have been "forsaken" by the Father because He would have contradicted Himself. After all, Jesus had said in John 16:32 –

"...and yet I am not alone, because the Father is with Me."

Although several other differences exist between Eastern and Western texts, let it be emphatically stated that NONE of these variations in any way alters the Gospel doctrine of Salvation exclusively available through Messiah, Jesus of Nazareth.

The debate concerning whether "superior authority" of Scripture belongs to the Aramaic or the Greek manuscripts has been long, bitter and arduous. Certainly, it has engaged many sincere and highly qualified scholars. Readers must be left to reach their own conclusions after evaluating the material presented here and elsewhere, as they are guided by the Holy Spirit. It is likely that most readers of this book will have learned here of even the existence of the *Peshitta* for the very first time.

Common sense, as well as remarks from Josephus, would seem to indicate that Judeans from Galilee would have conversed and written "in the language of the people," which certainly was Aramaic and not Greek. It is entirely likely, however, that by the time of the canonization of the Scriptures: O.T. (4th century B.C.E.) and N.T. (3rd century C.E.), most if not all 66 books of Western texts had been transcribed in Greek. It should be emphatically remembered also that no punctuation existed in any written language until the 9th century C.E.– and even then, in Latin only.

Practical common sense also would indicate that Paul had preached to the Greeks of Thessalonica, Athens, Corinth, and the other Greek cities in their own language. Having been raised in the community of Tarsus, especially, Paul would be expected to have been bilingual and even fluent both in Greek and in Aramaic. This expectation derives from the fact that Tarsus was located at the point where Mediterranean nations adjoined nations of Asia Minor. Both the Greek and the Aramaic cultures coexisted in that region during several centuries. Some evidence of that characteristic exists in the region today.

A "practical" summary as to the languages of "original" Scriptural manuscripts, aside from traditional theological and denominational influences, is therefore proposed as follows:

- Old Testament: Aramaic (Also known as *Chaldee* or *Syriac*)
- New Testament Gospels: Aramaic
- New Testament Pauline Epistles: Greek
- New Testament Remaining Epistles and Books: Uncertain, but Aramaic or Greek

In the main body of this book we have made the case that the New Testament had been written before the Jewish Rebellion of 66 C.E. on basis of there being no mention of *three* major Biblical Events that occurred after that date. Specifically, these were:

- 66 C.E. – Withdrawal of Israel's *Shekhinah* (Divine Presence) from the Temple
- 70 C.E. – Ascension of *Shekhinah* from the Mount of Olives summit.
- 70 C.E. – Destruction of the Holy Temple and Jerusalem

Many mainline Christian theologians, and even some conservative theologians, insist that the first New Testament Scriptures were written in about the 2nd or 3rd century C.E. However, merely by applying common sense, we find it extremely doubtful that, if they had been writing *after* those events occurred, the writers of the N.T. would have neglected to point out, to their Pharisaic persecutors especially, that ALL *three* Events were in fact prophesied and ordained by Almighty God. It is plainly inconceivable that these stalwarts and martyrs would have failed to confront their Jewish adversaries to announce to ALL within hearing that these *three* Events were Holy Judgments against Israel for having rejected Messiah, Son of David, when they had His Visitation. There can be no sensible rationale for such an omission, if these things had happened before their writings. We remain confident that our refuting of the "traditional" claim of 2nd or 3rd century New Testament writings stands the test of common sense.

Lamsa's Bible along with his claim for Aramaic origin in Scripture are not without critics. There is great resistance and/or ignorance throughout both Protestantism and Roman Catholicism concerning Lamsa's translation. This resistance appears in a large part because Western theology and teaching has for so long been deeply rooted in the King James Version – often named: "The Authorized Version." This recognition has been consistently firm among Protestant Evangelical theologians, having a solid reputation for conservatism toward their traditional doctrine and teaching. These are not easily steered from Tradition to Truth. In fact, most elect not even to hear anything unless they have heard it before! It is interesting to note that Lamsa further departs from "tradition" in that he joins those other scholars who believe that Paul was the writer of the Book of Hebrews.

Let it be said that there is no dogmatic conclusion for this question. Furthermore, it is indeed certain that Conservative/Evangelical/Traditionalist acceptance of Lamsa's work is not going to arrive any time soon. Nevertheless, Lamsa offers many new insights to Scripture that, although they differ from Western "traditional" teaching, do deserve evaluation and consideration. We have demonstrated that some of Lamsa's text produces profound and edifying impact on our concepts of Scriptural knowledge and, with no alteration or compromise of that simplest, but most effective Gospel message. Witness this in Lamsa's version of John 3:16 –

"For God so loved the world that he even gave his only begotten Son, so that whoever believes in him should not perish, but have eternal life."

Appendix G – Temple Site

Detailed discussion pointing out multiple, irrefutable flaws in claims that the Holy Temple was located at the present site of The Dome of the Rock.

Demonstrates vital importance of the Law of the Red Heifer in such analyses. Convincing evidence from Mt. of Olives contours.

Details concerning Temple articles, cubit lengths, archaeological finds and "threshingfloor" function bring emphatic evidence to force an obvious conclusion on this question.

Various scholars have challenged Asher Kaufman's conclusion that the Holy of Holies was located at the present position on the Temple Mount identified as the Dome of the Tablets, about 100 meters northwest of the traditional position at the Dome of the Rock. Despite the "mountain" of evidence that overwhelmingly convinces in favor of Kaufman's analysis, two respected scholars, Dr. Leen Ritmeyer and Dr. David Jacobson, – identified as "Central Theorists" – have insisted that the traditional site is correct. However, each of these supports a slightly different conclusion as to the exact position of the *Shethiyah*; i.e., the Foundation Stone where the Holy Ark rested in Solomon's Temple.

We endeavor to demonstrate why neither Ritmeyer's nor Jacobson's conclusion is valid, based upon the Law of the Red Heifer as well as a few other factors. We are submitting several items of data that indicate positively toward accepting Asher Kaufman's proposed site at the Dome of the Tablets. Still, we can present no concrete *proof* that Prof. Kaufman's conclusion is correct. – Nevertheless, we remain confident that the evidence we are presenting shows that surely the Dome of the Rock *cannot* be the correct site.

- The most obvious and the most disqualifying defect in Central Theorist proposals is lack of compliance with rituals in the *Talmudic* Law of the Red Heifer ceremony. Major contributions to their errors are incurred through their choices of cubit measurements that far exceed Jewish historians' descriptions of that unit of length. It will be shown that the accuracy of the cubit measurement is vitally critical to this analysis.

- Principal among these objections within The Law is the *kohen's* (priest's) inability to view the doors of the *H'ekhal* from the point on the Mount of Olives where Ritmeyer's and Jacobson's analyses would position the *Miphkad* Altar. That is the point where the priest *must* stand in order to view the Temple Veil *as he sprinkles the heifer's blood "directly toward the Tabernacle."* Ritmeyer's analysis, as well as that of Jacobson or Joshua Schwartz* position the *kohen*, as he stands behind the *Miphkad* Altar, actually on the reverse (eastern) slope of the Mount of Olives! We present details of terrain contours to illustrate this problem in Illus. 26: Temple Mt., Contoured Mt. of Olives, Page 324. Again, this feature alone is the most serious failing in Central Theorist proposals reviewed to date. (*See Reference List at conclusion of Appendix.)

- Ritmeyer's entire thesis is founded upon a "Royal" cubit dimension = 20.67 in. = 52.5 cm. There is no foundation for use of a Royal cubit, of more than seven handbreadths in length, in any Jewish Temple construction. Many other cultures existing throughout ancient history had what were termed as "Royal cubits" – having greatly diverse lengths. The cubit of Arye ben David at 22.08 in = 56.08 cm., has been mentioned by certain scholars, and is in fact nearly *eight* handbreadths in length! *Talmud* specifies that Solomon's Temple was based upon the "Standard" Moses' cubit = six handbreadths and the Second Temple was built with a slightly (1/2 "fingerbreadth") longer cubit. This was done in order to reduce possibility that a Temple contractor might even unintentionally fabricate a piece that would be short. – A sort of tolerance "pad" – if you will – in order that he would avoid an "offence" against The House through *"liability to a trespass offering."* (*Pesachim* 86a) (See Glossary: Cubit)

- Jacobson stated that he used a cubit length = 0.465 meters, and which he says is "about 18 inches." Actually, it is 18.307 in. Considering the critical effects of the cubit dimension in these analyses, *"about"* is a poor choice of words in Dr. Jacobson's statement. It is apparent that his analysis did not consider the Sabbath Limit distance to the *kohen's* station. The cubit length at that distance of almost 2000 cubits is obviously critical. This is especially important regarding the impact of *Olivet* contours in these analyses.

- The *Miphkad* Altar was located at the spot on the Mount of Olives where ALL of the burnt offerings as well as ALL of the ashes and scorched remains, etc. from the sacrifices at the Temple Altar were *"poured out."* These ashes were to *"naturally pour down"* toward the Temple. Whereas, from evidence of Ritmeyer's and Jacobson's positions on that same map for the *kohen* and the *Miphkad* Altar, the ashes would most certainly not *"naturally pour down"* toward the Temple. In fact, they would just stream downhill in an indiscriminate direction, if anything – southeastwardly and *away* from the Temple! (Ref. Ex. 29:14, Lev. 4:11 – 12, 16:27 – *Yoma* 68 and *Zebahim* 105b)

- *Middoth* 2:3 states that all Temple steps were half a cubit in height. Using Ritmeyer's Royal cubit would result in Temple steps being 10 to 11 in. high. Anthropological data as well as archaeological evidence shows that, typically, Jewish men of the 1st century were very short in stature. There were no railings or banisters on the steps leading up to the Temple. Steps of such a height then certainly would have been difficult for short Judean legs to climb, especially without the support of a rail or banister. Even six-footers of today would find such stairs an "exerting" challenge.

- *Yoma* 5:4 states that the *Shethiyah* (Foundation Stone upon which the Holy Ark rested) was a projection extending three fingers *above* ground. – The spot that Ritmeyer proposes is actually a rectangular *depression* in the rock at *es-Sakhra*, purportedly the same size as the Holy Ark (using Royal cubit size), and having been cut several centimeters deep into the rock. That rectangular depression must therefore be rejected as the *Shethiyah*.

- One of the most convincing archaeological features of the Temple Mount that supports Kaufman's proposal, while simultaneously and equally convincingly negating the claims for the Dome of the Rock, is what must be considered the obvious near proximity of the Fortress of Antonia. Surviving ruins of that structure are supported by most scholars as an "authenticated" site. The tower nearest the Temple courts was the southeast tower, about 150 meters north of the Dome of the Tablets. (See Contoured Map – Illus. 26: Temple Mt., Contoured Mt. of Olives, Page 324.)

- That tower, according to Josephus, *Wars* 5.5.8/242 – 244, *was erected adjacent to the north wall of the Temple* and was much taller (70 cubits vs. 50 cubits) than the other three towers. In this way, the activities of Jews in the Tempe courts below could be monitored for formation of plots for mischief and rebellions, just by noting "who" was talking to "whom," "when," etc.

- The distance to the Dome of the Rock from an estimated location of the Antonia SE tower is about 250 meters. This could hardly be considered *"adjacent to the north wall of the Temple."* Compare this distance with the estimated 150 meters to the Dome of the Tablets from that tower.

- Moreover, it is obvious that a sentry, from a parapet of that SE tower, would not be able to observe much of anything in the Temple courts from a distance of 250 meters – or, certainly much less than could be seen in the courts of Kaufman's Temple site at 150 meters.

- *Menahoth* 98a states that the Ark was oriented with the longer axis extending parallel to the Temple width; i.e., north - south. The rectangular depression proposed by Ritmeyer is oriented with the long axis parallel to the Temple length, east – west. Ritmeyer attempts to rationalize that orientation, saying of the "staves" (or "poles") that were used by the bearers to carry the Holy Ark: *"The only way to remove the staves was by keeping the short side facing the partition that separated the Holy of Holies from the Holy Place."*. Exodus 25:15 as well as *Talmud Yoma* 72a and *Makkoth* 22a confirm that the staves were *permanently* installed through the support rings and were *never* to be removed.

- Further, diagrams are provided (Illus. 48: Appendix G – Comparison of Ark Orientations and Illus. 49: Appendix G – Diagram of Ark and Staves, Pages 597 and 598.) to demonstrate it would be "profane" to face the Ark as Ritmeyer proposes. This is because the cherubim were at the ends of the Ark. Ritmeyer's arrangement would have one of the cherubim *standing in front of the Lord's Presence!* – Never! – Again, on basis of historical records of Temple details, the rectangular depression does not qualify as the *Shethiyah*.

Appendix G — Temple Site

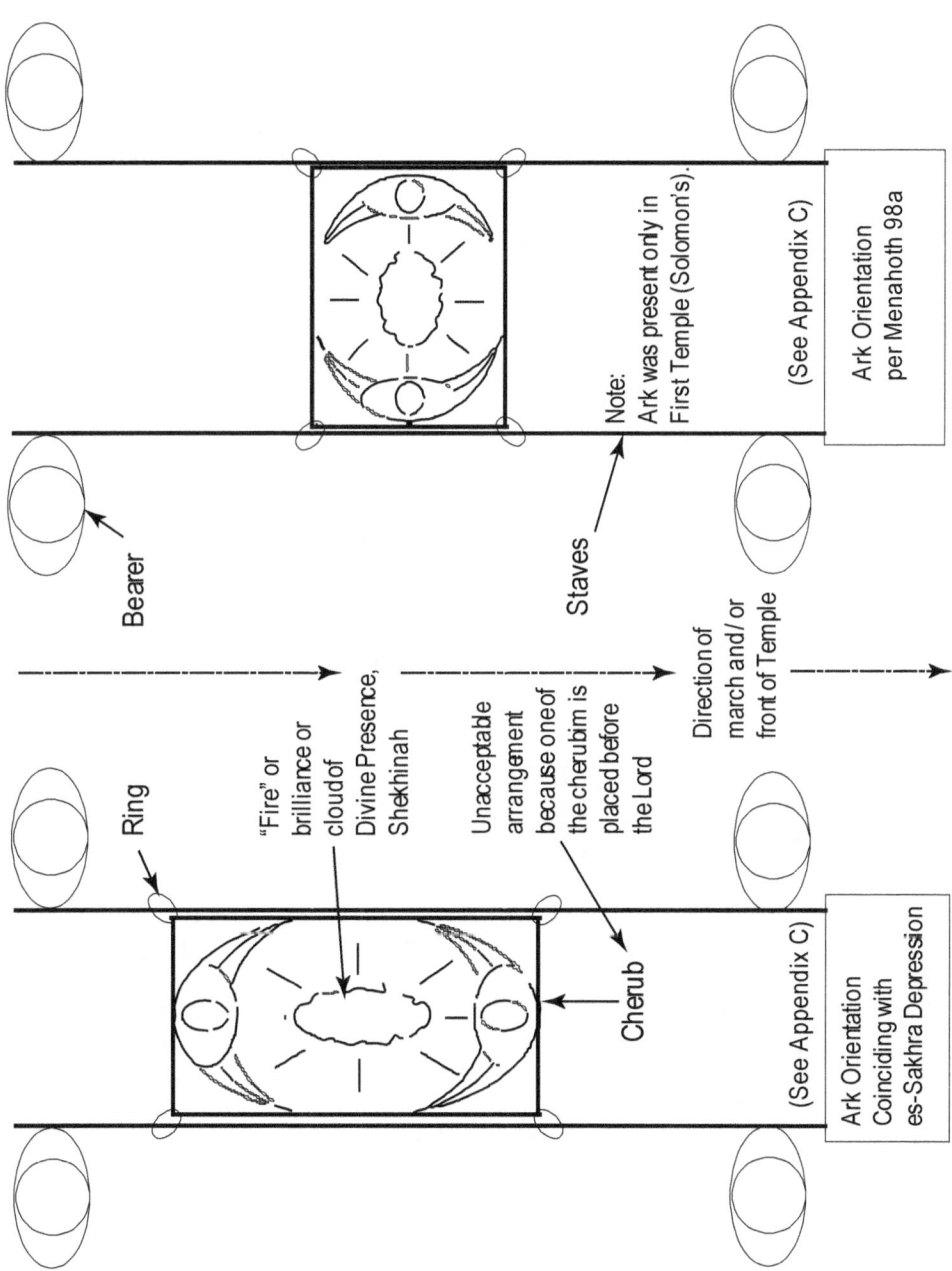

Illus. 48: Appendix G — Comparison of Ark Orientations

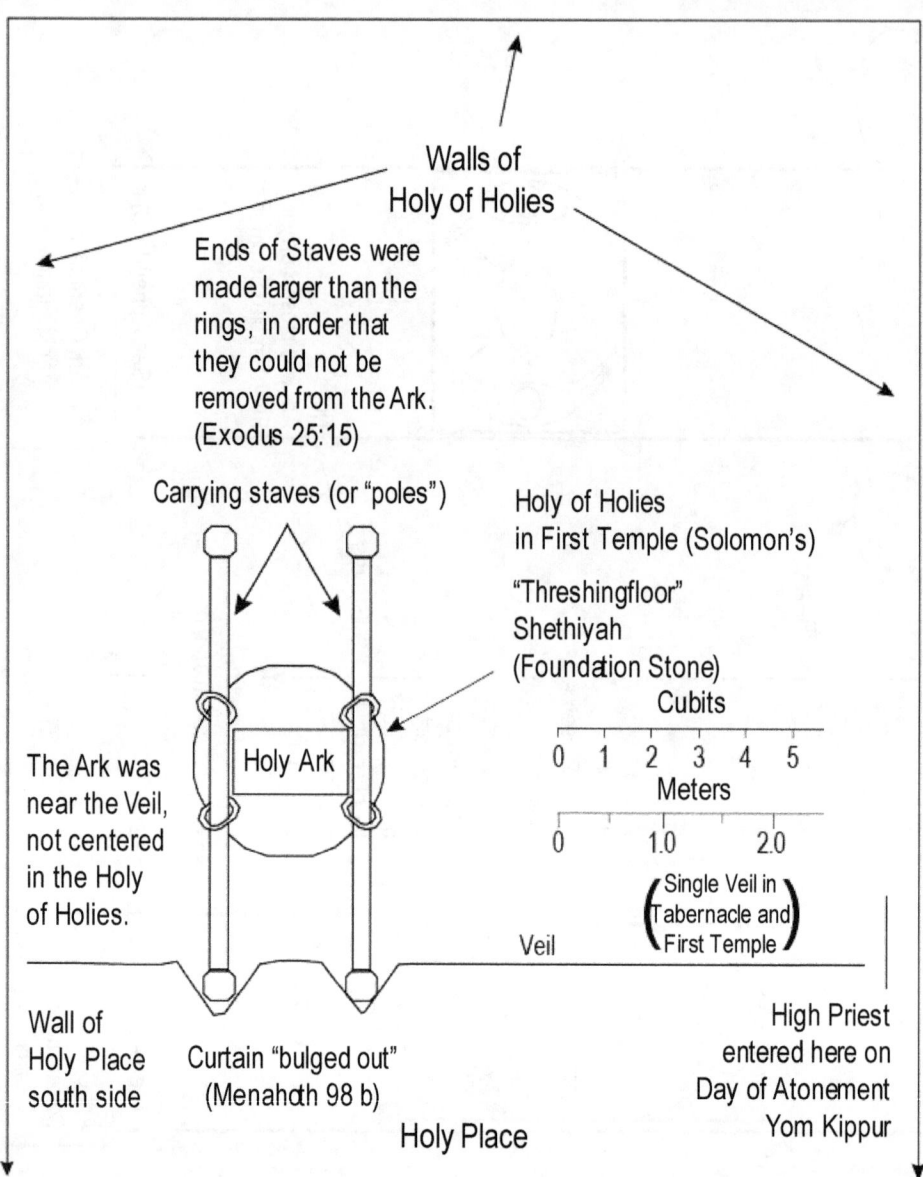

Illus. 49: Appendix G – Diagram of Ark and Staves

- The seismic fault of Zechariah 14:4 extends along "the right side of the House" (Ezekiel 47:1). Today that fault runs straight through The Dome of the Rock! The "House" therefore *must* be farther to the "left" of the fault (north); which is where Kaufman's Temple site is located. The fault line and subsequent earthquakes at Kaufman's locale will in fact *"cleave"* along *"the right side of the House."* Whereas, the Central Theorist Temple site, being right on the fault line, is going to become river-bottom "on that day."

- II Chronicles 3:1 states that the Temple was built by King Solomon on the *threshingfloor* that his father, King David, had purchased from Araunah, the Jebusite. *Es-Sakhra* could not qualify as a "threshingfloor." There is hardly a spot at any point on *es-Sakhra* that could qualify as a "threshingfloor." Even more to-the-point, we stated earlier that Ritmeyer's proposed *Shethiyah* is actually a *depression* of several centimeters deep into the Rock. It would be useless as a "threshingfloor" because the chaff, hulls and straw drop down into the depressed area and would not be able to be blown or swept off to reveal the grain. Whereas, the flat rock beneath The Dome of the Tablets is a Perfect threshingfloor. That is why David purchased it for the Holy Ark to rest upon. (II Samuel 24:24)

- A report from a study of the Temple Mount by J.E. Hanauer reports having made examinations of *"more than forty rock levels"* on the Temple Mount. Hanauer states that these have *"proved"* that the rock surface north of the Dome of the Rock was a *"naturally and fairly level rock floor."* He adds that it *"would be admirably suited"* as an oriental threshingfloor – such as was owned by Araunah, the Jebusite – later selling it to David.

- Dr. Ritmeyer says his proposed *Shethiyah* at *es-Sakhra* was "prepared" and leveled to a flat, smooth surface. The "threshingfloor" that Araunah, the Jebusite, sold to King David did not need to be "prepared." (II Samuel 24:24 and II Chronicles 3:1) It was already smooth and flat and level – like a "threshingfloor," having been "prepared" by The Creator at The Creation of course. Nevertheless, Ritmeyer did observe accurately that the proposed rectangular spot had been "quarried" for souvenirs, etc. by Crusaders and other visitors. Also, there can be no doubt that the depression itself was originally "prepared" by chiseling; i.e., "cutting" several centimeters down into the rock. Cutting that deep into such a rock almost unquestionably would have been accomplished using iron implements.

Middoth 3:4 states a stern warning that if iron tools even so much as *touch* a Temple stone, it is "disqualified!" We can be confident that there were no Jewish authorities present to make certain that no iron implements were used during the "quarrying" by Crusaders, early Christian pilgrims, etc. Moreover, if that were the correct location, it is certain that God would *never* have permitted any "preparing" or "quarrying!" of His place with iron tools -- thereby defiling His Holy House that He will again occupy -- "in that day!" The quarried rectangular depression at *es-Sakhra,* and indeed the entirety of The Dome of the Rock, is therefore definitely "disqualified" and could *never* have been the site of the Holy Temple because of the reasons stated.

So far, not *one* of Kaufman's opponents has so much as even mentioned the miraculous discovery of Dr. James Fleming's "Lower Arch." The presence of a more ancient arch and gate directly beneath the present "Golden Gate" indicates a powerful "clue" that the earlier gate was in fact the East Gate to The City. Mentioned earlier, it is even *much* lower than the present gate and therefore even much less of a block to the *kohen's* line-of-sight to the door of the *H'ekhal*. Fleming's Lower Arch indicates the Dome of the Tablets as the Temple site with much the same credibility as would a hunter's prey be revealed by a faithful and reliable bird dog!

Summary Critique of "Central Location Theorists" Proposals

1. Analyses of Asher Kaufman's opponents are based on cubits of seven – or even eight -- handbreadths, contradicting *Kelim* 17:9 and correct translation of Ezekiel 40:5 from the Aramaic *Peshitta*, resulting in approx. 16% – 17% errors.

2. Altar cubit was 5 handbreadths – not 6 handbreadths – resulting in 54% error for Altar calculations from at least one of Kaufman's opponents.

3. The "Royal" cubit results in Temple steps, at ½ cubit being over 10 in. high, or ½ of the Arye ben David cubit would have steps 11 in. high. It would have been certainly difficult for short Hebrew legs of 1st century Judean men to climb such steps, especially without support from railings or banisters – which were non-existent at the Temple.

4. The "rock" under the Dome of the Rock is several feet higher than ground level on the Temple Mount platform. With that rock as the Foundation Stone for the Ark of the Covenant, most of Ritmeyer's Temple would have been above present ground level. *Talmud* Rabbis confirm that the entire Sanctuary was built at the level of the Foundation Stone.

5. All proposals of Kaufman's opponents, thus far reviewed, have completely ignored Dr. James Fleming's discovery of a "Lower Arch" of a much earlier City Wall, and which is directly in line with Kaufman's proposed Temple site, – "*Pointing*" to it, as it were.

6. Ritmeyer claims Dome of the Tablets is above a "pavement slab." Kaufman quotes Israeli sources, who verify it is in fact bedrock.

7. Importance of compatibility with topographical requirements for the priest's view of the Temple doors as he sprinkles the blood of the Heifer cannot be over emphasized. Central Theorists' proposals therefore impose gross error because, using much longer cubits at a distance of almost 2000 cubits from the Temple, the priest actually would stand on the rear (eastern) slope of the Mount of Olives! – The priest cannot even *see* the Temple Mount from such a vantage.

8. Ashes and remains "*poured out*" from the *Miphkad* Altar, as proposed for the Central Theorists, would not "*naturally pour down*" toward the Temple. Rather,

from those locations, the ashes would "pour down" actually *away* from the Temple. Whereas, from Kaufman's position, the ashes in fact would pour *directly* toward the Temple. – (See Illus. 26: Temple Mt., Contoured Mt. of Olives, Page 324.)

9. *Yoma* 5:4 states that the *Shethiyah* (Foundation Stone for the Holy Ark) extended three fingers *above* ground. – Ritmeyer's proposed location is actually a *depression* several centimeters deep into the rock surface.

10. *Menahoth* 98a states that the Ark was oriented with the longer axis extending parallel to the Temple width. – Ritmeyer's proposed long axis is instead parallel to Temple length. Besides this contradiction of *Talmudic* historical record, other reasons have been presented to refute such an orientation for the Holy Ark in the Temple. (See Diagrams – Illus. 48: Appendix G – Comparison of Ark Orientations andIllus. 49: Appendix G – Diagram of Ark and Staves, Pages 597 and 598.)

11. Ritmeyer disputes Kaufman's "*trapezium*" shape at the rear of the Temple. *Middoth* 4:7 confirms the H'ekhal was "narrow behind and broad in front."

12. The seismic fault of Zechariah 14:4 extends along "*the right side of the House*" (Ezekiel 47:1). Today that fault runs right through The Dome of the Rock! The "House" is therefore farther to the "left" (North); whereas, Ritmeyer's Temple is going to be river bottom "on that day."

13. It follows from Centralists' proposals, the fault goes through the Jewish Cemetery. Since the 5th century B.C.E., and even to this day, Jewish people continue to trust God's Promise in Zechariah 14:4 that Messiah will arrive at that point. It is doubtful that 5th century B.C.E. Jews would have placed their cemetery as it is presently; i.e., in line with "the right side" of proposed Central Theorists' Holy House, to be "*cleaved*" by the earthquake to come "on that day." Logically and sensibly, therefore, the cemetery was placed at a safe distance south of "*the right side of the House.*"

14. *Es-Sakhra* does not in any way resemble a "*threshingfloor;*" whereas, the rock beneath The Dome of the Tablets is a Perfect threshingfloor, which David purchased it for the Holy Ark to rest upon. (II Samuel 24:24)

15. Ritmeyer says the *Shethiyah* was "prepared" and leveled to a flat, smooth surface. The "threshingfloor" that Araunah, the Jebusite, sold to King David did not need to be "prepared." It was already smooth and flat and level – like a "threshingfloor."

16. Ritmeyer states that the proposed rectangular spot had been "*quarried*." The Law states that if iron tools so much as *touch* a Temple stone, it is "disqualified!"

17. The "*Lower Arch*," discovered by Dr. James Fleming, is directly east of the Dome of the Tablets. Presence of the earlier City Gate at that point lends excellent

credibility to the Dome of the Tablets as the verified Temple site – *"pointing"* to it like a faithful and reliable "Bird Dog!"

18. Josephus wrote that the southeast tower of the Fortress of Antonia was *"adjacent to the north wall of the Temple."* This presently authenticated location is much nearer a court that would have been north of the Dome of the Tablets, than for such a court to have been north of the Dome of the Rock. It is obvious, considering the function of the SE tower for surveillance of the courts, that the courts for a Temple at *es-Sakhra* would have been far too distant for effective surveillance.

SEE ALSO:

- "Where the Ancient Temple of Jerusalem Stood" – Kaufman, Professor Asher S. – Biblical Archaeology Review, Biblical Archaeology Society, 4710 41st Street NW, Washington DC 20016 – March/April 1983

- "Locating the Original Temple Mount" – Ritmeyer, Dr. Leen – Biblical Archaeology Review, Biblical Archaeology Society, 4710 41st Street NW, Washington DC 20016 – March/April 1992

- "The Ark of the Covenant: Where it Stood in Solomon's Temple" – Ritmeyer, Dr. Leen – Biblical Archaeology Review, Biblical Archaeology Society, 4710 41st Street NW, Washington DC 20016 – January/February 1996

- "Sacred Geometry – Unlocking the Secret of the Temple Mount – Part 1" – Jacobson, Dr. David, Biblical Archaeology Review, Biblical Archaeology Society, 4710 41st Street NW, Washington DC 20016 – July/August 1999

- "Sacred Geometry – Unlocking the Secret of the Temple Mount – Part 2" – Jacobson, Dr. David, Biblical Archaeology Review, Biblical Archaeology Society, 4710 41st Street NW, Washington DC 20016 – September/October 1999

- *The Temple Mount – Where is The Holy of Holies?* – Kaufman, Professor Asher S. – Har Ye'ra'eh Press – Jerusalem – Distributed by Rubin Mass, Ltd. – P.O. Box 91009 – Jerusalem 91009 Israel – 2004

- Book Review of: *The Temple Mount – Where is The Holy of Holies?* – Schwartz, Professor Joshua – Biblical Archaeology Review, Biblical Archaeology Society, 4710 41st Street NW, Washington DC 20016 – September/October 2005

- *Walks In and Around Jerusalem* – J.E. Hanauer – 1926 2nd Revised Ed., pp. 260 (Facsimile) – Ariel Publishing House, Jerusalem 1981

Glossary

— A —

Aboth

Sayings of the fathers. Title of *Talmud* tractate. (Hebrew)

Adar

Twelfth month of Jewish religious calendar, sixth month of the civil year. Feast of *Purim* on 14th day. (Hebrew)

Afikoman

Festive procession – Larger piece from *matzah* wafer broken and hidden away, later to be found and eaten as a sort of *Seder* "dessert." (Greek)

Apochrypha

Group of fourteen books that were not accepted by the Canonical Council, considered doubtful in authenticity. (From the Greek *Apokryphos*: Hidden, unknown, spurious)

Aramaic

Ancient and still functional language, principally in Asia Minor and sometimes called "*Syriac*." Aramaic is presently in use by the Maronites and other scattered remnants of Eastern Christians in regions of Azerbaijan, Cyprus, Egypt, Iran, Lebanon, Syria, Iraq and Turkey. Many scholars believe this to have been the language of everyday usage among the common people of Judea (Palestine) during the time of Jesus.

Av

Fifth month of Jewish religious calendar, eleventh month of the civil year. – Both the First Temple and the Second Temple were destroyed on the ninth day of the eleventh month of the civil year. That mournful observance is called *Tisha B'Av*. (Hebrew)

Azarah

Easternmost outer court of the Temple. Also called "The Court of the Women" – beyond which only "clean" Jewish men were permitted to advance. (Hebrew)

Azazel

The rare Hebrew noun, meaning: "dismissal" or "entire removal." The name is assigned to the he-goat that is released "to the wilderness" on *Yom Kippur*; whereas, the other he-goat "For the Lord" is the one that is slain to atone for Israel's sins. (Pronounced: Az-ah-zale`)

— B —

Baba Bathra

The Last Gate. Title of *Talmud* Tractate. (Hebrew)

Bath Kol

Literally, "the daughter of a voice;" i.e., a feminine voice. (See Appendix B and/ or Reference 13, pp. 51) This was a female voice, having been described in ancient Jewish writings as "the Divine voice" such as spoke to Moses and the children of Israel. This voice spoke from "a pillar of fire and a pillar of cloud" and during many later times as reported in Jewish writings, including the departure of Israel's *Shekhinah*, as has been described in this work. (Hebrew – Pronounced: BAT-COAL)

Beinonim

Those in the middle. Term used to describe persons who are neither wholly righteous nor wholly wicked; i.e., the "intermediate." (See *Tshuvah* and *Yamim Nora'im*.) (Hebrew)

Berakoth

Benedictions. – Title of *Talmud* tractate. (Hebrew)

Bezah

Egg. – Rules for preparing food for festivals. Title of *Talmud* tractate. (Hebrew)

— C —

Centurion

Roman officer commanding unit of one-hundred soldiers.

Chagigah

Festal Offering – Title of *Talmud* tractate. (Hebrew) (Pronounced: *Kha'gig-ah or Kha-gig'-ah*)

Chanukah (or Hanukkah)

Dedication, for the Feast of Dedication or Festival of Lights, in commemoration of the miraculous burning of the *Menorah* candlesticks for eight days after the oil had been depleted. This miracle occurred during the rededication of the Temple, 167 B.C.E., after it had been desecrated by Antiochus IV Epiphanes. (Hebrew)

Cherubim

Angelic beings. (Hebrew)

Cheshvan (or Heshvan)

Eighth month of Jewish religious calendar, second month of the civil year. (Hebrew)

Chukkah

(Pronounced: *Khuk'ah*) – A Divine ordinance or commandment, that will not be understood by man until he enters the World to come. (Hebrew)

Chutzpah

(Pronounced *khutz'pah*) Expression describing traits of a person as: effrontery, impudence, audacity, boldness, presumption, brass, cheek. (Slang: "gall," "nerve," "crust.") (Yiddish)

City

The City is the City of Jerusalem, the Holy City.

Cohain or Cohen

(See Kohen)

Coup de Grace

Literally: a blow of mercy. – A final blow, a finishing, decisive stroke. (French)

Cubit

Talmud specifies that Holy precincts of Solomon's Temple were based upon the "Standard" Moses' cubit = six handbreadths and the Second Temple was built with a slightly (1/2 "fingerbreadth") longer cubit. *Pesahim* 86a and *Menahoth* 98a explain that, although the cubit was specified longer; contractors' bids were based upon the shorter Moses' cubit. In that way, if the contractor should unintentionally make an "error," he would avoid the "trespass" or "sacrilege" of having "benefited" or "profited" through his privilege of building the Temple.

— E —

Eastern Gate

Gate to the Court of the Temple Sanctuary, or "Nicanor's Gate" (Illus. 15: Plan of Second Temple (by Dr. A.S. Kaufman), Illus. 16: Isometric View of 2nd Temple and Illus. 21: Detail of the 2nd Temple, Pages 148, 149 and 154); Not to be confused with the East Gate in the City wall.

Elul

Sixth month of Jewish religious calendar, twelfth month of the civil year. (Hebrew)

Ephod

A binding or sash. – A sacred vestment worn originally by the High Priest (Exodus 28:4) afterwards by the ordinary priest (I Sam 22:18) and characteristic of his office. (I Samuel 2:18,28 14:3) It was made of fine linen, and featured clasps or buckles of gold or precious stones, and was fastened round the waist by a "curious girdle of gold, blue, purple, and fine twined linen." (Exodus 28:6-12 The breastplate, with the twelve jewels (*Urim and Thummim*), was attached to the *Ephod*. (Hebrew)

Eretz Israel

The Land of Israel. (Hebrew)

Erub – (or Eruv)

Mixture. – A quantity of food, enough for two meals, placed on the day preceding the Sabbath within 2000 cubits from an intended Sabbath day destination. This is done in order to keep the Law limiting travel – i.e., "work" – to within one Sabbath Limit from one's "personal domain." (Hebrew)

Erubin (or Eruvin)

Mingling. *Talmud* tractate. Regulations interpreted from the Law permitting movement beyond normal limits. (Hebrew)

— F —

Fingerbreadth

This was the measurement that contributed to Jewish dimensions in the shorter categories. It was based upon the width of a man's middle finger and was especially important in makeup of certain cubit lengths. (See Cubit)

— G —

Gemara

A completion or learning. A discussion and/or debate of interpretations of the Law and traditions of Judaism. Sometimes following and elaborating on items from a *Mishnah* preceding. An example of scholarly notation form is *Yoma* 32a, denoting the 32nd portion of the *Gemara* in *Yoma* tractate. (Hebrew)

Golgotha

Skull and/or Place of the Skull. Jerusalemites' local jargon for the place that became the locale of The Crucifixion. (Aramaic)

— H —

Haftorah

Conclusion – Portion of Scripture from the Prophets to be read on Sabbaths and Feast Days, corresponding to the portion read from the *Torah* on those same occasions in synagogues. (See *Sedrah*) (From the Hebrew: *haphtarah*)

Haggadah

Narrative or story. – Order of ritual or liturgy (instructions) for Passover meal (*Seder*). Plural: *Haggadoth*. (Hebrew)

Hallah

Dough, in particular, referring to the portion of dough that was given to the Temple priests. *Talmud* tractate. (Hebrew)

Ham

Noah's youngest son, considered to be the ancestor of African peoples.

Hametz

Leaven, fermentation – Any product containing even a slight amount of fermented material, thereby being symbolic of sin. Must be removed from Jewish households in preparation for the Passover. (Hebrew)

Hamantaschen

"Haman's Pockets" – Triangular-shaped cakes filled with fruits and eaten during *Purim*, to commemorate and celebrate the demise of the villainous Persian Chief Minister, Haman. This Biblical villain filled his pockets with the Jews' money and is believed to have worn a three-cornered hat as symbolic of his office. (*Yiddish*)

Hannuth

Talmud defines this only as "a place on the Temple Mount" presumably the location of the "trade halls" (moneychangers," etc.) - See *Shabbath* 15a.

H'ekhal

Literally, "Ark" – The main building of the Temple, the Sanctuary, comprised principally of the Holy Place and the Holy of Holies. Earthly dwelling place of the Divine Presence or *Shekhinah* Glory of Almighty God the Father, "I AM". (Hebrew)

Heshvan

(See Cheshvan)

Hoshana Rabba

Last day of *Sukkoth*.

Hosheannah (or Hosanna)

Please deliver us. (Or, save us.) (Aramaic)

Hukkah

A law or statute that is not to be questioned. A Divine ordinance or commandment that will not be understood by man until he enters the world to come. (Hebrew)

Hullin

Profane (unhallowed) – Laws relating to slaughtering consecrated animals. – Title of *Talmud* tractate. (Hebrew)'

— I —

Islam

Religion of followers of the prophet, Mohammed. (Muslims)

Iyar

Second month of Jewish religious calendar, eighth month of the civil year. (Hebrew)

— J —

Japheth

Second son of Noah, ancestor of European peoples.

Josephus, Flavius

Jewish historian, most respected and renowned of all historians of the first century.

— K —

Kalal

Ritually pure urn that contains the ashes of the Red Heifer.

Katepetasmah

That which spreads outward and downward. New Testament word for the Veil of the Temple. (Greek)

Kelim

Vessels, utensils. Title of *Talmud* Tractate. (Hebrew)

Kerithoth

Cutting off. *Talmud* tractate dealing with violations of the Levitical Laws requiring that one "*shall be cut off from his people.*" (Hebrew)

Kethuboth

Written. Specifically dealing with the sum that is due a wife when she is divorced. Title of *Talmud* tractate. (Hebrew)

Kibbutzim

Gatherings – Israeli cooperative farm communities. (Hebrew)

Kiddushin

Consecrations – *Talmud* tractate dealing principally with the ritual, process, traditions and laws of betrothal, marriage, servants, etc. (Hebrew)

Kingdom Age

(See " Millennial.")

Kislev

Ninth month of Jewish religious calendar. Includes *Chanukah* (or *Hanukkah*), Festival of Lights on Twenty-fifth day. Third month of the civil year. (Hebrew)

KJV

Abbreviation for the King James Version, Bible translation, dated 1611, as commissioned by England's King James I, and as published by the Revisers in their Parallel Bible in 1886.

Kodesh Ha-Kodashim

Holy of Holies, the inner sanctuary and dwelling place of God (*Shekhinah*) in the Temple. (Hebrew)

Kohen

Male descendant of Aaron. – A priest. – The word from which the popular Jewish surname, Cohen, is derived. Sometimes also spelled as: *cohain*. (Hebrew)

Koran

Book, specifically the Holy Book of the Muslim religion, Islam. (From Arabic equivalent: *Quran*)

Kreplach

Triangular-shaped dumplings made with chopped meat or cheese, chopped onion and seasoning. This delight is eaten as a pre-fast meal before *Yom Kippur* and is also eaten at *Shavuot, Purim* and *Hoshana Rabba*.

— L —

Le Shanah Tova Tikataivu

"May you be inscribed (in the Book of Life) for a good year." Jewish greeting during the Days of Awe. (Hebrew)

— M —

Maccabees (or "Maccabean")

Pertaining to the Jewish revolt of 167 B.C.E. led by Judas Maccabeus and his brothers against Syrian oppressor, Antiochus IV Epiphanes.

Maronites

Sect of Eastern Christians that separated from Western affiliation during the 7th century, dwelling principally in Asia Minor.

Matzah (or "matzoh," "mazzah," etc.)

Unleavened bread, similar to soda crackers, eaten at the Passover meal (*Seder*). (Hebrew)

Megeg

Type of reed used to make ritually "clean" rope for binding the legs of the Red Heifer as it was slain. (Hebrew)

Megillah

A scroll. Also a term commonly applied in Judaism for the rules for reading the Book of Esther during *Purim*. Title of *Talmud* tractate. (Hebrew)

Menahoth

Meal offerings. Rules for conducting the meal offerings specified in the *Torah*. Title of *Talmud* tractate. (Hebrew)

Menorah

Large golden candelabrum with seven candlesticks or "lights," and which stood along the south wall of the Holy Place in the Temple.

Middoth

Dimensions. *Talmud* tractate detailing dimensions of the Second Temple. (Hebrew)

Midrash

Explanation. – A Rabbinical commentary on Jewish Scripture, including the five books of Moses plus five other books of the so-called Old Testament books from the Hebrew *Tanakh*. (Hebrew)

Mikweh

Ritual bath consisting of complete immersion in naturally flowing ("living") water, tradition of which led to baptism. (Hebrew)

Millennial

Pertaining to the one thousand year reign of Messiah after He arrives at *Olivet* summit to conquer Israel's enemies. Also referring to the "Third" Temple that will be the next legitimate or Holy consecrated Temple, which will be occupied by the Lord at His Coming.

Miphkad Altar

Place of the slaying and burning of the Red Heifer, due east of the Temple and at or near the summit of the Mount of Olives.

Mishnah

To learn. – A collection of statements and Rabbinical interpretations (rulings) on the Law and Jewish tradition, listed as the most formal of the entries in the *Talmud*. The conventional notations applied in scholarly work are, for example: *Middoth* 2:4, indicating the fourth *Mishnah* of Chapter 2 in *Middoth* tractate. (Hebrew)

In some tractates each *Mishnah* is followed by a *Gemara* providing further discussion.

Muslim

(See Islam).

— N —

NASA

National Aeronautics and Space Administration, United States federal supervising agency for aeronautical and space sciences.

NASB

New American Standard Bible, modern Bible translation.

NEB

New English Bible, modern Bible translation.

Nicanor's Gate (Or Nĕquanor's Gate)

The East Gate of entry from the Court of the Women into the Court of the Israelites. (See Illus. 15: Plan of Second Temple (by Dr. A.S. Kaufman), Illus. 16: Isometric View of 2nd Temple, Illus. 17: Detailed Elevation of 2nd Temple, Illus. 18: Elevation Profile of Temple and Temple Mt., Illus. 19: Elev. Profile: Temple Mt., Kidron VLY., Mt. Olivet and Illus. 21: Detail of the 2nd Temple, Pages 148, 149, 150, 151, 152 and 154.)

Nisan

First month of the Jewish Sacred Calendar and seventh month of the Jewish Secular Calendar. Jewish Passover (Hebrew: *Pesach*) occurs during the month of *Nisan*.

NIV

New International Version, modern Bible translation.

— O —

Omer

Sheaf. About one tenth of a bushel. (Hebrew)

— P —

Parah

Heifer or young cow, especially the Red Heifer and Law relating thereto. Title of *Talmud* tractate. (Hebrew)

Parah adumah

Red Heifer. (Hebrew)

Parokhet

Veil or Vail, in some translations – (Also see *Katapetasmah*) (Hebrew)

Patibulum

Horizontal cross-piece member that supported the arms of the victim in crucifixion. (Latin: Transverse Beam)

Perutah

The smallest copper Roman coin. Valued at $1/128^{th}$ of a *denarius*, a Roman coin. (Latin)

Pesach

Pass over or "skip" over. (Hebrew)

Pesahim

Paschal or Passover Lambs. Title of *Talmud* tractate dealing with the Law for conduct of the Passover rite. (Hebrew)

Peshitta

Simple, true, original. – A somewhat remote or "unadvertised" version of the Bible, having been subjected to very little change over the past twenty centuries. It has been scrupulously preserved in its original form by the Church of the East, an obscure Christian minority – not to be confused with the Eastern Orthodox Church. These peoples still use the Aramaic language and are living in countries such as Afghanistan, Iraq, Turkey, Iran, India, Syria and other nations east of the Caucasus. (See Vol. II, Appendix B) (Aramaic)

Pogrom

Devastation. – Term frequently used to describe Gentiles' violent persecutions of Jewish communities and villages in Russia and Eastern Europe. (Russian)

Purim

Lots. – Jewish holiday, Feast of Lots, celebrating the Jews' deliverance in the Book of Esther. (Hebrew)

— Q —

Qetoret

Incense. – Cinnamon based material burned in the Altar of Incense in the Holy Temple. (Hebrew)

Quran

(See *Koran*)

— R —

Rapture

Term applied in theology – and especially, eschatology – to describe the "gathering up" or "taking away" of Believers, particularly Christians, both dead and living; resurrected to be with the Lord sometime before the seven years of "Tribulation" that will immediately precede the arrival of Jesus as Messiah. (Luke 21:36; I Corinthians 15:51 – 57; I Thessalonians 4:16 – 18; Revelation 3:10)

Rosh Hashanah

New Year. Title of *Talmud* tractate dealing with the calendar connection with the New Moon, especially the New Moon at the beginning of the New Year. (Hebrew)

— S —

Sanhedrin

A council of leaders. Title of *Talmud* tractate prescribing the various court levels for administering the Mosaic Law. (Greek)

Seah

Dry measure, about one-third of a bushel. (Hebrew)

Seder

Order. – The Passover meal, taken after sundown as 15 *Nisan* begins, commemorating the flight of the Jewish people from slavery in Egypt. (Hebrew)

Sedrah (or Sidra; plural: sedrim)

Portion. Portion of Scripture from the *Torah* to be read in synagogues on specific dates during Sabbaths and Feast Days. (See *Haftorah*) (Hebrew)

Shabbath, (or Shabbot)

Sabbath. – Title of *Talmud* tractate. (Hebrew)

Shavuot

Weeks. – The feast taking place seven weeks after Passover. (Also called "Pentecost.") (Hebrew)

Shebat

Eleventh month of the Jewish religious year, fifth month of the civil year. (Hebrew)

Shekhinah (or Shechinah)

Presence. The visible Divine Presence of Almighty God, "*Yahweh*" or "*YHWH*" or "I AM", who spoke to Moses from the bush and was seen by the Jewish people at the Temple or the Tabernacle as a *"pillar of cloud by day"* or as *"a pillar of fire by night"*. Most English Bible translations refer to the Divine Presence as *"the Glory of the Lord"*. Some Jewish teachers refer to the *Shekhinah* as "The Holy Spirit." (Hebrew)

Shekalim

Shekels (coins). Title of *Talmud* tractate relating to rules for paying the annual poll tax for maintenance of the Temple. (Hebrew)

Shem

Eldest son of Noah, ancestor of Semitic and Oriental peoples.

Shemen Afarshimon

Holy anointing oil used for anointing priests and the Kings of Judah. (Hebrew)

Shethiyah

Foundation. – Term used to denote the Foundation Stone; the resting place of the Ark of the Covenant in the Holy of Holies. Literally, *even* (stone) and *Shethiyah* (Foundation). (Hebrew)

Shiva

Seven. Under Rabbinical law, Jewish mourners are required to sit as mourners for seven days following the burial. They sit on a low stool during the *shiva* week. This is described as "sitting *shiva*." (Hebrew)

Shofar

Horn. Used as a trumpet during Temple worship. Usually made from a ram's horn. (Hebrew)

Sukkah (or Succah)

Booths – Regulations for the Feast of Tabernacles. Title of *Talmud* tractate. (Hebrew)

Suleiman

Sixteenth-century Turkish Sultan and conqueror, Suleiman I, the Magnificent.

— T —

Ta'anith

Fasts. Title of *Talmud* tractate, presenting rules for special fasts decreed upon a community because of drought. (Hebrew)

Talmud

Teaching or lesson. – Jewish Rabbinical commentary on the Law and Jewish traditions. (Hebrew)

Tammuz

Fourth month of Jewish religious calendar, tenth month of the civil year. (Hebrew)

Tanakh (or Ta-nakh')

Hebrew word derived from an acronym "TNK" describing the Scriptures, formed from: the *Torah* – (the first five books), *Nebhi'im* – (the Prophets), *Kethubhim* – ("other writings," including the Psalms). Christian Gentiles call this "The Old Testament."

Targum

Interpretation – (Plural: *targumim*) – Paraphrased versions for various of the books of the Hebrew *Tanakh* (Old Testament). (Hebrew)

Tebeth

Tenth month of the Jewish religious calendar, fourth month of the civil year.

Tetragrammaton

Having four letters. – Refers to the Name of God: "*YHWH*" – "Jehovah" – "I AM" – *"The Ineffable Name"* (Greek)

Tisha B'Av

Ninth day of *Av*. – Woeful anniversary of destruction of both the First Temple and the Second Temple. (Hebrew)

Tishri

Seventh month of the Jewish religious calendar, first month of the civil year. *Rosh Hashanah* on first day, *Yom Kippur* on tenth day, Feast of Tabernacles (*Sukkoth*) on fifteenth day of this month. (Hebrew)

Torah

Law. The first five books of the Holy Scriptures. (Hebrew)

Touché

Touched – An expression from fencing, to indicate a touch on an opponent. Also used as acknowledgement of a telling remark or response. (French)

Tractate

A treatise or tract of writing, as used here denoting various sections of the Babylonian *Talmud*.

Tshuvah

Repent, return. Name for the Jewish High Holidays season of forty days leading up to Day of Atonement, *Yom Kippur*. Sometimes called the Days of Awe. (See *Yamim Nora'im*) (Hebrew)

— U —

Urim and Thummim

(See Ephod)

— W —

Waqf

Legal authority under Islamic law. (Arabic)

— Y —

Yebamoth

Deceased brother's widow. – *Talmud* Tractate. (Hebrew)

Yeshiva

Sitting place. A Jewish school for students of the Holy Scriptures, Judaism, *Talmudic* Law, Judaic tradition, etc. (Hebrew)

Yom Kippur

Day of Atonement. Most sacred Jewish Feast holiday.

Yoma

Day. Title of *Talmud* tractate dealing primarily with the Day of Atonement, *Yom Kippur*. (Hebrew)

— Z —

Zabim

They that suffer a flux (a flow). Title of *Talmud* tractate. (Hebrew)

Zebahim (or Zevahim)

Animal offerings (sacrifices). *Talmud* tractate. (Hebrew)

Indexes

Scripture References

Genesis

1:5	497
1:14	354
1:15	354
1:16	354
1:17	354
1:18	354
1:19	354
1:24	354
3:4	438
5:5	399
6	529
8	529
9:27	177
18:27	293
22:2	120
22:4	357, 473
22:7	120
22:8	120, 343, 357, 481
22:13	121
22:14	121
42:17	473

Exodus

1:22	298
2:4	275
2:5	275
2:6	275
2:7	275
2:8	275
2:9	275
2:10	275
3:2	4, 163
6:6	425
6:7	425
6:8	495
12	265
12:1	480
12:2	480, 484
12:3	86, 98, 242, 349, 474, 480
12:4	349, 474, 480
12:5	98, 349, 361, 474, 480
12:6	86, 98, 242, 318, 349, 361, 465, 474, 476, 480, 487, 490
12:7	349, 490
12:8	98, 349, 469, 490
12:14	482
12:15	475, 476
12:18	469, 491
12:22	297, 361
12:34	431
12:43	426, 427
12:46	87
12:48	105, 427, 475
13:2	236
13:8	415
13:9	422
13:12	236
13:21	4, 518
14:13	134, 405
14:19	525
19:9	4
20:22	276
21:32	243
23:19	228
24:11	94
25	248
26	248
26:31	175
26:35	175
26:36	83, 326
27	248

Reference	Page
28	248
29	248
29:14	319
30	248
30:31	514
30:34	287, 510
30:34	
31	248
32	248, 275
33	248
33:16	140
34	248
34:26	228
34:29	4
34:30	4
35	248
36	248
36:37	313
37	248
38	248
38:13	327
38:14	327
38:15	327
39	248
40	248
40:36	23, 24, 255, 294
40:37	255, 294
40:38	23, 24, 255

Leviticus

Reference	Page
1:4	269
4:6	83
4:11	319
4:12	83, 319, 335, 337, 374
4:17	83
6:10	336
6:11	336
12:2	236
12:3	236, 237
12:4	236
12:5	236
12:6	236
12:7	236
12:8	236
13	306, 307
13:13	534
13:47	307
13:48	307
13:49	307
13:50	307
13:51	307
13:52	307
13:53	307
13:54	307
13:55	307
13:56	307
13:57	307
13:58	307
13:59	307
14:1	53, 298
14:2	53, 298
14:3	53, 298
14:4	53, 298, 307
14:5	298
14:6	298
14:7	298
14:8	298
14:9	298
14:10	298
14:11	298
14:12	298
14:13	298
14:14	298
14:15	298
14:16	298
14:17	298
14:18	298
14:19	298
14:20	298
14:21	298
14:22	298
14:23	298
14:24	298
14:25	298
14:26	298
14:27	298
14:28	298
14:29	298
14:30	298
14:31	298
14:32	298
14:37	307
16	481
16:1	4
16:2	4, 5
16:3	4
16:4	4

Reference	Page
16:5	4
16:6	4
16:7	4
16:8	4
16:9	4
16:10	4
16:11	4, 5
16:12	4, 5
16:13	4, 5
16:14	4, 5
16:15	4, 5
16:16	4
16:17	4
16:21	359
16:22	359
16:27	319
16:34	4
17:11	53
23:5	469, 481, 490
23:6	469, 481, 490
23:7	99, 100, 481, 489
23:8	481
23:9	481
23:10	100, 102, 481, 495
23:11	99, 100, 481, 483, 492, 495
23:12	100, 102
23:15	102, 467, 481
23:16	100, 102, 467, 486
23:17	100, 138, 486
23:18	486
23:19	486
23:20	486
23:21	486
23:22	486
23:23	486
23:24	486
23:25	486
23:26	486
23:27	103, 486
23:28	103, 486
23:29	103, 486
23:30	103, 486
23:31	486
23:32	103, 486
23:34	103
23:35	103
23:36	103
24:14	246, 278, 317
24:16	308
24:23	317
25:2	436
25:5	436
26:44	17, 140

Numbers

Reference	Page
1:3	238
1:18	238
3:23	327
3:38	55, 327
5:17	293
5:18	293
5:19	293
5:20	293
5:21	293
5:22	293
5:23	293
5:24	293
5:25	293
5:26	293
5:27	293
5:28	293
5:29	293
5:30	293
5:31	293
7:19	298, 299
12:1	275
12:2	275
12:3	275
12:4	275
12:5	275
12:6	275
12:7	275
12:8	275
12:9	275
12:10	275
12:11	275
12:12	275
12:13	275
12:14	275
12:15	275
12:16	275
13:31	238
13:32	238
13:33	238
15:35	317
18	239
18:15	273

19 ... 40, 92, 262, 265, 267, 268, 271, 350, 398, 481
19:1 ... 268
19:2 ... 268, 293
19:3 ... 268
19:4 ... 268, 275
19:5 ... 268
19:6 ... 52, 268
19:7 ... 268, 281
19:8 ... 268, 274, 281
19:9 ... 268, 317, 329, 330, 337, 351, 396
19:10 ... 92, 268, 328, 389, 398
19:11 ... 268, 398
19:12 ... 268, 398
19:13 ... 268, 351, 398
19:14 ... 268, 398
19:15 ... 268, 398
19:16 ... 268, 393, 398
19:17 ... 268, 294, 398
19:18 ... 268, 398
19:19 ... 268, 398
19:20 ... 268, 351
19:21 ... 268, 351, 398
19:22 ... 268
20:1 ... 275
20:3 ... 275
20:4 ... 275
20:5 ... 275
20:6 ... 275
20:7 ... 275
20:8 ... 275
20:9 ... 275
20:13 ... 275
20:23 ... 275
20:24 ... 275
20:25 ... 275
20:26 ... 275
20:27 ... 275
20:28 ... 275
20:29 ... 275
26:65 ... 238
31:23 ... 351
32:11 ... 238
35:5 ... 321

Deuteronomy

4 ... 127
4:2 ... 555
4:7 ... 127, 143
4:8 ... 143
4:23 ... 525
4:24 ... 525
4:25 ... 525
4:26 ... 525
4:27 ... 525
4:27 ... 143
4:28 ... 143
4:29 ... 143, 555
4:30 ... 143, 555
4:31 ... 143, 555
4:32 ... 143
4:33 ... 128, 143, 168, 517
4:34 ... 128, 143
4:35 ... 128, 143
4:36 ... 128, 143
4:37 ... 128, 143
4:38 ... 128, 143
4:39 ... 128, 143
4:40 ... 143
6:4 ... 416, 423
6:5 ... 231
14:21 ... 228
16:16 ... 237, 250
18:5 ... 277
19:15 ... 242
21:22 ... 247, 330, 332
21:23 ... 172, 247, 330, 332
23:10 ... 281
23:11 ... 281
23:18 ... 242
23:19 ... 242, 243
26:2 ... 483
30:3 ... 110
32:30 ... 535
33:16 ... 163

Joshua

3:15 ... 122
3:16 ... 122
3:17 ... 122
4:19 ... 350

I Samuel

4:4 ... 10
4:5 ... 10

4:6...10
4:7...10
4:8...10
4:9...10
4:10...10
4:11...10
4:12...10
4:13...10
4:14...10
4:15...10
4:16...10
4:17...10
4:18...10
4:19...10
4:20...10
4:21...10
4:22...10
5:9...188
11:1...239
11:2...239
11:3...239
11:4...239
11:5...239
11:6...239
11:7...239
11:8...239
11:9...239
11:10...239
11:11...239
12:22...239
16:7...305
16:12...129
17:42...129

II Samuel

7:12...428
7:13...428
7:16...428
7:18...277
24:21...20
24:22...20
24:23...20
24:24...20
24:25...20

II Chronicles

3:1..50, 120

5:10...52
5:13...519
5:14...164
7:1...184
24:20...278
24:21...278
24:22...278

Ezra

6:12..169, 182

Nehemiah

2:1.................................72, 73, 286, 392
2:2...72, 73, 392
2:3...72, 73, 392
2:4...72, 73, 392
2:5...72, 73, 392
2:6...72, 73, 392
2:7...72, 73, 392
2:8...72, 73, 392
2:9...72, 392
2:10...72, 392
3:31...40
8..5, 182, 520
9..5, 182, 520
9:38...520
12...5
10..5, 182, 520
10:21...520
11...5
12:43......................................5, 183, 185

Esther

3..421
3:7...484

Job

6:24...553
6:25...553
11:20...141
12:22...557
14:22...474
33:14...146
38:6...385
38:37...385

38:38...385

Psalms

2:7...428
8:5...217
12:6...263
12:7...263
16:10........................247, 331, 481
22:18...315
34:20......................................87, 315
35:19...226
48..228
48:8...227
48:9...227
50:1...385
50:2...385
51:7...297
51:9...297
69:21...315
72:1...354
72:17...354
80:2...211
80:3...211
89:52...534
90:4...535
92:1...535
118:26..72
119:80...265

Proverbs

1:7...549
2:1...549
2:2...549
2:3...549
2:4...549
2:5...549
2:6...549
6:23...225
25:2...264

Song of Solomon

1:13...10
2:9...17
17:21...536

Isaiah

1:18...521
2:11...535
7:14...428
11:12..17
13:10...110
27:12...485
27:13.....................................485, 534
29:1...50
34:4...110
43:5...106
43:5...105
43:6.......................................105, 106
53:5...423
59:15...534
64:3...532

Jeremiah

3:16..........................5, 385, 386, 388
3:17.......................................381, 385
7..165
10:2...132
21..142, 165
22:19...235
23:3...106
23:4.......................................106, 113
30:7...114
31:31...............................201, 202, 208
31:32.....................................201, 208
31:33.....................................201, 208
31:34.....................................201, 208
31:35...208
31:36...208
31:37...208
36:30...235
36:31...235
36:32...235
52:12...368
52:13...368
52:14...368
52:15...368
52:16...368
52:17...368
52:18...368
52:19...368
52:20...368
52:21...368

52:22...368
52:23...368

Ezekiel

3:16...386
8..164, 180, 186
8:1...165, 180
8:16....................40, 55, 75, 81, 97, 192, 312
8:17...97
8:2..165, 180
8:3..165, 180, 551
8:4...180
9...164, 169, 180, 186
9:5...180
10.......12, 164, 169, 180, 186, 196, 526, 524
10:19...55
11.......12, 164, 169, 180, 186, 196, 524, 526
11:23...22, 169
11:24...12, 165
18:20...438
20:38...530
26:14...182
36:16...268
36:17...268
36:18...268
36:19...268
36:20...268
36:21...268
36:22...268
36:23...268
36:24...268
36:25...268
36:26...268
36:27...268
36:28...268
36:29...268
36:30...268
36:31...268
36:32...268
36:33...268
36:34...268
36:35...268
36:36...268
36:37...268
36:38...268
37..............................106, 143, 181, 182, 548
37:13..106, 181
37:14...106

37:21...551
37:22..182, 551
37:25...384
38...93, 355, 364
38:6...364
38:15...364
39...93, 355, 364
39:2...93, 364
39:4...93
39:6...541
39:11...93
39:12...93, 364
39:13...93, 364
40...29, 329, 388, 389
40:1..186, 551
40:5...54, 377
41...................................29, 329, 385, 388, 389
41:2...94
41:23...386
41:24...386
42...................................29, 329, 385, 388, 389
43...................................29, 329, 385, 388, 389
43:1...17
43:2...17, 109, 181, 186, 551
43:3...17, 180, 186
43:4...17, 96, 97
43:5...17
43:6...17
43:7..17, 97
44...................................29, 329, 385, 388, 389
44:1...47, 51, 94
44:2...47, 51, 94, 96, 97
44:3...47, 48, 51, 94, 186
45...385, 388, 389
46...385, 388, 389
46:1..81, 95
46:8...97
46:9...97
47...385, 389
47:1....................................59, 61, 95, 381, 386, 392
47:10...59, 95
47:2...59, 61, 95, 386
47:3...59
47:4...59
47:5...59
47:6...59
47:7...59
47:8...59
47:9...59

Daniel

4:34..88
4:35..88
4:36..88
4:37..88
5:1..368
5:2..368
7:13...110
9:21...537
9:22...537
9:23...537
9:24...72, 115, 132, 211, 286, 356, 388, 392, 393, 429, 521, 536, 537, 549
9:25.......72, 73, 95, 115, 211, 286, 356, 388, 392, 393, 429, 521, 536, 537, 549
9:26.....73, 95, 115, 116, 211, 286, 356, 388, 392, 393, 429, 521, 532, 536, 537, 549
9:27.......29, 91, 93, 111, 115, 211, 265, 267, 344, 356, 363, 364, 369, 378, 381, 388, 392, 393, 429, 521, 536, 537, 542
11:31...211, 378
11:41...542
12:1..107, 231, 315, 352
12:2..........103, 107, 108, 315, 339, 352, 530
12:4...193, 539
12:7..116
12:11...181, 378

Hosea

5:15...16, 113, 115, 120, 143, 169, 181, 255, 352, 435, 436, 522, 525
6:1.....................113, 143, 255, 436, 525, 555
6:2...113, 115, 116, 143, 207, 352, 436, 438, 473, 535
6:3..113, 143, 522

Joel

2:10...110
2:32...108
3:5..108
3:15...110

Amos

4:7..533
8:11...539

9:11...383
9:12...383
9:13...383
9:14...383
9:15...383

Micah

5:2..428

Habakkuk

2:3..204

Zephaniah

3..401

Haggai

1:4..183
1:8..184, 387, 518, 551
2..186
2:3...164, 183
2:4..164, 169, 183, 551
2:5...164, 169, 183
2:6...164, 169
2:7:5, 164, 169, 185, 187, 189, 387, 518, 551
2:8...164, 169
2:9...164, 169, 185

Zechariah

1:16............29, 164, 169, 186, 187, 189, 387
1:20...210
2:6..110
8:23...215
9:9...72
9:14...485
9:15...485
9:16...485
9:17...485
11:1...140
11:12..243
11:13..243
12...254, 315, 316
12:2..60
12:3...315
12:9...315

12:10.....31, 65, 78, 105, 111, 181, 208, 211, 315, 320, 423, 442, 486
12:11...................................111, 316
12:12...................................208, 316
12:13...316
12:14...316
13.......................................254, 316
13:6....................31, 65, 209, 316, 442
13:9...114
14......................................254, 315, 316
14:4.......22, 31, 58, 64, 65, 76, 78, 105, 279, 315, 320, 322, 343, 432, 485, 486, 523, 525, 531
14:5..58
14:8......................................59, 316
14:16....................................60, 105
14:17...105

Malachi

3:7....................................215, 525
4:5...425

Matthew

1:1..210
1:2..210
1:3..210
1:4..210
1:5....................................210, 234
1:6....................................210, 428
1:7..............................210, 235, 428
1:8....................................210, 428
1:9....................................210, 428
1:10..................................210, 428
1:11..................................210, 428
1:12..................................210, 428
1:13..................................210, 428
1:14..................................210, 428
1:15..................................210, 428
1:16............................210, 235, 428
1:18...428
1:19...428
1:20....................................428, 522
1:21..................................236, 428
1:22...428
1:24...234
1:25...234
2:15...428

3:1..425
3:3..425
3:4..425
3:5..425
3:6..425
3:7..425
3:8..425
3:9..425
3:10..425
3:11..425
3:12..425
3:13..425
3:14..425
3:15..425
3:16..425
3:17..425
4:5....................................379, 380
4:6..379
4:7..379
5:17............................73, 479, 494
9:20..241
11:21..182
12:10..241
12:11..241
12:12..241
12:13..241
12:40........462, 469, 497, 498, 499, 500, 502
13:31..354
16...235
16:21......................492, 493, 497, 499
17:1..24
17:2..24
17:3..24
17:4..24
17:5..24
17:23..499
18:20..241
20:19..............................498, 499, 500, 502
21:1..................................471, 488
21:2..................................471, 488
21:3...471
21:4...471
21:5...471
21:6...471
21:7...471
21:8..................................471, 492
21:9......................72, 212, 471, 480
21:10..72
21:11..72

21:12	470, 480
21:14	492
21:18	470
21:19	470
22:23	6, 531
22:24	6
22:25	6
22:26	6
22:27	6
22:28	6
22:29	6
22:30	6
22:37	206
22:38	206
22:39	206
22:46	480
23:21	5, 24, 165, 169, 188, 189, 214, 387, 551
23:24	167, 497
23:37	22, 471
23:38	189
24:2	62, 73, 182
24:6	145
24:7	145
24:8	146
24:14	534
24:15	211, 378, 379, 380, 381
24:16	378
24:17	378
24:18	378
24:19	378
24:20	378
24:21	107, 378
24:22	108, 378
24:30	105, 109
24:31	105, 107
24:36	117, 440
24:44	111
25:13	117
25:30	111
26:2	490
26:5	482
26:15	243
26:17	477, 490
26:36	70, 320
26:37	70
26:38	70
26:39	70, 352, 436
26:40	70
26:41	70
26:42	70
26:43	70
26:44	70
26:45	70
26:46	70
26:47	70
26:48	70
26:49	70
26:50	70
26:57	310
26:58	310
26:59	310, 480
26:60	73, 310
26:61	73, 310
26:62	310
26:63	310
26:64	310
26:65	310
26:66	310
27	362
27:1	244
27:2	244
27:3	243
27:4	243
27:5	243
27:6	243
27:7	243
27:8	243
27:9	243
27:10	243
27:17	359
27:24	430
27:38	487
27:44	362
27:45	194
27:45	131
27:46	436, 480
27:47	436
27:48	436
27:49	436
27:50	84, 192, 436
27:51	42, 43, 75, 172, 173, 192, 313, 316
27:52	43, 75, 76, 172, 173, 192, 313
27:53	43, 75, 76, 172, 173, 192, 313
27:54	43, 75, 86, 172, 173, 192, 313
27:59	432, 464
27:60	464
27:61	464

Reference	Page
27:62	464
27:63	501
28:1	465
28:2	465
28:3	465
28:4	465
28:5	465
28:6	465
28:7	465
28:11	465
28:12	339
28:13	339
28:14	339
28:15	339

Mark

Reference	Page
1:30	201
6:4	227
7:5	273
8:31	498, 499, 500
9:31	499
10:34	499
10:46	472
11:1	472
11:10	470
11:11	470
11:12	470
11:13	470
11:14	470
11:15	470, 488
11:18	480
11:20	470
12:18	531
12:26	163
13:2	49, 62, 63
13:3	55, 75, 81, 312
13:8	145
13:20	93
13:24	109, 110, 485
13:25	110, 485
13:26	110, 485, 528
13:27	110, 485
14:1	491
14:1	490
14:1	489
14:3	54
14:12	477, 490, 491
14:25	207
14:50	171
14:51	171
14:52	171
14:61	309
14:62	309
14:63	309
15	362
15:1	244
15:7	359
15:25	84, 328
15:27	487
15:33	84
15:34	84
15:37	84, 195
15:38	42, 173, 313
15:39	173
15:42	330, 482
15:43	330
15:46	432
16:1	331
16:9	99, 399, 462, 464, 465, 466, 491, 498, 499, 500, 502
16:14	61

Luke

Reference	Page
2:22	273
2:23	273
2:24	273
2:25	237, 273
2:26	237, 273
2:27	237, 273
2:28	237, 273
2:29	237, 273
2:30	237, 273
2:31	237, 273
2:32	237, 273
2:33	273
2:34	273
2:41	237
2:42	237
2:43	237
2:44	237
2:45	237
2:46	237
2:47	237
2:48	237
2:49	237
2:51	237

Reference	Page(s)
2:52	237
3:23	210, 235
3:24	210, 235
3:25	210, 235
3:26	210, 235
3:27	210, 235
3:28	210, 235
3:29	235
3:30	235
3:31	235
3:32	235
3:33	235
3:34	235
3:35	235
3:36	235
3:37	235
3:38	235
4:16	239
4:17	238, 239
4:18	238, 239, 240
4:19	238, 239, 240
4:20	238, 239
4:21	238, 239, 240
4:22	240
4:23	240
4:24	240
4:25	240
4:26	240
4:27	240
4:28	240
4:29	240
4:30	240
6:5	68, 308, 308, 493
6:5	308
9:22	499
10:13	182
11:29	142
11:36	68
11:37	68
11:38	68
11:51	278
12:40	111, 485
13:34	471
14:11	402
16:20	307
16:21	307
16:22	307
16:23	307
16:24	307
16:25	307
16:26	307
16:27	307
16:28	307
16:29	307
16:30	307
16:31	307
18:33	499
19:11	471
19:29	488
19:30	488
19:31	488
19:32	488
19:33	488
19:34	488
19:35	488
19:36	488
19:37	70, 319, 488
19:38	70, 311, 488
19:39	70, 311
19:40	72
19:42	526
19:43	526
19:44	526
19:45	470
19:47	190, 472
21:6	62
21:9	146
21:10	146
21:11	146, 378
21:26	111
21:28	146
21:36	107, 117, 147
22:7	477
22:8	477
22:12	311
22:39	320
22:39	68
22:40	68
22:41	68
22:42	68
22:43	68
22:44	68
22:66	244
23	362
23:1	74
23:2	74
23:18	137, 358
23:24	526

23:33...361
23:34.........................166, 215, 361, 555
23:35...361
23:36...361
23:37...361
23:38...361
23:39...361
23:39...361
23:40....................................361, 362, 487
23:41....................................361, 362, 487
23:42....................................361, 362, 487
23:43....................................361, 362, 487
23:44...131, 194
23:45......................................42, 173, 313
23:46...173
23:47...173
23:50....................................332, 462, 468
23:51...............................332, 462, 468, 481
23:52...462, 468, 481
23:53..............330, 432, 462, 468, 481, 498
23:54..............462, 465, 466, 468, 481, 498
23:55....................................462, 465, 468, 481
23:56....................................462, 465, 468, 481, 500
24:7..499
24:31...340
24:32...340
24:33...340
24:34...340
24:35...340
24:36...340
24:37...340
24:38...340
24:39...340
24:40...340
24:41...340
24:42...340
24:43...340
24:44...340
24:45...340
24:46..340, 499
24:47...340
24:48...340
24:50....................................62, 248, 322, 523
24:51...63
24:52...63, 169
24:53.............................63, 169, 189, 387

John

1:1..354
1:2..354
1:3..354
1:14...291
2:13...475
2:15...471
2:16......................................169, 190, 387
3:16..428, 558
3:17...428
4:7..308
4:8..308
4:9..308
4:10......................................68, 268, 308
4:27...242
5:1..241
5:2..241, 304
5:3..241, 304
5:4..241, 304
5:5..241, 304
5:6..241, 304
5:7..241, 304
5:8..241, 304
5:9..241, 304
5:10...241
5:11...241
5:12...241
5:13...241
5:14...241
5:15...241
5:16...241
5:17...241
5:18...241
6:70...312
6:71...312
8:17...242
8:58...309
9:23...238
10:16..124
10:30...24, 206
11:39...55
11:44..432
11:55..475
12:1............72, 471, 472, 473, 476, 487, 493
12:2..................................72, 472, 473, 487, 493
12:3..72, 73, 472, 492, 493
12:4..72, 493
12:5..72, 472, 493
12:6..72, 472, 493
12:7..72, 472, 493

12:8	72, 493	19:35	87, 172, 173
12:8	472	19:36	78, 87, 173, 315
12:9	72, 472, 493	19:37	78, 87, 181, 315, 320
12:10	72, 472, 493	19:41	320
12:11	72, 472, 493	19:42	465, 466
12:12	72, 472, 473, 493	20:1	465, 487, 497
12:13	53, 69, 72, 473, 493	20:4	79
12:14	72, 473	20:5	285
12:15	72, 473	20:6	285
12:40	143	20:7	285
13:5	479		
13:26	437	**Acts**	
14:6	206, 478		
14:9	89	1:9	523
14:16	105	1:10	64, 523
14:26	105	1:11	62, 64, 322, 523
15:25	226	1:12	40, 62, 64, 322, 523
15:26	105	1:13	61
16:7	105	2:9	365
18:1	320	2:14	517
18:2	320	2:15	517
18:3	320	2:16	517
18:36	74	2:17	517
18:37	73	2:18	517
19:4	312	2:19	517
19:7	312	2:20	517
19:8	312	2:21	517
19:9	312	2:22	517
19:10	312	2:23	517
19:11	312	2:24	517
19:12	312	2:25	517
19:13	312	2:26	517
19:14	312, 465	2:27	517
19:15	312	2:28	517
19:16	312	2:29	517
19:18	362, 487	2:30	517
19:19	74	2:31	517
19:20	74, 246, 311	2:32	517
19:21	74	2:33	517
19:22	74	2:34	517
19:24	315	2:36	517
19:27	171	2:37	517
19:28	315	2:38	517
19:29	288, 341	2:39	517
19:30	172, 173, 195	2:40	517
19:31	99, 173, 247, 465, 482, 487	2:41	517
19:32	87, 172, 173	2:46	189
19:33	87, 173	2:46	63
19:34	87, 173	3:1	63, 189

3:3...189
3:8..63, 189
5:17..63, 189
5:18..63, 189
5:19..63, 189
5:20..63, 189
5:21...63
5:25..63, 189
5:33..556
5:34..88
5:35..88, 556
5:36..88, 556
5:37..88, 556
5:38....................................88, 523, 556
5:39....................................88, 523, 556
5:40..556
5:42..63, 189
6:7..........................142, 168, 198, 523
6:13..379
7...517
8:1..339, 523
8:2..339, 523
8:3..339, 523
8:39..109
8:40..109
9:1..523
9:2..523
20:7..441
21:26..63, 189
21:27..189
21:39..204
22:17..63, 189
24:12..63, 189
24:13..63
24:14..63
24:15..63
24:16..63
24:17..63
24:18..63, 189
26:21..63, 189

Romans

1:16..501
2:29..205
6:14..232
9:4........................5, 165, 169, 189, 552
10:12..205
11:11..200

11:26..530

I Corinthians

3:17..380
4:6..167
6:19..380
9:20..205
9:21..205
11:20..426
11:21..426
11:22..426
11:23..426, 440
11:24....................................426, 438, 441
11:25..426, 441
11:26..426, 440
11:27..426
11:28..426
11:29..426
13:12..10
15:4..340, 499
15:5..340
15:6..340
15:7..340
15:8..340
15:51..147, 397
15:52..147, 397
15:53..147, 397
15:54..147, 397
15:55..147
15:56..147

II Corinthians

4:6..168
5:21..403

Galatians

Galatians 3:28....................................204

Ephesians

Ephesians 5:26....................................292

Philippians

Philippians 1:21..................................199

I Thessalonians

3:13....................................109, 112, 528
4:15..528
4:16..............................105, 147, 484, 528
4:17..............................107, 147, 292, 528
4:18..146, 147

II Thessalonians

2:13..200
2:4...380

II Timothy

4:8...404

Hebrews

6:20..334
8:13..202
9:4...386
9:12..379, 403
9:13..403
9:14..403
9:15..403
9:25..379
10:20..196
11:6...205
11:28..361
13:12..311

I Peter

1:1...366
4:8...544

II Peter

3:9...117

I John

1:8...397
3:2...399
5:1...206

Jude

1:14..528

Revelation

1:7...528
3:10..107, 147
3:20..139
6:14..381
7:5...145
7:6...145
7:7...145
7:8...145
9:13..365
9:14..365
9:15..365
9:16..365
11:2.......................................59, 111, 116
11:3..111
11:19..386
12:6..116
12:14..116
13:15..102
13:16..102
13:17..102
13:18..102
16:16..29
16:17..29
16:18..29, 381
16:19..29, 381
16:20..29, 381
19:7..112
19:8..112
19:9..112
19:12..354, 355
19:14..112
19:15...60, 112
19:16...60, 532
19:20..109
20:4..114
20:6..112
20:12..231
20:13..400
20:13..231
20:14..400
20:15..400

Talmud References

Berakoth

I:5	532
6a	242
12b	532
17a	94, 532
28b	199
34b	405
43b	242
51b	6
62b	97

Hallah

1:8	54, 248, 320, 523

Shabbath

Shabbath	532
15a	140
22b	138
33b	103
63a	532
117b	241
118	241
119	241
120a	241
132a	237, 241
138b	539

Erubin

3b	230
21a	246
23a	248, 321
52b	229
54a	227, 228
58a	281
59b	229
105a	496

Pesachim

1:1	104
4a	468
57a	88
61a	86
96a	86, 242
118a	93, 536
119b	98

Yoma

2a	295
3:5	281
3b	292
4:1	135, 358
4:2	136
5:4	50, 385
6:1	358
9a	88, 134
9b	6, 364
15a	341, 479
15b	519
16a	40
19b	288, 510
21a	519
21b	184
25b	277
26b	521
35b	358
37a	135
38a	51, 130, 519
39	133
39a	136, 282, 521
39b	39, 81, 130, 140, 192, 214, 293
42a	285
51	387
51	81
51a	313
51b	313
52a	191

52b...519
53b...385, 479
54b...385
63b...138
68...319
68b.....................69, 136, 335, 336, 374
69a..133, 520
69b...309
72a...10
82a...468
85b...103

Sukkah

2a...94
21..296
21a..337
29a...131, 132
41a..391
48b..519
52..209, 355
52a...................................208, 356, 521
53b..81

Bezah

5b..391

Rosh Hashanah

3b..422
16b..112
17a..103
30a..391
31..17
31a............16, 114, 140, 180, 293, 381, 524
31b...140, 170

Ta'anith

17..391
26b..391
29a..143

Shekalim

Shekalim..395
6:3..386
8:4..............................45, 177, 194, 395

8:5.......................................176, 177, 314

Megillah

III..239
3a...393
4:5..268
20..496
20a...332, 398, 468, 495, 497, 500, 501, 502
20b...350, 495
30a..350

Chagigah

2..237, 238

Yebamoth

122a..45, 328
39..238
45b..234

Kethuboth

106a..313
l06a...295
111a..352, 355
111b..77, 352
112b..355

Sotah

5a...6, 163
16b..294
44b..276
48a..276

Gittin

68a..276

Kiddushin

31a..273
68b..234

Talmud References

Baba Kama

38a..258

Baba Metzia

73b..234

Baba Bathra

55a..234
60b..143
127b...234

Sanhedrin

19b..234
34b..244
35...244
35a..244
36b...51
39b..437
42a..334
42b.................................246, 278, 279
47a..330
55b..309
56a.................................233, 309, 310
58a..234
59a..258
65b..141
94a..364
97...521
97a................110, 115, 210, 356, 533
97b................115, 203, 211, 356, 393, 522
98a..355, 384
106b...305

Abodah Zerah

23b..273

Horayoth

11b..513

Shebuoth

11b..273

Aboth

3:2..242
5:6..................................86, 318, 476
8:21...238

Zebahim

40a...43
55b..313
93b...43
105b...319
106a...69, 335
113a...296

Menahoth

6:3...99
9:1..100
27a..389
64a..495
65a..496
98a...7, 51
98b...10

Hullin

7b...331
90b..177

Kerithoth

5b...513
6:b..287
6a...287, 509

Tamid

29b..313

Middoth

1:1..5, 385
1:3..280
2:2..., 518
2:2..187
2:4........40, 41, 42, 43, 44, 48, 49, 280, 326

2:5...51
3:3...280
3:4...276
4:1..............................94, 192, 386
4:7...50

Niddah

43b...234

Kelim

17:9.............................54, 323, 377

Parah

1:1...273

2:5...53, 273
3...281
3:1..............................92, 276, 295
3:10............................40, 286, 289
3:11............................53, 291, 336
3:2......................................295, 296, 337
3:3...296
3:5..........................44, 53, 92, 282, 292
3:6....................................71, 279, 337
3:8...285
3:9..................................53, 69, 358
4:2........................40, 46, 84, 282, 374
5:2...294
9...281
11:7...289
11:9...297

Zabim

Zabim..71

Midrash References

Genesis

100:7...473

Exodus

2:1...17
2:2...17
17:2...403
19:2.......................................265, 414
23:5...17
46:5...235

Leviticus

16:3...306
16:3...54
16:4...306
18:1..473, 474

Numbers

9:15...293
12:15...298
13:15...298
13:16...298
14:1...211
19:2...262
19:3...69
19:5...350
19:7...272
19:8...273

Deuteronomy

1:15...273

Ecclesiastes

Ecclesiastes 12:6............................473

Ecclesiastes 12:7............................473
Ecclesiastes 7:36............................263

Lamentations

Lamentations 1:54.............................17
Lamentations, Part 24 (Prologue)...........437
Lamentations, Part 25 (Proems)......16, 170, 293

Eichah

Eichah 25..524

Alphabetical Index

Aaron. .132, 136, 262, 271, 274p., 282, 298, 426, 514

Abraham.....114, 120p., 163, 233, 235, 293, 309, 343, 356p., 420, 426, 473, 521, 532, 535

Absalom's Pillar..40

Acts. 40, 61pp., 88, 109, 142, 144, 168, 189, 198, 204, 322, 334, 339, 365, 379, 387, 441, 511, 517, 523, 556

Afikoman.....196, 207, 247, 344, 413, 419p., 424, 429pp., 436pp., 440, 478, 481

Alexander......................133, 182, 220, 520p.

Alexandria................................51, 486, 519

Almighty God...3p., 6, 12, 60, 85, 87, 127p., 164, 173, 188, 195, 248, 281, 313, 334, 382, 387, 404, 518, 550, 552, 554

Altar.16, 40p., 43p., 46p., 52p., 55p., 58, 61, 68pp., 72, 74, 79, 91p., 97, 120p., 136, 138, 166, 175, 181, 184, 191, 248, 265p., 276pp., 284pp., 299, 306, 308, 311p., 314p., 318p., 321, 325, 327, 335pp., 340p., 346, 349p., 358, 368pp., 373pp., 383, 400p., 479, 509, 519, 521p.

Altar of Incense.52, 191, 248, 287, 368, 509

Altar of Sacrifice.......16, 136, 138, 166, 266, 285, 299, 336, 377, 383, 519

Amillennialists...29

Anderson................................116, 219, 550

Angel....6, 98, 163, 361, 430, 459, 465, 477, 490

Angel of Death..................98, 361, 430, 490

Angels..6, 322

Angelus..290

anti-Semitism. 168, 201, 227, 232, 251, 256, 351

Antichrist. .30, 59p., 91, 93, 104, 108p., 111, 115pp., 124, 145, 181, 211, 363p., 378pp., 389, 392, 528, 540pp.

Antiochus................................134, 166, 181

Antipatris..133

Antonia...168, 194p.

Apocryphal Books............................4, 188

Apostle. 5, 62, 114, 143, 165, 171, 189, 199, 304, 315, 339, 397, 440, 523

Apostolic Fathers..12

Arab...............21, 129, 321, 325, 372p., 541

Aramaic...42, 84, 121, 137, 176p., 182, 189, 219, 236, 263, 307, 313, 319p., 351, 357, 359p., 381, 408

Araunah..20

Arch..50, 55p., 368

Ark 3pp., 7, 10, 20, 50pp., 141, 188, 367, 371, 384pp., 408, 513

Ark of The Covenant...................3, 367, 385

Armageddon.......................29, 60, 93, 364

Artaxerxes...72p., 116, 211, 286, 388, 392p.

Ascension 4, 21p., 37p., 42, 47, 56pp., 61p., 64p., 70, 98, 120p., 123, 169p., 175, 182, 186, 218, 248, 250, 254p., 264, 293, 321p., 329, 342, 373, 375, 433, 435, 517, 523p., 526, 551

Ascension of Jesus......4, 22, 121, 123, 218, 254, 264, 293, 517, 551

Ascension of Shekhinah................4, 22, 120

assumptions............168, 170, 180, 376, 552

Atonement.......4p., 72, 87, 93, 96, 100, 103, 105, 109pp., 115, 121, 123, 135pp., 191, 243, 249, 254, 266, 268, 281, 285, 299, 319, 341, 343p., 354, 358pp., 377, 383, 385, 414, 481, 483, 485p., 519, 521, 540, 543

Awe..103, 112
Azazel.........................135pp., 358pp., 521
Babylon...13, 30, 129, 140, 144, 165, 179p., 182pp., 282p., 294, 329, 337, 368, 385p., 388, 393pp., 475, 491, 520, 550p.
Balfour Declaration................................345
Barabbas.........................74, 137p., 359p.
Barkay..80, 219, 408
Barnabas..114, 202
Bethany............54p., 62, 64, 71p., 172, 303, 306pp., 311, 322, 470pp., 477, 487pp., 492p., 523
Bethesda..................................241, 303pp.
Bethlehem.....87, 130, 170, 209, 333, 359p., 428
Blessed Assurance........107, 112, 199, 202, 205p., 231, 556
Boaz..234
Book of Life....103, 107, 112, 231, 485, 528, 531, 544
Caesar................70, 74, 84p., 278, 312, 470
Caesarea..63, 557
Caiaphas..68, 70, 74, 87p., 134, 187, 309p., 334, 339, 408, 476, 489, 520, 531
Caleb..238
Calvary.....75, 122, 168, 174, 247, 254, 278, 318p., 323, 325, 336, 338, 345p., 361, 488, 557
Capernaum......................................238, 320
Cave of the Column........287, 349, 369, 509
CD-ROM......................259, 409p., 460, 508
Cedar.......................................163, 264, 402
cedarwood....40, 100, 262, 286, 288p., 307, 400, 496
Cemetery 76, 80, 279, 342, 352, 485p., 492, 531
Chanukah.....16, 25, 98, 105, 110, 131, 134, 141, 190, 282, 514
Children of Israel.239, 247, 262p., 330, 332, 361, 427p., 431, 443, 484
China...365

Church Age.....23p., 98, 124, 145, 186, 203, 207, 215, 255, 435p., 518, 543, 547
Church of Mary Magdalene.......................58
cinnamon............................52, 287p., 509p.
cohain...374, 376
Cohen............................101, 210, 217pp.
Communion..................414, 426, 440p., 443
Conservative...162, 351, 391, 427, 459, 475
Constantine.......................174, 345p., 557
Copper Scroll......................................368p.
Corinthian......................................130, 519p.
Creation......102, 123, 217, 245, 354p., 385, 400p., 419
Crimson Strap................87, 136, 184, 521p.
Crusades..27p., 556
cubit. 40, 46, 53p., 95, 191, 229p., 337, 342, 374pp., 386, 389
curtain...10, 42p., 45p., 81pp., 176p., 191p., 194p., 299, 313, 326, 375p., 384, 395, 552
Dama...274
Damascus Gate Bus Station...................174
Daniel...29, 72p., 88, 91, 93, 95, 103, 107p., 110p., 115p., 132, 181, 193, 211, 220, 231, 265, 267, 286, 315, 339, 344, 352, 356, 363p., 368p., 378, 381, 388, 392p., 409, 429, 521, 528, 530, 532, 536pp., 542, 548p.
Davka...259, 409
Day of Preparation........435, 475pp., 489pp.
Dayenu...437
De Mille..344
Dead Sea 59, 95, 262, 265, 368p., 509, 513, 543
December.....................16, 45, 131, 327, 468
Descent of the Mount of Olives.53, 69p., 72, 311, 319
Desire of All Nations.............185p., 284, 354
Diaspora................................101, 475, 485
Divine Number............................122p., 416
Dome of the Rock....17, 20, 42, 44, 49, 278, 326, 341p., 372pp., 377, 379p.

Dome of the Spirits..........................20, 51p.
Dome of the Tablets.....20pp., 37pp., 42, 47, 50pp., 61, 78, 170, 278, 284, 317, 323, 325, 342, 372pp., 376p., 524
Eastern Gate...41, 50, 55, 94, 237, 284, 383
Egypt....3, 98, 106, 123, 128, 142, 183, 229, 238, 255, 298, 332, 357, 360, 415, 422, 424p., 430p., 437, 441, 477, 517, 528, 532
El Aqsa..61
Eleazar.....92, 262, 274p., 281pp., 292, 295, 372, 389
Eli 10
Elijah....207, 209p., 262, 425, 440, 519, 536
Elohim............................6, 24, 210, 217, 309
Emmaus...333
En Gedi.....................................59, 95, 543
End of Days.........................146, 355, 440
England............................143p., 408, 458p.
Enoch...530
Ephraim..211
Equinox...45, 327
Eretz Israel.......72, 141, 144, 352, 355, 370, 388, 536
Essene....................................71, 265, 346
Et Tur..21
Eucharist....................414, 426, 441, 443
Eusebius....16, 80, 170, 220, 254, 316, 322, 345, 407, 525, 557
Evil Inclination..............144p., 208, 250, 544
Ezra................................169, 182, 282, 536
Feasts....28, 45, 98, 101p., 104p., 111, 196, 414, 483pp., 492, 501p., 540
Fiddler on the Roof................................143
First Fruits...99pp., 104, 138, 344, 438, 481, 483p., 492p., 495
Fleming........48, 50p., 55p., 219, 371, 376p.
Flood...........................146, 198, 529p., 544
Foundation Stone.................20, 38, 50, 385

Galilean......24, 68, 73, 85, 88, 97, 132, 193, 195, 332, 477, 489, 491, 521, 523, 525, 549
Galilee.140, 240, 320, 334, 340, 475p., 491, 523, 534
Gamaliel....................88, 101, 431, 523, 556
Garden Tomb..75, 79p., 168, 174, 192, 219, 317p., 323, 325, 337p., 346, 408, 552
Gate..16, 20, 39, 41, 43pp., 47pp., 55p., 61, 70p., 75, 81, 83, 87, 94pp., 130, 170p., 174, 192, 195, 219, 237, 278, 280, 284, 311, 314, 319, 326pp., 371, 376p., 383, 519p., 525
Gehenna..103, 354p.
Gemara..132, 136, 211, 277, 313, 352, 358, 385, 495
Gethsemane....44, 54, 68, 70, 74, 137, 308, 311, 321p., 436
Gibson...248, 274
Gilgal..349
Global Warming.......................................146
Gog.................93, 211, 355, 364pp., 541
Golden Calf.......................................238, 275
Golgotha......67, 69, 83, 171, 195, 220, 254, 303, 314, 319p., 336, 345, 361, 407, 471, 478, 487p.
Gordon.....75, 168, 174, 247, 278, 318, 323, 325, 338, 345p., 458
Goron..92, 367
Great Trumpet........................534, 539, 543
Greece......................................17, 352, 431
Greek..121, 134, 177, 204p., 208, 220, 265, 282, 288p., 319, 357, 378pp., 387, 407, 425, 431, 501, 520
Gregory IX...28, 252
Gregory XIII...133
H'ekhal.......10, 41pp., 48pp., 79, 82, 94, 96, 139p., 166, 168, 176, 185, 188, 191p., 194p., 214, 248, 299, 313, 326pp., 374pp., 379p., 382, 386p., 518p., 551
HafTorah..239p., 268
Hag Hamatzah................................98, 483

Haggadah...99, 221, 391, 413, 415pp., 420, 422, 424, 429, 431, 436pp., 458pp., 482, 508

Haggadoth.......413, 415p., 419p., 425, 427, 431, 434, 439p.

Ham..177
Hamantaschen..................................420p.
Hannuth..140
Hanukkah..............................16, 514, 525
Heifer's Gangway Bridge........53, 68, 70, 72, 279p., 295, 308, 311, 319, 394
Helena....................................174, 345, 557
Herod..........5, 29, 74, 167, 187p., 190, 192, 213p., 334, 376, 392p., 489, 519p.
Hewn Stone.........................140, 276p., 292
High Priest. 4p., 12, 40, 43p., 48, 74p., 82p., 87p., 95p., 128p., 133pp., 168, 183p., 191, 195, 258, 266, 274pp., 284, 286, 289p., 296, 299, 309p., 314, 326, 334, 336p., 339, 342, 358, 360, 374, 383, 385, 396, 400, 489, 519, 531, 551
High Sabbath............................99, 474, 482
Hillel II...133, 240
Holocaust..............................93, 143p., 556
Holy House. .12, 17, 23, 37, 74, 82, 97, 142, 185, 187p., 190, 214, 248, 277, 280, 327, 380, 382p., 387, 524, 555
Hophni...10
Hyrcanus................44, 129, 133p., 282, 520
incense..........22, 52, 284, 287p., 370, 509p.
Isaac 120p., 123, 163, 217, 232p., 246, 354, 357p., 420, 459, 473, 534
Isaiah.....17, 50, 94, 105p., 109p., 114, 136, 141, 143, 146, 204, 208p., 235, 239p., 291, 356, 405, 423, 428, 485, 509, 521, 532, 534p.
Islam..................18, 175, 346, 370pp., 378p.
Islamic 48, 256, 266, 345, 372p., 378, 380p., 389, 540p.
Israel.......5p., 10, 12, 17, 29, 31p., 44, 46p., 51p., 60, 62, 69, 73, 77, 86pp., 92pp., 97p., 100, 103pp., 113pp., 122pp., 127pp., 131pp., 138, 140, 142pp., 180pp., 186, 188, 191, 193, 197pp., 202p., 207p., 210p., 214p., 217, 220p., 233, 236, 238pp., 246pp., 256, 262p., 271, 284, 287, 291, 293, 298, 318, 325p., 330, 332p., 339, 353, 355pp., 361, 364p., 367pp., 374, 382pp., 386, 388pp., 394, 403p., 408pp., 415, 419, 422, 424p., 427pp., 431pp., 443, 459p., 473, 475p., 478, 480, 484, 486, 490, 508p., 513, 517pp., 530p., 535, 537, 540pp., 548, 555p.

Israelite...............................103, 294, 426, 430
issue..100, 116, 241p., 256p., 316, 386, 496
Jacob. 61, 94, 110, 114, 163, 233, 235, 356, 420, 458, 541p.
Jacob's Trouble............................110, 541p.
Jacobson..375p., 408
James..........24, 48, 55, 63p., 121, 165, 201, 209p., 219, 236, 247, 278, 304, 357, 376p., 379, 381, 407, 499, 524
Japheth...177, 365
Jechoniah..235
Jehoiakim..235
Jehoshaphat...111
Jehovah. 6, 28, 98, 105, 111, 163, 218, 308, 483pp., 492, 540
Jeremiah......4p., 106, 113p., 132, 142, 165, 188, 201p., 208, 235, 243, 368, 381, 385p., 388
Jericho...234, 288, 472p., 477, 487pp., 493, 510
Jerusalem 3, 17, 21pp., 37, 39p., 44, 46, 48, 51, 53pp., 59pp., 68, 71pp., 75, 79p., 88, 96p., 100p., 103pp., 108pp., 116, 124, 129pp., 137, 139pp., 146, 165, 168p., 171, 174, 176, 179pp., 183, 185p., 188, 190, 192, 195, 201, 211p., 215p., 219pp., 237p., 246, 250, 254p., 267, 280, 283p., 286, 288, 294p., 304, 306, 308, 310pp., 315pp., 325p., 329, 333, 338pp., 343, 345p., 350, 353, 356pp., 364, 366, 368, 371, 373, 377pp., 381pp., 385, 387p., 390, 392, 394pp., 407pp., 422, 438, 459p., 465, 470pp., 478, 480p., 483pp., 488p.,

491p., 495p., 508, 510, 518, 520pp., 528, 530p., 537pp., 543p., 548, 551, 553p.

Jerusalem Post..........................40, 219, 286

Jewish Rapture........................485, 527, 530

John.........12, 24, 44, 53, 55, 60, 62p., 68p., 72pp., 78p., 87, 89, 99, 105, 124, 129, 133p., 143, 165, 168p., 171pp., 181, 189p., 195, 206p., 209, 226, 238, 241p., 246p., 268, 285, 288, 291, 304p., 308p., 311p., 315pp., 320, 341, 354, 362, 387, 397, 399, 425, 428, 432, 437, 459, 465p., 471pp., 475p., 478p., 482, 487p., 492p., 495, 497, 508, 532, 540, 558

Jonah...............................122, 354, 357, 498

Jones...........27, 31, 38, 52, 92, 219, 286pp., 349p., 367pp., 394, 409, 416, 459, 513, 556

Jordan..................122, 146, 367p., 425, 542

Joseph...80, 131, 208pp., 214, 221, 234pp., 240, 247, 249, 259, 273, 316, 326, 329pp., 337pp., 341, 354pp., 398, 405, 409, 432, 460, 466pp., 473, 481, 507, 522, 528, 531, 533

Josephus....5, 13, 15p., 23p., 38p., 41p., 44, 48, 86, 95, 125, 128pp., 141p., 164p., 167, 169pp., 176, 180, 182, 189p., 192, 194, 216, 219, 251, 259, 263, 275, 293p., 313, 318, 366, 385, 388, 392, 407, 519p., 524p., 550p.

Judas................................70, 243, 312, 437

Judgment Day..106

Judgment Seat................................231, 297

June....................16, 45, 131, 327, 460, 468

Kalal............92, 287, 363, 368p., 371, 394p.

Kaufman..........15, 17, 20, 37p., 40p., 49pp., 53pp., 58, 141, 161, 170, 219, 284, 317, 323, 373pp., 386, 407, 409, 524, 549

Khartoum...174, 345

Kidron Valley..16, 22, 40p., 56, 59, 64, 70p., 81, 85, 121, 285, 325, 342, 373, 379, 524, 550

King of Kings.30, 102, 122p., 199, 355, 366, 388, 543

Kingdom..29, 60, 72, 74, 94, 96, 102p., 105, 111pp., 123p., 136, 186, 207, 209, 215, 235, 240, 250, 261, 265, 272, 283, 290pp., 310, 347, 353pp., 362, 366, 381, 388p., 392, 398pp., 429, 432, 435, 483, 485p., 528, 531, 534, 539, 544

kohain...375p.

kohanim...299

kohen..266

Kolatch.................251, 259, 409, 460, 507p.

Koran...372, 408

Lamsa Bible............169, 182, 189, 191, 304

Larkin.......................................122, 220, 507

Last Supper....207, 311, 437, 440, 469, 474, 476p., 491

Latin.................................52, 121, 248, 265

Lazarus...55, 72p., 306p., 432, 472pp., 487, 492

Lebanon..............52, 93, 140, 390, 401, 541

Levi.................................101, 188, 424, 431

Lights.................................16, 131, 134, 514

Lower Arch..50, 55p.

Luke..62, 64, 70, 173, 191, 235p., 244, 307, 320, 322, 470pp., 488, 500

MacArthur..344

Maccabees..4, 188

Magdalene..............................58, 465, 498

Magen David.....................................418, 429

Magog................93, 211, 355, 364pp., 541

Maimonides....................326, 399, 409, 466

Mark.55, 110, 171, 173, 191, 195, 244, 320, 468, 470pp., 487, 489

Martin....15, 23p., 38p., 44, 47, 53p., 75, 80, 120, 133, 174, 216, 219p., 345, 375p., 407, 409

Mary.58, 172, 209p., 234pp., 465, 468, 483, 487, 492, 498

Masada.................................120, 357, 554

Masoretic Text.................211, 236, 299, 359

Matzah.................................421, 428p., 434

Megiddo...111, 543

Megillah.......239, 268, 332, 350, 393, 398p., 468, 495pp., 500pp.
Melchizedek..210
Menorah..........138, 191, 248, 368, 409, 521
Mercy Seat..385
Meshech..365
Messiah.....11, 22, 24, 28pp., 48, 51p., 59p., 62, 65, 69, 72p., 76p., 88, 91, 93, 95p., 101, 103pp., 107pp., 117, 124, 132, 135, 139, 142, 166pp., 175, 181, 185p., 189, 193, 197pp., 203p., 206pp., 214p., 217, 227, 237, 246, 250, 255pp., 261, 264p., 272, 279p., 282pp., 291, 297, 303, 305, 308pp., 314pp., 329, 331, 337pp., 344, 352pp., 363p., 368, 370p., 378, 381p., 384pp., 388p., 391pp., 398p., 403p., 409, 413p., 416, 424p., 428pp., 432pp., 438pp., 478, 480, 485p., 501, 508, 514, 517, 521p., 525pp., 530pp., 546, 548, 553, 555p.
Middle Ages...101, 232, 413, 416, 418, 421, 424, 546
Midian..198
Midrashic..164, 306
Millennial.......60, 95pp., 114, 146, 185, 187, 283, 392, 531, 544
Millennium..94, 398
Miphkad..........40p., 43p., 46p., 53, 55p., 58, 68pp., 72, 74, 79, 91p., 120p., 175, 266, 278pp., 284pp., 289, 299, 306, 308, 311p., 314p., 318p., 321, 325, 327, 335pp., 346, 373pp., 400p.
Miriam..238, 275
Mishna 45, 49, 53, 87, 136, 234, 238, 241p., 257, 272, 280p., 309, 313, 323, 326, 358, 395, 532, 537
Mohammed...372
Moriah....................120p., 124, 357, 473
Moscow..365
Moses....3p., 6, 10, 52, 92, 102, 104p., 123, 136, 140, 163, 198, 204p., 218, 225, 228, 230p., 238p., 247p., 262, 271p., 274p., 283, 287, 298, 303, 306, 323, 330, 332, 350pp., 363, 372, 375p., 383, 386, 409, 415pp., 426, 429, 487, 494, 513p., 542
Moslem...380
Mount. 4, 6, 12, 16p., 20pp., 30p., 37pp., 43, 45p., 48, 50pp., 60pp., 64p., 68pp., 75pp., 83, 85, 94, 102, 107pp., 115pp., 120pp., 130pp., 140, 170, 181p., 190, 194p., 206, 218, 220p., 238, 240, 247p., 254p., 265p., 275, 278pp., 284, 286, 291, 295, 299, 306, 311pp., 319p., 322p., 325, 327pp., 331, 333, 336p., 339, 341p., 344p., 352p., 356pp., 371pp., 384, 389p., 392, 396, 400, 408p., 432, 472, 485p., 523pp., 531, 533, 539p., 543, 555
Muslim...18, 39, 48pp., 56p., 61, 127, 372p., 377p., 394, 396, 414, 540
Muslims................268, 345, 373, 378p., 558
Nazareth. .24, 101, 104, 121, 123, 137, 139, 166, 203, 205p., 209, 213, 215, 228, 239p., 245, 250, 254pp., 282, 285p., 293, 330, 334, 344, 352, 356, 360, 392, 423, 428, 431p., 435, 484, 486, 522p., 536p., 546, 553
Nazi...143
Nebuchadnezzar..4, 88, 186, 188, 246, 293, 368, 388
Nehemiah...5, 72p., 185, 286, 521, 534, 536
next Temple................................30, 59, 384
Nicanor's.......43pp., 48p., 51, 81, 87, 94pp., 130, 170, 192, 284, 311, 328, 519p.
Nicodemus..234
Nicodemus..531
Nisan.....16, 45, 64, 86, 93, 98pp., 104, 111, 131, 171, 180, 212, 242, 286, 298, 343p., 349p., 392, 435p., 438, 442, 464p., 467pp., 480pp., 487pp., 495pp., 500, 524, 542
Noahide...233
Number....122p., 248, 282p., 416, 419, 425, 484
Olives. .4, 12, 15pp., 20pp., 31, 37p., 40, 43, 46, 48, 51, 53, 55, 57p., 62, 64p., 68pp., 75pp., 80p., 83, 85, 94, 107pp., 115pp., 120pp., 130pp., 170, 181p., 194p., 206,

Alphabetical Index

218, 220, 240, 248, 254p., 265p., 278pp., 284, 286, 291, 299, 306, 311pp., 319p., 322p., 325, 327pp., 331, 333, 336p., 339, 341p., 344, 349, 352p., 356, 358, 373pp., 400, 408p., 432, 472, 485p., 523pp., 527, 531, 533, 539, 543, 555

Olivet..15, 22, 28, 40p., 43pp., 49pp., 54pp., 58, 64p., 69p., 74pp., 83pp., 88, 95p., 105, 107pp., 111, 116, 120p., 123p., 131, 138p., 168p., 175, 180, 192, 194p., 203, 210, 216, 254, 278pp., 293, 299, 306, 308, 311, 314p., 317pp., 325p., 329, 333, 336pp., 340pp., 345p., 353, 357p., 371, 374p., 377, 392p., 400, 485, 523, 525, 530, 552, 557

Online Bible......................................259, 409
Origen..137, 359
Ornan...20
Orthodox..........61, 100, 143, 228, 349, 366, 371p., 381, 389, 391, 394, 427, 475, 514
Ovid...31
Palestine.........................134, 355, 384, 431
Palestinian......................342, 369, 541, 557
Paschal Lamb....86, 98, 242, 298, 318, 350, 361, 404, 434p., 437, 440, 469, 474pp., 480p., 490, 492
Paschal's Wager......................................527
Passover 16, 45, 79, 81, 86p., 93, 98p., 101, 104p., 111, 115, 117, 122, 131p., 136, 171, 196, 198, 207, 209p., 221, 237p., 240, 247, 249p., 254, 265pp., 298, 314, 318, 327p., 332p., 341, 343p., 350, 354, 358, 361, 381, 391, 404, 413pp., 422, 424pp., 429pp., 436, 440pp., 458pp., 465, 469p., 472pp., 480pp., 487, 489pp., 493, 495p., 507, 524, 538, 542, 558

Paul..5, 12, 62pp., 88, 101, 114, 165, 167p., 189, 199pp., 232pp., 339, 380, 407, 426, 440p., 471, 517, 523, 551p., 555
Pentagon...144

Pentecost......16, 25, 27, 51, 97p., 100, 102, 105, 122, 124, 131, 185, 238, 250, 483p., 524, 549
Peshitta..189, 219, 236, 304, 307, 377, 381, 408, 499
Peter....24, 63, 79, 122, 189, 201, 471, 517, 540
Petra..542
Philistines..................................188, 256
Phillip..............................89, 109, 458, 530
Phinehas..10
Pia 285
Pilate......70p., 74, 86, 128, 137, 172, 243p., 247, 312, 330pp., 360, 430, 476, 498
Pinnacle.......201, 247, 278, 379p., 390, 524
Pompey...166
Pope.................................28, 133, 251p.
Potiphar...357
Purim...............105, 268, 350, 420, 424, 478
Qumran.........................265, 349, 369, 514
Quran..372p., 410
Rahab...234
Rashi.92, 229, 232, 276, 295, 355, 385, 426
Reconstructionist...................................391
Red Cow................261, 268, 288, 351, 372
Red Heifer......37p., 40p., 43p., 47, 50, 52p., 68pp., 86, 91p., 96, 100, 120p., 128p., 175, 193, 210, 223, 229, 244, 254, 257, 261pp., 271pp., 280p., 283, 285, 287p., 290pp., 298p., 303p., 307p., 311, 317pp., 322p., 326pp., 334pp., 338, 340p., 343p., 346, 349pp., 354, 358, 362pp., 367p., 370, 372pp., 383p., 389p., 393, 396, 398, 400p., 403pp., 409, 414, 481, 496, 509, 513, 533, 540, 558
Red Sea...59, 287
Redeemer......115, 193, 199, 203, 206, 232, 239, 284, 310, 315, 339, 355, 362, 388, 438, 501, 526, 531, 549
Reformed...............................391, 427, 475
reidel..423, 434

Replacement Theology....27, 109, 166, 197, 201, 256

Resurrection............77, 99, 101, 104p., 109, 122pp., 132, 169, 186, 195, 264, 279, 285, 293, 303, 315p., 331p., 337, 339, 353, 388, 396, 399, 405, 427, 431, 435, 438, 463pp., 479, 483, 485, 487, 493, 497, 525, 530, 551

Reuchlin.........................245, 252

Ritmeyer......................373pp., 408

Roots............................118

Rosh Hashanah. .98, 102p., 105pp., 109pp., 133, 240, 314, 475, 483pp., 543

Sabbath Day's journey. 54, 64, 78, 193, 277, 317, 333, 342, 523

Sabbath Limit.....50, 229p., 246p., 266, 278, 280, 299, 317, 321pp., 329, 373, 375p., 496

Saducean...339, 481p., 493, 496, 527, 531

Sadducees. 6, 12, 99pp., 339, 480, 496, 531

Sanhedrin 68, 80, 88, 140, 214, 240, 243pp., 252, 277, 330p., 338, 356, 476, 556

Satan.......24, 92, 144p., 175, 201, 208, 211, 228, 281, 350, 379, 433, 437p., 479, 544

Satanic........................145

Saul.................129, 239, 431, 523

Scaliger........................131

Scapegoat..............100, 136p., 359p., 521p.

Scapegoat's Gangway.................135

Scythians........................365

Second Temple 5, 7, 10p., 13, 20, 24, 28pp., 38p., 45, 49p., 53pp., 63, 67, 70, 80p., 88, 95p., 103, 134, 142, 162pp., 169, 176, 179, 181pp., 192, 196, 248, 282p., 287, 293, 306, 313, 319, 330, 337p., 359, 368, 384pp., 392, 509, 514, 519p., 530, 550pp.

Seder....98p., 101, 105, 122, 196, 207, 209, 247, 249, 391, 413pp., 418pp., 424p., 427pp., 439pp., 458p., 469, 472, 474pp., 481p., 489pp., 558

Sedrah.....................239p., 268

Selah............................227

Sennacherib.....................246

Septuagint......................379

Shamir..........................276

Shanks..........................408

Shavuot.......16, 98, 100pp., 420, 475, 483p.

Shekhinah..1, 3pp., 10pp., 15pp., 20pp., 24, 27pp., 37pp., 51p., 55p., 58, 61pp., 87p., 91, 97p., 109pp., 115pp., 120p., 123p., 127, 131, 133p., 138, 140p., 163pp., 168pp., 173p., 179pp., 195p., 201, 207, 212pp., 218, 254p., 293, 313, 318, 326, 386pp., 392, 401, 517p., 521p., 524pp., 530, 543, 547pp., 551pp.

Shem........................177, 365

Shemen Afarshimon...............52, 349, 513p.

Shethiyah.....................50, 382, 385

Shroud of Turin.............247, 285, 331, 432

Shulcan Aruch..................477

Sign...........................130, 133

Signs.....56, 72, 127pp., 133, 139, 146, 213, 367, 520

Siloam.................295pp., 376, 395, 422

Simeon.....44, 133pp., 138, 184p., 237, 273, 282, 496, 520pp.

Simon 54p., 71, 73, 201, 306, 437, 458, 460, 489, 491, 507, 520

Sinai. .4, 6, 23, 52, 92, 102p., 198, 287, 333, 350, 382, 431, 458, 513, 517p.

Six Day War......................345

Solomon..4, 10, 17, 30, 69, 142, 184, 235p., 248, 259, 261pp., 275p., 284, 289, 303, 319, 343, 349, 387, 397, 403p., 408p., 507, 513, 519, 523, 536

Son of David.....60, 72, 96, 101, 104p., 107, 110, 115, 132, 206, 212, 272, 282, 286, 305, 316, 329, 344, 353, 355p., 364, 384, 386, 388, 436, 438, 440, 442, 485, 526, 530p., 533, 536, 538, 540p.

Son of Joseph....................208, 356

Soviet..........................364pp.

Spain...........................143p.

Spielberg......................344, 367

Alphabetical Index

Star of David............................413, 418, 429
Stauber.................................415p., 421, 436
Stephen......................................247, 278, 517
Sukkoth...103, 105, 250, 422, 484, 486, 544
Suleiman..............48, 51, 55p., 97, 373, 377
Syriac..............................236, 304, 351, 499
Tabernacle...4, 6p., 10, 23, 41, 43p., 60, 82, 92, 96p., 105, 123, 176, 229, 248, 255, 262, 267, 271, 276, 282p., 294, 298, 313, 321, 326p., 341, 363, 367, 372, 378, 380pp., 386, 389pp., 396, 514, 519, 540
Tabernacles.....60, 103, 105, 111, 122, 238, 250, 422, 483pp., 544
Tanakh 110, 114, 183, 208p., 232, 351, 353, 438, 539
Tetragrammaton............................236, 308
Tevyeh..143
Third Temple.......17, 29p., 59p., 95pp., 103, 105, 185, 187, 261, 371, 381, 386, 390, 392, 527, 558
Thomas..163, 407
Thursday..461p., 464, 477, 488, 493p., 496, 499, 502
Tisha B'Av..142p.
Tishri. .93, 102p., 109, 111, 468, 475, 483p., 486, 539p., 543p.
Titus 17, 24, 135, 142, 165p., 181, 368, 514, 522, 524p.
Tobolsk..365
Torah.....28, 115, 136, 225p., 233, 239, 242, 248, 258p., 263, 268, 293, 298, 306, 332, 350p., 354, 359, 386, 408, 417, 421, 424, 426p., 464, 481, 484, 490, 507, 520, 533, 535
Transfiguration..24
Tribulation. 91pp., 105, 107pp., 113pp., 146, 344, 364, 369, 388, 485, 528pp., 536, 540p.
Trinity. 25, 51, 101, 122, 169, 217, 297, 354, 416, 418, 423, 428pp., 433pp., 443
Triumphal Entry53, 55, 68p., 72p., 286, 311, 350, 470, 472p., 479, 488, 493

Triune.........6, 101, 207, 217, 297, 416, 423, 429p., 435
Trumpets.......91, 98, 105, 109pp., 115, 483, 485, 534, 543
Tshuvah...103, 531
Tubal..365p.
Tyre...182
Unleavened Bread.....86, 98, 104, 216, 436, 463, 469, 480, 482p., 489pp.
Urim and Thummim........................129, 245
Uzziah..58
Uzziel, Rabbi Jonathan ben...393, 404, 544, 546, 589
Vatican..368
Waqf..............................50, 345, 378, 396
Water...61
Wednesday......461p., 464, 466, 477, 487p., 502
Weeks....97, 100, 102, 124, 250, 393, 483p.
Western Wall..............................17, 61, 390
Whiston.........................129, 219, 259, 407
World Trade Center................................144
Y'israel...........................101, 421, 424, 431
Y'shua.........137, 236, 255p., 329, 354, 425, 440pp., 480, 486, 523
Yadin............................54p., 219, 338, 407
Yahatz..434
Yahweh................................6, 218, 272, 308
Yamim Nora'im..112
Yeshu...359p.
Yeshu bar Abbas......................................360
Yeshu bar Yusef.......................................360
YHWH 6, 134, 217, 236, 239, 272, 298, 308, 391, 487
Yom Kippur....4, 12, 93, 96, 103pp., 108pp., 115, 117, 138, 143, 188, 191, 249, 285, 358, 360, 383, 414, 420, 475, 483pp., 519, 540, 543
Zakkai..................................17, 140, 199p.
Zerubbabel........5, 29, 95, 169, 180, 183pp., 385pp., 551

Zion. 108, 120, 183, 341, 357, 385, 390, 473 72, 141, 144, 352, 355, 370, 388, 536

Rosh Hashanah................................483

Yom Kippur........................483

"Signs.....................127

Please Tell Others About

Jesus and the Third Temple

The Complete Guide to the Ancient History and Secret Rituals of the Red Heifer Ceremony

jesusandthethirdtemple.com

yowbooks.com

www.ingramcontent.com/pod-product-compliance
Lightning Source LLC
Chambersburg PA
CBHW080527300426
44111CB00017B/2634